Essentials of Sociology

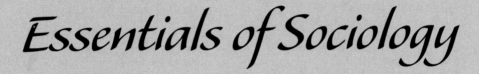

Essentials of Sociology

A Down-to-Earth Approach

▼

Second Edition

James M. Henslin
Southern Illinois University, Edwardsville

Allyn and Bacon

Boston London Toronto Sydney Tokyo Singapore

Editor-in-Chief, Social Sciences:
  Karen Hanson
Series Editorial Assistant: Elissa Schaen
Marketing Manager: Karon Bowers
Signing Representative: Ward Moore
Cover Administrator: Linda Knowles

Manufacturing Buyer: Megan Cochran
Photo Researcher: Stephen Forsling
Fine Art Researcher: Laurie Frankenthaler
Editorial-Production Service: The Book Company
Text Designer: Wendy Calmenson/By Design
Page Layout: Omegatype

Copyright © 1998, 1996 by James M. Henslin
Allyn and Bacon
A Viacom Company
Needham Heights, Massachusetts 02194

www.abacon.com
America Online: Keyword: College Online

Library of Congress Cataloging-in-Publication Data
Henslin, James M.
    Essentials of sociology : a down-to-earth approach / James M.
Henslin. -- 2nd ed.
      p.   cm.
    Includes bibliographical references and index.
    ISBN 0-205-26557-X
    1. Sociology.   I. Title.
HM51.H39794   1997
301–dc21
                                              97-20060
                                              CIP

Chapter Opener Art Credits

Chapter 1: *Too Many Crowds*, Diana Ong. Diana Ong/Superstock.

Chapter 2: *Beauty of the Continuum*, 1987 by Dan V. Lomahaftewa. Acrylic on canvas, 48" x 36". Courtesy of El Cerro Graphics.

Chapter 3: *Modern Madonna*, 1995 by Christian Pierre. Private Collection/Superstock.

Chapter 4: *Patria B*, 1925 by Alejandro Xul Solar. Water color, crayon, and pencil. Cristie's Images/Superstock.

Chapter 5: *Friends*, 1995 by Diana Ong. Private Collection/Superstock.

Chapter 6: *Bombardment*, 1991 by Tsing-Fang Chen. Lucia Gallery, New York City/TF Chen/Superstock.

Chapter 7: *If My Friends Could See Me Now*, 1991 by Pacita Abad. Mixed media, 95" x 69". Photo by Paul Tanedo.

Chapter 8: *City Gleaners*, Tsing-Fang Chen. Paul Lee Collection TF Chen/Superstock.

Chapter 9: *Stagger Lee*, 1984 by Frederick Brown. © 1984 COPYRIGHT Frederick J. Brown. National Museum of American Art, Washington, DC/Art Resource, NY.

Chapter 10: *The Sisters*, 1991 by Deidre Scherer. Fabric and thread, 31" x 33". © 1992 Deidre Scherer. Photo by Jeff Baird.

Chapter 11: *Masters of the Universe*, 1992 by Pacita Abad. Mixed media, 97" x 58". Photo by Paul Tanedo.

Chapter 12: *Making Tamales (Tamalada)*, 1987 by Carmen Lomas Garza. Gouache painting, 20" x 27". © 1987 Carmen Lomas Garza. Photo by Wolfgang Dietze. Collection of Leonila Ramirez, Don Ramon's Restaurant, San Francisco, California.

Chapter 13: *Take Me to the Water*, 1994 by Jessie Coates. Jessie Coates/Superstock.

Chapter 14: *Lower East Side* from *Scenes of New York*, 1938 by Kindred McLeary. Mural study, Madison Square Postal Station, New York City. © 1938. Tempera on fiberboard, 23.75" x 20". National Museum of American Art, Washington DC/Art Resource, NY.

Chapter 15: *Power Book Girl*, 1996 by Christian Pierre. Acrylic on canvas. Private Collection/Christian Pierre/Superstock.

Art and photo credits continue on page 487, which is a continuation of this copyright page.

Printed in the United States of America
13 12 11 10 9 8 7 6 5 4   00 VHP 99 98

To my son, Paul,
who is inheriting a world not of his making.
May his contributions to it be of value to those who follow.

BRIEF CONTENTS

CONTENTS

▼

▼▲▼▼▲▼▲▼▲▼▲▼▲▼▲▼▲▼▲▼▲▼▲▼▲▼▲▼▲▼▲▼▲▼
Part One   The Sociological Perspective

Part Two Social Groups and Social Control

Part Three   Social Inequality

Part Four Social Institutions

Part Five Social Change

▼

If you like to watch people and try to figure out why they do what they do, you will like sociology. Sociology pries open the doors of society so you can see what goes on behind them.

Essentials of Sociology: A Down-to-Earth Approach stresses how all of us are profoundly influenced by the society in which we live and the specific experiences we have. Social class, for example, sets us on different paths in life. For some, these paths lead to better health, more education, and higher income, whereas for others they result in poverty, dropping out of school, and even a higher risk of illness and disease. These paths are so significant that they even affect our chances of making it to our first birthday, as well as of getting in trouble with the police. They even influence how our marriages work out, the number of children we will have—and whether or not we will read this book in the first place.

When I took my first course in sociology, I was "hooked." Seeing how marvelously my life had been affected by these larger social influences opened my eyes to a new world, one that has been fascinating to explore. I hope that this will be your experience also.

From how people become homeless to how they become presidents, from why women are treated as second-class citizens to why people commit suicide—all are part of sociology. This breadth, in fact, is what makes sociology so intriguing. We can place the sociological lens on broad features of society, such as social class, gender, and race, and then immediately turn our focus on the small-scale level. If we look at two people interacting—whether quarreling or kissing—we see how these broad features of society are being played out in their lives.

We aren't born with instincts. We don't come into this world with preconceived notions of what life should be like. At birth, we have no ideas of race, gender, age, or social class. We have no idea, for example, of how people "ought" to act because they are male or female. Yet we all learn such things as part of growing up in our society. Uncovering the "hows" and the "whys" of this process is also part of sociology's fascination.

One of sociology's many pleasures is that as we study life in groups (which can be taken as a definition of sociology), whether those groups be in some far-off part of the world (if there still are far-off places) or in some nearby corner of our own society, we constantly gain insights into our own selves. As we see how *their* customs affect *them*, effects of our own society on ourselves become more visible.

This book, then, can be part of an intellectual adventure, for it can lead you to a new way of looking at your social world—and in the process, help you to better understand both society and yourself.

I wish you the very best in college—and in your career afterward. It is my sincere hope that *Essentials of Sociology: A Down-to-Earth Approach* will contribute to that success.

James M. Henslin
Department of Sociology
Southern Illinois University
Edwardsville, IL 62026

P.S. If you want to comment on your experiences with this text, don't hesitate to write me. I enjoy communicating with students. I can also be reached at henslin@aol.com by email.

Also, three other items that might interest you:

1. You may want to look at the website at http://www.abacon.com/henslin/ for this text.

2. At the end of each chapter is a section on how to use the Internet to learn more about the chapter's topics. *Before* you begin a project, be sure to read through the entire assignment to see what you are expected to produce, such as what kind of report you should write.

3. If you like using a study guide, check out the *Study Guide Plus*, prepared by Profesor Gwendolyn E. Nyden. It will help you review the chapters, and even provides self-tests so you can see how you are doing.

P R E F A C E

As instructors of sociology, we have set formidable tasks for ourselves—to teach both social structure and social interaction, to introduce students to the main sociological literature, to both the classic theorists and contemporary research—and to do so in ways that enliven the classroom, encourage critical thinking, and stimulate the sociological imagination. Although formidable, these goals are attainable. This book, based on many years of classroom experience, is designed to help you reach these goals.

The subtitle of this text, *A Down-to-Earth Approach*, is not proposed lightly. The goal is to share the fascination of sociology with students. Remember when you first got "hooked" on sociology, how the windows of perception opened and you began to see life-in-society through the sociological lens? For most of us, that was an eye-opening experience. This text is designed to open those windows onto social life, so students can see clearly the vital effects of group membership on their lives. Although few students will get into what Peter Berger calls "the passion of sociology," we can at least provide them the opportunity.

Sociology is like a huge jigsaw puzzle. Only very gradually do the intricate pieces start to fit together. As they do so, our perspective changes as we shift our eyes from the many small, disjointed pieces onto the whole that is being formed. Although this analogy is imperfect, it indicates a fascinating process of sociological discovery. Of all the endeavors we could have entered, we chose sociology because of the ways in which it joins together the "pieces" of society and the challenges it poses to "ordinary" thinking. To share the sociological perspective with students is our privilege.

Over the years, I have found the introductory course especially enjoyable. It is especially satisfying to see students' faces light up as they begin to see how separate pieces of their world fit together, as they gain insight into how their social experiences have given shape to even their innermost desires. This is precisely what this text is designed to do—to stimulate the sociological imagination so students can better perceive how the "pieces" of society fit together, and what that means for their own lives.

Filled with examples from around the world as well as from our own society, this text helps make today's multicultural, global society come alive for the student. From the international elite dividing up global markets to the intimacy of friendship and marriage, the student can see how sociology is the key to explaining contemporary life—and his or her own role in it.

In short, this text is designed to make your teaching easier. There simply is no justifiable reason for students to have to wade through cumbersome approaches to sociology. I am firmly convinced that the introduction to sociology should be enjoyable, and that the introductory textbook can be an essential tool in sharing the discovery of sociology with students.

The Organization of This Text

The text is laid out in five parts. Part I focuses on the sociological perspective. After introducing the sociological perspective in the first chapter, in Chapter 2 we then look at how culture influences us, examine socialization in Chapter 3, and compare macrosociology and microsociology in Chapter 4. Part II, which focuses on groups and social control, adds to the students' understanding of how significantly social groups influence our lives. In Chapter 5, we examine the different types of groups in society, looking also at the fascinating area of group dynamics. Then, in Chapter 6, we focus on how groups "keep us in line" and sanction those who violate their norms.

In Part III, we examine how social inequality pervades society and how those inequalities have an impact on us. Because social stratification is so significant, I have written two chapters on this topic. The first (Chapter 7), with its global focus, presents an overview of the principles of stratification. The second (Chapter 8), with its emphasis on variations in social class, focuses on stratification in U.S. society. After establishing this broader context, in Chapter 9 we examine inequalities in race and ethnicity, and in Chapter 10 those of gender and age.

Part IV makes students more aware of how social institutions encompass their lives. In Chapter 11, we look at how the economy and politics are the overarching social institutions in contemporary society. In Chapter 12, we turn our focus on the family, and in Chapter 13 we examine education and religion. Throughout, we look at how these social institutions are changing, and how these changes, in turn, influence our orientations and decisions.

With its focus on broad social change, Part V provides an appropriate ending for the book. Here we examine why our world is changing so rapidly, as well as catch a glimpse of what is yet to come. Chapter 14 opens this concluding part with an analysis of population and urbanization. Then, in Chapter 15 our focus on technology, social movements, and the environment takes us to the "cutting edge" of the changes that engulf us all.

Themes and Features

Four central themes run throughout the text. Three of these themes—cultural diversity, down-to-earth sociology, and critical thinking—were in the first edition. New to this edition is the timely—and fascinating—theme of technology and society.

The first theme, cultural diversity, explores the cultures of peoples worldwide, as well as subgroups that make up the United States. The second theme, down-to-earth sociology, examines sociological processes that underlie everyday life. The third theme, critical thinking, focuses on controversial social issues and engages students in examining the various sides of those issues. The fourth theme, sociology and the new technology, investigates how technol-

ogy both shapes society and is shaped by it. Let's look at these four themes in more detail.

Cultural Diversity and Globalization

In the new global economy, the interdependent fates of nations affect our lives in many crucial areas—from influencing the kinds of skills and knowledge we need, types of work available to us, and costs of the goods and services we consume, to whether our country is at war or peace. This text has a strong emphasis on global issues, such as a separate chapter on global stratification, extensive coverage in the chapters on social institutions, and a global focus in the final chapters on social change: technology, population, urbanization, social movements, and the environment.

Because we live in a global society, our sociological interpretations must take into account this broader perspective. What occurs in Russia and Japan, as well as in much smaller nations such as Chechen and Bosnia, has direct and far-reaching consequences on our own lives. Consequently, in addition to this global focus throughout the text, a series of boxes headed "A Global Glimpse" focuses on dimensions of social issues as they are played out in other societies. These include the relativity of deviance (Chapter 6), urbanization in the Least Industrialized Nations (Chapter 14), and the loss to humanity of the disappearing rain forests (Chapter 15). One of my favorites is in Chapter 9, which recounts an attempt to kill or maim an ethnic offender (with myself the victim!).

In addition, the text recurringly highlights key issues of multicultural diversity within U.S. society. A prime example is the boxes headed "The Immigrant Experience." Each year over a million people from around the world legally immigrate to the United States, with the number of illegal entrants perhaps as large. Currently about one American in four defines him- or herself as Latino or nonwhite. In the next few years, the population of Asian Americans and Latinos is expected to increase by about 22 percent, that of African Americans by 12 percent, but whites by a mere 2 percent. In some places the future has already arrived. In New York City, for example, 40 percent of all primary and secondary students belong to an ethnic minority, while in California that figure stands at 51 percent.

A sociology textbook that does not explore this fundamental demographic shift cannot adequately introduce the realities of life in a multicultural society. Thus "The Immigrant Experience" boxes introduce students to how immigrants' fundamental orientations of the world are challenged and modified as they are immersed in their new culture. For example, we examine how education can force huge gaps between young immigrants and their families (Chapter 3), how the rules for life in the new society conflict so greatly with what immigrants had previously learned that they get in trouble with the law (Chapter 6), how they confront prejudice (Chapter 9), and how Latin American wives become much less submissive after they are introduced to North American culture (Chapter 10). See the inside front cover for a complete listing of this feature.

This focus on cultural diversity, as well as the many discussions of multiculturalism throughout the text, helps develop the student's sociological imagination. By stimulating a broader perception of their society, it helps students see the connections between key sociological concepts such as culture, socialization, norms, race, gender, and social class. As your students' sociological imagination grows, they will be able to apply these ideas to their own and others' experiences—and to their understanding of the social structure of U.S. society.

Down-to-Earth Sociology

The second theme is highlighted by a series of "Down-to-Earth Sociology" boxes, in which we explore the sociological implications of everyday life and their application to social issues. Using this feature, we consider such issues as the relationship between heredity and environment (Chapter 3), the discrimination faced by heavy people (Chapter 4), how society is being "McDonaldized" (Chapter 5), how welfare ravages the self-concept (Chapter 8), the racist mind (Chapter 9), urban fears (Chapter 14), and the main types of propaganda designed to deceive us (Chapter 15).

I have reinforced the "down-to-earth" theme throughout the text by a friendly, accessible writing style. As many years of teaching have shown me, all too often textbooks are written to appeal to the adopters of texts rather than to the students who must learn from them. Thus, a central concern in writing this book has been to present sociology in a manner that not only facilitates understanding but also shares its excitement. During the course of writing other texts, I often have

been told that my explanations and writing style are "down-to-earth," or accessible and inviting to students—so much so that I have used the phrase in the title of this text. The term is also highlighted in my introductory reader, *Down to Earth Sociology*, 9th edition (New York: Free Press, 1997).

This down-to-earth quality is also present in the chapters' opening vignettes, which invite the student into each chapter. Several of these vignettes are based on my own sociological investigations. It also shows up in the absence of unnecessary jargon, concise explanations, the use of clear and simple (but not reductive) language, and by student-relevant examples that illustrate key concepts.

Critical Thinking

The third feature, "Thinking Critically about Social Controversy," can help enliven your classroom with a vibrant exchange of ideas. These sections address pressing and often controversial social issues, such as the "Mommy Track" (Chapter 5); our tendency to conform to evil authority, as uncovered by the Milgram experiments (Chapter 5); bounties paid to kill homeless children (Chapter 7); the "deserving" versus the "undeserving" in our hotly contested welfare debate (Chapter 8); racial segregation (by choice) on college campuses (Chapter 9); and abortion as a social movement (Chapter 15).

These sections, based on controversy that either affects the student's own life or is something he or she is vitally interested in, stimulate critical thinking and lively class discussions. For a full listing of this feature, see the inside front cover.

A New Theme: Sociology and the New Technology

New to this edition is a focus on technology and society. One of the most profound social forces that we face is an accelerated rate of technological change. Today "sci fi"-like technologies are being used to aid reproduction. In just a single generation, computers have become integrated in our daily lives, online services have become common, and millions now feel an urgent need to be connected to the Internet. Such topics are explored in a new boxed feature entitled "Sociology and the New Technology." Other topics, selected both for their relevance and timeliness, include cybercommunications and the creation of electronic communities (Chapter 5), how pornography has gone high tech (Chapter 6), the dilemma of medical rationing (Chapter 10), how technology affects democracy (Chapter 11), and opposition to technology (Chapter 15).

This theme is introduced in Chapter 2, where technology is defined and presented as a major aspect of culture. The box in this chapter, "Technology and Culture—Is Technology the Cart or the Horse?" harkens back to the French sociologist Jacques Ellul's fear that technology was destroying civilization and to Marshall McLuhan's celebration of "the global village." For a complete listing of the technology boxes, see the inside front cover.

Technology is also discussed throughout the text. Examples include the implications of technology for maintaining global stratification (Chapter 7); how the consequences of technology differ by social class (Chapter 8); how technology often outpaces norms (Chapter 10); and new technologies, world peace, and Big Brother (Chapter 14). The final chapter, "Technology, Social Change, and the Environment," concludes the book with an emphasis on this new theme.

On Sources and Terms

Sociological data are found in an amazingly wide diversity of sources, and this text reflects that variety. Cited throughout this text are standard journals such as the *American Journal of Sociology*, *Social Problems*, and *Journal of Marriage and the Family*, as well as more esoteric journals such as the *Bulletin of the History of Medicine*, *Chronobiology International*, and *Western Journal of Black Studies*. I also have drawn heavily from standard news sources such as the *New York Times* and *Wall Street Journal*, as well as more unusual sources such as *El País*. In addition, I have cited numerous unpublished papers by sociologists.

The boxes are one of my favorite features. They are especially valuable for introducing the provocative and controversial materials that make sociology such a lively activity.

Finally, a note on terms. The terms First World, Second World, and Third World, although still used, are severely problematic. Even though it is unintentional, to use the term First World inevitably connotes superiority of some sort—a sort of coming in first place, with other nations in lesser, inferior positions. To substitute the terms Most Developed Countries, Less Developed Countries, and Least Developed Countries, as some do, carries the same

ethnocentric burden. These terms indicate that our economic state is superior: *We* are "developed," but *they* are not. To overcome this problem, I introduce neutrally descriptive terms: the Most Industrialized Nations, the Industrializing Nations, and the Least Industrialized Nations. These terms do not carry an ethnocentric value burden, for they indicate only that a nation's amount of industrialization is measurable and relative, without a connotation that industrialization is desirable.

Intext Learning Aids

Essentials of Sociology: A Down-to-Earth Approach includes other pedagogical aids that are especially helpful in the teaching/learning process.

Summary and Review. Each chapter closes with a question-and-answer format that highlights and reinforces the most important concepts and issues discussed in the chapter. The question-and-answer format is pedagogically superior to the traditional summary as it more effectively engages students in a thinking process.

Internet Projects. New to this edition is an in-text learning aid that reinforces the text's new technology theme, and the role the Internet is playing in social change. Two Internet projects for each chapter, titled Sociology and the Internet, written by Robert Thompson of Minot State University, guide the students into the Internet so they can learn more about major topics introduced in the chapter. You, too, might enjoy these fascinating projects.

Suggested Readings. A list of suggested readings is included for each chapter. These readings are useful for wider background reading on the chapter's topics, as well as a guide for students as they write papers. Sociological journals are also listed.

Comprehensive Glossary. A comprehensive glossary at the end of the book gathers into a single, accessible format the key terms and concepts introduced throughout the text.

Supplements to Help Your Teaching

Instructor's Manual and Test Bank. This manual, thoroughly revised for the second edition by

Gary Scott Smith, contains chapter summaries, outlines, key terms with definitions, author suggestions for interactive teaching, class discussion questions, essay questions, projects, guest speaker suggestions, and suggestions for using videos and transparencies. The Test Bank portion of the manual contains over 2,000 questions in multiple-choice, true/false, fill-in, and essay formats.

Computerized Instructor's Manual. The complete Instructor's Manual is also available on disk for Macintosh and IBM.

Test Bank. The Test Bank is available in a computerized format (Macintosh, and IBM-DOS, Windows) utilizing Allyn and Bacon Custom Test, from ESA-TEST, the best-selling, state of the art test generation software program.

Call-in Testing. Allyn and Bacon can run your tests for you and have a finished, ready-to-duplicate test on its way to you by mail or fax within 48 hours.

Transparencies. This package includes 100 color acetates featuring illustrations from both the text and from other sources. The majority of these transparencies are also found on the new *Allyn and Bacon Digital Archive for Sociology* (CD-ROM).

PowerPoint. A complete PowerPoint presentation for introductory sociology is available to adopters. Consisting of approximately 300 colorful graphic and text images, this supplement is ideal for the instructor interested in incorporating multimedia technology into his or her lectures. It is available on disk (IBM and Macintosh) and comes packaged with an informative user's guide offering details on how to use PowerPoint, including how to customize the images.

Website. Both professors and students can now enjoy access to the Allyn and Bacon web page at http://www.abacon.com and the specific site to accompany this book at http://www.abacon.com/henslin/. There is a variety of resources here, including SocLinks, a massive collection of links to sociological resources for all major subfields of sociology.

Allyn and Bacon Quick Guide to the Internet for Sociologists, 1998 edition. This handy reference acquaints users with the Internet and the World Wide Web, and provides a multitude of sociology-specific resources. Each guide comes packaged with a Sprint Internet Passport (CD-ROM), which allows one month of Internet access.

Video. Specifically designed for use with this text, this video brings current sociological issues to the classroom by focusing on issues and events directly related to text content. An accompanying Video Guide provides detailed descriptions of the video, specific tie-ins to the text, and suggested discussion questions and projects.

A&B Video Library. The Allyn and Bacon Video Library offers qualified adopters an impressive selection of videos from such sources as Films for the Humanities, and Annenberg/CPB.

CD-ROM Library. New to this edition are several fascinating CD-ROM's available to qualified adopters of this text—*Material World: A Global Family Portrait, Our Times: Multimedia Encyclopedia of the 20th Century, Faces of Conflict*, and the *Allyn and Bacon Digital Archive for Sociology.* A User's Guide provides links to the text.

Just-in-Time Publishing. Allyn and Bacon uses the newest printing and computer technology to offer you this program, whereby you have the opportunity to build your own textbook or supplements to fit your own course, choosing materials from our database, and adding your own materials.

Sociology Digital Image Archive. This exciting new CD-ROM contains hundreds of images to incorporate in multimedia presentations. It includes original images, as well as selected art from Henslin's texts and many other Allyn & Bacon sociology texts, providing a broad selection of graphs, charts, and tables to use to illustrate key sociological concepts.

College Newslink. As a subscriber to College Newslink, you receive daily e-mail delivery of customized information and unlimited access to articles that interest you.

Acknowledgments

The gratifying response to the first edition indicates that my efforts at making sociology down to earth have succeeded. The years that have gone into writing this text are a culmination of the many more years that preceded its writing—from graduate school to that equally demanding endeavor known as classroom teaching. No text, of course, comes solely from its author. Although I am responsible for the final words on the printed page, I have depended heavily on feedback from instructors who used the first edition and to earlier feedback from many sociologists. I am especially grateful to

Sandra L. Albrecht *The University of Kansas*
Kenneth Ambrose *Marshall University*
Alberto Arroyo *Baldwin-Wallace College*
Karren Baird-Olsen *Kansas State University*
Linda Barbera-Stein *The University of Illinois*
Richard D. Clark *John Carroll University*
John K. Cochran *The University of Oklahoma*
Russell L. Curtis *University of Houston*
John Darling *University of Pittsburgh-Johnstown*
Ray Darville *Stephen F. Austin State University*
Nanette J. Davis *Portland State University*
Paul Devereux *University of Nevada*
Lynda Dodgen *North Harris Community College*
James W. Dorsey *College of Lake County*
Helen R. Ebaugh *University of Houston*
Obi N. Ebbe *State University of New York-Brockport*
Margaret C. Figgins–Hill *University of Massachusetts—Lowell*
David O. Friedrichs *University of Scranton*
Norman Goodman *State University of New York-Stony Brook*
Donald W. Hastings *The University of Tennessee—Knoxville*
Michael Hoover *Missouri Western State College*
Charles E. Hurst *The College of Wooster*
Mark Kassop *Bergen Community College*
Alice Abel Kemp *University of New Orleans*
Dianna Kendall *Austin Community College*
Gary Kiger *Utah State University*
Patricia A. Larson *Cleveland State University*
Abraham Levine *El Camino Community College*

Ron Matson *Wichita State University*
Armaund L. Mauss *Washington State University*
Evelyn Mercer *Southwest Baptist University*
Robert Meyer *Arkansas State University*
W. Lawrence Neuman *University of Wisconsin—Whitewater*
Charles Norman *Indiana State University*
Laura O'Toole *University of Delaware*
Phil Piket *Joliet Junior College*
Adrian Rapp *North Harris Community College*
Howard Robboy *Trenton State College*
Walt Shirley *Sinclair Community College*
Marc Silver *Hofstra University*
Roberto E. Socas *Essex County College*
Susan Sprecher *Illinois State University*
Randolph G. Ston *Oakland Community College*
Kathleen Tiemann, *University of North Dakota*
Larry Weiss *University of Alaska*
Douglas White *Henry Ford Community College*
Stephen R. Wilson *Temple University*
Stuart Wright *Lamar University*

I also am indebted to the capable staff of Allyn and Bacon. I wish to thank Karen Hanson, who has strongly supported this project from the beginning to the present; to Dusty Davidson of The Book Company, for her capable handling of both the routine and the urgent; and to Hannah Rubenstein, who made such vital contributions to the text on which this one is based.

Since this text, then, is based on the contributions of many, I would count it a privilege if you also would share with me your teaching experiences with this book, including any suggestions for improving the text.

I wish you the very best in your teaching. It is my sincere desire that *Essentials of Sociology: A Down-to-Earth Approach* contributes to that success.

James M. Henslin
Department of Sociology
Southern Illinois University
Edwardsville, IL 62026

henslin@aol.com

Essentials of Sociology

Diana Ong, Too Many Crowds.

C H A P T E R

1

The Sociological Perspective

VEN FROM THE DIM GLOW of the faded red-and-white exit sign, its light barely reaching the upper bunk, I could see that the sheet was filthy. Resigned to another night of fitful sleep, I reluctantly crawled into bed—tucking my clothes firmly around my body like a protective cocoon.

The next morning, I joined the long line of disheveled men leaning against the chain-link fence. Their faces were as downcast as their clothes were dirty. Not a glimmer of hope among them.

No one spoke as the line slowly inched forward. When my turn came, I was handed a styrofoam cup of coffee, some utensils, and a bowl of semiliquid that I couldn't identify. It didn't look like any food I had seen before. Nor did it taste like anything I had ever eaten.

My stomach fought the foul taste, every spoonful a battle. But I was determined. "I will experience what they experience," I kept telling myself. My stomach reluctantly gave in and accepted its morning nourishment.

The room was eerily silent. Hundreds of men were eating, but each was sunk deeply into his own private hell, his head aswim with disappointment, remorse, bitterness.

As I stared at the styrofoam cup holding my solitary postbreakfast pleasure, I noticed what looked like teeth marks. I shrugged off the thought, telling myself that my long weeks as a sociological observer of the homeless were finally getting to me. "That must be some sort of crease from handling," I concluded.

I joined the silent ranks of men turning in their bowls and cups. When I saw the man behind the counter swishing out styrofoam cups in a washtub of water, I began to feel sick to my stomach. I knew then that the jagged marks on my cup really had come from a previous mouth.

How much longer did this research have to last? I felt a deep longing to return to my family—to a welcome world of clean sheets, healthy food, and "normal" conversations.

The Sociological Perspective

Why were these men so silent? Why did they receive such despicable treatment? What was I doing in that homeless shelter? After all, I hold a respectable, secure professional position, and I have a home and family.

Sociology offers a perspective, a view of the world. The sociological perspective (or imagination) opens a window onto unfamiliar worlds, and offers a fresh look at familiar worlds. In this text you will find yourself in the midst of Nazis in Germany, chimpanzees in Africa, and warriors in South America. But you will also find yourself looking at your own world in a different light. As you look at other worlds, or your own, the sociological perspective casts a light that enables you to gain a new vision of social life. In fact, this is what many find appealing about sociology.

The sociological perspective certainly has been a motivating force in my own life. Ever since I took my first introductory course in sociology, I have been enchanted by the perspective that sociology offers. I have enjoyed both observing other groups and questioning my own assumptions about life. I sincerely hope the same happens to you.

Seeing the Broader Social Context

The **sociological perspective** stresses the social contexts in which people live. It examines how these contexts influence their lives. At the center of the sociological perspective is the question of how people are influenced by their **society**—a group of people who share a culture and a territory.

To find out why people do what they do, sociologists look at **social location,** where people are located in a particular society. Sociologists consider their jobs, income, education, gender, and race. Take, for example, how growing up identified with a group called females or a group called males affects our ideas of what we should attain in life. Growing up as

4

a male or a female influences not only our aspirations, but also how we feel about ourselves and how we relate to others in dating and marriage and at work.

Sociologist C. Wright Mills (1959) put it this way: "The sociological perspective enables us to grasp the connection between history and biography." Because of its history, each society has certain broad characteristics—such as its ideas of the proper roles of men and women. By biography, Mills referred to the individual's specific experiences in society. In short, people don't do what they do because of inherited internal mechanisms, such as instincts. Rather, *external* influences—our experiences—become part of our thinking and motivations. The society in which we grow up, and our particular corners in that society, then, lie at the center of our behavior.

Consider a newborn baby. If we were to take the baby away from its U.S. parents and place that infant with a Yanomamo Indian tribe in the jungles of South America, you know that when the child begins to speak, his or her sounds will not be in English. You also know that the child will not think like an American. He or she will not grow up wanting credit cards, for example, or designer jeans, a new car, and the latest video game. Equally, the child will take his or her place in Yanomamo society—perhaps as a food gatherer, a hunter, or a warrior—and will

not even know about the world left behind at birth. And, whether male or female, that child will grow up, not debating whether to have one, two, or three children, but assuming that it is natural to want many children.

This brings us to *you*—to how your social groups have shaped your ideas and desires. Over and over in this text you will see that how you look at the world is the result of your exposure to certain groups rather than others. I think you will enjoy the process of self-discovery that sociology offers. (For an overview of the groups sociologists study, see pages 108–114.)

The Development of Sociology

Tradition versus Science

Just how did sociology begin? In some ways this is a difficult question to answer. Even ancient peoples tried to figure out social life. They, too, asked questions about why there was war, why some people became more powerful, or why some were richer. They often based their answers on superstition, myths, or even the position of the stars, however, and did not *test* their assumptions.

Science, in contrast, requires the development of theories that can be tested by systematic research. Measured by this standard, sociology only recently appeared on the human scene. It emerged about the middle of the nineteenth century, when social observers began to use scientific methods to test their ideas.

Sociology emerged out of social upheaval. The Industrial Revolution had just begun, and masses of people were moving to cities in search of work. Their ties to the land—and to a culture that provided them ready answers—were broken. The city greeted them with horrible working conditions: low pay, long, exhausting hours, dangerous work. To survive, even children had to work in these conditions. Some children were even chained to factory machines to make certain they did not run away. Life no longer looked the same, and tradition, which had provided the answers to social life, no longer could be counted on.

Tradition was to receive yet further blows. The success of the American and French revolutions encouraged people to rethink social life. The result was new ideas, such as the conviction that individuals possess inalienable rights. As this new idea caught fire, many traditional Western monarchies gave way to more democratic forms. This further upset the ready answers of tradition.

About this same time, the *scientific method*—objective, systematic observations to test theories—was being used in chemistry and physics. The result was an uncovering of secrets locked in nature. With tradition no longer holding the answers to social life, the logical step was to apply this method to the ques-

tions now being raised about the social world. The result was the birth of sociology.

Auguste Comte

This idea of applying the scientific method to the social world, known as **positivism,** was apparently first proposed by Auguste Comte (1798–1857). With the French Revolution still fresh in his mind, Comte left the small, conservative town in which he had grown up and moved to Paris. The change he himself experienced, combined with those France underwent in the revolution, led Comte to become interested in what holds society together. What brings social order, he wondered, instead of anarchy or chaos? And then, once society *does* become set on a particular course, what causes it to change?

As he considered these questions, Comte concluded that the right way to answer them was to apply the scientific method to social life. Just as this method had revealed the law of gravity, so, too, it would uncover the laws that underlie society. Comte called this new science **sociology**—"the study of society" (from the Greek *logos*, "study of," and the Latin *socius*, "companion," or "being with others"). Comte stressed that this new science not only would discover social principles but also would apply them to social reform, to making society a better place to live.

To Comte, applying the scientific method to social life apparently referred to "armchair philoso-

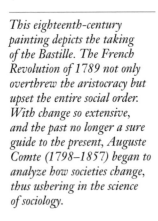

This eighteenth-century painting depicts the taking of the Bastille. The French Revolution of 1789 not only overthrew the aristocracy but upset the entire social order. With change so extensive, and the past no longer a sure guide to the present, Auguste Comte (1798–1857) began to analyze how societies change, thus ushering in the science of sociology.

phy"—drawing conclusions from informal observations of social life. He did not do what today's sociologists would call *research*, and his conclusions have been abandoned. Nevertheless, Comte's insistence that we must observe and classify human activities in order to uncover society's fundamental laws is well taken. Because he developed this idea and coined the term *sociology*, Comte is often credited with being the founder of sociology.

Herbert Spencer

Herbert Spencer (1820–1903), a native of England, is sometimes called the second founder of sociology. Unlike Comte, Spencer stood firmly against social reform. In fact, he was convinced that no one should intervene in the evolution of society. Spencer was convinced that societies evolve from lower ("barbarian") to higher ("civilized") forms. As generations pass, he said, the most capable and intelligent ("the fittest") members of the society survive, while the less capable die out. Thus, over time, societies steadily improve. Helping the lower classes interferes in this natural process. The fittest members will produce a more advanced society—unless misguided do-gooders get in the way and help the less fit survive.

Spencer called this principle "the survival of the fittest." Although Spencer coined this phrase, it usually is attributed to his contemporary, Charles Darwin, who proposed that organisms evolve over time as they adapt to their environment. Because of their similarities, Spencer's views of the evolution of societies became known as *social Darwinism*.

Like Comte, Spencer was more of a social philosopher than a sociologist. Also like Comte, Spencer did not conduct scientific studies, but simply developed ideas about society and based his conclusions on those ideas. Eventually, after gaining a wide following in England and the United States, Spencer's ideas about social Darwinism were discredited.

Karl Marx

The influence of Karl Marx (1818–1883) on world history has been so great that even that staunch advocate of capitalism, the *Wall Street Journal*, has called him one of the three greatest modern thinkers (the other two being Sigmund Freud and Albert Einstein).

Marx, who came to England after being exiled from his native Germany for proposing revolution, believed that the key to human history was **class conflict.** According to Marxist theory, the *bourgeoisie* (the controlling class of *capitalists*, those who own the means to produce wealth—capital, land, factories, and machines) are locked in inevitable conflict with the *proletariat* (the exploited class, the mass of workers who do not own the means of production). This bitter struggle can end only when members of the working class unite in revolution and throw off their chains of bondage. The result will be a classless society, one free of exploitation in which everyone will work according to their abilities and receive according to their needs (Marx and Engels 1848/1967).

Marxism is not the same as communism. Although Marx stood firmly behind revolution as the way for the proletariat to gain control of society, he did not develop the political system called *communism*, which was a later application of his ideas (and rapidly changing ones at that). Indeed, Marx himself felt disgusted when he heard debates about his insights into social life. After listening to some of the positions attributed to him, he even declared, "I am not a Marxist" (Dobriner 1969:222).

Emile Durkheim

The primary professional goal of Emile Durkheim (1858–1917), who grew up in France, was to get sociology recognized as a separate academic discipline. Up to this time, sociology was viewed as part of history and economics. Durkheim achieved this goal when he received the first academic appointment in sociology, at the University of Bordeaux in 1887 (Coser 1977).

Another of Durkheim's goals was to show how social forces affect people's behavior. To do so, he did rigorous research. In a study still quoted today, he compared the suicide rates of several European countries. He (1897/1966) found that each country's suicide rate was different and that it remained remarkably stable year after year. He also found that different groups within a country had different suicide rates. For example, Protestants, males, and the unmarried killed themselves at a higher rate than did Catholics, Jews, females, and the married. From this, Durkheim drew the highly insightful conclusion that suicide is not simply a matter of individuals

Auguste Comte (1798–1857), who is identified as the founder of sociology, began to analyze the bases of the social order. Although he stressed that the scientific method should be applied to the study of society, he did not apply it himself.

Karl Marx (1818–1883) believed that the roots of human misery lay in the exploitation of the proletariat, or propertyless working classes, by the capitalist class, those who own the means of production. Social change, in the form of the overthrow of the capitalists by the proletariat, was inevitable from Marx's perspective. Although Marx did not consider himself a sociologist, his ideas have profoundly influenced many in the discipline, particularly conflict theorists.

The French sociologist Emile Durkheim (1858-1917) contributed many important concepts to sociology. His systematic study comparing suicide rates among several countries revealed an underlying social factor: People are more likely to commit suicide if their ties to others in their communities are weak. Durkheim's identification of the key role of social integration in social life remains central to sociology today.

here and there deciding to take their lives for personal reasons. Rather, *social factors underlie suicide,* and this is what keeps those rates fairly constant year after year.

Durkheim identified **social integration,** the degree to which people are tied to their social group, as a key social factor in suicide. He concluded that people with weaker social ties are more likely to commit suicide. This factor, he said, explained why Protestants, males, and the unmarried have higher suicide rates. It works this way, Durkheim argued: Protestantism encourages greater freedom of thought and action, males are more independent than females, and the unmarried lack the ties and responsibilities of marriage. In other words, because their social integration is weaker, people in these groups have fewer social ties that keep them from committing suicide.

A hundred years later, Durkheim's work is still quoted. His research was so thorough that the prin-ciple he uncovered still applies: People who are less socially integrated have higher rates of suicide. Even today, those same categories of people that Durkheim identified—Protestants, males, and the unmarried—are still more likely to kill themselves.

Like Comte, Durkheim (1893/1933) also proposed that sociologists intervene in society. He suggested that new social groups be created. Standing somewhere between the state and the family, those groups would help meet people's need for a sense of belonging. Central to all of Durkheim's studies was the idea that human behavior cannot be understood simply in individualistic terms, that it must be understood within its larger social context.

Max Weber

Max Weber (Mahx VAY-ber) (1864–1920), a German sociologist and a contemporary of Durkheim, also held professorships in the new academic disci-

Max Weber (1864–1920) was another early sociologist who left a profound impression on sociology. He used cross-cultural and historical materials in order to trace the causes of social change and to determine how extensively social groups affect people's orientations to life.

pline of sociology. He was a renowned scholar who, like Marx, wrote in several academic fields. Weber agreed with much of what Marx wrote, but he strongly disagreed with Marx's claim that economics is the central force in social change. That role, he said, belongs to religion. Weber (1904/1958) theorized that the Roman Catholic belief system encouraged Roman Catholics to hold onto traditional ways of life, while the belief system of Protestantism encouraged its members to embrace change.

To test his theory, Weber compared the extent of capitalism in Roman Catholic and Protestant countries. He concluded that because Protestantism (specifically, Calvinism) encouraged people to work hard and to save and invest money, it was the central factor in the rise of capitalism. This conclusion was controversial when Weber made it, and it continues to be debated today (Zou 1994).

◤ Sexism and Early Sociology

Attitudes of the Time

As you may have noticed, we have discussed only men sociologists. In the 1800s, sex roles were rigidly defined, with women assigned the roles of wife and mother. In the classic German phrase, women were expected to devote themselves to the four *K*'s: *Kirche, Küchen, Kinder,* and *Kleider* (church, cooking, children, and clothes). To try to break out of this mold brought severe social disapproval.

Few people, either men or women, received any education beyond basic reading and writing. Higher education, rare at that time, was reserved for men. A handful of women from wealthy families, however, did pursue higher education. A few even managed to study sociology, although deeply entrenched sexism in the university stopped them from obtaining advanced degrees or becoming professors. In line with the times, their research was almost entirely ignored.

Harriet Martineau

Harriet Martineau (1802–1876) is a classic example of this situation. Born into a wealthy English family, she had opportunities that few women—or men—had. When Martineau first began to analyze social life, she would hide her writing beneath her sewing when visitors arrived, for *writing was "masculine" and sewing "feminine"* (Gilman 1911:88). Martineau persisted in her interests, however, and she eventually studied social life in both Great Britain and the United States. In 1837, two or three decades before Durkheim and Weber were born, Martineau published *Society in America,* in which she reported on this new nation's customs—family, race, gender, politics,

Interested in social reform, Harriet Martineau (1802–1876) turned to sociology, where she discovered the writings of Comte. An active advocate for the abolition of slavery, she traveled widely and wrote extensively.

and religion. In spite of her insightful examination of U.S. life, which is still worth reading today, Martineau's research met the fate of that of other early women sociologists and, until recently, has been ignored. Instead, she is primarily known for translating Comte's ideas into English.

Sociology in North America

Early History

Transplanted to U.S. soil in the late nineteenth century, sociology first took root at the University of Kansas, University of Chicago, and Atlanta University, then an all-black school. At first, U.S. sociology was dominated by the department at the University of Chicago, founded by Albion Small (1854–1926), who also founded the *American Journal of Sociology* and was its editor from 1895 to 1925. Members of this first sociology department whose ideas continue to influence today's sociologists include Robert Park (1864–1944), Ernest Burgess (1886–1966), and George Herbert Mead (1863–1931), who developed the symbolic interactionist perspective to be examined later.

The Tension between Social Reform and Sociological Analysis

While many North American sociologists combined the role of sociologist with that of social reformer, few were so active as Jane Addams (1860–1935), who founded Hull-House in Chicago in 1889. She came from a privileged background and attended The Women's Medical College of Philadelphia, dropping out due to illness. On one of her many trips to Europe, Addams was impressed with work being done on behalf of London's poor. From then on, she tirelessly worked for social justice, concentrating on housing, education, and the working conditions of the poor, especially immigrants. Hull-House, located in the midst of Chicago's slums, was open to people who needed refuge—immigrants, the sick, the aged, the poor. Sociologists from the nearby University of Chicago were frequent visitors at Hull-House. With her piercing insights into the exploitation of workers and how peasant immigrants adjust to city life, Addams strived to bridge the gap between the powerful and powerless. Her efforts at social reform were so outstanding that in 1931 she was a co-winner of the Nobel Peace Prize (Addams 1910/1981).

Jane Addams, 1860–1935, a recipient of the Nobel Peace Prize, tirelessly worked on behalf of poor immigrants. With Ellen G. Starr, she founded Hull-House, a center to help immigrants in Chicago. She was also a leader in women's rights (women suffrage) and in the peace movement.

Another sociologist who combined sociology and social reform is W. E. B. Du Bois (1868–1963), an African American who completed his education at the University of Berlin. Coming to Atlanta University in 1897, his lifetime research interest was relations between whites and African Americans. He published a book on this subject every year between

W(illiam) E(dward) B(urghardt) Du Bois (1868–1963) spent his lifetime studying relations between African Americans and whites. Like many early North American sociologists, Du Bois combined the role of academic sociologist with that of social reformer. He was also the editor of Crisis, *an influential journal of the time.*

Early North American Sociology: Du Bois and Race Relations

THE WORKS OF W. E. B. Du Bois, who expressed sociological thought more like an accomplished novelist than a sociologist, have been neglected in sociology. To help remedy this omission, I reprint the following excerpts from pages 66–68 of *The Souls of Black Folk* (1903). In this book, Du Bois analyzes changes that occurred in the social and economic conditions of African Americans during the thirty years following the Civil War. For two summers, while he was a student at Fisk, Du Bois taught in a log-hut, segregated school "way back in the hills" of rural Tennessee. The following excerpts help us understand conditions at the turn of the last century.

It was a hot morning late in July when the school opened. I trembled when I heard the patter of little feet down the dusty road, and saw the growing row of dark solemn faces and bright eager eyes facing me. . . . There they sat, nearly thirty of them, on the rough benches, their faces shading from a pale cream to deep brown, the little feet bare and swinging, the eyes full of expectation, with here and there a twinkle of mischief, and the hands grasping Webster's blue-black spelling-book. I loved my school, and the fine faith the children had in the wisdom of their teacher was truly marvelous. We read and spelled together, wrote a little, picked flowers, sang, and listened to stories of the world beyond the hill. . . . On Friday nights I often went home with some of the children,—

sometimes to Doc Burke's farm. He was a great, loud, thin Black, ever working, and trying to buy the seventy-five acres of hill and dale where he lived; but people said that he would surely fail and the "white folks would get it all." His wife was a magnificent Amazon, with saffron face and shiny hair, uncorseted and barefooted, and the children were strong and barefooted. They lived in a one-and-a-half-room cabin in the hollow of the farm near the spring. . . .

I liked to stay with the Dowells, for they had four rooms and plenty of good country fare. Uncle Bird had a small, rough farm, all woods and hills, miles from the big road; but he was full of tales,—he preached now and then,—and with his children, berries, horses, and wheat he was happy and prosperous. Often, to keep the peace, I must go where life was less lovely; for instance, 'Tildy's mother was incorrigibly dirty, Reuben's larder was limited seriously, and herds of untamed insects wandered over the Eddingses' beds. Best of all I loved to go to Josie's, and sit on the porch, eating peaches, while the mother bustled and talked: how Josie had bought the sewing-machine; how Josie worked at service in winter; but that four dollars a month was "mighty little" wages; how Josie longed to go away to school, but that it "looked like" they never could get far enough ahead to let her; how the crops failed and the well was yet unfinished; and, finally, how "mean" some of the white folks were.

For two summers I lived in this little world. . . . I have called my tiny community a world, and so its isolation made it; and yet there was among us

but a half-awakened common consciousness, sprung from common joy and grief, at burial, birth, or wedding; from common hardship in poverty, poor land, and low wages, and, above all, from the sight of the Veil* that hung between us and Opportunity. All this caused us to think some thoughts together; but these, when ripe for speech, were spoken in various languages. Those whose eyes twenty-five and more years had seen "the glory of the coming of the Lord," saw in every present hindrance or help a dark fatalism bound to bring all things right in His own good time. The mass of those to whom slavery was a dim recollection of childhood found the world a puzzling thing: it asked little of them, and they answered with little, and yet it ridiculed their offering. Such a paradox they could not understand, and therefore sank into listless indifference, or shiftlessness, or reckless bravado. There were, however, some—such as Josie, Jim, and Ben—to whom War, Hell, and Slavery were but childhood tales, whose young appetites had been whetted to an edge by school and story and half-awakened thought. Ill could they be content, born without and beyond the World. And their weak wings beat against their barriers,— barriers of caste, of youth, of life; at last, in dangerous moments, against everything that opposed even a whim.

*"The Veil" is shorthand for the Veil of Race, referring to how race colors all human relations. Du Bois's hope was that "sometime, somewhere, men will judge men by their souls and not by their skins" (p. 261).

1896 and 1914. The Down-to-Earth Sociology box above is taken from one of his books.

At first, Du Bois was content to collect and interpret objective data. Later, frustrated at the continuing exploitation of blacks, Du Bois turned to social action and helped found the National Association for the Ad-

vancement of Colored People (NAACP). Continuing to battle racism both as a sociologist and as a journalist, he finally embraced revolutionary Marxism. Dismayed that so little improvement had been made in race relations, when he was 93 he moved to Ghana, where he is buried (Du Bois 1968; Broderick 1974).

In the 1800s, poverty was widespread in the United States. Most people were so poor that they expended their life energies on just getting enough food, fuel, and clothing to survive. Formal education beyond the first several grades was a luxury. This photo depicts the conditions of the people Du Bois worked with.

During the 1940s, the emphasis shifted from social reform to social theory. Talcott Parsons (1902–1979), for example, developed abstract models of society that exerted great influence on sociology. These detailed models of how the parts of society harmoniously work together did nothing to stimulate social activism.

C. Wright Mills (1916–1962) deplored the theoretical abstractions of this period, which he said were accompanied by empty research methods. Mills (1956) urged sociologists to get back to social reform, seeing imminent danger to freedom in the coalescing of interests of a group he called the *power elite*—the top leaders of business, politics, and the military. After his death, the turbulence in U.S. society in the 1960s and 1970s, fueled by the Vietnam War, also disturbed U.S. sociology. As interest in social activism revived, Mills's ideas became popular among a new generation of sociologists.

This tension between analyzing society and working toward its reform remains today. Some sociologists believe that their proper role is to analyze some aspect of society and to publish their findings in sociology journals. Others say that this is not enough, that sociologists have an obligation to use their expertise to try to make society a better place in which to live.

Applied Sociology

Sociology has recently developed a blending of sociological knowledge and practical results, known as **applied sociology.** This term refers to the use of sociology to solve problems. Applied sociologists may make recommendations on how to solve problems in the workplace, or they may investigate pornography, rape, environmental pollution, or the spread of AIDS. To better understand applied sociology, see the Down-to-Earth Sociology box on page 13.

Some sociologists not only make recommendations for change, but they also become directly involved in trying to solve problems. This type of applied sociology is called **clinical sociology.** Clinical sociologists who do research in an office or factory, for example, may try to change work conditions to reduce job turnover. Other clinical sociologists work with drug addicts, ex-convicts, and runaway youths.

Applied sociology, however, is not the same as social reform. For the most part, it is an application of sociology in some specific setting, not an attempt

▼▲▼▲▼▲▼▲▼▲▼▲▼▲▼▲▼▲▼▲▼▲▼▲▼▲▼▲▼▲▼

Down-to-Earth Sociology

Sociologists at Work: What Applied Sociologists Do

APPLIED SOCIOLOGISTS WORK in a wide variety of settings—from counseling children to improving work relationships. To give you an idea of that variety, let's look over the shoulders of three sociologists.

Leslie Green, who does marketing research at Vanderveer Group in Philadelphia, Pennsylvania, earned her bachelor's degree in sociology at Shippensburg University. To develop marketing strategies so doctors will choose to prescribe a particular drug, her company has physicians meet in groups to discuss prescription drugs. Green sets up the meetings, locates moderators for the discussion groups, and arranges payments to the physicians who participate in the research. "My training in sociology," she says, "helps me in 'people skills.' It helps me to understand the needs of different groups, and to interact with them."

Laurie Banks, who received her master's degree in sociology from Fordham University, works for the New York City Health Department, where she analyzes vital statistics. By examining death certificates, she identified high- and low-cancer areas in the city. She found that a Polish neighborhood had high rates of stomach cancer. Follow-up interviews by the Centers for Disease Control traced the cause to eating large amounts of sausage. In another case, Banks compared birth certificates and school records and found that problems at birth— low birth weight, lack of prenatal care, and birth complications— were linked to low reading skills and behavior problems in school.

Ross Cappell, whose doctorate is from Temple University, runs his own research company, Social Research Corporation, in Philadelphia. His work, too, is filled with variety—from surveying the customers of a credit card company so the company can understand its market, to analyzing the impact of fare increases in public transportation. In one case, Cappell was asked to evaluate the services that unemployed workers received when a steel mill closed down. He found that the services and training were not particularly helpful. Too many workers were retrained in a single field, such as air conditioner repair, and the local market was flooded with more specialists than it could use. When Cappell testified before Congress, he recommended that the training given to displaced workers match the needs of the local labor market.

From just this small sample, you can catch a glimpse of the variety of work that applied sociologists do. You can see that some applied sociologists work for corporations, some work for government and private agencies, and others operate their own firms. You also can see that a doctorate is not necessary to work as an applied sociologist.

---

to rebuild society, as early sociologists envisioned. Clinical sociology has taken contemporary sociology closer to its roots, however, and a new vision may yet emerge of the role of sociology in bringing about social change.

Theoretical Perspectives in Sociology

Facts never interpret themselves. People interpret what they observe by placing their observations into a framework of some sort. That conceptual framework is called a *theory*. A **theory** is a general statement about how some parts of the world fit together and how they work. It is an explanation of how two or more facts are related to one another. By providing a framework in which to fit observations, each theory interprets reality in some way.

Sociologists use three major theories: symbolic interactionism, functional analysis, and conflict theory. Let's first examine the main elements of these theories. Then let's see how each theory helps us understand why the divorce rate in the United States is so high.

Symbolic Interactionism

We can trace the origins of **symbolic interactionism** to the Scottish moral philosophers of the eighteenth century, who noted that people evaluate their own conduct by comparing themselves with others (Stryker 1990). This perspective was brought into sociology by sociologists Charles Horton Cooley (1864–1929), William I. Thomas (1863–1947), and George Herbert Mead (1863–1931).

Symbolic interactionists stress that *symbols*— things to which we attach meaning—make social life possible. What do they mean by this? First, without symbols we would be limited to a simple animal existence. Strange as it may seem, for example, without symbols we would not have brothers, sisters, or parents in any sense that we now know them. That is, these symbols tell us that we are "related" to other people, and because of this we "owe" them certain "obligations" and, in return, can expect designated "privileges." So it is with the symbols of boss, teacher, neighbor, friend, and so on. Second, without symbols we could not coordinate our actions with those of others. We would be unable to make plans for a future date, time, and place. Unable to specify times, materi-

als, sizes, or goals, we could not build bridges and highways. Without symbols, there would be no books, movies, or musical instruments. We would have no schools or hospitals, no government, no religion.

Symbolic interactionists also point out that even the *self* is a symbol, for it consists of the ideas we have about who we are. And it is a changing symbol, for as we interact with others we constantly adjust our views of the self based on how we interpret the reactions of others.

In short, symbolic interactionists analyze how symbols—such as our definitions of ourselves and others—underlie our behavior. For example, if you think of someone as an aunt or uncle, you behave in a certain way, but if you think of that person as a boyfriend or girlfriend you behave quite differently. In a sense, then, we are different persons as we change our behaviors to match people's expectations. It is as though we are on a stage, switching roles to suit our audiences. Symbolic interactionists primarily examine face-to-face interaction, looking at how people work out their relationships and make sense out of life and their place in it.

Applying Symbolic Interactionism To explain why the U.S. divorce rate increased (see Figure 1.1 on page 15), symbolic interactionists look at how changing symbols change people's expectations and behavior. They note that until the early part of this century, people thought of marriage as sacred and divorce as evil. To divorce was to abandon adult responsibilities, to break a lifelong commitment. Divorce was seen as immoral and a flagrant disregard for public opinion.

Then, slowly, came a change in the meaning of marriage. In 1933, sociologist William Ogburn observed that personality was becoming more important in mate selection. In 1945, sociologists Ernest Burgess and Harvey Locke noted the growing importance of mutual affection, understanding, and compatibility. These trends have changed marriage from lifelong commitment based on duty and obligation to an often temporary arrangement based on feelings of intimacy.

Changes in the meanings of divorce also encouraged the breakup of marriages. From a symbol of everything despicable, divorce has been transformed into an indication of freedom and new beginnings. This new meaning has shattered what had been a strong barrier to breaking up a marriage.

George Herbert Mead (1863–1931) is one of the founders of symbolic interactionism, a major theoretical perspective in sociology. He taught at the University of Chicago, where his lectures were very popular. Though he wrote very little, after his death his students compiled his lectures into an influential book, Mind, Self, and Society.

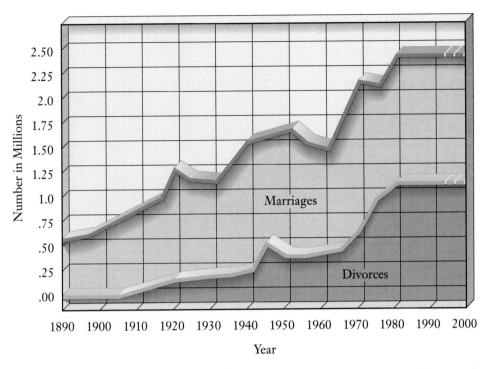

Source: For 1995, "Population Update" 1996; for 1950–1990, *Statistical Abstract 1994:* Table 146; and 1996: Table 146; earlier editions for earlier years. The broken lines indicate the author's estimates.

FIGURE 1.1

U.S. Marriage, U.S. Divorce

Symbolic interactionists also note that a variety of related symbols has changed—and that none of the changes strengthens marriage. An example is marital roles, what is expected of a husband or wife. Previously, due to tradition, each knew what was expected, but today the matter is confusing. As they work out their own arrangements, trying to balance conflicting expectations, many flounder in the process. Similarly, the meaning of children has changed. Parents used to have little responsibility beyond providing food, clothing, shelter, and moral guidance—and children began contributing to the family income early in life. Today's parents have much greater responsibility much longer, for children are now thought of as being more vulnerable, and needing to depend on their parents even into their twenties. These changed ideas place greater burdens on parents, and, with it, more strain on marriage.

Symbolic interactionists, then, look for how changes in people's ideas have put pressure on today's married couples. No single change is *the* cause of a higher divorce rate, but taken together these changes provide a strong "push" toward divorce.

Functional Analysis

The central idea of **functional analysis** is that society is a whole unit, made up of interrelated parts that work together. Functional analysis, also known as *functionalism* and *structural functionalism*, is rooted in the origins of sociology (Turner 1978). Auguste Comte and Herbert Spencer viewed society as a kind of living organism. Just as a biological organism has tissues and organs that function together, they wrote, so does society. Like an organism, if society is to function smoothly, its various parts must work together in harmony.

Emile Durkheim also saw society as composed of many parts, each with its own function. When all the parts of society fulfill their functions, society is in a "normal" state. If they do not fulfill their functions, society is in an "abnormal" or "pathological" state. To understand society, then, functionalists say we need to examine both *structure* (how the parts of a society fit together to make the whole) and *function* (how each part contributes to society).

Although Robert Merton dismissed the organic analogy, he continued the essence of functionalism—the image of society as a whole composed of interrelated parts. Merton used the term *functions* to refer to the beneficial consequences of people's actions that help keep a group (society, social system) in equilibrium. In contrast, *dysfunctions* are consequences that undermine a system's equilibrium.

Functions can be either manifest or latent. If an action is intended to help some part of a system, it is a *manifest function.* For example, suppose that the government is worried about our slowing rate of child birth. It offers a $10,000 bonus for every child born to a married couple. The intention, or manifest function, of the bonus is to increase childbearing. Merton pointed out that people's actions also can have *latent functions*, unintended consequences that help a system adjust. Let's suppose that the bonus works, that the birth rate jumps. As a result, the sale of diapers and baby furniture booms. Because the benefits to these businesses were unintended, they are latent functions of the bonus.

Of course, human actions can also hurt a system. Because such consequences usually are unintended, Merton called them *latent dysfunctions.* Let's assume that the government has failed to put a stopping point on its bonus system. To collect the bonus, some people keep on having children. The more they have, however, the more they need the next bonus to survive. Large families become common, and poverty increases. The welfare bill skyrockets, taxes jump, and the nation erupts in protest. Because these results were not intended, and actually harmed the social system, they represent latent dysfunctions of the bonus program.

Applying Functional Analysis Now that the basic terms are clear, let's see how functional analysis explains the U.S. divorce rate. Functionalists stress that industrialization and urbanization undermined the traditional functions of the family. For example, prior to industrialization the family was a sort of economic team. On the farm, for example, each family member had jobs or "chores" to do. The wife

Sociologists who use the functionalist perspective stress how industrialization and urbanization undermined the traditional functions of the family. Before industrialization, members of the family worked together as an economic unit. As production moved away from the home, it took with it first the father, and more recently the mother. One consequence is a major dysfunction, the weakening of family ties.

was in charge not only of tasks within the house, but also of small animals such as chickens. Milk, eggs, and butter were also her responsibility, as well as cooking, baking, sewing, washing, and cleaning. Female children helped her. The husband was responsible for large animals, such as horses and cattle, for planting and harvesting, and for building and tool maintenance. Male children helped him. *Together* they formed an economic unit in which each depended on the others for survival.

The functions that bonded members to one another also included educating the children, home-based recreation, and care of the sick and elderly. To see how sharply family functions have changed, look at this example:

> When Phil became sick, he was nursed by Ann, his wife. She cooked for him, fed him, changed the bed linen, bathed him, read to him from the Bible, and gave him his medicine. (She did this in addition to doing the housework and taking care of their six children.) Phil was also surrounded by the children, who shouldered some of his chores while he was sick.
>
> When Phil died, the male neighbors and relatives made the casket while Ann, her mother, and female friends washed and dressed the body. Phil was then "laid out" in the front parlor (the formal living room), where friends, neighbors, and relatives paid their last respects. From there, friends moved his body to the church for the final message, and then to the grave they themselves had dug.

As you can see, the family used to have more functions. They even included many aspects of life and death that we assign to outside agencies. Similarly, economic production is no longer a cooperative, home-based matter, where husbands and wives depend on one another for their interlocking contributions to a mutual endeavor. Today, in contrast, husbands and wives earn paychecks, often part of an impersonal, multinational, and even global system. For functions to be taken over by outside agencies is to weaken the "ties that bind," with higher divorce the consequence.

Conflict Theory

Conflict theory provides a third and sharply different perspective on social life. Unlike the functionalists who view society as a harmonious whole, with its parts working together, conflict theorists see society as composed of groups fiercely competing for scarce resources. Although alliances or cooperation may prevail on the surface, beneath that surface is a struggle for power.

Karl Marx, the founder of conflict theory, witnessed the Industrial Revolution that transformed Europe. He saw that peasants who had left the land to seek work in cities had to work at wages that barely gave them enough to eat. Shocked by the suffering and exploitation he witnessed, Marx began to analyze society and history. As he did so, he developed **conflict theory,** concluding that the key to human history is class struggle. In each society, some small group controls the means of production and exploits those who do not. In industrialized societies the struggle is between the *bourgeoisie*, the small group of capitalists who own the means to produce wealth, and the *proletariat*, the mass of workers exploited by the bourgeoisie.

When Marx made his observations, capitalism was in its infancy, and workers were at the mercy of their employers. Workers had none of what we take for granted today—the right to strike, minimum wages, eight-hour days, coffee breaks, five-day work weeks, paid vacations and holidays, medical benefits, sick leave, unemployment compensation, Social Security. Marx's analysis reminds us that these benefits came not from generous hearts, but by workers forcing concessions from their employers.

Some current conflict sociologists use conflict theory in a much broader sense. Ralf Dahrendorf (b. 1929) sees conflict as inherent in all relations that have authority. He points out that **authority,** or power that people consider legitimate, runs through all layers of society—whether small groups, a community, or the entire society. People in positions of authority try to enforce conformity, which in turn creates resentment and resistance. The result is a constant struggle throughout society to determine who has authority over what (Turner 1978).

Another sociologist, Lewis Coser (b. 1913), pointed out that conflict is especially likely to develop among people who are in close relationships. Such people are connected by a network of responsibilities, power, and rewards, and to change something can easily upset arrangements that they have so carefully worked out. Consequently, we can think even of close relationships as a balancing act—of maintaining and reworking a particular distribution of responsibilities, power, and rewards.

Applying Conflict Theory To explain the current high rate of divorce, conflict theorists stress that for millennia men exploited women, but that today male–female relationships are undergoing fundamental change. Unlike in agrarian societies, industrialization has made it easier to meet basic survival needs outside marriage. It also has fostered a culture in which females participate in social worlds beyond the home. Consequently, today's women refuse to bear burdens their grandmothers accepted as inevitable, and now are much more likely to dissolve a marriage that becomes intolerable.

In short, the traditional imbalance of power between men and women has been upset as women have gained power, especially through the paycheck. One consequence is higher divorce as wives attempt to resolve basic inequalities and husbands resist those efforts. From the conflict perspective, then, the increase in divorce is not a sign that marriage has weakened, but, rather, an indication that women are making headway in their historical struggle with men.

Levels of Analysis: Macro and Micro

A major difference among these three theoretical perspectives is their level of analysis (see Table 1.1). Functionalists and conflict theorists focus on the **macro level;** that is, they examine large-scale patterns of society. In contrast, symbolic interactionists focus on the **micro level,** on **social interaction,** or on what people do when they are in one another's presence.

Let's return to the example of homelessness to make this distinction between micro and macro levels clearer. In studying homeless people, symbolic interactionists would focus on the micro level. They would analyze what homeless people do when they are in shelters and on the streets. They also would analyze their communications, both their talk and their **nonverbal interactions** (how they communicate by gestures, silence, use of space, and so on). The observations that I made at the beginning of this chapter about the despair and silence in the homeless shelter, for example, would be of interest to symbolic interactionists.

This micro level, however, would not interest functionalists and conflict theorists. They would focus instead on the macro level. Functionalists would examine how changes in society have increased homelessness. They might look at how changes in the family (smaller, more divorce) and economic conditions (higher rents, fewer unskilled jobs, loss of jobs overseas) cause homelessness among people who are unable to find jobs and do not have a family to fall back on. For their part, conflict theorists would emphasize the struggle between social classes, especially how the policies of the wealthy push certain groups into unemployment and homelessness. That, they would point out, accounts for the disproportionate number of African Americans who are homeless.

Table 1.1

Major Theoretical Perspectives in Sociology

Perspective	Usual Level of Analysis	Focus of Analysis	Key Terms	Applying the Perspectives to the U.S. Divorce Rate
Symbolic Interactionism	Microsociological—examines small-scale patterns of social interaction	Face-to-face interaction; how people use symbols to create social life	Symbols Interaction Meanings Definitions	Industrialization and urbanization lead to a redefinition of love, marriage, children, and divorce
Functional Analysis (also called functionalism and structural functionalism)	Macrosociological—examines large-scale patterns of society	Relationships among the parts of society; how these parts are *functional* (have beneficial consequences) or *dysfunctional* (have negative consequences)	Structure Functions (manifest and latent) Dysfunctions Equilibrium	As social change erodes the traditional functions of the family, family ties are weakened and the divorce rate increases
Conflict Theory	Macrosociological—examines large-scale patterns of society	The struggle for scarce resources by groups in a society; how dominant elites use power to control the less powerful	Inequality Power Conflict Competition Exploitation	When men control economic life, the divorce rate is low because women find few alternatives to a bad marriage; the rising divorce rate reflects a shifting balance of power between men and women

Putting the Theoretical Perspectives Together

Which theoretical perspective should we use to study human behavior? Which level of analysis is the correct one? As you have seen, these theoretical perspectives provide contrasting pictures of human life. In the case of divorce, those interpretations are quite different from the commonsense understanding of "They were incompatible." Because no theory or level of analysis encompasses all of reality, it is necessary to use all three theoretical lenses to analyze human behavior. By putting their contributions together, we gain a more comprehensive picture of social life.

Sociology and Common Sense

Around the globe, people make assumptions about the way the world "is." *Common sense*, these things that "Everyone knows are true," may or may not be true, however. It takes research to find out. To test your own "common sense," read the Down-to-Earth Sociology box below.

Before we look at how sociologists do research, consider Renée, who was raped on a dark country road. She won't even talk about that night, and common sense tells us that her rape has ongoing effects, that it can trigger fears and anxieties, and that it can make women distrust men. These commonsense notions are substantiated by research.

But common sense also tells some people that one reason men rape is women's revealing clothing. Research, however, shows that men who rape don't care what a woman wears. (Most men who rape don't even care who the woman is; she is simply an object to satisfy their sexual lust and drive for power.) Common sense tells others that men who rape are sexually deprived. And some rapists are sexually deprived, but others are not—the same as men who do not rape. Many rapists, in fact, have a wife or girlfriend with whom they have an ongoing sexual relationship.

Down-to-Earth Sociology

Enjoying a Sociology Quiz— Sociological Findings versus Common Sense

SOME FINDINGS OF SOCIOLOGY support commonsense understandings of social life, while others contradict them. Can you tell the difference? If you want to enjoy this quiz fully, before looking at the next page to check your answers complete *all* the questions.

1. *True/False* The earnings of U.S. women have just about caught up with those of U.S. men.

2. *True/False* When faced with natural disasters such as floods and earthquakes, people panic and social organization disintegrates.

3. *True/False* Revolutions are more likely to occur when conditions are consistently bad than when they are improving.

4. *True/False* Most people on welfare are lazy and looking for a handout. They could work if they wanted to.

5. *True/False* Compared with men, women touch each other more while they are conversing.

6. *True/False* Compared with women, men maintain more eye contact while they are conversing.

7. *True/False* The more available alcohol is (as measured by the number of places to purchase alcohol per one hundred people), the more alcohol-related injuries and fatalities occur on U.S. highways.

8. *True/False* Couples who live together before marriage are usually more satisfied with their marriages than couples who do not live together before marriage.

9. *True/False* The reason why people discriminate against minorities is prejudice; unprejudiced people don't discriminate.

10. *True/False* African Americans in the South are more likely to live in segregated housing than are African Americans in the North.

▲▼▲▼▲▼▲▼▲▼▲▼▲▼▲▼▲▼▲▼▲▼▲▼▲▼▲▼▲▼

Down-to-Earth Sociology

Sociological Findings versus Common Sense—
Answers to the Sociology Quiz

1. *False* Over the years, the income gap has narrowed, but only slightly. On average, full-time working women earn only about 65 percent of what full-time working men earn; this low figure is actually an improvement, for in the 1970s women's incomes averaged about 60 percent of men's.

2. *False* Following such disasters, people develop greater cohesion, cooperation, and social organization to deal with the catastrophe.

3. *False* Just the opposite is true. When conditions are consistently bad, people are more likely to be resigned to their fate. Rapid improvement causes their aspirations to outrace their circumstances, which can increase frustrations and foment revolution.

4. *False* Most people on welfare are children, the old, the sick,

the mentally and physically handicapped, or young mothers with few skills. Less than 2 percent meet the common stereotype of an able-bodied man—and many of these are actively looking for jobs.

5. *False* Men touch each other more during conversations (Henley et al. 1985; Whyte 1989).

6. *False* Female speakers maintain considerably more eye contact (Henley et al. 1985).

7. *False* In California, researchers compared the number of alcohol outlets per population with the alcohol-related highway injuries and fatalities. They found that counties in which alcohol is more readily available do not have more alcohol-related injuries and fatalities (Kohfeld and Leip 1991).

8. *False* The opposite is true. The reason, researchers suggest, is that many couples who marry after cohabiting are less committed to marriage in the first place—and a key to marital success is firm commitment to one another (Larson 1988).

9. *False* When racial discrimination was legal in the United States, sociologists found that due to business reasons and peer pressure some unprejudiced people did discriminate (LaPiere 1934). For these same reasons, some prejudiced people do not discriminate, although they want to.

10. *False* Although racial segregation in housing is high in the South, it is higher in the North. This is true of all income levels (Massey and Denton 1993).

If neither provocative clothing nor sexual deprivation is the underlying cause of rape, then what is? This brings us to the need to move beyond common sense and conduct sociological research. To explain how sociologists do their research, we shall continue with the example of rape.

▲ A Research Model   — not on test * Project *

As shown in Figure 1.2 on the next page, scientific research follows eight basic steps. This is an ideal model, however, and in the real world of research some of these steps may be collapsed or even omitted.

1 *Selecting a topic.* First, what do you want to know more about? In this case, it will be rape.

2 *Defining the problem.* Second, you must narrow the topic, focusing on a specific area or problem. For example, you may want to know why men rape, or what can be done to reduce rape.

3 *Reviewing the literature.* Third, you must review the literature to see what is already known about the problem.

4 *Formulating a hypothesis.* The fourth step is to formulate a *hypothesis*, a statement of what you expect to find according to predictions from a theory. A hypothesis predicts a relationship between or among *variables*, factors that change, or vary, from one person or situation to another. For example, the statement "Men who are more socially isolated are more likely to rape than are men who are more socially integrated" is a hy-

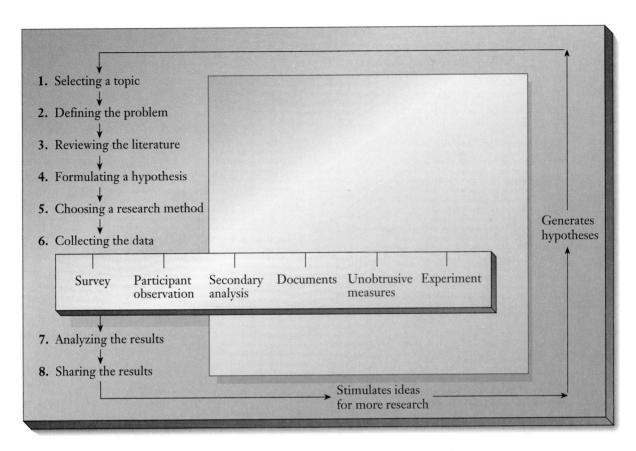

1. Selecting a topic
2. Defining the problem
3. Reviewing the literature
4. Formulating a hypothesis
5. Choosing a research method
6. Collecting the data

Survey | Participant observation | Secondary analysis | Documents | Unobtrusive measures | Experiment

Generates hypotheses

7. Analyzing the results
8. Sharing the results

Stimulates ideas for more research

Source: Modification of Schaefer 1989: Fig. 2–2.

FIGURE 1.2

The Research Model

pothesis. Your hypothesis will need *operational definitions*, that is, precise ways to measure the variables. In this example, you would need operational definitions for three variables: social isolation, social integration, and rape.

5 *Choosing a research method.* The means by which sociologists collect data are called *research methods.* Sociologists use six basic research methods, outlined in the next section. You will want to choose the method that will best answer your particular questions.

6 *Collecting the data.* When you gather your data, you will have to take great care to assure their *validity;* that is, your operational definitions must measure what they are intended to measure. In this case, you must be certain that you really are measuring social isolation, social integration, and

rape—and not something else. For example, in some states a particular act of forced sex is classified as rape; in others, it isn't. Which will you count as rape? In other words, you must be so precise that no one has any question about what you are including in your measures.

You must also be sure your data are reliable. *Reliability* means that other researchers who use your operational definitions will come up with findings that are consistent with yours. If your operational definitions are sloppy, some men who have done the same act will be excluded from another study, and the findings are likely to differ from yours. This would make your study unreliable.

7 *Analyzing the data.* After you have gathered the data, you will choose from a variety of techniques to analyze them. If a hypothesis has been

part of your research—and not all social research has a hypothesis—it is during this step that it is tested. You probably will use the computer, for in an instant this powerful tool can perform tests on your data that used to take tedious days, or even weeks. The basic program that sociologists, even many undergraduates, learn is the Statistical Package for the Social Sciences (SPSS). Another is Microcase.

8 *Sharing the results.* In this last step, you write a report to share your findings with the scientific community. This report reviews how you did the research, including your operational definitions, so others can judge your findings. It also shows how your findings are related to the literature, what others have published on the problem. As Table 1.2 on the next page illustrates, sociologists often summarize their findings in tables.

Let's look in greater detail at the fifth step and examine the research methods that sociologists use.

Six Research Methods

Not on Quiz 5/18

As we review the six research methods (or "research designs") that sociologists use, we shall continue our example of rape. As you will see, your choice of method will depend on the questions you want to answer. Since many research methods require that

you determine what "average" is in order to have a yardstick for comparison, the measures of average are discussed in Table 1.3 (on page 24).

Surveys

Suppose you want to know how many females are raped each year. The *survey*, asking people a series of questions, would be appropriate. Before you begin your research, however, you must deal with practical matters that face all researchers. Let's look at these problems.

Selecting a Sample Ideally, you may want to learn about all the females in the world. Obviously, however, your resources will not permit such a study, and you must narrow your *population*, the target group that you will study.

Let us assume that your resources allow you to investigate rape only on your campus. Let us also assume that your college enrollment is large, making it impractical to survey all the women who are enrolled. Now you must select a *sample*, individuals from among your target population. How you choose a sample is crucial, for the choice will affect the results of your study. For example, to survey only first-year students—or only seniors, or only women enrolled in introductory sociology courses, or only those in advanced physics classes—would produce skewed results.

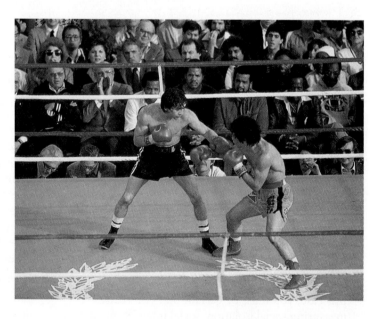

Because sociologists usually cannot interview or observe every member of a group they wish to study, such as the spectators at this boxing match, they must select a sample that will let them generalize to the entire group. The text explains how samples are selected.

Table 1.2

How to Read a Table

Rapists' Accounts of Alcohol and Drug Use Prior to Their Crime

These are the results of interviews with men imprisoned for rape in seven prisons in Virginia. *Admitters* are men who define their acts as rape, *deniers* those who do not define their acts as rape.

Use of Alcohol and Drugs	Admitters n = 39	Deniers n = 25
Neither the rapist nor the victim used alcohol or drugs.	23%	16%
The rapist used alcohol or drugs.	77%	72%
The rapist was affected by the alcohol or drugs.	69%	40%
The victim used alcohol or drugs.	26%	72%
The victim was affected by the alcohol or drugs.	15%	56%
Both the rapist and the victim used and were affected by alcohol or drugs.	15%	16%

Source: Modification of Scully and Marolla 1984, Table 2.

A table is a concise way of presenting information. Because sociological findings are often presented in tabular form, it is important to understand how to read a table. Tables contain six elements: title, headnote, headings, columns, rows, and source. When you understand how these elements work together, you know how to read a table.

1. The *title* states the topic of a table. It is located at the top of the table. What is the title of this table? Please determine your answer before looking at the correct answer below.

2. A *headnote* is not always included in a table. When it is, it is located just below the title. Its purpose is to give more detailed information about how the data were collected or how data are presented in the table. What are the first seven words of the headnote of this table?

3. The *headings* of a table tell what kind of information is contained in the table. There are three headings in this table. What are they? In the second heading, what does $n = 39$ mean?

4. The *columns* in a table present vertically arranged information. What is the fourth number in the second column and the second number in the third column?

5. The *rows* in a table present information arranged horizontally. In the sixth row, who is listed as using and being affected by alcohol or drugs?

6. The *source* of a table, usually listed at the bottom, provides information on where the data shown in the table originated. Often, as in this instance, the information is specific enough for you to consult the original source. What is the source for this table?

Some tables are much more complicated than this one, but all follow the same basic pattern. To apply these concepts to a table with more information, see Tables 9.2 and 9.3 on page 231.

Answers

1. "How to Read a Table: Rapists' Accounts of Alcohol and Drug Use Prior to Their Crime."

2. "These are the results of interviews with."

3. "Use of Alcohol and Drugs," "Admitters," "Deniers." The *n* is an abbreviation for *number*, and "*n* = 39" means that 39 men were admitters.

4. 26%, 72%.

5. Both the rapist and the victim.

6. A 1984 article by Scully and Marolla (listed in the References section of this text).

Table 1.3

Three Ways to Measure "Average"

The Mean

The term *average* seems clear enough. As you learned in grade school, to find the average you add a group of numbers and then divide the total by the number of cases that were added. For example, assume that the following numbers represent men convicted of rape who are incarcerated in seven different prisons

321
229
57
289
136
57
1,795

The total is 2,884. Divided by 7 (the number of cases), the average is 412. Sociologists call this form of average the *mean*.

The mean can be deceptive because it is strongly influenced by extreme scores, either low or high. Note that six of the seven cases are less than the mean.

Two other ways to compute averages are the median and the mode.

The Median

To compute the second average, the *median*, first arrange the cases in order—either from the highest

to the lowest or the lowest to the highest. In this example, that arrangement will produce the following distribution:

57
57
136
229
289
321
1,795

Then look for the middle case, the one that falls halfway between the top and bottom. That figure is 229, for three numbers are lower and three numbers higher. When there are an even number of cases, the median is the halfway mark between the two middle cases.

The Mode

The third measure of average, the *mode* is simply the cases that occur the most often. In this instance the mode is 57, which is way off the mark. Because the mode is often deceptive, and only by chance comes close to either of the other two averages, sociologists seldom use it. In addition, it is obvious that not every distribution of cases has a mode. And if two or more different numbers appear with the same frequency, you can have more than one mode.

Since you want to generalize your findings to your campus, you need a sample that is representative of the campus. How do you get a representative sample?

The best is a *random sample*. This does *not* mean that you stand on some campus corner and ask questions of whoever happens to walk by. *In a random sample, everyone in the population has the same chance of being included in the study.* In this case, since the population is every woman enrolled in your college, all such women—whether first-year or graduate students, full or part time—must have the same chance of being included in your sample.

How can you get a random sample? First, you need a list of all the women enrolled in your college. Then you would assign a number to each name on the list and, using a table of random numbers, determine which students become part of your sample.

(Random numbers are available in tables in statistics books, or they can be generated by a computer.) Because a random sample represents the population—in this case women enrolled at your college—you will be able to generalize your findings to all the women students on your campus, whether they were included in the sample or not.

If you want to know only about certain subgroups, such as freshmen and seniors, you may want to use a *stratified random sample*. You would need a list of these students and then use random numbers to select subsamples from each group. This would allow you to generalize to all the freshmen and seniors at your college, but you could say nothing about the sophomores or juniors.

Asking Neutral Questions After you have decided on your population and sample, your next task is to

Because sociologists consider all human behavior to be valid research topics, they research both socially approved and disapproved behaviors. Rape, which reaches far back into antiquity, is among these topics. This painting by Peter Paul Rubens (1577–1640), "Abduction of the Daughters of Leukippos," depicts an event that is supposed to have occurred in the fifth century B.C.

make certain that your questions are neutral. Your questions must allow *respondents*, people who respond to a survey, to express their own opinions. Otherwise you will end up with biased findings. For example, if you were to ask, "Don't you agree that rapists deserve the death penalty?" you would be tilting the answers toward agreement with the death penalty. As with the findings reviewed in the Down-to-Earth Sociology box on the next page, biased findings are worthless.

You must also decide whether to use open- or closed-ended questions. *Closed-ended questions* are followed by a list of possible answers. This is OK for questions about someone's age, but how would you know all possible opinions that people hold, for example, on what causes rape? The alternative is *open-ended questions*, which people can answer in their own words. Although this allows you to tap their full range of opinions, it makes it difficult to compare answers. For example, how would you compare these answers to the question "What do you think causes rape?"

"Rapists are sick."

"I think they must have had problems with their mother."

"We ought to string them up!"

Establishing Rapport   Will rape victims really talk to researchers? The answer is yes, but you first must establish *rapport* ("ruh-pour"), a feeling of trust, with your respondents. This is true in all research, but especially in sensitive matters such as rape. We know that once rapport is established (such as by first asking nonsensitive questions), victims will talk about rape. For example, researchers conduct national crime surveys in which they interview a random sample of 100,000 Americans. They ask them if they have been victims of burglary, robbery, and so on. After gaining rapport, the researchers then ask questions about rape. They find that rape victims will talk about their experiences. The national crime surveys show that rape is twice as high as the official statistics—and that most rape is committed by someone the victim knows (Schafran 1995).

Participant Observation (Fieldwork)

In *participant observation*, the researcher *participates* in a research setting while *observing* what is happening in that setting. Obviously this method does not mean that you would be present during a rape. But if you wanted to learn how rape has affected the victims' hopes and goals, their dating patterns, or their relationship with a spouse, you could use participant observation.

For example, if your campus has a rape crisis center, you may be able to observe rape victims from the time they first report the attack to their participation in counseling. With good rapport, you may even be able to spend time with victims outside this setting, observing other aspects of their lives. Their statements and other behaviors may be the keys that help you unlock answers about how the rape has affected their lives. This, in turn, might allow you to make suggestions about how to improve college counseling services.

Secondary Analysis

If you were to analyze data that someone else has already collected, you would be doing *secondary analysis*. For example, sociologists Diana Scully and Joseph

▲▼▲▼▲▼▲▼▲▼▲▼▲▼▲▼▲▼▲▼▲▼▲▼▲▼▲▼▲▼▲▼▲▼▲▼

Down-to-Earth Sociology

Loading the Dice: How *Not* to Do Research

THE METHODS OF SCIENCE lend themselves to distortion, misrepresentation, and downright fraud. Consider the following information. Surveys show that

- *Americans overwhelmingly prefer Toyotas to Chryslers.*
- *Americans overwhelmingly prefer Chryslers to Toyotas.*

- *Americans think that cloth diapers are better for the environment than disposable diapers.*
- *Americans think that disposable diapers are better for the environment than cloth diapers.*

Obviously such opposites cannot both be true. In fact, both sets of findings are misrepresentations, although each does come from surveys conducted by so-called independent researchers. These researchers, however, are biased, not independent and objective.

It turns out that some consumer researchers load the dice. Hired by firms that have a vested interest in the outcome of the research, they deliver the results their clients are looking for. There are six basic ways of loading the dice.

1. **Choose a biased sample.** For example, if you want to know if Americans prefer Chryslers or Toyotas, and you choose as your sample unemployed union workers who trace their job loss to Japanese imports, the answer is fairly predictable.
2. **Ask biased questions.** Even if you choose an unbiased sample, you can phrase questions in such a way that most people see only one logical choice. The diaper survey just cited is a case in point. When the dis-

posable diaper industry paid for the survey, the researchers used an excellent sample, but they worded the question this way: "It is estimated that disposable diapers account for less than 2 percent of the trash in today's landfills. In contrast, beverage containers, third-class mail and yard waste are estimated to account for about 21 percent. Given this, in your opinion, would it be fair to ban disposable diapers?"

Is it surprising, then, that 84 percent of the respondents said that disposable diapers are better for the environment than cloth diapers? Similarly, when the cloth diaper industry funded its survey, the wording of their questions loaded the dice in their favor.

Consider the following finding, which is every bit as factual as those just cited:

- *80 percent of Americans support foreign aid.*

It is difficult to get 80 percent of Americans to agree on anything, but as loaded as this question was it is surprising that there was *only* 80 percent agreement. Incredibly, the question was phrased this way: *"Should the U.S. share at least a small portion of its wealth with those in the world who are in great need?"*

This question is obviously designed to channel people's thinking toward a predetermined answer—quite contrary to the standards of scientific research.

3. **List biased choices.** Another way to load the dice is to use closed-ended questions that

push people into the answers you want. Consider this finding:

- *U.S. college students overwhelmingly prefer Levis 501 to the jeans of any competitor.*

Sound good? Before you rush out to buy this product, note what the researchers for Levis did: In asking a sample of students which clothes would be the most popular in the coming year, their list of choices included *no jeans* but Levis 501!

4. **Discard undesirable results.** Researchers can simply keep silent about findings they find embarrassing, or they can even continue to survey samples until they find one that matches what they are looking for.

As stressed in this chapter, research must be objective before it can be considered scientific. Obviously, none of the preceding results qualifies. The underlying problem with the research cited here—and with so many similar surveys that are bandied about in the media—is that survey research has become big business. Simply put, the vast sums of money offered by corporations have corrupted some researchers.

The beginning of the corruption is subtle. Paul Light, dean at the University of Minnesota, put it like this: "A funder will never come to an academic and say, 'I want you to produce finding *X*, and here's a million dollars to do it.' Rather, the subtext is that if the researchers produce the right finding, more work—and funding—will come their way." He adds, "Once you're on that treadmill, it's hard to get off."

(continued)

▼▲▼▲▼▲▼▲▼▲▼▲▼▲▼▲▼▲▼▲▼▲▼▲▼▲▼▲▼▲▼▲▼▲▼▲

Down-to-Earth Sociology (Continued)

These first four sources of bias are inexcusable. They constitute intentional fraud. The next two sources of bias that we shall examine reflect sloppiness—which is also inexcusable in science.

5. **Misunderstand the subjects' world.** This route can lead to errors every bit as great as those just cited. Even researchers who use an adequate sample, word their questions properly, and offer adequate choices can end up with skewed results. For example, surveys show that 80 percent of Americans are environmentalists. Most Americans, however, are probably embarrassed to tell a stranger otherwise. Today, that would be like going against the flag, motherhood, and apple pie.

6. **Analyze the data incorrectly.** Even when researchers strive for objectivity, the sample and wording are correct, and respondents answer the questions honestly, the results can still be skewed—the researchers may simply err in their calculations, such as entering incorrect data into computers.

Sources: Based on Crossen 1991; Goleman 1993; Barnes 1995.

Marolla (1984, 1985) interviewed men who were in prison for rape. They found that these men were *not* sick, but rather were rational men who engaged in calculated behavior. If you were to examine Scully and Marolla's original data to see what else you could find, you would be doing secondary analysis.

Documents

Documents include books, newspapers, bank records, immigration files, and so on. To study rape, you might examine police reports to find out how many men in your community have been arrested for rape. You might also want to find out what proportion of those men were charged, convicted, and sentenced.

But if you wanted to know about the social and emotional adjustment of rape victims, these documents would tell you nothing. Other documents, however, might help answer such questions. For example, a rape crisis center might have records that contain key information. Or the center might ask rape victims to keep diaries that you can study later.

Unobtrusive Measures

Researchers sometimes use *unobtrusive measures* to observe people who do not know they are being studied. To use this technique, you could observe rapists in prison when they do not know they are being watched. For example, you could arrange for the leader of a therapy group for rapists to be called out of the room and, using a one-way mirror and video camera, record the men's interactions. This probably would tell you more about their real attitudes than most other techniques.

Experiments

Let's suppose that you want to know if therapy with rapists actually works. You could conduct an *experiment* to find out. See Figure 1.3 on page 29. Your *independent variable*, something that causes a change in another variable, would be therapy. Your *dependent variable*, the variable that is changed, would be the men's behavior, whether or not they rape after they get out of prison. For that, you would need to rely on a somewhat sloppy operational definition—whether or not the men are rearrested for rape. This is sloppy because some of the men will rape and not be caught, but it may be the best you can do.

You would randomly divide your subjects into two groups. Those in the *experimental group* would be exposed to the independent variable; that is, they would attend therapy sessions. Those in the *control group* would not go to therapy. It is essential that the men be divided randomly in order to assure that their individual characteristics (number of convictions, severity of crimes, length of prison sentence, education, race, age, and so on) are evenly distributed between the groups. If you find that the men who received therapy are less likely to be rearrested for rape, you can attribute the difference to the therapy. Your study may show no difference in rearrest

Because sociologists find any human behavior a valid research topic, their research runs from the unusual to the routines of everyday life. On the macro level, they study how voting patterns are related to religion, and on the micro level they study tattoo conventions, such as this one in Elizabeth, New Jersey. Their analyses range from such intensely individual acts as suicide to such broad-scale social change as the globalization of capitalism.

rates, however, meaning that therapy was ineffectual. Or you may even find that the men who received the therapy have a higher rearrest rate!—meaning that the therapy backfired.

Frankly, no one yet knows how to change rapists, and such experiments are badly needed.

Ethics in Sociological Research

In addition to choosing an appropriate research method, we must also follow the ethics of sociology, which center on assumptions of science and morality. Research ethics require openness (sharing findings with the scientific community), honesty, and truth. Ethics clearly forbid the falsification of results or plagiarism; that is, stealing someone else's work. Another ethical guideline is that research subjects should not be harmed by the research. Ethics further require that researchers protect the anonymity of people who provide private, sometimes intimate, and often potentially embarrassing or otherwise harmful information. Finally, although not all soci-

ologists agree, it generally is considered unethical for researchers to misrepresent themselves.

Sociologists take these ethical criteria seriously. To illustrate the extent to which sociologists will go to protect their respondents, consider the research conducted by Mario Brajuha and Rik Scarce.

The Brajuha Research

Mario Brajuha, a graduate student at the State University of New York at Stony Brook, was doing participant observation of restaurant work (Brajuha and Hallowell 1986). He lost his job as a waiter when the restaurant where he was working burned down. The fire turned out to be of "suspicious origin," and the police investigated it. During their investigation, detectives learned that Brajuha had taken extensive field notes, and they asked to see them. Brajuha refused. The district attorney then subpoenaed the notes. Brajuha still refused to hand them over. The district attorney then threatened to send Brajuha to jail. By this time, Brajuha's notes had become rather famous, and unsavory characters, perhaps those who had set the fire, also began to wonder what was in them. They, too, demanded to see them—accompanying their demands with threats of a different nature. Brajuha unexpectedly found himself in a very disturbing double bind.

For two years Brajuha refused to hand over his notes, even though he had to appear at numerous court hearings and became filled with anxiety. Finally, the district attorney dropped the subpoena. Happily, when the two men under investigation for setting the fire died, so did the threats to Brajuha, his wife, and their children.

The Scarce Research

In 1993, a group calling itself the Animal Liberation Front broke into a research facility at Washington State University, released animals, and did extensive damage to computers and files. Rik Scarce, a doctoral student in sociology at the university who was doing research on radical environmental groups, was called before a federal grand jury investigating the break-in. Scarce was not a suspect, but law enforcement officers thought that during his research Scarce might have come across information that would help lead them to the guilty parties.

Scarce answered scores of questions about himself and topics related to the raid, but he refused to answer questions that would violate his agreements

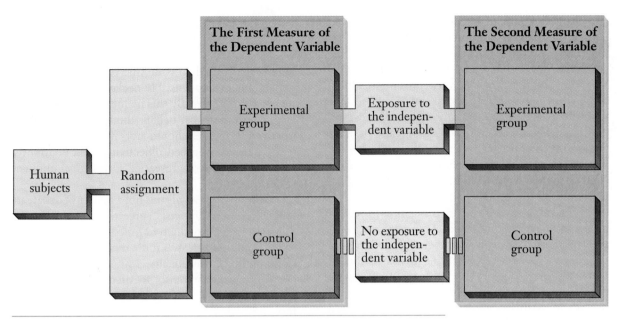

FIGURE 1.3

The Experiment

of confidentiality with research subjects. He cited the American Sociological Association's Code of Ethics (1989):

> "Confidential information provided by research participants must be treated as such by sociologists, even when this information enjoys no legal protection or privilege and legal force is applied."

A federal judge did not agree and put Scarce in the Spokane County Jail for contempt of court. Although Scarce could have obtained his freedom at any time simply by testifying, he maintained his laudable ethical stance and continued to refuse, in his words, "to be bludgeoned into becoming an agent of the state." Scarce served 159 days in jail. The longest any scholar before this had been held in contempt was one week (Scarce 1993, 1994).

The Humphreys Research

Sociologists agree on the necessity to protect respondents, and they applaud the professional manner in which Brajuha and Scarce handled themselves. Although there is less complete agreement on the requirement that researchers not misrepresent themselves, sociologists who violate this norm can become embroiled in ethical controversy. An example is the research of Laud Humphreys, which forced sociologists to rethink and refine their ethical stance.

Laud Humphreys (1970, 1971, 1975), a classmate of mine at Washington University in St. Louis, was an Episcopal priest who decided to become a sociologist. For his Ph.D. dissertation, Humphreys decided to study social interaction in "tearooms," places where some men go for quick, anonymous sex with other men.

Humphreys found that some restrooms in Forest Park, just across from the campus, were tearooms. He first did a participant observation study, just hanging around these restrooms. He found that three people were involved, the two having sex and a third person—called a "watchqueen"—who stayed on the lookout for police and other unwelcome strangers. Humphreys took the role of watchqueen, not only watching for strangers but also watching and systematically recording what the men did.

Humphreys decided that he wanted to know more about the regular lives of these men. For example, what was the significance of the wedding rings that many of the men wore? He hit on an ingenious technique. Many of the men parked their cars near the tearooms, and Humphreys recorded their license numbers. Through the help of a friend in the St. Louis police department, Humphreys obtained each man's address. About a year later, he arranged for these men to be included in a medical survey conducted by some of the sociologists on our faculty.

Disguising himself with a different hairstyle and clothing, and driving a different car, Humphreys visited some of these at their homes. He then interviewed them, supposedly for the medical study. He found that these men led very conventional lives. They voted, mowed their lawns, and took their kids to Little League games. Many reported, however, that their wives were not aroused sexually or were afraid of getting pregnant because their religion did not allow them to use birth control. Humphreys concluded that heterosexual men were also using the tearooms for an alternative form of quick sex.

This study stirred controversy among sociologists and nonsociologists alike. Humphreys was severely criticized by many sociologists, and a national columnist even wrote a scathing denunciation of "sociological snoopers" (Von Hoffman 1970). As the controversy grew more heated, Humphreys feared that the list of his respondents might be subpoenaed (a court case was being threatened). He then gave me the list to take from Missouri to Illinois, where I had begun teaching. When he called and asked me to destroy it, I burned it in my back yard.

Was the research ethical? This question is not easily decided. Although many sociologists sided with Humphreys and his book reporting the research won a highly acclaimed award, the criticisms mounted. At first, Humphreys vigorously defended his position, but five years later, in a second edition of his book (1975), he stated that he should have identified himself as a researcher.

How Research and Theory Work Together

Research is closely related to sociological theory. On the one hand, as sociologist C. Wright Mills (1959) so forcefully argued, research without theory is of little value, simply a collection of meaningless "facts." On the other hand, if theory is unconnected to research it is abstract and empty, unlikely to represent the way life really is.

Research and theory go hand in hand. Theory stimulates research, for every theory that sociologists develop must be tested. Research also stimulates theory, for as sociologists do research they often come up with surprising findings. Those findings, in turn, need theory to explain them. As sociologists study social life, then, they combine research and theory.

The Dilemma of Values in Social Research

Max Weber raised an issue that remains controversial among sociologists. He declared that sociology should be *value free*. By this he meant that a sociologist's *values*, personal beliefs about what is good or worthwhile in life, should not affect research. Instead, he said, we need objectivity, total neutrality, for if values influence research, sociological findings will be biased.

Objectivity as an ideal is not a matter of debate in sociology. All sociologists agree that no one should distort data to make them fit preconceived notions or values, and that research must report actual, not desired, findings. It is equally clear, however, that, like everyone else, sociologists are members of a particular society at a given point in history and are, therefore, infused with values of all sorts. These values inevitably play a role in our research. For example, values are part of the reason that one sociologist chooses to do research on rapists, while another turns a sociological eye on kindergarten students.

To overcome the distortions that values can cause, and that unwittingly can become part of our research, sociologists stress *replication*, the repetition of a study by other researchers to compare results. If values have influenced research findings, replication should uncover this problem and correct it.

In another sense, however, values remain a hotly debated topic in sociology. This debate centers on the tension in sociology we discussed earlier—the goal of understanding social life versus social reform. Some sociologists are convinced that research should be directed along paths that will help reform society, that will alleviate poverty, racism, sexism, and so on. Other sociologists lean strongly toward **basic (or pure) sociology,** research that has no goal beyond understanding social life and testing social theories. They say that nothing but their own interests should direct sociologists to study one topic rather than another.

In the midst of this tension, sociologists study the major issues facing our society at this crucial juncture of world history. From racism and sexism to the globalization of capitalism—these are all topics that sociologists study, and that will show up in the pages to come. Sociologists also examine face-to-face interaction—talking, touching, gestures, clothing—and these, too, will show up in the coming chapters. This beautiful variety in sociology—and the contrast of going from the larger picture to the smaller picture and back again—is part of the reason that sociology holds such fascination for me. I hope that you also find this variety appealing as you read the rest of this book.

Summary and Review

The Sociological Perspective

What is the sociological perspective?

The **sociological perspective** stresses that people's social experiences—the groups to which they belong and their experiences within these groups—underlie their behavior. C. Wright Mills referred to this as the intersection of biography (the individual) and history (social factors influencing the individual). Pp. 4–5.

The Development of Sociology

When did sociology first appear as a separate discipline?

Sociology emerged as a separate discipline in the mid-1800s in western Europe, during the onset of the Industrial Revolution. Industrialization affected all aspects of human existence—where people live, the nature of their work, and interpersonal relationships. Early sociologists who focused on these social changes include Auguste Comte, Herbert Spencer, Karl Marx, Emile Durkheim, and Max Weber. Pp. 5–9.

Sexism and Early Sociology

Sociology appeared during a historical period of heavy sexism. Consequently, few women received the advanced education required to become sociologists, and those who did, such as Harriet Martineau, were ignored. Pp. 9–10.

Sociology in North America

When were academic departments of sociology first established in the United States?

The earliest departments of sociology were established around the turn of the nineteenth century at the universities of Chicago, Kansas, and Atlanta. During the 1940s, sociology was dominated by the University of Chicago. Today, no single university or theoretical perspective dominates. P. 10.

U.S. sociology has shown a tension between **pure** or **basic sociology** and attempts to use sociology to reform society. Today, these contrasting orientations exist dynamically side by side. **Applied sociology** is the use of sociology to solve problems. Pp. 10–13.

Theoretical Perspectives in Sociology

What is a theory?

A **theory** is a statement about how facts are related to one another. A theory provides a conceptual framework to interpret facts. P. 13.

What are the major theoretical perspectives?

Sociologists use three primary theoretical frameworks to interpret social life. **Symbolic interactionism** examines how people use symbols to develop and share their views of the world. Symbolic interactionists usually focus on the **micro level**—on small-scale, face-to-face interaction. **Functional analysis,** in contrast, focuses on the **macro level**—on large-scale patterns of society. Functional theorists stress that a social system is made up of various parts. When working properly, each part contributes to the stability of the whole, fulfilling a function that contributes to a system's equilibrium. **Conflict theory** also focuses on large-scale patterns of society. Conflict theorists stress that society is composed of competing groups struggling for scarce resources. Pp. 13–18.

Because no single theory encompasses all of reality, at different times sociologists may use any or all of the three theoretical lenses. With each perspective focusing on certain features of social life and each providing its own interpretation, their combined insights yield a more comprehensive picture of social life. P. 19.

Sociology and Common Sense

Why do we need sociology when we have common sense?

Common sense is undependable. Objective research often shows that commonsense ideas are highly limited or false. Pp. 19–20.

A Research Model

What are eight basic steps in sociological research?

1. Selecting a topic
2. Defining the problem
3. Reviewing the literature
4. Formulating a hypothesis
5. Choosing a research method
6. Collecting the data
7. Analyzing the results
8. Sharing the results

These steps are explained on pp. 20–22.

Six Research Methods

How do sociologists gather data?

Sociologists use six research methods (or research designs) for gathering data: surveys, participant observation, secondary analysis, documents, unobtrusive measures, and experiments. Pp. 22–28.

Ethics in Sociological Research

How do ethics affect sociological research?

Ethics are of fundamental concern to sociologists, who are committed to openness, honesty, truth, and protecting their subjects from harm. The Brajuha research on restaurants, the Scarce research on the environmental movement, and the Humphreys research on "tearooms" were cited to illustrate ethical issues of concern to sociologists. Pp. 28–30.

How Research and Theory Work Together

What is the relationship between theory and research?

Theory and research are interdependent. Sociologists use theory to interpret the data they gather. Theory also generates questions that need to be answered by research, while research, in turn, helps to generate theory. Theory without research is not likely to represent real life, while research without theory is merely a collection of empty facts. P. 30.

The Dilemma of Values in Social Research

What value dilemma do sociologists face?

Max Weber stressed that social research should be *value free:* the researcher's personal beliefs must be set aside in order to permit objective findings. But like everyone else, sociologists are members of a particular society at a given point in history and therefore are infused with values of all sorts. To overcome the distortions that values can cause, sociologists stress *replication*, the repetition of a study by other researchers to compare results. Values present a second dilemma for researchers—whether to do research solely to understand (**pure sociology**) or to reform harmful social arrangements. Pp. 30–31.

Where can I read more on this topic?

Suggested readings for this chapter are listed on page 435.

Glossary

applied sociology the use of sociology to solve problems—from the micro level of family relationships to the macro level of war and pollution (p. 12)

authority power that people accept as rightly exercised over them; also called legitimate power (p. 17)

basic (or pure) sociology sociological research whose only purpose is to make discoveries about life in human groups, not to make changes in those groups (p. 30)

class conflict Karl Marx's term for the struggle between owners (the bourgeoisie) and workers (the proletariat) (p. 7)

clinical sociology the direct involvement of sociologists in bringing about social change (p. 12)

conflict theory a theoretical framework in which society is viewed as composed of groups competing for scarce resources (p. 17)

functional analysis a theoretical framework in which society is viewed as composed of various parts, each with a function that, when fulfilled, contributes to society's equilibrium; also known as functionalism and structural functionalism (p. 15)

macro-level analysis an examination of large-scale patterns of society (p. 18)

micro-level analysis an examination of small-scale patterns of society (p. 18)

nonverbal interaction communication without words through gestures, space, silence, and so on (p. 18)

positivism the application of the scientific approach to the social world (p. 6)

social integration the degree to which people feel a part of social groups (p. 8)

social interaction what people do when they are in one another's presence (p. 18)

social location people's group memberships because of their location in history and society (p. 4)

society a group of people who share a culture and a territory (p. 4)

sociological perspective an approach to understanding human behavior by placing it within its broader social contexts (p. 4)

sociology the scientific study of society and human behavior (p. 6)

symbolic interactionism a theoretical perspective in which society is viewed as composed of symbols that people use to establish meaning, develop their views of the world, and communicate with one another (p. 13)

theory a general statement about how some parts of the world fit together and how they work; an explanation of how two or more facts are related to one another (p. 13)

Sociology and the Internet

All URLs listed are current as of the printing of this book. URLs are often changed. Please check our Website http://www.abacon.com/henslin for updates.

1. The Challenge of Objectivity

As you discovered when you read the section in the text headed "The Dilemma of Values in Social Research," to maintain objectivity is a challenge to researchers. This is especially true when sociologists study people whose values and living patterns are vastly different from their own. It is equally true when they study societies around the world, as anthropologists have discovered in the last 100 years.

To examine a wide variety of peoples and to see whether you can maintain your own objectivity, go to the NativeWeb homepage (http://www.maxwell.syr. edu/nativeweb). (*Instructor:* For help in how to navigate the Internet, refer to the booklet "Allyn and Bacon Quick Guide to the Internet for Sociologists.") When you arrive at NativeWeb, page down until you see I Isubject I I geographic regions I I nations/peoples I I (and so on). Click on geographic regions. You will see a list of areas on the new page. Browse through a number of societies. What do most of them have in common? What are their most widely different elements? Decide on four rather different peoples, and take notes for a three-to four-page paper in which you discuss the following questions: (1) Which elements of the societies are you comfortable with? (2) Which ones make you most uncomfortable? (3) How objective do you think you could be doing field research in each of the four? (4) Briefly describe as objectively as possible what you see as the most important elements in each society.

2. Constructing a Table

Go to the 1990 Census Lookup page (http://www.census.gov/cdrom/lookup/). Select the data base "STF#c—Part 1." At the Retrieval Area page, click on the Submit bar. At the Data Retrieval Option page, click on the Submit bar. At the page headed "Select the tables you wish to retrieve," page down to "P70—Sex and Employment Status," and click on the circle in front of the entry. Then go to the top of the page and click on the Submit bar. You should see a table showing the employment status of males and females. Depending on your Web browser, you either can save the table or print it. (Netscape will allow both.) Use these data to construct a table, as described in Table 1.2 on page 23, "How to Read a Table." Your instructor may want you to use another census table, and to figure percentages to enter into your table. Be sure to include all the elements in a typical table when you prepare the final version of your own table for your instructor.

Dan V. Lomahaftewa, Beauty of the Continuum, 1987.

CHAPTER

2

Culture

I HAD NEVER FELT HEAT LIKE *this before. If this was northern Africa, I wondered what it must be like closer to the equator. The sweat poured off me as the temperature soared past 110° Fahrenheit.*

As we were herded into the building—without air conditioning—hundreds of people lunged toward the counter at the rear of the building. With body crushed against body, we waited as the uniformed officials behind the windows leisurely examined each passport. At times like this I wondered what I was doing in Africa.

When I had arrived in Morocco, I found the sights that greeted me exotic—not far removed from my memories of Casablanca, Raiders of the Lost Ark, *and other movies that over the years had become part of my collective memory. The men, the women, and even the children did wear those white robes that reached down to their feet. What was especially striking was the fact that the women were almost totally covered. In spite of the heat, every woman wore not only a full-length gown, but also a head covering that reached down over the forehead and a veil that covered her face from the nose down. All you could make out were their eyes—and every eye the same shade of brown.*

And how short everyone was! The Arab women looked to be on average 5 feet, and the men only about three or four inches more. As the only blue-eyed, blonde, 6-foot-plus person around, wearing jeans and a pullover shirt, in a world of white-robed short people, I stood out like a sore thumb. Everyone stared. No matter where I went, they stared. Wherever I looked, I found brown eyes watching intensely. Even staring back at those many dark brown eyes had no effect. It was so different from home, where, if you caught someone staring at you, the person would immediately look embarrassed and glance away.

And lines? The concept apparently didn't even exist. Buying a ticket for a bus or train meant pushing and shoving toward the ticket man (always a man—no women were visible in any public position), who just took the money from whichever outstretched hand he decided on.

And germs? That notion didn't seem to exist here either. Flies swarmed over the food in the restaurants and the unwrapped loaves of bread in the stores. Shopkeepers would considerately shoo off the flies before handing me a loaf. They also had home delivery of bread. I still remember a bread vendor delivering an unwrapped loaf to a woman standing on a second-floor balcony. She first threw her money to the bread vendor, and he then threw the unwrapped bread up to her. Only, his throw was off. The bread bounced off the wrought-iron balcony railing and landed in the street filled with people, wandering dogs, and the ever-present burros. The vendor simply picked up the loaf and threw it again. This certainly wasn't his day, for again he missed. But the man made it on his third attempt. And the woman smiled, satisfied, as she turned back into her apartment, apparently to prepare the noon meal for her hungry family.

As I stood in the oppressive heat of the Moroccan–Algerian border, the crowd had once again become unruly. Another fight had broken out. And once again, the little man in uniform appeared, shouting and knocking people aside as he forced his way to the little wooden box nailed to the floor. Climbing onto this makeshift platform, he would shout at the crowd, his arms flailing about him. The people would become silent. But just as soon as the man would leave, the shoving and shouting would begin again as the people clamored to get their passports stamped.

The situation had become unbearable. Pressed body to body, the man behind me had decided that this was a good time to take a nap. Determining that I made a good support, he placed his arm against my back and leaned his head against his arm. Sweat streamed from my back at the point that his arm and head touched me.

Finally, I realized that I had to abandon U.S. customs. I pushed my way forward, forcing my frame into every space I could make. At the counter, I shouted in English. The official looked up at the sound of this strange tongue, and, thrusting my long arms over the heads of three people, I shoved my passport into his hand.

What Is Culture?

What is culture? The concept is sometimes easier to grasp by description than by definition. For example, suppose you meet a young woman who has just arrived in the United States from India. That her culture is different from yours is immediately evident. You first see it in her clothing, jewelry, make-up, and hairstyle. Next you hear it in her language. It then becomes apparent by her gestures. Later, you may hear her express unfamiliar beliefs about the world and opinions about what is valuable in life. All these characteristics are indicative of **culture,** the language, beliefs, values, norms, behaviors, and even material objects that are passed from one generation to the next. *It's what makes one person different from the rest*

In northern Africa, I was surrounded by a culture quite alien to my own. It was evident in everything I saw and heard. The **material culture**—such things as jewelry, art, buildings, weapons, machines, and even eating utensils, hairstyles, and clothing—provided a sharp contrast to what I was used to seeing. There is nothing inherently "natural" about material culture. That is, it is no more natural (or unnatural) to wear gowns on the street than it is to wear jeans.

I also found myself immersed in a contrasting **nonmaterial culture,** that is, a group's ways of thinking (its beliefs, values, and other assumptions about the world) and doing (its common patterns of behavior, including language, gestures, and other forms of interaction). North African assumptions about crowding to buy a ticket and staring in public are examples of nonmaterial culture. So are U.S. assumptions about not doing either of these things. Like material culture, neither custom is "right." People simply become comfortable with the customs they learn during childhood, and—as in the case of my visit to northern Africa—uncomfortable when their basic assumptions about life are challenged.

Culture and Taken-for-Granted Orientations to Life

To develop a sociological perspective, we must understand how culture affects people's lives. Although meeting someone from a different culture may make us aware of culture's pervasive influence, attaining the same level of awareness regarding our own culture is quite another matter. *Our* speech, *our* gestures, *our* beliefs, and *our* customs are usually taken for granted. We assume they are "normal" or "natural," and we almost always follow them without question. As anthropologist Ralph Linton (1936) remarked, "The last thing a fish would ever notice would be water." So also with people: except in unusual circumstances, the effects of our own culture generally remain imperceptible to us.

Yet culture's significance is profound; it touches almost every aspect of who and what we are. We came into this life without a language, without values and morality, with no ideas about religion, war, money, love, use of space, and so on. We possessed none of these fundamental orientations that we take for granted and that are so essential in determining the type of people we are. Yet as adults we all have acquired them. Sociologists call this culture *within* us. These learned and shared ways of believing and of doing (another definition of culture) penetrate our being at an early age and quickly become part of our taken-for-granted assumptions concerning normal behavior. *Culture becomes the lens through which we perceive and evaluate what is going on around us.* Seldom do we question these assumptions, for, like water to a fish, the framework from which we view life remains largely beyond our ordinary perception.

The rare instances in which these assumptions are challenged, however, can be upsetting. Although as a sociologist I should be able to look at my own culture "from the outside," my trip to Africa quickly revealed how fully I had internalized my own culture. My upbringing in Western industrialized society had given me strong assumptions about aspects of social life that had become deeply rooted in my being—staring, hygiene, and the use of space. But in this part of Africa these assumptions were useless for helping me get through daily life. No longer could I count on people to stare only surreptitiously, to take precautions against invisible microbes, or to stand in an orderly way one behind the other, on the basis of arrival time, to obtain a service.

As you can tell from the opening vignette, I personally found these different assumptions upsetting, for they violated my basic expectations of "the way people *ought* to be"—although I did not even know I held these expectations until they were so abruptly challenged. When my nonmaterial culture failed me—when it no longer enabled me to make sense out of the world—I experienced a disorientation known as **culture shock.** In the case of buying tickets, the fact that I was several inches taller than most

Moroccans and thus able to outreach almost everyone helped me adjust partially to their different ways of doing things. But I never did get used to the idea that pushing ahead of others was "right," and I always felt guilty when I used my size to receive preferential treatment.

An important consequence of culture within us is **ethnocentrism,** a tendency to use our own group's ways of doing things as the yardstick for judging others. All of us learn that the ways of our own group are good, right, proper, and even superior to other ways of life. As sociologist William Sumner (1906), who developed this concept, said, "One's own group is the center of everything, and all others are scaled and rated with reference to it."

Ethnocentrism has both positive and negative consequences. On the positive side, it creates in-group loyalties. On the negative side, ethnocentrism can lead to harmful discrimination against people whose ways differ from ours.

The effects of culture on our lives fascinate sociologists. By examining more explicitly just how profoundly culture affects everything we are, this chapter will serve as a basis from which you can start to analyze your previously unquestioned assumptions of reality and thus help you gain a different perspective on social life and your role in it.

▼ **In Sum** To avoid losing track of the ideas under discussion, let's pause for a moment to summarize, and in some instances clarify, the principles we have covered:

1 There is nothing "natural" about material culture. Arabs wear gowns on the street and feel it is natural to do so; Americans do the same with jeans.

2 There is nothing "natural" about nonmaterial culture; it is just as arbitrary to stand in line as to push and shove.

3 Culture engulfs our thinking, becoming a taken-for-granted lens through which we see the world and obtain our perception of reality.

4 Culture provides implicit instructions that tell us what we ought to do in various situations; it provides a fundamental basis for our decision making.

5 Culture also provides a "moral imperative"; that is, by internalizing a culture, people learn ideas of right and wrong. (I, for example, deeply believed that it was unacceptable to push and shove to get ahead of others.)

6 Coming into contact with a radically different culture challenges our basic assumptions of life.

The material culture in which we are reared becomes a taken-for-granted part of our lives. It is no more natural, or unnatural, for the Arab women in the photo above to wear gowns in public than it is for the U.S. women in the photo on the right to appear on the beach in scanty attire. For Americans, the scene above appears strange, and for some, distressful, for they see this clothing as a sign of female subservience in a male-dominated society. For many Moroccans, the scene on the right is not only strange, but distressful, as they consider it a sign of moral depravity.

(I experienced culture shock when I discovered that my deeply ingrained cultural ideas about hygiene and the use of space no longer applied.)

7 Although the particulars of culture differ from one group of people to another, culture itself is universal. That is, all people have culture. There are no exceptions. A society cannot exist without developing shared, learned ways of dealing with the demands of life.

8 All people are *ethnocentric*, which has both positive and negative consequences.

Practicing Cultural Relativism

To counter our tendency to use our own culture as a standard to judge another culture, we can practice cultural relativism; that is, we can try to understand a culture on its own terms. **Cultural relativism** is looking at how the elements of a culture fit together, without judging those elements as superior or inferior to one's own way of life.

Because we tend to use our own culture to judge others, cultural relativism presents a challenge to ordinary thinking. For example, most U.S. citizens appear to have strong feelings against raising bulls for the purpose of stabbing them to death in front of crowds shouting "Olé!" According to cultural relativism, however, bullfighting must be viewed from the framework of the culture in which it takes place—*its* history, *its* folklore, *its* ideas of bravery, and *its* ideas of sex roles.

You may still regard bullfighting as wrong, of course, since U.S. culture, which lies deep within us, has no history of bullfighting. We possess culturally specific ideas about cruelty to animals, ideas that have evolved slowly and that match other elements of our culture. Consequently, practices that once were common—cock fighting, dog fighting, bear–dog fighting, and so on—have been gradually weeded out (Bryant 1993).

None of us can be entirely successful at practicing cultural relativism; we simply cannot help viewing a contrasting way of life through the lens that our own culture provides. Cultural relativism, however, is an attempt to refocus that lens and thereby appreciate other ways of life rather than simply asserting, "Our way is right."

Although cultural relativism is a worthwhile goal and helps us avoid cultural smugness, this view has come under attack. Anthropologist Robert Edgerton, in a provocative book, *Sick Societies* (1992), points out that some cultures endanger their people's health, happiness, or survival. He suggests that we develop a scale to evaluate cultures on their "quality of life," much as we do for U.S. cities. He also asks why we should consider cultures that practice female genital mutilation, gang rape, wife beating, or that sell daughters into prostitution as morally equivalent to those that do not. Cultural values that result in exploitation, he says, are inferior to those that enhance people's lives.

Edgerton's sharp questions and incisive examples bring us to a point that comes up repeatedly in

Many Americans perceive bullfighting, which is illegal in the United States, as a cruel activity that should be abolished everywhere in the world. To Spaniards and those who have inherited Spanish culture, however, bullfighting is a beautiful, artistic sport in which matador and bull blend into a unifying image of power, courage, and glory. Cultural relativism *requires the suspension of our own perspectives in order to grasp the perspectives of others, much easier described than attained.*

this text—disagreements that arise among scholars as they confront changing views of reality. It is such questioning of assumptions that keeps sociology interesting.

Components of Culture

The Symbolic Basis of Culture

Sociologists sometimes refer to nonmaterial culture as **symbolic culture** because a central component is the symbols that people use. A **symbol** is something to which people attach meaning and which they then use to communicate with one another. Symbols are the basis of culture. They include gestures, language, values, norms, sanctions, folkways, and mores. Let's look at each of these components of symbolic culture.

Gestures

Gestures, using one's body to communicate with others, are useful shorthand ways to give messages without using words. Although people in every culture of the world use gestures, their meaning may change completely from one culture to another. North Americans, for example, communicate a succinct message by raising the middle finger in a short, upward-stabbing motion. I stress "North Americans," for that gesture does not convey the same message in South America or most other parts of the world.

I was once surprised to find that this particular gesture was not universal, having internalized it to such an extent that I thought everyone knew what it meant. When I was comparing gestures in Mexico, however, this gesture drew a blank look from friends. After I explained its intended meaning, they laughed and showed me their rudest gesture—placing the hand under the armpit and moving the upper arm up and down. To me, they simply looked as if they were imitating a monkey, but to them the gesture meant "Your mother is a whore," absolutely the worst possible insult in that culture.

Gestures thus not only facilitate communication but, since they differ around the world, can also lead to misunderstandings, embarrassment, or worse. Once in Mexico, for example, I raised my hand to a certain height to indicate how tall a child was. My hosts began to laugh. It turns out that Mexicans have a more complicated system of hand gestures to indi-

Although most gestures are learned, and therefore vary from culture to culture, some gestures that represent fundamental emotions such as sadness, anger, and fear appear to be inborn. This crying Masai child in Kenya differs little from a crying child in China or the United States or anywhere else on the globe. In a few years, however, this child will demonstrate a variety of gestures highly specific to Masai culture.

cate height: separate ones for people, animals, and plants. (See Figure 2.1.) What had amused them was that I had ignorantly used the plant gesture to indicate the child's height.

To get along in another culture, then, it is important to learn the gestures of that culture. If you don't, you will not only fail to achieve the simplicity of communication that gestures allow but you will also miss much of what is happening, run the risk of appearing foolish, and possibly offend people. In many cultures, for example, you would provoke deep offense if you offered food or a gift with your left hand, because the left hand is reserved for dirty tasks, such as wiping after going to the bathroom. Left-handed Americans visiting Arabs, please note!

Now suppose for a moment that you are visiting southern Italy. After eating one of the best meals in your life, you are so pleased that when you catch the waiter's eye, you smile broadly and use the standard U.S. "A-OK" gesture of putting your thumb and forefinger together and making a large "O." The waiter looks horrified, and you are struck speechless when the manager asks you to leave. What have you done? Nothing on purpose, of course, but in that culture that gesture refers to a part of the human

Indicates animal height   Indicates plant height   Indicates human height

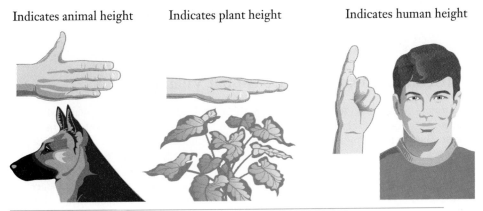

FIGURE 2.1
Gestures to Indicate Height, Southern Mexico

body that is not mentioned in polite company (Ekman et al. 1984).

Gestures, which tend to vary remarkably around the world, can create emotions. Some gestures are so associated with emotional messages that the gesture itself summons up an emotion. For example, my introduction to Mexican gestures took place at a dinner table. It was evident that my husband-and-wife hosts were trying to hide their embarrassment at actually using their culture's obscene gesture at their dinner table. And I felt the same way—not about their gesture, of course, which meant absolutely nothing to me—but about the one I was teaching them.

Language

The primary way in which people communicate with one another is through **language**—a system of symbols that can be strung together in an infinite number of ways for the purpose of communicating abstract thought. Each word is actually a symbol, a sound to which we have attached a particular meaning so that we can then use it to communicate with one another. Language itself is universal in the sense that all human groups have language, but there is nothing universal about the meanings given to particular sounds. Thus, like gestures, in different cultures the same sound may mean something entirely different—or may have no meaning at all. This can lead to some strange situations, as indicated in the Global Glimpse box on the next page.

The significance of language for human life is difficult to overstate, as will become apparent from the following discussion on how language allows culture to exist.

Language Allows Human Experience to Be Cumulative By means of language, one generation can pass significant experiences on to the next and allow that next generation to build on experiences it may not itself undergo. This building process enables humans to modify their behavior in the light of what previous generations have learned. Hence the central sociological significance of language: *Language allows culture to develop by freeing people to move beyond their immediate experiences.*

Without language, human culture would be little more advanced than that of the lower primates. People would be limited to communicating by some system of grunts and gestures, which would greatly shorten the temporal dimension of human life and limit communication to a small time zone surrounding the immediate present: events now taking place, those which have just taken place, or those which will immediately take place—a sort of "slightly extended present." You can grunt and gesture, for example, that you want a drink of water, but in the absence of language how could you share ideas concerning past or future events? There would be little or no way to communicate to others what event you had in mind, much less the greater complexities that humans communicate—ideas and feelings about events.

Language Provides a Social or Shared Past Even without language an individual would still have

▲ ▲ ▲ ▲ ▲ ▲ ▲ ▲ ▲ ▲ ▲ ▲ ▲ ▲ ▲ ▲ ▲

A Global Glimpse

Miscommunicating in the Global Village

VIEWED FROM AFAR, cultural differences among human groups may be only a matter of interest. But when there is **culture contact**—that is, when we come into contact with people from different cultures—those differences can lead to problems in communication.

It is not only travelers who face this problem. Increasingly, business is going global, making cultural differences a practical problem for businesspeople. And at times, even highly knowledgeable and experienced firms don't quite

manage to break through those cultural barriers. General Motors, for example, was very successful in marketing its automobile, the Nova, in the United States. When they decided to export that success south of the border, they were perplexed when people snickered and the car sold very, very slowly. Finally, someone let them in on the secret: In Spanish, *"No va"* is an entire sentence that means "It does not go."

Similarly, the Japanese find English a cultural hurdle, but at

least they have a plain-talking phrase book to learn from. In this book, called *New York English* (Hardy 1993), they learn how "real" Americans talk, memorizing such phrases as "suck face" and "chill out." But what about the subtle differences, such as when *not* to say the phrase (which this book teaches) "Get outta my face, you lying bag of scum!"? (Probably at this point the Japanese value of skill in martial arts comes in handy.)

---

memories of experiences and events. Those memories, however, would be extremely limited, for people associate experiences with words and then use words to recall the experience. Such memories as would exist in the absence of language would also be highly individualized, for they could be but rarely and incompletely communicated to others, much less discussed and agreed on. With language, however, events can be codified, that is, attached to words and then recalled so they can be discussed in the present.

Language Provides a Social or Shared Future Language also extends our time horizons forward. When people talk about past events, they share meanings that allow them to decide how they will or should act in similar circumstances in the future. Because language enables people to agree with one another concerning times, dates, and places, it also allows them to plan activities with one another.

Think about it for a moment. Without language, how could people ever plan future events? How could they possibly communicate goals, purposes, times, and plans? Whatever planning could exist would have to be limited to extremely rudimentary communications, perhaps to an agreement to meet at a certain place when the sun is in a certain position. But think of the difficulty, perhaps impos-

sibility, of conveying a change in this simple arrangement, such as "I can't make it tomorrow but my uncle can come, if that's all right with you."

Language Allows Shared Perspectives or Understandings Our ability to speak, then, provides a social past and future. These two vital aspects of our humanity represent a watershed that distinguishes us from animals. But speech does much more than this. When humans talk with one another, they are exchanging ideas about events, that is, exchanging perspectives. Their words are the embodiment of their experiences, distilled and codified into a readily exchangeable form, mutually intelligible for people who have learned that language. Talking about events allows people to arrive at the shared understandings that form the essence of social life. To not share a language, however, while living alongside one another, is to open up suspicions and miscommunications. This risk, which comes with a multicultural society, is discussed in the box on the next page.

Language Allows Complex, Shared, Goal-Directed Behavior Common understandings further enable people to establish a *purpose* for getting together. Let us suppose you want to go on a picnic. You use speech not only to plan the picnic but also to decide on reasons for the picnic—which may be any-

Our Multicultural Society

Miami—Language in a Changing City

IN THE YEARS since Castro seized power in Cuba, the city of Miami has been transformed from a quiet southern city to a Latin-American mecca. Few things better capture Miami today than its ethnic divisions, especially its long-simmering fight over language: English versus Spanish. Half of the city's 360,000 residents have trouble speaking English—possibly the highest proportion in any large U.S. city. Only 25 percent of Miami residents speak English at home.

As this chapter stresses, language is a primary means by which people learn—and communicate—their social worlds. Consequently, language differences in Miami reflect not just cultural diversity but people who live in separate worlds.

Although the ethnic stew makes Miami culturally one of the richest cities in the United States, the language gap sometimes creates anger and misunderstanding.

The aggravation felt by Anglos —tinged with hostility—is seen in the bumper stickers reading, "Will the Last American Out Please Bring the Flag?"

But Latinos, now a majority in Miami, are equally frustrated. Many feel Anglos should be able to speak at least some Spanish. Nicaraguan immigrant Pedro Falco, for example, is studying English and wonders why more people won't try to learn his language. "Miami is the capital of Latin America," he says. "The population speaks Spanish."

Language and cultural flare-ups sometimes make headlines in Miami. Latinos were outraged when an employee at the Coral Gables Board of Realtors lost her job for speaking Spanish at the office. And protesters swarmed a Publix supermarket after a cashier was fired for chatting with a friend in Spanish.

What's happening in Miami, says University of Chicago sociol-

ogist Douglas Massey, is what happened in cities such as Chicago at the beginning of the century. Then, as now, the rate of immigration exceeded the speed with which new residents learned English, creating a pile-up effect in the proportion of non-English speakers. Becoming comfortable with English is a slow process, he points out, whereas immigration is fast.

Massey expects the city's proportion of non-English speakers to rise with continuing immigration. But he says that this "doesn't mean in the long run that Miami is going to end up being a Spanish-speaking city." Instead, Massey believes, bilingualism will prevail. "Miami is the first truly bilingual city," he says. "The people who get ahead are not monolingual English speakers or monolingual Spanish speakers. They're people who speak both languages."

Source: Copyright 1992, *USA Today.* Reprinted by permission.

thing from "because it's a nice day and it shouldn't be wasted studying" to "because it's my birthday." Language permits you to blend individual activities into an integrated sequence. In other words, through discussion you decide where you will go; who will drive; who will bring the hamburgers, the potato chips, the soda; where you will meet; and so on. Only because of language can you participate in such a picnic—or build bridges and roads, or have college classes.

▼ **In Sum** The sociological significance of language is that it takes us beyond the world of apes and allows culture to develop. Language frees us from the present by providing a past and a future, giving us the capacity to share understandings about the

past and to develop common perceptions about the future, as well as to establish underlying purposes for our current activities.

Language and Perception: The Sapir–Whorf Hypothesis

In the 1930s, two anthropologists, Edward Sapir and Benjamin Whorf, became intrigued when they noted that the Hopi Indians of the southwestern United States had no words to distinguish between the past, the present, and the future. English, in contrast, as well as German, French, Spanish, and so on, distinguishes carefully just when something takes place. From this observation, Sapir and Whorf concluded that the commonsense idea that words are merely labels people attach to things was wrong. Language, they concluded, has embedded within it ways of looking at the world. Thus thinking and perception are not only expressed through language but are also shaped by language. When we learn a language, then, we learn not only words but also particular ways of thinking and perceiving (Sapir 1949; Whorf 1956).

The implications of the **Sapir–Whorf hypothesis,** which alerts us to how extensively language affects us, are far-reaching. *The Sapir–Whorf hypothesis reverses common sense:* It indicates that rather than objects and events forcing themselves onto our consciousness, it is our very language that determines our consciousness, and hence our perception, of objects and events. Eskimos, for example, have many words for snow. As Eskimo children learn their language, they learn distinctions among types of snowfalls that are imperceptible to non-Eskimo speakers. Others might learn to see heavy and light snowfalls, wet and dry snowfalls, and so on; but not having words for "fine powdery," "thicker powdery," and "more granular" snowfalls prevents them from perceiving snow in the same way that Eskimos do.

Although Sapir and Whorf's observation that the Hopi do not have tenses was incorrect (Edgerton 1992:27), we still need to take their conclusion seriously, for the classifications that we humans develop as we try to make sense of our worlds do direct our perception. Sociologist Eviatar Zerubavel (1991) gives a good example: Hebrew, his native language, does not differentiate between jam and jelly. Only when Zerubavel learned English could he "see" this difference, which is "obvious" to native English speakers. Similarly, if you learn to classify students as "dweebs," "dorks," "nerds," "brains," and so on, you will perceive a student who asks several questions during class in an entirely different way from someone who does not know these classifications. In short, *language is the basis of culture.*

Values, Norms, and Sanctions

To learn a culture is to learn people's **values,** their ideas of what is desirable in life. When we uncover people's values, we learn a great deal about them, for values are the standards by which people define good and bad, beautiful and ugly. Values underlie their preferences, guide their choices, and indicate what they hold worthwhile in life.

Every group develops both values and expectations concerning the right way to reflect them. Sociologists use the term **norms** to describe those ex-

pectations, or rules of behavior, that develop out of a group's values. They use the term **sanctions** to refer to positive or negative reactions to the ways in which people follow norms. The term **positive sanction** refers to an expression of approval given for following a norm, while a **negative sanction** is disapproval for breaking a norm. Positive sanctions can be material, such as a money reward, a prize, or a trophy, but in everyday life they usually consist of hugs, smiles, a clap on the back, soothing words, or even handshakes. Negative sanctions can also be material—a fine is one example—but they, too, are more likely to consist of gestures, such as frowns, stares, harsh words, or raised fists. Being awarded a raise at work is a positive sanction, indicating that the norms clustering around work values have been followed, while being fired is a negative sanction, indicating the opposite. The North American finger gesture discussed earlier is, of course, a negative sanction.

Folkways and Mores

Norms that are not strictly enforced are called **folkways.** We expect people to comply with folkways, but we are likely to shrug our shoulders and not make a big deal about it if they don't. If someone insists on passing you on the left side of the sidewalk, for example, you are unlikely to take corrective action—although if the sidewalk is crowded and you must move out of the way, you might give the person a dirty look.

Other norms, however, are taken much more seriously. We think of them as essential to our core values, and we insist on conformity. These are called **mores** ("MORE-rays"). A person who steals, rapes, and kills has violated some of society's most important mores. As sociologist Ian Robertson (1987:62) put it,

> A man who walks down a street wearing nothing on the upper half of his body is violating a folkway; a man who walks down the street wearing nothing on the lower half of his body is violating one of our most important mores, the requirement that people cover their genitals and buttocks in public.

It should also be noted that one group's folkways may be another group's mores. Although a man walking down the street with the upper half of his body uncovered is deviating from a folkway, a woman doing the same thing is violating a more. In addition, the folkways and mores of a subculture (the topic of

The violation of mores is usually a very serious matter. In this case, it is serious enough that the police at this international rugby tournament have swung into action— to protect the public from seeing a "disgraceful" sight—at least so designated by this group. Yet, unlike the reactions to most violations of mores, this scene also shows barely suppressed laughter.

the next section) may be the opposite of the general culture. For example, to walk down the sidewalk in a nudist camp with the entire body uncovered would conform to that subculture's folkways.

A **taboo** refers to a norm so strongly ingrained that even the thought of its violation is greeted with revulsion. Eating human flesh and having sex with one's parents are examples of such behaviors (Benales 1973; Read 1974; Henslin 1997).

Many Cultural Worlds: Subcultures and Countercultures

> We can make epistemically subjective statements about entities that are ontologically objective, and similarly, we can make epistemically objective statements about entities that are ontologically subjective. . . . Mental phenomena are ontologically subjective; and the observer-relative features inherit that ontological subjectivity. (Searle 1995:8, 12–13)

My best guess is that you are unable to decipher the meaning of these statements. They might as well

be written in Greek for all they mean to most of us. Philosophers, however, write like this, and—to them—the author's intent is clear. Philosophers form a **subculture,** *a world within the larger world of the dominant culture.* Each subculture has some distinctive way of looking at life. Even if we cannot understand the preceding quote, it makes us aware that the philosopher's view of life is not quite the same as ours.

U.S. society contains tens of thousands of subcultures. Some are as broad as the way of life we associate with teenagers, others as narrow as those we associate with body builders—or with philosophers. Some U.S. ethnic groups also form subcultures: Their values, norms, and foods set them apart. So might their religion, language, and clothing. Occupational groups also form subcultures, as anyone who has hung out with cab drivers (Davis 1959; Henslin 1993), artists (McCall 1980), or construction workers (Haas 1972) can attest. Even sociologists form a subculture, who, as you are learning, use a unique language for carving up the world.

Consider this quote from another subculture:

> If everyone applying for welfare had to supply a doctor's certificate of sterilization, if everyone who had committed a felony were sterilized, if anyone who had mental illness to any degree were sterilized—then our economy could easily take care of these people for the rest of their lives, giving them a decent living standard—but getting them out of the way. That way there would be no children abused, no surplus population, and, after a while, no pollution. . . .

> Now let's talk about stupidity. The level of intellect in this country is going down, generation after generation. The average IQ is always 100 because that is the accepted average. However, the kid with a 100 IQ today would have tested out at 70 when I was a lad. You get the concept . . . the marching morons. . . .

> When the . . . present world system collapses, it'll be good people like you who will be shooting people in the streets to feed their families. (Zellner 1995:58, 65)

Welcome to the world of the survivalists—where the message is much clearer than that of the philosophers, and much more disturbing.

The values and norms of most subcultures are compatible with the larger society to which they belong. In some cases, however, such as these survivalists, the group's values and norms place it in opposition to the dominant culture. Sociologists use the

Each subculture provides its members with sets of values and distinctive ways of viewing the world. Subcultures can form around almost any activity, including, as shown here, the human body itself.

term **counterculture** to describe such groups. Heavy metal music adherents who glorify satanism, hatred, cruelty, rebellion, sexism, violence, and death are another example of a counterculture. Countercultures do not have to be negative, however. Back in the 1800s, the Mormons were a counterculture, challenging the culture's core value of monogamy.

Often members of the broader culture feel threatened by a counterculture, and they sometimes move against it in the attempt to affirm their own values. The Mormons, for example, were driven out of several states before they finally settled in Utah, which was then a wilderness. Even there the federal government would not let them practice polygyny (one man having more than one wife), and Utah's statehood was made conditional on its acceptance of monogamy (Anderson 1942/1966). Today, the federal and state governments have taken steps against various survivalist groups.

Values in U.S. Society

An Overview of U.S. Values

As you know, the United States is a **pluralistic society,** made up of many different groups. The United States has numerous religious, racial, and ethnic groups, as well as countless interest groups centering on such divergent activities as collecting dolls and hunting animals. This state of affairs makes the job of specifying U.S. values difficult. Nonetheless, sociologists have tried to identify the underlying core values that are shared by most of the groups that make up U.S. society. Sociologist Robin Williams (1965) identified the following:

1 *Achievement and success.* Americans place a high value on personal achievement, especially outdoing others. This value includes getting ahead at work and school, and the goal of attaining wealth, power, and prestige.

2 *Individualism.* Americans prize success through individual efforts and initiative. They cherish the ideal that an individual can rise from the bottom to the very top of society. If someone fails to "get ahead," Americans generally find fault with that individual, rather than with the social system for placing roadblocks in his or her path.

3 *Activity and work.* Americans expect people to work hard and to be busily engaged in some activity even when not at work.

4 *Efficiency and practicality.* Americans award high marks for getting things done efficiently. Even in everyday life, Americans consider it important to do things as fast or as well as possible, and constantly seek changes to increase efficiency.

5 *Science and technology.* Americans have a passion for applied science, for using science to control nature—to tame rivers and harness winds—and to develop new technology, from improved carburetors to the World Wide Web.

6 *Progress.* Americans expect rapid technological change. They believe that they should constantly build "more and better" gadgets that will help them move toward some vague goal called "progress."

7 *Material comfort.* Americans expect a high level of material comfort. This comfort includes not only nutrition, medical care, and housing, but

Why Do Native Americans Like Westerns?

U.S. AUDIENCES (and even German, French, and Japanese) devour westerns. In the United States, it is easy to see why Anglos might like westerns, for it is they who seemingly defy odds and emerge victorious. It is they who are portrayed as heroically taming a savage wilderness, who defend themselves from cruel, barbaric Indians intent on their destruction. But why would Indians like westerns?

Sociologist JoEllen Shively, a Chippewa who grew up on Indian reservations in Montana and North Dakota, found that westerns are so popular that Native Americans bring bags of paperbacks into taverns to trade with one another. They even call one another "cowboy."

Intrigued, Shively decided to investigate the matter by showing a western movie to adult Native Americans and Anglos in a reservation town. To select the movie,

Shively (1991, 1992) previewed over seventy westerns and then chose a John Wayne movie, *The Searchers*, because it not only focuses on conflict between Indians and cowboys but also shows the cowboys defeating the Indians. After the movie, she had the viewers fill out questionnaires and interviewed them. The Native Americans and Anglos were matched on education, age, income, and percentage of unemployment.

Shively found something surprising: *all* Native Americans and Anglos identified with the cowboys; *none* identified with the Indians. The ways in which Anglos and Native Americans identified with the cowboys, however, were quite different, for each projected a different fantasy onto the story. While Anglos saw the movie as an accurate portrayal of the Old West and a justification of their own status in the social system, Native

Americans saw it as embodying a free, natural way of life. In fact, Native Americans said that they were the "real cowboys." They said, "Westerns relate to the way I wish I could live"; "The cowboy is free"; "He's not tied down to an eight-to-five job, day after day."

Shively (1992) adds,

What appears to make Westerns meaningful to Indians is the fantasy of being free and independent like the cowboy. . . . Indians . . . find a fantasy in the cowboy story in which the important parts of their ways of life triumph and are morally good, validating their own cultural group in the context of a dramatically satisfying story.

In other words, values, not ethnicity, are the central issue. Thus, says Shively, Native American viewers make cowboys "honorary Indians," for the cowboys express their values of bravery, autonomy, and toughness.

also late-model cars and recreational playthings—from boats to computer games.

8 *Humanitarianism.* Americans emphasize helpfulness, personal kindness, aid in mass disasters, and organized philanthropy.

9 *Freedom.* This core value pervades U.S. life. It underscored the American Revolution, and Americans today bristle at the suggestion of any limitation on personal freedom. The box above highlights some interesting research on how this core value applies to Native Americans.

10 *Democracy.* By this term, Americans refer to majority rule, to the right of everyone to express an opinion, and to representative government.

11 *Equality.* It is impossible to understand Americans without being aware of the central role that the value of equality plays in their lives.

12 *Racism and group superiority.* Although it contradicts freedom, democracy, and equality, Ameri-

cans value some groups more than others and have done so throughout their history. The institution of slavery in earlier U.S. society is the most notorious example.

In an earlier publication (Henslin 1975), I updated Williams's analysis by adding the following three values.

13 *Education.* Americans are expected to go as far in school as their abilities and finances allow. Over the years, the definition of an "adequate" education has changed sharply, and today the expectation of a college education is held as an appropriate goal for most Americans.

14 *Religiosity.* There is a feeling that every true American ought to be "religious." This does not mean that everyone is expected to join a church or synagogue, but that everyone ought to acknowledge a belief in a Supreme Being and follow some set of matching precepts. This value is

so pervasive that Americans stamp "In God We Trust" on their money and declare in their national pledge of allegiance that they are "one nation under God."

15 *Romantic love.* Americans feel that the only proper basis for marriage is romantic love. Songs, literature, mass media, and "folk beliefs" all stress this value, and sometimes include the theme that "love conquers all."

Value Clusters

As you can see, values are not independent units; some cluster together to form a larger whole. In the **value cluster** surrounding success, for example, we find hard work, education, efficiency, material comfort, and individualism all bound up together. Americans are expected to go far in school, to work hard afterward, to be efficient, and then to attain a high level of material comfort, which, in turn, demonstrates success. Success is attributed to the individual's own efforts, the lack of success to his or her own faults.

Value Contradictions and Social Change

Not all values fall into neat, integrated packages. Some even contradict one another. The **value con-**

tradition noted earlier—group superiority—contradicts freedom, democracy, and equality. There simply cannot be full expression of freedom, democracy, equality, racism, and sexism all at the same time. Something has to give. One way in which Americans sidestepped this contradiction in the past was to say that freedom, democracy, and equality apply only to some groups. The contradiction was bound to surface over time, however, as it did with the Civil War and the women's liberation movement. *It is precisely at the point of value contradictions, then, that one can see a major force for social change in a society.*

Emerging Values

A value cluster of three interrelated core values—leisure, physical fitness, and self-fulfillment—appears to be emerging in the United States. A fourth emerging core value—concern for the environment—can also be identified.

1 *Leisure.* The emergence of leisure as a value is reflected in the rapid growth of a huge recreation industry—from computer games, boats, and motor homes, to sports arenas, vacation homes, and a gigantic travel and vacation industry.

2 *Physical fitness.* Physical fitness is not a new U.S. value, but increased emphasis is moving it into

Values, though firmly held, are changeable, both those held by individuals and those that represent a nation or people. It is difficult for many of us today to grasp the pride with which earlier Americans destroyed trees that took thousands of years to grow, are located only on one tiny speck of the globe, and are part of the nation's and world's heritage. But this is a value statement, representing current views. The pride on these woodcutters' faces represents another set of values entirely.

the core. This trend can be seen in the "natural" foods craze; brew bars; obsessive concerns about weight and diet; the many joggers, cyclists, and backpackers; and the mushrooming of health clubs and physical fitness centers.

3   *Self-fulfillment*. This value is reflected in the "human potential" movement, a concern with becoming "all one can be," "self-help," "relating," and "personal development."

This emerging value cluster is a response to new needs and interests resulting from fundamental changes in U.S. society. Americans used to be largely preoccupied with forging a nation and fighting for economic survival. They now have come to a point in their economic development where millions of people are freed from long hours of work, and millions more are able to retire from work when they can still expect decades of life ahead of them. This value cluster centers around enabling them to enjoy those years of retirement, or to maintaining their health and vigor during their younger years while they look forward to a life of leisure.

4   *Concern for the environment*. During most of U.S. history, the environment was seen as a challenge—a wilderness to be settled, forests to be chopped down, rivers and lakes to be fished, and animals to be hunted. The lack of concern for the environment that characterized earlier Americans is illustrated by the near extinction of the bison and the extinction in 1915 of the passenger pigeon, a bird previously so numerous that its annual migration would darken the skies for days. Today, Americans have developed a genuine, and (we can hope) long-term, concern for the environment.

This emergent value of environmental concern is also related to the current stage of U.S. economic development, a point that becomes clearer when we note that people act on environmental concerns only after basic needs are met. At this point in their development, for example, the world's poor nations have a difficult time "affording" this value.

Reactions to Changes in Core Values

Core values do not change without meeting strong resistance from traditionalists who hold them dear. Consequently, many people are upset at the changes

swirling around them, seeing their way of life challenged and their future growing insecure. A major criticism of the emerging value cluster of leisure, physical fitness, and self-fulfillment is that it encourages individualism at the cost of social responsibility. Critics fear that these values will stimulate self-indulgence, break down community, and ultimately undermine the family, religion, and the economy (Etzioni 1982; Bellah et al. 1985).

The new concern for the environment has also come under attack, but for quite different reasons. Among the traditionalists who are threatened by this emergent value are hunters, contractors, and developers who feel that their rights of individual choice are being trampled on by extremists.

Values as Blinders

Values and their supporting beliefs paint a unique picture of reality, as well as forming a view of what life *ought* to be like. Because Americans value individualism so highly, for example, they tend to see people as free to pursue whatever legitimate goals they desire. This value blinds them to the many social circumstances that impede people's efforts. The dire consequences of family poverty, parents' low education, and dead-end jobs tend to drop out of sight. Instead, Americans cling to the notion that anyone can make it—with the right amount of effort. And to prove it, dangled before their eyes are success stories of individuals who have succeeded in spite of huge handicaps.

← what we *ought* think   → what is actual

"Ideal" versus "Real" Culture

Many of the norms that surround cultural values are only partially followed. Differences always exist between what a group holds out as its cultural ideal and what its members actually do. Consequently, sociologists use the term **ideal culture** to refer to a group's ideal values and norms, to the goals they hold out for themselves. The idea of success, for example, is part of ideal culture. Americans glorify academic progress, hard work, and the display of material goods as signs of individual achievement. What people actually do, however, usually falls short of the cultural ideal. Compared with their capacities, for example, most people don't go as far as they could in school or work as hard as they can. Sociologists call the norms and values that people actually follow **real culture.**

Part of Americans' ideal culture is individualism, financial success, and the display of material goods as a sign of having "made it" in society. The family on the left represents this value cluster, but the family on the right is a sorry reminder that ideal culture often fails to reflect reality.

Technology, Culture, and the Global Village

New Technologies

The gestures, language, values, folkways, and mores that we have discussed—these all are part of symbolic or nonmaterial culture. Culture, as you recall, also has a material aspect, a group's *things*, from its houses to its toys. Central to a group's material culture is its technology. In its simplest sense, **technology** can be equated with tools. In its broader sense, technology also includes the skills or procedures necessary to make and use those tools.

We can use the term **new technologies** to refer to the emerging technologies of an era. Many minor technologies appear from time to time, but most are slight modifications of existing technologies. Occasionally, however, technologies appear that make a major impact on human life. It is primarily these to which the term *new technologies* refers. For people 500 years ago, the new technology was the printing press. For us, these new technologies are computers, satellites, and various forms of the electronic media.

The sociological significance of technology is that its importance goes far beyond the tool itself. *The type of technology a group has sets a framework for its nonmaterial culture.* Technology even influences the way people think and how they relate to one another, a focus of the box (page 52) on Sociology and the New Technology.

An example is gender relations. Through the centuries and throughout the world, it has been the custom (a group's nonmaterial culture) for men to dominate women. Today, with instantaneous communications (the material culture), this custom has become much more difficult to maintain. For example, when women from many nations gathered in Beijing for a U.N. conference in 1995, satellites instantly transmitted their grievances around the globe. Such communications both convey and create

"COOL! A KEYBOARD THAT WRITES WITHOUT A PRINTER."

Technological advances are now so rapid that the technology of one generation is practically unrecognizable by the next generation.

discontent, sometimes a feeling of sisterhood, and women agitate for social change.

In today's world, the long-accepted idea that it is proper to withhold rights on the basis of someone's sex can no longer hold. What is usually invisible in this revolutionary change is the role of technology, which joins the world's nations into a global communication network. Until recent technological advances, this was impossible.

focus on Technology

Cultural Lag and Cultural Change

A couple of generations ago, sociologist William Ogburn (1922/1938), a functional analyst, coined the term **cultural lag.** By this, Ogburn meant that not all parts of a culture change at the same pace. When some part of a culture changes, other parts lag behind.

Ogburn pointed out that *a group's material culture usually changes first, with the nonmaterial culture lagging behind,* playing a game of catch up. For example, when we get sick, we can type our symptoms into a computer and get an immediate printout of our diagnosis and best course of treatment. In fact, in some tests computers outperform physicians (Waldholz 1991). Yet our customs have not caught up with our technology, and we continue to visit doctors' offices.

Sometimes nonmaterial culture never does catch up. Instead, we may rigorously hold on to some outmoded form, one that once was needed, but long ago has been bypassed by new technology. A striking example is our nine-month school year. Have you ever wondered why it is nine months long, and why we take off the summers? For most of us, this is "just the way it's always been," and we've never questioned it. But there is more to this custom than meets the eye, for it is an example of cultural lag.

In the nineteenth century, when universal schooling came about, the school year matched the technology of the time, which was labor intensive. For survival, parents needed their children's help at the critical times of planting and harvesting. Although the invention of highly productive farm machinery eliminated the need for the school year to be so short, generations later we live with this cultural lag.

Technology and Cultural Leveling

For most of human history, communication was limited and travel slow. Consequently, in their relative isolation human groups developed highly distinctive ways of life as they responded to the particular sit-

Shown here is a Masai Barbie Doll. Mattel Toys, the U.S. manufacturer, has modified Barbie to match Masai (Kenya) culture by dressing her in a traditional "shuka" dress, beads, shawl, headdress, and anklets. As objects diffuse from one culture to another, they are modified to meet the tastes and specific needs of the adoptive culture. In this instance, the modification has been done intentionally as part of the globalization of capitalism. Now that Barbie is a Masai, can a Masai Ken be far behind?

uations they faced. The unique characteristics they developed, which distinguished one culture from another, tended to change little over time. The Tasmanians, who lived on an inaccessible island off the coast of Australia, provide an extreme example. For thousands of years, they had no contact with any other people. They were so isolated that they did not even know how to make clothing or fire (Edgerton 1992).

Except in such rare instances, humans always had *some* contact with other groups. During these contacts, people learned from one another, adapting some part of the other's way of life. In this process, called **cultural diffusion,** groups are most open to a change in their technology or material culture. They usually are eager, for example, to adopt superior weapons and tools. In remote jungles in South

Is Technology the Cart or the Horse?

WARNING! This machine is subject to breakdowns during periods of critical need. A special circuit in the machine called a "critical detector" senses the operator's emotional state, in terms of how desperate he or she is to use the machine. The "critical detector" then creates a malfunction proportional to the desperation of the operator. Threatening the machine with violence only aggravates the situation. Keep cool and say nice things to the machine. Nothing else seems to work. Never let the machine know you are in a hurry.

All over the country, users of copiers have laughed at some version of this attempt to turn frustration into humor. This sign comes close to a point of view called **technological determinism,** the idea that technology is the single greatest force in shaping our lives. Like the preceding warning, some technological determinists believe that machines have become an independent force that is out of human control (Chandler 1995). For them, technology is more important than anything else—politics, economics, religion, or any other social factor—in creating the kind of society we live in.

In 1954, long before the personal computer and most other forms of modern communications appeared on the scene, Jacques Ellul, a French sociologist, wrote an influential book, *The Technological Society*. In it, he (1965) claimed that technology had begun to dominate civilization. Technology, he said, is rapidly taking charge, and we humans are in danger of losing our freedom to the machines we have built.

Neil Postman echoes this negative sentiment. He (1992) argues that television's emphasis on immediate gratification and quick responses has ruined children's attention spans. Countless hours in front of television's "short bursts" of imagery have made it difficult for children to "organize their thought into logical structure, even in a simple paragraph."

Not all technological determinists are pessimists. While maintaining the emphasis on technology as the driving force in social change, the late media guru Marshall McLuhan (1911–1980) was optimistic about our technological future. McLuhan sought to understand the impact of the electronic media on symbolic culture. Coining a term that has become part of our common vocabulary, McLuhan (1964) noted that electronic communications are transforming the world into a "global village." By allowing people around the world to share experiences, the media shrink geographical boundaries and bring diverse peoples and ideas together.

Other analysts switch the emphasis. Instead of concentrating on how technology transforms culture, they stress how culture shapes technology. This view, called **the social construction of technology,** emphasizes how values and special interests shape the development and use of technology (Bijker 1987). For decades after the technology was available, for example, Los Angeles did not build a mass transit system. Why? Because the oil industry, which wielded immense political power, wanted to protect the profits they were reaping from the use of private automobiles.

Let's look at another example of the social construction of technology (Volti 1995). In the 1500s, guns were imported to Japan. The Japanese copied them, modified their design, and manufactured them. The use of guns, however, threatened the Samurai, the warrior class that used swords and followed ancient rituals in hand-to-hand combat. Now, from a distance, anyone with a gun, even cowards and social inferiors, could kill the best-trained and bravest Samurai. The Japanese government then centralized the production of guns and sold them only by license—which they refused to grant. Eventually the skills to make guns were lost, and guns disappeared from Japan. People and culture—in this case the Samurai and adherence to Japanese rituals of bravery—dominated technology.

In short, the *social constructionists* emphasize how people control, influence, or use technology. People, or culture, are "the horse" that drives technology. The *technological determinists*, in contrast, emphasize how technology affects people's customs, lifestyles, relationships, and even ideas. They see technology as "the horse" and culture as "the cart."

For Your Consideration

The technological determinists and the social constructionists bring us to a significant issue: Does technology free us, or is it yet another force of society that programs us? In other words, are we in control of technology, or is technology in control of us? Which is the cart, and which the horse?

Perhaps the truth consists of a combination of these views; perhaps technology both liberates and constrains. If so, can you provide examples from your own experience of how people mold technology, and how it, in turn, molds us?

America one can find metal cooking pots, steel axes, and even bits of clothing spun in mills in South Carolina. Although the direction of cultural diffusion today is primarily from the West to other parts of the world, cultural diffusion is not a one-way street, as bagels, woks, and hammocks in the United States show.

With today's technology in travel and communications, cultural diffusion is occurring rapidly. Air travel has made it possible to journey around the globe in a matter of hours. In the not-so-distant past, a trip from the United States to Africa was so unusual that only a few hardy people made it, and newspapers would herald their feat. Today, hundreds of thousands make the trip each year.

The changes in communication are no less vast. Communication used to be limited to face-to-face speech and to visual signals such as smoke, light reflected from mirrors, and written messages passed from hand to hand. In spite of newspapers, people in some parts of the United States did not hear about the end of the Civil War until weeks and even months after it was over. Today's electronic communications transmit messages across the globe in a matter of seconds, and we learn almost instantaneously what is happening on the other side of the world.

In fact, travel and communication unite us to such an extent that there almost is no "other side of the world" anymore. One result is **cultural leveling,** a process in which cultures become similar to one another as the globalization of capitalism brings not only technology but also Western culture to the rest of the world. Japan, for example, has adapted not only Western economic production but also Western forms of dress and music. These changes, superimposed on Japanese culture, have turned Japan into a blend of Western and Eastern cultures.

Cultural leveling, occurring rapidly around the world, is apparent to any traveler. The Golden Arches of McDonald's welcome today's visitors to Tokyo, Paris, London, Madrid, and even Moscow, Beijing, and Hong Kong. In the Indian Himalayan town of Dharmsala, a Buddhist monk and two Indian boys, sitting on benches in a shack with a dirt floor waiting for a videotaped U.S. movie to begin, watch a Levis commercial on MTV (Brauchli 1993). In a remote part of China, a peasant farmer in a mud hut with pigs running freely from room to room tunes in to "The Rich and the Famous"—thanks to a satellite dish perched atop his wood-planked roof ("Of Channel Jockeys and Tyrants," 1993). "Thanks to MTV," says an Indian girl in Calcutta, "I can wear a miniskirt to a disco" (Brauchli 1993).

Although the bridging of geography and culture by electronic signals does not in itself mark the end of traditional cultures, it inevitably results in some degree of cultural leveling, some blander, less distinctive way of life—U.S. culture with French, Japanese, and Bulgarian accents, so to speak. Although the "cultural accent" remains, something is lost forever.

Summary and Review

What Is Culture?

All human groups possess **culture**—language, beliefs, values, norms, and material objects passed from one generation to the next. **Material culture** consists of objects (art, buildings, clothing, tools). **Nonmaterial** (or symbolic) **culture** is a group's ways of thinking and patterns of behavior. **Ideal culture** is the values and norms that a group holds out for itself. **Real culture** is their actual behavior, which often falls short of their cultural ideals. Pp. 37–39.

What are cultural relativism and ethnocentrism?

People are naturally **ethnocentric;** that is, they use their own culture as a yardstick for judging the ways of others. In contrast, those who embrace **cultural relativism** try to understand other cultures on those cultures' own terms. Pp. 39–40.

Components of Culture

What are the components of nonmaterial culture?

The central component is **symbols,** anything to which people attach meaning and use to communicate with others. Universally, the symbols of nonmaterial culture are **gestures, language, values, norms, sanctions, folkways,** and **mores.** Pp. 40–41.

Why is language so significant to culture?

Language allows human experience to be goal directed, cooperative, and cumulative. It also lets humans move beyond the present and share past, future, and other common perspectives. According to the **Sapir–Whorf hypothesis,** language even shapes our thoughts and perceptions. Pp. 41–44.

How do values, norms, sanctions, folkways, and mores reflect culture?

All groups have **values,** standards by which they define what is desirable or undesirable, and **norms,** rules or expectations about behavior. Groups use **positive sanctions** to show approval of those who follow their norms, and **negative sanctions** to show disapproval of those who do not. Norms that are not strictly enforced are called **folkways,** while **mores** are norms to which groups demand conformity because they reflect core values. Pp. 44–45.

Subcultures and Countercultures

How do subcultures and countercultures differ?

A **subculture** is a group whose values and related behaviors distinguish its members from the general culture. A **counterculture** is a subculture that has some values that stand in opposition to those of the dominant culture. Pp. 45–46.

Values in U.S. Society

What are the dominant U.S. values?

Although the United States is a **pluralistic society,** made up of many groups, each with its own sets of val-

ues, certain values dominate: chiefly achievement and success, individualism, activity and work, efficiency and practicality, science and technology, progress, material comfort, equality, freedom, democracy, humanitarianism, racism and group superiority, education, religiosity, and romantic love. Some values cluster together (**value clusters**) to form a larger whole. **Value contradictions** (such as equality and racism) indicate areas of social tension, which are likely points of social change. Leisure, physical fitness, self-fulfillment, and concern for the environment are emerging core values. Changes in a society's values do not come without opposition. Pp. 46–49.

Technology and the Global Village

How is technology changing culture?

Ogburn coined the term **cultural lag** to refer to a group's nonmaterial culture lagging behind its changing technology. With today's technological advances in travel and communications, **cultural diffusion** is occurring rapidly. This leads to **cultural leveling,** whereby many groups are adopting Western culture in place of their own customs. Much of the richness of the world's diverse cultures is being lost in the process. Pp. 50–53.

Where can I read more on this topic?

Suggested readings for this chapter are listed on page 436.

Glossary

counterculture a subculture whose values place its members in opposition to the values of the broader culture (p. 46)

cultural diffusion the spread of cultural characteristics from one group to another (p. 51)

cultural lag William Ogburn's term for a situation in which nonmaterial culture lags behind changes in the material culture (p. 51)

cultural leveling the process by which cultures become similar to one another, especially by which Western industrial culture is imported and diffused into the Least Industrialized Nations (p. 53)

cultural relativism understanding a people from the framework of their own culture (p. 39)

culture the language, beliefs, values, norms, behaviors, and even material objects that are passed from one generation to the next (p. 37)

culture contact when people from different cultures come into contact with one another (p. 42)

culture shock the disorientation that people experience when they come in contact with a fundamentally different culture and can no longer depend on their taken-for-granted assumptions about life (p. 37)

ethnocentrism the use of one's own culture as a yardstick for judging the ways of other individuals or societies, generally leading to a negative evaluation of their values, norms, and behaviors (p. 38)

folkways norms that are not strictly enforced (p. 44)

gestures the ways in which people use their bodies to communicate with one another (p. 40)

ideal culture the ideal values and norms of a people, the goals held out for them (p. 49)

language a system of symbols that can be combined in an infinite number of ways to communicate abstract thought (p. 41)

material culture the material objects that distinguish a group of people, such as their art, buildings, weapons, utensils, machines, hairstyles, clothing, and jewelry (p. 37)

mores norms that are strictly enforced because they are thought essential to core values (p. 44)

negative sanction an expression of disapproval for breaking a norm; ranging from a mild, informal reaction such as a frown to severe formal reactions such as a prison sentence, banishment, or death (p. 44)

new technology a technology introduced into a society that has a significant impact on that society (p. 50)

nonmaterial culture (also called *symbolic culture*) a group's ways of thinking (including its beliefs, values, and other assumptions about the world) and doing (its common patterns of behavior, including language and other forms of interaction) (p. 37)

norms the expectations, or rules of behavior, that develop out of values (p. 44)

pluralistic society a society made up of many different groups (p. 46)

positive sanction a reward or positive reaction for following norms, ranging from a smile to a prize (p. 44)

real culture the norms and values that people actually follow (p. 49)

sanction an expression of approval or disapproval given to people for upholding or violating norms (p. 44)

Sapir–Whorf hypothesis Edward Sapir and Benjamin Whorf's hypothesis that language creates ways of thinking and perceiving (p. 44)

social construction of technology the view (opposed to *technological determinism*) that culture (people's values and special interests) shape the development and use of technology (p. 52)

subculture the values and related behaviors of a group that distinguish its members from the larger culture; a world within a world (p. 45)

symbol something to which people attach meanings and then use to communicate with others (p. 40)

symbolic culture another term for nonmaterial culture (p. 40)

taboo a norm so strong that it brings revulsion if violated (p. 45)

technological determinism the view that technology is the driving force behind culture; in its extreme form, technology is seen as taking on a life of its own, forcing human behavior to follow (p. 52)

technology in its narrow sense, tools; in its broader sense, the skills or procedures necessary to make and use those tools (p. 50)

value cluster a series of interrelated values that together form a larger whole (p. 48)

value contradiction values that contradict one another; to follow the one means to come into conflict with the other (p. 48)

values the standards by which people define what is desirable or undesirable, good or bad, beautiful or ugly (p. 44)

Sociology and the Internet

All URLs listed are current as of the printing of this book. URLs are often changed. Please check our Website http://www.abacon.com/henslin for updates.

1. Identifying Subcultures

One of the fascinating aspects of studying culture is the concept of subculture. As you have learned from reading this chapter, subcultures are groups whose norms, roles, and lifestyles deviate significantly from those in their society's general culture. In this project, you will look at the characteristics of some religious groups to see if they are subcultures.

To begin, direct your computer to Sociosite's Religion and Spirituality page (http://www.pscw.uva.nl/sociosite/TOPICS/Religion.html). Under "Eastern Religions," click on "Bahai." Click on several of the listed subjects and read the material, looking for how their beliefs and behaviors deviate from the dominant U.S.

culture. When you finish, you should be able to explain how Bahai is a subculture. Now, go back to the Religion and Spirituality page and choose three religions. Follow the procedure you used in studying Bahai. When you have completed your research, write a paper of three to five pages comparing the groups as possible subcultures.

2. Core Values

As discussed in this chapter, freedom is a core value in U.S. society. Compare the eleven excerpts from the "Declarations on Religious Freedom" (http://www.kosone.com/people/ocrt/humright.htm). Write a one- to two-page report on the common principles and differences that you find. Also discuss whether you think people in our society agree on what religious freedom means. Do you think this core value is changing?

Christian Pierre, Modern Madonna, 1995.

CHAPTER

3

Socialization

T HE OLD MAN WAS HORRIFIED *when he found out. Life never had been good since his daughter had lost her hearing when she was just two years old. She couldn't even talk—just fluttered her hands around trying to tell him things. Over the years, he had gotten used to that. But now . . . he shuddered at the thought of her being pregnant. No one would be willing to marry her, he knew that. And the neighbors, their tongues would never stop wagging. Everywhere he went, he could hear people talking behind his back.*

If only his wife were still alive, maybe she could come up with something. What should he do? He couldn't just kick his daughter out into the street.

After the baby was born, the old man tried to shake his feelings, but they wouldn't let loose. Isabelle was a pretty name, but every time he looked at the baby he felt sick to his stomach.

He hated doing it, but there was no way out. His daughter and her baby would have to live in the attic.

. . . Unfortunately, this is a true story. Isabelle was discovered in Ohio in 1938 when she was about 6½ years old, living in a dark room with her deaf-mute mother. Isabelle couldn't talk, but she did use gestures to communicate with her mother. An inadequate diet and lack of sunshine had given Isabelle a disease called rickets. *Her legs*

> *were so bowed that as she stood erect the soles of her shoes came nearly flat together, and she got about with a skittering gait. Her behavior toward strangers, especially men, was almost that of a wild animal, manifesting much fear and hostility. In lieu of speech she made only a strange croaking sound. (Davis 1995:122)*

When the newspapers reported this case, sociologist Kingsley Davis decided to find out what happened to Isabelle after her discovery. We'll come back to that later, but first let's use the case of Isabelle to gain some insight into human nature.

What Is Human Nature?

For centuries, people have been intrigued with the question of what is human about human nature. How much of people's characteristics comes from "nature" (heredity) and how much from "nurture" (the **social environment,** contact with others)? One way to answer this question is to study identical twins who have been reared apart. See the Down-to-Earth Sociology box on the next page for a fascinating account of identical twins. Another way is to study children who have had little human contact. Let us begin with the case of Isabelle.

Isolated Children

On occasion, an unfortunate, isolated child is discovered. What can they tell us about human nature? We can first conclude that humans have no natural language, for Isabelle, and others like her, are unable to speak.

But maybe Isabelle was not normal. This is what people first thought, for when given an intelligence test she scored practically zero. But after intensive language training, in only two months Isabelle was able to speak in short sentences. In about a year, she could write a few words, do simple addition, and retell stories after hearing them. Seven months later, she had a vocabulary of almost 2,000 words. It took only two years for Isabelle to reach the intellectual level normal for her age. She then went on to school, where she was "bright, cheerful, energetic . . . and participated in all school activities as normally as other children" (Davis 1995:123).

Institutionalized Children

But what besides language is required if a child is to develop into what we consider a healthy, balanced, intelligent human being? We find part of the answer in an interesting experiment from the 1930s. Back then, orphanages dotted the United States,

Down-to-Earth Sociology

Heredity or Environment?
The Case of Oskar and Jack, Identical Twins

IDENTICAL TWINS SHARE exact genetic heredity. One fertilized egg divides to produce two embryos. If heredity is the cause of personality (or of people's attitudes, temperament, and basic skills), then identical twins should be identical not only in their looks but also in these characteristics.

The fascinating case of Jack and Oskar helps us to unravel this mystery. From their experience, we can see the far-reaching effects of the environment—how social experiences override biology.

Jack Yufe and Oskar Stohr are identical twins born in 1932 to a Jewish father and a Catholic mother. They were separated as babies after their parents divorced. Oskar was reared in Czechoslovakia by his mother's mother, who was a strict Catholic. When Oskar was a toddler, Hitler annexed this area of Czechoslovakia, and Oskar learned to love Hitler and to hate Jews. He became involved with the Hitler Youth (a sort of Boy Scout organization designed to instill the "virtues" of patriotism, loyalty, obedience—and hatred).

Jack's upbringing provides almost total contrast. Reared in Trinidad by his father, he learned loyalty to Jews and hatred of Hitler and the Nazis. After the war, Jack emigrated to Israel, where, at the age of 17, he joined a kibbutz. Later, Jack served in the Israeli army.

In 1954, the two brothers met. It was a short meeting, and Jack had been warned not to tell Oskar that they were Jews. Twenty-five years later, in 1979, when they were 47 years old, social scientists at the University of Minnesota

The question of the relative influence of heredity and the environment on human behavior has fascinated and plagued researchers. Identical twins reared apart provide an opportunity to examine this relationship. Almost all identical twins, however, as is the case with these girls, are reared together, frustrating efforts to separate heredity and environment.

brought them together again. These researchers figured that since Jack and Oskar had the same genes, whatever differences they showed would have to be due to the environment—to their different social experiences.

Not only were Oskar's and Jack's attitudes toward the war, Hitler, and Jews different, so, too, were their other basic orientations to life. In their politics, Oskar is conservative, while Jack is more liberal. Oskar enjoys leisure, while Jack is a workaholic. And, as you

can predict, Jack is very proud of being a Jew. Oskar, however, won't even mention it.

That would seem to settle the matter. But there is another side to the findings. The researchers also found that Oskar and Jack both like sweet liqueur and spicy foods, excelled at sports as children but had difficulty with math, and have the same rate of speech. Each even flushes the toilet both before and after using it.

For Your Consideration

Heredity or environment? How much influence does each have? The question is not yet settled, but at this point it seems fair to conclude that the *limits* of certain physical and mental abilities are established by heredity (such as ability at sports and mathematics), while such basic orientations to life as attitudes are the result of the environment. We can put it this way: For some parts of life, the blueprint is drawn by heredity; but even here the environment can redraw those lines. For other parts, the individual is a blank slate, and it is entirely up to the environment to determine what is written on that slate.

Sources: Based on Begley 1979; Chen 1979; Wright 1995.

and children reared in orphanages tended to have difficulty establishing close bonds with others—and to have lower IQs. "Common sense" (which we noted in Chapter 1 is unreliable) told everyone that the cause of mental retardation is biological ("They're just born that way"). Two psychologists, H. M. Skeels and H. B. Dye (1939), however, began to suspect another cause. For background on their experiment, look at this account of a good orphanage in Iowa during the 1930s, where they were consultants:

> Until about six months, they were cared for in the infant nursery. The babies were kept in standard hospital cribs that often had protective sheeting on the sides, thus effectively limiting visual stimulation; no toys or other objects were hung in the infants' line of vision. Human interactions were limited to busy nurses who, with the speed born of practice and necessity, changed diapers or bedding, bathed and medicated the infants, and fed them efficiently with propped bottles. (Skeels 1966)

Perhaps, they thought, the absence of stimulating social interaction is the basic problem, not some biological incapacity on the part of the children. To test their controversial idea, they placed thirteen infants whose mental retardation was so obvious that no one wanted to adopt them in an institution for the mentally retarded. Each infant, then about 19 months old, was assigned to a separate ward of women ranging in mental age from 5 to 12 and in chronological age from 18 to 50. The women were pleased with this arrangement. They not only did a good job taking care of the infants' basic physical needs—diapering, feeding, and so on—but they also loved to play with the children, to cuddle them, and to shower them with attention. They even competed to see which ward would have "its baby" walking or talking first. One woman would become

> particularly attached to him [or her] and figuratively "adopted" him [or her]. As a consequence, an intense one-to-one adult–child relationship developed, which was supplemented by the less intense but frequent interactions with the other adults in the environment. Each child had some one person with whom he [or she] was identified and who was particularly interested in him [or her] and his [or her] achievements. (Skeels 1966)

The researchers left a control group of twelve infants, also retarded but higher in intelligence, at the orphanage, where they received the usual care. Two and a half years later, Skeels and Dye tested all the children's intelligence. Their findings were startling: Those assigned to the retarded women had gained an average of 28 IQ points while those who remained in the orphanage had lost 30 points.

What happened after these children were grown? Did these initial differences matter? Twenty-one years later, Skeels and Dye did a follow-up study. Those in the control group who had remained in the orphanage averaged less than third grade in education. Four still lived in state institutions, while the others held low-level jobs. Only two had married. In contrast, the average level of education for the thirteen individuals in the experimental group was 12 grades (about normal for that period). Five had completed one or more years of college. One had not only earned a B.A. but had gone on to graduate school. Eleven had married. All thirteen were self-supporting and had higher-status jobs or were homemakers (Skeels 1966). Apparently, then, one characteristic we take for granted as being a basic "human" trait—high intelligence—results from early close relations with other humans.

Let's consider one other case, the story of Genie:

> In 1970, California authorities found Genie, a 13½-year-old girl who had been kept locked in a small room and tied to a chair since she was 20 months old. Apparently her 70-year-old father hated children, and had probably caused the death of two of Genie's siblings. Her 50-year-old mother was partially blind and frightened of her husband. Genie could not speak, did not know how to chew, and was unable to stand upright. On intelligence tests, she scored at the level of a 1-year-old. After intensive training, Genie learned to walk and use simple sentences (although they were garbled). As she grew up, her language remained primitive, she took anyone's property if it appealed to her, and she went to the bathroom wherever she wanted. At the age of 21, Genie went to live in a home for adults who cannot live alone. (Pines 1981)

From the pathetic story of Genie, we can conclude that not only intelligence but also the ability to establish close bonds with others are dependent on early interaction. In addition, apparently there is a period prior to age 13 in which language and human bonding must occur for humans to develop high intelligence and the ability to be sociable and follow social norms.

Deprived Animals

A final lesson can be gained by looking at animals that have been deprived of normal interaction. In a series of experiments with rhesus monkeys, psychologists Harry and Margaret Harlow demonstrated the importance of early learning. The Harlows (1962) raised baby monkeys in isolation. They gave each monkey two artificial mothers, shown in the photograph on this page. One "mother" was only a wire frame with a wooden head, but it did have a nipple from which the baby could nurse. The frame of the other "mother," which had no bottle, was covered with soft terrycloth. To obtain food, the baby monkeys nursed at the wire frame.

When the Harlows (1965) frightened them with a mechanical bear or dog, the babies did not run to the wire frame "mother." Instead, they would cling pathetically to their terrycloth "mother." The Har-

Like humans, monkeys also need interaction to thrive. Those raised in isolation are unable to interact satisfactorily with others. In this photograph, we see one of the monkeys described in the text. Purposefully frightened by the experimenter, the monkey has taken refuge in the soft terrycloth draped over an artificial "mother."

lows concluded that infant–mother bonding is due not to feeding but, rather, to what they termed "intimate physical contact." To most of us, this phrase means cuddling.

In one of their many other experiments, the Harlows isolated baby monkeys for different lengths of time. They found that monkeys isolated for short periods (about three months) were able to overcome the effects of their isolation. Those isolated for six months or more, however, were unable to adjust to normal monkey life. They could not play or engage in pretend fights, and the other monkeys rejected them. In other words, as in the case of Genie, the longer the isolation, the more difficult it is to overcome its effects.

Because humans are not monkeys, we must always be careful about extrapolating from animal studies to human behavior. The Harlow experiments, however, strongly corroborate what we know about children who are reared in isolation.

▼ **In Sum: Society Makes Us Human** Apparently, babies do not "naturally" develop into human adults. Although their bodies get bigger, if raised in isolation they become little more than big animals. Without the concepts of language, they can't experience or even grasp relations between people (the "connections" we call brother, sister, parent, friend, teacher, and so on). And without warm, intimate interaction, they aren't "friendly" in the accepted sense of the term, nor do they cooperate with others. In short, it is through human contact that people learn to be members of the human community. This process by which we learn the ways of society (or of particular groups), called **socialization,** is what sociologists have in mind when they say, "Society makes us human." *how to interact with other*

◤ Socialization into the Self, Mind, and Emotions

At birth, we have no idea that we are a separate being. We don't even know that we are a he or a she. How do we develop a **self,** the picture that we have of how others see us, our view of who we are?

Cooley and the Looking-Glass Self

Back in the 1800s, Charles Horton Cooley (1864–1929), a symbolic interactionist who taught at the

University of Michigan, concluded that this unique aspect of "humanness" is socially created; that is, *our sense of self develops from interaction with others.* Cooley coined the term **looking-glass self** (1902) to describe the process by which a sense of self develops. He summarized this idea in the following couplet:

> Each to each a looking-glass
> Reflects the other that doth pass.

The looking-glass self contains three elements:

1 *We imagine how we appear to those around us.* For example, we may think that others see us as witty or dull.

2 *We interpret others' reactions.* We come to conclusions about how others evaluate us. Do they like us being witty? Do they dislike us for being dull?

3 *We develop a self-concept.* Based on our interpretations of how others react to us, we develop feelings and ideas about ourselves. A favorable reflection in this "social mirror" leads to a positive self-concept, a negative reflection to a negative self-concept.

Note that the development of the self does not depend on accurate evaluations. Even if we grossly misinterpret how others think about us, those misjudgments become part of our self-concept. Note also that although the self-concept begins in childhood, *its development is an ongoing, lifelong process.* The three steps of the looking-glass self are part of our everyday lives: As we monitor how other people react to us, we continually modify the self. The self, then, is never a finished product, but is always in process, even into old age.

Mead and Role Taking

Another symbolic interactionist, George Herbert Mead (1863–1931), who taught at the University of Chicago, added that play is crucial to the development of the self. In play, children learn to **take the role of the other,** that is, to put themselves in someone else's shoes—to understand how someone else feels and thinks and to anticipate how that person will act.

Young children attain this ability only gradually (Mead 1934; Coser 1977). In a simple experiment, psychologist J. Flavel (1968) asked 8- and 14-year-olds to explain a board game to some children who were blindfolded and to others who were not. The 8-year-olds gave the same instructions to everyone, while the 14-year-olds gave more detailed instructions to those who were blindfolded. The younger children could not yet take the role of the other, while the older children could.

Mead analyzed taking the role of the other *as an essential part of learning to be a full-fledged member of society. At first, we are only able to take the role of* significant others, *as these children are doing. Later we develop the capacity to take the role of* the generalized other, *which is essential not only for extended cooperation but also for the control of antisocial desires.*

To help his students understand what the term generalized other *means, Mead used baseball as an illustration. The text explains why team sports and organized games are excellent examples to explain this concept.*

As they develop this ability, at first children are able to take only the role of **significant others,** individuals who significantly influence their lives, such as parents or siblings. By assuming their roles during play, such as dressing up in their parents' clothing, children cultivate the ability to put themselves in the place of significant others.

As the self gradually develops, children internalize the expectations of more and more people. The ability to take roles eventually extends to being able to take the role of "the group as a whole." Mead used the term **generalized other** to refer to this, our perception of how people in general think of us.

To take the role of others is essential if we are to become a cooperative member of human groups—whether our family, friends, or co-workers. This ability allows us to modify our behavior by anticipating the reactions of others—something Genie never learned.

Learning to take the role of the other goes through three stages:

1 *Imitation.* Children under 3 do not yet have a sense of self separate from others, and they can only imitate people's gestures and words. (This stage is actually not role taking, but it prepares the child for it.)

2 *Play.* From the age of about 3 to 6, children pretend to take the roles of specific people. They might take the role of firefighter, wrestler, Supergirl, Batman, and so on. They also like costumes at this stage and enjoy dressing up in their parents' clothing, or tying a towel around their necks to "become" Superman or Wonder Woman.

3 *Games.* This third stage, organized play, or team games, begins roughly with the early school years. The significance for the self is that to play these games the individual must be able to take multiple roles. One of Mead's favorite examples was that of a baseball game, in which each player must be able to take the role of all the other players. To play baseball, the child not only must know his or her own role but also must be able to anticipate who will do what when the ball is hit or thrown.

Mead also distinguished between the "I" and the "me" in the development of the self. The *"I" is the self as subject,* the active, spontaneous, creative part of the self. In contrast, the *"me" is the self as object,* made up of attitudes internalized from our interactions with others. Mead chose pronouns to indicate these two aspects of the self because in our language "I" is the active agent, as in "I shoved him," while "me" is the object of action, as in "He shoved me." Mead stressed that we are not passive in the socialization process. We are not like computerized robots, simply absorbing the responses of others. Rather, our "I" evaluates the reactions of others and organizes them into a unified whole.

Mead also drew a conclusion that some find startling—that *not only the self but also the human mind is a social product.* Mead stressed that we cannot think without symbols. But where do these symbols come from? Only from society, which gives us our symbols by giving us language. If society did not provide the symbols, we would not be able to think, and thus would not possess what we call the mind. Mind, then, like language, is a product of society.

Piaget and the Ability to Reason

An essential part of our minds is our ability to reason. How do we learn to reason? This question bothered Swiss psychologist Jean Piaget (1896–1980), who noticed that when young children take intelligence tests they give similar wrong answers. He thought that younger children might be using some sort of incorrect rule to figure out their answers. This could mean that children go through a common process as they acquire reasoning skills (Piaget 1950, 1954; Phillips 1969).

Through systematic testing, Piaget discovered that children go through these four stages as they develop the ability to reason. (If you equate the term *operational* with "reasoning skills," Piaget's findings are easier to understand.)

1 **The sensorimotor stage** (from birth to about age 2) During this stage, understanding is limited to direct contact with the environment—sucking, touching, listening, seeing. Infants do not think, in any sense we understand. They, for example, cannot recognize cause and effect.

2 **The preoperational stage** (from about age 2 to age 7) During this stage, children *develop the ability to use symbols.* They do not yet understand common concepts, however, such as numbers, size, speed, weight, volume, and causation. Although they can count, they do not really understand what numbers mean. For example, if you spread out six flowers and six pennies, a child will count each to six and say that the flowers and pennies are equal in number. But if you place the pennies in a single pile, the child will say there are more flowers than pennies (Phillips 1969). Nor do they yet have the ability to take the role of the other. Piaget asked preoperational children to describe a clay model of a mountain range and found they could do so. But when he asked them to describe how the mountain range looked from where another child was sitting, they could not do so. They could only repeat what they saw from their view.

3 **The concrete operational stage** (from the age of about 7 to 12) Although reasoning abilities are more developed, they remain *concrete.* Children can now understand numbers, causation, and speed, and they are able to take the role of the other and to participate in team games. Without concrete examples, however, they are unable to talk about concepts such as truth, honesty, or justice. They can explain why Jane's answer was a lie, but they cannot describe what truth itself is.

4 **The formal operational stage** (after the age of about 12) During this stage, children are capable of abstract thinking. They can talk about concepts, come to conclusions based on general principles, and use rules to solve abstract problems.

Global Considerations: Developmental Sequences

Cooley's conclusions about the looking-glass self and Mead's conclusions about role taking appear to be universal. There is less agreement, however, that Piaget's four stages are globally true. Some child development specialists, for example, suggest that the stages are much less distinct, that children develop reasoning skills much more gradually than Piaget indicated (Berk 1994).

Consider how the *content* of what children learn varies from one culture to another, and how this influences their thinking. For example, Brazilian street children have little or no schooling. Yet through selling candy they develop sophisticated mathematical and bargaining abilities (Saxe 1995). Similarly, in southern Mexico Zinacanteco Indian girls become expert weavers at an early age (Childs and Greenfield 1982). With experiences and abilities so unlike those learned by our children, and with thinking processes that revolve around these activities, we

Basic thought processes may be the same around the world, but the content of thinking and the development of abilities differ markedly from one culture to another. South American street children, for example, learn how to bargain and compute basic mathematics at an early age. Shown here are Brazilian children whose experiences and abilities differ dramatically from those of most children in the industrialized nations.

cannot assume that the developmental sequences observed in our children are true of children around the globe (Berk 1994).

Freud and the Development of Personality

Along with the development of the mind and the self comes the development of personality. Let's look at a theory that has influenced the Western world.

In Vienna at the turn of the century, Sigmund Freud (1856–1939), a physician, founded *psychoanalysis*, a technique for treating emotional problems through long-term, intensive exploration of the subconscious mind. We shall look at that part of his thought that applies to the development of personality.

Freud believed that personality consists of three elements. Each child is born with the first, an **id**, Freud's term for inborn drives for self-gratification. The id of the newborn is evident in cries of hunger or pain. The pleasure-seeking id operates throughout life, demanding the immediate fulfillment of basic needs: attention, safety, food, sex, aggression, and so on.

But the id's drive for immediate and complete satisfaction runs directly against the needs of other people. As the child comes up against norms and other constraints (usually represented by parents), he or she must adapt to survive. To help adapt to these constraints that block his or her desires, a second component of the personality emerges, which Freud called the ego. The **ego** is the balancing force between the id and the demands of society that suppress it. The ego also serves to balance the id and the **superego,** the third component of the personality, more commonly called the *conscience.*

The superego represents *culture within us*, the norms and values we have internalized from our social groups. As the *moral* component of the personality, the superego gives us feelings of guilt or shame when we break social rules, or pride and self-satisfaction when we follow them.

According to Freud, when the id gets out of hand, we follow our desires for pleasure and break society's norms. When the superego gets out of hand, we become overly rigid in following those norms, finding ourselves bound in a straitjacket of rules that inhibit our lives. The ego, the balancing force, tries to prevent either the superego or the id

from dominating. In the emotionally healthy individual, the ego succeeds in balancing these conflicting demands of the id and the superego. In the maladjusted individual, however, the ego cannot control the inherent conflict between the id and the superego, and the result is internal confusion and problem behaviors.

Sociological Evaluation What sociologists appreciate about Freud is his emphasis on socialization—that the social group into which we are born transmits norms and values that restrain our biological drives. Sociologists, however, object to the view that inborn and unconscious motivations are the primary reasons for human behavior, for this denies *the central principle of sociology:* that social factors such as roles, religion, and social class (income, education, and occupation) underlie people's behaviors (Epstein 1988; Bush and Simmons 1990). Feminist sociologists have been especially critical of Freud. Although what we just summarized applies to both females and males, Freud assumed that what is "male" is "normal." He even analyzed females as inferior, castrated males (Chodorow 1990).

Global Considerations: Socialization into Emotions

As we have seen, the mind is a social product, and through socialization we acquire the particulars that go into human reasoning. Emotions, too, are not simply the results of biology. They also depend on socialization (Hochschild 1975; Johnson 1992; Wouters 1992).

This conclusion may sound strange. Don't all people get angry? Doesn't everyone cry? Don't we all feel guilt, shame, sadness, remorse, happiness, fear? What has socialization to do with emotions?

Let's start with the obvious. Certainly people around the world feel these particular emotions, but the ways in which they express them vary from one culture to another. This variation becomes evident when we compare cultures. Let's consider, for example, the case of very close adult male friends reunited after a long separation. Americans might shake hands vigorously or even pat each other on the back. Japanese might bow, while Arabs will kiss. A good part of childhood socialization centers on learning to express emotions, for each culture has "norms of emotion" that demand conformity (Clark 1991).

How we learn to express emotions depends not only on culture but also on our social location. Consider gender. When two U.S. female friends are reunited after a long separation, they are much more likely to hug than to merely shake hands or to give each other a pat on the back. African Americans, Asian Americans, Latinos, Native Americans, and whites also may react differently. And all of this is modified by social class. That is, on seeing a friend after a long absence, lower-class women, men, African Americans, and so on, are likely to express emotions of delight in different ways than do upper-class women, men, African Americans, and so on.

But the matter goes deeper than this. In some cultures people even learn to experience emotions quite unlike ours. For example, the Ifaluk, who live on the Western Caroline Islands of Micronesia, use the word *fago* to refer to feelings evoked by seeing someone suffer or in need of help, something close to what we refer to as sympathy or compassion. But they also use this term to describe their feelings when they are around someone who has high status, someone who is highly admired or respected (Kagan 1984). To us, these are two distinct emotions, and they require distinct terms.

▼ **In Sum** As we are socialized into a culture, we learn not only how to express our emotions, but also what emotions to feel. Because feelings influence behavior, to understand emotions is to broaden our understanding of human behavior.

The Self and Emotions as Social Control—Society within Us

Much of our socialization is intended to turn us into conforming members of society. Socialization into the self and emotions is essential in this process, for both mold our behavior. Although we like to think we are "free," consider for a moment just some of the factors that influence how we act: the expectations of friends, parents, and teachers; classroom norms; college rules; and federal and state laws. For example, if for some reason, such as a moment of intense frustration or a devilish desire to shock people, you wanted to tear off your clothes and run naked down the street, what would stop you?

The answer is your socialization—*society within you.* Your experiences in society have resulted in a self that thinks along certain lines and feels particular emotions. This helps keep you in line. Thoughts such as "Would I be kicked out of school?" and "What would my friends (parents) think if they found out?" represent an awareness of the self in relationship to others. So does the desire to avoid feelings of shame and embarrassment. Our *social mirror,* then—the result of being socialized into a self and emotions—sets up effective controls over our behavior. In fact, socialization into self and emotions is so effective that some people experience embarrassment just thinking about running nude in public!

Socialization into Gender

Society also channels our behavior through **gender socialization.** By expecting different attitudes and behaviors from us *because* we are male or female, the human group nudges boys and girls in separate directions in life. This foundation of contrasting attitudes and behaviors is so thorough that, as adults, most of us think, act, and feel according to our culture's guidelines.

How do we learn gender messages? Because the significance of gender in social life is emphasized throughout this book, with a special focus in Chapter 10, for now let's briefly consider the influence of just the family and the mass media.

Gender, the Family, and Sex-Linked Behaviors

Our parents are the first significant others who teach us our part in this symbolic division of the world. Their own gender orientations are so firmly established that they do much of this teaching without even being aware of what they are doing. This is illustrated by a classic study done by psychologists Susan Goldberg and Michael Lewis (1969). They asked mothers to bring their 6-month-old infants into their laboratory, supposedly to observe the infants' development. Secretly, however, these researchers also observed the mothers. They found that the mothers kept their daughters closer to them. They also touched and spoke more to their daughters.

By the time the children were 13 months old, the girls stayed closer to their mothers during play, and they returned to them sooner and more often than did the boys. When Goldberg and Lewis set up a barrier to separate the children from their mothers, who

Although males are socialized to express less emotion than are females, such socialization apparently goes against their nature. In certain settings, especially sports, males are allowed to be openly emotional, even demonstrative, with one another. Shown here is U.S. sprinter Michael Johnson ("the world's fastest man") being congratulated after winning the Olympics gold medal in the-200 meter dash.

were holding toys, the girls cried and motioned for help more than the boys, who attempted to circumvent the barrier more actively. Goldberg and Lewis concluded that in our society mothers unconsciously reward their daughters for being passive and dependent, their sons for being active and independent.

These lessons continue throughout childhood. On the basis of their sex, children are given different kinds of toys. Preschool boys are allowed to roam farther from home than their preschool sisters, and they are subtly encouraged to participate in more rough-and-tumble play—even to get dirtier and to be more defiant (Gilman 1911/1971; Henslin 1997).

Such experiences in socialization lie at the heart of the sociological explanation of male–female differences. We should note, however, that some sociologists consider biology to be a cause. For example,

were the infants in the Goldberg–Lewis study demonstrating built-in biological predispositions, with the mothers merely reinforcing—not causing—those differences? We shall return to this controversial issue in Chapter 10.

Gender and the Mass Media

Sociologists stress how this sorting process that begins in the family is reinforced as the child is exposed to other aspects of society. Especially important today are the **mass media,** forms of communication directed to large audiences. Let's look at how the powerful images of the sexes in television and music reinforce society's expectations of gender.

Television Children's television overwhelmingly features more males than females. In cartoons, males outnumber females by four or five to one (Morgan 1982, 1987). Adult television picks up this message of male dominance. On prime-time television, male characters outnumber female characters by two to one, with the male characters more likely to be portrayed in higher-status positions (Vande Berg and Streckfuss 1992). Although there are some exceptions—Murphy Brown is depicted as stronger than her weak, sniveling boss—females are more likely to be portrayed as passive and indecisive. In commercials women's voices are rarely used as the voice-over. The significance of these images is not lost on viewers, for the more television that people watch, the more they tend to have restrictive ideas about women's role in society (Signorielli 1989, 1990).

Music Music also helps to form our images of the sexes. Many songs directed toward teenagers give boys the message that they should dominate male–female relationships, and girls that they should be sexy, dependent, and submissive. In music videos, males are more likely to be portrayed as aggressive and domineering, females as affectionate and dependent (Seidman 1992). On MTV, three-quarters of music videos show only male performers (Vincent et al. 1987). Of those that do show females, 10 percent portray violence against women and three-fourths either "put women down" or "keep them in their place." Perhaps the most damning finding, however, is that females are generally irrelevant, usually presented as background ornaments for male action.

▼ **In Sum** All of us are born into a society in which "male" and "female" are significant symbols. Sorted into separate groups from childhood, girls and boys come to have sharply different ideas of themselves and of one another, beginning within the family and later reinforced by other social institutions. Each of us learns the meanings that our society associates with the sexes. These symbols become integrated into our views of the world, forming a picture that forces an interpretation of the world in terms of gender.

Agents of Socialization

People and groups that influence our self-concept, emotions, attitudes, and behavior are called **agents of socialization.** Of the many agents of socialization that prepare us to take our place in society, we shall examine the family, religion, day care, school and peers, and the mass media.

The Family

One of the main findings of sociologists is how socialization depends on a family's social class. Let's compare how working-class and middle-class parents rear their children. Sociologist Melvin Kohn (1959, 1963, 1976, 1977; Kohn et al. 1986) found that the main concern of working-class parents is that their children be obedient, neat, and clean, follow the rules, and stay out of trouble. They are likely to use physical punishment to make their children obey. Middle-class parents, in contrast, show greater concern about developing their children's curiosity, self-expression, and self-control. They stress the reasons for their children's behavior and are more likely to reason with their children than to use physical punishment.

These findings were a sociological puzzle. Just why should working-class and middle-class parents rear their children so differently? Kohn knew that life experiences of some sort held the key, and he found that key in the world of work. Blue-collar workers are usually supervised very closely. Their bosses expect them to do exactly as they are told. Since blue-collar parents expect their children's lives

to resemble their own, they stress obedience and conformity. Middle-class parents, in contrast, have more independence at work, and are encouraged to take the initiative. Expecting their children to work at similar jobs, they, in turn, socialize them into the qualities they have found valuable.

Kohn still felt puzzled, however, for some working-class parents act more like middle-class parents, and vice versa. He found the answer to this part of the puzzle in the parents' specific type of job. Middle-class office workers, for example, have little freedom and are closely supervised. Kohn found that they follow the working-class pattern of child rearing, for they stress outward conformity. In contrast, some blue-collar workers, such as those who do home repairs, have a good deal of freedom. These workers follow the middle-class model in rearing their children (Pearlin and Kohn 1966; Kohn and Schooler 1969).

Religion

By influencing morality, religion becomes a key component in people's ideas of right and wrong. Religion is so important to Americans that 65 percent of Americans belong to a local congregation, and during a typical week 40 percent attend a religious service (*Statistical Abstract* 1995:83). Religion is significant even for people reared in nonreligious homes, for religious ideas pervade U.S. society, providing basic ideas of morality that become significant for us all.

The influence of religion extends to other areas of our lives as well. For example, participation in religious services teaches us not only beliefs about the hereafter but also ideas about the dress, speech, and manners appropriate for formal occasions. Religion is so significant that we shall spend a separate chapter on this social institution.

Day Care

With more mothers working for wages today than ever before, day care has become a significant agent of socialization. Concerns about its effects have propelled day care into the center of controversy. Researchers find that the effects of day care largely depend on the child's background (Scarr and Eisenberg 1993). Children from poverty-stricken homes, as well as those from dysfunctional families (such as with alcoholic, inept, or abusive parents), appear to benefit from day care. For example, the language skills of children from low-income homes increase. In contrast, day care may slow these skills in middle-class children, who would have received more intellectual stimulation at home. As you would expect, much depends on the quality of day care: high-quality day care (safe, small numbers, warm interaction, with low turnover of a trained staff) benefits children, while low-quality care has negative effects.

At this point, however, findings are preliminary, many even contradictory. For example, some studies show that children in day care are more cooperative and secure, while others show that they are more aggressive and insecure. Perhaps the fairest summary of current knowledge is that children from stable families receive no clear benefit or detriment from day care, and children in poverty and from dysfunctional families benefit from quality day care.

The School and Peer Groups

As a child's experiences with agents of socialization broaden, the influence of the family lessens. Entry into school marks only one of many steps in this transfer of allegiance. Here children move away from a world in which they may have been the almost exclusive focus of doting parents, and learn to be part of a large group of people of similar age. The Immigrant Experience box on the next page illustrates how vital schools can be in the socialization process.

One of the most significant aspects of education is that it exposes children to peer groups. A **peer group** is a group of individuals of roughly the same age who are linked by common interests. Examples of peer groups are friends, clubs, gangs, and "the kids in the neighborhood."

Sociologists Patricia Adler, Steven Kless, and Peter Adler (1992) document how the peer group provides an enclave in which boys and girls resist the efforts of parents and schools to socialize them their way. Observing children at two elementary schools in Colorado, they saw how the children separate themselves by sex and develop their own worlds with unique norms. The norms that make boys popular are athletic ability, coolness, and toughness. For girls, they are family background, physical appearance (clothing and the use of makeup), and the ability to

Schools are one of the primary agents of socialization. One of their chief functions is to sort young people into the adult roles thought appropriate for them, as well as to teach them the attitudes and skills that match those roles. What sorts of attitudes and adult roles do you think these "Redskinettes" are being socialized into? Is this a manifest or a latent function? Is it a dysfunction?

The Immigrant Experience

Caught between Two Worlds

JUST AS AN INDIVIDUAL is socialized into becoming a member of a culture, so a person can lose a culture through socialization. If you are exposed to a new culture as an adult, as older immigrants are, you can selectively adopt aspects of the new culture without entirely relinquishing your native culture. If the immersion occurs as a child, however, the second culture will vie for dominance with your native heritage. This, in turn, can lead to inner turmoil. To cut ties with your first culture—one way of handling the conflict—can create a sense of loss that may be recognized only later in life.

Richard Rodriguez, a literature professor and essayist, was born in the 1950s to working-class Mexican immigrants. Like other children of Mexican immigrants, Richard's first language was Spanish—a rich mother tongue that provided his orientation to the world. Until the age of 5 when he began school, he knew but fifty words in English. He describes what happened when he began school.

The change came gradually but early. When I was beginning grade school, I noted to myself the fact that the classroom environment was so different in its styles and assumptions from my own family environment that survival

would essentially entail a choice between both worlds. When I became a student, I was literally "remade"; neither I nor my teachers considered anything I had known before as relevant. I had to forget most of what my culture had provided, because to remember it was a disadvantage. The past and its cultural values became detachable, like a piece of clothing grown heavy on a warm day and finally put away.

Like millions of immigrants before him, whose parents spoke German, Polish, Italian, and so on, learning English eroded family ties and ate away at his ethnic roots. Language and education were not simply devices that eased Richard's transition to the dominant culture. Instead, they transformed him into a *pocho,* "a Mexican with gringo aspirations." They slashed at the roots that had given him life.

To face such inner turmoil is to confront a fork in the road. Some turn one way and withdraw from the new culture—a clue to the high dropout rate of Latinos from U.S. schools. Others go in the opposite direction and, cutting ties with their family and cultural roots, wholeheartedly adopt the new culture.

Rodriguez took the second road. He performed well in his

new language—so well, in fact, that he graduated from Stanford University and then became a graduate student in English at the University of California at Berkeley. He was even awarded a prestigious Fulbright fellowship to study English Renaissance literature at the British Museum.

But the past wouldn't let Rodriguez alone. Prospective employers were impressed with his knowledge of Renaissance literature. Yet at job interviews, they would ask if he would teach the Mexican novel in translation and be an adviser to Latino students. Rodriguez was haunted by the image of his soft-spoken grandmother, the culture he had left behind, the language to which he was now a stranger.

Richard Rodriguez represents millions of immigrants—not just those of Latino origin but millions from other cultures, too—who want to be a part of the United States without betraying their past. They fear that to integrate into U.S. culture is to lose their roots. They are caught between two cultures, each beckoning, each offering rich rewards.

Sources: Based on Rodriguez 1975, 1982, 1990, 1991, 1995.

attract popular boys. In this children's subculture, academic achievement pulls in opposite directions: for boys, to do well academically hurts popularity, while getting good grades increases a girl's standing among her peers.

As you well know from personal experience, peer groups are compelling. It is almost impossible

to go against a peer group, whose cardinal rule seems to be "conformity or rejection." Anyone who doesn't do what the others want becomes an "outsider," a "nonmember," an "outcast." For preteens and teens just learning their way around in the world, it is not surprising that the peer group is king.

concentration camps, convents, some religious cults, and some boarding schools, such as West Point, are total institutions.

The Mass Media

As already noted concerning gender socialization, the mass media do not merely entertain us. They also shape our attitudes, values, and other basic orientations to life. Since children sit transfixed for hours before television's dancing images, it is not surprising that some social analysts have become concerned about the *content* of what children see. As Joshua Meyrowitz (1984) points out, to use television as an electronic baby-sitter

> is equivalent to a broad social decision to allow young children to be present at wars and funerals, courtships and seductions, criminal plots and cocktail parties . . . television exposes children to many topics and behaviors that adults have spent several centuries trying to keep hidden from them.

By the age of 18, the average U.S. adolescent has watched about 18,000 people being strangled, smothered, stabbed, shot, poisoned, beaten to death, or otherwise ingeniously done in (Volti 1995). He or she has also watched about 160,000 rapes, robberies, and assaults.

Apparently, television teaches lasting lessons. In a longitudinal study (the same people are studied over time), researchers measured the television viewing and aggression of all the 8-year-olds in a county in New York (Comstock and Strasburger 1990). The children who watched more television were also the more violent. When the children turned 19, the researchers again measured their antisocial behavior. They were surprised to find the same results. At age 30, they measured their levels of aggression once more. This time they were stunned to find results as strong as those that show cigarettes cause lung cancer. The adults who had watched the most television at the age of 8 had more arrests for drunk driving and more arrests for violent crime. They even had more aggressive children.

If these findings are supported by further research, we still must deal with the question of how televised violence can have such effects. Some researchers suggest that television teaches scripts. One researcher put it this way:

> In a new social situation, how do you know how to behave? You search for scripts to follow. Where is a likely place for those scripts to come from? From what you've observed others doing in life, films, TV. So, as a child, you see (violence on television). . . . Even years later, the right kind of

scene can trigger that script and suggest a way to behave that follows it. . . . Moreover, we find that watching TV violence affects the viewer's beliefs and attitudes about how people are going to behave. (Institute for Social Research 1994)

Resocialization

What does a woman who has just become a nun have in common with a man who has just divorced? The answer is that they both are undergoing **resocialization;** that is, they are learning new norms, values, attitudes, and behaviors to match their new situation in life. In its most common form, resocialization occurs each time we learn something contrary to our previous experiences. A new boss who insists on a different way of doing things is resocializing you. Most resocialization is mild, only a slight modification of things we already have learned.

Resocialization can be intense, however. People who join Alcoholics Anonymous (AA), for example, expose themselves to a barrage of testimony about the destructive effects of excessive drinking. Some students also find the process of leaving high school and entering college to be an intense period of resocialization—especially during those initially scary, floundering days before becoming comfortable and fitting in. Even more so is psychotherapy or joining a cult, for they expose people to ideas that conflict with their previous ways of looking at the world. If these ideas "take," not only does the individual's behavior change, but he or she also learns a fundamentally different way of looking at life.

Total Institutions

Relatively few of us experience the powerful mechanism Erving Goffman (1961) called the **total institution.** He coined this term to refer to a place in which people are cut off from the rest of society and where they come under almost total control of the officials who run the place. Boot camps, prisons, concentration camps, convents, some religious cults, and some boarding schools, such as West Point, are total institutions.

A person entering a total institution is greeted with a **degradation ceremony** (Garfinkel 1956), an attempt to remake the self by stripping away the individual's current identity and stamping a new one in its place. This unwelcome greeting may in-

Down-to-Earth Sociology

Boot Camp as a Total Institution

THE BUS ARRIVES at Parris Island, South Carolina, at 3 A.M. This is no accident. The recruits are groggy, confused. Up to a few hours ago, the boys had been civilians. Now, as a sergeant sneeringly calls them "maggots" and their heads are buzzed (25 seconds per recruit), they are quickly and deeply thrust into the heart of Marine life.

After eleven weeks here, the Beavises and Butt-heads emerge self-disciplined, physically fit, and even courteous to their elders. Each time they see a superior, they automatically respond with "Good day, sir." Even skinheads and black separatists have been known to lay aside antagonistic identities and to live and work together as a team.

Every intense moment of those eleven weeks reminds them that they are joining a subculture of self-discipline. Here pleasure is suspect and sacrifice is good. As they learn the Marine way of talking, walking, and thinking, they are denied the diversions they knew: television, cigarettes, cars, candy, soft drinks, video games, music, alcohol, drugs, and sex.

Buzzing their hair is just the first step in stripping away their previous identities so a new one can be stamped in its place. The uniform serves the same purpose. There is a ban on using the first person, and even simple requests must be made in precise Marine style or they will not be acknowl-

edged. ("Sir, Recruit Jones requests permission to make a head call, sir.")

Lessons are given with utter intensity. When Sgt. Carey checks brass belt buckles, Recruit Robert Shelton nervously blurts, "I don't have one." Sgt. Carey's face grows red as his neck cords bulge. "I?" he says, his face just inches from the recruit. With spittle flying from his mouth, he screams, "'I' is gone!"

"Nobody's an individual, understand?" is the lesson that is driven home again and again. "You are a team, a Marine. Not a civilian. Not black or white, but a Marine. You will live like a Marine, fight like a Marine, and, if necessary, die like a Marine."

Each day begins before dawn with close order formations. The rest of the day is filled with training in hand-to-hand combat, marching, running, calisthenics, and Marine history.

The pressure to conform is intense. Those sent packing for insubordination or suicidal tendencies are mocked in cadence during drills. ("Hope you like the sights you see / Parris Island casualty.") Exhausted, as lights go out at 9 P.M. the recruits perform the day's last task: the entire platoon, in unison, shouts the virtues of the Marines.

Recruits are constantly scrutinized. Subperformance is not accepted, whether it be a dirty rifle

or a loose thread on a uniform. The subperformer is shouted at, derided, humiliated.

The group suffers for the individual. If a recruit is slow, the entire platoon is punished with additional exercise.

The system works.

"Pick your nose!" Simultaneously fifty-nine index fingers shoot into nostrils.

"An M-16 can blow someone's head off at 500 meters," Sgt. Norman says. "That's beautiful, isn't it?"

"Yes, sir!" shout the platoon's fifty-nine voices.

In the Marine vocabulary, the highest praise is "intense" and "motivated." Their opposites are "undisciplined" and "civilian."

At the end of the eleven weeks, one Marine (until graduation, they are recruits, not Marines) says, "I feel like I've joined a new society or religion."

For Your Consideration

Of what significance is the recruits' degradation ceremony? Why are recruits not allowed video games, cigarettes, or calls home? Why are the Marines so unfair as to punish an entire platoon for the failure of an individual? Use concepts in this chapter to explain why the system works.

Source: Based on Garfinkel 1956; Goffman 1961; "Anybody's Son Will Do," 1990; Ricks 1995.

volve fingerprinting, photographing, shaving the head, and banning the person's *personal identity kit* (items such as jewelry, hairstyles, clothing, and other body decorations used to express individual-

ity). Newcomers may be ordered to strip, be examined (often in humiliating, semipublic settings), and then be given a uniform to designate their new status.

Resocialization is often a gentle process as we are usually gradually exposed to different ways of thinking and doing. Sometimes, however, it can be sudden and brutal, as with these recruits in basic training. What new values, behaviors, and ways of looking at the world do you think they are learning?

Total institutions are isolated from the public (the walls, bars, or other barriers not only keep the inmates in but also keep outsiders from interfering). They closely supervise the entire lives of the residents—eating, sleeping, showering, recreation are all standardized. They suppress pre-existing statuses (inmates learn that their previous roles such as spouse, parent, worker, or student mean nothing, and that the only thing that counts is their current role).

As a result, no one leaves a total institution unscathed, for the experience brands an indelible mark on the individual's self that colors the way he or she sees the world. Boot camp, as described in the Down-to-Earth Sociology box on the facing page, is brutal, but swift. Prison, in contrast, is brutal and prolonged. Neither recruit nor prisoner, however, has difficulty in pinpointing how the institution affected the self.

Socialization through the Life Course

Some compare the stages of our lives from birth to death, called the **life course** (Elder 1975), to the seasons of the year. Whatever analogy is used, the sociological significance of the life course is twofold. First, we all pass through major stages that affect our behaviors and orientations to life. Second, the life course differs by social location. Social class, ethnicity, and gender, for example, separate people into different worlds of experience. Consequently the typical life course differs for males and females, the rich and poor, and so on. To emphasize this major sociological point, in the sketch that follows I stress the *historical* setting of people's lives. Because of your particular social location, your own life course may differ from this sketch, which is a composite of stages others have suggested (Levinson 1978; Carr et al. 1995).

Childhood (from birth to about age 12)

To begin, consider how different your childhood would have been if you had grown up during the Middle Ages. When historian Philippe Ariès (1965) examined European paintings from the Middle Ages, such as the one on page 74, he noticed that children were always dressed up in adult clothing. If children were not stiffly posed for a family portrait, they were depicted as engaging in adult activities.

Ariès concluded that at that time and in that place childhood was not regarded as a special time of life. Rather, children were seen as miniature adults. Ariès pointed out that boys were apprenticed at very early ages. At the age of 7, for example, a boy might leave home for good to learn to be a jeweler or a

In contemporary Western societies such as the United States, children are viewed as innocent and in need of protection from adult demands such as work and self-support. Historically and cross-culturally, however, ideas of childhood vary. For instance, as illustrated by this painting of Sir Walter Raleigh and son (artist unknown), in fifteenth-century Europe children were viewed as miniature adults who assumed adult roles at the earliest opportunity.

hanging there as an example of what happens to bad children when they grow up. Whole classes were taken out of school to witness hangings, and parents would often whip their children afterwards to make them remember what they had seen. (DeMause 1975)

Such practices have not disappeared from the world. Vivid in my memory is a Moroccan black-smith standing next to an open furnace, nude from the waist up. Sweating profusely in the insufferable heat, his hammer beat rhythmically on glowing, red-hot metal. The blacksmith was about 12 years old.

Industrialization's economic surplus brings fundamental change to the role of children. When children have the leisure to go to school, they come to be thought of as tender and innocent, as needing more adult care, comfort, and protection. Over time, such attitudes of dependency grow, and today we view children as needing gentle guidance if they are to develop emotionally, intellectually, morally, even physically. We take our view for granted—after all it is only "common sense." Yet, as you can see, our view is not "natural," but geographically and historically rooted.

Childhood, then, is much more than biology. The point in history in which we live, as well as our social location at that time, lay a framework over our biology. Although a child's *biological* characteristics (such as small and dependent) are universal, the child's *social* experiences (what others expect of the child) are not.

Adolescence (ages 13–17)

In earlier centuries, societies did not mark out adolescence as a distinct time of life. People simply moved from childhood into young adulthood, with no stopover in between. The Industrial Revolution brought such an abundance of material surpluses, however, that for the first time millions of teenagers were able to remain outside the labor force. At the same time, the demand for education grew. The convergence of these two forces in industrialized societies created a gap between childhood and adulthood. In the early part of this century, the term *adolescence* was coined to indicate this new stage in life (Hall 1904), one that has become renowned for inner turmoil.

To ground the self-identity and mark the passage of children into adulthood, preliterate societies

stonecutter. A girl, in contrast, stayed home until she married, but by the age of 7 she had to do her full share of household tasks.

To keep children in line, parents and teachers also felt it their moral duty to use psychological terror. They would lock children in dark closets, frighten them with tales of death and hellfire, and force them to witness gruesome events.

A common moral lesson involved taking children to visit the gibbet [an upraised post on which executed bodies were left hanging from chains], where they were forced to inspect rotting corpses hold initiation rites (Gilmore 1990). In the industrialized world, however, adolescents must "find" themselves on their own. As they attempt to carve out an identity distinct from both the "younger" world being left behind and the "older" world still out of range, adolescents develop distinctive standards of clothing, hairstyles, language, and music. What we usually fail to realize about adolescence is that it is contemporary society, not biological age, that has created the period of inner turmoil that we call *adolescence*.

Young Adulthood (ages 18–29)

If society invented adolescence, can it also invent new periods of life? Historian Kenneth Keniston thinks so. He notes that industrialized societies seem to be adding a period of prolonged youth to the life course, in which people postpone adult responsibilities past adolescence. For millions, the end of high school marks a period of extended education with continued freedom from needing to support oneself. During this time, people are "neither psychological adolescents nor sociological adults" (Keniston 1971). Somewhere during this period of extended youth, young adults gradually ease into adult responsibilities. They finish school, take a full-time job, engage in courtship rituals, get married—and go into debt.

The Middle Years (ages 30–65)

The Early Middle Years (ages 30–49) During the early middle years most people are much surer of themselves and of their goals in life. As with any point in the life course, however, the self can receive severe jolts—in this case from such circumstances as divorce or being fired. It may take years for the self to stabilize after such ruptures.

Because of recent social change, the early middle years pose a special challenge for U.S. women, who increasingly have been given the message, especially by the media, that they can "have it all." They can be superworkers, superwives, and supermoms—all rolled into one. The reality, however, is likely to consist of highly conflicting pressures, of too little time and too many demands. Something has to give. Attempts to resolve this dilemma often are compounded by another hard reality—that during gender socialization their husbands learned that child care and housework are not "masculine." In

In many societies, manhood is not bestowed upon males simply because they reach a certain age. Manhood, rather, is a standing in the community that must be achieved. Shown here is an initiation ceremony in Indonesia, where boys, to lay claim to the status of manhood, must jump over this barrier.

short, adjustments continue in this and all phases of life.

The Later Middle Years (ages 50–65) During the later middle years, health and mortality begin to loom large as people feel their bodies change, especially if they watch their parents become frail, fall ill, and die. The consequence is a fundamental reorientation in thinking—from *time since birth* to *time left to live* (Neugarten 1976). With this changed orientation, people attempt to evaluate the past and to come to terms with what lies ahead. They compare what they have accomplished with how far they had hoped to get. Many people also find themselves caring for not only their own children but also their aging parents. Because of this often crushing set of twin burdens, people in the later middle years sometimes are called the "sandwich generation."

Life during this stage, however, is far from filled only with such concerns. Many people find this period the most comfortable of their entire lives as they enjoy job security and a standard of living higher than ever before, a bigger house (perhaps paid for), newer cars, and more exotic vacations. The children are grown, the self is firmly planted, and fewer upheavals are likely to occur.

As they anticipate the next stage of life, however, most people do not like what they see.

The Older Years (about 65 on)

In industrialized societies, the older years begin around the mid-60s. This, too, is recent, for in preindustrial societies, when most people died early, old age was thought to begin around age 40. Today, in contrast, especially for those in good health, being over 65 is often experienced more as an extension of the middle years than being old. Older people who continue to work or to be active in other rewarding social activities are unlikely to see themselves as old (Neugarten 1977). Although frequency of sex declines, most men and women in their 60s and 70s are sexually active (Denney and Quadagno 1992).

Because we have a self and can reason abstractly, we can contemplate death. Initially death is something vaguely "out there," but as people see their friends die and their own bodies no longer functioning as before, death becomes less abstract. Increasingly, people feel that "time is closing in" on them.

Are We Prisoners of Socialization?

From our discussion of socialization, you might conclude that sociologists think of people as little ro-

bots: The socialization goes in, and the behavior comes out. People cannot help what they do, think, or feel, for everything is a result of their exposure to socializing agents.

Sociologists do *not* think of people in this way. Although socialization is powerful, and profoundly affects us all, we have a self. Laid down in childhood and continually modified by later experience, the self is dynamic. It is not a sponge that passively absorbs influences from the environment but a vigorous, essential part of our being that allows us to act upon our environment (Couch 1989).

Indeed, it is precisely because individuals are not little robots that their behavior is so hard to predict. The countless reactions of other people merge in each of us. As the self develops, we internalize or "put together" these innumerable reactions, producing a unique whole that we call the *individual*. Each unique individual uses his or her own mind to reason and to make choices in life.

In this way, *each of us is actively involved in the social construction of the self.* For example, although our experiences in the family lay down the basic elements of our personality, including fundamental orientations to life, we are not doomed to keep those orientations if we do not like them. We can purposely expose ourselves to groups and ideas that we prefer. Those experiences, in turn, will have their own effects on our self. In short, although socialization is powerful, within the limitations of the framework laid down by our social location we can change even the self. And that self—along with the options available within society—is the key to our behavior.

Summary and Review

What Is Human Nature?

How much of our human nature characteristics comes from "nature" (heredity) and how much from "nurture" (the social environment)?

Observations of isolated and institutionalized children help answer this question, as do experiments with monkeys that have been raised in isolation. Language and intimate social interaction—functions of "nurture"—are essential to the development of

what we consider to be human characteristics. Pp. 58–61.

Socialization into the Self, Mind, and Emotions

How do we acquire a self?

Humans are born with the capacity to develop a **self**, but the self must be socially constructed; that is, its contents depend on social interaction. According to Charles Horton Cooley's concept of the **looking-glass**

self, our self develops as we internalize others' reactions to us. George Herbert Mead identified the ability to **take the role of the other** as essential to the development of the self. Mead concluded that even the mind is a social product. Pp. 61–63.

How do children develop reasoning skills?

Jean Piaget identified four stages that children go through as they develop the ability to reason: (1) *sensorimotor,* in which understanding is limited to sensory stimuli such as touch and sight; (2) *preoperational,* the ability to use symbols; (3) *concrete operational,* in which reasoning ability is more complex but not yet capable of complex abstractions; and (4) *formal operational,* or abstract thinking. Researchers have found that emotions also develop in an orderly sequence. Pp. 63–65.

How do sociologists evaluate Freud's psychoanalytic theory of personality development?

Freud viewed personality development as the result of self-centered inborn desires, the **id,** clashing with social constraints. The **ego** develops to balance the id as well as the **superego,** the conscience. Sociologists, in contrast, do not examine inborn and unconscious motivations, but, rather, how social factors—social class, gender, religion, education, and so forth—underlie personality development. P. 65.

How does socialization influence emotions?

Socialization influences not only how we express our emotions, but also what emotions we feel. Socialization into emotions is a major means by which society produces conformity. Pp. 65–66.

Socialization into Gender

How does gender socialization affect our sense of self?

Gender socialization—sorting males and females into different roles—is a primary means of controlling human behavior. Children learn gender roles beginning in infancy. A society's ideals of sex-linked behaviors are reinforced by its social institutions. Pp. 66–68.

Agents of Socialization

What are the main agents of socialization?

The main **agents of socialization** are family, religion, day care, school, **peer groups,** and the **mass media.** Each has its particular influences in socializing us into becoming full-fledged members of society. Pp. 68–71.

Resocialization

What is resocialization?

Resocialization is the process of learning new norms, values, attitudes, and behaviors. Most resocialization is voluntary, but some, as with prisoners in **total institutions,** is involuntary. Pp. 71–73.

Socialization through the Life Course

Does socialization end when we enter adulthood?

Socialization occurs throughout the **life course.** In industrialized societies, the life course can be divided into childhood, adolescence, young adulthood, the middle years, and the older years. Typical patterns include obtaining education, becoming independent from parents, building a career, finding a mate, rearing children, and confronting aging. Life course patterns vary by social location such as gender, ethnicity, and social class. Pp. 73–76.

Are We Prisoners of Socialization?

Although socialization is powerful, we are not merely the sum of our socialization experiences. Just as socialization influences human behavior, so humans act on their environment and influence it. P. 76.

Where can I read more on this topic?

Suggested readings for this chapter are listed on page 436.

Glossary

agents of socialization people and groups that influence our self-concept, emotions, attitudes, and behavior (p. 68)

degradation ceremony a term coined by Harold Garfinkel to describe rituals designed to strip an individual of his or her identity as a group member; for example, a court martial or the defrocking of a priest (p. 71)

ego Freud's term for a balancing force between the id and the demands of society (p. 65)

gender socialization the ways in which society sets children onto different courses in life because they are male or female (p. 66)

generalized other taking the role of a large number of people (p. 63)

id Freud's term for the individual's inborn basic drives (p. 65)

life course the stages of our life as we go from birth to death (p. 73)

looking-glass self a term coined by Charles Horton Cooley to refer to the process by which our self develops through internalizing others' reactions to us (p. 62)

mass media forms of communication directed to huge audiences (p. 67)

peer group a group of individuals of roughly the same age who are linked by common interests (p. 69)

resocialization the process of learning new norms, values, attitudes, and behaviors (p. 71)

self the concept, unique to humans, of being able to see ourselves "from the outside"; to gain a picture of how others see us (p. 61)

significant other an individual who significantly influences someone else's life (p. 63)

social environment the entire human environment, including direct contact with others (p. 58)

socialization the process by which people learn the characteristics of their group—the attitudes, values, and actions thought appropriate for them (p. 61)

superego Freud's term for the conscience, which consists of the internalized norms and values of our social groups (p. 65)

taking the role of the other putting oneself in someone else's shoes; understanding how someone else feels and thinks and thus anticipating how that person will act (p. 62)

total institution a place in which people are cut off from the rest of society and are almost totally controlled by the officials who run the place (p. 71)

Sociology and the Internet

All URLs listed are current as of the printing of this book. URLs are often changed. Please check our Website http://www.abacon.com/henslin for updates.

1. Considering Sociobiology

In this chapter, you have read about the nature–nurture controversy—whether biology or society is the main factor in human behavior. You now can apply what you learned by critiquing a graduate student's paper on sociobiology, a controversial theory that looks at biological factors as almost completely determining human social behavior. You should be able to make some general arguments about this paper, even though you know little or nothing about sociobiology itself.

Go to the Internet site at http://www.clas.ufl.edu/anthro/scholarly/bio-creative.html where you will find an article by Steve Mizrach. After you have read the article, address each of the following questions in a short paper: (1) What is your general impression of the validity of Mizrach's paper? (Does it "ring true"?) Why? (2) How well does the sociobiological theory explain genius and madness? What does it fail to explain? (3) Is Mizrach fair to sociobiology in his conclusions? Bring your paper to class. Your instructor may want the class to exchange papers or to form small groups to share their ideas.

2. The Socialization of Children

Child rearing and child care vary widely from one society to another. To explore some of these differences on the Internet, enter the search term "child rearing." You might also try "child care." Try to discover some of the varieties of values and practices within the United States. Can you identify any of the social characteristics of those proposing a particular point of view? Try the same exercise by looking at different countries. Look at the term after the last address "dot"—for example, http://www.ucalg.ca/. You might try ca (Canada), uk (England), and au (Australia) for a start. Japan (jp) is interesting if you can find text in English. Be prepared to share your findings with the class in whatever form your instructor assigns.

Alejandro Xul Solar, Patria B, 1925.

CHAPTER

4

Social Structure and Social Interaction

(212) or (718)
555-1212

WHEN THE SOCIOLOGY CONVENTION FINISHED, *I climbed aboard the first city bus that came along. I didn't know where the bus was going, and I didn't even know where I was going to spend the night.*

"Maybe I overdid it this time," I thought as the bus began winding down streets I had never seen before. Actually, since this was my first visit to Washington, D.C., I hadn't seen any of the streets before. I had no direction, no plans, not even a map. I carried no billfold, just a driver's license shoved into my jeans for emergency identification, some pocket change, and a $10 bill tucked into my socks. My goal was simple: If I see something interesting, I'll get off and check it out.

"Nothing but the usual things," I mused, as we passed row after row of apartment buildings and stores. I could see myself riding buses the entire night. Then something caught my eye. Nothing spectacular—just groups of people clustered around a large circular area where several streets intersected.

I climbed off the bus and made my way to what turned out to be Dupont Circle. I took a seat on a sidewalk bench and began to observe. As the scene came into focus, I noted several street corner men drinking and joking with one another. One of the men broke from his companions and sat down next to me. As we talked, I mostly listened.

As night fell, the men said that they wanted to get another bottle of wine. I contributed. They counted their money and asked if I wanted to go with them.

Although I felt a churning inside—emotions combining hesitation and fear—I heard a confident "Sure!" coming out of my mouth. As we left the circle, the three men began to cut through an alley. "Oh, no," I thought. "That's not what I had in mind."

I had but a split second to make a decision. I found myself continuing to walk with the men, but holding back half a step so that none of the three was behind me. As we walked, they passed around the remnants of their bottle. When my turn came, I didn't know what to do. I shuddered to think about the diseases lurking within that bottle. I made another decision. In the semidarkness I faked it, letting only my thumb and forefinger touch my lips and nothing enter my mouth.

When we returned to Dupont Circle, the men finished their new bottle of Thunderbird. I couldn't fake it in the light, so I passed, pointing at my stomach to indicate that I was having problems.

Suddenly one of the men jumped up, smashed the emptied bottle against the sidewalk, and thrust the jagged neck in a menacing gesture. He stared straight ahead at another bench, where he had spotted someone with whom he had some sort of unfinished business. As the other men told him to cool it, I moved slightly to one side of the group—ready to flee, just in case.

Levels of Sociological Analysis

On this sociological adventure, I almost got myself in over my head. Fortunately, it turned out all right. The man's "enemy" didn't look our way, the broken bottle was set down next to the bench "just in case he needed it," and until dawn I was introduced to a life that up to then I had only read about.

Sociologists Elliot Liebow (1967) and Elijah Anderson (1978) have written fascinating accounts about men like these. Although street corner men may appear disorganized, simply coming and going as they please and doing whatever feels good at the moment, these sociologists have analyzed how, like us, these men are also influenced by the norms and beliefs of our society. This will become more apparent as we examine the two levels of analysis that sociologists use.

Macrosociology and Microsociology

The first level, **macrosociology,** places the focus on broad features of society. Sociologists who use this approach analyze such things as social class and how groups are related to one another. If macrosociologists were to analyze street corner men, for example, they would stress that these men are located at the bottom of the U.S. social class system. Their low status means that many opportunities are closed to them: The men have few skills, little education, hardly anything to offer an employer. As "able-bodied" men, however, they are not eligible for welfare, so they hustle to survive. As a consequence, they spend their lives on the streets.

Conflict theory and functionalism, both of which focus on the broader picture, are examples of this macrosociological approach. In these theories, the goal is to examine the large-scale social forces that influence people.

The second approach sociologists use is **microsociology.** Here the emphasis is placed on **social interaction,** what people do when they come together. Sociologists who use this approach are likely to focus on the men's survival strategies ("hustles"); their rules for dividing up money, wine, or whatever

other resources they have; their relationships with girlfriends, family, and friends; where they spend their time and what they do there; their language; their pecking order; and so on. With its focus on face-to-face interaction, symbolic interactionism is an example of microsociology.

With their different emphases, macrosociology and microsociology yield distinctive perspectives, and both are needed to gain a more complete understanding of social life. We cannot adequately understand street corner men, for example, without using *macrosociology*. It is essential that we place the men within the broad context of how groups in U.S. society are related to one another—for, as with ourselves, the social class of these men helps to shape their attitudes and behavior. Nor can we adequately understand these men without *microsociology*, for their everyday situations also form a significant part of their lives.

To see how these two approaches in sociology help us to understand social life, let's take a look at each.

The Macrosociological Perspective: Social Structure

To better understand human behavior, we need to understand **social structure,** the framework of so-

Sociologists use both macro and micro levels of analysis to study social life. Those who use macrosociology to analyze the homeless—or any human behavior—focus on broad forces, such as the economy and social classes. Sociologists who use the microsociological approach analyze how people interact with one another. Note how this scene invites both levels of analysis: here you have both social classes (power and powerlessness) and social interaction.

ciety that was already laid out before you were born. Social structure is the typical patterns of a group, such as its usual relationships between men and women or students and teachers. *The sociological significance of social structure is that it guides our behavior.*

Because this term may seem vague, let's consider how you experience social structure in your own life. As I write this, I do not know if you are African American, white, Latino, Native American, Asian American. I do not know your religion. I do not know if you are young or old, tall or short, male or female. I do not know if you were reared on a farm, in the suburbs, or in the inner city. I do not know if you went to a public high school or an exclusive prep school. But I do know you are in college. And that, alone, tells me a great deal about you.

From this one piece of information, I can assume that the social structure of your college is now shaping what you do. For example, let us suppose that today you felt euphoric over some great news. I can be fairly certain (not absolutely, mind you, but relatively certain) that when you entered the classroom, social structure overrode your mood. That is, instead of shouting at the top of your lungs and joyously throwing this book into the air, you entered the classroom fairly subdued and took your seat.

The same social structure influences your instructor, even if, on the one hand, he or she is facing a divorce or has a child dying of cancer, or, on the other, has just been awarded a promotion or a million-dollar grant. The instructor may feel like either retreating into seclusion or celebrating wildly, but it is most likely that he or she will conduct class. In short, personal feelings and desires tend to be overridden by social structure.

Just as social structure influences you and your instructor, so it also establishes limits for street people. They, too, find themselves in a specific social location in the U.S. social structure—although it is quite different from yours or your instructor's. Consequently, they are affected differently—and nothing about their social location leads them to take notes or to lecture. Their behaviors are as logical an outcome of where they find themselves in the social structure, however, as are your own. It is just as "natural" in their position in the social structure to drink wine all night as it is for you to stay up studying all night for a crucial examination. It is just as "natural" for you to nod and say, "Excuse me," when you enter

a crowded classroom late and have to claim a desk on which someone has already placed books or a coat as it is for them to break off the head of a wine bottle and glare at an enemy.

In short, people learn certain behaviors and attitudes because of their location in the social structure (whether privileged, deprived, or in between), and they act accordingly. This is equally true of street people and of ourselves. *The difference in behavior and attitudes is not due to biology (race, sex, or any other supposed genetic factors), but to people's location in the social structure.* Switch places with street people and watch your behaviors and attitudes change!

To better understand social structure, read the Down-to-Earth Sociology box on football on page 85. Because social structure so critically affects who we are and what we are like, let us look in more detail at its major components: culture, social class, social status, roles, groups, social institutions, and societies.

Culture

In Chapter 2, we examined how culture affects us. At this point, let's simply review the main impact of culture, the largest envelope that surrounds us. Sociologists use the term *culture* to refer to a group's language, beliefs, values, behaviors, and even gestures. Culture also includes the material objects used by a group. Culture is the broadest framework that determines what kind of people we become. If we are reared in Eskimo, Japanese, Russian, or U.S. culture, we will grow up to be like most Eskimos, Japanese, Russians, or Americans. On the outside, we will look and act like them; and on the inside, we will think and feel like them.

Social Class

To understand people, we must examine the particular social locations that they hold in life. Especially significant is social class, which is based on income, education, and occupational prestige. Large numbers of people who have similar amounts of income and education and who work at jobs that are roughly comparable in prestige make up a **social class.** It is hard to overemphasize this aspect of social structure, for our social class heavily influences not only our behaviors but even our ideas and attitudes. We have this in common, then, with the street people de-

▼▲▼▲▼▲▼▲▼▲▼▲▼▲▼▲▼▲▼▲▼▲▼▲▼▲▼▲▼▲▼▲▼▲▼▲▼▲

Down-to-Earth Sociology

College Football as Social Structure

To GAIN A better idea of what social structure is, think of college football (see Dobriner 1969). You know the various positions on the team: center, guards, tackles, ends, quarterback, and running backs. Each is a *status*; that is, each is a recognized social position. For each of these statuses, there is a *role*; that is, each of these positions has particular expectations attached to it. The center is expected to snap the ball, the quarterback to pass it, the guards to block, the tackles to tackle or block, the ends to receive passes, and so on. These *role expectations* guide each player's actions; that is, the players try to do what their particular role requires.

Let's suppose that football is your favorite sport and you never miss a home game at your college. Let's also suppose that you graduate and move across the country. Five years later you return to your campus for a nostalgic visit. The climax of your visit is the biggest football game of the season. When you get to the game, you might be surprised to see a different coach, but you are not surprised that each playing position is occupied by people you don't know, for all the players you knew have graduated, and their places have been filled by others.

This scenario mirrors *social structure*, which is the framework around which a group exists. In this football example, that framework consists of the coaching staff and the eleven playing positions. The game does not depend on any particular individual, but rather on statuses, the positions that the individuals occupy. When someone leaves a position, the game can go on because someone else takes over the position and plays the role. The game will continue even though not a single individual remains the same from one period of time to the next. Notre Dame's football team endures today even though Knute Rockne, the Gipper, and his teammates are long dead.

Even though you may not play football, you nevertheless live your life within a clearly established social structure. The statuses you occupy and the roles that you play were already in place before you were born. You take your particular positions in life, others do the same, and society goes about its business. Although the specifics change with time, the game—whether of life or of football—goes on.

scribed in the opening vignette—both they and we are influenced by our location in the social class structure. Theirs may be a considerably less privileged position, but it has no less influence on their lives. Social class is so significant that we shall spend an entire chapter (Chapter 8) on this topic.

Social Status

When you hear the word *status*, you are likely to think of prestige. These two words are welded together in common thinking. Sociologists, however, use **status** in a different way: to refer to the *position that an individual occupies*. That position may carry a great deal of prestige, as in the case of a judge or an astronaut, or it may bring very little prestige, as in the case of a gas station attendant or a hamburger flipper at a fast-food restaurant. The status may also be looked down on, as in the case of a street corner man, an ex-convict, or a bag lady.

All of us occupy several positions at the same time. You may be simultaneously a son or daughter, a worker, a date, and a student. Sociologists use the term *status set* to refer to all the statuses or positions that you occupy. Obviously your status set changes as your particular statuses change; for example, if you graduate from college and take a full-time job, get married, buy a home, have children, and so on, your status set changes to include the positions of worker, spouse, homeowner, and parent.

Like other aspects of social structure, statuses are part of our basic framework of living in society. The example given earlier of students and teachers doing what others expect of them in spite of their temporary moods is an illustration of how statuses affect our actions—and those of the people around us. Our statuses—whether daughter or son, worker or date—serve as guides for our behavior.

Ascribed Statuses and Achieved Statuses The first type, **ascribed statuses,** is involuntary. You do not ask for them, nor can you choose them. Some you inherit at birth such as your race, sex, and the social class of your parents, as well as your statuses as female or male, daughter or son, niece or nephew, and granddaughter or grandson. Others, such as teenager and senior citizen, are given to you later in life.

The second type, **achieved statuses,** is voluntary. These you earn or accomplish. As a result of your efforts you become a student, a friend, a spouse, a rabbi, minister, priest, or nun. Or, for lack of effort (or efforts that others fail to appreciate), you become a school dropout, a former friend, an ex-spouse, or a defrocked rabbi, priest, or nun. In other words, achieved statuses can be either positive or negative; both college president and bank robber represent achieved statuses.

Each status provides guidelines for how people are to act and feel. Like other aspects of social structure, they set limits on what people can and cannot do. Because social statuses are an essential part of social structure, they are found in all human groups.

Status Symbols People who are pleased with their particular social status may want others to recognize that they occupy that status. To gain this recognition, they use **status symbols,** signs that identify a status. For example, people wear wedding rings to announce their marital status; uniforms, guns, and badges to proclaim that they are police officers (and to not so subtly let you know that their status gives them authority over you); and "backward" collars to declare that they are Lutheran ministers or Roman Catholic or Episcopal priests.

Some social statuses are negative, and so, therefore, are their status symbols. The scarlet letter in Nathaniel Hawthorne's book by the same title is one example. Another is the CONVICTED DUI (driving under the influence) bumper sticker that some U.S. counties require convicted drunk drivers to display if they wish to avoid a jail sentence.

All of us use status symbols to announce our statuses to others and to help smooth our interactions in everyday life. You might consider your own status symbols. For example, how does your clothing announce your statuses of sex, age, and college student?

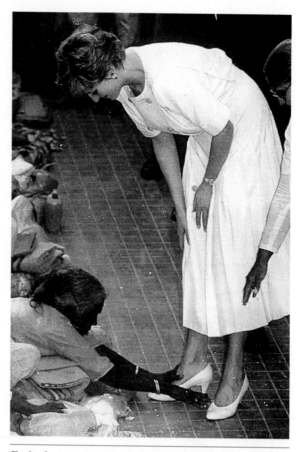

Each of us occupies several statuses. Among the achieved statuses of Diana Spencer are wife and mother. Because she gained the status of Princess of Wales by marrying into the Royal Family, this status, which she retained after her divorce from Prince Charles, is an achieved rather than ascribed status. The woman touching Diana's feet is a member of India's Untouchable caste. This woman's caste status is ascribed, or involuntary.

Master Statuses A **master status** is one that cuts across the other statuses you hold. Some master statuses are ascribed. An example is your sex. Whatever you do, people perceive you as a male or as a female. If you are working your way through college by flipping burgers, people see you not only as a burger flipper and a student but as a *male* or *female* burger flipper and a *male* or *female* college student. Other master statuses are race and age.

Some master statuses are achieved. If you become very, very wealthy (and it does not matter if your wealth comes from an invention or the lottery—it is still *achieved* as far as sociologists are con-

Master statuses *overshadow our other statuses. Shown here is Stephen Hawking, who is severely disabled by Lou Gehrig's disease. For many, his master status is that of a disabled person. Because Hawking is one of the greatest physicists who has ever lived, his astounding accomplishments have given him another master status, that of world-class physicist in the ranking of Einstein. Thus, Hawking occupies two master statuses simultaneously, the one ascribed and the other achieved.*

cerned), your wealth is likely to become a master status. No matter what else, people are likely to say, "She is a very rich burger flipper." (Or, more likely, "She's very rich, and she used to flip burgers!")

Similarly, people who become disabled or disfigured find, to their dismay, that their condition becomes a master status. For example, a person whose face is extremely scarred will be viewed through this unwelcome master status no matter what the individual's occupation or accomplishments. People confined to wheelchairs can attest to how "disabled" overrides all their other statuses and determines others' perceptions of everything they do.

Although our statuses usually fit together fairly well, sometimes a contradiction or mismatch between statuses occurs; this is known as **status inconsistency** (or discrepancy). A 14-year-old college student is an example. So is a 40-year-old married woman on a date with a 19-year-old college sophomore.

From these examples you can understand an essential aspect of social statuses: Like other components of social structure, they come with a set of built-in *norms* (that is, expectations) that provide guidelines for behavior. When statuses mesh well, as they usually do, we know what to expect of people. Status inconsistency, however, upsets our expectations. In the preceding examples, how are you supposed to act? Are you supposed to treat the 14-year-old as you would a teenager, or as you would your college classmate? The married woman as the mother of your friend, or as a classmate's date?

Roles

All the world's a stage
And all the men and women merely players.
They have their exits and their entrances;
And one man in his time plays many parts . . .
(William Shakespeare, *As You Like It*, Act II, Scene 7)

Like Shakespeare, sociologists, too, see roles as essential to social life. When you were born, **roles**—the behaviors, obligations, and privileges attached to a status—were already set up for you. Society was waiting with outstretched arms to teach you how it expected you to act as a boy or a girl. And whether you were born poor, rich, or somewhere in between, certain behaviors, obligations, and privileges were attached to your statuses.

The difference between role and status is that you *occupy* a status, but you *play* a role (Linton 1936). For example, being a son or daughter is your status, but your expectations of receiving food and shelter from your parents—as well as their expectations that you show respect to them—is your role.

Our roles are a sort of fence that helps keep us doing what society wants us to do. That fence leaves us a certain amount of freedom, but for most of us that freedom doesn't go very far. Suppose a female decides that she is not going to wear dresses—or a male that he will not wear suits and ties—regardless of what anyone says. In most situations they won't. When a formal occasion comes along, however, such as a family wedding or a funeral, they are likely to cave in to norms they find overwhelming. Almost all of us stay within the fences that mark out what is "appropriate" for our roles. Most of us are little troubled by such constraints, for our socialization is so thorough that we usually *want* to do what our roles indicate is appropriate.

The sociological significance of roles is that they lay out what is expected of people. As individuals throughout society perform their roles, those roles mesh together to form this thing called *society.* As Shakespeare put it, people's roles provide "their exits and their entrances" on the stage of life. In short, roles are remarkably effective at keeping people in line—telling them when they should "enter" and when they should "exit," as well as what to do in between.

Groups

A **group** consists of people who regularly and consciously interact with one another. Ordinarily, the members of a group share similar values, norms, and expectations. Just as our actions are influenced by our social class, statuses, and roles, so, too, the groups to which we belong represent powerful forces in our lives. In fact, *to belong to a group is to yield to others the right to make certain decisions about our behavior.* If we belong to a group, we assume an obligation to act according to the expectations of other members of that group. Groups are so significant for our lives that they shall be the focus of our next chapter.

Social Institutions

At first glance, the term *social institution* may appear far removed from our personal lives. The term seems so cold and abstract. In fact, however, **social institutions**—the organized means that each society develops to meet its basic needs—involve concrete and highly relevant aspects of our lives.

Sociologists have identified nine social institutions: the family, religion, law, politics, economics, education, medicine, science, and the military. In industrialized societies social institutions tend to be more formal, in preliterate societies more informal. For example, in industrialized societies education is highly structured, while in preliterate societies education may consist of informally learning expected roles. Figure 4.1 summarizes the basic social institutions. Note that each institution has its own set of

Functional theorists have identified five key functional requisites for the survival of a society. One, providing a sense of purpose, is often met through religion. To most people, snake handling, as in this church service in Jolo, West Virginia, is nonsensical. From a functional perspective, however, it makes a great deal of sense. Can you identify some of its sociological meanings?

roles, values, and norms. Their sociological significance is that they, too, set limits and provide guidelines for our behavior. The social institutions are so significant for our lives that Part IV of this book focuses on them.

Societies: The Four Social Revolutions

Society, which consists of people who share a culture and a territory, is the largest and most complex group that sociologists study. Because the values, beliefs, and cultural characteristics of our society affect us profoundly, it is useful to understand how contemporary society came into being. As we review the evolution of societies portrayed in Figure 4.2, note how technology underlies each type of society. Also picture yourself as a member of each society, and see how each would have changed your life—how even your thoughts and values would be different.

Social Institution	Basic Needs	Some Groups or Organizations	Some Values	Some Roles	Some Norms
Family	Regulate reproduction, socialize and protect children	Relatives, kinship groups	Sexual fidelity, providing for your family, keeping a clean house, respect for parents	Daughter, son, father, mother, brother, sister, aunt, uncle, grandparent	Have only as many children as you can afford; be faithful to your spouse
Religion	Concerns about life after death, the meaning of suffering and loss; desire to connect with the Creator	Congregation, synagogue, denomination, charitable association	Reading and adhering to holy texts such as the Bible, the Koran, and the Torah; honoring God	Priest, minister, rabbi, worshipper, teacher, disciple, missionary, prophet, convert	Attend worship services, contribute money, follow the teachings
Law	Maintain social order	Police, courts, prisons	Trial by one's peers, innocence until proven guilty	Police officer, judge, lawyer, defendant, prison guard	Give true testimony, follow the rules of evidence
Politics	Establish a hierarchy of power and authority	Political parties, congresses, parliaments, monarchies	Majority rule, the right to vote as a sacred trust	President, senator, lobbyist, spin doctor, candidate	One vote per person, voting as privilege and a right
Economics	Produce and distribute goods and services	Credit unions, banks, credit bureaus, buying clubs	Making money, paying bills on time, producing efficiently	Worker, boss, buyer, seller, creditor, debtor, advertiser	Maximize profits, "the customer is always right," work hard
Education	Transmit knowledge and skills across the generations	School, college, student senate, sports team, PTA, school board	Academic honesty, good grades, being "cool"	Teacher, student, dean, principal, football player, cheerleader	Do homework, prepare lectures, don't snitch on classmates
Science	Master the environment	Local, state, regional, national, and international associations	Unbiased research, open dissemination of research findings	Scientist, researcher, technician, administrator	Follow scientific method, fully disclose research findings
Medicine	Heal the sick and injured, care for the dying	AMA, hospitals, pharmacies, HMOs, insurance companies,	Hippocratic oath, staying in good health, following doctor's orders	Doctor, nurse, patient, pharmacist, medical insurer	Don't exploit patients, give best medical care available
Military	Protection from enemies, support of national interests	Army, navy, air force, marines, coast guard, national guard	To die for one's country is an honor, obedience unto death	Soldier, recruit, enlisted person, officer, prisoner, spy	Be ready to go to war, obey superior officers, don't question orders
Mass Media (an emerging institution)	Disseminate information, mold public opinion, report events	Television networks, radio stations, publishers	Timeliness, accuracy, large audiences, freedom of the press	Journalist, newscaster, author, editor, publisher	Be accurate, fair, timely, and profitable

FIGURE 4.1

Social Institutions in Industrialized Societies

FIGURE 4.2

**The Social
Transformations
of Society**

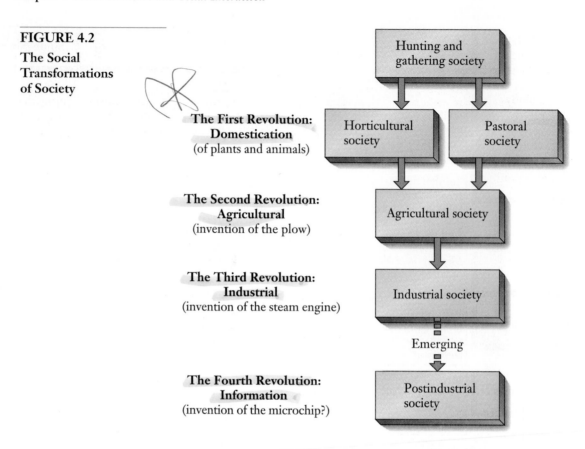

**The First Revolution:
Domestication**
(of plants and animals)

**The Second Revolution:
Agricultural**
(invention of the plow)

**The Third Revolution:
Industrial**
(invention of the steam engine)

**The Fourth Revolution:
Information**
(invention of the microchip?)

Hunting and Gathering Societies The simplest societies are called **hunting and gathering societies.** As the name implies, these groups depend on hunting and gathering for their survival. Because an area cannot support a large number of people who hunt animals and gather plants (they do not plant, only gather what is already there), hunting and gathering societies are small, usually consisting of twenty-five to forty members. They are also nomadic, moving from one place to another as the food supply of an area gives out (Lenski and Lenski 1987).

Of all societies, hunters and gatherers are the most egalitarian. Because what the people hunt and gather are perishable, they can't accumulate possessions. Consequently, no one becomes wealthier than anyone else. There are no rulers, and most decisions are arrived at through discussion.

Pastoral and Horticultural Societies About ten thousand years ago, hunting and gathering societies branched in one of two directions. Some groups found that they could tame and breed some of the animals they hunted, others that they could cultivate plants. The key to understanding the first branching is the word *pasture;* **pastoral societies** are based on the *pasturing of animals.* Groups that took this turn remained nomadic, for they followed their animals to fresh pasture. The key to understanding the second branching is *horticulture,* or plant cultivation. **Horticultural societies** are based on the *cultivation of plants by the use of hand tools.* No longer having to abandon an area as the food supply gave out, these groups developed permanent settlements.

We can call the domestication of animals and plants the *first social revolution,* for, as shown in Figure 4.3, it transformed human society. With a more dependable food supply, human groups became larger. Because not everyone had to produce food, a specialized division of labor evolved: Some became makers of jewelry, others of tools, weapons, and so on. This production of objects, in turn, stimulated trade, and people began to accumulate gold, jewelry, and utensils, as well as herds of animals.

The primary significance of these changes is that they set the stage for social inequality. Feuds and wars erupted, for groups now had material goods to

The simplest forms of societies are called hunting and gathering societies. Members of these societies face severe hardships, but have adapted well to their environments. They have the most leisure of any type of society. The man shown here is a member of a hunting and gathering society in the Brazilian Amazon.

fight about. War, in turn, let slavery enter the human picture, for people found it convenient to let captives do their drudge work. As individuals passed on their possessions to their descendants, wealth grew more concentrated and power more centralized. Forms of leadership also changed as chiefs emerged.

Agricultural Societies When the plow was invented about five or six thousand years ago, it ushered in a *second social revolution*. The huge agricultural surplus allowed the population to increase, cities to develop, and many people to engage in activities other than farming—to develop the things popularly known as "culture," such as philosophy, art, literature, and architecture. The changes during this period in history were so profound that they sometimes are referred to as "the dawn of civilization."

Social inequality, previously only a tendency, became a fundamental feature of social life. Some people managed to gain control of the growing surplus resources. To protect their expanding privileges and power, this elite surrounded itself with armed

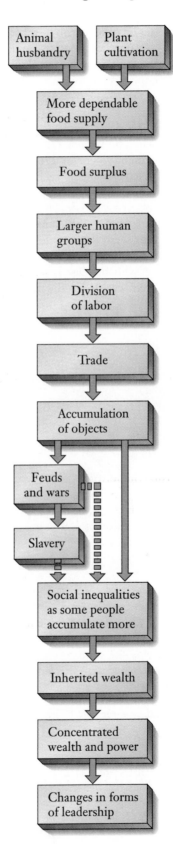

FIGURE 4.3

How Animal Husbandry and Plant Cultivation Changed Social Life

men. They even levied taxes on others, who now had become their "subjects." As conflict theorists point out, this concentration of resources and power, along with the oppression of people not in power, was the forerunner of the state.

Industrial Societies   The *third social revolution* also turned society upside down. The **Industrial Revolution** began in Great Britain, where in 1765 the steam engine was first used to run machinery. Before this time a few machines had harnessed nature (such as wind and water mills), but most had depended on human and animal power. Far more efficient than anything the world had ever seen, this new form of production brought even greater surplus and social inequality. The individuals who first used the new technology accumulated great wealth, but the masses

The sociological significance of the four social revolutions discussed in the text is that the type of society in which we live determines the kind of people we become. It is obvious, for example, that the orientations to life of this worker would differ markedly from those of the man shown on page 91.

The machinery that ushered in industrial society was met with ambivalence. On one hand, it brought a multitude of welcomed goods. On the other hand, factory time clocks and the incessant production line made people slaves to the very machines they built. The idea of machines dominating workers is illustrated by this classic scene of Charlie Chaplin's in Modern Times.

of people, thrown off the land as feudal society broke up, moved to the cities, where they faced the choice of stealing, starving, or working for starvation wages (Michalowski 1985).

Through a bitter struggle too long to review here, workers gradually won their demands for better working conditions, reversing the earlier pattern of growing inequality. The indicators of greater equality in later industrial societies are extensive: widespread ownership of homes and automobiles, access to libraries and education, better housing, greater variety of food, and much longer lives for the average person. On an even broader level, indicators include the abolition of slavery, the shift from monarchies and dictatorships to more representative political systems, the right to vote, the right to be tried by a jury of one's peers and to cross-examine witnesses, and greater rights for women and minorities.

Postindustrial Societies   Today, an entirely new type of society is emerging. The basic trend in advanced industrial societies is away from production and manufacturing to service industries. The United States was the first country to have more than half its work force employed in service industries—health, education, research, the government, counseling, banking and investments, sales, law, and the mass media. Australia, New Zealand, western Europe, and Japan soon followed. The term *postindustrial society* refers to this emerging society—one based on information, services, and high technology rather than on raw materials and manufacturing (Bell 1973; Lipset 1979; Toffler 1980).

The basic component of the postindustrial society is information. People who offer services either provide or apply information. Teachers pass on knowledge to students, while lawyers, physicians, bankers, and interior decorators sell their specialized knowledge of law, the body, money, and color schemes. Unlike factory workers in an industrial society, they don't *produce* anything. Rather, they transmit or use knowledge to provide services that others are willing to pay for.

Perhaps in years to come social analysts will refer to these changes as the *fourth social revolution*. Based on the computer chip, the information revolution is transforming society—and with it, our social relationships. Because of this tiny device, we can talk to people in other countries while we drive our automobiles, we can peer farther into space than ever before, and, at home and in the arcades, millions of children spend countless hours struggling against video enemies. Although the full implications of the information explosion are still unknown, as history is our guide, the changes will be so extensive that even our attitudes about the self and life will be transformed.

▼ **In Sum** The type of society in which we live sets boundaries around our lives. It especially determines the type and extent of inequality that prevails, which, in turn, governs relationships between men and women, the young and elderly, racial and ethnic groups, the rich and poor, and so on.

It is difficult to overstate the sociological principle that the type of society in which we live is the fundamental reason why we become who we are. It is obvious that you would not be taking this course if it were not for the state of your society. On a deeper level, you would not feel the same about life or hold your particular aspirations for the future.

What Holds Society Together?

With its many, often conflicting groups, and its exposure to social change, how can a society manage to hold together? Let us examine two answers sociologists have proposed.

Mechanical and Organic Solidarity Sociologist Emile Durkheim (1893/1933) found the key to **social cohesion**—the degree to which members of a society feel united by shared values and other social bonds—in what he called **mechanical solidarity.** By this term Durkheim meant that people who perform similar tasks develop a shared consciousness, a sense of similarity that unites them into a common whole. Think of an agricultural society, in which everyone is involved in planting, cultivating, and harvesting. Members of this group have so much in common that it is possible for them to know how most others feel about life.

As societies increase in size, their **division of labor** (how they divide up work) becomes more specialized. Some people mine gold, others turn it into jewelry, while still others sell it. This division of labor makes people depend on one another—for the work of each contributes to the whole.

Durkheim called this new form of solidarity based on interdependence **organic solidarity.** To see why he used this term, think about how you depend on your teacher to guide you through this introductory course in sociology. At the same time, to have a job your teacher needs you and other students. The two of you are *like organs* in the same body. Although each of you performs different tasks, your dependence on one another creates a form of unity.

Gemeinschaft **and** ***Gesellschaft*** Ferdinand Tönnies (1887/1988) also analyzed this major change in society. He used the term ***Gemeinschaft*** ("Guh-MINE-shoft"), or "intimate community," to describe the traditional type of society in which everyone knows

The text contrasts Gesellschaft *and* Gemeinschaft *societies. The French café represents a* Gemeinschaft *approach to life, while the cybernet café, where people ignore one another in favor of concentrating on electronic interactions via the Internet, represents a* Gesellschaft *orientation. The Internet interactions do not easily fit into standard sociological models— another instance of cultural lag.*

everyone else. He noted that in the emerging society short-term relationships, individual accomplishments, and self-interests were crowding out personal ties, family connections, and lifelong friendships. Tönnies called this new type of society **Gesellschaft** ("Guh-ZELL-shoft"), or "impersonal association."

▼ **In Sum** Whether the terms are *Gemeinschaft* and *Gesellschaft* or *mechanical solidarity* and *organic solidarity*, they indicate that societies change, and that as they do the people living within them also change. The sociological point is that social structure sets limits on what we do, feel, and think. Ultimately, social structure lies at the basis of what kind of people we become. This becomes more evident in the box on the next page, which describes the Amish, one of the few remaining *Gemeinschaft* societies in the United States.

The Microsociological Perspective: Social Interaction in Everyday Life

Where the macrosociological approach stresses the broad features of society, the microsociological approach has a narrower focus, placing its emphasis on *face-to-face interaction*, on what people do when they are in one another's presence. Let's examine some of the areas of social life that microsociologists study.

Personal Space

Each of us surrounds ourselves with a "personal bubble" that we go to great lengths to protect. We open the bubble to intimates—to close friends, children, parents, and so on—but are careful to keep most people out of this space. When we stand in lines, for example, we make certain there is enough room so we don't touch the person in front of us and we aren't touched by the person behind us.

The amount of space that people prefer varies from one culture to another. Anthropologist Edward Hall (1959) recounts a conversation with a man from South America who had attended one of his lectures:

> He came to the front of the class at the end of the lecture. . . . We started out facing each other, and as he talked I became dimly aware that he was standing a little too close and that I was beginning to back up. . . . By experimenting I was able to observe that as I moved away slightly, there was an associated shift in the pattern of interaction. He had more trouble expressing himself. If I shifted to where I felt comfortable (about twenty-one inches), he looked somewhat puzzled and hurt.

After Hall (1969) analyzed such situations, he observed that North Americans use four different "distance zones":

1 *Intimate distance.* This is the zone that the South American unwittingly invaded. It extends to about 18 inches from our bodies. We reserve this

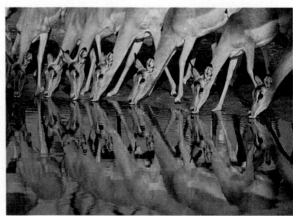

Among the many aspects of social life studied by sociologists with a microsociological focus is personal space. What do you see in common in these two photos?

The Amish: *Gemeinschaft* Community in a *Gesellschaft* Society

U.S. SOCIETY EXHIBITS all the characteristics Ferdinand Tönnies identified as those of a *Gesellschaft* society. Impersonal associations pervade everyday life. Local, state, and federal governments regulate many activities. Impersonal corporations hire people not on the basis of personal relationships, but on their value to the bottom line. And, perhaps even more significantly, millions of Americans do not even know their neighbors.

Within the United States, a handful of small communities exhibit characteristics that depart from those of the larger society. One such example is the Old Order Amish, followers of a sect that broke away from the Swiss-German Mennonite church in the late 1600s, settling in Pennsylvania around 1727. Today, more than 130,000 Old Order Amish live in the United States. The largest concentration, about 14,000, reside in Lancaster County, Pennsylvania.

To the nearly five million tourists who pass through Lancaster County each year, the quiet pastures and almost identical white farmhouses, simple barns, horse- or mule-drawn carts, and clothes flapping on lines to dry convey a sense of peace and wholeness reminiscent of another era. Although just sixty-five miles from Philadelphia, "Amish country" is a world away.

The Amish faith rests on separation from the world, taking Christ's Sermon on the Mount literally. This rejection of worldly concerns, Donald Kraybill writes in *The Riddle of Amish Culture*,

"provides the foundation of such Amish values as humility, faithfulness, thrift, tradition, communal goals, joy of work, a slow-paced life, and trust in divine providence."

The village life that Tönnies identified as fostering *Gemeinschaft* communities—and that he correctly predicted was fast being lost to industrialization—is very much

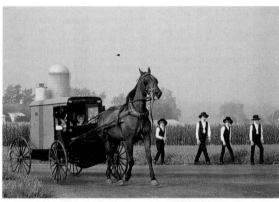

alive among the Amish. The Amish make their decisions in weekly meetings, where, by consensus, they follow a set of rules, or *Ordnung*, to guide their behavior. Religion and the discipline it calls for are the glue that holds these communities together. Brotherly love and the welfare of the community are paramount values. Most Amish farm plots of a hundred acres or less, keeping their farms small so that horses can be used instead of tractors and neighbors can pitch in with the chores. In these ways, intimacy—a sense of community—is maintained.

The Amish are bound by many other communal ties, including language (a dialect of German known as Pennsylvania Dutch), a distinctive style of plain dress that has remained unchanged for almost 300 years, and church-sponsored schools. Nearly all Amish marry, and divorce is forbidden. The family is a vital ingredient in Amish life; all major events take place in the home, including weddings and worship services, even births and funerals. Most Amish children attend church schools only until the age of 13. To go to school beyond the eighth grade would expose them to "worldly concerns" and give them information considered of no value to farm life. They believe that all violence is bad, even in personal self-defense, and register as conscientious objectors during times of war.

The Amish cannot resist all change, of course. Instead, they attempt to adapt to social change in ways that will cause the least harm to their core values. Because of the high cost of land due to urban sprawl, about 30 percent of married Amish men work at jobs other than farming, most in farm-related businesses or in woodworking trades. They go to great lengths to avoid leaving the home. The Amish believe that when the husband works away from the home, all aspects of life change—from the marital relationship to the care of the children—certainly an excellent sociological insight. They also believe that if a man receives a paycheck he will think that his work is of more value than his wife's. For the Amish, intimate, or *Gemeinschaft*, society is absolutely essential to maintain their way of life.

Sources: Hostetler 1980; Kraybill 1989; Bender 1990; Raymond 1990; Ziegenhals 1991; Kephart and Zellner 1994; Savells 1997.

space for lovemaking and wrestling, comforting and protecting.

2 *Personal distance.* This zone extends from 18 inches to 4 feet. We reserve it for friends and acquaintances and ordinary conversations. This is the zone in which Hall would have preferred speaking with the South American.

3 *Social distance.* This zone, extending out from us about 4 to 12 feet, marks impersonal or formal relationships. We use this zone for such things as job interviews.

4 *Public distance.* This zone, extending beyond 12 feet, marks even more formal relationships. It is used to separate dignitaries and public speakers from the general public.

Let's now turn to dramaturgy, a special focus of microsociology.

Dramaturgy: The Presentation of Self in Everyday Life

It was their big day, two years in the making. Jennifer Mackey wore a white wedding gown adorned with an 11-foot train and 24,000 seed pearls that she and her mother had sewn onto the dress. Next to her at the altar in Lexington, Kentucky, stood her intended, Jeffrey Degler, in black tie. They said their vows, then turned to gaze for a moment at the four hundred guests.

That's when groomsman Daniel Mackey collapsed. As the shocked organist struggled to play Mendelssohn's "Wedding March," Mr. Mackey's unconscious body was dragged away, his feet striking—loudly—every step of the altar stairs.

"I couldn't believe he would die at my wedding," the bride said. (Hughes 1990)

Sociologist Erving Goffman (1922–1982) added a new twist to microsociology when he developed **dramaturgy** (or dramaturgical analysis). By this term he meant that social life is like a drama or the stage: Birth ushers us onto the stage of everyday life, and our socialization consists of learning to perform on that stage. The self that we studied in the previous chapter lies at the center of our performances: we have definite ideas of how we want others to think of us, and we use our roles to communicate those ideas. Goffman calls these efforts to manage the impressions that others receive of us **impression management.**

Everyday life, Goffman said, involves playing our assigned roles. We have *front stages* on which to perform them, as did Jennifer and Jeffrey. (By the way, Daniel Mackey didn't really die—he had just passed out from the excitement of it all.) But we don't have to look at weddings to find front stages. Everyday life is filled with them. Where your teacher lectures is a front stage. And if you make an announcement at the dinner table, you are using a front stage. In fact, you spend most of your time on front stages, for a front stage is wherever you deliver your lines. We also have *back stages*, places where we can retreat and let our hair down. When you close the bathroom or bedroom door for privacy, for example, you are entering a back stage.

Everyday life brings with it many roles. The same person may be a student, a teenager, a shopper, a worker, a date, as well as a daughter or a son. Ordinarily our roles are sufficiently separated that conflict between them is minimized. Occasionally, however, what is expected of us in one role is incompatible with what is expected of us in another role. This problem, known as **role conflict,** makes us very uncomfortable, as illustrated in Figure 4.4, in which family, friendship, student, and work roles come clashing together. Usually, however, we manage to avoid role conflict by segregating our roles, which in some instances may require an intense juggling act.

Sometimes the *same* role presents inherent conflict, a problem known as **role strain.** Suppose that you are exceptionally prepared for a particular class assignment. Although the instructor asks an unusually difficult question, you find yourself knowing the answer when no one else does. If you want to raise your hand, yet don't want to make your fellow students look bad, you will experience role strain. As illustrated in Figure 4.4, the difference between role conflict and role strain is that role conflict is conflict *between* roles, while role strain is conflict *within* a role.

To show ourselves as adept role players brings positive recognition from others, something we all covet. To accomplish this, we often use **teamwork**—two or more people working together to make certain a performance goes off as planned. When a performance doesn't come off quite right, however, it may require **face-saving behavior.** We may, for example, ignore someone's flaws in perfor-

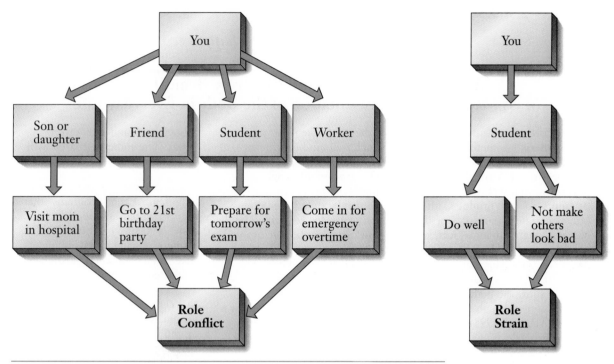

FIGURE 4.4
Role Strain and Role Conflict

mance, which Goffman defines as *tact*. Suppose your teacher is about to make an important point. Suppose also that her lecturing has been outstanding and the class is hanging on every word. Just as she pauses for emphasis, her stomach lets out a loud growl. She might then use a face-saving technique by remarking, "I was so busy preparing for class that I didn't get breakfast this morning." It is more likely, however, that both the class and the teacher will simply ignore the sound, both giving the impression that no one heard a thing—a face-saving technique called *studied nonobservance*. This allows the teacher to make the point, or as Goffman would say, it allows the performance to go on.

Since our own body is so strongly identified with the self, a good part of impression management centers around "body messages." Usually people accept our intended messages, but as the Down-to-Earth Sociology box on the next page describes, a conflict sometimes exists between the impressions people try to make and those which others are willing to accept.

Ethnomethodology: Uncovering Background Assumptions

Certainly one of the strangest words in sociology is *ethnomethodology*. To understand this term, consider its three basic components. "*Ethno*" means folk or people; "*method*" means how people do something; "*ology*" means "the study of." Putting them together, then, *ethno/method/ology* means "the study of how people do things." Specifically, **ethnomethodology** is the study of how people use commonsense understandings to get through everyday life.

Let's suppose that during an office visit, your doctor remarks that your hair is rather long, then takes out a pair of scissors and offers to give you a haircut. You would feel strange about this situation—for your doctor has violated **background assumptions,** your ideas about the way life is and the way things ought to work. These assumptions, which lie at the root of daily life, are so deeply embedded in our consciousness that most of us fulfill them unquestioningly. Thus, your doctor does not

▲▼▲▼▲▼▲▼▲▼▲▼▲▼▲▼▲▼▲▼▲▼▲▼▲▼▲▼▲▼▲▼▲▼

Down-to-Earth Sociology

Disgusting, Pathetic, and Bizarrely Beautiful: Mass Media and the Presentation of the Body in Everyday Life

A COMMON MESSAGE of advertisers is that there is something wrong with our bodies. Although we may try to shrug off these messages, knowing that they are clear attempts to sell products, they still penetrate our images of the way we "ought" to look. Such advertising is not limited to the West. In both Japan and China advertisers push a soap that supposedly slims the body by "sucking up fat through the skin's pores" (Marshall 1995).

Today, television programs rank high among the mass media's influences on how we feel about our bodies. Sociologist Karen Honeycutt (1995) studied television talk shows that feature women and weight. She identified these patterns of how obese women feel about themselves and how audiences react to them:

- *Disgusting.* In this, the most prevalent category, disgust about obese people prevails. As one guest said, "What really offends me about obese people

is that they take up way too much room in buses and at concerts—and they smell." The overweight people sometimes cry as they are confronted by rude stares and nasty personal remarks. The host may play the role of the sympathizer, sometimes even with a closeup of her or him wiping away a tear.

- *Pathetic.* Although this category is sometimes difficult to separate from disgusting, it contains an element of compassion. When obese children are featured, for example, the guests express sympathy, even a bit of hope for change.
- *Bizarrely beautiful.* These shows feature obese people and guests who find them sexually attractive. The women, who often say they are happy with their weight, may strike provocative poses. The audience still views them as freaks, however. In one show, one of the male guests asked the 300-pound women if their

boyfriends and lovers were sick. The audience roared with laughter.

Always, there is the matter of judgment. Even programs that are presented as neutral ("the issue is health") contain hidden assumptions and moral judgments that women's bodies need to be remolded. Even the term *overweight* is not neutral, for it implies that certain people have too much weight, while most of us are the "right" weight from which we measure their "over" weightness.

For Your Consideration

Most advertising and television shows focusing on weight are directed at women. Is this because women are more concerned than men about weight, more likely to have eating disorders, and more likely to express dissatisfaction with their bodies (Honeycutt 1995)? Or does this targeting of women create these attitudes and behaviors? Or is it a bit of both; that is, does one feed the other?

---

offer you a haircut, even if he or she is good at cutting hair and you need a haircut!

The founder of ethnomethodology, sociologist Harold Garfinkel, conducted some interesting exercises to uncover our background assumptions. Garfinkel (1967) asked his students to act as though they did not understand the basic rules of social life. Some tried to bargain with supermarket clerks; others would inch closer to people and stare directly at them. They were met with surprise, bewilderment, even anger. In one exercise Garfinkel asked students to take words and phrases literally. One conversation went like this:

Acquaintance: How are you?

Student: How am I in regard to what? My health, my finances, my schoolwork, my peace of mind, my . . . ?

Acquaintance (red in the face): Look! I was just trying to be polite. Frankly, I don't give a damn how you are.

Students who are given the assignment to break background assumptions can be highly creative. The young children of one of my students were surprised one morning when they came down for breakfast to find a sheet spread across the living

All of us contrast the reality we see when we look in the mirror with our culture's ideal body types. The ultrathin (some would say skinny) French model represents an ideal body type that has developed in some parts of Western culture. Partly because of such cultural images, large women sometimes find themselves social outcasts. Consequently, as in the photo on the left, some now band together in support groups to help overcome the emotional impact of their status.

room floor. On it were dishes, silverware, candle holders with lit candles—and ice cream. They, too, wondered what was going on—but they dug eagerly into the ice cream before their mother could change her mind.

▼ **In Sum** Ethnomethodologists explore background assumptions, our taken-for-granted ideas about the world, which underlie our behavior and are violated only with risk. These basic rules of social life are an essential part of the social structure. Deeply embedded in our minds, they give us basic directions for living everyday life.

The Social Construction of Reality

Usually we assume that reality is something "out there," that it hits us in the face with its independent existence. Symbolic interactionists, however, point out that we define our own realities and then live within those definitions. As sociologist W. I. Thomas said, in what has become known as the **Thomas theorem,** "If people define situations as real, they are real in their consequences." Consider the following incident:

On a visit to Morocco, in northern Africa, I decided to buy a watermelon. When I indicated to the street vendor that the knife he was going to use to cut the watermelon was dirty (encrusted with filth would be more apt), he was very obliging. He immediately bent down and began to swish the knife in a puddle on the street. I shuddered as I looked at the passing burros, freely defecating and urinating as they went. Quickly, I indicated by gesture that I preferred my melon uncut after all.

For that vendor, germs did not exist. For me, they did. And each of us acted according to our definition of the situation. My perception and behavior did not come from the fact that germs are real but *because I grew up in a society that teaches they are real.* Microbes, of course, *objectively* exist, and whether or not germs are part of our thought world makes no difference to whether we are infected by them. Our behavior, however, does not depend on the *objective* existence of something but, rather, on our *subjective interpretation,* on our *definition of reality.* In other words, it is not the reality of microbes that impresses itself on us, but society that impresses the reality of microbes on us.

The process by which we take the various elements available in our society and put them together to develop a view of reality is called the **social construction of reality.** The definitions that we learn from our culture, and that we help construct, underlie not only what we do but also what we perceive, feel, and think. Let me provide an example common to our society, although one that is difficult for men to identify with.

A gynecological nurse, Mae Biggs, and I did research on vaginal examinations. Reviewing about 14,000 cases, we looked at how the medical profession constructs social reality in order to define this examination as nonsexual (Henslin and Biggs 1997). We found that the pelvic examination unfolds much as a stage play does. I will use "he" to refer to the physician because only male physicians participated in this study. Perhaps the results would be different with women gynecologists.

Scene 1 (the patient as person) In this scene, the doctor maintains eye contact with his patient, calls her by name, and discusses her problems in a professional manner. If he decides that a vaginal examination is necessary, he tells a nurse, "Pelvic in room 1." By this statement, he is announcing that a major change will occur in the next scene.

Scene 2 (from person to pelvic) This scene is the depersonalizing stage. In line with the doctor's announcement, the patient begins the transition from a "person" to a "pelvic." The doctor leaves the room, and a female nurse enters to help the patient make the transition. The nurse prepares the "props" for the coming examination and answers any questions the woman might have.

What occurs at this point is essential for the social construction of reality, for *by absenting himself the doctor removes even the suggestion of sexuality.* To undress in front of him could suggest either a striptease or intimacy, thus undermining the reality being so carefully defined, that of nonsexuality.

Patients also want to remove any hint of sexuality, and during this scene many express concern about what to do with their panties, perhaps muttering to the nurse, "I don't want him to see these." Most women solve the problem by either slipping their panties under their clothes or placing them in their purse.

Scene 3 (the person as pelvic) This scene opens when the doctor enters the room. Before him is a woman lying on a table, her feet in stirrups, her knees tightly together, and her body covered by a drape sheet. The doctor seats himself on a low stool before the woman, tells her, "Let your knees fall apart" (rather than the sexually loaded "Spread your legs"), and begins the examination.

The drape sheet is crucial in this process of desexualization, for *it dissociates the pelvic area from the person:* Bending forward and with the drape sheet above his head, the physician can see only the vagina, not the patient's face. Thus dissociated from the individual, the vagina is dramaturgically transformed into an object of analysis. If the doctor examines the patient's breasts, he also dissociates them from her person by examining them one at a time, with a towel covering the unexamined breast. Like the vagina, each breast becomes an isolated unit dissociated from the person.

In this crucial scene, the patient cooperates in being an object, becoming for all practical purposes a pelvis to be examined. She withdraws eye contact from the doctor, usually from the nurse as well, is likely to stare at the wall or at the ceiling, and avoids initiating conversation.

Scene 4 (from pelvic to person) In this scene the patient is "repersonalized." The doctor has left the examining room; the patient dresses and takes care of any problems with her hair and makeup. Her reemergence as person is indicated by such statements to the nurse as "My dress isn't too wrinkled, is it?" indicating a need for reassurance that the metamorphosis from "pelvic" back to "person" has been completed satisfactorily.

Scene 5 (the patient as person) In this scene, the patient is once again treated as a person rather than an object. The doctor makes eye contact with her and addresses her by name. She, too, makes eye contact with the doctor, and the usual middle-class interaction patterns are followed. She has been fully restored.

▼ **In Sum** To an outsider to our culture, the custom of women going to a male stranger for a vaginal examination might seem bizarre. But not to us. We learn that pelvic examinations are nonsexual. To sustain this definition requires teamwork—patients, doctors, and nurses working together to *socially construct reality.*

It is not just pelvic examinations or our views of microbes that make up our definitions of reality. Rather, *all of our reality is socially constructed.* These constructions are so important that they form the essence of society, providing the bases for what we do and how we feel about life.

The Need for Both Macrosociology and Microsociology

As noted earlier, both microsociology and macrosociology make vital contributions to our understanding of human behavior. Our understanding of social life would be vastly incomplete without one or the other.

To illustrate this point, let's consider the research on two groups of high school boys conducted by sociologist William Chambliss (1973/1997). Both groups attended Hanibal High School. In one group were eight middle-class boys who came from "good" families and were perceived by the community as "going somewhere." Chambliss calls this group the "Saints." The other group consisted of six lower-class boys who were seen as headed down a dead-end road. Chambliss calls this group the "Roughnecks."

Both groups skipped school, got drunk, and did a lot of fighting and vandalism. The Saints were actually somewhat more delinquent, for they were truant more often and they did more vandalism. Yet the Saints had a good reputation, while the Roughnecks were seen by teachers, the police, and the general community as no good and heading for trouble.

These reputations followed the boys throughout life. Seven of the eight Saints went on to graduate from college. Three studied for advanced degrees: one finished law school and became active in state politics, one finished medical school, and one went on to earn a Ph.D. The four other college graduates entered managerial or executive training with large firms. After his parents divorced, one Saint failed to graduate from high school on time and had to repeat his senior year. Although this boy tried to go to college by attending night school, he never finished. He was unemployed the last time Chambliss saw him.

In contrast, only four of the Roughnecks even finished high school. Two of these boys did exceptionally well in sports and received athletic scholarships to college. They both graduated from college and became high school coaches. Of the two others who graduated from high school, one became a small-time gambler and the other disappeared "up north," where he was last reported to be driving a

Can you tell which of these photos is of upper-middle-class youth and which portrays working-class youth? In spite of similarities of social identifiers by which both groups of students proclaim that they are U.S. teenagers, they also use status markers to signal their social class background. As the text explains, this information is of crucial importance, for it affects perception, social interaction, and, ultimately, life chances.

truck. Of the two who did not complete high school, each was sent to state penitentiaries for separate murders.

To understand what happened to the Saints and the Roughnecks, we need to grasp *both* social structure and social interaction. Using *macrosociology*, we can place these boys within the larger framework of the U.S. social class system. This context reveals how different opportunities open or close to youngsters and how people learn different goals as they grow up in vastly different groups. We can then use *microsociology* to follow their everyday lives. We can see how the Saints manipulated their "good" reputa-

tions to skip classes repeatedly and how their access to automobiles allowed them to transfer their troublemaking to different communities and thus prevent damage to their local reputations. In contrast, lacking access to automobiles, the Roughnecks were highly visible. Their lawbreaking activities, limited to a small area, readily came to the attention of the community. Microsociology also reveals how their respective reputations opened doors of opportunity to the first group of boys while closing them to the other.

Thus we need both kinds of sociology, and both are stressed in the following chapters.

Summary and Review

Levels of Sociological Analysis

What two levels of analysis do sociologists use?

Sociologists use macro- and microsociological levels of analysis. In **macrosociology,** the focus is placed on large-scale features of social life, while in **microsociology,** the focus is on **social interaction.** Functionalists and conflict theorists tend to use a macrosociological approach, while symbolic interactionists are more likely to use a microsociological approach. Pp. 82–83.

The Macrosociological Perspective: Social Structure

How does social structure influence behavior?

The term **social structure** refers to a society's framework, which forms an envelope around us and establishes limits on our behavior. Social structure consists of culture, social class, social statuses, roles, groups, and social institutions. Together these serve as foundations for how we view the world. Pp. 83–84.

Our location in the social structure underlies our perceptions, attitudes, and behaviors. *Culture* lays the broadest framework, while **social class** divides people according to income, education, and occupational prestige. Our behaviors and orientations are further influenced by the **statuses** we occupy, the **roles** we play, the **groups** to which we belong, and our experiences with the institutions of our society. These components

of society work together to help maintain social order. Pp. 84–88.

What are social institutions?

Social institutions are the organized and standard means that a society develops to meet its basic needs. As summarized in Figure 4.1, sociologists have identified nine social institutions—the family, religion, law, politics, economics, education, medicine, science, and the military. P. 88.

What are the four social revolutions?

The discovery that animals and plants could be domesticated marked the first social revolution, transforming hunting and gathering societies into pastoral and horticultural societies. The invention of the plow brought about the second social revolution, as societies became agricultural. The invention of the steam engine allowed industrial societies to develop, the third social revolution. Today, we are witnessing the fourth social revolution, being ushered in by the invention of the microchip. As in the previous three social revolutions, little will remain the same. Our attitudes, ideas, expectations, behaviors, relationships—all will be transformed. Pp. 88–93.

What holds society together?

In agricultural societies, said Emile Durkheim, people are united by **mechanical solidarity** (similar views and feelings). With industrialization comes **organic solidarity** (people depend on one another to do their jobs). Ferdinand Tönnies pointed out that the informal means of control of *Gemeinschaft* (small, intimate) societies are replaced by formal mechanisms in *Gesellschaft* (larger, more impersonal) societies. P. 94.

The Microsociological Perspective: Social Interaction in Everyday Life

Do all human groups share a similar sense of personal space?

In examining how people use physical space, symbolic interactionists stress that each of us is surrounded by a "personal bubble" that we carefully protect. People from different cultures have "personal bubbles" of varying sizes, so the answer to the question is no. Americans typically use four different "distance zones": intimate, personal, social, and public. Pp. 94–96.

What is dramaturgy?

Erving Goffman developed **dramaturgy** (or dramaturgical analysis), which analyzes everyday life in terms of the stage. At the core of this analysis is **impression management,** our attempts to control the impressions we attempt to make on others. Our performances often call for **teamwork** and **face-saving behavior.** Pp. 96–97.

What is the social construction of reality?

The phrase **the social construction of reality** refers to how we construct our views of the world, which, in turn, underlie our actions. **Ethnomethodology** is the study of how people make sense of everyday life. Ethnomethodologists try to uncover our **background assumptions,** our basic ideas about the way life is. Pp. 97–101.

The Need for Both Macrosociology and Microsociology

Why are both levels of analysis important?

Because each focuses on different aspects of the human experience, both microsociology and macrosociology are necessary for us to understand social life. Pp. 101–102.

Where can I read more on this topic?

Suggested readings for this chapter are listed on page 437.

Glossary

achieved statuses positions that are earned, are accomplished, or involve at least some effort or activity on the individual's part (p. 86)

ascribed statuses positions an individual either inherits at birth or receives involuntarily later in life (p. 86)

background assumptions deeply embedded common understandings, or basic rules, concerning our view of the world and of how people ought to act (p. 97)

division of labor how work is divided among the members of a group (p. 93)

dramaturgy an approach, pioneered by Erving Goffman, analyzing social life in terms of drama or the stage (p. 96)

ethnomethodology the study of how people use background assumptions to make sense of life (p. 97)

face-saving behavior techniques used to salvage a performance that is going sour (p. 96)

Gemeinschaft a type of society in which life is intimate; a community in which everyone knows everyone else and people share a sense of togetherness (p. 93)

Gesellschaft a type of society dominated by impersonal relationships, individual accomplishments, and self-interest (p. 94)

group people who regularly and consciously interact with one another; in a general sense, people who have something in common and who believe that what they have in common is significant (p. 88)

horticultural society a society based on cultivating plants by the use of hand tools (p. 90)

hunting and gathering society a society dependent on hunting and gathering for survival (p. 90)

impression management the term used by Erving Goffman to describe people's efforts to control the impressions that others receive of them (p. 96)

Industrial Revolution the third social revolution, occurring when machines powered by fuels replaced most animal and human power (p. 92)

macrosociology analysis of social life focusing on broad features of social structure, such as social class and the relationships of groups to one another; an approach usually used by functionalists and conflict theorists (p. 83)

master status a status that cuts across the other statuses that an individual occupies (p. 86)

mechanical solidarity Durkheim's term for the unity or shared consciousness that comes from being involved in similar occupations or activities (p. 93)

microsociology analysis of social life focusing on social interaction; an approach usually used by symbolic interactionists (p. 83)

organic solidarity Durkheim's term for the interdependence that results from people needing others to fulfill their jobs; solidarity based on the division of labor (p. 93)

pastoral society a society based on the pasturing of animals (p. 90)

role the behaviors, obligations, and privileges attached to a status (p. 87)

role conflict conflicts that someone feels between roles because the expectations attached to one role are incompatible with the expectations of another role (p. 96)

role strain conflicts that someone feels within a role (p. 96)

social class a large number of people with similar amounts of income and education who work at jobs that are roughly comparable in prestige (p. 84)

social cohesion the degree to which members of a group or a society feel united by shared values and other social bonds (p. 93)

social construction of reality the use of background assumptions and life experiences to define what is real (p. 100)

social institution the organized, usual, or standard ways by which society meets its basic needs (p. 88)

social interaction what people do when they are in one another's presence (p. 83)

social structure the relationship of people and groups to one another (Pp. 83–84)

society a group of people who share a culture and a territory (p. 88)

status the position that someone occupies; one's social ranking (p. 85)

status inconsistency a contradiction or mismatch between statuses; a condition in which a person ranks high on some dimensions of social class and low on others (p. 87)

status symbols items used to identify a status (p. 86)

teamwork the collaboration of two or more persons who, interested in the success of a performance, manage impressions jointly (p. 96)

Thomas theorem basically, that people live in socially constructed worlds; that is, people jointly build their own realities; summarized in William I. Thomas's statement "If people define situations as real, they are real in their consequences." (p. 99)

Sociology and the Internet

All URLs listed are current as of the printing of this book. URLs are often changed. Please check our Website http://www.abacon.com/henslin for updates.

1. Statuses (Positions in Organizations)

In this chapter you learned about the statuses and roles found in groups. Although formal organizations are explored in the next chapter, in this project you will be looking at the organization charts of large organizations to see what the various positions (statuses) are and how they differ from group to group.

Point your computer to http://www.yahoo.com and enter the search term "organization chart" (without the quotation marks). Go to the bottom of the page, and click on the AltaVista bar. On the new page you will see the first ten of hundreds of sites containing organization charts. Your task is to describe and compare statuses. Start by clicking on two or three sites, and note the similarities of the positions. Are there any major differences? Once you get a feel for the charts, select several sites in each of two types of organizations. For example, you might look at military, government, education, or religion. Take notes on the general similarities of statuses among the various types of organizations, as well as differences among them. Then select a third site involving another type of organization, and make similar notes concerning it. (You may also want to get an organization chart of your college or university if it is available and compare it with what you noted about these other organizations.) Write a two- or three-page paper on your findings.

2. Intentional Communities

The creation of "intentional communities" is an attempt to restore *Gemeinschaft* to modern living. Access the list of intentional communities of the Web at http://www.well.com/user/cmty/index.html and browse several of the sites. Look for *Gemeinschaft* elements featured in the descriptions, as well as any *Gesellschaft* components that may be there. Write a report comparing the particular *Gesellschaft* emphases of the communities you explored. Be sure to discuss the factors of postindustrial societies that you think draw people to these new intentional communities.

Diana Ong, Friends, 1994.

C H A P T E R 5

Social Groups in a Socially Diverse Society

OHNNY SMILED AS HIS FINGER tightened on the trigger. The explosion was pure pleasure to his ears. His eyes glistened as the bullet ripped into the dog. With an exaggerated swagger, Johnny walked away, surrounded by five buddies, all wearing Levis, Air Jordans, and jackets emblazoned with the logo of Satan's Servants.

Johnny never had felt as if he belonged. His parents were seldom home, and when they were, one drunken quarrel followed another. Many times Johnny had huddled in a corner while the police separated his parents. One of Johnny's recurring memories was of his handcuffed father being taken away in a police cruiser. School was a hassle, too, for he felt that the teachers were out to get him and that most of his classmates were jerks. It wasn't unusual for Johnny to spend most of his time in detention for disrupting classes.

Johnny didn't want to be a loner, but that seemed to be what fate held in store. He once tried a church group, but that lasted just one meeting. He was lousy at rollerblading and had given that up after the guys laughed at him. It was the same with baseball and other sports.

But Satan's Servants—now, that was different. For the first time in his life, Johnny felt welcome—even appreciated. All the guys got in trouble in school, and none of them got along with their parents. He especially liked the jackets, with the skull and crossbones and "Satan's Servants" emblazoned on the back. And finally, with the "Satan's Servettes," there were girls who looked up to him.

The shooting assured Johnny, now known as J.B., of a firm place in the group. The old man wouldn't bother them anymore. He'd get the message when he found his dog.

When they returned to the abandoned building that served as their headquarters, Johnny had never felt so good in his entire life. This was what life was all about. "There isn't anything I wouldn't do for these guys," he thought, as they gathered around him and took turns pointing the pistol.

The groups we form have profound effects on us. We can trace our attitudes and even opinions about life to our groups, for they lie at the basis of the socialization that we studied in Chapter 3. Sociologist Emile Durkheim (1893/1933) said they serve as a buffer that helps keep us from feeling oppressed by that huge, amorphous entity known as *society*. Sometimes, as with Satan's Servants, small groups stand in opposition to the larger society, but in most instances they reinforce society's dominant values.

Before we examine groups in detail, we should distinguish among groups, aggregates, and categories. An **aggregate** consists of individuals who temporarily share the same physical space but who do not see themselves as belonging together. People waiting in a checkout line or drivers parked at the same red light are an aggregate. A **category** consists of people who share similar characteristics, such as all college women who wear glasses or all men over 6 feet tall. Unlike groups, the individuals who make up a category neither interact with one another nor take one another into account.

In contrast, the members of a **group** think of themselves as belonging together, and they interact with one another. To better understand this essential feature of social life, let's look at the types of groups that make up our society and at how they affect our lives.

Primary Groups

Johnny never felt as though he belonged anywhere until Satan's Servants welcomed him. With them he found the friendship and admiration he longed for. For him, Satan's Servants was what sociologist Charles Cooley calls a **primary group**. As Cooley (1909) put it,

> By primary groups I mean those characterized by intimate face-to-face association and cooperation.

They are primary in several senses, but chiefly in that they are fundamental in forming the social nature and ideals of the individual.

Producing a Mirror Within

It is significant that Cooley calls primary groups the "springs of life." By this, he means that primary groups, such as the family, friendship groups, and even gangs, are essential to our emotional well-being. As humans, we have an intense need for face-to-face interaction that provides feelings of self-esteem. By offering a sense of belonging, a feeling of being appreciated, and sometimes even love, primary groups are uniquely equipped to meet this basic need.

Another reason why primary groups are so significant is that their values and attitudes become fused into our identity. We internalize their views,

Primary groups such as the family, a major focus of sociological investigation, play a key role in the development of the self. As a small group, the family also serves as a buffer from the often-threatening larger group known as society. The family has been of primary significance in helping this couple from Nicaragua adjust to their new life in the United States.

which become the lens through which we view life. Even as adults, no matter how far we may have come from our childhood roots, early primary groups remain "inside" us, where they continue to form part of the perspective from which we look out onto the world. Ultimately, then, it is difficult, if not impossible, for us to separate the self from our primary groups, for the self and our groups merge into a "we."

Secondary Groups

Compared with primary groups, **secondary groups** are larger, more anonymous, formal, and impersonal. Such groups are based on some interest or activity, and their members are likely to interact on the basis of specific roles, such as president, manager, worker, or student. Examples are a college classroom, the American Sociological Association, a factory, and the Democratic Party. Contemporary society could not function without secondary groups. They are part of the way we get our education, make our living, and spend our money and leisure.

As necessary as they are for contemporary life, secondary groups often fail to satisfy our deep needs for intimate association. Consequently, *secondary groups tend to break down into primary groups.* For example, at school and work we form friendship cliques, which provide such valued interaction that we sometimes feel if it weren't for them, school or work "would drive us crazy." Just as small groups serve as a buffer between us and the larger society, so the primary groups we form within secondary groups serve as a buffer between us and the demands secondary groups place on us.

Voluntary Associations

A special type of secondary group is a **voluntary association,** a group made up of volunteers who organize on the basis of some mutual interest. Some are local, consisting of only a few volunteers; some are national, with a paid professional staff; and others are in between.

Americans love voluntary associations, using them to pursue a wide variety of interests. A visitor entering any of the thousands of small towns that dot the U.S. landscape will be greeted with a highway sign boasting its particular volunteer associations: Girl Scouts, Boy Scouts, Lions, Elks, Eagles, Knights of Columbus, Chamber of Commerce, Ju-

Relationships in secondary groups are more formal and temporary than those in primary groups. In order to satisfy basic emotional needs, members of secondary groups, such as members of the military (or of college classes), form smaller primary groups.

nior Chamber of Commerce, Future Farmers of America, American Legion, Veterans of Foreign Wars, and perhaps a host of others. One form of voluntary association is so prevalent that a separate sign usually indicates which varieties are present in the town: Roman Catholic, Baptist, Lutheran, Methodist, Episcopalian, and so on. Not listed on these signs are many other voluntary associations, such as political parties, unions, health clubs, the National Organization for Women, Alcoholics Anonymous, Gamblers Anonymous, Association of Pinto Racers, and Citizens United For or Against This and That.

The Inner Circle, the Iron Law of Oligarchy, and Social Diversity

An interesting, and disturbing, aspect of voluntary associations is that the leaders are likely to grow distant from their members and to become convinced that they can trust only an inner core to make the group's

important decisions. To see this principle at work, let's look at the Veterans of Foreign Wars (VFW).

Sociologists Elaine Fox and George Arquitt (1985) studied three local posts of the VFW, a national organization of former U.S. soldiers who have served in foreign wars. They found that the leaders, although careful to conceal their attitudes, view the rank and file as a bunch of ignorant boozers. Because the leaders can't stand the thought that such people might represent them to the community and at national meetings, a curious situation arises. Although the VFW constitution makes rank-and-file members fully eligible for top leadership positions, they never become leaders. In fact, the leaders are so effective in controlling these top positions that even before an election they can specify who is going to win. "You need to meet Jim," the sociologists were told. "He's the next post commander after Sam does his time."

At first the researchers found this statement puzzling. How could the elite be so sure? As they investigated further, they found that leadership is actually decided behind the scenes. The elected leaders appoint their favored people to chair the key committees. This makes the members aware of their accomplishments, and they elect them as leaders. The inner core, then, maintains control over the entire organization simply by appointing members of their inner circle to highly visible positions.

Like the VFW, most organizations are run by only a few of their members (Cnaan 1991). Building on the term *oligarchy*, a system in which many are ruled by a few, sociologist Robert Michels (1876–1936) coined the term **the iron law of oligarchy** to refer to how organizations come to be dominated by a small, self-perpetuating elite. The majority of an organization's members become passive, and an elite inner circle keeps itself in power by passing the leading positions from one clique member to another.

In a socially diverse society, this means that people who are not representative of the appearances, values, or background of the inner circle may be excluded from leadership. Even organizations strongly committed to democratic principles have fallen prey to the iron law of oligarchy. U.S. political parties, for example, supposedly the backbone of the nation's representative government, are run by an inner group that passes leadership positions from one elite member to another. This principle is demonstrated by the U.S. Senate. With their control of statewide political machinery and access to free mailing, in an average election about 97 percent of U.S. senators who choose to run are re-elected (*Statistical Abstract* 1994: Table 436).

In-Groups and Out-Groups

Groups toward which we feel loyalty are called **in-groups;** those toward which we feel antagonisms, **out-groups.** For Johnny, Satan's Servants was an in-group, while the police, teachers, welfare workers, and all those associated with school represented out-groups. This fundamental division of the world has far-reaching consequences for our lives.

Producing Loyalty and a Sense of Superiority

To identify with a group can generate not only a sense of belonging, but also loyalty and feelings of superiority. These, in turn, often produce rivalries. Usually the rivalries are mild, such as sports rivalries among nearby towns, where the most extreme act is likely to be the furtive invasion of the out-group's territory in order to steal a mascot, paint a rock, or uproot a goal post. The consequences of in-group membership, however, can also be discrimination, hatred, and violence.

Implications for a Socially Diverse Society

It is not surprising that in-group membership leads to discrimination, for, with our strong identifications and loyalties, we favor members of our in-groups. This aspect of in- and out-groups is, of course, the basis of many problems in contemporary society and underlies many gender and racial and ethnic divisions. As sociologist Robert Merton (1968) observed, one consequence is an interesting double standard. The traits of our in-group come to be viewed as virtues, while those *same* traits in out-groups are seen as vices. For example, men may perceive an aggressive man as assertive, but an aggressive woman as pushy. A male employee who doesn't speak up may be thought of as "knowing when to keep his mouth shut," but a quiet woman as too timid to make it in the business world.

To divide the world into "we" and "them" poses a danger for a pluralistic society. An out-group can come to symbolize evil, arousing fear and hatred. During times of economic insecurity, for example,

"*I'm surprised, Marty. I thought you were one of us.*"
Drawing by Ziegler; © 1983 The New Yorker Magazine, Inc.

The role of social group membership in shaping the self-concept is a primary focus of symbolic interactionists. In this process, knowing who we are not is as significant as knowing who we are.

xenophobia, or fear of strangers, may grow. The out-group may represent jobs stolen from one's friends and relatives. The result may be attacks against immigrants, a national anti-immigration policy, or a local resurgence of the Ku Klux Klan.

In short, to divide the world into in-groups and out-groups, a natural part of social life, brings with it both functional and dysfunctional consequences.

Reference Groups

Suppose you have just been offered a job that pays double what you hope to make even after you graduate from college. If you accept it, you will have to drop out of college. You have just three days to decide. As you consider the matter, thoughts like this may go through your mind: "My friends will say I'm a fool if I don't take the job . . . but Dad and Mom will practically go crazy. They've made sacrifices for me, and they'd be crushed if I didn't finish college. They've always said I've got to get my education first, that good jobs will always be there. . . . But, then, I'd like to see the look on the faces of those neighbors who said I'd never amount to much!"

This is an example of how people use **reference groups,** the groups we use as standards to evaluate ourselves. Your reference groups may include family,

All of us have reference groups—the groups we use as standards to evaluate ourselves. Although the groups by which we evaluate our own attitudes and behaviors certainly differ from the reference groups of these members of the KKK who are demonstrating in Chicago's Marquette Park, both ours and theirs serve the same sociological functions.

the members of a church or synagogue, your neighbors, teachers, classmates, and co-workers. Your reference group need not be one you actually belong to; it may include a group to which you aspire. For example, if you are thinking about going to graduate school, members of the profession you want to join may form a reference group as you evaluate your grades or writing skills.

Providing a Yardstick

Reference groups exert tremendous influence over our lives. For example, if you want to become the president of a corporation, you might start dressing more formally, try to improve your vocabulary, read the *Wall Street Journal*, take business and law courses, and join the local chamber of commerce. In contrast, if you want to become a rock musician, you might wear three earrings in one ear, dress in ways your parents and many of your peers consider outlandish, read *Rolling Stone*, drop out of college, and hang around clubs and rock groups.

Exposure to Contradictory Standards in a Socially Diverse Society

From these examples, you can see that the yardsticks provided by reference groups operate as a form of social control. When we see ourselves as measuring

up to the yardstick, there is no conflict, but if our behavior, or even aspirations, do not match the standards held by a reference group, the mismatch can lead to internal turmoil. For example, to want to become a corporate officer would present no inner turmoil for most of us, but it would if you had grown up in an Amish home, for the Amish strongly disapprove of such activities for their children. They ban high school and college education, three-piece suits, the *Wall Street Journal*, and corporate employment. Similarly, if you want to become a soldier and your parents are dedicated pacifists, you likely would experience deep conflict, as your parents would hold quite different aspirations for you.

Given the social diversity of our society as well as our social mobility, many of us are exposed to contradictory ideas and standards from the groups that become significant to us. The "internal recordings" that play contradictory messages from these reference groups, then, are one cost of social mobility. An example is highlighted in the Immigrant Experience box, "Caught between Two Worlds," in Chapter 3 (page 70).

Social Networks

If you are a member of a large group, there probably are a few people within that group with whom you regularly associate. In a sociology class I was teaching at a commuter campus, six women chose to work together on a project. They got along well, and they began to sit together. Eventually they planned a Christmas party at one of their homes. These clusters, or internal factions, are called **cliques.** The links between people—their cliques, as well as their family, friends, acquaintances, and even "friends of friends"—are called **social networks.** Think of a social network as ties that expand outward from yourself, gradually encompassing more and more people.

Familiar Worlds in a Sea of Strangers

Although we live in a huge society, we do not experience social life as an ocean of nameless, strange faces. Instead, we interact within social networks that connect us to the larger society. Social scientists have wondered just how extensive the connections are between social networks. If you list everyone you know, and each of those individuals lists everyone he or she knows, and you keep doing this, would almost everyone in the United States eventually be included on those lists?

It would be too cumbersome to test this hypothesis by drawing up such lists, but psychologist Stanley Milgram (1967) hit on an ingenious way to find out just how interconnected our social networks are. In what has become a classic experiment known as "the small world phenomenon," he selected names at random from across the United States. Some he designated as "senders," others as "receivers." Milgram addressed letters to the receivers and asked the senders to mail the letters to someone they knew on a first-name basis whom they thought might know the receiver. This person, in turn, was asked to mail the letter to someone he or she knew who might know the receiver, and so on. The question was, Would the letters ever get to the receivers, and if so, how long would the chain be?

Think of yourself as part of this experiment. What would you do if you are a sender, but the receiver lives in a state in which you know no one? You would send the letter to someone you know who might know someone in that state. This is just what happened. None of the senders knew the receivers, and in the resulting chains some links broke; that is, after receiving a letter, some people didn't send it on. Surprisingly, however, most letters did reach their intended receivers. Even more surprising, the average chain was made up of only *five* links.

Global Considerations Milgram's experiment shows just how small our world really is, and it gives us insight into why strangers from different parts of the country sometimes find they have a mutual acquaintance. If our social networks are so interrelated that most of us are connected to just about everyone else in the United States by just five links, how many links connect us to everyone on earth? This experiment is yet to be done.

Implications for Social Diversity

As we move in these smaller, familiar circles within our larger society, most of us find that our important social networks are made up of people who look much like ourselves—especially our race, age, and social class. Most jobs are secured through social networks, and as people tell others of an opening at the factory or office, the information seldom goes to people who have diverse characteristics. A notable example is the "old boy network," which tends to keep good jobs moving in the direction of male friends and acquaintances (Hall 1987; Abramson 1992).

Social networks, then, tend to perpetuate social inequalities. The term **networking,** which has appeared in popular speech, refers to people trying to overcome this barrier by using or even developing social networks, usually for career advancement (Speizer 1983). Hoping to establish a circle of acquaintances who will prove valuable to them, people go to parties, join clubs, churches, synagogues, and political parties. To break the "old boy network," many women do "gender networking," developing networks of working women to help advance their careers (Lin et al. 1981).

A New Group: Technology and the Emergence of Electronic Communities

In the 1990s, due to our new technology, a new type of human group, the **electronic community,** made its appearance. The Internet consists of tens of thousands of computers hooked together worldwide. On the Internet are thousands of newsgroups, called usenets, people who communicate on almost any conceivable topic—from donkey racing and bird watching to sociology and quantum physics. Most newsgroups are only an interesting, new way of communicating, but some meet our definition of *group:* people who interact with one another and who think of themselves as belonging together.

Some newsgroups pride themselves on the distinctive nature of their interest and knowledge, factors that bind them together and distinguish them from others. Some have even taken on the characteristics we associate with primary groups: People look forward to communicating daily with others in their newsgroup, with whom they share personal, sometimes intimate, matters about themselves—even though they have "met" only electronically. It is likely, then, that the electronic community heralds a new form of social intimacy, one in which people have closeness without permanence, have depth without commitment, and need not even meet one another to identify on a close, personal level (Cerulo et al. 1992).

Bureaucracies

Almost 100 years ago, sociologist Max Weber also noted the emergence of a new type of group, the *bureaucracy.* With the goal of achieving maximum efficiency and results, this new type of social organization changed the emphasis from personal loyalties to the "bottom line." Bureaucracies have become so common that we now take them for granted, unaware that they are fairly new on the human scene. Let's look at the characteristics of bureaucracies and consider their implications for our lives.

The Essential Characteristics of Bureaucracies

Although the army, a college, and General Motors may not seem to have much in common, they all are **bureaucracies.** As Weber (1913/1947) pointed out, they all have

1 *Clear-cut levels, with assignments flowing downward and accountability flowing upward.* Each level assigns responsibilities to the level beneath it, while each lower level is accountable to the level above for fulfilling those assignments. The bureaucratic structure of a typical university is shown in Figure 5.1.

2 *A division of labor.* Each worker has a specific task to fulfill, and all the tasks are then coordinated to

A central characteristic of formal organizations is the division of labor. Bureaucracies, for example, divide responsibilities into very small segments. Prior to capitalism and industrialization, however, there was little division of labor, and few formal organizations existed. In this woodcut of money coiners in Germany during the Middle Ages, you can see an early division of labor and the emergence of a formal organization.

accomplish the purpose of the organization. In a college, for example, a teacher does not run the heating system, the president does not teach, and a secretary does not evaluate textbooks. These tasks are distributed among people who have been trained to do them.

3 *Written rules.* In their attempt to become efficient, bureaucracies stress written procedures. In general, the longer a bureaucracy exists, the larger it grows and the more written rules it has.

4 *Written communications and records.* Records are kept of much of what transpires in a bureaucracy ("Fill that out in triplicate"), and workers spend a fair amount of time sending memos back and forth.

5 *Impersonality.* It is the office that is important, not the individual who holds the office. You work for

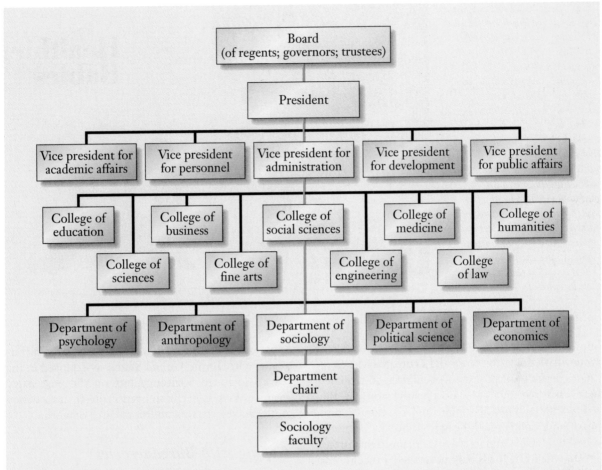

This is a scaled-down version of a university's bureaucratic structure. The actual lines of authority of a university are likely to be more complicated than those depicted here. A university may have a chancellor and several presidents under the chancellor, with each president responsible for a particular campus. Although extensions of authority are given in this figure only for the vice president for administration and the College of Social Sciences, each of the other vice presidents and colleges has similar positions. If the figure were to be extended, departmental secretaries would be shown, and eventually, somewhere, even students.

FIGURE 5.1

The Typical Bureaucratic Structure of a Medium-Size University

the organization, not for the replaceable person who heads some post in the organization.

The Perpetuation of Bureaucracies

Bureaucracies, which have become a standard feature of modern life, are a powerful form of social organization. They harness people's energies to reach specific goals, and once in existence, they tend to perpetuate themselves. One way they do this is by replacing old goals with new ones. In this process called **goal displacement,** even after the organization achieves its goal and no longer has a reason to continue, continue it does.

A classic example is the National Foundation for the March of Dimes, organized in the 1930s to fight polio (Sills 1957). At that time, the origin of polio was a mystery. The public was alarmed and fearful, for overnight a healthy child would be stricken with this crippling disease. Parents were fearful because no

The March of Dimes was founded by President Franklin Roosevelt in the 1930s. When a vaccine for polio was discovered in the 1950s, the organization did not declare victory and disband. Instead, it kept the organization intact by creating new goals—fighting birth defects. Sociologists use the term goal displacement *to refer to this process of adopting new goals. "Fighting birth defects" is now being replaced by an even vaguer goal, "campaigning for healthier babies." This last goal displacement may guarantee the organization's existence forever, for it is a goal so elusive it can never be reached.*

one knew whose child would be next. To solicit money to discover the cause and a cure, the March of Dimes began to place posters of children on crutches near cash registers in almost every store in the United States. The U.S. public took the campaign to heart and contributed heavily. The organization raised money beyond its wildest dreams. During the 1950s, when Dr. Jonas Salk developed a vaccine for polio, this threat was wiped out almost overnight. The public breathed a collective sigh of relief.

What then? Did the organization fold? After all, its purpose had been fulfilled. But, as you know, the March of Dimes is still around. Faced with the loss of their jobs, the professional staff that ran the organization quickly found a way to keep the bureaucracy intact by pursuing a new enemy—birth defects. Their choice of enemy is particularly striking, for it is doubtful that we will ever run out of birth defects—and thus unlikely that these people will ever run out of jobs.

The Rationalization of Society

Weber viewed bureaucracies as such a powerful form of social organization that he predicted they would come to dominate social life. He called this process the **rationalization of society,** meaning that bureaucracies, with their rules, regulations, and emphasis on results, would increasingly govern our lives. One of the best examples is how traditional

functions of the family have been taken over by bureaucracies. In the United States, as explored in the Down-to-Earth Sociology box on the next page, even cooking is becoming rationalized, as fast-food outlets take over this traditional area of work.

Coping with Bureaucracies

Although in the long run no other form of social organization is more efficient, as Weber recognized, bureaucracies also have a dark side. Let's look at some of their dysfunctions.

Red Tape: A Rule Is a Rule Bureaucracies can be so filled with red tape that they impede the purpose of the organization. Some rules (or "correct procedures" in bureaucratic jargon) are enough to try the patience of a saint.

> In the Bronx, Mother Teresa spotted a structurally sound abandoned building and wanted to turn it into a homeless shelter. But she ran head on into a rule: the building must have an elevator for the handicapped homeless. Not having the funds for the elevator, Mother Teresa struggled to get permission to bypass this rule. Two frustrating years later, she gave up. The abandoned building is still rotting away. (Tobias 1995)

Obviously this rule about elevators was not intended to stop Mother Teresa from ministering to the down and out. But, hey, rules is rules!

▼△

Down-to-Earth Sociology

The McDonaldization of Society

SOCIOLOGIST GEORGE RITZER (1993) sees the thousands of McDonald's restaurants that dot the U.S. landscape—and increasingly, the world—as having much greater significance than the convenience of fast hamburgers and milk shakes. He coined the term *the McDonaldization of society*, to refer to the increasing rationalization of the routine tasks of everyday life.

He points out that Ray Kroc, the founder of McDonald's, applied the principles developed by Henry Ford to the preparation and serving of food. A 1958 operations manual spelled out the exact procedure:

It told operators exactly how to draw milk shakes, grill hamburgers, and fry potatoes. It specified precise cooking times for all products and temperature settings for all equipment. It fixed standard portions on every food item, down to the quarter ounce of onions placed on each hamburger patty and the thirty-two slices per pound of cheese. It specified that french fries be cut at nine-thirty-seconds of an inch thick. . . . Grill men . . . were instructed to put hamburgers down on the grill moving from left to right, creating six rows of six patties each. And because the first two rows were farthest from the heating element, they were instructed (and still are) to flip the third row first, then the fourth, fifth, and sixth before flipping the first two.

Ritzer stresses that "McDonaldization" does not refer just to the robotlike assembly of food. Rather, this process, occurring throughout society, is transforming our lives. Shopping malls are controlled environments of approved design, logo, colors, and opening and closing hours. Travel agencies transport middle-class

Americans to ten European capitals in fourteen days, each visitor experiencing exactly the same hotels, restaurants, and other predictable settings. No one need fear meeting a "real" native. *USA Today* produces the same bland, instant news—in short, unanalytic pieces that can be read between gulps of the McShake or the McBurger.

Is all this bad? Not necessarily. Efficiency does bring reduced prices. But at a cost, a loss of something difficult to define, a quality of life washed away by rationalization. In my own travels, for example, had I taken packaged tours, I never would have had the enjoyable, eye-opening experiences that have added to my appreciation of human diversity.

In any event, the future has arrived. The trend is strongly toward the McDonaldization of human experience. For good or bad, our social destiny is to live in such prepackaged settings. When education becomes rationalized—which is now in process—our children will no longer have to put up with the idiosyncrasies of real professors, those people who think that ideas must be discussed endlessly and who never come to decisive answers anyway. What we want are instant, preformed solutions to social issues, like those we find in mathematics and engineering. Fortunately, our children will be able to be instructed in computerized courses, in which everyone learns the same answers, the approved, "politically correct," precise, and proper ways to think about social issues. This certainly will be efficient—and the "iron cage" of bureaucracy that Weber said would entrap us.

Alienation Treated in terms of roles, rules, and functions rather than as individuals, many workers begin to feel more like objects than people. Marx termed these reactions **alienation**, which he said comes from being cut off from the finished product of one's labor. He pointed out that before industrialization, workers used their own tools to produce an entire product, such as a chair or table. Now the

Bureaucracies are so powerful and overwhelming that even Mother Teresa, one of the most famous religious figures of the late twentieth century, was not able to overcome bureaucratic rules in order to help the U.S. homeless.

capitalists own the tools (machinery), and assign each worker only a single step or two in the entire production process. Relegated to repetitive tasks disassociated from the final product, workers lose a sense of identity with what they produce. They come to feel estranged not only from their products but from their whole work environment.

Because workers want to feel valued and to have a sense of control over their work, they resist alienation. Forming primary groups at work is a major form of that resistance. Workers band together in informal settings—at lunch, around desks, or for a drink after work. There they give one another approval for jobs well done and express sympathy for the shared need to put up with cantankerous bosses, meaningless routines, and endless rules. Here they relate to one another not just as workers, but as people who value one another. They flirt, laugh and tell

jokes, and talk about their families and goals. Adding this multidimensionality to their work relationships restores their sense of value as persons rather than as cogs in an endlessly moving machine.

Consider a common sight. You are visiting an office, and you see work areas decorated with family and vacation photos. The sociological implication is that of workers attempting to resist alienation. By staking a claim to individuality, the workers are rejecting an identity as machines functioning at a particular job.

The "Hidden" Corporate Culture and Social Diversity

Who gets ahead in a large corporation? Although we might like to think that success comes from intelligence and hard work, as sociologist Rosabeth Moss Kanter (1977, 1983) stresses, many factors other than merit underlie salary increases and promotions. She explains how the **corporate culture,** the orientations that characterize corporate work settings, contains "hidden values" that create a self-fulfilling prophecy.

It works like this: The elite have ideas about who are the best workers and colleagues. People who fit this mold—backgrounds similar to the elite and who look like them—receive better access to information, networking, and "fast track" positions. These people then perform better and become more committed to the organization, thus confirming the initial expectation. In contrast, those judged to be outsiders find opportunities closing up. They tend to work at a level beneath their capacity, come to think poorly of themselves, and become less committed to the organization. What is visible are people with superior performances and greater commitment to the company being promoted, not the self-fulfilling prophecy that has produced these attitudes and work performances.

This process is part of the iron law of oligarchy we just reviewed: Because of the self-fulfilling prophecy, the corporation reproduces itself with people who "look" like the elite's stereotypes. In these days of affirmative action, women and minorities, who don't match this stereotype, often are "showcased"—placed in highly visible positions with little power in order to demonstrate how progressive the company is (Benokraitis and Feagin 1991). There, however, they often hold "slow track" positions, where accomplishments seldom come to the attention of top management.

To understand the hidden corporate culture is helpful, for almost all of us who graduate from college will work within bureaucracies. It is even more significant now that the U.S. work force is being transformed by diversity, as discussed in the following Thinking Critically section.

▼▲▼▲▼▲▼▲▼▲▼▲▼▲▼▲▼

Thinking Critically about Social Controversy

Managing Diversity in the Workplace

SOME OF THE SIGNS: More than half of U.S. workers are minorities, immigrants, and women. Of new workers, only 15 percent are non-Latino white males. In San Jose, California, families with the Vietnamese surname Nguyen outnumber the Joneses by nearly 50 percent. Diversity in the workplace is much more than skin color. Diversity also includes ethnicity, gender, age, religion, social class, and sexual orientation.

The huge successes of the women's movement and civil rights activism have encouraged pride in one's heritage and made many Americans comfortable with being different from the dominant group. Consequently, people are now less amenable to *assimilation*, the process by which minorities are absorbed into the dominant culture. People who assimilate relinquish distinctive cultural patterns in favor of those of the dominant culture. As Roosevelt Thomas, president of the American Institute for Managing Diversity, says, "You don't have to aspire to be a white male or a member of the dominant group. People are willing to be part of a team, but they won't jump into the melting pot anymore."

Realizing that assimilation is probably not the wave of the future, 40 percent of U.S. companies have begun programs on managing diversity. These programs are designed to uncover and root out biases and prejudices about people's differences, to increase awareness and appreciation of those differences, and to teach "people skills," especially communication and negotiation skills, for working with diverse groups. The bottom line of these programs is to develop leaders who can mold people of diverse backgrounds into a team that will cooperate to attain corporate goals.

Sources: Thomas 1990; Piturro 1991; Sowell 1993a; Reich 1995.

Gender is an essential part of the social diversity of today's corporations. Because wives are more likely than husbands to be the caretakers of the marriage, to nurture it through the hard times, as well as to take greater responsibility for the children and to spend considerably more time doing housework (see Chapter 12), most employed wives face greater role conflict than do their husbands. The "mommy track," discussed in the following Thinking Critically section, has been proposed to help resolve this conflict.

▼▲▼▲▼▲▼▲▼▲▼▲▼▲▼▲▼

Thinking Critically about Social Controversy

The "Mommy Track"

FELICE SCHWARTZ (1989) SUGGESTED that corporations offer women a choice of two parallel career paths. The "fast track" consists of high-powered, demanding positions that may require sixty or seventy hours of work per week—regular responsibilities, emergencies, out-of-town meetings, and a briefcase jammed with work at night and on weekends. With such limited time outside of work, family life often suffers. Women can choose this "fast track" if they wish. Or instead they may choose a "mommy track," which would stress both career and family. Less would be expected of a woman on the "mommy track," for her commitment to the firm would be lower and her commitment to her family higher.

That, of course, say critics, is exactly what is wrong with this proposal. A "mommy track" will encourage women to be satisfied with lower aspirations and fewer promotions and confirm men's stereotypes of women executives. Because there is no "daddy track," it also assumes that child rearing is women's work (Starrels 1992). To encourage women to slow up in the race to climb the corporate ladder would perpetuate, or even increase, the executive pay gap. The "mommy track," conclude critics, would keep men in executive power and relegate women to an inferior position in corporate life.

Schwartz replied that what she really is proposing is a "zigzag track" (Shellenbarger 1995). "In my ideal world," she said, "people, including men, would slow down during a period when their kids are small. Later they would be readmitted to the mainstream. If you choose this intermittent route upward, you would make it to the top more slowly than someone equally able who took the straight vertical route. The goal is to balance family and career."

What do you think?

Global Bureaucracies in Competition: Japanese and U.S. Corporations

How were the Japanese able to arise from the defeat of World War II, including the nuclear destruction of two of their main cities, to become such a giant in today's global economy? Some analysts trace part of the answer to the way in which their major corporations are organized. Let's look at the conclusions of William Ouchi (1981), who pinpointed five major ways in which Japanese corporations differ from those in the United States.

Hiring and Promotion   In *Japan*, college graduates hired by a corporation are thought of as a team working toward the same goal, namely, the success of the organization. They all are paid about the same starting salary, and they are rotated through the organization to learn its various levels. Not only do they work together as a team, but they also are promoted as a team. Team members cooperate with one another, for the welfare of one represents the welfare of all. They also develop intense loyalty to one another and to their company. Only in later years are individuals singled out for recognition. When there is an opening in the firm, outsiders are not even considered.

In the *United States*, an employee is hired on the basis of what the firm thinks that individual can contribute. Employees try to outperform others, regarding salary and position as a sign of success. The individual's loyalty is to himself or herself, not to the company. When there is an opening in the firm, outsiders are considered.

Lifetime Security   In *Japan*, lifetime security is taken for granted. Once hired, employees can expect to work for the same firm for the rest of their lives. Similarly, the firm expects them to be loyal to the company, to stick with it through good and bad times. On the one hand, employees will not be laid off or fired; on the other hand, they do not go job shopping, for their careers—and many aspects of their lives—are wrapped up in this one firm.

In the *United States*, lifetime security is unusual, being limited primarily to some college professors (who receive what is called *tenure*). A company is expected to lay off workers in slow times, and if it reorganizes it is not unusual for whole divisions to be fired. Given this context, workers "look out for

number one," and that includes job shopping and job hopping, constantly seeking better pay and opportunities elsewhere.

Almost Total Involvement   In *Japan*, work is like a marriage: The employee and the company are committed to each other. The employee supports the company with loyalty and long hours of dedicated work, while the company, in turn, supports its workers with lifetime security, health services, recreation, sports and social events, even a home mortgage. Involvement with the company does not stop when the workers leave the building. They are likely to spend evenings with co-workers in places of entertainment, and perhaps to be part of a company study or exercise group.

In the *United States*, the work relationship is assumed to be highly specific. An employee is hired to do a specific job, and employees who have done their jobs have fulfilled their obligation to the company. The rest of their hours are their own. They go home to their private lives, which are highly separated from the firm.

Broad Training   In *Japan*, employees move from one job to another within the corporation. Not only are they not stuck doing the same thing over and over for years on end, but they gain a broader picture of the corporation and how the specific jobs they are assigned fit into the bigger picture.

In the *United States*, employees are expected to perform one job, to do it well, and then to be promoted upward to a job with more responsibility. Their understanding of the company is largely tied to the particular corner they occupy, and it may be difficult for them to see how their job fits into the overall picture.

Decision Making by Consensus   In *Japan*, decision making is a lengthy process. The Japanese think it natural that after lengthy deliberations, to which each person to be affected by a decision contributes, everyone will agree on which suggestion is superior. This process broadens decision making, allowing workers to feel that they are an essential part of the organization, not simply cogs in a giant wheel.

In the *United States*, whoever has responsibility for the unit in question does as much consulting with others as he or she thinks necessary and then makes the decision.

Limitations of the Model This model of corporate life in Japan has always struck some sociologists as too idealized to accurately reflect reality. And, indeed, to peer beneath the surface does give a different view. Look at the following statements:

- The Japanese are more productive than Americans.
- The living standard of Americans has fallen behind that of the Japanese.
- Japanese workers enjoy lifetime job security.
- The Japanese are paid less than Americans.

What is wrong with these statements? Nothing, except that they are untrue (Besser 1992; Naj 1993; Schlesinger et al. 1993; Shill 1993; Shirouzu and Williams 1995). During the worldwide recession of the 1990s, Japan was hit hard, exposing cracks in the seamless surface—the image that Japan had so carefully cultivated. It turns out that only employees of major corporations have lifetime job security, perhaps a third of Japanese workers. And Japan has found that paying the same wages to almost everyone in the same age group is costly and inefficient. Diligent but uninspired executives are compensated more by seniority than by output. Japanese labor costs have soared past those in the United States,

while their much-vaunted productivity actually lags behind that of U.S. industry.

In a surprise move, Japan has turned to U.S. corporations to see why they are more efficient. Flying in the face of their traditions, Japanese corporations have begun to lay off workers and to use merit pay. Although this is standard U.S. practice, it was unthinkable in Japan just a few years ago. Some firms have even cut salaries and demoted managers who don't meet goals. Perhaps the biggest surprise was Ford's takeover of Mazda. After huge losses, Mazda creditors decided that Ford knew more about building and marketing cars than Mazda and invited Ford to manage the company (Reitman and Suris 1994).

The real bottom line is that we live in a global marketplace—of ideas as well as products. The result of global competition will likely be that both the West and Japan will feed off each other—the one learning greater cooperation in the production process, the other greater internal competitiveness.

Group Dynamics

As you know from your personal experience, the lively interaction *within* groups—who does what with whom—has profound consequences for how you adjust to life. Sociologists use the term **group**

The text contrasts U.S. and Japanese corporate life. One of the main distinctions is that Japanese who work for the same firm think of themselves more as a group or team, Americans more as individuals. Japanese corporations such as this Coca Cola bottling plant in Asahikawa, Japan, use many techniques to encourage group identity, such as making group exercise a part of the work day. Sociologically, similarity of appearance and activity help to fuse group identity and company loyalty.

dynamics to refer to how groups affect us and how we affect groups. Let's first consider the differences that the size of a group makes, and then examine leadership, conformity, and decision making.

Before doing this, we should see what sociologists mean by the term **small group.** This is a group small enough for everyone to interact directly with all the other members. Small groups can be either primary or secondary. A wife, husband, and children, as well as workers who take their breaks together, is an example of primary small groups, while bidders at an auction and passengers on a flight from Chicago to Saint Louis are examples of secondary small groups.

Group Size

How Group Size Affects Group Stability and a Sense of Intimacy Writing at the turn of the century, sociologist Georg Simmel (1858–1918) noted the significance of group size. He used the term **dyad** for the smallest possible group, which consists of two people. Dyads, he noted, which include marriages, love affairs, and close friendships, show two distinct qualities. First, they are the most intense or intimate of human groups. Because only two people are involved, the interaction is exclusively between

them. Second, because dyads require the continuing active participation and commitment of both members, they are the most unstable of social groups. If one member loses interest, the dyad collapses. In larger groups, in contrast, even if one member withdraws the group can continue, for its existence does not depend on any single member (Simmel 1950).

A **triad** is a group of three people. As Simmel noted, the addition of a third person fundamentally changes the group. For example, with the birth of a child hardly any aspect of a couple's relationship goes untouched (Rubenstein 1992). Despite difficulties that couples experience adjusting to their first child, however, their marriage is usually strengthened. Simmel's principle that groups larger than a dyad are inherently stronger helps explain this effect. Like dyads, triads are also intense, for interaction is shared by only three people; but because interaction is shared with an additional person, the intensity lessens.

Simmel also pointed out that triads, too, are inherently unstable. Because relationships among a group's members are seldom neatly balanced, **coalitions** tend to form; that is, some group members align themselves against others. In a triad, it is not uncommon for two members to feel stronger bonds

Group size has a significant influence on how people interact. When a group changes from a dyad (two people) to a triad, the relationships among each of the participants undergo a shift.

with one another, leading them to act as a dyad and leaving the third feeling hurt and excluded. In addition, triads sometimes produce an arbitrator or mediator, someone who tries to settle disagreements between the other two.

The general principle is that *as a small group grows larger its intensity, or intimacy, decreases while its stability increases.* To see why, look at Figure 5.2. The addition of each person to a group greatly increases the connections among people. In a dyad, there is only 1 relationship; in a triad, 3; in a group of four, 6; in a group of five, 10. If we expand the group to six, we have 15 relationships; while a group of seven yields 21 relationships. If we continue adding members, we soon are unable to follow the connections, for a group of eight has 28 possible relationships; a group of nine, 36 relationships; a group of ten 45; and so on.

It is not only the number of relationships that makes larger groups more stable. As groups grow, they tend to develop a more formal structure to accomplish their goals. For example, leaders emerge and more specialized roles come into play, ultimately resulting in such familiar offices as president, secretary, and treasurer. This structure provides a framework that helps the group survive over time.

How Group Size Affects Attitudes and Behaviors Imagine that you are taking a class with social psychologists John Darley and Bibb Latané (1968), and they have asked you to join a few students to discuss your adjustment to college life. When you arrive, they tell you that to make things anonymous, they would like you to sit unseen in a booth and participate in the discussion over an intercom. You are to speak when your microphone comes on. The professors say they will not listen in, and they leave.

You find the format somewhat strange, to say the least, but you go along with it. You have not seen the other students in their booths, but when they begin to talk about their experiences, you find yourself becoming wrapped up in the problems they are sharing. One student even mentions how frightening he has found college because of his history of epileptic seizures. Later, this individual begins to breathe heavily into the microphone. Then he stammers and cries for help. A crashing noise follows, and you imagine him lying helpless on the floor. Then there is nothing but an eerie silence.

What do you do? The researchers staged the whole thing, but you don't know that. In fact, no students were even in other booths. Everything, except your comments, was on tape.

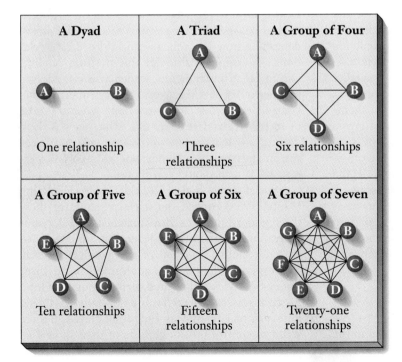

FIGURE 5.2

The Incremental Effects of Group Size on Relationships

Some participants were told they would be discussing the topic with just one other student, others with two, others with three, and so on. Darley and Latané found that all students who thought they were part of a dyad rushed out to help. If they thought they were part of a triad, only 80 percent went to help—and they were slower in leaving the booth. In six-person groups, only 60 percent went to see what was wrong—and they were even slower in doing so.

This experiment demonstrates how deeply group size influences our everyday lives, that it even affects our willingness to help one another. Darley and Latané concluded that in the dyad, the students clearly knew it was up to them. The professor was gone, and if they didn't help there would be no help. In the triad, students felt less personal responsibility, while in the larger groups they felt a *diffusion of responsibility:* it was no more up to them than it was up to anyone else.

You probably have observed the second consequence of group size firsthand. When a group is small, its members are informal, but as the group grows they lose their sense of intimacy and become more formal. No longer can the members assume that the others are "insiders" in sympathy with what they say. Now they must take a "larger audience" into consideration, and instead of merely "talking," they begin to "address" the group. Just as their speech becomes more formal, their body language stiffens, too.

A third aspect of group dynamics is also one that you probably have observed many times. In the very early stages of a party, when only a few people are present, almost everyone talks with everyone else. But as others arrive, the guests break into smaller groups. The hosts, who may want all their guests to mix together, sometimes make a nuisance of themselves trying to achieve *their* ideas of what a group should be like. The division into small groups is inevitable, however, for it follows the basic sociological principles we have just reviewed. Because the addition of each person rapidly increases connections (in this case, "talk lines"), it makes conversation more difficult. The guests then break into smaller groups where they can see each other and comfortably interact directly with one another.

Leadership

All groups, no matter what their size, have leaders, although they may not hold a formal position in the group. A **leader** is someone who influences the behaviors, opinions, or attitudes of others. Some people are leaders because of their personalities, but leadership involves much more than this, as we shall see.

Types of Leaders Groups have two types of leaders (Bales 1950, 1953; Cartwright and Zander 1968). The first is easy to recognize. This person, called an **instrumental leader** (or task-oriented leader), tries to keep the group moving toward its goals. These leaders try to keep group members from getting sidetracked, reminding them of what they are trying to accomplish. The **expressive leader** (or socio-emotional leader), in contrast, is not usually recognized as a leader, but he or she certainly is. This person is likely to crack jokes, to offer sympathy, or to do other things that help lift the group's morale. Both types of leadership are essential: the one to keep the group on track, the other to increase harmony and minimize conflicts.

It is difficult for one person to be both an instrumental and an expressive leader, for these roles contradict one another. Because instrumental leaders are task oriented, they sometimes create friction as they prod the group to get on with the job. Their actions often cost them popularity. Expressive leaders, in contrast, being peacemakers who stimulate personal bonds and reduce friction, are usually more popular (Olmsted and Hare 1978).

Leadership Styles Let's suppose that the president of your college has asked you to head a task force to determine how the college can improve race relations on campus. Although this position requires you to be an instrumental leader, you can adopt a number of **leadership styles,** or ways of expressing yourself as a leader. The three basic styles are those of **authoritarian leader,** one who gives orders; **democratic leader,** one who tries to gain a consensus; and **laissez-faire leader,** one who is highly permissive. Which should you choose?

Social psychologists Ronald Lippitt and Ralph White (1958) carried out a classic study of these three leadership styles. Boys matched for IQ, popularity, physical energy, and leadership were assigned to "craft clubs" made up of five youngsters each. The experimenters trained adult males in the three leadership styles and rotated them among the clubs. As the researchers peered through peepholes, taking notes and making movies, each adult played all three styles to control possible effects of their individual personalities.

The authoritarian leaders assigned tasks to the boys and set the working conditions. They also praised or condemned their work arbitrarily, giving no explanation for why it was good or bad. The democratic leaders held group discussions and outlined the steps necessary to reach the group's goals. They also suggested alternative approaches to these goals and let the children work at their own pace. When they evaluated the children's projects, they gave "facts" as the bases for their decisions. The laissez-faire leaders were passive, giving the boys almost total freedom to do as they wished. They stood ready to offer help when asked, but made few suggestions. They did not evaluate the children's projects, either positively or negatively.

The results? The boys who had authoritarian leaders grew dependent on the leader and showed a high degree of internal solidarity. They also became either aggressive or apathetic, with the aggressive boys growing hostile toward their leader. In contrast, the boys with democratic leaders were friendlier, more "group minded," and looked to one another for mutual approval. They did less scapegoating, and when the leader left the room they continued to work at a steadier pace. The boys with laissez-faire leaders asked more questions, but they made fewer decisions. They were notable for their lack of achievement. The researchers concluded that the democratic style of leadership worked best. Their conclusions, however, may have been biased, as the researchers themselves favored a democratic style of leadership, and they did the research during a highly charged political period (Olmsted and Hare 1978).

You may have noted that only males were involved in this experiment. It is interesting to speculate how the results might differ if the experiment were repeated with all-girl groups and with groups of both girls and boys and used both men and women as leaders. Perhaps you will become the sociologist to study such variations.

Adapting Leadership Styles to Changing Situations It is important to note that different situations require different styles of leadership. Suppose, for example, that you are leading a dozen backpackers in California's Sierra Madre mountains, and it is time to make dinner. A laissez-faire style would be appropriate if everyone had brought their own food—or perhaps a democratic style if the meal were to be communally prepared. Authoritarian leadership—you telling everyone how to prepare their meals—would probably create resentment. This, in turn, would likely interfere with meeting the primary goals of the group, in this case, having a good time while enjoying nature.

Now assume the same group but a different situation: one of your party is lost, and a blizzard is on its way. This situation calls for you to take charge and be authoritarian. To simply shrug your shoulders and say, "You figure it out," would invite disaster.

Who Becomes a Leader? Are leaders born with characteristics that propel them to the forefront of a group? No sociologist would agree with such a premise. In general, people who become leaders are seen as strongly representing the group's values or as able to lead a group out of a crisis (Trice and Beyer 1991). Leaders also tend to be more talkative and to express determination and self-confidence.

These findings may not be surprising, as such traits appear related to a leadership role. Researchers, however, have also discovered that traits seeming to have no bearing whatsoever on ability to lead are also significant. For example, taller people and those judged better looking are more likely to become leaders (Stodgill 1974; Crosbie 1975). The taller and more attractive are also likely to earn more, but that is another story (Deck 1968; Feldman 1972; Katz 1995).

Many other factors underlie people's choice of leaders, most of which are quite subtle. A simple experiment performed by social psychologists Lloyd Howells and Selwyn Becker (1962) uncovered one of these factors. They formed groups of five people each who did not know one another, seating them at a rectangular table, three on one side and two on the other. After each group had discussed a topic for a set period of time, they chose a leader. Their findings are startling: Although only 40 percent of the people sat on the two-person side, 70 percent of the leaders emerged from that side. The explanation is that we tend to direct more interactions to people facing us than to people to the side of us.

Conformity: The Asch Experiment

How influential are groups in our lives? To answer this, let's look first at *conformity* in the sense of going along with our peers. They have no authority over us, only the influence that we allow.

Imagine that you are taking a course in social psychology with Dr. Solomon Asch and you have agreed to participate in an experiment. As you enter his laboratory, you see seven chairs, five of them already filled by other students. You are given the sixth. Soon the seventh person arrives. Dr. Asch stands at the front of the room next to a covered easel. He explains that he will first show a large card with a vertical line on it, then another card with three vertical lines. Each of you is to tell him which of the three lines is identical to the line on the first card (see Figure 5.3).

Dr. Asch then uncovers the first card with a single line and the comparison card with the three lines. The correct answer is easy, for two of the lines are obviously wrong, and one is exactly right. Each person, in order, states his or her answer aloud. You all answer correctly. The second trial is just as easy, and you begin to wonder what the point is of your being here. Then on the third trial something unexpected happens. Just as before, it is easy to tell which lines match. The first student, however, gives a wrong answer. The second gives the same incorrect answer. So do the third and the fourth. By now you are wondering what is wrong. How will the person next to you answer? You can hardly believe it when he, too, gives the same wrong answer. Then it is your turn, and you give what you know is the right answer. The seventh person also gives the same wrong answer. On the next trial, the same thing happens. You know the choice of the other six is wrong, yet they give what to you are obviously wrong answers. You don't know what to think. Why aren't they seeing things the same way you are? Sometimes they do, but in twelve trials they don't. Something is seriously wrong, and you are no longer sure what to do.

When the eighteenth card is finished, you heave a sigh of relief. The experiment is finally over, and you are ready to bolt for the door. Dr. Asch walks over to you with a big smile on his face, thanks you for participating in the experiment, and then explains that you were the only real subject in the experiment! "The other six were all stooges! I paid them to give those answers," he says. Now you feel real relief. Your eyes weren't playing tricks on you after all.

What were the results? Asch (1952) tested fifty people. About 33 percent gave in to the group half the time and gave what they knew to be wrong answers. Another 40 percent also gave wrong answers, but not as often. And 25 percent stuck to their guns and always gave the right answer. I don't know how

FIGURE 5.3
Asch's Cards

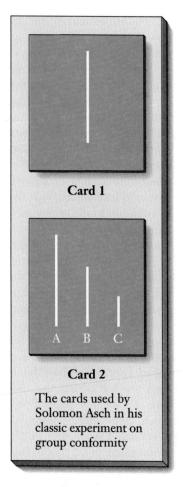

Card 1

Card 2

The cards used by Solomon Asch in his classic experiment on group conformity

Source: Asch 1952:452–453.

I would do on this test (if I knew nothing about it in advance), but I like to think that I would be part of the 25 percent. You probably feel the same way. But why should we feel that we wouldn't be like *most* people?

The results are disturbing. In our "land of individualism," the group is so powerful that most people are willing to say things that they know do not match objective reality. And this was simply a group of strangers! How much more can we expect the group to enforce conformity when it consists of friends, people we value highly and depend on for getting along in life? Again, perhaps you will become the sociologist to run that variation of Asch's experiment, and perhaps to use female subjects.

Even more disturbing are the results of an experiment featured in the following Thinking Critically section.

If Hitler Asked You to Execute a Stranger, Would You? The Milgram Experiment

IMAGINE THAT YOU are taking a course with Dr. Stanley Milgram (1963, 1965), a former student of Dr. Asch's. Assume that you did not take part in the Asch experiment and have no reason to be wary of these experimenters. You arrive at the laboratory to participate in a study on punishment and learning. You and a second student draw lots for the roles of "teacher" and "learner." You are to be the teacher, he the learner. When you see the learner's chair, with its protruding electrodes, you are glad that you are to be the teacher. Dr. Milgram shows you the machine you will run. You see that one side of the control panel is marked "Mild Shock, 15 volts," the center says "Intense Shock, 350 Volts," while the far right side reads "DANGER: SEVERE SHOCK."

"As the teacher, you will read aloud a pair of words," explains Dr. Milgram. "Then you will repeat the first word, and the learner will reply with the second word. If the learner can't remember the word, you press this lever on the shock generator. The shock will serve as punishment, and we can then determine if punishment improves memory." You nod, now ex-tremely relieved that you haven't been designated a learner.

"Every time the learner makes an error, increase the punishment by 15 volts," instructs Dr. Milgram. Then, seeing the look on your face, he adds, "The shocks can be extremely painful, but they won't cause any permanent tissue damage." He pauses, and then says, "I want you to see." You then follow him to the "electric chair," and Dr. Milgram gives you a shock of 45 volts. "There. That wasn't too bad, was it?" "No," you mumble.

The experiment begins. You hope for the learner's sake that he is bright, but unfortunately he turns out to be rather dull. He gets some answers right, but you have to keep turning up the dial. Each turn makes you more and more uncomfortable. You find yourself hoping that the learner won't miss another answer. But he does. When he received the first shocks, he let out some moans and groans, but now he is screaming in agony. He even protests that he suffers from a heart condition. *How far do you turn that dial?*

By now, you probably have guessed that there was no electricity attached to the electrodes and the "learner" was a stooge, only pretending to feel pain. The purpose of the experiment, of course, was to find out at what point people refuse to participate. Does anyone actually turn the lever all the way to "DANGER: SEVERE SHOCK"?

Milgram wanted the answer because of the Nazi slaughter of Jews, gypsies, homosexuals, and others they designated as "inferior." That millions of ordinary people did nothing to stop the deaths seemed bizarre,

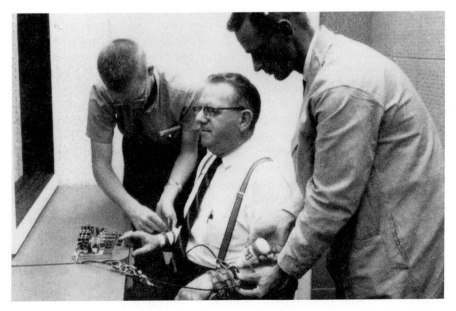

In the 1960s, U.S. social psychologists ran a series of creative but controversial experiments. Among these were Stanley Milgram's experiments described above. From this photo of the "learner" being prepared for the experiment, you can get an idea of how convincing the situation would be for the "teacher."

and Milgram wanted to see how ordinary, intelligent Americans might react in an analogous situation.

Milgram was upset by what he found. Many "teachers" broke into a sweat and protested to the experimenter that this was inhuman and should be stopped. But when the experimenter, supposedly recording how the "learner" was performing, calmly replied that the experiment must go on, this assurance from the "authority" ("scientist, white coat, university laboratory") was enough for most "teachers" to continue, even though the learner screamed in agony. Even "teachers" who were "reduced to twitching, stuttering wrecks" continued to follow orders.

Milgram varied the experiments (Miller 1986). He used both males and females and put some "teachers" and "learners" in the same room, where the "teacher" could clearly see the suffering. He had some "learners" pound and kick on the wall during the first shocks and then go silent. The results varied from situation to situation. The highest proportion of "teachers" who pushed the lever all the way to 450 volts—65 percent—occurred when there was no verbal feedback from the "learner." Of those who could see the "learner," 40 percent turned the lever all the way. When Milgram added a second "teacher," a stooge who refused to go along with the experiment, only 5 percent carried out the "severe shocking," a result that bears out some of Asch's findings.

Milgram's experiments became a stormy basis for rethinking research ethics. Not only were researchers surprised, and disturbed, at what Milgram found, but they also were alarmed at his methods. Universities began to require that subjects be informed of the nature and purpose of social research. Researchers agreed that to reduce subjects to "twitching, stuttering wrecks" was unethical, and almost all deception was banned.

For Your Consideration

Considering how significant these findings are, do you think that the scientific community overreacted to Milgram's experiments? Should we allow such research? Considering both the Asch and Milgram experiments, use symbolic interactionism, functionalism, and conflict theory to explain why groups have such influence over us.

Global Consequences of Group Dynamics: Groupthink and Decision Making

In this era of rapid communications and powerful weapons, one of the disturbing implications of the Asch and Milgram experiments is **groupthink.** Sociologist Irving Janis (1972) coined this term to refer to a sort of collective tunnel vision, when a group of people think alike and any suggestion of alternatives becomes a sign of disloyalty. Even moral judgments must be put aside, for the "team" is convinced that its welfare depends on a particular course of action. Groupthink may lead to overconfidence and a disregard for the risks that the group is taking (Hart 1991).

The Asch and Milgram experiments let us see how groupthink can develop. Suppose you are a member of the president's inner circle. It is midnight, and the president has just called an emergency meeting to deal with a national crisis. At first, various options are presented. Eventually, these are narrowed to only a few choices, and at some point everyone seems to agree on what now seems "the only possible course of action." At that juncture, expressing doubts will bring you into conflict with *all* the other important people in the room, while actual criticism may mark you as not being a "team player." So you keep your mouth shut, with the result that each step commits you—and them—more and more to the "only" course of action.

We can choose from a variety of examples from around the globe, but U.S. history provides a fertile field to illustrate groupthink: the refusal of President Franklin D. Roosevelt and his chiefs of staff to believe that the Japanese might attack Pearl Harbor and the subsequent decision to continue naval operations as usual; President Kennedy's invasion of Cuba; and U.S. policies in Vietnam. Watergate is especially noteworthy, for it plunged the United States into political crisis and for the first time in history a U.S. president was forced to resign.

In each of these cases, options closed as officials committed themselves to a single course of action. To question this course would mark someone as disloyal, as not a "team player". Those in power plunged ahead, no longer able to see different perspectives, no longer trying to objectively weigh evidence as it came in, interpreting everything as supporting their one "correct" decision. Like Milgram's subjects, they became mired deeper and deeper in actions that as individuals they would have considered unacceptable, and found themselves pursuing policies they may have found morally repugnant.

Preventing Groupthink

Groupthink is a danger that faces any government, for if leaders are isolated at the top they become cut off from information that does not support their own opinions. Leaders also foster groupthink by surrounding themselves with an inner circle that closely reflects their own views. Perhaps the key to preventing the mental captivity and intellectual paralysis known as groupthink is the widest possible circulation—especially among a nation's top government officials—of research that has been freely conducted by social scientists and information that has been freely gathered by media reporters.

If this conclusion comes across as an unabashed plug for sociological research and the free exchange of ideas, it is. Giving free rein to diverse opinions can effectively curb groupthink, which—if not prevented—can lead to the destruction of a society and, in today's world of sophisticated weapons, the obliteration of the earth's inhabitants.

Summary and Review

Social Groups in a Socially Diverse Society

What is a group?

Sociologists have many definitions of groups, but, in general, **groups** are people who have something in common and who believe that what they have in common is significant. Societies are the largest and most complex groups that sociologists study. P. 108.

How do sociologists classify groups?

Sociologists divide groups into primary, secondary, in-groups, out-groups, reference groups, and networks. The cooperative, intimate, long-term, face-to-face relationships provided by **primary groups** are fundamental to our sense of self. **Secondary groups** are larger, more anonymous, formal, and impersonal than primary groups. **In-groups** provide members with a strong sense of identity and belonging. **Out-groups** also help create this identity by showing in-group members what they are *not*. **Reference groups** are groups we use as standards to evaluate ourselves. **Social networks** consist of social ties that link people together. The new technology has given birth to a new type of group, the **electronic community**. Pp. 108–114.

What is the "iron law of oligarchy"?

Sociologist Robert Michels noted that formal organizations have a tendency to become controlled by a small group that limits leadership to its own inner circle. The dominance of a formal organization by an elite inner circle that keeps itself in power is called the **iron law of oligarchy**. P. 110.

Bureaucracies

What are bureaucracies?

A **bureaucracy** consists of a hierarchy, a division of labor, written rules, written communications, and impersonality of positions—characteristics that allow bureaucracies to be efficient and enduring. Pp. 114–118.

How does the corporate culture affect workers?

The term **corporate culture** refers to an organization's traditions, values, and unwritten norms. Much of corporate culture, such as its hidden values, is not readily visible. People who match a corporation's hidden values are put on tracks that enhance their chances of success, while those who do not match these values are set on a course that minimizes their performance. Pp. 118–119.

How do Japanese and U.S. corporations differ?

The Japanese corporate model contrasts sharply with the U.S. model in its hiring and promotion practices, lifetime security, worker involvement outside the work setting, broad training of workers, and collective decision making. This model, however, has been idealized and does not adequately reflect the reality of Japanese corporate life. Pp. 120–121.

Group Dynamics

How does a group's size affect its dynamics?

The term **group dynamics** refers to how individuals affect groups and how groups influence individuals. In a **small group**, everyone can interact directly with everyone else. As a group grows larger, its intensity decreases and its stability increases. A **dyad**, consisting of two persons, and the most unstable of human groups, provides the most intense or intimate relationships. The addition of a third person, forming a **triad**, fundamentally alters relationships. Triads are unstable, as **coalitions** tend to form. Pp. 121–124.

What characterizes a leader?

A **leader** is someone who influences others. **Instrumental leaders** try to keep the group moving toward its goals, even at the cost of causing friction. **Expressive leaders** focus on creating harmony and raising group morale. Both types are essential to the functioning of groups. P. 124.

What are the three main leadership styles?

Authoritarian leaders give orders, **democratic leaders** try to lead by consensus, and **laissez-faire leaders** are highly permissive. An authoritarian style appears to be more effective in emergency situations, a demo-cratic style works best for most situations, and a laissez-faire style is usually ineffective. Pp. 124–125.

How do groups encourage conformity?

The Asch experiment was cited to illustrate the power of peer pressure, the Milgram experiment the influence of authority. Both experiments demonstrate how easily we can succumb to **groupthink,** a kind of collective tunnel vision. Preventing groupthink requires the free circulation of contrasting ideas. Pp. 125–129.

Where can I read more on this topic?

Suggested readings for this chapter are listed on page 437.

Glossary

aggregate people who temporarily share the same physical space but do not see themselves as belonging together (p. 108)

alienation Marx's term for the experience of being cut off from the product of one's labor, which results in a sense of powerlessness and normlessness (p. 117)

authoritarian leader a leader who leads by giving orders (p. 124)

bureaucracies formal organizations with a hierarchy of authority, a clear division of labor, impersonality of positions, and emphasis on written rules, communications, and records (p. 114)

category people who have similar characteristics (p. 108)

clique a cluster of people within a larger group who choose to interact with one another; an internal faction (p. 113)

coalition the alignment of some members of a group against others (p. 122)

corporate culture the orientations that characterize corporate work settings (p. 118)

democratic leader a leader who leads by trying to reach a consensus (p. 124)

dyad the smallest possible group, consisting of two persons (p. 122)

electronic community people who more or less regularly interact with one another on the Internet (p. 113)

expressive leader an individual who increases harmony and minimizes conflict in a group; also known as a *socioemotional leader* (p. 124)

goal displacement a goal displaced by another, such as an organization adopting new goals (p. 115)

group people who think of themselves as belonging together and who interact with one another (p. 108)

group dynamics the ways in which individuals affect groups and groups influence individuals (pp. 121–122)

groupthink Irving Janis's term for a narrowing of thought by a group of people, leading to the perception that there is only one correct answer, in which the suggestion of alternatives becomes a sign of disloyalty (p. 128)

in-groups groups toward which one feels loyalty (p. 111)

instrumental leader an individual who tries to keep the group moving toward its goals; also known as a *task-oriented leader* (p. 124)

iron law of oligarchy Robert Michels's term for the tendency of formal organizations to be dominated by a small, self-perpetuating elite (p. 110)

laissez-faire leaders individuals who lead by being highly permissive (p. 124)

leader someone who influences other people (p. 124)

leadership styles ways in which people express their leadership (p. 124)

networking the process of consciously using or cultivating networks for some gain (p. 113)

out-groups groups toward which one feels antagonisms (p. 111)

primary group a group characterized by intimate, long-term, face-to-face association and cooperation (p. 108)

(the) rationalization of society the increasing influence of bureaucracies in society, which makes the "bottom line" of results dominant in social life (p. 116)

reference group Herbert Hyman's term for the groups we use as standards to evaluate ourselves (p. 111)

secondary group compared with a primary group, a larger, relatively temporary, more anonymous, formal, and impersonal group based on some interest or activity (p. 109)

small group a group small enough so everyone can interact directly with all the other members (p. 122)

social network the social ties radiating outward from the self, that link people together (p. 113)

triad a group of three persons (p. 122)

voluntary association a group made up of volunteers who organize on the basis of some mutual interest; the Girl Scouts, Baptists, and Alcoholics Anonymous are examples (p. 109)

Sociology and the Internet

All URLs listed are current as of the printing of this book. URLs are often changed. Please check our Website http://www.abacon.com/henslin for updates.

1. The McDonaldization of Society

In this chapter, you are introduced to George Ritzer's concept of "the McDonaldization of society," which involves the rationalization of the routine tasks of everyday life. First, read the Down-to-Earth Sociology box on page 117, and go to the McDonaldization home page (http://www.wam.umd.edu/~allan/mcdonald.html). Read the page, and then click on the italicized word *"rationalization."* After reading the new page, go back to the McDonaldization home site, click on "Efficiency," "Calculability," "Predictability," and "Control," and read each page. Next, click on the "frontiers of McDonaldization" at the bottom of the first screen, and check out the Max Headroom episode. Finally, click on "irrationality of rationality" on the second screen, and read the page. (If you are hooked, click on the Dilbert button and see if you can find any cartoons involving the irrationality of rationality in the workplace.)

After you have finished your research, write a two-part paper. In Part 1, discuss the general idea of McDonaldization and its specific elements. In Part 2, apply this concept to some aspect of your college or university, and discuss the degree to which each of the McDonaldization concepts you learned from your Web research applies to the situation.

2. Formal Organizations

The U.S. government bureaucracy is the largest and most complex in the world. Explore a small portion of its organization by accessing the Secretary of Defense's Web page. Go to http://www. dtic.dla.mil/defenselink/ and select Office of the Secretary. On the Secretary's page, select the Organization Chart.

Browse through the chart, looking for elements that are bureaucratic. What are the advantages of these bureaucratic features? What are the drawbacks? Can you think of alternative ways of organizing the Department of Defense? Print the chart, and bring it to class for discussion.

Tsing-Fang Chen, Bombardment, 1930.

CHAPTER

6

Deviance and Social Control

I N JUST A FEW MOMENTS *I was to meet my first Yanomamo, my first primitive man. What would it be like? . . . I looked up (from my canoe) and gasped when I saw a dozen burly, naked, filthy, hideous men staring at us down the shafts of their drawn arrows. Immense wads of green tobacco were stuck between their lower teeth and lips, making them look even more hideous, and strands of dark-green slime dripped or hung from their noses. We arrived at the village while the men were blowing a hallucinogenic drug up their noses. One of the side effects of the drug is a runny nose. The mucus is always saturated with the green powder, and the Indians usually let it run freely from their nostrils. . . . I just sat there holding my notebook, helpless and pathetic. . . . The whole situation was depressing, and I wondered why I ever decided to switch from civil engineering to anthropology in the first place. . . . (Soon) I was covered with red pigment, the result of a dozen or so complete examinations. . . . These examinations capped an otherwise grim day. The Indians would blow their noses into their hands, flick as much of the mucus off that would separate in a snap of the wrist, wipe the residue into their hair, and then carefully examine my face, arms, legs, hair, and the contents of my pockets. I said (in their language), "Your hands are dirty"; my comments were met by the Indians in the following way: they would "clean" their hands by spitting a quantity of slimy tobacco juice into them, rub them together, and then proceed with the examination.*

So went Napoleon Chagnon's eye-opening introduction to the Yanomamo tribe of the rain forests of Brazil. His ensuing months of fieldwork continued to bring surprise after surprise, and often Chagnon (1977) could hardly believe his eyes—or his nose.

Where would we start to list the deviant behaviors of these people? Appearing naked in public? Using hallucinogenic drugs? Letting mucus hang from their noses? Rubbing hands filled with mucus, spittle, and tobacco juice over a frightened stranger who doesn't dare to protest? Perhaps. But it isn't this simple, for deviance, as we shall see, is relative.

Gaining a Sociological Perspective on Deviance

No human group can exist without norms, for *norms make social life possible by making behavior predictable.* What would life be like if you could not predict what others would do? Imagine for a moment that you have gone to a store to purchase milk:

Suppose the clerk says, "I won't sell you any milk. We are overstocked with soda, and I'm not going

to sell anyone milk until our soda inventory is reduced."

You don't like it, but you decide to buy a case of soda. At the checkout, the clerk says, "I hope you don't mind, but there's a $5 service charge on each fifteenth customer." You, of course, are the fifteenth.

Just as you start to leave, another clerk stops you and says, "We're not working anymore. We decided to party." Suddenly a stereo begins to blast, and everyone in the store is dancing. "Oh, good, you've brought the soda," says one clerk, who takes your package and passes sodas all around.

But life is not like this. You can depend on grocery clerks to sell you milk. You also can depend on paying the same price as everyone else, and not being forced to attend a party in the store. Why can you depend on this? Because we are socialized to follow norms, to play the basic roles as society indicates we should.

Without norms we would have social chaos. Norms lay out the basic guidelines for how we play our roles and how we interact with others. In short, norms allow **social order,** a group's customary social arrangements. Our lives are based on those arrangements, and this is why deviance is often seen as so threatening, for it undermines predictability, the foundation of social life.

The Relativity of Deviance *anything that violates the norm is deviance*

Sociologists use the term **deviance** to refer to any violation of norms, whether the infraction is as minor as jaywalking, as serious as murder, or as humorous as Chagnon's experience. This deceptively simple definition takes us to the heart of the sociological perspective on deviance, which sociologist Howard S. Becker (1966) identified this way: *It is not the act itself, but the reactions to the act, that make something deviant.* In other words, people's behaviors must be viewed from the framework of the culture in which they take place. To Chagnon, the behaviors were frighteningly deviant, but to the Yanomamo they represented normal, everyday life. What was deviant to Chagnon was *conforming* to the Yanomamo. From their viewpoint,

you *should* check out strangers as they did—and nakedness is good, as are hallucinogenic drugs and letting mucus be "natural."

Chagnon's abrupt introduction to the Yanomamo allows us to see the *relativity of deviance*. Because different groups have different norms, *what is deviant to some is not deviant to others.* This principle holds *within* a society as well as across cultures. Thus acts perfectly acceptable in one culture—or in one group within a society—may be considered deviant in another culture, or by another group within the same society. This idea is explored in the Global Glimpse box below.

This principle also applies to a specific form of deviance known as **crime,** the violation of rules that have been written into law. In the extreme, an act applauded by one group may be so despised by another group that it is punishable by death. An example is making a huge profit in a business deal. Americans who do so are admired, and may even write a book

deviance does not mean something is bad, it is how people react to it.

▲ ▲ ▲ ▲ ▲ ▲ ▲ ▲ ▲ ▲ ▲ ▲ ▲ ▲ ▲ ▲ ▲ ▲ ▲

A Global Glimpse

Human Sexuality in Cross-Cultural Perspective

ANTHROPOLOGIST ROBERT EDGERTON (1976) reports how differently human groups react to similar behaviors. Of the many examples he cites, let's look at sexuality to illustrate how a group's *definitions* of a behavior, not the behavior itself, determine whether or not it will be considered deviant.

Norms of sexual behavior vary so widely around the world that what is considered normal in one society may be considered deviant in another. The Pokot people of northwestern Kenya, for example, place high emphasis on sexual pleasure and fully expect that both a husband and his wife will reach orgasm. If a husband does not satisfy his wife, he is in serious trouble. Pokot men often engage in adulterous affairs, and should a husband's failure to satisfy his

wife be attributed to his adultery, when her husband is asleep the wife will bring in female friends and tie him up. The women then shout obscenities at him, beat him, and, as a final gesture of their utter contempt, slaughter and eat his favorite ox before releasing him. His hours of painful humiliation are assumed to make him henceforth more dutiful concerning his wife's conjugal rights.

People can also become deviants for failing to understand that the group's ideal norms may not be its real norms. As with many groups, the Zapotec Indians of Mexico expect sexual activity to take place exclusively between husband and wife. Yet the only person in one Zapotec community who had had no extramarital affairs was considered deviant. Ev-

idently these people have a covert, commonly understood norm that married couples will engage in discreet extramarital affairs, for when a wife learns that her husband is having an affair she does the same thing. One Zapotec wife, however, did not follow this informal pattern. Instead, she continually threw her virtue into her husband's face—and claimed headaches. Worse, she also informed the other husbands and wives in the village who their spouses' other partners were. As a result, this virtuous woman was condemned by everyone in the village. In other words, the official norms do not always represent the real norms—another illustration of the gap between ideal and real culture.

From a sociological viewpoint, deviance is relative. In U.S. culture, for instance, taking hallucinogenic drugs is deviant. Among the Yanomamo Indians (introduced in Chapter 10), however, the normal route to initiation into manhood is accomplished through the administration of hallucinogens by a shaman, or holy man.

about it or seek public office. In China, however, until recently this same act was a crime called profiteering. Anyone found guilty was publicly hung.

Unlike the general public, sociologists use the term *deviance* nonjudgmentally, to refer to any act to which people respond negatively. When sociologists use this term, it does not mean that they agree that an act is bad, just that people judge it negatively. To sociologists, then, we all are deviants of one sort or another, for we all violate norms from time to time.

To be considered deviant, a person may not even have to *do* anything. Sociologist Erving Goffman (1963) used the term **stigma** to refer to characteristics that discredit people. These include violations of norms of ability (blindness, deafness, mental handicaps) and norms of appearance (a facial birthmark, obesity). They also include involuntary memberships, such as being a victim of AIDS or the brother of a rapist. The stigma becomes a person's master status, defining him or her as deviant. Recall from Chapter 4 that a master status cuts across all other statuses that a person occupies.

Sanctions

As discussed in Chapter 2, people do not strictly enforce folkways, but they become very upset when mores are broken. Disapproval of deviance, called **negative sanctions,** ranges from frowns and gossip

for breaking folkways to imprisonment and capital punishment for breaking mores. **Positive sanctions,** in contrast—from smiles to formal awards—are used to reward people for conforming to norms. Getting a raise is a positive sanction, being fired a negative sanction. Getting an *A* in basic sociology is a positive sanction, getting an *F* a negative one.

Most negative sanctions are informal. You probably will merely stare when someone dresses in what you consider inappropriate clothing, or just gossip if a married person you know spends the night with someone other than his or her spouse. Whether you consider the breaking of a norm simply an amusing matter that warrants no severe sanctions or a serious infraction that does, however, depends on your perspective. If a woman appears at your college graduation ceremonies in a swimsuit, you may stare and laugh, but if it is *your* mother you are likely to feel that different sanctions are appropriate. Similarly, if it is *your* father who spends the night with an 18-year-old college freshman, you are likely to do more than gossip.

▼ **In Sum** In sociology, the term *deviance* refers to all violations of social rules, regardless of their seriousness. The term is not a judgment about the behavior. Deviance is relative, for what is deviant in one group may be conforming behavior in another. Consequently, we must consider deviance from

When Cultures Clash—How Should We Define Deviance?

THE HMONG OF LAOS fought fiercely on the side of the U.S. forces in Vietnam. When the war ended, 100,000 Hmong were flown to U.S. cities.

The Hmong had been tribal mountain dwellers whose agricultural life was light-years removed from the bewildering world they encountered in the United States. Their remote villages had no cars, telephones, televisions, or faxes, not even plumbing or electricity. They did not even have a written language until American and French missionaries invented one in the mid-1950s.

Just as their material culture was radically different, so was their nonmaterial culture. Its norms, developed during centuries of village tribal life, and matching their unique culture, provided ill-suited guidelines for life in the new culture.

Take choosing a bride as an example. Having decided that it was time to marry, a young Hmong refugee in Fresno, California, named Kong Moua went to a local college campus along with a group of friends and forced the girl he had selected as his mate to his house. He then had sex with her.

In the Hmong culture, Kong Moua had performed *zij poj niam*, marriage by capture. While this method of obtaining a marriage partner is not the only, or even the most frequent, way of marrying among traditional Hmong, neither is it a rare occurrence. Universal to Hmong courtship is the idea that men appear strong, women resistant and virtuous.

The apparent sincerity of Kong Moua presented a dilemma to the judge who heard his case. Under the U.S. legal system, Kong Moua had committed two crimes: kidnap and rape. Given Moua's cultural background, however, the judge felt uncomfortable simply applying U.S. law. In an attempt to balance matters, he allowed Moua to plead to a lesser charge of false imprisonment, thus giving the court the leeway "to get into all these cultural issues and try to tailor a sentence that will fulfill both our needs and the Hmong needs." Moua was ordered to pay $1,000 to the girl's family and serve a ninety-day jail term.

For Your Consideration

Do you think the judge's decision was right? Does this mean that we should have two legal standards, one for citizens and another for immigrants? If you had been the judge, what would you have decided?

Sources: Based on Sherman 1988; Trueba et al. 1990.

---

within a group's own framework, for it is *their* meanings that underlie their behavior. The Immigrant Experience box on this page, focuses on this issue.

Comparing Biological, Psychological, and Sociological Explanations

Since norms are essential for society, why do people violate them? To better understand the reasons, it is useful to know how sociological explanations differ from biological and psychological ones.

Psychologists and *sociobiologists* explain deviance by looking for answers *within* individuals. They assume that something in the makeup of people leads them to become deviant. By contrast, sociologists look for answers in factors *outside* the individual. They assume that something in the environment influences people to become deviant.

Biological explanations focus on **genetic predispositions** to such deviances as juvenile delinquency and crime (Lombroso 1911; Sheldon 1949; Glueck and Glueck 1956; Wilson and Hernstein 1985). Biological explanations include (but are not restricted to) the following three theories: (1) intelligence—low intelligence leads to crime; (2) the "XYY" theory—an extra Y chromosome in males leads to crime; and (3) body type—people with "squarish, muscular" bodies are more likely to commit **street crime**, acts such as mugging, rape, and burglary.

How have these theories held up? Not very well. Most people with these supposedly "causal" characteristics do not become criminals. Some criminals are very intelligent, and most people of low intelligence do not commit crimes. Most criminals have the normal "XY" chromosome combination, and most men with the "XYY" combination do not become criminals. Criminals also run the range of the body types exhibited by humanity, and most people with "squarish, muscular" bodies do not become street criminals. In addition, no women have this combination of genes, so it wouldn't even deal with female criminals.

137

Unlike biology and psychology, which look within individuals for their explanations of human behavior, sociological explanations focus on external experiences, such as people's associations or group memberships. Sociological explanations of human behavior have become widely accepted, and now permeate society, as illustrated by this teenager whom I photographed as we were exiting the Staten Island Ferry in New York City.

Psychological explanations of deviance focus on abnormalities *within* the individual, on what are called **personality disorders**. The supposition is that deviating individuals have deviating personalities (Kalichman 1988; Stone 1989; Heilbrun 1990), that various unconscious devices drive people to deviance. No specific negative childhood experience, however, is invariably linked with deviance. Nor is there any particular personality that results in deviance. For example, children who had "bad toilet training," "suffocating mothers," or "emotionally aloof fathers" may become embezzling bookkeep-

ers—or good accountants. Just as students, teachers, and police officers represent a variety of bad—and good—childhood experiences, so do deviants. In short, there is no inevitable outcome of particular childhood experiences.

Sociologists, in contrast, search for factors *outside* the individual. They look for social influences that "recruit" some people rather than others to break norms. To account for why people commit crimes, for example, sociologists examine such external influences as socialization, subcultural membership, and social class. *Social class,* a concept discussed in depth in Chapter 8, refers to people's relative standing in terms of education, occupation, and especially income and wealth.

Knowing how relative deviance is, sociologists ask this telling question: Why should we expect to find something constant within people to account for a behavior that is conforming in one society and deviant in another?

To see how sociologists study deviance, we shall contrast the three sociological perspectives—symbolic interactionism, functionalism, and conflict theory.

The Symbolic Interactionist Perspective

As we examine symbolic interactionism, it will become more evident why sociologists are not satisfied with explanations rooted in biology and personality. A basic principle of symbolic interactionism is that each of us interprets life through the symbols that we learn from the groups to which we belong. Let's consider the extent to which membership in groups influences our behaviors and views of life.

Differential Association Theory

The Theory Contrary to theories built around biology and personality, sociologist Edwin Sutherland stressed that people *learn* deviance. He coined the term **differential association** to indicate that we learn to deviate or to conform to society's norms mostly by the people with whom we associate (Sutherland 1924, 1947; Sutherland and Cressey 1974; Sutherland et al. 1992). On the most obvious level, boys and girls who join Satan's Servants learn a way of looking at the world that is more likely to get them in trouble with the law than boys and girls who join the Scouts.

Sutherland's theory is actually more complicated than this, but he stressed that learning deviance is like learning anything else—which goes directly against the thinking that deviance is biological or due to deep personality needs. Sutherland said that the key to differential association is learning "definitions" (which you can translate as ideas or attitudes) favorable to following the law or favorable to breaking it. From the various people we associate with, each of us learns both, and the end result is an imbalance—attitudes that tilt us more in one direction than the other. Consequently, we conform or deviate.

Families The extent to which some families teach their members to violate the norms of society is well documented. Demographers Allen Beck, Susan Kline, and Lawrence Greenfeld (1988), for example, studied the family histories of a representative sample of the 25,000 delinquents confined in high-security state institutions nationwide. They found that 25 percent have a father who has been in prison, 25 percent a brother or sister, 9 percent a mother, and 13 percent some other relative. Apparently families involved in crime tend to set their children on a lawbreaking path.

Friends, Neighbors, and Subcultures The neighborhood is also likely to be influential, for sociologists have long observed that delinquents tend to come from neighborhoods in which their peers are involved in crime (Miller 1958; Wolfgang and Ferracuti 1967). Sociologist Ruth Horowitz (1983, 1987), who did participant observation in a lower-class Chicano neighborhood in Chicago, discovered how associating with people who have a certain concept of "honor" can propel young men to deviance. The formula is simple. In this group an insult is defined as a threat to one's manliness. Honor requires a man to stand up to an insult. Not to stand up to someone is to be less than a real man.

Now suppose you are a young man growing up in this neighborhood. You would likely do a fair amount of fighting, for you would see many statements and acts as infringing on your honor. You might make certain that you carry a knife or have access to a gun, for words and fists won't always do. Along with members of your group, you would define fighting, knifing, and shooting quite differently from the way most Americans do.

For members of the Mafia, killing, manliness, and honor are also intertwined. For them, *to kill is a measure of their manhood*. Not all killings are accorded the same respect, however, for "the more awesome and potent the victim, the more worthy and meritorious the killer" (Arlacchi 1980). Some killings are very practical matters. A member of the Mafia who gives information to the police, for example, has violated the Mafia's *omerta* (the vow of secrecy its members take). Such an offense can never be tolerated, for it threatens the very existence of the group. This exam-

When I graduated from a large high school a few miles from San Bernardino, California, where this photo was taken, many of my classmates wore similar gang jackets. At that simpler time, however, students carried no guns, threats between rival groups, often on a racial basis, usually dissipated after heated exchanges of words and physical gestures, and violence consisted of an occasional fist fight. Although we now live in an era of drive-by shootings, the sociological principles that underlie gang membership have not changed.

ple further illustrates just how relative deviance is. Although killing is deviant to mainstream society, for them, *not* killing after certain rules are broken, such as "squealing" to the cops, is the deviant act.

Prison or Freedom?   As symbolic interactionists stress, we are not mere pawns in the hands of others, destined by our group memberships to think and behave as our groups dictate. Rather, we *help produce our own orientations to life*. Our choice of membership (differential association), for example, helps shape the self. For instance, one college student may join a feminist group that is trying to change the treatment of women in college; another may associate with a group of women who shoplift on weekends. Their choice of groups points them in two different directions. The one who associates with shoplifters may become even more oriented toward deviant activities, while the one who joins the feminist group may develop an even greater interest in producing social change.

Control Theory

Inside most of us, it seems, are strong desires to do things that would get us in trouble—inner drives,

temptations, urges, hostilities, and so on. Yet most of us most of the time stifle these desires. Why?

Sociologist Walter Reckless (1973), who developed **control theory,** stresses that two control systems work against our motivations to deviate. Our *inner controls* include our internalized morality—conscience, ideas of right and wrong, and reluctance to violate religious principles. Inner controls also include fears of punishment, feelings of integrity, and the desire to be a "good" person (Hirschi 1969; Rogers 1977). Our *outer controls* consist of groups and individuals—such as family, friends, and the police—who influence us not to deviate. Control theory is sometimes classified as a functional theory, because when our outer controls operate well, we conform to social norms and thereby do not threaten the status quo. Because symbols and meanings are central to this theory, however, it can also be classified as a symbolic interactionist theory.

As sociologist Travis Hirschi (1969) noted, the more that we feel bonds with society, the more effective our inner controls are. Bonds are based on *attachments* (in this case, affection and respect for people who conform to society's norms), *commitments* (having a stake in society that you don't want to risk,

When O. J. Simpson was arrested and charged with killing his former wife and her friend, Ronald Goldman, because of O. J.'s celebrity status the news made instant headlines around the world. For over a year, Simpson's criminal trial was followed closely by the national media, its revelations at times even bumping international events into second place. For more than a year after the trial, a major television program, Rivera Live, *continued to review various aspects of the trial and then to cover the civil suit against O. J. for wrongful death. For O. J., the stigma of the accusation of murder—being found not guilty in the criminal trial and guilty in the civil trial—has become a master status.*

such as a respected place in your family, a good standing at college, a good job), *involvements* (putting time and energy into approved activities), and *beliefs* (holding that certain actions are morally wrong).

The likelihood that we will deviate from social norms, for example by committing a crime, depends on the strength of these two control systems relative to the strength of the pushes and pulls toward the deviance. If our control systems are weak, we deviate. If they are strong enough, however, we do not commit the deviant act. This theory can be summarized as *self*-control, says Hirschi. The key to learning high self-control is socialization, especially in childhood. Parents help their children develop self-control by supervising them and punishing their deviant acts (Gottfredson and Hirschi 1990).

Labeling Theory

Symbolic interactionists have developed **labeling theory,** which focuses on the significance of the labels (names, reputations) given to people. Labels tend to become a part of the self-concept, which helps to set people on paths that propel them into or divert them from deviance. Let's look at how people react to society's labels—from whore and pervert to cheat and slob.

Rejecting Labels: How People Neutralize Deviance Most people resist the labels that others try to pin on them. Some are so successful that even though they persist in deviance, they still consider themselves conformists. For example, even though they beat up people and vandalize property, some delinquents consider themselves conforming members of society. How do they do it?

Sociologists Gresham Sykes and David Matza (1988) studied boys in this exact situation. They found that they used five **techniques of neutralization** to deflect society's norms.

Denial of Responsibility The youths frequently said, "I'm not responsible for what happened because . . ." and then were quite creative about the "becauses." The act may have been an "accident," or they may see themselves as "victims" of society, with no control over what happened—like billiard balls shot around the pool table of life.

Denial of Injury Another favorite explanation of the boys was "What I did wasn't wrong because no one got hurt." They would define vandalism as "mis-

The term mainstreaming of deviance *refers to activities generally disapproved of that move into the mainstream, or become more socially acceptable. An example is Snoop Doggy Dog's receiving a Soul Train award for songs that in years past would have brought him expulsion from school.*

chief," gang fighting as a "private quarrel," and stealing cars as "borrowing." They might acknowledge that what they did was illegal, but claim that it was "just having a little fun."

Denial of a Victim Sometimes the boys thought of themselves as avengers. To vandalize a teacher's car is only to get revenge for an unfair grade, while to shoplift is to even the score with "crooked" store owners. In short, if the boys did accept responsibility and even admit that someone did get hurt, they protected their self-concept by claiming that the people "deserved what they got."

Condemnation of the Condemners Another technique the boys used was to deny that others had the right to judge them. They might accuse people who pointed their fingers at them of being "a bunch of hypocrites": the police are "on the take," teachers have "pets," and parents cheat on their taxes. In short, they say, "Who are *they* to accuse *me* of something?"

Appeal to Higher Loyalties A final technique the boys used to justify antisocial activities was to consider loyalty to the gang more important than following the norms of society. They might say, "I had to help my friends. That's why I got in the fight." Not incidentally, the boy may also have shot two members of the rival group as well as a bystander!

These five techniques of neutralization have implications far beyond these boys, for it is not only delinquents who try to neutralize the norms of mainstream society. Look again at these five techniques: (1) "I couldn't help myself"; (2) "Who really got hurt?" (3) "Don't you think she deserved that, after what *she* did?" (4) "Who are *you* to talk?" and (5) "I had to help my friends—wouldn't you have done the same thing?" Don't such statements have a familiar ring? All of us attempt to neutralize the moral demands of society, for such neutralizations help us sleep at night.

Inviting Labels: Outlaw Bikers and the Embrace of Deviance Although most of us resist being labeled deviant, there are those who revel in a deviant identity. Some teenagers, for example, make certain by their clothing, choice of music, and hairstyle that no one misses their purposeful rejection of adult norms. Their status among fellow members of a subculture, within which they are almost obsessive conformists, is vastly more important than any status outside it.

One of the best examples of a group that embraces deviance is motorcycle gangs. Sociologist Mark Watson (1988) did participant observation with outlaw bikers. He rebuilt Harleys with them, hung around their bars and homes, and went on "runs" (trips) with them. He concluded that outlaw bikers see the world as "hostile, weak, and effeminate," while they pride themselves on looking "dirty, mean, and generally undesirable"—and take great pleasure in provoking shocked reactions to their appearance. Holding the conventional world in contempt, they also pride themselves on getting into trouble, laughing at death, and treating women as lesser beings whose primary value is to provide them with services—especially sex. Outlaw bikers also look at themselves as losers, a factor that becomes woven into their unusual embrace of deviance.

The Power of Labels: The Saints and the Roughnecks We can see how powerful labeling is by referring back to the study of the "Saints" and the "Roughnecks" cited in Chapter 4 (pages 101–102). As you recall, both groups of high school boys were "constantly occupied with truancy, drinking, wild parties, petty theft, and vandalism." Yet their teachers looked on the Saints as "headed for success" and the Roughnecks as "headed for trouble." By the time they finished high school, not one Saint had been arrested, while the Roughnecks had been in constant trouble with the police.

Why did the community see these boys so differently? Chambliss (1997) concluded that this double vision was due to their family background, especially social class. The Saints came from respectable, middle-class families, while the Roughnecks came from less respectable, working-class families. Because of their respective backgrounds, teachers and other authorities expected good, law-abiding behavior from the Saints and trouble from the Roughnecks. And like the rest of us, both teachers and police see what they expect to see.

Social class had allowed the Saints' lawbreaking to be *less visible.* The Saints had automobiles, and they made their drinking and vandalism inconspicuous by spreading it around neighboring towns. Without cars, the Roughnecks could not even make it to the edge of town. Day after day, they hung around the same street corners, where their boisterous behavior made them conspicuous, confirming the negative ideas that the community held about them.

Another significant factor was also at work. The boys' different social backgrounds had equipped them with distinct *styles of interaction.* When questioned by police or teachers, the Saints put on apologetic and penitent faces. Their deferential behavior elicited such positive reactions that they escaped legal problems. In contrast, the Roughnecks' attitude was "almost the polar opposite." They expressed open hostility to the authorities, and even when they pretended to show respect, the veneer was so thin that it fooled no one. Consequently, while the police let the Saints off with warnings, they came down hard on the Roughnecks, interrogating and arresting them when they had the chance.

While a lifetime career is not determined by a label alone, the Saints and the Roughnecks did live up to the labels that the community gave them. As you recall, all but one of the Saints went on to college, after which one earned a doctorate and one be-

Sociology and the New Technology

Pornography Goes High Tech

NOT LONG AFTER photography was invented (in 1839), photographic pornography appeared. Today, computers allow pornography to be exchanged electronically. The University of Delft in the Netherlands, which offered a picture archive that included a data base of digitized pornography, had to pull the plug on the collection because Internet users overwhelmed the system by pulling down 30,000 pornographic images a day.

Some Internet "newsgroups"—people clustered around any topic of interest, from Roman architecture to rap music—focus on explicit discussions about sex. Sexually explicit electronic exchanges certainly seem to fall within guidelines of adult conversations. In addition, codes are needed to open files and participate. The codes, although readily available, prevent anyone from "accidentally" stumbling on these discussions.

Yet some people are upset. Some are bothered because users are exchanging provocative drawings and photographs. Others are upset that subgroups have formed to discuss such topics as bestiality and bondage. Some are especially concerned about the files that contain accounts of how to torture women. And then there are the groups that like to discuss having sex with children.

Some sanctions are informal. When software producers held their annual trade show in Las Vegas and some CD-ROM makers began to show nude performers in kinky situations, the sponsor declared them out of order and kicked them out. They now hold their own trade show, where posters advertise new CD-ROMs: "Bad Girls II: The Strip Search," and "Club 21: Our Deck Is Stacked."

Other sanctions are formal. A Tennessee court convicted a California couple of violating Tennessee obscenity laws. Yet the couple's sexually oriented electronic bulletin board was located in Milpitas, California. The jury applied the community standards of Tennessee because the photographs were downloaded there. This ruling may mean that no one can put anything racier on the Internet or any other system of electronic communication than would be tolerated in the most conservative community in the United States.

The sociological questions are, Whose norms? Whose sanctions? And who has the power to make them stick?

Source: Based on Pearl 1995; Sandberg 1995; Ziegler 1995; Henslin 1996.

---

came a lawyer, one a doctor, and the others business managers. In contrast, only two of the Roughnecks went to college, both on athletic scholarships, after which they became coaches. The other Roughnecks did not fare so well. Two of them dropped out of high school, later became involved in separate killings, and received long prison sentences. One became a local bookie, and no one knows the whereabouts of the other.

How do labels work? While the matter is extremely complex since it involves the self-concept and individual reactions, we can note that labels open and close the doors of opportunity. Being labeled a "deviant" (certainly far from a nonjudgmental term in everyday life!) can lock people out of conforming groups and force them into almost exclusive contact with people who have similar labels.

▼ **In Sum** Symbolic interactionists examine how people's definitions of the situation underlie their deviation from or conformance to social norms. They focus on group membership (differential association), how people balance pressures to conform and to deviate (control theory), and the significance of the labels placed on people (labeling theory).

The Sociology and the New Technology box above explores a central point of symbolic interactionism, that to call something deviant involves competing definitions and reactions to the same behavior.

▲ The Functionalist Perspective

When we think of deviance, its dysfunctions are likely to come to mind. Functionalists, in contrast,

We perceive—and are perceived—not directly, but, rather, through intermediary concepts. This abstract principle of symbolic interactionists, which may seem obtuse, is really a down-to-earth principle of everyday life. In short, we tend to see people through the labels we place on them. In these photos, what different sets of labels are we likely to apply? What consequence are these labels likely to have on how we "see" the people in these photos?

are as likely to stress the functions of deviance as its dysfunctions.

How Deviance Is Functional for Society

Most of us are upset by deviance, especially crime, and assume that society would be better off without it. The classic functionalist theorist Emile Durkheim (1893/1933, 1893/1964), however, came to a surprising conclusion. Deviance, he said, including crime, is functional for society, for it contributes to the social order. Its three main functions are

1 *Deviance clarifies moral boundaries and affirms norms.* A group's ideas about how people should act and think mark its *moral boundaries.* Deviance challenges those boundaries. To call a deviant member to account, saying in effect, "You broke an important rule, and we cannot tolerate that," affirms the group's norms and clarifies the distinctions between conforming and deviating behavior. To punish deviants is to assert what it means to be a member of the group.

2 *Deviance promotes social unity.* To affirm the group's moral boundaries by punishing deviants fosters a "we" feeling among the group's members. In saying, "You can't get by with that," the group collectively affirms the rightness of its own ways.

3 *Deviance promotes social change.* Groups do not always agree on what to do with people who push beyond their acceptable ways of doing things. Some group members may even approve the rule-breaking behavior. Boundary violations that gain enough support become new, acceptable behaviors. Thus, deviance may force a group to rethink and redefine its moral boundaries, helping groups, and whole societies, to change their customary ways.

Strain Theory: How Social Values Produce Crime

Functionalists argue that crime is a *natural* part of society, not an aberration or some alien element in our midst. Indeed, they say, some crime represents values that lie at the very core of society. This concept sounds strange at first. To understand how the acceptance of mainstream values can generate crime, consider what sociologists Richard Cloward and Lloyd Ohlin (1960) identified as the crucial problem of the industrialized world: the need to locate and train the most talented people of every generation—whether born in wealth or in poverty—so they can take over the key technical jobs of modern society. When children are born, no one knows which ones will have the abilities to become dentists, nuclear physicists, or engineers. To get the most talented people to compete with one another, society tries to motivate *everyone* to strive for success. It does this by arousing discontent—making people feel dissatisfied with what they have so they will try to "better" themselves.

Four Deviant Paths Most people, then, end up with strong desires to achieve **cultural goals,** the objectives held out as desirable for them, such as wealth or high status. Not everyone, however, has equal access to society's **institutionalized means,** the legitimate ways of achieving success. Some people, for example, find their path to education and good jobs blocked. These people experience *strain* or frustrations, which may motivate them to take a deviant path.

This perspective, known as **strain theory,** was developed by sociologist Robert Merton (1956, 1968). People who experience strain, he said, are likely to feel *anomie,* a sense of normlessness. Because mainstream norms (work, education) don't seem to be getting them anywhere, they have a difficult time identifying with them. They may even feel wronged by the system, and its rules may seem illegitimate (Anderson 1978).

Table 6.1 compares people's reactions to cultural goals and institutionalized means. The first reaction, which Merton said is the most common, is *conformity,* using socially acceptable, legitimate means to strive to reach cultural goals. In industrialized so-

cieties most people try to get good jobs, a good education, and so on. If well-paid jobs are unavailable, they take less desirable jobs. If they are denied access to Harvard or Stanford, they go to a state university. Others take night classes and attend vocational schools. In short, most people take the socially acceptable road.

The remaining four types of responses are deviant. Let's look at each. *Innovators* are people who accept the goals of society but use illegitimate means to achieve them. Drug dealers, for instance, accept the goal of achieving wealth but reject the legitimate avenues for doing so. Other examples are embezzlers, robbers, and con artists.

The second deviant path is taken by people who become discouraged and give up on achieving cultural goals. Yet they still cling to conventional rules of conduct. Merton called this response *ritualism.* Although ritualists have given up on excelling and advancing in position, they survive by following the rules of their job. Teachers who suffer from "burnout" but continue to go through the motions of classroom performance after their idealism is shattered are an example. Their response is considered deviant because they cling to the job although they actually have abandoned the goal, such as stimulating young minds and, possibly, making the world a better place.

People who choose the third deviant path, *retreatism,* reject both cultural goals and the institutionalized means of achieving them. Those who drop out of the pursuit of success by way of alcohol or drugs are retreatists. Such people do not even try to appear as though they share the goals of their society.

The final type of deviant response is *rebellion.* Convinced that their society is corrupt, rebels, like retreatists, reject both society's goals and its institutionalized means. Unlike retreatists, however, they

Table 6.1

How People Match Their Goals to Their Means

Feel Strain That Leads to Anomie?	Mode of Adaptation	Cultural Goals	Institutionalized Means
No	Conformists	Accept	Accept
Yes	Innovators	Accept	Reject
	Ritualists	Reject	Accept
	Retreatists	Reject	Reject
	Rebels	Reject/Accept	Reject/Accept

seek to replace existing goals with new ones. Revolutionaries are the most committed type of rebels.

Strain theory underscores the main sociological point about deviance, namely, that each society produces its deviants. Due to their social location, some people experience greater pressures to deviate from society's norms, others much less. Simply put, if a society emphasizes the goal of material success, groups deprived of access to this goal will be more involved in property crime.

Illegitimate Opportunity Structures: Explaining Social Class and Crime

One of the more interesting sociological findings in the field of deviance is that the social classes have distinct styles of crime. Let's see how unequal access to the institutionalized means to success helps to explain this.

Street Crime Functionalists point out that industrialized societies have no trouble socializing the poor into wanting to own things. Like others, they, too, are bombarded with messages urging them to purchase everything from designer jeans to new cars. Television portrays vivid images of the middle class enjoying luxurious lives, reinforcing the myth that all full-fledged Americans can afford the goods and services portrayed in movies and on television and offered in commercials (Silberman 1978).

The school system, however, which constitutes the most common route to success, fails the poor. It is run by the middle class, and when the children of the poor enter it, they confront a bewildering world for which their background ill prepares them. Their grammar and nonstandard language—liberally punctuated by what the middle class considers obscene words and phrases—their ideas of punctuality and neatness, and their lack of preparation in paper-and-pencil skills are a mismatch with their new environment. Facing such barriers, the poor drop out of school in larger numbers than their more privileged counterparts. Educational failure, in turn, closes the door on many legitimate avenues to financial success.

Not infrequently, however, a different door opens to them, one that sociologists Richard Cloward and Lloyd Ohlin (1960) called **illegitimate opportunity structures.** Woven into the texture of life in urban slums, for example, are robbery, burglary, drug dealing, prostitution, pimping, gambling, and other remunerative crimes, commonly called "hustles" (Liebow 1967; Anderson 1978, 1990; Bourgois

Shown in this nineteenth-century lithograph are some of London's hungry unemployed as they lunge forward to receive a free meal ticket. Conflict theorists stress that the marginal working class provides the temporary workers who are hired during economic booms and then discharged to their misery during economic downturns. Until these workers are needed, they are kept alive at substandard conditions. Whether in early or late capitalism, is it surprising that most street criminals come from the marginal working class?

1994). For many of the poor, the "hustler" is a role model—glamorous, in control, the image of "easy money," one of the few people in the area who comes close to the cultural goal of success. For some, then, such illegal income-producing activities are functional—they provide income—and they attract disproportionate numbers of the poor.

Youth Gangs Gangs are one way that this illegitimate opportunity structure opens to disadvantaged youth. For over ten years, sociologist Martín Sánchez Jankowski (1991) did participant observation of thirty-seven African American, Central American, Chicano, Dominican, Irish, Jamaican, and Puerto Rican gangs in Boston, Los Angeles, and New York City. The gangs earn money by gambling, arson, mugging, armed robbery, making and wholesaling drugs to pushers, and selling moonshine, guns, stolen car parts, and protection. Jankowski ate, slept, and sometimes fought with the gangs, but by mutual agreement did not participate in drugs or other illegal activities. He was seriously injured twice during the study.

Surprisingly, Jankowski did not find that the motive for joining was to escape broken homes (there were as many members from intact as broken homes) or to seek a substitute family (as many members said they were close to their families as said they were not). Rather, the boys joined to gain access to steady money, recreation (including access to females and drugs), anonymity in criminal activities, protection, and to help the community. This last reason may seem surprising, but in some neighborhoods gangs protect residents from outsiders. The gang was also seen as an alternative to the dead-end—and deadening—jobs held by the working parents.

The residents of a gang's turf are ambivalent about gangs. On the one hand, they don't like the violence. On the other hand, many adults once belonged to the same gangs, gang members are the children of neighborhood residents, and the gangs often provide better protection than do the police.

Particular gangs will come and go, but gangs will likely always be part of the city, for from a functional standpoint gangs fulfill needs for poor youth who live on the margins of society.

White-Collar Crime The more privileged social classes are not crime free, of course, but they find different illegitimate opportunities beckoning. For them, *other forms* of crime are functional. Rather than mugging, pimping, and burglary, the more privileged encounter "opportunities" for income tax evasion, bribery of public officials, embezzlement, false advertising, and so on. Physicians, for example, never hold up cabbies, but many do cheat Medicare. Sociologist Edwin Sutherland (1949) coined the term **white-collar crime** to refer to crimes that people of respectable and high social status commit in the course of their occupations.

Although the general public seems to think that the lower classes are more crime prone, numerous studies show that white-collar workers also commit many crimes (Weisburd et al. 1991; Zey 1993). The difference in public perception is largely based on visibility. While crimes committed by the poor are given much publicity, the crimes of the more privileged classes seldom make the evening news and go largely unnoticed. Yet the dollar cost of "crime in the suites" is considerably higher than "crime in the streets." It actually totals several hundred billion dollars a year. Just the overbilling of insurance companies and Medicare by "respectable" physicians runs about $100 billion a year (Davis 1996). These totals refer only to dollar costs. No one has yet figured out a way to compare, for example, the suffering of a rape victim with the pain experienced by an elderly couple who lose their life savings to white-collar fraud.

In terms of dollars, perhaps the most costly crime in U.S. history is the plundering of the savings and loan industry. Corporate officers, who had the trust of their depositors, systematically looted these banks of billions of dollars. The total cost may run as high as $500 billion—a staggering $2,000 for every man, woman, and child in the entire country (Kettl 1991; Newdorf 1991). Of the thousands involved, the most infamous culprit was Neil Bush, son of the president of the United States and an officer of Silverado, a Colorado savings and loan. Bush approved loans totaling $100 million to a company in which he secretly held interests, an act that helped bankrupt his firm (Tolchin 1991).

Future generations will continue to suffer from the wholesale looting of this industry. The interest alone will be exorbitant (at 5 percent, a year's interest on an increase of $500 billion in the national deficit would be $25 billion, at 10 percent $50 billion). Since the government does not pay its debt, but merely keeps borrowing more to pay the compounding interest, this extra $500 billion will double in just a few years. As the late Senator Everett Dirkson once said, "A billion here and a billion there, and pretty soon you're talking about real money."

▼ **In Sum** Functionalists conclude that much street crime is the consequence of socializing the less privileged social classes into equating success with material possessions, while denying them the means to attain that success. People from higher social classes encounter different opportunity structures to commit crimes.

The Conflict Perspective

Have you ever wondered what is going on when you read that top-level executives who defraud the public of millions through price fixing, insider trading, or stock manipulation receive only small fines and suspended sentences? In the same newspaper, furthermore, you may read that some young man who stole an automobile worth $5,000 was sentenced to several years in prison. An example is the Grumman Corporation, which, accused of defrauding the federal government of millions of dollars, agreed to pay a fine so no one would go to jail and the company could bid on more federal contracts (Pasztor 1993). How can a legal system that is supposed to provide "justice for all" be so inconsistent? According to conflict theorists, this question is central to the analysis of crime and the **criminal justice system**— the police, courts, and prisons that deal with people who are accused of having committed crimes.

Power and Inequality

Conflict theorists look at power and social inequality as the primary characteristics of society. They stress that the state's machinery of social control represents the interests of the wealthy and powerful. This group determines the basic laws whose enforcement is essential to preserving its own power. Other norms, such as those that govern informal behavior (chewing with a closed mouth, appearing in public with combed hair, and so on), may come from other sources, but they simply do not count for much. Although such norms influence our everyday behavior, they do not determine prison sentences.

Conflict theorists see the most fundamental division in industrial society as that between the few who own the means of production and the many who do not, those who sell their labor and the privileged few who buy it. Those who buy labor, and thereby control workers, make up the **capitalist class;** those who sell their labor form the **working class.** Toward the most depressed end of the working class is the **marginal working class,** people with few skills, who are subject to unexpected layoffs, and whose jobs are low paying, part time, or seasonal. This class is marked by unemployment and poverty, and from its ranks come most of the prisoners in the United States. Desperate, these people commit street crimes, and because their crimes threaten the social order, they are severely punished.

A Dual Structure of Social Control: The Law as an Instrument of Repression

According to conflict theorists, the idea that the law is a social institution that operates impartially and administers a code shared by all is a cultural myth promoted by the capitalist class. In contrast, they see the law as an instrument of repression, a tool designed to maintain the powerful in their privileged position (Spitzer 1975; Turk 1977; Ritzer 1992). Because the working class holds the potential of rebelling and overthrowing the current social order, when its members get out of line, they are arrested, tried, and imprisoned.

For this reason, the criminal justice system does not focus on the owners of corporations and the harm they do to the masses with unsafe products, wanton pollution, and price manipulations but, instead, directs its energies against violations by the working class (Gordon 1971; Platt 1978; Coleman 1989). The violations of the capitalist class cannot be totally ignored, however, for if they became too outrageous or oppressive, the working class might rise up in revolution. To prevent this, a flagrant violation by a member of the capitalist class is occasionally prosecuted. The publicity given to the case helps to stabilize the social system by providing visible evidence of the "fairness" of the criminal justice system.

Usually, however, the powerful bypass the courts altogether, appearing instead before some agency with no power to imprison (such as the Federal Trade Commission). Most cases of illegal sales of stocks and bonds, price fixing, restraint of trade, collusion, and so on are handled by "gentlemen overseeing gentlemen," for such agencies are directed by people from wealthy backgrounds who sympathize with the intricacies of the corporate world. It is not surprising, then, that the typical sanction is a token fine. In contrast, the property crimes of the masses are handled by courts that do have the power to imprison. The burglary, armed robbery, and theft by the poor threaten not only the sanctity of private property but, ultimately, the positions of the powerful.

▼ **In Sum** From the perspective of conflict theory, the small penalties imposed for crimes committed by the powerful are typical of a legal system designed to mask injustice, to control workers, and, ultimately, to stabilize the social order. From this perspective, law enforcement is a cultural device through which the capitalist class carries out self-protective and repressive policies (Silver 1977).

Street Crime and Imprisonment

The public is demanding that street criminals be locked up, and as Figure 6.1 shows, the number of Americans in prison is now *five times* what it was in 1970. Today, more than a million Americans are in

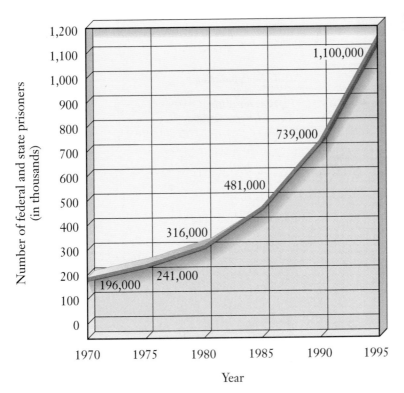

FIGURE 6.1

Growth in the U.S. Prison Population

Note: To better understand the significance of this phenomenal growth, it is useful to compare it with the change in the general population during this same period. Between 1970 and 1995, the population of the United States grew 28 percent, while the prison population grew *20 times as fast*, increasing by 560 percent. If the number of prisoners had increased at the same rate as the general population, there would be 250,000 people in prison, less than one-fourth of the actual number. Or, conversely, the U.S. population would total 4 billion if it had increased as fast as the U.S. prison population!

Source: Statistical Abstract 1995:Table 349; "What's News?" 1995.

prison. Another half million are locked up in city and county jails (*Statistical Abstract* 1995:Table 348). As Table 6.2 shows, about 95 percent of prisoners are men, and about half are African Americans. As noted, because social class funnels some people into the criminal justice system and others away from it, official statistics on crime have an inherent social class bias.

Among the severe problems with imprisonment is that prisons fail to teach their clients to stay away from crime. Four out of every five prisoners have been in prison before (*Statistical Abstract* 1995: Table 351). The **recidivism rate** (the proportion of people who are rearrested) runs as high as 85 to 90 percent (Blumstein and Cohen 1987). Within just six years of their release from prison 69 percent are re-arrested, most within just three years (Zawitz 1988).

Perhaps an underlying reason for this high recidivism rate is that Americans do not agree on *why* people should be put in prison. There appears to be widespread agreement that offenders should be imprisoned, but not on the reasons for doing so. Let's examine the four primary reasons for imprisoning people.

Retribution The purpose of **retribution** is to right a wrong by making offenders suffer, or to pay back what they have stolen. The offense is thought to have upset a moral balance; the punishment is an attempt to restore that balance (Cohen 1940). Attempts to make the punishment "fit the crime," such as sentencing someone who has stolen from a widow to work a dozen weekends in a geriatric center for the poor, are rooted in the idea of retribution.

Table 6.2			
Inmates in U.S. State Prisons			
	Prisoners		*U.S. Population*
	Their Characteristics	*Percentage with These Characteristics*	*Percentage with These Characteristics*
Age	Under 18	0.6	25.9%
	18–24	21.3	10.2
	25–34	45.7	16.6
	35–44	22.7	15.7
	45–54	6.5	10.7
	55–64	2.4	8.2
	65 and over	0.7	12.7
Race	White[a]	49.1	83.4
	African American	47.3	12.4
	Other races	3.5	4.2
Sex	Male	94.5	48.8
	Female	5.5	51.2

Note: [a]The category "white" includes Latinos.
Source: Statistical Abstract 1995: Tables 14, 18, 22, 350.

Need to know

Deterrence The purpose of **deterrence** is to create fear so that others won't break the law. The belief underlying deterrence is that if people know that they will be punished, they will refrain from committing the crime. Sociologist Ernest van den Haag (1975), a chief proponent of deterrence, believes, like many Americans, that the criminal justice system is too soft. He advocates that juveniles who commit adult crimes be tried as adults, that parole boards be abolished, and that prisoners be forced to work.

Does deterrence work? Evidence is mixed, but those who claim that it does not like to recall an example from the nineteenth century. When English law meted out the death penalty for pickpockets, other pickpockets looked forward to the hangings—for people whose attention was riveted on the gallows made easy victims (Hibbert 1963). At this point, no firm evidence resolves the issue.

Rehabilitation The focus in **rehabilitation** switches from punishing offenders to resocializing them so they can become conforming citizens. One example of rehabilitation is teaching prisoners skills so they can support themselves after their release. Other examples include college courses in prison, encounter groups for prisoners, and *halfway houses*—community support facilities where ex-prisoners supervise many aspects of their own lives, such as household tasks, and still report to authorities.

Incapacitation To remove offenders from circulation is called **incapacitation.** "Nothing works," some say, "but we can at least keep them off the streets." Criminologist James Wilson (1975, 1992) supports incapacitation, calling it the only policy that works. He proposes what he calls *added incapacitation*, increasing an offender's sentence each time he or she is convicted of a crime.

In the United States, the public is fearful of crime and despairing of solutions. Increasing dependence on prisons (see Figure 6.1) may indicate that Americans are throwing up their hands as far as criminals are concerned and just trying to "keep them off the streets." It also may indicate attempts at retribution and deterrence. It certainly does not indicate efforts toward rehabilitation, for U.S. prisons

Degradation ceremonies are intended to humiliate norm violators and mark them as "not members" of the group. This photo was taken by the U.S. army in 1945 after U.S. troops liberated Cherbourg, France. Members of the French resistance shaved the heads of these women, who had "collaborated" with (had sex with) the occupying Nazis. They then marched the shamed women down the streets of the city, while the public shouted insults and spat on them.

are basically just holding tanks, offering few, if any, programs of rehabilitation.

The Medicalization of Deviance: Mental Illness

Another way in which society deals with deviance is to "medicalize" it. Let us look at what this entails.

Neither Mental Nor Illness?

To *medicalize* something is to make it a medical matter, to classify it as a form of illness that properly belongs in the care of physicians. For the past hundred years or so, especially since the time of Sigmund Freud (1856–1939), the Viennese physician who founded psychoanalysis, there has been a growing tendency toward the **medicalization of deviance.** In this view, deviance, including crime, is a sign of mental sickness. Rape, murder, stealing, cheating, and so on are external symptoms of internal disorders, consequences of a confused or tortured mind.

Thomas Szasz (1986, 1996), a renegade in his profession of psychiatry, argues that *mental illnesses are neither mental nor illnesses. They are simply problem behaviors.* Some forms of so-called mental illnesses have organic causes; that is, they are *physical* illnesses that result in unusual perceptions and behavior. Some depression, for example, is caused by a chemical imbalance in the brain, which can be treated by drugs. The depression, however, may show itself as

crying, long-term sadness, and the inability to become interested in anything. When a person becomes deviant in ways that disturb others, and these others cannot find a satisfying explanation for why the person is "like that," they conclude that a "sickness in the head" causes the inappropriate, unacceptable behavior.

All of us have troubles. Some of us face a constant barrage of problems as we go through life. Most of us continue the struggle, encouraged by relatives and friends, motivated by job, family responsibilities, and life goals. Even when the odds seem hopeless, we carry on, not perfectly, but as best we can.

Some people, however, fail to cope well with the challenges of daily life. Overwhelmed, they become depressed, uncooperative, or hostile. Some strike out at others, while some, in Merton's terms, become retreatists and withdraw into their apartments or homes and won't come out. These are *behaviors, not mental illnesses,* stresses Szasz. They may be inappropriate coping devices, but they are coping devices, nevertheless, not mental illnesses. Thus, Szasz concludes that "mental illness" is a myth foisted on a naive public by a medical profession that uses pseudoscientific jargon in order to expand its area of control and force nonconforming people to accept society's definitions of "normal."

Szasz's extreme claim forces us to look anew at the forms of deviance called mental illness. To explain behavior that people find bizarre, he does not point to causes hidden deep within the "subconscious," but, instead, to how people learn such be-

People whose behaviors violate norms often are called mentally ill. "Why else would they do such things?" is a common response to deviant behaviors that we don't understand. Mental illness is a label that contains the assumption that there is something wrong "within" people that "causes" their disapproved behavior. Outlaw bikers reject such labels, and in an "in-your-face" approach replace them with their own labels of approval.

haviors. To ask, "What is the origin of inappropriate or bizarre behavior?" then becomes similar to asking, "Why do some women steal?" "Why do some men rape?" "Why do some teenagers cuss their parents and stalk out of the room slamming doors?" *The answers depend on people's particular experiences in life, not an illness in their mind.* In short, some sociologists find Szasz's renegade analysis refreshing because it indicates that *social experiences*, not some illness of the mind, underlies bizarre behaviors—as well as deviance in general.

The Homeless Mentally Ill

Jamie was sitting on the low wall surrounding the landscaped open-air eating area of an exclusive restaurant. She appeared unaware of the stares elicited by her many layers of mismatched clothing, her dirty face, and the ever-present shopping cart overflowing with her meager possessions.

Every once in a while Jamie would pause, concentrate, and point to the street, slowly moving her finger horizontally. I asked her what she was doing.

"I'm directing traffic," she replied. "I control where the cars go. Look, that one turned right there," she said, now withdrawing her finger.

"Really?" I said.

After a while she confided that her cart talked to her.

"Really?" I said again.

"Yes," she replied. "You can hear it, too." At that, she pushed the shopping cart a bit.

"Did you hear that?" she asked.

When I shook my head, she demonstrated again. Then it hit me. She was referring to the squeaking wheels!

I nodded.

When I left Jamie, she was pointing to the sky, for, as she told me, she also controlled the flight of airplanes. To most of us, Jamie's behavior and thinking are bizarre. They simply do not match any reality we know.

Could you or I become Jamie? Suppose for a bitter moment that you are homeless and have to live on the streets. You have no money, no place to sleep, no bathroom, do not know *if* you are going to eat, much

The homeless are located at the bottom of the U.S. social class ladder. One might even say that their status is so low that they are a step below its lowest rung. Why do you think that such a wealthy society as the United States has homeless people?

152

less where, have no friends or anyone you can trust, and live in constant fear of rape and violence. Do you think this might be enough to drive you over the edge?

Consider just the problems involved in not having a place to bathe. (Shelters are often so dangerous that the homeless prefer to take their chances sleeping in public settings.) At first, you try to wash in the toilets of gas stations, bars, the bus station, or a shopping center. But you are dirty, and people stare when you enter, and they call the management when they see you wash your feet in the sink. You are thrown out, and told in no uncertain terms never to come back. So you get dirtier and dirtier. Eventually you come to think of being dirty as a fact of life. Soon, maybe, you don't even care. No longer do the stares bother you, at least not as much.

No one will talk to you, and you withdraw more and more into yourself. You begin to build a fantasy life. You talk openly to yourself. People stare, but so what? They stare anyway. Besides, they are no longer important to you.

Jamie might be mentally ill. Some organic problem, such as a chemical imbalance in her brain, might underlie her behavior. But perhaps not. How long would it take us to show bizarre behaviors if we were homeless and hopeless for years? The point is that *just being on the streets can cause mental illness*—or whatever we want to label socially inappropriate behaviors that we find difficult to classify (McCarthy 1983; Belcher 1988; Nelson 1989). *Homelessness and mental illness are reciprocal*: just as "mental illness" can cause homelessness, so the trials of being homeless, of living on cold, hostile streets, can lead to unusual and unacceptable thinking and behaviors.

The Need for a More Humane Approach

As Durkheim (1895/1964:68) pointed out, deviance is inevitable—even in a group of saints.

> Imagine a society of saints, a perfect cloister of exemplary individuals. Crimes, properly so called, will there be unknown; but faults which appear [invisible] to the layman will create there the same scandal that the ordinary offense does in ordinary [society].

With deviance inevitable, one measure of a society is how it treats its deviants. Our prisons certainly say little good about U.S. society. Filled with the poor, they are warehouses of the unwanted, reflecting patterns of broad discrimination in the larger society. White-collar criminals continue to get by with a slap on the wrist while street criminals are severely punished. Some deviants, failing to meet current standards of admission to either prison or mental hospital, take refuge in shelters and cardboard boxes in city streets. Although no one has *the* answer, it does not take much reflection to see that there are more humane approaches than these.

With deviance inevitable, the larger issues are how to protect people from deviant behaviors that are harmful to themselves or others, to tolerate those that are not, and to develop systems of fairer treatment for deviants. In the absence of the fundamental changes that would bring about a truly equitable social system, most efforts are, unfortunately, Band-Aid work. What we need is a more humane social system, one that would prevent the social inequalities that are the focus of the next four chapters.

Summary and Review

Gaining a Sociological Perspective on Deviance

How do sociologists view deviance?

From a sociological perspective, **deviance**—defined as the violation of norms—is relative. What people consider deviant varies from one culture to another and from group to group within the same society. Consequently, as symbolic interactionists stress, it is not the act itself, but the reactions to the act, that make something deviant. All groups develop systems of social control to punish those who violate its norms. Pp. 134–137.

How do biological, psychological, and sociological explanations of deviance differ?

To explain why people deviate, biologists and psychologists look for reasons *within* the individual, such as **genetic predispositions** or **personality disorders.** Sociologists, in contrast, look for explanations *outside* the individual, in social relations. Pp. 137–138.

The Symbolic Interactionist Perspective

How do symbolic interactionists explain deviance?

Symbolic interactionists have developed several theories to explain deviance such as **crime** (the violation of norms written into law). According to **differential association theory,** people learn to deviate by associating with others. According to **control theory,** each of us is propelled toward deviance, but most of us conform because of an effective system of **inner** and **outer controls.** People who have less effective controls deviate. From the perspective of **labeling theory,** acts are deviant only because people label them as such. Pp. 138–143.

How do people neutralize the norms of society?

Many people commit deviant acts and still think of themselves as conformists. They apparently use five **techniques of neutralization.** Although most people resist being labeled deviant, some embrace deviance. Pp. 141–142.

The Functionalist Perspective

How do functionalists explain deviance?

Functionalists point out that deviance, including criminal acts, is functional for society. Functions include affirming norms and promoting social unity and social change. According to **strain theory,** societies socialize their members into desiring **cultural goals,** but many people are unable to achieve these goals in socially acceptable ways—by **institutionalized means.** *Deviants,* then, are people who either give up on the goals or use deviant means to attain them. Merton identified five types of responses to cultural goals and institutionalized means: conformity, innovation, ritualism, retreatism, and rebellion. **Illegitimate opportunity theory** stresses that some people have easier access to illegal means of achieving goals. Pp. 143–147.

The Conflict Perspective

How do conflict theorists explain deviance?

Conflict theorists take the position that the group in power (the **capitalist class**) imposes its definitions of deviance on other groups (the **working class** and the **marginal working class**). From the conflict perspective, the law is an instrument of oppression used to maintain the power and privilege of the few over the many. The marginal working class has little income, is desperate, and commits highly visible property crimes. The ruling class directs the **criminal justice system,** using it to punish the crimes of the poor while it diverts its own criminal activities away from this punitive system. Imprisonment is motivated by the goals of **retribution, deterrence, rehabilitation,** and **incapacitation.** Pp. 147–151.

The Medicalization of Deviance: Mental Illness

How does society medicalize deviance?

The medical profession has attempted to **medicalize** many forms of deviance, claiming that they represent mental illnesses. Thomas Szasz disagrees, claiming that they are just problem behaviors, not mental illnesses. Research on homeless people illustrates how problems in living can lead to bizarre behavior and thinking. Pp. 151–153.

The Need for a More Humane Approach

Deviance is inevitable, so the larger issues are how to protect people from deviance that harms themselves and others, to tolerate deviance that is not harmful, and to develop systems of fairer treatment for deviants. P. 153.

Where can I read more on this topic?

Suggested readings for this chapter are listed on page 438.

Glossary

capitalist class the wealthy who own the means of production and buy the labor of the working class (p. 148)

control theory the idea that two control systems—inner controls and outer controls—work against our tendencies to deviate (p. 140)

crime the violation of norms that are written into law (p. 135)

criminal justice system the system of police, courts, and prisons set up to deal with people who are accused of having committed a crime (p. 148)

cultural goals the legitimate objectives held out to the members of a society (p. 145)

deterrence creating fear so people will refrain from an act (p. 150)

deviance the violation of rules or norms (p. 135)

differential association Edwin Sutherland's term to indicate that associating with some groups results in learning an "excess of definitions" of deviance (attitudes favorable to committing deviant acts), and, by extension, in a greater likelihood that their members will become deviant (p. 138)

genetic predisposition inborn tendencies (p. 137)

illegitimate opportunity structure opportunities for crimes that are woven into the texture of life (p. 146)

incapacitation the removal of offenders from "normal" society; taking them "off the streets," thereby removing their capacity to commit crimes against the public (p. 150)

institutionalized means approved ways of reaching cultural goals (p. 145)

labeling theory the view, developed by symbolic interactionists, that the labels people are given affect their own and others' perceptions of them, thus channeling their behavior either into deviance or into conformity (p. 141)

marginal working class the most desperate members of the working class, who have few skills, have little job security, and are often unemployed (p. 148)

medicalization of deviance to make some deviance a medical matter, a symptom of some underlying illness that needs to be treated by physicians (p. 151)

negative sanction an expression of disapproval for breaking a norm; ranging from a mild, informal reaction such as a frown to a formal prison sentence or even capital punishment (p. 136)

personality disorders as a theory of deviance, the view that a personality disturbance of some sort causes an individual to violate social norms (p. 137)

positive sanction a reward or positive reaction for following norms, ranging from a smile to a prize (p. 136)

recidivism rate the proportion of people who are re-arrested (p. 149)

rehabilitation the resocialization of offenders so that they can become conforming citizens (p. 150)

retribution the punishment of offenders in order to restore the moral balance upset by an offense (p. 149)

social order a group's usual and customary social arrangements (p. 134)

stigma "blemishes" that discredit a person's claim to a "normal" identity (p. 136)

strain theory Robert Merton's term for the strain engendered when a society socializes large numbers of people to desire a cultural goal (such as success) but withholds from many the approved means to reach that goal; one adaptation to the strain is deviance, including crime, the choice of an innovative means (one outside the approved system) to attain the cultural goal (p. 145)

street crime crimes such as mugging, rape, and burglary (p. 137)

techniques of neutralization ways of thinking or rationalizing that help people deflect society's norms (p. 141)

white-collar crime Edwin Sutherland's term for crimes committed by people of respectable and high social status in the course of their occupations (p. 147)

working class people who sell their labor to the capitalist class (p. 148)

Sociology and the Internet

All URLs listed are current as of the printing of this book. URLs are often changed. Please check our Website http://www.abacon.com/henslin for updates.

1. Criminal Justice

As you discovered in this chapter, criminal behavior is only one part of deviance. Still, it is an important part. To pursue this topic further, go to Cecil Greek's criminal justice home page (http://www.fsu.edu/~crimdo/cj. html), and browse through the topics. (This is probably the most complete criminal justice site on the Internet.) First, form a research question. (What do you want to know more about?) Then follow links relating to your topic, taking notes as if you were working in a library.

When you finish, write a paper according to your instructor's directions. (Don't forget, a good paper has an introduction and a conclusion, and is well organized into topical sections and paragraphs.)

2. Using FBI Statistics

Investigate changes in the crime index for major cities. Go to the FBI's home page (http://www. fbi.gov/), and page down to the Uniform Crime Reporting Program. At "Preliminary 199—Statistics," select "Report." On the Report page, select "Table 4—OFFENSES KNOWN TO THE POLICE." (The table number may change.) Select "Proceed to Table 4" at the top of the page. Save or print the table.

Note the changes in index crimes from the previous year in the column "Crime Index total" for several different-size cities in various regions of the country. Are there patterns in the changes, or is each city fairly unique? Why do you think this is? (Your instructor may want you to figure the percentage change for each of the cities you use in your report.)

Pacita Abad, If My Friends Could See Me Now, 1991.

C H A P T E R

7

Social Stratification in Global Perspective

*L*ET'S CONTRAST TWO "AVERAGE" FAMILIES.

For Getu Mulleta, 33, and his wife, Zenebu, 28, of rural Ethiopia, life is a constant struggle to keep themselves and their seven children from starving. They live in a 320-square-foot manure-plastered hut with no electricity, gas, or running water. They have a radio, but the battery is dead. Surviving on $130 a year, the family farms teff, a cereal grain.

The Mulletas' poverty is not due to a lack of hard work. Getu works about 80 hours a week, while Zenebu puts in even more hours. "Housework" for Zenebu includes fetching water, making fuel pellets out of cow dung for the open fire over which she cooks the family's food, and cleaning animal stables. Like other Ethiopian women, she eats after the men.

In Ethiopia, the average male can expect to live to 48, the average female to 50.

The Mulletas' most valuable possession is their oxen. Their wishes for the future: more animals, better seed, and a second set of clothing.

Springfield, Illinois, is home to the Kellys—Rick, 36, Patti, 34, Julie, 10, and Michael, 7. The Kellys live in a four-bedroom, 2,100-square-foot, carpeted ranch-style house, with central heating and air conditioning, a basement, and a two-car garage. Their home is equipped with a refrigerator, washing machine, clothes dryer, dishwasher, garbage disposal, vacuum cleaner, food processor, microwave, and toaster. They also own three radios, two stereos (one a CD player), four telephones (one cellular), two televisions, a camcorder, VCR, tape recorder, Gameboy, Nintendo, computer and printer, not to mention two blow dryers, an answering machine, an electric can opener, and an electric toothbrush. This doesn't count the stereo-radio-cassette players in their pickup and car.

Rick works 40 hours a week as a cable splicer for the local telephone company. Patti teaches school part time. Together they make $32,857, plus benefits. The Kellys can choose from among dozens of superstocked supermarkets. They spend $3,986 for food they eat at home, and another $2,287 eating out, a total of 19 percent of their annual income.

In the United States, the average life expectancy is 72 for males, 79 for females.

On the Kellys' wish list are car phones, a new Bronco, a 2 gigabyte computer, a fax machine, a boat, a camping trailer, and, oh yes, farther down the road, a vacation cabin.

Sources: *Menzel 1994; Population Reference Bureau, 1995; Statistical Abstract 1995:*Tables 719, 730.

What Is Social Stratification?

Some of the world's nations are wealthy, others poor, and some in between. This layering of nations, or of groups of people within a nation, is called *social stratification.* Social stratification is one of the most significant topics we shall discuss, for it affects our life chances—from our access to material possessions to the age at which we die.

Social stratification also affects our orientations to life. If you had been born into the Ethiopian family, for example, you would be illiterate and expect your children to be the same. You also would expect hunger

to be a part of life and not be too surprised when people die young. To be born into the U.S. family would give you quite a different picture of the world.

Social stratification is a system in which people are divided into layers according to their relative power, property, and prestige. It is important to emphasize that social stratification does not refer to individuals. It is a *way of ranking large groups of people into a hierarchy that shows their relative privileges.*

Let's examine how the nations of the world became so stratified that, as with these two families, it profoundly affects our chances in life. But first let's review the major systems of social stratification.

"Worlds Apart" could be the title for these photos, which illustrate how life chances depend on global stratification. On the left is the Mulleta family of Ethiopia, featured in the opening vignette, standing in front of their home with all their material possessions. On the right is the Skeen family of Texas, surrounded by their possessions.

Systems of Social Stratification

Every society stratifies its members. Some societies have greater inequality than others, but the existence of social stratification is universal. Let us consider three major systems of social stratification: slavery, caste, and class.

Slavery

As we examine the major causes and conditions of slavery, you will see how remarkably slavery has varied around the world.

Causes of Slavery **Slavery,** whose essential characteristic is *ownership of some people by others,* has been common in world history. The Old Testament even lays out rules on how the Israelites should treat their slaves. The Romans had slaves, as did the Africans and the Greeks. Slavery was least common among nomads, especially hunters and gatherers, and most common in agricultural societies (Landtman 1938/1968).

Contrary to popular assumption, slavery was not usually based on racism, but on one of three other factors. The first was debt. In some cultures, an individual who could not pay a debt could be enslaved by the creditor. The second was a violation of the law. Instead of being killed, a murderer or thief might be enslaved by the family of the victim as compensation for their loss. The third was war and conquest. When one group of people conquered another, it was often convenient to enslave at least some of the vanquished (Starna and Watkins 1991). Historian Gerda Lerner (1986) notes that the first people enslaved through this practice were women. When premodern men raided a village or camp, they killed the men, raped the women, and then brought the women back as slaves. The women were valued for sexual purposes, for reproduction, and for extra labor.

Roughly twenty-five hundred years ago when Greece was but a collection of city-states, slavery was common. A city that became powerful and conquered other cities would enslave some of the vanquished. Both slaves and slaveholders were Greek. Similarly, when Rome became the supreme power of the Mediterranean area about two thousand years ago, following the custom of the time the Romans enslaved some of the Greeks they had conquered. More educated than their conquerors, some of these slaves served as tutors in Roman homes. Slavery, then, was a sign of defeat in battle, of crime, or of debt, not the sign of some supposedly inherently inferior status.

Conditions of Slavery The conditions of slavery have varied widely around the world. *In some cases, slavery was temporary.* After serving a set number of years, slaves were free to return to their home coun-

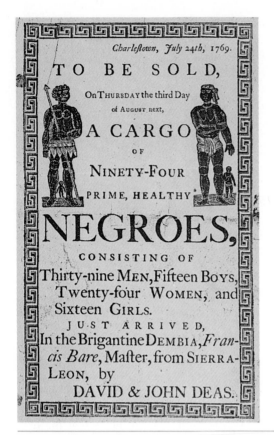

Charleftown, July 24th, 1769.

TO BE SOLD,

On THURSDAY the third Day
of AUGUST next,

A CARGO

OF

NINETY-FOUR

PRIME, HEALTHY

NEGROES,

CONSISTING OF

Thirty-nine MEN, Fifteen BOYS,
Twenty-four WOMEN, and
Sixteen GIRLS.

JUST ARRIVED,

In the Brigantine DEMBIA, *Francis Bare*, Mafter, from SIERRA-
LEON, by

DAVID & JOHN DEAS.

Slavery is an age-old system of social stratification. This 1769 broadside from Charleston, South Carolina, reminds us that this form of stratification was once the custom in the United States.

try. Slaves of the Israelites were set free in the year of jubilee, which occurred every fifty years. Roman slaves ordinarily had the right to buy themselves out of slavery. They knew what their purchase price was, and some were able to meet this price by striking a bargain with their owner and selling their services to others. In most instances, however, slavery was life-long. Some criminals, for example, became slaves when they were given life sentences as oarsmen on Roman war ships. There they served until death, which under this exhausting service often did not take long.

Slavery was not necessarily inheritable. In most places, the children of slaves were automatically slaves themselves. But in some instances, the child of a slave who served a rich family might even be adopted by that family, becoming an heir who bore the family name along with the other sons or daughters of the household. In ancient Mexico, the chil-

dren of slaves were always free (Landtman 1938/ 1968:271).

Slaves were not necessarily powerless and poor. In almost all instances, slaves owned no property and had no power. Among some slaveholding groups, however, slaves could accumulate property and even rise to high positions in the community. Occasionally, a slave might even become wealthy, loan money to the master, and, while still a slave, own slaves himself or herself (Landtman 1938/1968). Such instances, however, were not typical.

Slavery in the New World With a growing need for labor, some colonists tried to enslave Indians. This attempt, however, failed miserably. Among other reasons, when Indians escaped they knew how to survive in the wilderness and were able to make their way back to their tribe. The colonists then turned to Africans, who were being brought to North and South America by the Dutch, English, Portuguese, and Spanish.

Given this broad background of slavery's causes, some analysts have concluded that racism didn't lead to slavery, but, rather, slavery led to racism. Finding it profitable to make people slaves for life, U.S. slave owners developed an **ideology,** a system of beliefs that justifies social arrangements. Essential to an ideology that would justify lifelong slavery was the view that the slaves were inferior. Some concluded that they were locked into a childlike, helpless state, which meant that they needed to be taken care of by superior people—white colonists, of course. Others said that they were not even fully human. In short, the colonists developed elaborate justifications for slavery on the presumed superiority of their own race.

To make slavery even more profitable, slave states passed laws that made slavery *inheritable;* that is, the babies born to slaves became the property of the slave owners (Stampp 1956). These children could be sold, bartered, or traded. To strengthen their control, slave states passed laws making it illegal for slaves to hold meetings or to be away from the master's premises without carrying a pass (Lerner 1972). As sociologist W. E. B. Du Bois (1935/ 1966:12) noted, "gradually the entire white South became an armed camp to keep Negroes in slavery and to kill the black rebel."

Patterns of legal discrimination did not end after the Civil War. For example, until 1954 the states operated two separate school systems. Even until the 1950s, to keep the races from "mixing," it was illegal in Mississippi for a white and an African

American to sit together on the same seat of a car! The reason there was no outright ban on both races being in the same car was to allow for African-American chauffeurs.

Slavery Today Slavery has again reared its ugly head, this time in Sudan and Mauritania (Horwitz 1989; Jacobs 1995; Liben 1995). Apparently villages are raided and the men killed. The captive children are sold for a few dollars, sometimes for just a couple of chickens. The women, sold to the highest bidder for work and sex, bring more. Public television (PBS) has even run film footage of captured children in chains. In spite of this, representatives of these governments strongly deny the accusations (Abdullah 1995).

Caste

The second system of social stratification is caste. In a **caste system,** a society is divided into strata, and one's status is determined by birth and is lifelong. Someone born into a low-status group will al-

ways have low status, no matter how much that person may accomplish in life. In sociological terms the basis of a caste system is ascribed status. Achieved status cannot change an individual's place in this system.

Societies with this form of stratification try to make certain that the boundaries between castes remain firm. They practice **endogamy,** marriage within their own group, and prohibit intermarriage. To prevent contact between castes, they even develop elaborate rules about *ritual pollution*, teaching that contact with inferior castes contaminates the superior caste.

India India provides the best example of a caste system. Based not on race but on religion, it has existed for almost three thousand years (Chandra 1993a, b). India's four main castes, or *varnas*, are depicted in Table 7.1. The four main castes are subdivided into thousands of specialized subcastes, or *jati*, with each *jati* working in a specific occupation. For example, knife sharpening is done only by members of a particular subcaste.

In a caste system, status is determined at birth and is lifelong. Members of lower castes suffer deprivation in virtually all aspects of life. In the Indian caste system, even occupation is determined by birth. Just as this man's father fixed shoes, so will his son. Gender cuts across every form of social stratification. Birth gave the woman in the photo on the left membership in a lower caste, as well as a secondary status within that caste. So it will be for her daughter. The photo on the right illustrates gender stratification in the division of labor that has been found in all societies. As the text discusses, this system has come under attack.

Table 7.1

India's Caste System

Caste	Occupation
Brahman	Priests or scholars
Kshatriya	Nobles and warriors
Vaishya	Merchants and skilled artisans
Shudra	Common laborers
Harijan	The outcastes; degrading labor

The lowest group listed on Table 7.1, the Harijan, is actually so low that it is beneath the caste system altogether. The Harijans, along with some of the Shudras, make up India's "untouchables." If someone of a higher caste is touched by one of them, that person becomes unclean. In some cases, even the shadow of an untouchable is contaminating. Early morning and late afternoons are especially risky, for the long shadows of these periods pose a danger to everyone higher up the caste system. Consequently, Harijans are not even allowed in some villages during these times. If anyone becomes contaminated, their religion specifies *ablution*, or washing rituals, to restore purity (Lannoy 1975).

Although the Indian government declared the caste system abolished in 1949, the force of centuries-old practices cannot be so easily eliminated, and the caste system remains part of everyday life in India (Sharma 1994). The ceremonies one follows at births, marriages, and deaths, for example, are dictated by caste (Chandra 1993a). Due to industrialization and urbanization, this system is gradually breaking down, for it is difficult to maintain caste divisions in crowded and anonymous cities (Robertson 1976).

A U.S. Racial Caste System Before leaving the subject of caste, we should note that when slavery ended in the United States it was replaced by a *racial caste system*, in which birth marked a person for life (Berger 1963/1997). In this system, *all* whites, no matter if they were poor and uneducated, considered themselves higher than *all* African Americans. Even into the earlier parts of this century, long after slavery had ended, this attitude persisted. When any white met any African American on a southern sidewalk, for example, the African American had to move aside. And as in India, the upper caste feared pollution from the lower, insisting on separate schools, hotels, restaurants, and even toilets and drinking fountains in public facilities.

Class

As we have seen, stratification systems based on slavery and caste are rigid. The lines marking the divisions between people are so firm that there is little or no movement from one group to another. A **class system,** in contrast, which is based primarily on money or material possessions, is much more open. It, too, begins at birth, when an individual is ascribed the status of his or her parents, but, unlike in slavery and caste, one's social class may change due to what one achieves (or fails to achieve) in life. In addition, there are no laws that specify occupations on the basis of birth or that prohibit marriage between the classes.

A major characteristic of this third system, then, is its relatively fluid boundaries. A class system allows **social mobility,** that is, movement up or down the class ladder. The potential for improving one's social circumstances, or class, is one of the major forces that drives people to go far in school and to work hard. In the extreme, the family background that an individual inherits at birth may bring such deprivation that the child has little chance of climbing very far—or it may provide such privileges that it is almost impossible to fall down the class ladder.

A Note on Global Stratification and the Status of Females

In every society of the world, gender is a basis for social stratification. In no society is gender the sole basis for stratifying people, but gender cuts across *all* systems of social stratification—whether slavery, caste, or class (Huber 1990). On the basis of their gender, people in every society are sorted into categories and given different access to the good things offered by their society. Apparently these distinctions always favor males. Because gender is so important to what happens to us in life, we shall examine its implications in detail in Chapter 10.

What Determines Social Class?

In the early days of sociology, a disagreement arose about the meaning of social class in industrialized societies. Let's compare how Marx and Weber saw the matter.

Karl Marx: The Means of Production

As discussed in Chapter 1, when the feudal system broke up, masses of peasants were displaced from their traditional lands and occupations. Fleeing to cities, they competed for the few available jobs. Offered only a pittance for their labor, they dressed in rags, went hungry, and slept under bridges and in shacks. In contrast, the factory owners built mansions, hired servants, and lived in the lap of luxury. Seeing this great disparity between owners and workers, Marx concluded that social class depends on a single factor—the **means of production**—the tools, factories, land, and investment capital used to produce wealth (Marx 1844/1964; Marx and Engels 1848/1967).

Marx argued that the distinctions people often make between themselves—such as their clothing, speech, education, or relative salary—are superficial matters. They camouflage the only real significant dividing line: people (the **bourgeoisie**) either own the means of production or they (the **proletariat**) work for those who do. This is the only distinction that counts, for these two classes make up modern society. In short, according to Marx, people's relationship to the means of production determines their **social class.**

Marx did recognize that other groups were part of industrial society: farmers and peasants; a *lumpenproletariat* (marginal people such as migrant workers, beggars, vagrants, and criminals); and a middle class (self-employed professionals). Marx did not consider these groups social classes, however, for they lacked **class consciousness**—a common identity based on their position in the means of production. They did not see themselves as exploited workers whose plight could be solved only by collective action. Consequently, Marx thought of these

These photos, taken at the end of the last century, illustrate the different worlds that social classes produce within the same society. The boys on the left worked full time—when they could get work. They did not go to school, and they had no home. The children on the right, Cornelius and Gladys Vanderbilt, are shown in front of their parents' estate. They went to school and did not work. You can see how the life situations illustrated in these photos would have produced different orientations to life—and, therefore, politics, ideas about marriage, values, and so on—the stuff of which life is made.

groups as insignificant in the coming workers' revolution that would overthrow capitalism.

Capital will become ever more concentrated, Marx said, which will make capitalists and workers increasingly hostile to one another. When the workers realize that capitalists are their common source of oppression, they will unite and throw off the chains of their oppressors. In a bloody revolution, they will seize the means of production and usher in a classless society, where no longer will the few grow rich at the expense of the many. What holds back the workers' unity and their revolution is **false consciousness,** workers mistakenly identifying with capitalists. For example, workers with a few dollars in the bank may forget that they are workers and instead see themselves as investors, or as capitalists who are about to launch a successful business.

The only distinction worth mentioning, then, is whether a person is an owner or a worker. This decides everything else, Marx stressed, for property determines people's lifestyles, shapes their ideas, and establishes their relationships with one another.

Max Weber: Property, Prestige, and Power

Max Weber (1864–1920) became an outspoken critic of Marx. He said that to see property as the whole picture is shortsighted. **Social class,** said Weber, is actually made up of three components—property, prestige, and power (Gerth and Mills 1958; Weber 1922/1968). Some call these the three *P*'s of social class. (Although Weber used the terms *class*, *status*, and *power*, some sociologists find *property*, *prestige*, and *power* to be clearer terms. To make them even clearer, you may wish to substitute *wealth* for *property*.)

Property (or wealth), said Weber, is certainly significant in determining a person's standing in society. On that he agreed with Marx. But, added Weber, ownership is not the only significant aspect of property. For example, some powerful people, such as managers of corporations, *control* the means of production although they do not *own* them. If managers can control property for their own benefit—awarding themselves huge bonuses and magnificent perks—it makes no practical difference that they do not own the property they so generously use for their own benefit.

Prestige, the second element in Weber's analysis, is often derived from property, for people tend to look up to the wealthy. Prestige, however, may be based on

other factors. Olympic gold medalists, for example, may not own property, yet they have very high prestige. Some are even able to exchange their prestige for property—such as being paid a small fortune for saying that they start their day with "the breakfast of champions." In other words, property and prestige are not one-way streets: although property can bring prestige, prestige can also bring property.

Power, the third element of social class, is the ability to control others, even over their objections. Weber agreed with Marx that property is a major source of power, but he added that it is not the only source. Position, for instance, can also lead to power. A notable example is J. Edgar Hoover, who headed the FBI for forty-eight years, from 1924 to 1972. Hoover wielded such enormous power that even presidents Johnson and Kennedy were fearful of him. Hoover's power, however, did not come from ownership of property, for he lived simply and did not accumulate property. Rather, his power derived from his position as the head of this powerful government agency. Not only did he direct a well-trained secret police, but he also maintained files on presidents and members of Congress, documenting their sexual indiscretions, files they knew he could leak to the public if they crossed him.

▼ **In Sum** For Marx, social class was based solely on a person's position in relationship to the means of production—as a member of either the bourgeoisie or the proletariat—while Weber argued that social class is a combination of property, prestige, and power.

Why Is Social Stratification Universal?

What is it about social life that makes all societies stratified? We shall first consider the explanation proposed by functionalists, which has aroused much controversy in sociology, followed by criticisms of this position. We then explore explanations proposed by conflict theorists.

The Functionalist View of Davis and Moore: Motivating Qualified People

Functionalists take the position that whatever patterns of behavior characterize a society are functional for that society. Since social inequality is universal, then inequality must help societies survive. Using this principle, sociologists Kingsley Davis and Wilbert Moore (1945, 1953) concluded that stratification is inevitable for the following reasons:

1 Society must make certain that its positions are filled.

2 Some positions are more important than others.

3 The more important positions must be filled by the more qualified people.

4 To motivate the more qualified people to fill these positions, society must offer them greater rewards.

Let's look at an example to flesh out this functionalist argument. The position of college president is deemed much more important than that of a student because the president's decisions affect many more people. Any mistakes he or she makes carry implications for a large number of people, including many students. So it is with the general of an army versus privates. The decisions of a college president and a general affect careers, paychecks, and, in some cases, even determine life and death.

Positions with greater responsibility require greater accountability. College presidents and army generals are accountable for how they perform—to boards of control and the leader of a country, respectively. How can society motivate highly qualified people to enter such high-pressure positions? What keeps people from avoiding them and seeking only less demanding jobs?

The answer, said Davis and Moore, is that society offers greater rewards for its more responsible, demanding, and accountable positions. If they didn't offer higher prestige, salaries, and benefits, why would anyone strive for them? Thus, a salary of $2 million, country club membership, a chauffeured limousine, and a private jet may be necessary to get the most highly qualified people to compete with one another for a certain position, while a $30,000 salary without fringe benefits is enough to get hundreds of people to compete for a less demanding position. Similarly, higher rewards are necessary to recruit people to positions that require rigorous training.

The functionalist argument is simple and clear. Society works better if its most qualified people hold its most important positions. For example, to get highly talented people to become surgeons—to undergo many years of rigorous training and then cope

with the tensions of life-and-death situations on a daily basis, as well as withstand the Sword of Damocles known as malpractice suits—requires a high payoff.

Tumin: A Critical Response

Note that the Davis–Moore thesis is an attempt to explain *why* social stratification is universal, not an attempt to *justify* social inequality. Note also that their view nevertheless makes many sociologists uncomfortable, for they see it as coming close to justifying the inequalities in society.

Melvin Tumin (1953) was the first sociologist to point out what he saw as major flaws in the functionalist position. Here are three of his arguments.

First, how do you measure the importance of a position? You can't measure importance by the rewards a position carries, for that argument is circular. You must have an independent measure of importance to test whether the more important positions actually carry higher rewards. For example, is a surgeon really more important to society than a garbage collector, since the garbage collector helps prevent contagious diseases?

Second, if stratification worked as Davis and Moore described it, society would be a **meritocracy;** that is, all positions would be awarded on the basis of merit. Ability, then, should predict who goes to college. Instead, the best predictor of college entrance is family income—the more a family earns, the more likely their children are to go to college. Similarly, while some people do get ahead through ability and hard work, others simply inherit wealth and the opportunities that go with it. Moreover, a stratification system that places half the population above the other half solely on the basis of sex does not live up to the argument that talent and ability are the bases for holding important positions. In short, factors far beyond merit give people their relative positions in society.

Third, if social stratification is so functional, it ought to benefit almost everyone. In actual fact, however, social stratification is *dysfunctional* for many. Think of the people who could have made invaluable contributions to society had they not been born in a slum and had to drop out of school, taking menial jobs to help support the family; or the many who, born female, are assigned "women's work," ensuring that they do not maximize their mental abilities (Huber 1988).

Mosca: A Forerunner of the Conflict Perspective

In 1896 Italian sociologist Gaetano Mosca wrote an influential book entitled *The Ruling Class.* He argued that every society will be stratified by power, for three main reasons:

1 A society cannot exist unless it is organized. This requires politics of some sort in order to coordinate people's actions and get society's work done.

2 Political organization always results in inequalities of power, for it requires that some people take leadership positions, while others follow.

3 It is human nature to be self-centered. Therefore, people in positions of power will use their positions to bring greater rewards for themselves.

There is no way around these facts of life, said Mosca. Social stratification is inevitable, and every society will stratify itself along lines of power. Because the ruling class is well organized and enjoys easy communication among its relatively few members, it is extremely difficult for the majority they govern to resist (Marger 1987). Mosca's argument is a forerunner of explanations developed by conflict theorists.

The Conflict Perspective: Class Conflict and Competition for Scarce Resources

Conflict theorists such as William Domhoff (1990, 1997), C. Wright Mills (1956), and Irving Louis Horowitz (1966) sharply disagree with the functionalist position. They stress that conflict, not function, is the basis of social stratification. They point out that in every society groups struggle with one another for their society's limited resources. Whenever some group gains power, it uses that power to extract what it can from the groups beneath it. It also uses the social institutions to keep other groups weak and itself in power.

All ruling groups—whether slave masters or modern elites—develop an ideology to justify their position at the top. The view that "we receive more because we hold the more important, demanding positions" is an ideology. Ideology often seduces the oppressed into believing that their welfare depends on keeping society stable. Consequently, the oppressed may support laws that work against their own interests and even sacrifice their children as soldiers in wars designed to enrich the bourgeoisie.

Marx predicted that the workers would revolt. The day will come, he claimed, when class consciousness will overcome ideology, and the workers, their eyes finally opened, will throw off their oppressors. At first, this struggle for control of the means of production may be covert, showing up as work slow-downs or industrial sabotage, but ultimately it will break out into open resistance. The struggle will be difficult, for the bourgeoisie control the police, the military, and even education (where they implant false consciousness in the workers' children).

Some sociologists have refocused conflict theory. C. Wright Mills (1956), Ralf Dahrendorf (1959), and Randall Collins (1974, 1988), for example, stress that groups within the *same class* also compete for scarce resources—for power, wealth, education, housing, and even prestige—whatever benefits society has to offer. The result is conflict not only between labor unions and corporations, but also between the young and the old, women and men, and racial and ethnic groups. Unlike functionalists, then, conflict theorists hold that just beneath the surface of what may appear to be a tranquil society lies overt conflict—only uneasily held in check.

Toward a Synthesis

In spite of vast differences between the functionalist and conflict views, some analysts have tried to synthesize them. Sociologist Gerhard Lenski (1966), for example, used the development of surpluses as a basis for reconciling the two views. He said that the functionalists are right if you look at societies that have only basic resources and do not accumulate wealth. In hunting and gathering societies, the limited resources are channeled to people as rewards for taking on important responsibilities. The conflict theorists are right, however, when it comes to societies with a surplus. Because humans pursue self-interest, they struggle to control those surpluses, and a small elite emerges. To protect its position, the elite builds social inequality into the society, which results in a full-blown system of social stratification.

How Do Elites Maintain Stratification?

Suppose that you are part of the ruling elite of your society. What can you do to maintain your privileged position? The key lies in controlling ideas and information, in social networks, and in the least effective of all, the use of force.

Ideology versus Force

Medieval Europe provides a good example of the power of ideology. At that time, land, which was owned by only a small group of people, was the primary source of wealth. With the exception of the clergy and some craftsmen, almost everyone was a peasant working for this small group of powerful landowners, called the aristocracy. The peasants farmed the land, took care of the cattle, and built the roads and bridges. Each year, they had to turn over a designated portion of their crops to their feudal lord. Year after year, for centuries, they did so. Why?

Controlling Ideas Why didn't the peasants rebel and take over the land themselves? There were many reasons, not the least of which is that the army was controlled by the aristocracy. Coercion, however, only goes so far, for it breeds hostility and nourishes rebellion. How much more effective it is to get the people to *want* to do what the ruling elite desires. This is where *ideology* comes into play, and the aristocracy of that time used it to great effect. They stressed the **divine right of kings**—the idea that the king's authority comes directly from God—which can be traced back several thousand years to the Old Testament. The king could delegate authority to nobles, who as God's representatives also had to be obeyed. To disobey was a sin against God; to

rebel meant physical punishment on earth and a sentence to suffer in eternal hell.

The control of ideas, then, can be remarkably more effective than brute force. Although this particular ideology no longer governs people's minds today, the elite in every society develops ideologies to justify its position at the top. For example, around the world schools teach that their country's form of government—*whatever form of government that may be*—is the best. Each nation's schools also stress the virtues of governments past and present, not their vices. Religion also teaches that we owe obedience to authority, that laws are to be obeyed. To the degree that their ideologies are accepted by the masses, political arrangements are stable.

Controlling Information To maintain their positions of power, elites also try to control information. In dictatorships this is accomplished through the threat of force, for dictators can—and do—imprison editors and reporters for printing critical reports, sometimes even for publishing information unflattering to them (Timerman 1981). The ruling elites of democracies, lacking such power, accomplish the same purpose by manipulating the media through the selective release of information, withholding what they desire "in the interest of national security." But just as coercion has its limits, so does the control of information—especially given its new forms (from satellite communications to modems, fax machines, and the Internet) that pay no respect to international borders.

The divine right of kings *was an ideology that made the king God's direct representative on earth—to administer justice and punish evildoers. This theological-political concept was supported by the Roman Catholic Church, whose representatives crowned the king. Depicted here is the coronation of Charlemagne by Pope Leo III on Christmas day 800, thus establishing what became known as the Holy Roman Empire.*

Social Networks   Also crucial in maintaining stratification are social networks—the social ties that link people together (Higley et al. 1991). As discussed in Chapter 5, social networks—contacts expanding outward from the individual that gradually encompass more and more people—supply valuable information and tend to perpetuate social inequality. Sociologist William Domhoff (1983, 1990) has documented how members of the elite move in a circle of power that multiplies their opportunities. Contacts with people of similar backgrounds, interests, and goals allow the elite to pass privileges from one generation to the next. In contrast, the social networks of the poor perpetuate poverty and powerlessness.

Technology   The elite's desire to preserve its position is aided by recent developments in technology, especially monitoring devices. These devices—from "hot telephones," taps that turn your telephone into a microphone even when it is off the hook, to machines that can read the entire contents of your computer without leaving a trace—help the elite monitor citizens' activities without their even being aware that they are being shadowed. Dictatorships have few checks on how such technology will be employed, but the checks and balances of democracies, such as constitutional rights and the necessity of court orders, at least partially curb their use.

Comparative Social Stratification

Now that we have examined different systems of social stratification and considered why stratification is universal, let us look in turn at social stratification in Great Britain and in the former Soviet Union.

Social Stratification in Great Britain

Great Britain is often called England by Americans, but England is only one of the countries that make up the island of Great Britain. The others are Scotland and Wales. In addition, Northern Ireland is part of the United Kingdom of Great Britain and Northern Ireland.

Like other industrialized countries, Great Britain has a class system that can be divided into a lower, middle, and upper class. A little over half the population is in the lower or working class, while close to half the population is in the nation's very large middle class. A tiny upper class, perhaps 1 percent of the population, is powerful, highly educated, and extremely wealthy.

Compared with Americans, the British are extremely class conscious. Like Americans, the British recognize class distinctions on the basis of the type of car a person drives, or the stores that person patronizes. But the most striking characteristics of the British class system are language and education. Differences in speech still have a powerful impact on British life. Accent almost always betrays class, and as soon as someone speaks, the listener is aware of that person's class—and treats him or her accordingly.

Education is the primary way in which the British perpetuate their class system from one generation to the next. Almost all children go to neighborhood schools, but the children of Great Britain's more privileged 5 percent—who own *half* the nation's wealth—attend exclusive private boarding schools (known as "public" schools), where they are trained in subjects considered "proper" for members of the ruling class. An astounding 50 percent of the students at Oxford and Cambridge, the country's most prestigious universities, come from this 5 percent of the population. To illustrate how powerfully this system of stratified education affects the national life of Great Britain, sociologist Ian Robertson (1987) says,

> [E]ighteen former pupils of the most exclusive of them, Eton, have become prime minister. Imagine the chances of a single American high school producing eighteen presidents!

Social Stratification in the Former Soviet Union

Vladimir Ilyich Lenin (1870–1924) and Leon Trotsky (1879–1940) heeded Karl Marx's call for a classless society. They led a revolution in Russia to bring this about. They, and the nations that followed their banner, never claimed to have achieved the ideal of communism, in which all contribute their labor to the common good and receive according to their needs. Instead, they used the term *socialism* to describe the intermediate step between capitalism and communism, in which social classes are abolished but some individual inequality remains.

Although the socialist nations often manipulated the world's mass media to tweak the nose of Uncle Sam because of the inequalities in the United

States, they, too, were marked by huge disparities in privilege—much more than they ever acknowledged to the outside world. Their major basis of stratification—membership in the Communist Party—often was the determining factor in deciding who would gain admission to the better schools or obtain the more desirable jobs. The equally qualified son or daughter of a nonmember would be turned down, for such privileges came with demonstrated loyalty to the Party.

Divided into three layers, even the Communist Party was highly stratified. Most members occupied a low level, having such assignments as spying on other workers. For their services, they might be given easier jobs in the factory or occasional access to special stores to purchase hard-to-find goods. A smaller number were mid-level bureaucrats with better than average access to resources and privileges. The top level consisted of a small elite: party members who enjoyed not only power but also limousines, imported delicacies, vacation homes, and even servants and hunting lodges. As with other stratification systems around the world, women held lower positions in the Party, as was readily evident in each year's May Day photos of the top members of the Party reviewing the weapons paraded in Moscow's Red Square. The top officials were always men.

Struggling with a bloated bureaucracy, the gross inefficiencies of central planning, workers who did the minimum because they did not see a personal stake in their jobs, and the military grabbing one of every eight of the nation's rubles (*Statistical Abstract* 1993:1432), the leaders of the USSR became frustrated as they saw the West thrive. Their ideology did not intend their citizens to be deprived, and in an attempt to turn things around, the Soviet leadership initiated reforms. They sold to the public huge chunks of state-owned businesses and allowed elections with more than one candidate for an office (unlike earlier elections). With private investment and ownership, profits changed from a curse word to a respectable goal.

This transition to capitalism has taken a bizarre twist. To seize the newly opened opportunities to gain wealth and power, some Russians have organized into criminal groups. Taking advantage of a breakdown of authority, and sometimes with the complicity of disgruntled military officers, they have stolen vast amounts of state property, amassed wealth, and intimidated businesspeople. To enforce cooperation, this Russian Mafia also assassinates heads of banks and other business leaders (Bernstein 1994; Sterling 1994; "Russian Banker . . ." 1995).

Global Stratification: Three Worlds of Development

As noted at the beginning of this chapter, just as the people within a nation are stratified by power, prestige, and property, so are the world's nations. Until recently, a simple model consisting of First, Second, and Third Worlds was used to depict global stratification. *First World* referred to the industrialized capitalist nations, *Second World* to the communist nations, and *Third World* to any nation that did not fit into the first two categories. After the Soviet Union broke up in 1989, these terms became outdated. In addition, although *first*, *second*, and *third* were not supposed to mean "best," "better," and "worst," they sounded like it. An alternative classification some now use—developed, developing, and undeveloped nations—has the same drawback. By calling ourselves "developed," it sounds as though we are mature and the "undeveloped" nations somehow retarded.

Consequently, I have chosen more neutral, descriptive terms: "Most Industrialized," "Industrializing," and "Least Industrialized." One can measure industrialization, with no judgment, even implied, about whether a nation's industrialization represents "development," ranks them "first"—or is even desirable in the first place. (The oil-rich nations are unique—not industrialized but having many characteristics of the industrialized world. Consequently, they are detailed separately on the world map on pages 172–173.)

The intention is to depict on a global level social stratification's three primary dimensions: property, power, and prestige. The Most Industrialized Nations have much greater property (wealth), power (they do get their way in international relations), and prestige—they are looked up to as world leaders. The two families sketched in the opening vignette illustrate the far-reaching effects that global stratification has on people's lives.

The Most Industrialized Nations

The Most Industrialized Nations are the United States and Canada in North America; Great Britain,

Table 7.2		
Three Worlds of Development		
Percentage of the World's		
	Land	*Population*
Most Industrialized Nations	31%	16%
Industrializing Nations	20	16
Least Industrialized Nations	49	68

Source: Computed from Kurian 1990, 1991, 1992.

France, Germany, Switzerland, and the other industrialized nations of western Europe; Japan in Asia; and Australia and New Zealand in the area of the world known as Oceania. Although there are variations in their economic systems, these nations are capitalistic. As Table 7.2 shows, although these nations have only 16 percent of the world's people, they have 32 percent of the earth's land. Their wealth is so enormous that even their poor live better and longer lives than do average citizens of the Least Industrialized Nations. The map on pages 172–173 shows the tremendous disparities in income among nations.

The Industrializing Nations

The Industrializing Nations include most of the nations of the former Soviet Union and its former satellites in eastern Europe. These nations account for 20 percent of the earth's land and 16 percent of its people.

The dividing points between the three "worlds" are soft, making it difficult to know how to classify some nations. This is especially the case with the Industrializing Nations. Exactly how much industrialization must a nation have to belong in this category? Although soft, these categories do pinpoint essential differences. Most inhabitants of the Industrializing Nations have much lower incomes and standards of living than people who live in the Most Industrialized Nations, and most are better off than members of the Least Industrialized Nations. For example, on such measures as access to electricity, indoor plumbing, automobiles, telephones, and even food, citizens of the Industrializing Nations rank lower than those

in the Most Industrialized Nations, but higher than those in the Least Industrialized Nations.

The Least Industrialized Nations

In the Least Industrialized Nations, most people are peasant farmers living on farms or in villages, and living standards are low. These nations account for 49 percent of the earth's land and 68 percent of the world's people.

It is difficult to imagine the poverty that characterizes the Least Industrialized Nations. Although wealthy nations have their pockets of poverty, *most people in these nations live on less than $1,000 a year,* in many cases considerably less. Most of them have no running water, indoor plumbing, central water supply, or access to trained physicians. Because modern medicine has cut infant mortality but not births, the population grows fastest in these nations, thus placing even greater burdens on their limited facilities, and causing them to fall farther behind each year (Sweezy and Magdoff 1992). The twin specters of poverty and death at an early age continuously stalk these countries. Some conditions of these poor countries are gruesome, as discussed in the following Thinking Critically section.

The extent and depth of poverty in the Least Industrialized Nations is stunning to someone who has grown up in a Most Industrialized Nation. This photo of a slum in Bombay, India, illustrates not only poverty but also the gender segregation of work. What do you think the chances are that these women will escape from poverty? How do their chances compare with those of Americans in poverty or with poor people living in other industrialized nations? Why the difference?

▼▲▼▲▼▲▼▲▼▲▼▲▼▲▼▲▼

Thinking Critically about Social Controversy

Open Season: Children as Prey

WHAT IS CHILDHOOD like in the poor nations? The answer depends primarily on who your parents are. If you are the son or daughter of rich parents, childhood can be extremely pleasant—a world of luxuries and even servants. If you are born into poverty, but living in a rural area where there is plenty to eat, life can still be good—although there likely will be no books, no television, and little education. If you live in a slum, however, life can be horrible—worse even than in the slums of the wealthy nations. Let's take a glance at what is happening to children in the slums of Brazil.

Not having enough food, you can take for granted —as well as broken homes, alcoholism, drug abuse, and a high crime rate. From your knowledge of slums in the Most Industrialized Nations, you would expect these things. What you may not expect, however, are the brutal conditions in which Brazilian slum (*favela*) children live.

Sociologist Martha Huggins (1993) reports that poverty is so deep that children and adults swarm over garbage dumps to try to find enough decaying food to keep them alive. And you might be surprised to discover that in Brazil the owners of these dumps hire armed guards to keep the poor out—so they can sell the garbage for pig food. And you might be shocked to learn that poor children are systematically killed. Each year, the Brazilian police and death squads murder about 2,000 children. Some associations of shop own-

ers even put hit men on retainer and auction victims off to the lowest bidder! The going rate is half a month's salary—figured at the low Brazilian minimum wage.

Life *is* cheap in the poor nations—but death squads for children? To understand this situation, we must first note that Brazil has a long history of violence, an extremely high rate of poverty, only a tiny middle class, and is controlled by a small group of families who, under a veneer of democracy, make the country's major decisions. Hordes of homeless children, with no schools or jobs, roam the streets. To survive, they wash windshields, shine shoes, beg, and steal. These children, part of the "dangerous classes," as they are known, threaten the status quo.

The "respectable" classes see these children as nothing but trouble. They hurt business, for customers feel intimidated when they see a group of begging children clustered in front of stores. Some shoplift; others dare to sell items in competition with the stores. With no social institutions to care for these children, one solution is to kill them. As Huggins notes, murder sends a clear message—especially if it is accompanied by ritual torture—pulling out the eyes, ripping open the chest, cutting off the genitals, raping the girls, and burning the victim's body.

Not all life is bad in the poor nations, but this is about as bad as it gets.

For Your Consideration

Do you think there is anything the Most Industrialized Nations can do about this situation? Or is it any of their business? Is it, though unfortunate, just an "internal" affair that is up to the Brazilians to handle as they wish?

To help grasp how severe poverty can be in the Least Industrialized Nations, study this photo by Sebastião Salgado, which shows garbage pickers in Fortaleza, Brazil. The survival of these children and adults depends on plucking bits and pieces from the city's garbage dump. Note that they must even fight with vultures for scraps of spoiled food.

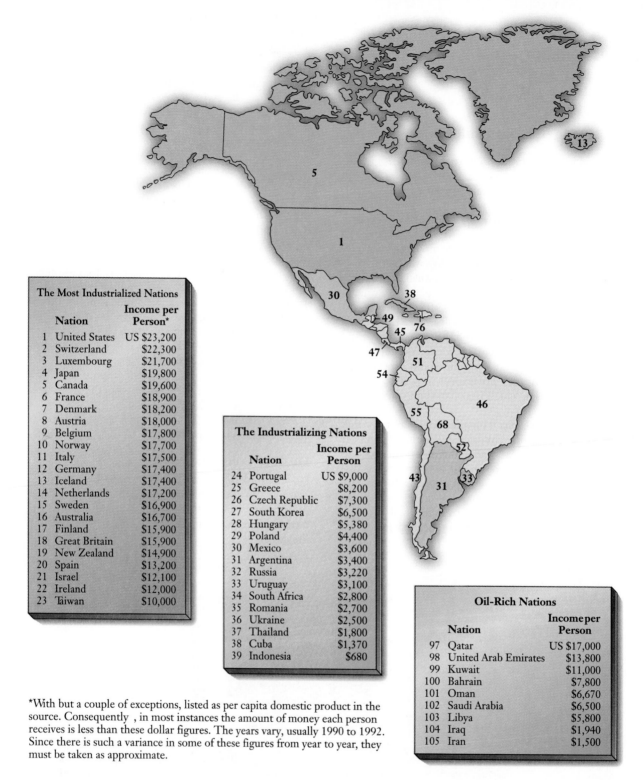

The Most Industrialized Nations

Nation	Income per Person*
1 United States	US $23,200
2 Switzerland	$22,300
3 Luxembourg	$21,700
4 Japan	$19,800
5 Canada	$19,600
6 France	$18,900
7 Denmark	$18,200
8 Austria	$18,000
9 Belgium	$17,800
10 Norway	$17,700
11 Italy	$17,500
12 Germany	$17,400
13 Iceland	$17,400
14 Netherlands	$17,200
15 Sweden	$16,900
16 Australia	$16,700
17 Finland	$15,900
18 Great Britain	$15,900
19 New Zealand	$14,900
20 Spain	$13,200
21 Israel	$12,100
22 Ireland	$12,000
23 Taiwan	$10,000

The Industrializing Nations

Nation	Income per Person
24 Portugal	US $9,000
25 Greece	$8,200
26 Czech Republic	$7,300
27 South Korea	$6,500
28 Hungary	$5,380
29 Poland	$4,400
30 Mexico	$3,600
31 Argentina	$3,400
32 Russia	$3,220
33 Uruguay	$3,100
34 South Africa	$2,800
35 Romania	$2,700
36 Ukraine	$2,500
37 Thailand	$1,800
38 Cuba	$1,370
39 Indonesia	$680

Oil-Rich Nations

Nation	Income per Person
97 Qatar	US $17,000
98 United Arab Emirates	$13,800
99 Kuwait	$11,000
100 Bahrain	$7,800
101 Oman	$6,670
102 Saudi Arabia	$6,500
103 Libya	$5,800
104 Iraq	$1,940
105 Iran	$1,500

*With but a couple of exceptions, listed as per capita domestic product in the source. Consequently , in most instances the amount of money each person receives is less than these dollar figures. The years vary, usually 1990 to 1992. Since there is such a variance in some of these figures from year to year, they must be taken as approximate.

Source: Famighetti 1994.

FIGURE 7.1

Comparative Income in the Three Worlds of Development

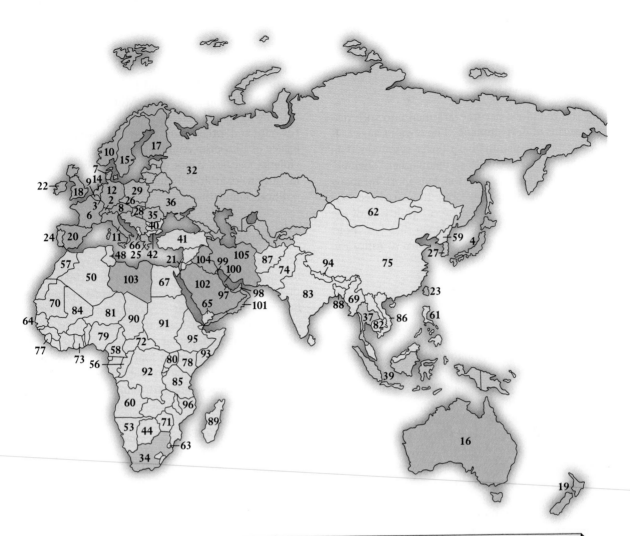

The Least Industrialized Nations

Nation	Income per Person	Nation	Income per Person	Nation	Income per Person
40 Bulgaria	US $3,800	59 North Korea	US $1,000	78 Kenya	US $320
41 Turkey	$3,670	60 Angola	$950	79 Nigeria	$300
42 Macedonia	$3,110	61 Philippines	$860	80 Uganda	$300
43 Chile	$2,550	62 Mongolia	$800	81 Niger	$290
44 Botswana	$2,450	63 Swaziland	$800	82 Cambodia	$280
45 Panama	$2,400	64 Senegal	$780	83 India	$270
46 Brazil	$2,350	65 Yemen	$775	84 Mali	$265
47 Costa Rica	$2,000	66 Albania	$760	85 Tanzania	$260
48 Tunisia	$1,650	67 Egypt	$730	86 Vietnam	$230
49 Belize	$1,635	68 Bolivia	$670	87 Afghanistan	$200
50 Algeria	$1,570	69 Myanmar (Burma)	$660	88 Bangladesh	$200
51 Colombia	$1,500	70 Mauritania	$555	89 Madagascar	$200
52 Paraguay	$1,500	71 Zimbabwe	$545	90 Chad	$190
53 Namibia	$1,300	72 Central African Republic	$440	91 Sudan	$184
54 Ecuador	$1,100	73 Ghana	$410	92 Zaire	$180
55 Peru	$1,100	74 Pakistan	$410	93 Somalia	$170
56 Congo	$1,070	75 China	$360	94 Nepal	$165
57 Morocco	$1,060	76 Haiti	$340	95 Ethiopia	$130
58 Cameroon	$1,010	77 Sierra Leone	$330	96 Mozambique	$115

FIGURE 7.1 (*Continued*)

What Caused Global Stratification?

How did the globe become stratified into such distinct worlds of development? The obvious answer is that the poorer nations have fewer resources than the richer nations. As with so many other "obvious" answers, however, this one, too, falls short, for many of the Industrializing and Least Industrialized Nations are rich in natural resources, while one of the Most Industrialized Nations, Japan, has few. Four competing theories explain how global stratification came about.

Colonialism

The first theory focuses on how European powers exploited weaker nations. The nations that industrialized earliest got the jump on the rest of the world. Beginning in Great Britain about 1750, industrialization spread throughout western Europe. Backed by the more powerful armaments developed by their new technology, the industrialized nations found weaker nations easy prey (Harrison 1993). The result was **colonialism;** that is, these more powerful nations made colonies out of weaker nations. After invading and subduing them, they left a controlling force to exploit their labor and natural resources. At one point, there was even a free-for-all among the industrialized European nations as they frantically rushed to divide up an entire continent. As Africa was sliced into pieces, even tiny Belgium got into the act and acquired the Congo, seventy-five times larger than itself.

Whereas the more powerful European nations would plant their national flags in a colony and send their representatives to directly run the government, the United States usually chose to plant corporate flags in a colony and let these corporations dominate the territory's government. Central and South America are prime examples of such "economic imperialism" on the part of the United States. No matter what the form, and whether it was benevolent or harsh, the purpose was the same—to exploit the nation's people and resources for the benefit of the "mother" country.

Western imperialism and colonialism, then, shaped the Least Industrialized Nations (Martin 1994). In some instances, the Most Industrialized Nations were so powerful that to divide their spoils, they drew lines across a map, creating new states without regard for tribal or cultural considerations (Kennedy 1993). Britain and France did just this in North Africa and parts of the Middle East, which is why the national boundaries of Libya, Saudi Arabia, Kuwait, and other nations are so straight. This legacy of European conquests still erupts into tribal violence because tribes with no history of national identity were arbitrarily incorporated into the same political boundaries.

World System Theory

To explain how global stratification developed, Immanuel Wallerstein (1974, 1979, 1984, 1990) noted that since the sixteenth century a **world system** has been developing. That is, economic and political connections expanded, and they now tie most of the world's countries together.

Wallerstein identified four groups of interconnected nations. The first are the *core nations* in which capitalism first developed (Britain, France, Holland, and later Germany). These nations grew rich and powerful. The second are the nations around the Mediterranean, called the *semiperiphery*. Becoming dependent on trade with the core nations, their economies stagnated. The third group, the *periphery*, or fringe, consists of the eastern European countries. Primarily limited to selling cash crops to the core nations, their economies developed even less. The fourth group, which Wallerstein calls the *external area*, includes most of Africa and Asia. These nations were left out of the development of capitalism and had few if any economic connections with the core nations.

Capitalism's relentless expansion has given birth to a **capitalist world economy** dominated by the Most Industrialized Nations. This economy is so all-encompassing that today even the nations in the external area are being drawn into its commercial web.

Globalization The extensive interdependence among the nations of the world ushered in by the expansion of capitalism is called **globalization** (Robertson 1992). Although globalization has been under way for the past several hundred years, today's new forms of communication and transportation have greatly speeded it up (Kennedy 1993). The interconnections are so extensive that events in remote parts of the world now affect us all—sometimes immediately, as when a revolution interrupts the flow of raw materials, or, perish the thought, if in

Russia's unstable political climate terrorists manage to seize an arsenal of earth-destroying nuclear missiles. At other times the effects arrive like a slow ripple, as when a government's policies impede its ability to compete in world markets. All of today's societies, then, no matter where they are located, are part of a global social system.

Dependency Theory

The third theory is sometimes difficult to distinguish from world system theory. **Dependency theory** attributes the lack of economic development in the Least Industrialized Nations to the dominance of the world economy by the Most Industrialized Nations (Cardoso 1972; Furtado 1984). According to this theory, the first nations to industrialize turned other nations into their plantations and mines, planting or extracting whatever they needed to meet their growing appetite for commodities and exotic foods. As a result, many of the Least Industrialized Nations began to specialize in a single cash crop. Brazil became the primary source for coffee; Nicaragua and other Central American countries specialized in bananas (hence the term *banana republic*); Chile became the primary source of tin; and the Belgian Congo (Zaire) was turned into a gigantic rubber plantation. The Mideast nations became the Most Industrialized Nations' supplier of oil. By becoming dependent on the Most Industrialized Nations, these other countries did not develop independent economies of their own.

Culture of Poverty

An entirely different explanation of global stratification was proposed by economist John Kenneth Galbraith (1979), who claimed that it was the Least Industrialized Nations' own culture that held them back. Building on the ideas of anthropologist Oscar Lewis (1966a, 1966b), Galbraith argued that some nations are crippled by a **culture of poverty,** a way of life that perpetuates poverty from one generation to the next. He explained it in this way: Most of the world's poor live in rural areas, where they barely eke out a living from the land. Their marginal life offers little room for error or risk, so they tend to stick closely to tried-and-true, traditional ways. Experimenting with new farming or manufacturing techniques is threatening, for if these fail they could

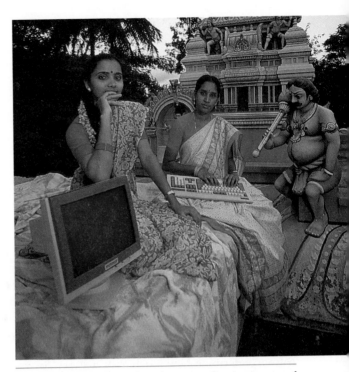

The world's people always have been part of an interconnected system of water and air, and, ultimately, of a food chain. Now they also are interconnected by a global system of telecommunications. These women in Bangalore, India, are computer programmers.

lead to hunger or death. Their religion also reinforces traditionalism, for it teaches fatalism, the acceptance of their lot in life as God's will.

Evaluating the Theories

Most sociologists find colonialism, world systems, and dependency theory preferable to an explanation based on a culture of poverty, for this theory places blame on the victim, the poor nations themselves. It points to characteristics of the poor nations, rather than to international arrangements that benefit the Most Industrialized Nations at the expense of the poor nations. But even taken together, these theories yield only part of the picture, as becomes evident from the example of Japan. None of these theories would lead anyone to expect that after World War II, Japan—with a religion that stressed fatalism, with two major cities destroyed by atomic bombs, and stripped of its colonies—would become an economic powerhouse able to turn the Western world on its head.

Each theory, then, yields but a partial explanation, and the grand theorist who will put the many pieces of this puzzle together has yet to appear.

Maintaining Global Stratification

Why are the same countries rich year after year, while some nations remain poor? Let us look at two explanations of how global stratification is maintained.

Neocolonialism

Sociologist Michael Harrington (1977) argued that colonialism fell out of style and was replaced by **neocolonialism.** By this term he meant that instead of soldiers and colonists the Most Industrialized Nations usually use the international markets to control the Least Industrialized Nations. These powerful nations determine how much they will pay for tin from Bolivia, copper from Peru, coffee from Brazil, and so forth. They also move hazardous industries into the Least Industrialized Nations.

As many of us to our sorrow learn, to owe a large debt and to fall behind on payments is to be dangled at the end of a string pulled by the one who holds the debt. So it is with neocolonialism. Selling weapons and other manufactured goods to the Least Industrialized Nations on credit turns those countries into eternal debtors. The debt continuously bloats with interest, impeding the ability of these countries to accumulate capital to develop their own industries. As debtors, they also are vulnerable to trading terms dictated by the neocolonialists (Tordoff 1992; Carrington 1993).

Thus although the Least Industrialized Nations have their own governments—whether elected or dictatorships—they remain almost as dependent on the Most Industrialized Nations as they were when those nations occupied them. For an example of neocolonialism today, see the Global Glimpse box on sex tourism.

Multinational Corporations

Multinational corporations, companies that operate across many national boundaries, also help to maintain the dominance of the Most Industrialized Nations. In some cases, multinational corporations exploit the Least Industrialized Nations directly. A prime example is the United Fruit Company, which for decades controlled national and local politics in Central America, running these nations as fiefdoms for the company's own profit while the U.S. Marines waited in the wings in case the company's interests needed to be backed up. Most commonly, however, multinational corporations help to maintain international stratification simply by doing business. A single multinational may do mining in several countries, do manufacturing in many others, and run transportation and marketing networks around the globe. No matter where the profits are made, or where they are reinvested, the primary beneficiaries are the Most Industrialized Nations, especially the one in which the multinational corporation has its world headquarters. As Michael Harrington (1977) stressed, the real profits are made in processing the products and in controlling their distribution—and these profits are withheld from the Least Industrialized Nations.

Multinational corporations try to work closely with the elite of the Least Industrialized Nations (Lipton 1979; Waldman 1995). This elite, which lives a sophisticated upper-class life in the major cities of its home country, sends its children to Oxford, the Sorbonne, or Harvard to be educated. The multinational corporations funnel investments to this small circle of power, whose members favor projects such as building laboratories and computer centers in the capital city, projects that do not help the vast majority of their people, who live in poor, remote villages where they eke out a meager living on small plots of land.

The end result is an informal partnership between multinational corporations and the elite of the Least Industrialized Nations. The elite benefits by receiving subsidies (or payoffs), and the corporations through access to the country's raw materials, labor, and market. Both benefit through political stability, necessary to keep the partnership alive.

This, however, is not the full story. As an unintentional by-product of their worldwide search for cheap resources and labor, multinational corporations also change international stratification. By moving manufacturing from the Most Industrialized Nations to the Least Industrialized Nations, they not only exploit cheap labor but in some cases also bring prosperity to those nations. Although workers

A Global Glimpse

Sex Tourism and the Patriotic Prostitute

"Holidays with the most beautiful women of the world. An exclusive tour by Life Travel. . . . You fly to Bangkok and then go to Pattaya. . . . Slim, sunburnt and sweet, they . . . are masters in the art of making love by nature, an art we European people do not know. . . . In Pattaya costs of living and loving are low." (from a Swiss pamphlet)

A new wrinkle in the history of prostitution is the "patriotic prostitute." These are young women who are encouraged by their governments to prostitute themselves to help the country's economy. Patriotic prostitution is one of the seediest aspects of global stratification. Some poor nations encourage prostitution to accumulate national income for industrial development and help pay their national debts. A consequence is that perhaps 10 percent of all Thai women between the ages of 15 and 30 have become prostitutes. Bangkok alone reports 100,000 prostitutes—plus 200,000 "masseuses."

Government officials encourage prostitution as a service to their country. In South Korea, prosti-

tutes are issued identification cards that serve as hotel passes. In orientation sessions, they are told, "Your carnal conversations [sic] with for-

eign tourists do not prostitute either yourself or the nation, but express your heroic patriotism." With such an official blessing, "sex tourism" has become big business. Travel agencies in Germany

openly advertise "trips to Thailand with erotic pleasures included in the price." Japan Air Lines hands out brochures that advertise the "charming attractions" of Kisaeng girls, advising men to fly JAL for a "night spent with a consummate Kisaeng girl dressed in a gorgeous Korean blouse and skirt."

What the enticing advertising fails to mention is the misery underlying this prostitution. Many of the prostitutes are held in bondage. Some are forced into prostitution to pay family debts. Some are kept under lock and key to keep them from escaping. The advertisements also fail to mention the incidence of AIDS. Somewhere between 25 percent and 50 percent of Nairobi's 10,000 prostitutes appear to be infected.

Women's groups protest this international sex trade, deploring its exploitation of the world's most impoverished and underprivileged women.

Sources: Based on Gay 1985; Cohen 1986; Shaw 1987; O'Malley 1988; Srisang 1989; Hornblower 1993.

in the Least Industrialized Nations are paid a pittance, it is more than they can earn elsewhere. With new factories come opportunities to develop new skills and a capital base. This does not occur in all

nations, but the Pacific Rim nations, nicknamed the "Asian tigers," are a remarkable case in point. They have now developed such a strong capital base that they have begun to rival the older capitalist nations.

Technology and the Maintenance of Global Domination

The race between the Most and Least Industrialized Nations to develop and apply the new information technologies is like a marathon runner competing with a one-legged man. Can the outcome be in doubt? The vast profits piled up by the multinational corporations allow the Most Industrialized Nations to invest huge sums in the latest technologies. Gillette, for example, is spending $100 million simply to adjust its output "on an hourly basis" (Zachary 1995). While these millions come from just one U.S. company, many Least Industrialized Nations would love to have $100 million to invest in their entire economy, much less to fine-tune the production of razor blades. In short, in the quest to maintain global domination, the new technologies pile up even more advantages for the Most Industrialized Nations.

▲ A Concluding Note

Let's go back to the two families in our opening vignette. Remember that these families represent distinct worlds of development, that is, global stratification. Their life chances—from access to material possessions to the opportunity for education and even the likely age at which they will die—are profoundly affected by the global stratification that we have reviewed in this chapter. This division of the globe into interconnected units of nations with more or less wealth and more or less power and prestige, then, is much more than a matter of mere theoretical interest. In fact, it is *your* life we are talking about.

Summary and Review

What Is Social Stratification?

The term **social stratification** refers to a hierarchy of relative privilege based on power, property, and prestige. Every society stratifies its members. P. 158.

Systems of Social Stratification

What are the three major systems of social stratification?

The major systems of **social stratification** are slavery, caste, and class. The essential characteristic of **slavery** is that some people own other people. Initially, slavery was based not on race but on debt, punishment, or defeat in battle. Slavery could be temporary or permanent, and was not necessarily passed on to one's children. In North America slaves had no legal rights, and the system was gradually buttressed by a racist ideology. In a **caste system,** status is determined by birth and is lifelong. People marry within their own group and develop rules about ritual pollution. A **class system** is much more open than these other systems, for it is based primarily on money or material possessions. Industrialization encourages the formation of class systems. Gender discrimination cuts across all forms of social stratification. Pp. 158–162.

What determines social class?

Karl Marx argued that a single factor determines **social class:** If you own **the means of production,** you belong to the **bourgeoisie;** if you do not, you are one of the **proletariat.** Max Weber argued that three elements determine social class: property, prestige, and power. Pp. 162–164.

Why is social stratification universal?

To explain why stratification is universal, functionalists Kingsley Davis and Wilbert Moore argued that to attract the most capable people to fill its important positions, society must offer them higher rewards. Melvin Tumin criticized this view, arguing that if it were correct, U.S. society would be a **meritocracy,** with all positions awarded on the basis of merit. Gaetano Mosca argued that stratification is inevitable because every society must have leadership, which by definition means inequality. Conflict theorists argue that stratification is due to resources being limited, and groups struggling against one another for them. Gerhard Lenski suggested a synthesis between the functionalist and conflict perspectives. Pp. 164–166.

Maintaining National Stratification

How do elites maintain stratification?

To maintain social stratification within a nation, the ruling class uses an ideology that justifies current arrangements. It also controls information, and, when all else fails, depends on brute force. The social networks of the rich and poor also perpetuate social inequality. Pp. 166–168.

Comparative Social Stratification

What are some key characteristics of stratification systems in other nations?

The most striking features of the British class system are differences in speech and in educational patterns. In Britain, accent nearly always betrays class standing, and virtually all of the elite attend "public" schools (the equivalent of our private schools). In what is now the former Soviet Union, communism was supposed to abolish class distinctions. Instead, it merely ushered in a different set of classes. Pp. 168–169.

Global Stratification: Three Worlds of Development

How are nations stratified?

The model presented here divides the world's nations into three groups: the Most Industrialized, the Indus-

trializing, and the Least Industrialized. This layering represents relative property, power, and prestige. Pp. 169–173.

What Caused Global Stratification?

Why are some nations rich and others poor?

The main theories that seek to account for global stratification are **colonialism, world system theory, dependency theory,** and the **culture of poverty.** Pp. 174–176.

Maintaining Global Stratification

How is global stratification maintained?

There are two basic explanations for why nations remain stratified. **Neocolonialism** is the ongoing dominance of the Least Industrialized Nations by the Most Industrialized Nations. The second explanation points to the influence of **multinational corporations.** The new technology gives further advantage to the Most Industrialized Nations. Pp. 176–178.

Where can I read more on this topic?

Suggested readings for this chapter are listed on page 438.

Glossary

bourgeoisie Karl Marx's term for capitalists, those who own the means of production (p. 163)

capitalist world economy the dominance of capitalism in the world, along with an interdependence of the world's nations that capitalism has created (p. 174)

caste system a form of social stratification in which one's status is determined by birth and is lifelong (p. 161)

class consciousness Karl Marx's term for awareness of a common identity based on one's position in the means of production (p. 163)

class system a form of social stratification based primarily on the possession of money or material possessions (p. 162)

colonialism the process by which one nation takes over another nation, usually for the purpose of exploiting its labor and natural resources (p. 174)

culture of poverty the values and behaviors of the poor that are assumed to make them fundamentally different from other people (p. 175)

dependency theory the view that the Least Industrialized Nations have been unable to develop their economies because they grew dependent on the Most Industrialized Nations (p. 175)

divine right of kings the idea that the king's authority comes directly from God (p. 167)

endogamy the practice of marrying within one's own group (p. 161)

false consciousness Karl Marx's term to refer to workers identifying with the interests of capitalists (p. 164)

globalization the extensive interconnections among nations due to the expansion of capitalism (p. 174)

ideology beliefs about the way things ought to be that justify social arrangements (p. 160)

means of production the tools, factories, land, and investment capital used to produce wealth (p. 163)

meritocracy a form of social stratification in which all positions are awarded on the basis of merit (p. 165)

multinational corporations companies that operate across many national boundaries (p. 176)

neocolonialism the economic and political dominance of the Least Industrialized Nations by the Most Industrialized Nations (p. 176)

proletariat Karl Marx's term for the people who work for those who own the means of production (p. 163)

slavery a form of social stratification in which some people own other people (p. 159)

social class a large number of people with similar amounts of income and education who work at jobs that are roughly comparable in prestige (p. 163)

social mobility movement up or down the social class ladder (p. 162)

social stratification the division of people into layers according to their relative power, property, and prestige; applies to both a society and nations (p. 158)

world system economic and political connections that tie the world's countries together (p. 174)

Sociology and the Internet

All URLs listed are current as of the printing of this book. URLs are often changed. Please check our Web-site http://www.abacon.com/henslin for updates.

1. Social Stratification in Global Perspective

Are the nations of the world stratified? If we classify countries as Most Industrialized, Industrializing, and Least Industrialized, we should be able to find variables that indicate levels of stratification. In this project you will be comparing an Industrializing Nation (Indonesia) with a Most Industrialized Nation (the U.S.). In order to do this you will be using two sources, the Internet and the library.

First go to the WEB site http://www.bps.go.id/soc wel/swtables.html where you will find a list of social welfare indicators. Either click on each one or just page down to look at the tables. (If you can, it would be a good idea to print the entire page.) Now go to the library and get the latest *Statistical Abstract of the U.S.* Find as many comparisons with Indonesia as you can. Look in the index at such topics as immunization, education, crime, etc. You should find enough information to make rough comparisons of several variables.

After you have completed your research, write a brief report of analysis and interpretation: What differences between the two nations did you find? Are any of these differences surprising? Why? What social forces do you think contribute to these differences between the two countries?

2. Poverty and Race/Ethnicity

To measure poverty in the United States, go to the 1990 Census Lookup page (http://www.census.gov/cdrom/ lookup/). Select the data base "STF#c—Part 1." At the Retrieval Area page, click on the Submit bar. At the Data Retrieval Option page, click on the Submit bar. At the page headed "Select the tables you wish to retrieve," page down to "P19—Poverty Status in 1989 by race and age," and click on the circle in front of the entry. Then go to the top of the page and click on the Submit bar. You should be presented with a table showing poverty status of five racial categories. Depending on your Web browser, you either can save the table or print it. (Netscape will allow both.) Next compute the percentages of those in poverty for each racial category. (Your instructor may ask you to do this for age groups as well.) Total those in "Income in 1989 above poverty level: White." (Use the most recent year available at the time you do this exercise.) Do the same for those in "Income in 1989 below poverty level: White." Add the two figures and divide the sum found in "Income in 1989 below poverty level: White" by the result. This is the percentage of white people whose income was below the poverty level in 1989. Repeat the process for the other four racial categories. After you have computed the percentages, construct a table of the results. (For help, refer to Table 1.2 on page 23, "How to Read a Table.") Then, write a short paper in which you use materials from this chapter to explain the data in your table. (Be sure to include your table in the paper.)

Tsing-Fang Chen, City Gleaners

C H A P T E R

8

Social Class in the United States

AH, NEW ORLEANS, THAT FABLED CITY on the Gulf. Images from its rich past floated through my head—pirates, wealth, intrigue. So did memories from a pleasant vacation—the exotic French Quarter with odors of Creole food and sounds of earthy jazz drifting through the air.

The shelter for the homeless, however, forced me back to an unwelcome reality. The shelter was the same as those I had visited in the North—as well as the West and the East—only dirtier. The dirt, in fact, was the worst that I encountered during my research, and this was the only shelter to insist on payment to sleep in one of its filthy beds. The men looked the same—disheveled and haggard, wearing that unmistakable expression of despair—just like the homeless anywhere in the country. Except for the accent, you wouldn't know where you were. Poverty wears the same tired face, I realized. The accent may differ, but the look remains the same.

The next morning, just a block or so from the shelter, I felt indignation growing within me. I had grown used to the sights of abject poverty. I had come to expect what I saw in the shelters and on the streets. Those no longer held surprises. But this was startling.

The almost life-sized posters mounted on the transparent plastic shelter that covered the bus stop seemed to glare at me. The fashionably thin men and women proudly strutting elegant suits, dresses, jewelry, and furs were obscenely out of joint with the despair I had just seen.

A wave of disgust swept over me as I stared at the display. "Something is cockeyed in this society," I thought, my mind refusing to stop juxtaposing the suffering I had witnessed in the shelter with these ads. I felt nauseated—and surprised at my urge to deface the sketches and photos of these people strutting their finery.

Occasionally the facts of social class hit home with brutal force. This was one of those moments. The disjunction that I felt in New Orleans was triggered by the ads, but it was not the first time that I had experienced this sensation. Whenever my research abruptly transported me from the world of the homeless to one of another social class, I felt unfamiliar feelings of disjointed unreality. Each social class has its own way of being, and because these fundamental orientations to the world contrast so sharply, the classes do not mix well.

What Is Social Class?

"There are the poor and the rich—and then there are you and I, neither poor nor rich." This is just about as far as most Americans' consciousness of social class goes. Let's try to flesh this out.

Our task is made somewhat difficult because sociologists have no clear-cut, single definition of social class. As noted in the last chapter, conflict sociologists (of the Marxist orientation) see only two social classes: those who own the means of production and those who do not. The problem with this view, say most sociologists, is that it lumps too many people together. Physicians and corporate executives with incomes of $300,000 a year are lumped together with hamburger flippers working at McDonald's for $10,000 a year.

Most sociologists agree with Weber that there are more components of social class than a person's relationship to the means of production. Consequently, most sociologists use the components Weber identified and define **social class** as a large group of people who rank closely to one another in wealth, power, and prestige. These three elements separate people into different lifestyles, give them different chances in life, and provide them with distinct ways of looking at the self and the world.

Let's look at how sociologists measure these three components of social class.

Wealth

The primary dimension of social class is wealth. **Wealth** consists of property and income. *Property* comes in many forms, such as buildings, land, animals, machinery, cars, stocks, bonds, businesses, and bank accounts. *Income* is money received as wages, rents, interest, royalties, or the proceeds from a business.

Distinction between Wealth and Income Wealth and income are sometimes confused with each other. They are not the same. Some people have much wealth and little income. For example, a farmer may own much land (a form of wealth), but with the high cost of fertilizers and machinery, a little bad weather can cause the income to disappear. Others have much income and little wealth. For example, an executive with $150,000 annual income may actually be debt ridden. Below the surface prosperity, he or she may be greatly overextended: unpaid bills for exotic vacations, country club membership, and the children's private schools, two sports cars just a payment away from being repossessed, and huge mortgage payments on the elite home in the exclusive suburb. Typically, however, wealth and income go together.

Distribution of Wealth Who owns the wealth in the United States? One answer, of course, is "everyone." Although this statement has some merit, it overlooks how the nation's wealth is divided among "everyone." Let's look how the two forms of wealth—property and income—are distributed among Americans.

Property Overall, Americans are worth a hefty sum, about $17 trillion (*Statistical Abstract* 1995: Table 749). Most of this wealth is in the form of real estate, corporate stocks, bonds, and business assets. As Figure 8.1 shows, this wealth is highly concentrated. The vast majority, 68 percent, is owned by only *10 percent* of the nation's families.

How concentrated is this wealth? The richest 36,000 Americans are worth $1 trillion—about 6 percent of all privately held wealth in the entire country (*Statistical Abstract* 1995:Tables 755, 759). Another way to grasp the extent of this vast inequality is to note that *the super-rich, the richest 1 percent of U.S. families, are worth more than the entire bottom 90 percent of Americans* (Beeghley 1996).

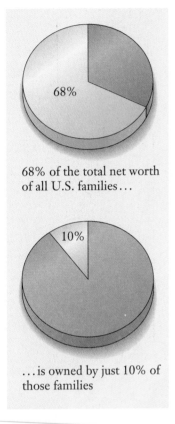

FIGURE 8.1

Distribution of Wealth of Americans

68% of the total net worth of all U.S. families...

...is owned by just 10% of those families

Source: Beeghley 1996.

Income How is income distributed in the United States? Economist Paul Samuelson (Samuelson and Nordhaus 1989:644) put it this way: "If we made an income pyramid out of a child's blocks, with each layer portraying $500 of income, the peak would be far higher than Mount Everest, but most people would be within a few feet of the ground."

Actually, if each block were 1½ inches tall, the typical American would be just *5 feet off the ground*, for the average per capita income in the United States is about $22,000 per year. See Figure 8.2. The typical family climbs a little higher, for most families have more than one worker, and together they average about $37,000 a year. Yet compared with the Mount Everest incomes of a few, the average family would find itself only 9 feet off the ground (*Statistical Abstract* 1995:Tables 713, 732).

The fact that some Americans live in the clouds above Mount Everest while most make it only 5 feet up the slope presents a striking image of income inequal-

FIGURE 8.2

Inequality of U.S. Income

Higher than Mount Everest 29,028 feet

(Some Americans)

If a 1½-inch child's block equals $500 of income, the average American is only 5 feet off the ground, the average family just 9 feet, while the income of some families propels them past the top of Mount Everest.

5 feet
Average American

9 feet
Average U.S. Family

ity in the United States. Another picture emerges if we divide the U.S. population into five equal groups and rank them from the highest to lowest income. As Figure 8.3 shows, the top 20 percent of the population acquires 44 percent of all income in the United States, while the bottom 20 percent of Americans receives less than 5 percent of the nation's income.

The most striking feature of Figure 8.3 is how consistent income inequality is. In spite of numerous antipoverty programs, *each fifth of the U.S. population receives the same proportion of the nation's income today as it did in 1945.* Some slight fluctuations have occurred over the years, such as a brief drop in the percentage going to the richest fifth of the population, but their proportion is now back to where it was 50 years ago. Also, some slight variations don't show up due to rounding. For example, in some years the bottom fifth received as low as 4.5 percent, in other years as high as 5.4 percent. These changes were so slight, however, that they did not change the poor's proportion by even 1 percent.

Apart from the very rich, whom we study later, the most affluent group in U.S. society consists of the chief executive officers (CEOs) of the nation's largest corporations. The *Wall Street Journal* ("The Boss's Pay," 1995), surveyed the 350 largest U.S. companies to determine what they paid their CEOs. Their median annual compensation, including salaries, bonuses, and stock options, came to $1,800,000. (Median means that half received more than this amount, and half less.) This figure does *not* include their income from investments—interest, dividends, rents, and capital gains.

Imagine how you could live with an income like this. And that is precisely the point. Beyond cold numbers lies a vibrant reality that profoundly affects people's lives. The difference in wealth between those at the top and the bottom of the U.S. class structure means vast differences in lifestyles. For example, a colleague of mine who was teaching at an exclusive eastern university piqued his students' curiosity when he lectured on poverty in Latin America. That weekend, one of his students borrowed his parents' corporate jet and pilot, and in Monday's class he and his friends reported on their personal observations on the problem. Other Americans, in contrast, must choose whether to spend the little they have at the laundromat or on milk for the baby. In short, divisions of wealth represent not "mere" numbers, but choices that make real differences in people's lives.

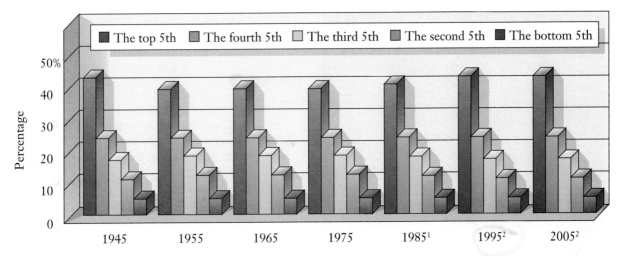

Note: The distribution of U.S. income—salaries, wages, and all other money received, except capital gains and government subsidies in the form of food stamps, health benefits, or subsidized housing. Because of rounding, totals for some years equal 101%.
[1]Because the 1985 data were not published, the average of the 1984 and 1986 figures is used.
[2]Author's estimate.

Sources: Statistical Abstract 1947, 1957, 1962, 1967, 1972, 1977, 1982, 1987, and 1995:Table 730.

FIGURE 8.3

The More Things Change, the More They Stay the Same: The Percentage of the Nation's Income Received by Each Fifth of U.S. Families since World War II

Power

Like many people, you may have said to yourself, "Sure, I can vote, but somehow the big decisions are always made in spite of what I might think. Certainly *I* don't make the decision to send soldiers to Vietnam, Grenada, Panama, Kuwait, Somalia, Haiti, or Bosnia. *I* don't decide to raise taxes. It isn't *I* who decides to change welfare benefits."

And then another part of you may say, "But *I* do it through my representatives in Congress." True enough—as far as it goes. The trouble is, it just doesn't go far enough. Such views of being a participant in the nation's "big" decisions are a playback of the ideology we learn at an early age—an ideology that Marx said is put forward by the elites to both legitimate and perpetuate their power. Sociologists Daniel Hellinger and Dennis Judd (1991) call this the "democratic façade" that conceals the real source of power in the United States.

Back in the 1950s, sociologist C. Wright Mills (1956) was criticized for insisting that **power**—the ability to carry out your will in spite of resistance—was concentrated in the hands of the few, for his

analysis contradicted the overpowering ideology of equality. As discussed in earlier chapters, Mills coined the term **power elite** to refer to those who make the big decisions in U.S. society.

Mills and others have stressed how wealth and power coalesce in a group of like-minded individuals. They share ideologies and values, belong to the same private clubs, vacation at the same exclusive resorts, and even hire the same bands for their daughters' debutante balls. These shared backgrounds and vested interests reinforce their view of the world and of their special place in it (Domhoff 1978, 1995). This elite wields extraordinary power in U.S. society. Although there are exceptions, *most* U.S. presidents have come from this group—millionaire white men from families with "old money" (Baltzell and Schneiderman 1988).

Sociologist William Domhoff (1990), continuing in the tradition of Mills, argues that this group is so powerful that no major decision of the U.S. government is made without its approval. He analyzed how this group works behind the scenes with elected officials to set both the nation's foreign and domestic policy—from establishing Social Security taxes to

Bill Gates, a founder of Microsoft Corporation, is the wealthiest person in the United States. His fortune of several billion dollars continues to increase as his company develops new products. He recently built a new home in Seattle, Washington, which cost about $25 million.

determining trade tariffs. Although Domhoff's conclusions are controversial—and alarming—they certainly follow logically from the principle that wealth brings power, and extreme wealth brings extreme power.

Prestige

Occupations and Prestige Table 8.1 illustrates how people rank occupations according to **prestige** (respect or regard). From this table, you can see how your parents' occupations, those of your neighbors, and the one that you are striving for all stack up. Because we are moving toward a global society, this table also shows how the rankings given by Americans compare with those of the residents of sixty other countries.

Why do people give some jobs more prestige than others? If you look at Table 8.1, you will notice that the jobs at the top share four elements:

1 They pay more.
2 They require more education.
3 They entail more abstract thought.
4 They offer greater autonomy (freedom, or self-direction).

If we turn this around, we can see that people give less prestige to jobs that are low paying, require less preparation or education, involve more physical

In the United States, a mere 0.5 percent of the population owns over a quarter of the nation's wealth. Very few minorities are numbered among this 0.5 percent. An outstanding exception is Oprah Winfrey, whose ultra successful career in entertainment, bringing her over $250 million a year, has made her one of the 400 richest Americans.

Table 8.1

Occupational Prestige: How the United States Compares with 60 Countries

Occupation	United States	Average of 60 Countries	Occupation	United States	Average of 60 Countries
Supreme Court justice	85	82	Undertaker	51	34
College president	82	86	Social worker	50	56
Physician	82	78	Electrician	49	44
Astronaut	80	80	Secretary	46	53
College professor	78	78	Real estate agent	44	49
Lawyer	75	73	Farmer	44	47
Dentist	74	70	Carpenter	43	37
Architect	71	72	Plumber	41	34
Psychologist	71	66	Mail carrier	40	33
Airline pilot	70	66	Jazz musician	37	38
Electrical engineer	69	65	Bricklayer	36	34
Civil engineer	68	70	Barber	36	30
Biologist	68	69	Truck driver	31	33
Clergy	67	60	Factory worker	29	29
Sociologist	65	67	Store sales clerk	27	34
Accountant	65	55	Bartender	25	23
Banker	63	67	Lives on public aid	25	16
High school teacher	63	64	Bill collector	24	27
Author	63	62	Cab driver	22	28
Registered nurse	62	54	Gas station attendant	22	25
Pharmacist	61	64	Janitor	22	21
Chiropractor	60	62	Waiter or waitress	20	23
Veterinarian	60	61	Bellhop	15	14
Classical musician	59	56	Garbage collector	13	13
Police officer	59	40	Street sweeper	11	13
Actor or actress	55	52	Shoe shiner	9	12
Athletic coach	53	50			
Journalist	52	55			
Professional athlete	51	48			

Sources: Treiman 1977, Appendices A and D; Nakao and Treas 1991.

labor, and are closely supervised. In short, the professions and white-collar jobs are ranked at the top of the list, blue-collar jobs at the bottom.

One of the more interesting aspects of these rankings is how consistent they are across countries and over time. For example, people in every country rank college professors higher than nurses, nurses higher than social workers, and social workers higher than janitors. Similarly, the occupations that were ranked high back in the 1960s still rank high in the 1990s—and likely will rank high in future decades.

Displaying Prestige To get a sense of payoff, people want others to acknowledge their prestige. In times past, some ruling elites even passed laws to signify their high status. In ancient Rome, only the emperor and his family were allowed to wear purple, while in France only the nobility could wear lace. In England, no one could sit while the king was on his throne. Some kings and queens required that subjects depart by walking backward—so that they never "turned their back" on the "royal presence."

Although we have much greater equality and no longer have consumption laws that specify who can and cannot wear particular clothing or colors, today's elites still manage to enforce their prestige. Western kings and queens expect curtsies and bows, while their Eastern counterparts expect their subjects to touch their faces to the ground. The U.S. president enters a room only after others are present (to show that *he* isn't the one waiting for *them*). If seated, the others rise when the president appears and remain standing until he is seated, or if he is going to speak without sitting first, until he signals (gives permission) for them to sit. Military officers surround themselves with elaborate rules about who must salute whom, while uniformed officers in the courtroom make certain that everyone stands when judges enter.

Most people are highly conscious of prestige, a fact that advertisers know well and exploit relentlessly. Consequently, some designers can charge more for clothing not because it is of better quality but simply because it displays their label. Similarly, people buy cars not only for transportation, but also for their prestige. (How does a BMW compare with a Geo—not for power, but for prestige?) People gladly spend many thousands of dollars more for a home with a "good address," that is, one in a prestigious neighborhood. For many, prestige is a primary factor in deciding which college to attend. Everyone knows how the prestige of a generic sheepskin from Regional State College compares with a degree from Harvard, Princeton, Yale, or Stanford.

Interestingly, status symbols vary with social class. Clearly, only the wealthy can afford certain items, such as yachts. But beyond affordability lies a class-based preference in status symbols. For example, Yuppies (young upwardly mobile professionals) are quick to flaunt labels and other material symbols to show that they have "arrived," while the rich, more secure in their status, often downplay such images. The wealthy see designer labels of the more "common" classes as cheap and showy. They, of course, flaunt their own status symbols, such as $30,000 Rolex watches.

Status Inconsistency

Ordinarily a person has a similar rank on all three dimensions of social class—wealth, power, and

Sociologists use income, education, and occupational prestige to measure social class. A mismatch of these components is referred to as status discrepancy *(or* status inconsistency*). What status inconsistency does Michael Jordan, shown here, experience?*

prestige. Such people are **status consistent.** The homeless men in the vignette are an example. Sometimes the match is not there, however, and someone has a mixture of high and low ranks, a condition called **status inconsistency.** This leads to some interesting situations.

Sociologist Gerhard Lenski (1954, 1966) pointed out that each of us tries to maximize our **status,** our social ranking. Thus individuals who rank high on one dimension of social class but lower on others expect people to judge them on the basis of their highest status. Others, however, concerned about maximizing their own position, may respond to them according to their lowest status.

A classic study of status inconsistency was done by sociologist Ray Gold (1952). He found that after apartment house janitors unionized, they made more money than some of the people whose garbage they carried out. Tenants became upset when they saw their janitors driving more expensive cars than they did, and some attempted to "put the janitor in his place" by making "snotty" remarks to him. On their part, the janitors took secret pride in knowing "dirty" secrets about the tenants, gleaned from their garbage.

Individuals with status inconsistency, then, are likely to confront one frustrating situation after another. They claim the higher status, but are handed the lower. The sociological significance of this condition, said Lenski, is that such people tend to be more politically radical. An example is college professors. Their prestige is very high, as we saw in Table 8.1, but their incomes are relatively low. Hardly anyone in U.S. society is more educated, and yet college professors don't even come close to the top of the income pyramid. In line with Lenski's prediction, the politics of most college professors are left of center. This hypothesis may also hold true *among* academic departments; that is, the higher a department's pay, the less radical are its politics. Teachers in departments of business and medicine, for example, are among the most highly paid in the university—and they also are the most politically conservative.

Sociological Models of Social Class

The question of how many social classes there are is a matter of debate. Sociologists have proposed vari-

ous models, but no model has gained universal support. There are two main models: one that builds on Marx, the other on Weber.

Updating Marx

Marx argued that there are just two classes—capitalists and workers—with membership based solely on a person's relationship to the means of production. Sociologists have criticized this view because these categories are too broad. For example, executives, managers, and supervisors are technically workers because they do not own the means of production. But what do they have in common with assembly-line workers? Similarly, the category of "capitalist" takes in too many types. For example, the decisions of someone who employs a thousand workers directly affect a thousand families. Compare this with a man I know in Godfrey, Illinois. Working on cars out of his own back yard, he gained a following, quit his regular job, and in a few years put up a building with five bays and an office. This mechanic is now a capitalist, for he employs five or six other mechanics and owns the tools and building (the "means of production"). But what does he have in common with a factory owner who controls the lives of one thousand workers? Not only is his work different, but so are his lifestyle and the way he looks at the world.

Sociologist Erik Wright (1985) resolved this problem by regarding some people as members of more than one class at the same time. They have what he called **contradictory class locations.** By this Wright means that people's position in the class structure can generate contradictory interests. For example, the automobile-mechanic-turned-business-owner may want his mechanics to have higher wages, since he, too, has experienced their working conditions. At the same time, his current interests—making profits and remaining competitive with other repair shops—lead him to resist pressures to raise wages.

Because of such contradictory class locations, Wright modified Marx's model. As summarized in Table 8.2, Wright identified four classes: (1) *capitalists,* business owners who employ many workers; (2) *petty bourgeoisie,* small business owners; (3) *managers,* who sell their own labor but also exercise authority over other employees; and (4) *workers,* who simply sell their labor to others. As you can see, this model allows finer divisions than the one Marx pro-

Table 8.2
Social Class and the Means of Production
Marx's Class Model *(based on the means of production)* 1. Capitalists (bourgeoisie) 2. Workers (proletariat)
Wright's Modification of *Marx's Class Model* *(to account for contradictory class locations)* 1. Capitalists 2. Petty bourgeoisie 3. Managers 4. Workers

posed, yet it maintains the primary distinction between employer and worker.

Updating Weber

Sociologists Dennis Gilbert and Joseph Kahl (1993) developed a six-class model to portray the class structure of the United States and other capitalist countries. Think of their model, illustrated in Figure 8.4, as a ladder. Our discussion will start with the highest rung and move downward. In line with Weber, on each lower rung you find less wealth, less power, and less prestige. Note that in this model education is also a primary criterion of class.

The Capitalist Class The super-rich, who occupy the top rung of the class ladder, consists of only about 1 percent of the population. As mentioned, this 1 percent is so wealthy that its members are worth more than the entire bottom 90 percent of the nation. Their power is so great that their decisions open or close jobs for millions of people. Through their ownership of newspapers and magazines, radio stations and television companies, together with their access to top politicians, this elite class even helps to shape the consciousness of the nation. Its members perpetuate themselves by passing on to their children their assets and influential social networks.

Old Money The capitalist class can be divided into "old" and "new" money (Aldrich 1989). The longer that wealth has been in a family, the more it adds to the family's prestige. Many people entering the capitalist class have found it necessary to cut moral corners, at least here and there. This "taint" to the money disappears with time, and the later generations of Kennedys, Rockefellers, Vanderbilts, Mellons, DuPonts, Chryslers, Fords, Morgans, Nashes, and so on are considered to have "clean" money sim-

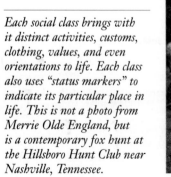

Each social class brings with it distinct activities, customs, clothing, values, and even orientations to life. Each class also uses "status markers" to indicate its particular place in life. This is not a photo from Merrie Olde England, but is a contemporary fox hunt at the Hillsboro Hunt Club near Nashville, Tennessee.

Need to know

Weath Power Prestige Education

Social Class	Education	Occupation	Income	Percentage of Population
Capitalist	Prestige university	Investors and heirs, a few executives	$500,000+	1%
Upper Middle	College or university, often with postgraduate study	Professionals and upper managers	$90,000+	14%
Lower Middle	At least high school; perhaps some college or apprenticeship	Semiprofessionals and lower managers, craftspeople, foremen	About $40,000	30%
Working Class	High school	Factory workers, clerical workers, retail sales, low-paid craftspeople	About $30,000	30%
Working Poor	Some high school	Laborers, service workers, low-paid salespeople	About $18,000	22%
Underclass	Some high school	Unemployed and part-time, on welfare	About $10,000	3%

Source: Based on Gilbert and Kahl 1993. Income estimates follow Duff 1995b.

FIGURE 8.4

The U.S. Social Class Ladder

ply by virtue of the passage of time. Able to be philanthropic as well as rich, they establish foundations and support charitable causes. Subsequent generations attend prestigious prep schools and universities, and male heirs are likely to enter law. These old-money capitalists wield vast power as they use extensive political connections to protect their huge economic empires (Persell et al. 1992; Domhoff 1990, 1995).

New Money Those at the lower end of the capitalist class also possess vast sums of money and power, but it is new, and therefore suspect. Although these people may have made fortunes in business, the stock market, inventions, entertainment, or sports, they have not attended the right schools and they lack the influential social networks that come with old money. Consequently, those with old money cannot depend on this newer group for adequate in-group loyalty. Their children, however, will ascend into the upper part of the capitalist class if they go to the right schools *and* marry old money.

The Upper Middle Class Of all the classes, the upper middle class is the one most shaped by education. Almost all members of this class have at least a bachelor's degree, and many have postgraduate degrees in business, management, law, or medicine. These people manage the corporations owned by the capitalist class or else operate their own business or profession. As Gilbert and Kahl (1982) say, these positions may not grant prestige equivalent to a title of nobility in the Germany of Max Weber, but they certainly represent the sign of having "made it" in contemporary America. . . . Their income is sufficient to purchase houses and cars and travel that become public symbols for all to see and for advertisers to portray with words and pictures that connote success, glamour, and high style.

Consequently, parents and teachers push children to prepare themselves for upper-middle-class jobs. About 14 percent of the population belong to this class.

The Lower Middle Class About 30 percent of the population belong to the lower middle class. Members of this class follow orders on the job given by those who have upper-middle-class credentials. Their technical and lower-level management positions bring them a good living—albeit one constantly threatened by taxes and inflation—and they enjoy a generally comfortable, mainstream lifestyle. They usually feel secure in their positions and anticipate being able to move up the social class ladder.

The distinctions between the lower middle class and the working class on the next lower rung are more blurred than those between other classes. In general, however, members of the lower middle class work at jobs that have slightly more prestige, and their incomes are generally higher.

The Working Class This class consists of relatively unskilled blue-collar and white-collar workers whose manual and clerical jobs are highly routinized and closely supervised. Most of these workers have a high school education, their incomes are lower than those of the lower middle class, and little prestige is attached to what they do. Their work is more insecure, and they are subject to layoffs during recessions. They feel vulnerable to larger forces such as the loss of jobs due to the North American Free Trade Agreement (NAFTA) and General Agreement on Trade and Tariffs (GATT). Their main hope is to support their families in a "simple but decent" manner. With only a high school diploma, the average member of the working class has little hope of climbing farther up the class ladder. Consequently, most concentrate on getting ahead by achieving seniority on the job rather than by changing their type of work. About 30 percent of the population belong to this class.

The Working Poor Members of this class, about 22 percent of the population, work at unskilled, low-paying, temporary and seasonal jobs, such as sharecropping, migrant farm work, house cleaning, and day labor. Although many members of this class have high school diplomas, they are likely to have received them simply for putting in time. Many are functionally illiterate, finding it difficult to read even

A husband and wife in their Virginia family estate and the migrant worker are both shown "at home." From the contrast evident in these photos, you can easily infer consequences of social class: from life chances to health, from family life to education. It also should be apparent why these people are not likely to see politics, religion, money, or much else in life in quite the same way.

the want ads. The working poor feel left out of politics and are not likely to vote (Gilbert and Kahl 1993). Most feel that no matter what party is elected to political office, their situation won't change.

With little education, low and undependable income, and low-prestige work, the working poor live from paycheck to paycheck—when there is a paycheck, that is. Constantly in debt, many depend on food stamps to supplement their meager incomes. In old age they rely on Social Security, since their jobs do not provide retirement benefits. Because they cannot save money or depend on steady work, many live with the daily fear of falling onto the lowest rung—of ending up "on the streets."

The Underclass On the lowest rung, and with next to no chance of climbing anywhere, is the **underclass** (Myrdal 1962; Wilson 1987; Bagguley and Mann 1992). Concentrated in the inner city, this group has little or no connection with the job market. Those who are employed, and some are, do menial, low-paying, temporary work. Welfare is their main support, and most members of other classes consider these people the "ne'er-do-wells" of society. About 3 percent of the population fall into this class.

Social Class in the Automobile Industry

The automobile industry illustrates the social class ladder. The Fords, for example, own and control a manufacturing and financial empire whose net worth is truly staggering. Their power matches their wealth, for through their multinational corporation their decisions affect plants, production, and employment in many countries. The family's vast accumulation of money, not unlike its accrued power, is now several generations old. Consequently, Ford children go to the "right" schools, know how to spend money in the "right" way, and can be trusted to make family and class interests paramount in life. They are without question at the top level of the *capitalist* class.

Next in line come top Ford executives. Although they may have an income of several hundred thousand dollars a year (and some, with stock options and bonuses, earn well over $1 million annually), most are new to wealth and power. Consequently, they would be classified at the lower end of the capitalist class.

A husband and wife who own a Ford agency are members of the *upper middle class*. Their income

clearly sets them apart from the majority of Americans, and their reputation in the community is enviable. More than likely they also exert greater-than-average influence in their community, but their capacity to wield power is limited.

A Ford salesperson, as well as people who work in the dealership office, belongs to the *lower middle class*. Although there are some exceptional salespeople, perhaps a few of whom make a lot of money selling prestigious, expensive cars to the capitalist class, salespeople at a run-of-the-mill local Ford agency are lower middle class. Compared with the owners of the agency, their income is less, their education is also likely to be less, and their work brings them less prestige.

Mechanics who repair customers' cars are members of the *working class*. If a mechanic is promoted to supervise the repair shop, that person has joined the lower middle class.

Those who "detail" used cars (making them appear newer by washing and polishing the car, painting the tires, spraying "new car scent" into the interior, and so on) belong to the *working poor*. Their income and education are low, the prestige accorded their work minimal. They are laid off when selling slows down.

Ordinarily, the *underclass* is not represented in the automobile industry. It is conceivable, however, that the agency might hire a member of the underclass to do a specific job such as raking the grass or cleaning up the used car lot. In general, however, personnel at the agency do not trust members of the underclass and do not want to associate with them—even for a few hours. They prefer to hire someone from the working poor for such jobs.

Below the Ladder: The Homeless

The homeless men described in the opening vignette of this chapter, and the women and children like them, are so far down the class structure that their position is even lower than that of the underclass. Technically, the homeless are members of the underclass, but their poverty is so severe and their condition in life so despairing that we can think of them as occupying an unofficial rung below the underclass.

These are the people whom most Americans wish would just go away. Their presence on our city streets bothers passersby from the more privileged social classes—which includes just about everyone. "What are those obnoxious, dirty, foul-smelling people doing here, cluttering up my city?" appears to be a common response. Some people respond with sympathy and a desire to do something. But what? Almost all of us just shrug our shoulders and look the other way, despairing of a solution and somewhat intimidated by the presence of the homeless.

The homeless are the "fallout" of industrialization, especially our developing postindustrial economy. In another era, they would have had plenty of work. They would have tended horses, worked on farms, dug ditches, shoveled coal, and run the factory looms. Some would have explored and settled the West. Others would have followed the lure of gold to California, Alaska, and Australia. Today, however, with no unsettled frontiers, factory jobs scarce, and even farms becoming technological marvels, we have little need for unskilled labor, and these people are left to wander aimlessly about the city streets.

Consequences of Social Class

Each social class can be thought of as a broad subculture with distinct approaches to life. Of the many ways that social class affects people's lives, we shall briefly review the new technology, family life, politics, religion, and health.

The New Technology

The new technology benefits some classes and hurts others. The higher one goes up the social class ladder, the more technology is a benefit. For the capitalist class, the new technology is a dream come true: global profits through global integration. No longer are national boundaries an obstacle. Rather, a product's components are produced in several countries, assembled in another, and the product marketed throughout the world. The new technology also benefits the upper middle class, for their education prepares them to take a leading role in managing this global system for the capitalist class, or for using the new technology to advance in their chosen professions.

Below these two classes, however, the new technology adds to the uncertainty of life, with the insecurity becoming greater the farther one moves down the ladder. As the new technology transforms the workplace, it eliminates jobs and outdates skills. People in lower management can transfer their skills from one job to another, although in shifting job

markets the times between periods of employment can be precarious. People in crafts are even less secure, for their training is more specific and the changing occupational world can reduce the need for their narrower, more specialized skills.

From this middle point in the ladder down, people are hit the hardest. The working class is ill prepared for the changes ushered in by the new technology, and they are haunted by the specter of unemployment. The low technical skills of the working poor make them even more vulnerable, for they have even less to offer in the new job market. As unskilled jobs dry up, more and more of the working poor are consigned to the industrial garbage bin. The underclass, of course, with no technical skills, is bypassed entirely.

The playing field is far from level. Some even fear that current trends in exporting U.S. jobs mean that U.S. workers are becoming an expendable luxury, destined to be replaced by low-paid, non-unionized—and more compliant—workers on other continents. In short, the new technology opens and closes opportunities for people largely by virtue of where they are located on the social class ladder.

Family Life

Social class plays an especially significant role in family life, affecting even our choice of marital partner and our chances of getting divorced.

Choice of Mate The capitalist class places strong emphasis on family tradition and even provides its children a sense of purpose or destiny in life (Baltzell 1979; Aldrich 1989). Children of this class learn that their choice of spouse affects not just themselves but the whole family unit, that their mate will have an impact on the "family line." Consequently, their field of "eligibles" is much narrower than it is for the children of any other social class. In effect, parents in this class play a greater role in their children's mate selection.

Divorce The more difficult life of the lower social classes, especially the many tensions and frustrations that come from insecure jobs and inadequate incomes, leads to high marital friction and a greater likelihood of both spouse and alcohol abuse. Consequently, the marriages of the poor are more likely to fail and their children to grow up in broken homes.

Politics

As has been stressed throughout this text, symbolic interactionists emphasize that people see events from their own corner in life. Political views are no exception to this principle, and the rich and the poor walk different political paths. The working class, which feels much more strongly than the classes above it that government should intervene in the economy to make citizens financially secure, is more likely to vote Democrat, those in the higher classes Republican. Although the working class is more liberal on *economic* issues (those that favor government spending), this class is more conservative on *social* issues (such as opposing abortion and the Equal Rights Amendment) (Lipset 1959; Houtman 1995). People toward the bottom of the class structure are also less likely to become politically active—to vote or to campaign for candidates (Gans 1991; Gilbert and Kahl 1993).

Religion

One area of social life that we might think would be unaffected by social class is religion. ("People are just religious, or they are not. What does class have to do with it?") As we shall see in Chapter 13, the classes tend to cluster in different denominations. Episcopalians, for example, are much more likely to recruit from the middle and upper classes, Baptists draw heavily from the lower classes, and Methodists are more middle class. Patterns of worship also follow class lines: those that attract the lower classes have more spontaneous worship services with louder music, while the middle and upper classes prefer more "subdued" worship.

Illness and Health Care

Social class also affects our health. As shown in Figure 8.5, the lower people's income, the more often they are sick. Even our chances of living and dying are related to social class. The principle is simple: the lower someone's class, the more likely that person is to die before the expected age. This principle holds true for all ages: infants born to the poor are more likely than other infants to die before their first birthday, while in old age—whether 70 or 90—a larger proportion of the poor die each year than do the wealthy. Part of the reason for these death rates is unequal access to medical care, a topic explored in the following Thinking Critically section.

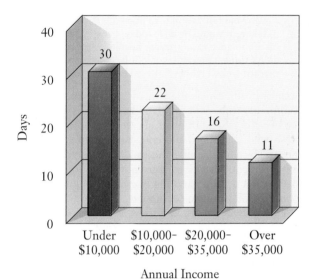

Note: Number of days people were so sick or injured that they cut down on their usual activities for more than half a day; includes days off work and school.

Source: Statistical Abstract 1995:Table 204.

FIGURE 8.5
Number of Days Sick

Thinking Critically about Social Controversy

Physical Illness and Inequality in Health Care

Terry Takewell (his real name) was a 21-year-old diabetic who lived in a small trailer park in Somerville, Tennessee. When Zettie Mae Hill, Takewell's neighbor, found the unemployed carpenter drenched with sweat from a fever, she called an ambulance. Takewell was rushed to nearby Methodist Hospital, where, it turned out, he had an outstanding bill of $9,400. A notice posted in the emergency room told staff members to alert supervisors if Takewell ever returned.

When the hospital administrator was informed of the admission, Takewell was already in a hospital bed. The administrator went to Takewell's room, helped him to his feet, and escorted him to the parking lot. There, neighbors found him under a tree and took him home.

Takewell died about twelve hours later.

Zettie Mae Hill is still torn up about it. She wonders if Takewell would be alive today if she had directed his ambulance to a different hospital. She said, "I didn't think a hospital would just let a person die like that for lack of money." (Based on Ansberry 1988)

Because health care in the United States is considered a commodity to be sold to the highest bidder, the result is a two-tier system of medical care—superior care for those who can afford the cost, and inferior care for those who cannot. Unlike the middle and upper classes, few poor people have a personal physician, and they are likely to spend hours waiting in crowded public health clinics. After waiting most of a day, some don't even get to see a doctor, but are told to come back the next day (Fialka 1993). Finally, when hospitalized, the poor are likely to find themselves in understaffed and underfunded public hospitals, where they are treated by rotating interns who do not know them and cannot follow up on their progress.

Why was Terry Takewell denied medical treatment and his life cut short? The fundamental reason is that in the United States health care is not the right of citizens, but a commodity for sale. As with potatoes, those with more money can buy the better quality, while, like Terry Takewell, the poor and uninsured can go without—or wait for handouts.

For Your Consideration

What do you think we can do to solve the problem of inequality in health care? Should medical care be a commodity to be sold to those who can afford it, or do citizens have some fundamental right that should guarantee high-quality health care to all?

It is easy to say that there is such a right, but this answer carries severe implications. For example, consider organ transplants. Should organs be assigned on the basis of age? If so, who should be first—the younger or the older? Or should they be given on the basis of the individual's potential to contribute to society? If so, who would decide people's "potential"? Or should all people needing transplants be put on a list and taken on a first-come, first-served basis? If so, would this include convicted murderers and rapists?

Mental health is also related to social class. From the 1930s until now, sociologists have found that the mental health of the lower classes is worse than that of the higher classes (Faris and Dunham 1939; Srole et al. 1978; Lundberg 1991; Miller 1994). Greater mental problems are part of a stress package that comes with poverty. Compared with middle- and upper-class Americans, the poor have less job security, lower wages, more unpaid bills, more divorce, more alcoholism, greater vulnerability to crime, more physical illnesses—all accompanied by the threat of eviction hanging over their heads. Such conditions certainly deal severe blows to people's emotional well-being.

People higher up the social class ladder experience stress in daily life, of course, but their stress is

In general, the time and activities of the rich are considered to be more valuable than those of the poor. One consequence is that the length of time that people wait is inversely related to social class. In other words, in most situations the poor wait longer than the rich. This principle is evident in "waiting rooms," such as this one in Los Angeles, California, where AFDC recipients fill out forms for the Department of Public Social Services.

generally less and their coping resources greater. Not only can they afford vacations, psychiatrists, and counselors, but their class position gives them greater control over their lives, a key to good mental health.

Social class is also a deciding factor in how the mentally ill are treated, a topic of the following Thinking Critically section.

▼▲▼▲▼▲▼▲▼▲▼▲▼▲▼▲▼

Thinking Critically about Social Controversy

Mental Illness and Inequality in Health Care

Standing among the police, I watched as the elderly, nude man, looking confused, struggled to put on his clothing. The man had ripped the wires out of the homeless shelter's main electrical box, and then led the police a merry chase as he had run from room to room.

I asked the officers where they were going to take the man, and they replied, "To Malcolm Bliss" (the state hospital). When I commented, "I guess he'll be in there for quite a while," they replied, "Probably for just a day or two. We picked him up last week—he was crawling under cars at a traffic light—and they let him out in two days."

The police then explained that a person must be a danger to others or to oneself to be admitted as a long-term patient. Visualizing this old man crawling under cars in traffic and the possibility of electrocution from ripping out electrical wires with bare hands, I marveled at the definitions of "danger" that the psychiatrists must be using. The two-tier system of medical care was readily visible, stripped of its coverings. Certainly a middle-class or rich person would receive different treatment, and would not, of course, be in this shelter in the first place.

Deinstitutionalization, the emptying of our mental hospitals, carried out in the 1960s, was intended to cut costs and integrate mental patients into the community. It backfired, however, for the community services to help these people were not set up. One consequence is that the poor—such as this confused nude man in the homeless shelter—find it difficult to get into mental hospitals. If they are admitted, they are sent to the dreaded state hospitals. In contrast, private hospitals serve the wealthy and those who have good insurance. The rich are also likely to be treated with "talk therapy" (various forms of psychotherapy), the poor with "medicinal straitjackets."

For Your Consideration

What do you think can be done to treat the poor mentally ill? Take into consideration that the United States has a huge national debt and the public does not want higher taxes.

Social Mobility

No aspect of life goes untouched by social class. Because life is so much more satisfying in the more privileged classes, people strive to climb the social class ladder. What affects their chances? Keep this question in mind as we examine social mobility.

Three Types of Social Mobility

There are three basic types of social mobility: intergenerational, structural, and exchange mobility. **Intergenerational mobility** is the change family members make in their social class from one generation to the next. Although children are initially assigned the social class of their parents, they can pass their parents. For example, if the child of a new-car salesperson goes to college and later becomes the manager of the dealership, that person has experienced **upward social mobility.** Conversely, if a child of the dealer's owners becomes an alcoholic, fails to get through college, and ends up selling cars, he or she experiences **downward social mobility.**

The second type is **structural mobility,** changes in society, largely due to changing technology, that cause huge numbers of people to move up or down the class ladder. In the preceding examples, the individual's change in social class was due to his or her own behavior—hard work, sacrifice, and ambition on the one hand, versus indolence and alcohol abuse on the other. Although some social mobility is due to such individual factors, sociologists consider structural mobility to be the crucial factor.

To better understand structural mobility, think of how opportunities opened when computers were invented. New types of jobs appeared overnight. Huge numbers of people took workshops and crash courses, switching from blue-collar to white-collar work. Although individual effort certainly was involved, the underlying cause was a change in the *structure* of work. Or consider the other side, the closing of opportunities in a depression, when millions of people are forced into downward mobility.

The term structural mobility *refers to changes in society that push large numbers of people either up or down the social class ladder. A remarkable example was the stock market crash of 1929, when hundreds of thousands of people suddenly lost immense amounts of wealth. People who once "had it made" found themselves standing on street corners selling apples, or, as depicted here, selling their possessions at fire-sale prices.*

In this instance, too, their changed status is due much less to individual behavior than to structural changes in the society that close opportunities.

The third type, **exchange mobility,** occurs when large numbers of people move up and down the social class ladder, but on balance, the proportions of the social classes remain about the same. Suppose that over a certain period of time a million or so working-class people are trained in computers, and they move up the class ladder. Suppose also that there is a vast surge in imports and about a million skilled workers have to take lower-status jobs. Although millions of people change their social class, there is in effect an *exchange* among large numbers of people. The net result more or less balances out, and the class system remains basically untouched.

Social Mobility in the United States

How Much Mobility? How much mobility is there on the U.S. social class ladder? The huge structural changes in the United States—especially from farming to blue-collar work in the earlier part of this century and, more recently, from blue-collar to white-collar occupations—allowed much intergenerational mobility. About half of sons passed their fathers; about one-third stayed at the same level, and only about one-sixth fell down the class ladder (Blau and Duncan 1967; Featherman and Hauser 1978; Featherman 1979).

Ignoring Women As you may have noticed, these studies refer only to sons, a matter that became controversial in sociology (Davis and Robinson 1988). Feminists objected that women were assumed to have no class position of their own and were simply assigned the class of their husbands. The defense was that too few women were in the labor force to make a difference.

With the large numbers of women now working for pay, more recent studies include women (Breen and Whelan 1995; Beeghley 1996). Sociologists Elizabeth Higginbotham and Lynn Weber (1992), for example, studied 200 women from working-class backgrounds who became professionals, managers, and administrators in Memphis. They found that almost without exception, when they were little girls their parents had encouraged them to postpone marriage and get an education. This study confirms findings of sociologists, that the family is of utmost importance in the socialization process and that the primary entry to the upper middle class is a college education. At the same time, note that if there had not been a *structural* change in society, the millions of new positions that women occupy would not exist.

Fears of the Future The ladder also goes down, of course, which is precisely what strikes fear in the hearts of many workers. If the United States does not keep pace with global change and remain highly competitive by producing low-cost, quality goods, its economic position will decline. The result will be shrinking opportunities—with U.S. workers facing fewer good jobs and lower incomes.

Certainly one of the goals of most Americans is to better their lot in life. In sociological terms, this

▼▲▼▲▼▲▼▲▼▲▼▲▼▲▼▲▼▲▼▲▼▲▼▲▼▲▼▲▼▲▼

The Immigrant Experience

Trying for a Better Life

IMMIGRANTS USUALLY COME to the United States hoping that their new lives will bring them upward social mobility. Most first-generation immigrants explain that they came here "for a better life," defined as a stable job, money for a car and a house, and a chance for their children to get a good education. The degree to which immigrants achieve their dream depends largely on the educational, technical, and language skills they bring with them—and their contacts in the world of work. Also significant are the state of the U.S. job market and the kinds of skills currently in demand.

For many of the post-1965 immigrants from India, most of whom came from urban, middle-class families, this hope of social mobility has been fulfilled. In general, the approximately 1 million Indian immigrants have been able to use their college education, their familiarity with Western-style technology and management techniques, and their fluency in English to find jobs in science and computing, medicine, college teaching and research, banking, finance, and business.

Consequently, the Indian immigrant community is more affluent and upper middle class than most immigrant communities.

Mr. Lal is such an immigrant. Reared in a westernized family of lawyers and civil servants, he grew up speaking English as well as local languages. After attending college in Bombay, he earned an MBA degree and became an executive in one of India's largest firms. When he moved to New York, friends employed in banking helped him land a job in finance. He was later promoted to vice president of a bank, and then formed a successful real estate and construction firm. Lal has done some exporting to India, and is now looking for ways to invest in Indian industry or real estate.

Not all Indian immigrants are so successful, of course, and some experience painful downward social mobility. Mr. Singh, for example, came from a family of teachers. He earned a master's degree and taught in a technical college in India. Dazzled by stories about Indians who came to the United States and became millionaires, Singh resigned his job

and moved to California, leaving his wife and son behind. While he looked for a better job, he worked as a farm hand for cousins who owned a fruit farm. Greeted by high unemployment, Singh was unable to find a teaching or technical job, and his rural cousins had no helpful connections.

Out of desperation, Singh took a bus to New York City, where the best job he could find was working for minimum wage at a subway newsstand from 6 A.M. to 7 P.M. six days a week. Describing his situation, Singh came close to tears: "We never hear about this part back home," he said. Unable to save enough to send for his wife and child and without the time or contacts to find a professional job in New York, Singh felt trapped and helpless. He grew depressed, and friends persuaded him to go back to India "for a visit"—a visit from which he never returned.

Johanna Lessinger
Senior Research Scholar
Southern Asian Institute
Columbia University
From the Ganges to the Hudson: Indian Immigrants in New York City, Allyn and Bacon (1996)

means that most Americans want a chance at upward social mobility. Indeed, this heartfelt desire is so common around the world that it drives many people to uproot themselves from their native lands and move to the United States. Some of the difficulties in that attempt to achieve upward mobility are discussed in the Immigrant Experience box above.

▶ ## Poverty

A lot of Americans find the "limitless possibilities" of the American dream rather elusive. As illustrated in

Figure 8.4 (on page 189), the working poor and underclass together form about 25 percent of the U.S. population. This percentage translates into a huge number, about 65 million people. Who are these people?

Drawing the Poverty Line

To define poverty, the U.S. government assumes that poor families spend one-third of their income on food and then multiplies a low-cost food budget by 3. Those whose incomes are lower than this amount are classified as below the **poverty line.** As sociologists observe, this definition is unrealistic. It does not allow for costs of child care for working mothers, and is the same amount across the nation, even though the cost of living is much higher in some states (Banerjee 1994; Michael 1995). Nevertheless, this is how the government draws the line that separates the poor from the nonpoor.

It is part of the magical sleight-of-hand of modern bureaucracy that a modification in this official measure of poverty instantly adds—or subtracts—millions of people from this category (Katz 1989; Ruggles 1990). Although the official definition of poverty does not make anyone poor, the way in which poverty is defined does have serious practical consequences. The government uses this definition to make choices about who will receive help and who will not. Based on this official definition of poverty, let's see who in the United States is poor.

Who Are the Poor?

The Feminization of Poverty The greatest predictor of whether a U.S. family is poor is the sex of the person who heads the family. Most poor families are headed by women. If a single-parent family is headed by a man, the poverty rate usually is less than the national average, but if a woman heads a family the chances of poverty soar. As Figure 8.6 shows, a mother-headed family is *two to six* times more likely to be poor than is a family headed by a married couple. The three major causes of this phenomenon, called **the feminization of poverty,** are divorce, births to unwed mothers, and the lower wages paid to women.

Race/Ethnicity Although two out of three poor people are white, in relationship to their numbers in the population most racial/ethnic minorities are more likely to be poor. As Figure 8.7 shows, only 12 percent of whites are poor, but 31 percent of Latinos and African Americans live in poverty. As we discuss in the next chapter, Asian Americans are an exception to this pattern.

Old Age As Figure 8.7 also shows, the elderly are less likely than the general population to be poor. It used to be that growing old increased one's chances of being poor, but changes in government policies concerning Social Security and subsidized housing, food, and medical care have significantly cut the rate of poverty among the elderly. The bottom line, however, is that the prevailing racial and ethnic patterns carry over into old age, and an elderly African American or Latino is more than twice as likely to be poor as an elderly white person.

FIGURE 8.6

Which Children Are Poor? Poverty Rates of U.S. Children Age 6 Years and Younger, by Family Type and Race/Ethnicity

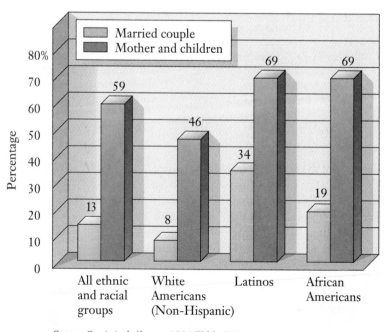

Source: Statistical Abstract 1994:Table 729.

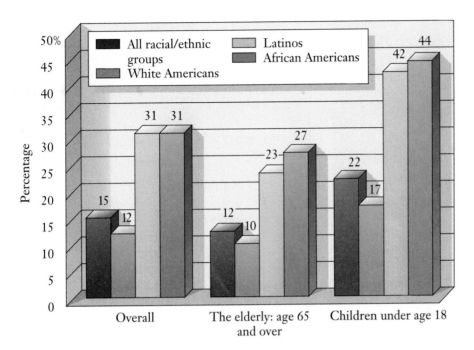

Note: The source includes data based only on money income. If food stamps, medical benefits, and government-subsidized housing were included, the percentages would be less.

Source: Statistical Abstract 1996:Table 733.

FIGURE 8.7

Poverty in the United States, by Age and Race/Ethnicity

The Rural Poor About 56 million Americans live in rural areas. Of these, 9 million are poor. At 16 percent, this is slightly higher than the national average shown in Figure 8.7. The rural poor reflect the nation's racial and ethnic patterns of poverty; that is, poverty is least among whites and greatest among African Americans, while Latinos rank in between. The rural poor, however, do differ from the national picture. They are less likely to be on welfare or to be single parents, and more likely to be married and to have jobs. Compared with urban Americans, the rural poor are less skilled and less educated, and the jobs available to them pay less than similar jobs in urban areas (Dudenhefer 1993).

Children of Poverty

Children are more likely to live in poverty than are adults or the elderly. This holds true regardless of race, but as Figures 8.6 and 8.7 show, poverty is much greater among Latino and African-American chil-

dren. That so many children are poor is shocking when one considers the wealth of this country and the supposed concern for the well-being of children. This new, and tragic, aspect of poverty in the United States is the topic of the following Thinking Critically section.

▼▲▼▲▼▲▼▲▼▲▼▲▼▲▼▲▼▲▼

Thinking Critically about
Social Controversy

The Nation's Shame: Children in Poverty

DURING THE PAST DECADE or two, children have slipped into poverty faster than any other age group. As Figure 8.7 shows, one of six white U.S. children, two of every five Latino children, and almost one of every two African-American children are poor. These figures translate into incredible numbers—approximately *18*

Beyond the awareness of most Americans are the rural poor, such as this West Virginia family and the thousands of similar families that live in what is known as Appalachia. As explained in the text, some of the characteristics of the rural poor differ from those of the urban poor.

Table 8.3
U.S. Births to Single and Married Women
Of Births to Women above the Poverty Line
94% are married
6% are single
Of Births to Women below the Poverty Line
56% are married
44% are single
Note: Figures were available only for white women.
Source: Murray 1993.

million children live in poverty: 9 million white children, 4 million Latino children, and 5 million African-American children.

According to sociologist and U.S. Senator Daniel Moynihan, this high rate of child poverty is due primarily to a general breakdown of the U.S. family. He points his finger at the sharp increase in births outside marriage. In 1960, 5 percent of all U.S. children were born to unmarried mothers. Today that figure is *six times higher*, and single women now account for 30 percent of all U.S. births. The relationship to social class is striking, for as Table 8.3 shows, births to unmarried mothers are not distributed evenly across the social classes. For women above the poverty line, only 6 percent of births are to single mothers, while for women below the poverty line this rate jumps to 44 percent.

Regardless of causes—and there are many—to say that millions of children live in poverty can be as cold and meaningless as saying that their shoes are brown. Easy to overlook is the significance of childhood poverty. Poor children are more likely to die in infancy, to go hungry and to be malnourished, to develop more slowly, and to have more health problems. They are more likely to drop out of school, to become involved in criminal activities, and to have children while still in their teens—thus perpetuating the cycle of poverty.

For Your Consideration

Many social analysts—liberals and conservatives alike—are alarmed at this increase in child poverty. They emphasize that it is time to stop blaming the victim, and instead to focus on the structural factors that underlie child poverty. To relieve the problem, they say, we must take immediate steps to establish national programs of child nutrition and health care. Solutions will require at least these fundamental changes: (1) removing obstacles to employment; (2) improving education; and (3) strengthening the family. To achieve these changes, what specific programs would *you* recommend?

Sources: Moynihan 1991; Murray 1993; Sandefur 1995; *Statistical Abstract* 1995:Tables 22, 745, 1367.

Short-Term, Long-Term, and Persistent Poverty

In the 1960s, Michael Harrington (1962) and Oscar Lewis (1966a, b) suggested that some of the poor are trapped in a **culture of poverty.** They assumed that the values and behaviors of the poor "make them fundamentally different from other Americans, and that these factors are largely responsible for their continued long-term poverty" (Ruggles 1989:7).

Economist Patricia Ruggles (1989, 1990) wanted to see if this were true. Is there a self-perpetuating culture, transmitted across generations, which keeps its members in poverty? If so, it would confirm common stereotypes of the poor as lazy people who bring poverty on themselves. After studying national statistics, Ruggles found that about half the poor are *short-term poor*; that is, they move out of poverty in less than eight years, some within a few months. About half are *long-term poor*, their poverty lasting at least eight years, for some, a lifetime. She also found that most children of the poor do *not* grow up to be poor. Only about 20 percent of people who are poor as children are still poor when they are adults (Corcoran et al. 1985; Sawhill 1988; Ruggles 1989). Contrary to popular belief, then, most poor families do not pass poverty across generations.

Since the number of people in poverty remains fairly constant year after year, however, this means that in any given year about as many people move into poverty as move out of poverty. In addition, although most people who are poor today will not be poor in just a few years, about 1 percent of the U.S. population lives in *persistent poverty*. These 2.5 million people were poor twenty years ago, and they are poor today. Ruggles found that this group has three primary characteristics: most are African American, unemployed, and live in female-headed households. About half are unmarried mothers with children.

Why Are People Poor? Individual versus Structural Explanations

Two explanations for poverty compete for our attention. The first, which sociologists adopt, focuses on *social structure*. Sociologists stress that *features of society* deny some people access to education or learning job skills. They emphasize racial, ethnic, age, and gender discrimination, as well as changes in the job market—the closing of plants, the drying up of unskilled jobs, and an increase in marginal jobs that pay poverty wages.

A competing explanation focuses on characteristics of *individuals* that are assumed to contribute to their poverty. Individualistic explanations that sociologists reject outright as worthless stereotypes are laziness and lack of intelligence. Individualistic explanations that sociologists reluctantly acknowledge include dropping out of school, bearing children at younger ages, and averaging more children than women in the other social classes. Most sociologists are reluctant to speak of such factors in this context, for they appear to blame the victim, something that sociologists bend over backward not to do.

The tension between these competing explanations is more than of mere theoretical interest, for explanations affect our perception and have practical consequences. Note how this works in the Down-to-Earth Sociology box on the next page and in the following Thinking Critically section.

▼▲▼▲▼▲▼▲▼▲▼▲▼▲▼▲▼▲▼▲▼
Thinking Critically about Social Controversy

The Welfare Debate: The Deserving and the Undeserving Poor

THROUGHOUT U.S. HISTORY, Americans have divided the poor into two types: the deserving and the undeserving. The deserving poor are people who, in the public mind, are poor through no fault of their own. Most of the working poor, such as the Lewises, are considered deserving:

> Nancy and Ted Lewis are married, in their late 30s, with two children. Ted works three part-time jobs; Nancy takes care of the children and house. Their total income is $12,000 a year. To make ends meet, the Lewises rely on food stamps, Medicaid, and housing subsidies. (Milbank 1995)

The undeserving poor, in contrast, are viewed as having brought on their own poverty. They are freeloaders who waste their lives in sloth, alcohol and drug abuse, and unwed motherhood. They don't deserve help, and, if given anything, will waste it on their dissolute lifestyles. Some would see Joan as an example:

> Joan's grandmother and her six children were supported by welfare. Joan's parents are alcoholics—and on welfare. Joan started having sex at 13, bore her first child at 15, and, now at 23, with three children, is expecting her fourth. Her first two children have the same father, the third a different father, and Joan isn't sure who fathered her coming child. Joan parties most nights, using both alcohol and whatever drugs are available. Her house is filthy, and social workers have threatened to take away her children.

This division of the poor into deserving and undeserving underlies the heated debate about welfare. "Why should we use *our* hard-earned money to help *them*? They are just going to waste it." "Of course, there are those who want to get on their feet, and helping them is okay."

For Your Consideration

Of what use is such a division of the poor into deserving and undeserving? Would we let some people starve

Down-to-Earth Sociology

Welfare: How to Ravage the Self-Concept

MY HUSBAND LEFT me shortly after I was diagnosed with multiple sclerosis. At the time, I had five children. My oldest child was 14, and my youngest was 7. My physician, believing I would be seriously disabled, helped get me on Social Security disability. The process took several months, and so it became necessary for me to go on public aid and food stamps.

By the time I needed to depend on my family in the face of a crisis, there weren't any resources left to draw on. My father had passed away and my mother was retired, living on a modest income based on Social Security and my father's pension. Isn't it funny how there is no social stigma attached to Social Security benefits for the elderly? People look at this money as an entitlement—"We worked for it." But people who have to depend on public aid for existence are looked at like vermin and accused of being lazy.

I can tell you from my own experience that a great deal of the lethargy that comes from long periods on welfare is due primarily to the attitudes of the people you have to come into contact with in these programs. I've been through the gamut: from rude, surly caseworkers at Public Aid, to patronizing nurses at the WIC [Women, Infants, and Children] clinic ("You have *how* many children?"), to the accusing tone of the food pantry workers when you have to go begging for a handout before the thirty-day time span has expired. After a while your dignity is gone, and you start to believe that you really are the disgusting human trash they all make you out to be.

Source: Christine Hoffman, a student in the author's introductory sociology class.

---

because they "brought poverty upon themselves?" Would we let children go hungry because their parents are unmarried and uneducated?

Try to go beyond such a simplistic division, and use the sociological perspective to explain poverty without blaming the victim. What *social* conditions (conditions of society) create poverty? What *social* conditions produce the lifestyles of which the middle class so violently disapproves? If the goal is to make people self-supporting and hard-working, how can welfare be restructured to produce such people? To be more attractive than welfare, what sort of jobs would have to be available? Considering the structural changes in work mentioned in this chapter, how could such jobs be made available?

A Matter of Perspective One consequence of a life of deprivation punctuated by emergencies—*and seeing the future as more of the same*—is a lack of **deferred gratification,** giving up things in the present for the sake of greater gains in the future. It is difficult to practice this middle-class virtue if one does not have a middle-class surplus—or middle-class hope.

Back in 1967, sociologist Elliot Liebow noted this precise problem among African-American street-corner men. Their jobs were low-paying and inse-cure, and their lives pitted with emergencies. With the future looking exactly like the present, and any savings they did manage gobbled up by emergencies, either theirs or their friends' and relatives', saving for the future was fruitless. The only thing that made sense from their perspective was to enjoy what they could at the moment. Immediate gratification, then, was not the cause of their poverty, but its consequence. Cause and consequence loop together, however, for their immediate gratification, in turn, helped perpetuate their poverty.

If both causes are at work, why do sociologists emphasize the structural explanation? Reverse the situation for a moment. Suppose that the daily routine of the middle class were an old car that ran only half the time, threats from the utility company to shut off the electricity and heat, and a choice between buying medicine and food and diapers or paying the rent. How long would they practice deferred gratification? Their orientations to life would likely make a sharp U-turn.

Sociologists, then, look at the behaviors of the poor as more driven by their poverty than as a cause of it. Poor people would love the opportunities that would allow them the chance to practice the middle-class virtue of deferred gratification.

Where Is Horatio Alger? The Social Functions of a Myth

Around the turn of the century, Horatio Alger was one of the most talked-about fictional heroes. The rags-to-riches exploits of this national character, and his startling successes in overcoming severe odds, motivated thousands of boys of that period. Although he has disappeared from U.S. literature, Horatio Alger remains alive and well in the psyche of Americans. From abundant real-life examples of people from humble origins who climbed far up the social class ladder, Americans know that anyone can get ahead by really trying. In fact, they believe that most Americans, including minorities and the working poor, have an average or better than average chance of getting ahead—obviously, a statistical impossibility (Kluegel and Smith 1986).

The accuracy of the **Horatio Alger myth** is less important than the belief itself in limitless possibilities for everyone. Functionalists would stress that this belief is functional for society. On the one hand, it encourages people to compete for higher positions, or, as the song says, "to reach for the highest star." On the other hand, it places blame for failure squarely on the individual. If you don't make it—in the face of ample opportunities to get ahead—the fault must be your own. The Horatio Alger belief helps to stabilize society, then, for since the fault is viewed as the individual's, not society's, current social arrangements are satisfactory. This reduces pressures to change the system.

As Marx and Weber pointed out, social class penetrates our consciousness, shaping our ideas of life and our proper place in society. When the rich look around, they sense superiority and control over destiny. In contrast, the poor see defeat, and a bitter

A culture's dominant ideology is reinforced in many ways, including its literature. In earlier generations, Horatio Alger was the inspirational hero for thousands of boys. The central theme of these many novels, immensely popular in their time, was rags to riches. Through rugged determination and self-sacrifice, a boy could overcome seemingly insurmountable obstacles to reach the pinnacle of success.

buffeting by unpredictable forces. Each knows the dominant ideology, that their particular niche in life is due to their own efforts, that the reasons for success—or failure—lie solely with the self. Like the fish not seeing water, people tend not to see the effects of social class on their own lives.

Summary and Review

What Is Social Class?

Most sociologists have adopted Weber's definition of **social class** as a large group of people who rank closely to one another in wealth, power, and prestige. **Wealth,** consisting of property and income, is concentrated in the upper classes. The distribution of wealth in the

United States has changed little over the past couple of generations, and the poorest and richest quintiles now receive the same share of the country's wealth as they did in 1945. **Power,** the ability to carry out one's will even over the resistance of others, is concentrated among the wealthy. C. Wright Mills coined the term **power elite** to refer to the small group that holds the reins of power in business, government, and the military. **Prestige** is often linked to occupational status. Pp. 184–188.

People's rankings of occupational prestige have changed little over the decades and are similar from country to country. Globally, occupations that pay more, require more education and abstract thought, and offer greater autonomy are accorded greater prestige. Pp. 188–190.

What is meant by the term status inconsistency?

Status is social ranking. Most people are **status consistent;** that is, they rank high or low on all three dimensions of social class. People who rank higher on some dimensions than on others are **status inconsistent.** The frustrations of status inconsistency tend to produce political radicalism. Pp. 190–191.

Sociological Models of Social Class

What models do sociologists use to portray the social classes?

Two models that portray the social class structure were described. Erik Wright developed a four-class model based on Marx: (1) capitalists or owners; (2) petty bourgeoisie or small business owners; (3) managers; and (4) workers. Gilbert and Kahl developed a six-class model based on Weber. At the top is the capitalist class. In descending order are the upper middle class, the lower middle class, the working class, the working poor, and the **underclass.** Pp. 191–196.

Consequences of Social Class

How does social class affect people?

Social class leaves no aspect of life untouched. Its primary significance is the determination of **life chances**—an individual's chances of such things as benefiting from the new technology, dying early, becoming ill, receiving good health care, and getting divorced. Class membership also affects child rearing, political participation, religious affiliation, and educational attainment. Pp. 196–199.

Social Mobility

What are the types of social mobility?

The term **intergenerational mobility** refers to change in social class from one generation to the next. **Exchange mobility** is the movement of large numbers of people from one class to another with the net result that the relative proportions of the population in the classes remain about the same. The term **structural mobility** refers to social changes that affect the social class membership of large numbers of people. Pp. 199–201.

Poverty

Who are the poor?

Poverty is unequally distributed in the United States. Latinos, African Americans, Native Americans, children, women-headed households, and rural Americans are more likely than others to be poor. The poverty rate of the elderly is about the same as for the general population. Pp. 201–205.

What are individual and structural explanations of poverty?

Some social analysts believe that characteristics of individuals, such as a desire for immediate gratification, cause poverty. Sociologists, in contrast, examine *structural* features of society, such as employment opportunities, to find the causes of poverty. Sociologists generally conclude that life orientations are a consequence, not the cause, of one's position in the social class structure. Pp. 205–206.

How is the Horatio Alger myth functional for society?

The **Horatio Alger myth,** the belief that anyone can get ahead if he or she tries hard enough, encourages people to strive to get ahead and deflects blame for failure from society to the individual. P. 207.

Where can I read more on this topic?

Suggested readings for this chapter are listed on page 439.

Glossary

contradictory class locations Erik Wright's term for a position in the class structure that generates contradictory interests (p. 191)

culture of poverty the values and behaviors of the poor that are assumed to make them fundamentally different from other people; these factors are assumed to be largely responsible for their poverty, and parents are assumed to perpetuate poverty across generations by passing these characteristics on to their children (p. 204)

deferred gratification forgoing something in the present in the hope of achieving greater gains in the future (p. 206)

downward social mobility movement down the social class ladder (p. 199)

exchange mobility about the same numbers of people moving up and down the social class ladder, such that, on balance, the social class system shows little change (p. 200)

feminization of poverty a trend in U.S. poverty whereby most poor families are headed by women (p. 202)

Horatio Alger myth belief that anyone can get ahead if only he or she tries hard enough; encourages people to strive to get ahead and deflects blame for failure from society to the individual (p. 207)

intergenerational mobility the change that family members make in social class from one generation to the next (p. 199)

poverty line the official measure of poverty; calculated as three times a low-cost food budget (p. 201)

power the ability to get your way, even over the resistance of others (p. 187)

power elite C. Wright Mills's term for the top leaders of corporations, military, and politics who make the nation's major decisions (p. 187)

prestige respect or regard (p. 188)

social class a large number of people with similar amounts of income and education who work at jobs that are roughly comparable in prestige (p. 184)

status the position that someone occupies in society or a social group; one's social ranking (p. 191)

status consistent people ranking high or low on all three dimensions of social class (p. 191)

status inconsistency a contradiction or mismatch between statuses; a condition in which a person ranks high on some dimensions of social class and low on others (p. 191)

structural mobility movement up or down the social class ladder that is attributable to changes in the structure of society, not to individual efforts (p. 199)

underclass a small group of people for whom poverty persists year after year and across generations (p. 195)

upward social mobility movement up the social class ladder (p. 199)

wealth property and income (p. 185)

Sociology and the Internet

All URLs listed are current as of the printing of this book. URLs are often changed. Please check our Website http://www.abacon.com/henslin for updates.

1. Extreme Inequality

Before you begin this project, review the section entitled "Wealth" (pages 185–186). Does the extreme difference between the rich and the poor surprise you? The disparities become even clearer if you look at more detailed data. With this in mind, go to "How the pie is sliced" (http://epn.org/prospect/22/ 22wolf.html) and read Wolff's article. (You may want to print it out so you can make notes on the copy.)

Write a one- or two-page paper based on this article, in which you address the following questions: (1) Of all of the growth in wealth and income in the 1980s, how much was gained by the richest 1 percent? by the bottom 80 percent? (2) What is the long-term trend in the distribution of wealth and income? (3) How does the level of inequalities in the United States compare with that of other industrialized nations? In the final two sections of your paper, discuss why the rich gained so much in the 1980s, and possible structural solutions to the problem of extreme inequality.

2. Welfare Reform

Welfare reform is an issue that continues to raise impassioned emotions, especially in presidential election years. Use Lycos (http://www.lycos.com) with the search words "welfare reform" to browse several sites related to the topic. What issues are currently being raised? How do the positions being taken seem to relate to social class differences in the United States? Explain why you think this is true. What is your view of these issues? Do you think your own social position has any influence on your views? Explain.

Fred Brown, Stagger Lee, 1984.

Inequalities of Race and Ethnicity

"M Y BROTHER-IN-LAW WAS A RELIGIOUS MAN," said Edmond. "When the militia came for him, he asked if he could pray first. They let him pray. After his prayers, he said he didn't want his family dismembered. They said he could throw his children down the latrine holes instead. He did. Then the militia threw him and my sister on top."

Shining a flashlight into the 40-foot-deep hole, Edmond said, "Look. You can still see the bones."

Between 800,000 and 1 million Rwandans died in the slaughter. Although the killings were low-tech—most were done with machetes—it took just 100 days in the summer of 1994 to complete the state-sanctioned massacres (Gourevitch 1995).

Rwanda has two major ethnic groups. The Hutus outnumber the Tutsis six to one. Hutus are stocky and round-faced, dark-skinned, flat-nosed, and thick-lipped. The Tutsis are lankier and longer-faced, lighter-skinned, narrow-nosed, and thin-lipped. But the two groups, who speak the same language, have intermarried for so long that they have difficulty telling Hutu from Tutsi. National identity cards, originally issued by the Belgians when Rwanda was its colony, are one way of knowing who is who.

During the genocide, a Tutsi card was a passport to death.

The Hutus, who controlled the government, called on all Hutus to kill all Tutsis. It was a national duty, said the Hutu leaders. Obediently, neighbors hacked neighbors to death in their homes. Colleagues hacked colleagues to death at work. Even teachers killed their students.

Opening stadiums and churches, local authorities offered refuge to Tutsis. There the largest executions occurred, supervised by these same local authorities.

While radio announcers urged their listeners to disembowel pregnant women, the government fortified armed men with alcohol and bused them from massacre to massacre.

Nkongoli, a Tutsi who is now the vice president of the National Assembly, says, "One expected to die. Not by machete, one hoped, but with a bullet. If you were willing to pay for it, you could ask for a bullet. Death was more or less normal, a resignation. You lose the will to fight" (Gourevitch 1995).

Laying the Sociological Foundation

Seldom do race and ethnic relations drop to such a brutal low as they did in Rwanda, but in our own society newspaper headlines and television news keep race relations constantly before us. Sociology can contribute greatly to our understanding of this aspect of social life. To begin, let us consider to what extent race itself is a myth.

Race: Myth and Reality

With its almost six billion people, the world offers a fascinating variety of human shapes and colors. People see one another as black, white, red, yellow, and brown. Eyes come in various shades of blue, brown, and green. Thick and thin lips. Straight hair, curly hair, kinky hair, black, white, and red hair—and, of course, all hues of brown.

As humans spread throughout the world, their adaptations to diverse climates and other living conditions resulted in this fascinating variety of complexions, colors, and shapes. Genetic mutations added distinct characteristics to the peoples of the globe. In this sense the concept of **race,** a group with inherited physical characteristics that distinguish it from another group, is a reality. Humans do, indeed, come in a variety of colors and shapes.

In two senses, however, race is a myth, a fabrication of the human mind. The *first* fabrication is the idea that any one race is superior to another. All

The gruesome events described in this chapter's opening vignette are symbolically depicted here. Survivors of the Rwandan holocaust view a pile of the machetes used for "ethnic cleansing."

races have their geniuses—and their idiots. As with language, no race is superior to another.

Ideas of racial superiority, however, abound. They are not only false, but also dangerous. Adolf Hitler, for example, believed that a superior race, the Aryan, was responsible for the cultural achievements of Europe. The Aryans, he said, were destined to establish a higher culture and institute a new world order. This destiny required them to avoid the "racial contamination" that would come from breeding with inferior races, and to isolate or destroy races that might endanger Aryan culture.

When Hitler's views were put into practice, the world was left an appalling legacy—the Nazi slaughter of people deemed inferior, Jews, Slavs, gypsies, and homosexuals. Dark images of gas ovens and emaciated bodies stacked like cordwood haunted the world's nations. At Nuremberg, the Allies, flush with victory, put the top Nazis on trial, exposing their heinous deeds to a shocked world. Their public executions, everyone assumed, marked the end of such grisly acts. Obviously, they didn't, as "ethnic cleansing" in Bosnia and the events recounted in our opening vignette sadly attest. **Genocide,** the attempt to destroy a people because of their presumed race or ethnicity, remains alive and well. Although the killings may lack swastika and goose-stepping, and even though machetes may replace poison gas and ovens, the goal is the same.

The *second* myth is that "pure" races exist. Humans show such a mixture of physical characteristics—in skin color, hair texture, nose shape, head shape, eye color, and so on—that there are no "pure" races. Instead of falling into distinct types clearly separate from one another, human characteristics flow endlessly together. These minute gradations make arbitrary any attempt to draw firm lines. As the box on the next page discusses, this makes it difficult for U.S. census takers.

Although large groupings of people can be classified by blood type and gene frequencies, even these classifications do not uncover "race." Rather, they are so arbitrary that biologists and anthropologists have drawn up many lists, each containing a different number of "races." Ashley Montagu (1964), a physical anthropologist, pointed out that some scientists have classified humans into only two "races" while others have found as many as two thousand. Montagu (1960) himself classified humans into forty "racial" groups.

The *idea* of race, of course, is far from a myth. That idea is very much alive. Firmly embedded in our culture, it is a social reality that we confront daily. As noted in Chapter 4, sociologist W. I. Thomas observed that "if people define situations as real, they are real in their consequences." The fact that no race is superior or that we cannot even decide how people should be biologically classified into races is not what counts. What makes a differ-

▼▲▼▲▼▲▼▲▼▲▼▲▼▲▼▲▼▲▼▲▼▲▼▲▼▲▼▲▼▲

Our Multicultural Society

Pity the Census Taker:
Racial Classifications in a Multicultural Society

EVERY TEN YEARS, the U.S. government takes a census of everyone living in the United States. Part of the job is to classify people by race. In the old days the categories were simple: Caucasian, Negro, Indian, and Oriental. Everyone was fit into one of them, based primarily on the census takers' judgment. Today's categories have expanded somewhat: White, Black, American Indian (including Eskimo and Aleut), Asian and Pacific Islander, and Hispanic.

Census takers are uncertain about how to classify Hispanics: Sometimes they count them separately; at other times, they include them as Whites. The *Statistical Abstract of the United States*, the official count of just about everyone in the country, even carries this warning: "*Note:* Hispanics may be of any race."

The job is certainly getting more difficult. Some Native Hawaiians, now counted as Pacific Islanders, want to be considered Native Americans. Some Arab-Americans want to be counted as Middle Eastern, not Whites. Others want to be listed simply as Multiracial (Wynter 1995). Still others want to be listed under the general, catch-all category of American.

For Your Consideration

Beyond such specifics lies a much broader issue: Just why do we want to count people by "race" anyway? Perhaps you can use materials in this chapter to answer this question. If we are going to continue to classify people by "race," what categories would you suggest? Why?

---

ence for social life, rather, is that people *believe* these ideas, for *people act on beliefs, not facts.* As a result, we always have people like the Hutu leaders, Hitler, and the Serbs in Bosnia. While few people hold such extreme views, most people appear to be ethnocentric enough to believe, at least just a little, that their *own* race is superior to others.

Ethnic Groups

Whereas the term *race* refers to biological characteristics that distinguish one people from another, **ethnicity** and **ethnic** apply to cultural characteristics. Derived from the Greek *ethnos*, meaning "people" or "nation," these terms refer to people who identify with one another on the basis of common ancestry and cultural heritage. Their sense of belonging centers on country of origin, distinctive foods, dress, family names and relationships, language, music, religion, and other customs.

Although this distinction between race and ethnicity is clear—one is biological, the other cultural—people often confuse the two. This confusion is due to the cultural differences people see *and* the way they define race. For example, many people consider the Jews a race—including many Jews. Jews, however, are more properly considered an ethnic group, for it is

their cultural characteristics, especially religion, that bind them together. Wherever Jews have lived in the world, they have intermarried. Consequently, Jews in China may look mongoloid, while some Swedish Jews are blue-eyed blonds. This matter is even more strikingly illustrated in the case of the Ethiopian Jews, who look so different from European Jews that when they immigrated to Israel some European Israelis felt that they could not *really* be Jews.

Minority and Dominant Groups

What These Terms Mean Sociologist Louis Wirth (1945) defined a **minority group** as people who are singled out for unequal treatment and who regard themselves as objects of collective discrimination. Worldwide, minorities share several conditions: Their physical or cultural traits are held in low esteem by the dominant group, who treats them unfairly, and they tend to marry within their own group (Wagley and Harris 1958). These conditions tend to create a shared sense of identity among minorities (a feeling of "we-ness"). In many instances, a sense of common destiny emerges (Chandra 1993b).

Surprisingly, a minority group is not necessarily a *numerical* minority. For example, before India's independence in 1947, a handful of British colonial

Fanning hatred for Jews as a scapegoat for Germany's problems and preaching the superiority of the supposedly racially pure Aryans, Adolf Hitler put his ideas of race into practice. The result was the Holocaust, the systematic slaughter of Jews and others deemed racially inferior. In the photo on the left, Hitler is addressing a group called Hitler Youth, a sort of Boy Scouts dedicated to serving Hitler and his ideas. The photo on the right shows the sight that greeted British troops when they entered the concentration camp in Bergen, Germany—60,000 people dying of starvation and diseases amidst piles of bodies awaiting burial.

rulers discriminated against millions of Indians. Similarly, when South Africa had apartheid, a small group of whites discriminated against the black majority. And all over the world females are a minority group. Accordingly, sociologists refer to those who do the discriminating not as the *majority* but, rather, as the **dominant group,** for they have greater power, privileges, and social status.

Being in a position of power and unified by shared physical and cultural traits, the dominant group uses its position to discriminate against those with different—and supposedly inferior—traits. The dominant group almost always considers its privileged position to be due to its own innate superiority.

Emergence of Minority Groups A group becomes a minority in one of two ways. The *first* is through the expansion of political boundaries. With the exception of females, tribal societies contain no minority groups, for everyone shares the same culture, including the same language, and belongs to the same physical stock. When a group expands its political boundaries, however, it produces minority groups, for it incorporates into a single political entity people with different customs, languages, values, and physical characteristics. For example, after defeating Mexico in war, the United States annexed the Southwest. The Mexicans living there, who had been the dominant group, were transformed into a minority group, a master status that has influenced their lives ever since. A *second* way in which a group becomes a minority is by migration. This can be voluntary, as with the millions of people who have chosen to move from Mexico to the United States, or involuntary, as with the millions of Africans forcibly transported to the United States. (The way females became a minority group represents a third way, but as will be reviewed in the next chapter, no one knows just how this occurred.)

Prejudice and Discrimination

Prejudice and discrimination are common throughout the world. In Northern Ireland, Protestants dis-

U.S. race relations have gone through many stages, some of them very tense. They sometime have even exploded into violence, as with the many lynchings in the South in the earlier part of this century. This photo was taken in Rayston, Georgia, on April 28, 1936. Earlier in the day, the 40-year-old victim, Lint Shaw, accused of attacking a white girl, had been rescued from a mob by National Guardsmen. After the National Guard left, the mob forced their way into the jail.

Racism is not limited to any country, people, or region of the world. Germany, however, has had more than its share of racial violence. With the recent migration of workers from some of the Least Industrialized Nations to Germany, racial violence has again flared up. Five Turks died in this home in Solingen, which was set afire while still occupied. Shown here are demonstrators mournfully protesting their deaths.

criminate against Roman Catholics; in Israel, Ashkenazi Jews, primarily of European descent, discriminate against Sephardi Jews from the Muslim world; and in Japan, the Japanese discriminate against just about anyone who isn't Japanese, especially immigrant Koreans and the descendants of the Eta caste. A stigma still attaches to the Eta, now renamed the Burakumin, who used to do the society's dirty work—working with dead animals (stripping the hides and tanning the leather) and serving as Japan's executioners and prison guards. In some places the elderly discriminate against the young, in others the young against the elderly. And all around the world men discriminate against women.

As you can see from this list, **discrimination** is an *action*—unfair treatment directed against someone. When the basis of discrimination is race, it is known as **racism**, but discrimination can be based on many characteristics other than race—including age, sex, height, weight, income, education, marital status, sexual orientation, disease, disability, religion, and politics. Discrimination is often the result of an *attitude* called **prejudice**—prejudging of some sort, usually in a negative way. There is also *positive prejudice*, which exaggerates the virtues of a group, such as thinking that some group (usually one's own) is more capable than others. Most prejudice, however, is negative, prejudging a group as inferior.

The Global Glimpse box on the next page discusses a severe instance of discrimination, one that I personally experienced.

The Extent of Prejudice You yourself may not be prejudiced, but sociologists have found that ethnocentrism is so common that each racial or ethnic group views other groups as inferior in at least some ways. In a random sample of adults in the Detroit area, sociologists Maria Krysan and Reynolds Farley (1993) found that whites and African Americans tend to judge Latinos as less intelligent than themselves. Using a probability sample (from which we can generalize), sociologists Lawrence Bobo and James Kluegel (1991) found that older and less educated whites are not as willing to have close, sustained interaction with other groups as are younger and more educated whites. Details of their findings are shown in Figure 9.1 on page 218. We must await

216

No One Ever Tried to Kill Me Before:
Ethnic Identity and the Perils of Global Travel

FOR SEVERAL REASONS, Barcelona is one of my least favorite cities. Within five minutes of arriving on the Ramblas, one of the city's more colorful areas, my 9-year-old son's backpack was stolen. I chased the thief into the subway station, but quickly lost him in a maze of tunnels. A few minutes later, a second thief, while talking to me and looking me straight in the face, tried to undo the zipper of my backpack.

A couple of days later, my wife, son, and I visited a cafeteria-style restaurant. An attractive display was filled with delectable foods, and, trying to be friendly and to show my appreciation of the culture, I haltingly said in broken Spanish that this was really good Spanish food and what a pleasure it was to be in Spain. Instead of getting the usual broad smile that such

remarks bring in a foreign country, a scowl spread over the waiter's face, and he mumbled something to the other waiter. When I had seconds, I found a fairly large piece of glass in my food.

Ethnicity, filled with emotion, self-identity, and often a history of hurts, is one of the most powerful concepts in social life. Without meaning to, I had offended this man's sense of ethnic identity. Unknown to me, the people in this part of northern Spain do not think of themselves as Spaniards. In fact, they detest Spaniards and everything Spanish. They identify themselves as Catalans, prefer to speak Catalonian, and only under protest remain part of Spain. During the Spanish civil war of the 1930s, at a high cost of life, Franco vanquished the rebels in this area of Spain.

Later, in the Prado museum in Madrid, when I saw Picasso's mural, *Guernica*, which depicts Franco's bombing of a defenseless town, I gained some idea of why the waiter feels as he does. This painting also helped me understand why, after a parade on the Ramblas on Spain's national day (the equivalent of our 4th of July), a group of masked men went down the street plucking the Spanish flags from their standards. They threw the flags on the ground, where hundreds of cheering followers stomped on them.

This insight doesn't change my opinion about Barcelona, however, although I do hope that a future visit will modify my experiences. And I still think the waiter was a _____, a word that I think is better left out of this text.

matching studies to test the prejudices of Latinos, Asian Americans, and Native Americans.

This finding does not mean, of course, that all people of the same age and education have the same amount of prejudice. At the University of Alabama, sociologist Donald Muir (1991) measured racial attitudes of white students who belonged to fraternities and sororities and compared them to those of

In the 1920s, the Ku Klux Klan became a powerful political force in the United States, especially in Indiana, where this photo was taken. Which theories, sociological and psychological, would be most useful to explain this upsurge in racism among ordinary citizens?

Percentage of white Americans who believe that different races should live in segregated housing, by education

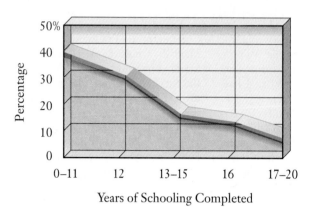

Percentage of white Americans who believe that racial intermarriage should be banned, by age

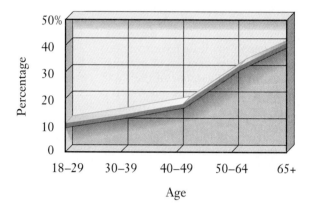

Source: Bobo and Kluegel 1991.

FIGURE 9.1

A Measure of Preferred Social Distance

nonmembers. He asked a variety of questions—from their ideas about dating African Americans to attending classes together. On all measures, fraternity members were more prejudiced than the non-frats. Research on other campuses supports this finding (Morris 1991). Let's take a closer look at race relations on U.S. campuses.

Thinking Critically about
Social Controversy

Self-Segregation: Help or Hindrance for Race Relations on Campus?

ONLY AFTER A long, bitter, and violent struggle was federal civil rights legislation prohibiting racial segregation on college campuses passed in the 1960s. These laws did not mark the end of self-segregation, however, such as areas of a cafeteria or lounge being used almost exclusively by a particular group. In recent years, minority students have requested separate dormitories and campus centers. At Brown University, an Ivy League school located in Providence, Rhode Island, the old rows of fraternity and sorority houses have been replaced by Harambee House (for African Americans), Hispanic House, Slavic House, East Asian House, and German House. Cornell University offers "theme dorms" for African Americans, Hispanics, and Native Americans.

Intense controversy surrounds this increasing segregation of racial/ethnic groups. On one side is William H. Gray III, the head of the United Negro College Fund. Both black and Latino students drop out of college at a much higher rate, Gray says, so colleges should do everything they can to make minority students feel welcome and accepted.

Critics call the trend toward separate housing a "separatist movement" that divides students into "small enclaves." The vice president of Brown compares separate college housing to the war in the former Yugoslavia (also known as the Balkan states) and worries that the result will be the "Balkanization of the campus." Administrators at the University of Pennsylvania also are concerned. A commission to study campus life concluded that when students self-segregate, they lose opportunities for wider interaction with diverse groups of students. Since students tend to socialize with the people they live with, separate housing inhibits the mixing of different groups, depriving students of the rich experiences that come through intercultural contacts.

Joshua Lehrer, a Brown University student who is white, says that various racial and ethnic groups "are separating themselves from everybody else, yet complain when society separates them. Can you really have it both ways?" he asks.

For Your Consideration

Compare separate racial/ethnic housing on college campuses with the patterns discussed in this chapter: segregation, assimilation, and multiculturalism. Is self-segregation permissible if minority students desire it, but not if desired by white students? Explain your position.

Sources: Bernstein 1993; "Racial Balkanization at Cornell" 1995; Jordon 1996.

Individual versus Institutional Discrimination

Sociologists stress that we need to move beyond thinking in terms of **individual discrimination,** the negative treatment of one person by another. Although such behavior certainly creates problems, it is primarily a matter of one individual treating another badly. With their focus on the broader picture, sociologists encourage us to examine **institutional discrimination,** that is, to see how discrimination is woven into the fabric of society. Let's look at two examples.

Home Mortgages Mortgage lending provides an excellent illustration. As shown in Figure 9.2, race/ethnicity is a significant factor in getting a mortgage. When bankers looked at the statistics shown in this figure, however, they cried foul. They said that it might *look* like discrimination, but the truth was that whites had better credit histories. To see if this were true, researchers went over the data again, comparing the credit histories of applicants. Not only did they check for late payments, but they also compared the applicants' debts, loan size relative to income, and even characteristics of the property they wanted to buy. The lending gap did narrow a bit, but the bottom line was that even when two mortgage applicants were identical in all these areas, African

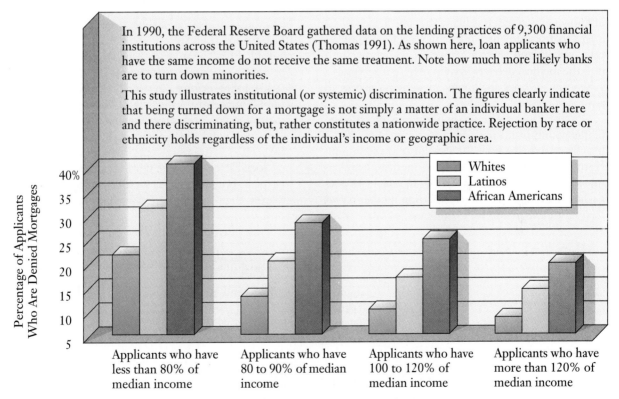

In 1990, the Federal Reserve Board gathered data on the lending practices of 9,300 financial institutions across the United States (Thomas 1991). As shown here, loan applicants who have the same income do not receive the same treatment. Note how much more likely banks are to turn down minorities.

This study illustrates institutional (or systemic) discrimination. The figures clearly indicate that being turned down for a mortgage is not simply a matter of an individual banker here and there discriminating, but, rather constitutes a nationwide practice. Rejection by race or ethnicity holds regardless of the individual's income or geographic area.

Note: The figures refer to applicants for conventional mortgages. Although applicants for government-backed mortgages had lower overall rates of rejection, the identical pattern showed up for all income groups. Median income is the income of each bank's local area.

FIGURE 9.2

Race/Ethnicity and Mortgages: An Example of Institutional Discrimination

Americans and Latinos were *60 percent* more likely to be rejected than whites (Thomas 1992). In short, the results do not show a banker here and there who discriminates, but, rather, that discrimination is built into the country's financial institutions.

Health Care Discrimination does not have to be deliberate. It can occur without the awareness of either the person doing the discriminating or those being discriminated against. An example is coronary bypass surgery. Physicians Mark Wenneker and Arnold Epstein (1989) studied all patients admitted to Massachusetts hospitals for circulatory diseases or chest pain. After comparing their age, sex, race, and income, they found that whites were 89 percent more likely to be given coronary bypass surgery. A national study of Medicare patients showed an even higher discrepancy—that whites were three times as likely as African Americans to receive this surgery (Winslow 1992).

The particular interracial dynamics that cause medical decisions to be made on the basis of race are unknown at present. It is likely that physicians *do not intend* to discriminate, but that in ways we do not yet fully understand discrimination is somehow built into the medical delivery system. There it serves as a subconscious basis for giving or denying access to advanced medical procedures.

Institutional discrimination, then, is much more than a matter of inconvenience, for it even translates into life and death. Table 9.1 also illustrates this point. Here you can see that an African-American baby has more than *twice* the chance of dying in infancy as does a white baby, that an African-American mother is *four*

times as likely to die in childbirth as a white mother, and that African Americans live six to eight years less than whites. The reason for these differences is not biology, but *social* factors, in this case largely income—the key factor in determining who has access to better nutrition, housing, and medical care.

Theories of Prejudice

Why are people prejudiced? The commonsense explanation is that some member of a group has done something negative to them or to someone they know, and they transfer their feelings to other members of the group. In some cases, this may be true, but as a classic piece of research by psychologist Eugene Hartley (1946) showed, much more is involved. Hartley asked people how they felt about various racial and ethnic groups. Besides blacks, Jews, and so on, his list included the Wallonians, Pireneans, and Danireans—names he had made up. Most people who expressed dislike for Jews and blacks also expressed dislike for these three fictitious groups. The significance of Hartley's study is twofold. First, people who are prejudiced against one racial or ethnic group tend to be prejudiced against other groups. Second, prejudice does not depend on negative experiences with others. People can be, and are, prejudiced against people they have never met—and even against groups that do not exist!

Social scientists have developed several theories to explain prejudice. Let's look first at psychological theories, then at sociological explanations.

Table 9.1

Race and Health

	Infant Mortality	Maternal Deaths	Life Expectancy	
			Males	Females
White Americans	6.9	5.0	73.2	79.8
African Americans	16.8	20.8	65.0	73.9

Note: The national data base used for this table does not list these figures for other racial/ethnic groups. *White* refers to non-Hispanic whites. The rate for infant mortality is the number of deaths per year of infants under 1 year old per 1,000 live births; for maternal deaths, it is the number per 100,000.

Source: Statistical Abstract 1995: Tables 116, 120.

Psychological Perspectives: Frustration, Scapegoats, and Authoritarian Personalities

Frustration and Scapegoats In 1939, psychologist John Dollard suggested that prejudice is the result of frustration. People who are unable to strike out at the real source of their frustration (such as low wages) find someone else to blame. This **scapegoat,** generally a racial, ethnic, or religious minority that they unfairly blame for their troubles, becomes a convenient—and safe—target on which to vent their frustrations. Gender and age also provide common bases for scapegoating.

Even mild frustration can increase prejudice. In an ingenious experiment, psychologists Emory Cowen, Judah Landes, and Donald Schaet (1959) measured the prejudice of a sample of students. They then gave the students two puzzles to solve, but made sure they did not have enough time to solve them. After the students had worked furiously on the puzzles, the experimenters shook their heads in disgust and said they couldn't believe they had not finished. They then retested the students and found higher scores on prejudice. The students had directed their frustrations outward, onto people who had nothing to do with their problem.

The Authoritarian Personality Have you ever wondered if personality is a cause of prejudice—if some people are more inclined to be prejudiced, and others more fair-minded? For psychologist Theodor Adorno, who had escaped from the Nazis, this was no idle speculation. With the horrors he had observed still fresh in his mind, Adorno wondered whether there was a certain type of individual who was more likely to fall for the racist utterances and policies of people like Hitler, Mussolini, and the Ku Klux Klan.

To test this idea, Adorno (1950) developed three scales: a series of statements that measured ethnocentrism, anti-Semitism, and support for strong, authoritarian leaders. Testing about two thousand people, ranging from college professors to prison inmates, Adorno found that people who scored high on one scale also scored high on the other two. For example, people who agreed with anti-Semitic statements also agreed that it was good for a government to be highly authoritarian and that foreign ways of life posed a threat to the "American" way.

Adorno concluded that highly prejudiced people are insecure, are highly conformist, have deep re-

spect for authority, and are highly submissive to superiors. He termed this the **authoritarian personality.** Such people see many threats to their world, believe that things are *either* right *or* wrong, and are disturbed by ambiguity, especially in matters of religion or sex. When such people confront norms and values that differ from their own, they become anxious. A scapegoat relieves their anxiety, for to define people who are different from themselves as inferior assures them that their own positions are right.

Adorno's research stirred the scientific community, and more than a thousand research studies followed. In general, the researchers found that people who are older, less educated, less intelligent, and from a lower social class are more likely to be authoritarian. Critics say that this merely shows that the less educated are more prejudiced—which we already knew (Yinger 1965; Ray 1991).

Sociological Perspectives: Functionalism, Conflict Theory, and Symbolic Interactionism

Sociologists find psychological explanations inadequate. They stress that the key to understanding prejudice is not the *internal* state of individuals, but factors *outside* the individual. Thus, sociological theories focus on how some environments foster prejudice, while others reduce it. Let's compare functionalist, conflict, and symbolic interactionist perspectives on prejudice.

Functionalism In a telling scene from a television documentary, journalist Bill Moyers interviewed Fritz Hippler, a Nazi intellectual who at age 29 was put in charge of the entire German film industry. Hippler said that when Hitler came to power the Germans were no more anti-Semitic than the French, probably less so. He was told to create anti-Semitism, which he did by producing movies that contained vivid scenes comparing Jews to rats—their breeding threatening to infest the population.

Why was Hippler told to create hatred? Prejudice and discrimination were functional for the Nazis, helping them come to power. The Jews provided a convenient scapegoat, a common enemy around which the Nazis could unite a Germany weakened by defeat in World War I and bled by war reparations and rampant inflation. In addition, the Jews had businesses, bank accounts, and other property to confiscate. They also held key positions (university professors, reporters, judges, and so on), which the Nazis could replace with their own flunkies as they fired Jews. In the end hatred also showed its dysfunctional side, as the Nazi officials who were sentenced to death at Nuremberg discovered.

To harness state machinery to hatred as the Nazis did—the schools, police, courts, mass media, and almost all aspects of the government—makes prejudice practically irresistible. Recall the identical twins featured in the Down-to-Earth Sociology box on page 59. Oskar and Jack had been separated as babies. Jack was brought up as a Jew in Trinidad, while Oskar was reared as a Catholic in Czechoslovakia. Under the Nazi regime, Oskar learned to hate Jews, although, unknown to himself, he was a Jew.

That prejudice is functional and shaped by the social environment was dramatically demonstrated by psychologists Muzafer and Carolyn Sherif (1953) in a simple but ingenious experiment. In a boys' summer camp, they first assigned friends to different cabins and then made the cabin the basic unit of competition. Each cabin competed against the others in sports and for status. In just a few days, strong in-groups had formed, and even former lifelong friends were calling one another "crybaby" and "sissy" and showing intense dislike for one another.

Sherif's study illustrates three major points. First, the social environment can be deliberately arranged to generate either positive or negative feelings about people. Second, prejudice, one product of pitting group against group in an "I win, you lose" situation, is functional in that it creates in-group solidarity and out-group antagonisms. Third, prejudice is dysfunctional in that it destroys social relationships.

Conflict Theory Conflict theorists stress that the capitalist class systematically pits group against group. If workers are united, they will demand higher wages and better working conditions. In contrast, groups that fear and distrust one another will work against one another. To reduce worker solidarity, then, is to weaken their bargaining power, drive down costs, and increase profits. Thus the capitalist class exploits racial and ethnic strife to produce a **split labor market,** workers divided along racial, ethnic, and gender lines (Du Bois 1935/1992; Reich 1972; Lind 1995).

Unemployment is a useful weapon to help maintain a split labor market. If everyone were employed, the high demand for labor would put workers in a position to demand pay increases and better

working conditions. Keeping some people unemployed, however, provides a **reserve labor force** from which owners can draw when they need to expand production. When the economy contracts, these workers are easily released to rejoin the ranks of the unemployed. Minority workers are especially useful for this manipulative goal, for white workers tend to see them as a threat (Willhelm 1980).

The consequences are devastating, say conflict theorists. Just like the boys in the Sherif experiment, African Americans, Latinos, whites, and so on see themselves as able to make gains only at one another's expense. This rivalry shows up along even finer racial and ethnic lines, such as Miami Haitians and African Americans who distrust each other as competitors. Thus, their frustration, anger, and hostility are deflected away from the capitalists and directed toward the scapegoats, whom they see as standing in their way. Pitted against one another, racial and ethnic groups learn to fear and distrust one another, instead of recognizing their common class interests and working for their mutual welfare (Blackwelder 1993).

Symbolic Interactionism Where conflict theorists focus on the role of the capitalist class in exploiting racial and ethnic inequalities, symbolic interactionists examine how labels produce prejudice. They stress that *the labels we learn color the way we see the world*. Labels cause **selective perception;** that is, they lead people to see certain things and blind them to others. Through labels, people look at the members of a group as though they were all alike. As sociologists George Simpson and Milton Yinger (1972) put it, "New experiences are fitted into old categories by selecting only those cues that harmonize with the prejudgment or stereotype."

Racial and ethnic labels are especially powerful. They are shorthand for emotionally laden stereotypes. The term *nigger*, for example, is not, like Romeo's *rose*, simply a neutral name. Nor are *honky, spic, mick, kike, limey, kraut, dago,* or any of the other scornful words people use to belittle ethnic groups. Such words overpower us with emotions, blocking out rational thought about the people to whom they refer (Allport 1954).

Symbolic interactionists stress that we are not born with prejudices. Instead, we learn our prejudices in interaction with others. At birth each of us joins some particular family and racial or ethnic group, where we learn beliefs and values. There, as part of our basic orientations to the world, we learn to like—or dislike—members of other groups and to perceive them positively or negatively. Similarly, if discrimination is the common practice, we learn to practice it routinely. Just as we learn any other attitudes and customs, then, so we learn prejudice and discrimination.

The stereotypes that we learn not only justify prejudice and discrimination, but they can even produce the behavior depicted in a stereotype. Let us consider Group X. Negative stereotypes, which characterize Group X as lazy, seem to justify withholding opportunities from this group ("because they are lazy and undependable") and placing its members in inferior positions. The result is a *self-fulfilling prophecy*. Denied jobs that require high dedication and energy, Group X members are confined to "dirty work," for it is seen as more fitting for "that kind" of people. Since much dirty work is irregular, members of Group X are also liable to be readily visible—standing around street corners. The sight of their idleness then reinforces the original stereotype of laziness, while the discrimination that created the "laziness" in the first place passes unnoticed.

One aspect of racism that has gained national attention and concern from citizens and government alike is the rise of neo-Nazi and Ku Klux Klan organizations. To understand the racist mind—and the appeal it has to some—see the Down-to-Earth Sociology box on the next page.

Patterns of Intergroup Relations

In any society that contains minorities, basic patterns develop between the dominant group and the minorities. Let us look at each of the patterns shown in Figure 9.3.

Genocide

This century's most notorious examples of genocide are Hitler's attempt to destroy all Jews and, as depicted in our opening vignette, the Hutus' attempt to destroy all Tutsis. One of the horrifying aspects of these events is that those who participated in the slaughters did not crawl out from under a rock someplace. Rather, they were ordinary citizens—whose participation was facilitated by labels that singled out the victims as enemies worthy of death (Huttenbach 1991; Browning 1993).

To better understand how ordinary people can participate in genocide, let's focus on an example from the last century. The U.S. government and white settlers chose the label "savages" to refer to Native Americans. This label, defining the Native Americans as less than human, made it easier to justify killing them in order to take over their resources. Although most Native Americans actually died from diseases brought by the whites, against which they had no immunity (Dobyns 1983; Thornton 1987), the settlers also ruthlessly destroyed the

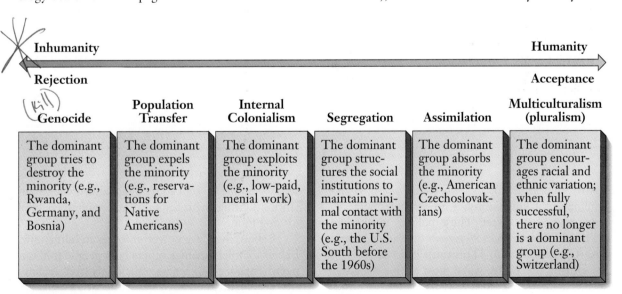

FIGURE 9.3

Patterns of Intergroup Relations: A Continuum

▼▲▼▲▼▲▼▲▼▲▼▲▼▲▼▲▼▲▼▲▼▲▼▲▼▲▼▲▼▲▼▲▼▲▼▲▼▲▼

Down-to-Earth Sociology

The Racist Mind

SOCIOLOGIST RAPHAEL EZEKIEL wanted to get an inside look at the racist mind. As a Jew, he faced a unique problem. The best way to examine racism from the inside is participant observation (see p. 25). Would this be possible for him? Openly identifying himself as a Jew, Ezekiel asked Ku Klux Klan and neo-Nazi leaders if he could interview them and attend their meetings. Surprisingly, they agreed. The results of his pathbreaking research were published in a book, *The Racist Mind*. Here Ezekiel (1995) shares some of the insights he gained during his fascinating sociological adventures:

[The leader] builds on mass anxiety about economic insecurity and on popular tendencies to see an Establishment as the cause of the economic threat; he hopes to teach people to identify that Establishment as the puppets of a conspiracy of Jews. [He has a] belief in exclusive categories. For the white racist leader, it is profoundly true . . . that the socially defined collections we call races represent fundamental categories. A man is black or a man is white; there are no in-betweens. Every human belongs to a racial category, and all the members of one category are radically different from all the members of other categories. Moreover, race represents the essence of the person. A truck is a

truck, a car is a car, a cat is a cat, a dog is a dog, a black is a black, a white is a white. . . . These axioms have a rockhard quality in the leaders' minds; the world is made up of racial groups. That is what exists for them.

Two further beliefs play a major role in the minds of leaders. First, life is war. The world is made of distinct racial groups; life is about the war between those groups. Second, events have secret causes, are never what they seem superficially. Events are caused by the complex scheming of tricksters. . . . Any myth is plausible, as long as it involves intricate plotting. . . . It does not matter to him what others say. . . . He lives in his ideas and in the little world he has created where they are taken seriously. . . . Gold can be made from the tongues of frogs; Yahweh's call can be heard in the flapping of the swastika banner. (pp. 66–67)

To whom do propagators of hate appeal? Here is what Ezekiel discovered about the recruits:

[There is a] ready pool of whites who will respond to the racist signal. . . . This population [is] always hungry for activity—or for the talk of activity— that promises dignity and meaning to lives that are working poorly in a highly competitive world. . . . Much as I don't want to believe it, [this] movement brings a sense of meaning—at least for a while—to some of the dis-

contented. To struggle in a cause that transcends the individual lends meaning to life, no matter how ill-founded or narrowing the cause. For the young men in the neo-Nazi group, . . . membership was an alternative to atomization and drift; within the group they worked for a cause and took direct risks in the company of comrades. . . .

When interviewing the young neo-Nazis in Detroit, I often found myself driving with them past the closed factories, the idled plants of our shrinking manufacturing base. The fewer and fewer plants that remain can demand better educated and more highly skilled workers. These fatherless Nazi youths, these high-school dropouts, will find little place in the emerging economy. . . . a permanently underemployed white underclass is taking its place alongside the permanent black underclass. The struggle over race merely diverts youth from confronting the real issues of their lives. Not many seats are left on the train, and the train is leaving the station. (pp. 32–33)

For Your Consideration

Use functionalism, conflict theory, and symbolic interactionism to explain (1) why some people are attracted to the message of hate mongers, and (2) how the world is viewed by leaders and followers of these hate groups.

Native Americans' food supply (buffalo, crops) and systematically killed those who resisted their advance toward the West. These policies resulted in the death of more than *90 percent* of Native Americans (Garbarino 1976; Thornton 1987).

During the 1800s, when most of this slaughter occurred, the same thing was happening in other places. In South Africa, the Boers, or Dutch settlers, looked on the native Hottentots as jungle animals and totally wiped them out. In Tasmania, the British

settlers ruthlessly stalked the local aboriginal population, hunting them for sport and sometimes even for dog food.

Labels, then, are powerful forces in human life. Labels that dehumanize others help people to **compartmentalize**—to separate their acts from feelings that would threaten their self-concept and make it difficult for them to participate in the act (Bernard et al. 1971; Markhusen 1995). Thus, *genocide is facilitated by labeling the targeted group as less than fully human.*

Population Transfer

Population transfer is of two types, indirect and direct. *Indirect* population transfer is achieved by making life so unbearable for members of a minority that they leave "voluntarily." Under the bitter conditions of czarist Russia, for example, millions of Jews made this "choice." *Direct* transfer takes place when a minority is expelled. Examples include the relocation of Native Americans to reservations and the transfer of Americans of Japanese descent to relocation camps during World War II.

In the 1990s, a combination of genocide and population transfer occurred in Bosnia, a part of the former Yugoslavia. A hatred bred for centuries, so carefully nurtured that no slight was overlooked, had been kept under wraps during Tito's iron-fisted rule. After the breakup of communism, Yugoslavia split into warring factions and these suppressed, smoldering hatreds broke to the surface. During protracted armed conflict, the Serbs vented their hatred by what they termed **ethnic cleansing,** that is, slaughtering Muslims and some Croatians who lived in areas the Serbs captured and forcing survivors to flee through fear inspired by the slaughter, rape, and torture.

Internal Colonialism

In Chapter 7, the term *colonialism* was used to refer to how the Most Industrialized Nations exploit the Least Industrialized Nations. Conflict theorists use the term **internal colonialism** to refer to how a country's dominant group exploits the country's minority groups. The "routine" form is to use the social institutions to deny minorities access to the society's full benefits. Slavery, reviewed in Chapter 7, is an extreme example of internal colonialism, as was the South African system of *apartheid*. Although the dominant Afrikaaners despised the minority, they found its presence necessary. As Simpson and Yinger (1972) put it, who else would do all the hard work?

Segregation

Segregation—the formal separation of racial or ethnic groups—accompanies internal colonialism. Segregation allows the dominant group to exploit the labor of the minority (butlers, chauffeurs, housekeepers, nannies, street cleaners) while maintaining social distance (Collins 1986). In the U.S. South until the 1960s, by law African Americans and whites had to use separate public facilities such as hotels, schools, swimming pools, bathrooms, and even drinking fountains. In thirty-eight states, laws prohibited interracial marriage. Violators could be punished by prison (Mahoney and Kooistra 1995).

Assimilation

Assimilation is the process by which a minority group is absorbed into the mainstream culture. There are two types. In *forced assimilation* the dominant group refuses to allow the minority to practice its religion,

Amid hysterical fears that Japanese Americans were "enemies within" who would sabotage industrial and military installations on the West Coast, in the early days of World War II Japanese Americans were transferred to "relocation camps." Many returned home after the war to find that their property had been vandalized.

▼▲▼▲▼▲▼▲▼▲▼▲▼▲▼▲▼▲▼▲▼▲▼▲▼▲▼▲▼▲▼▲▼▲▼▲

The Immigrant Experience

Pride against Prejudice: Haitian Assimilation

PHEDE WAS A teenage Haitian who had come to the United States when he was 12 years old. He quickly assimilated. He became a "cover-up," hiding his Haitian identity by Americanizing his name to Fred. He worked at McDonald's full time, sang in the church choir, and became an honors student in high school. He had a good-looking, steady girlfriend, an African American. One day she came to visit with Fred, to talk to him while he took his break at McDonald's. While they were talking Fred's sister arrived. She addressed Fred in Haitian Creole, the national language of Haiti. He was furious. She blew his cover, and he blew his cool. Fred screamed at her to never, ever speak Creole to him again. He did not want to be known as Haitian. Four days later he bought a .22 caliber revolver for $50, drove to an empty lot near his home, and put a bullet through his chest.

Six years after Phede committed suicide, Herve stood before his classmates at the same high school that Phede had attended. Herve, or Herb as he now called himself, tapped out a beat with his fists, shuffled a few dance steps, and rapped:

My name is Herb and I'm not poor . . .
I'm the Herbie that you're lookin' for,
like Pepsi,
a new generation

of Haitian education and
*   determination . . .*
I'm the Herb that you're lookin' for.

Fred and Herb embody two extreme reactions to a single problem, the integration of Haitians into the United States. All new immigrants must integrate into U.S. society in some way, but it is especially difficult for immigrants who are black. During the 1970s and 1980s, no other immigrant group suffered more prejudice and discrimination than Haitians—the Coast Guard attempting to intercept boats of Haitians before they left Haitian waters; the disproportionate incarceration of undocumented Haitians who made it to U.S. shores; the highest disapproval rating of any national group for political asylum requests. Repeatedly, local south Florida and national officials identified Haitians as a health threat: In the late 1970s, tuberculosis was allegedly endemic among Haitians; in the early 1980s, the CDC identified Haitians as one of the primary groups at risk for AIDS. Despite the removal of Haitians from that list, the FDA in the late 1980s refused to accept the donation of blood from those of Haitian descent.

These realities have created a tortured identity for Haitian adolescents. To avoid prejudice, many Haitian students quickly assimilate to U.S. culture and cover up

their Haitian roots. However, because they are black, the U.S. culture to which they assimilate is specifically African-American culture. They exemplify *segmentary assimilation*, assimilation not to mainstream U.S. culture, but to a particular segment of U.S. culture. Phede's becoming Fred permitted him to be accepted by his peers in the predominantly African-American neighborhood where he lived and attended school. He tragically believed that covering up was his only possible path to success.

Herb, however, resolved the tension differently. He adopted an African-American style, the rap song, but he expressed a distinctive immigrant ethic of hard work and success. He celebrated rather than concealed his Haitian culture.

Both Fred and Herb express segmentary assimilation. They both adopted a characteristically African-American expression of themselves. All Haitians initially want to be like Herb instead of Fred. Prejudice and discrimination, however, destroy the best intentions of many, while some do indeed realize their dreams of success in the United States.

Alex Stepick
Florida International University
Pride against Prejudice: Haitian
Refugees in the U.S., Allyn and Bacon
(1996)

speak its language, or follow its customs. Prior to the fall of the Soviet Union, for example, the dominant group, the Russians, required that Armenian schoolchildren be instructed in Russian and that Armenians honor Russian, not Armenian, holidays. In *permissible assimilation*, the minority is allowed to adopt the dom-

inant group's patterns in its own way and at its own speed. In Brazil, for example, an ideology favoring eventual blending of diverse racial types into a "Brazilian stock" encourages its racial and ethnic groups to intermarry. Difficulties of assimilation are discussed in the Immigrant Experience box above.

Multiculturalism (Pluralism)

A policy of **multiculturalism,** also called **pluralism,** permits or even encourages racial and ethnic variation. The minority groups are able to maintain their separate identities, yet participate in the country's social institutions, from education to politics. Switzerland provides an outstanding example of multiculturalism. The Swiss are made up of three separate ethnic groups—French, Italians, and Germans—who have kept their own languages, and live peacefully in political and economic unity. Multiculturalism has been so successful that none of these groups can properly be called a minority.

Race and Ethnic Relations in the United States

Each of us belongs to a racial or ethnic group, and the consequences of that membership are felt in virtually all areas of social life. As shown in Figure 9.4 on the next page, the major racial/ethnic groups in the United States are European Americans, African Americans, Latinos, Asian Americans, and Native Americans. Let's explore some of the implications of racial and ethnic identity.

Constructing an Ethnic Identity

Although each of us is a member of an ethnic group, some of us have a greater sense of ethnicity than others. For some, the boundaries between "us" and "them" are firm, while others have assimilated so extensively into the mainstream culture that they are only vaguely aware of their ethnic origins. With extensive interethnic marrying, some do not even know the countries from which their families originated—nor do they care. If asked to identify themselves ethnically, they respond with something like "I'm German and Irish, with a little Italian and French thrown in—and I think someone said something about being 1/16 Native American."

Why do some people feel an intense sense of ethnic identity, while others feel hardly any? Figure 9.5 on page 229 portrays four factors identified by sociologist Ashley Doane (1993) that heighten or reduce a sense of ethnic identity. From this figure, you can see that the keys are relative size, power, appearance, and discrimination. If your group is relatively small, has little power, looks different from most people in society, and is an object of discrimina-

tion, you will have a heightened sense of ethnic identity. In contrast, if you belong to the numerical majority that holds most of the power, look like most people in the society, and feel no discrimination, you are likely to feel a sense of "belonging," and wonder why ethnic identity is such a big deal.

We can use the term **ethnic work** to refer to how people construct their ethnicity. For people who have a strong ethnic identity, this term refers to how they enhance and maintain their group's distinctions—from clothing, food, and language to religion and holidays. For people with a weak sense of ethnicity, it refers to attempts to recover their ethnic heritage, such as trying to trace family lines. Millions of Americans are engaged in ethnic work, which has confounded the experts who thought that the United States would be a **melting pot,** its many groups quietly blending into a sort of ethnic stew. In recent years, however, Americans have become fascinated with their "roots" and increasingly assertive and prideful of their ethnic background (Karnow and Yoshihara 1992; Wei 1993). Consequently, some analysts think the term "tossed salad," "ethnic mosaic," or even "pizza" more appropriate than "melting pot."

White Europeans

The term **WASP** stands for white Anglo-Saxon Protestant. The WASP colonists were highly ethnocentric, and they viewed white Europeans from countries other than England as inferior. They greeted **white ethnics**—immigrants from Europe whose language and other customs differed from theirs—with negative stereotypes. They viewed the Irish as dirty, lazy drunkards, and they painted Germans, Poles, Jews, Italians, and so on with similarly broad brush strokes.

The cultural and political dominance of the WASPs placed great pressure on immigrants to blend into the mainstream culture. The children of most immigrants embraced the new way of life and quickly came to think of themselves as Americans rather than as Germans, French, Hungarians, and so on. They dropped their distinctive customs as quickly as they could, especially their language. This second generation of immigrants was sandwiched between two worlds, that of their parents from "the old country" and their new home. With fewer inconsistencies and with fewer customs to discard, it was their children, the third generation, who made the easier adjustment. As immigrants from other parts of Europe assimilated into this Anglo culture,

FIGURE 9.4

U.S. Racial and Ethnic Groups

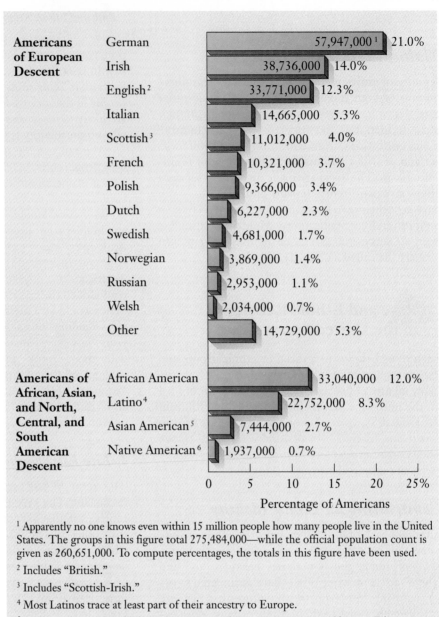

Americans of European Descent		
German	57,947,000 [1]	21.0%
Irish	38,736,000	14.0%
English [2]	33,771,000	12.3%
Italian	14,665,000	5.3%
Scottish [3]	11,012,000	4.0%
French	10,321,000	3.7%
Polish	9,366,000	3.4%
Dutch	6,227,000	2.3%
Swedish	4,681,000	1.7%
Norwegian	3,869,000	1.4%
Russian	2,953,000	1.1%
Welsh	2,034,000	0.7%
Other	14,729,000	5.3%

Americans of African, Asian, and North, Central, and South American Descent		
African American	33,040,000	12.0%
Latino [4]	22,752,000	8.3%
Asian American [5]	7,444,000	2.7%
Native American [6]	1,937,000	0.7%

Percentage of Americans

[1] Apparently no one knows even within 15 million people how many people live in the United States. The groups in this figure total 275,484,000—while the official population count is given as 260,651,000. To compute percentages, the totals in this figure have been used.

[2] Includes "British."

[3] Includes "Scottish-Irish."

[4] Most Latinos trace at least part of their ancestry to Europe.

[5] In descending order, the largest six groups of Asian Americans are Chinese, Filipinos, Japanese, Koreans, Asian Indians, and Vietnamese.

[6] Includes Native American, Eskimo, and Aleut.

Source: Statistical Abstract 1995:Tables 49, 50, 52, 53, 56.

the meaning of WASP expanded to include people of this descent.

Because the English settled the colonies, they established the institutions to which later immigrants had to conform—from the dominant language to the dominant religion and family form. Following their ethnocentric bent, they considered the customs of any group that differed from theirs as inferior. In short, it was the European colonists who, taking power and determining the national agenda, controlled the destiny of the nation and dominated and exploited other ethnic groups. Throughout the years, other ethnic groups have had to react to this institutional and cultural dominance of western Europeans, which still sets the stage for current ethnic relations.

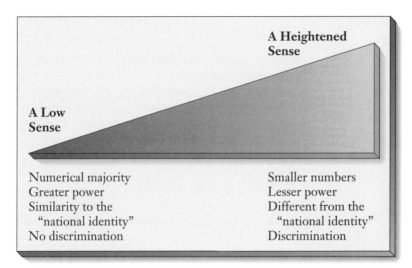

FIGURE 9.5
What Determines Our Sense of Ethnicity?
Source: Based on Doane 1993.

A Heightened Sense

A Low Sense

Numerical majority	Smaller numbers
Greater power	Lesser power
Similarity to the "national identity"	Different from the "national identity"
No discrimination	Discrimination

African Americans

Discrimination was once so integral a part of U.S. life that it was not until 1944 that the U.S. Supreme Court decided that African Americans could vote in southern primaries, and not until 1954 that they had the legal right to attend the same public schools as whites (Carroll and Noble 1977; Polenberg 1980). Well into the 1950s, the South was still openly—and legally—practicing segregation.

The Struggle for Civil Rights

It was 1955, in Montgomery, Alabama. As specified by law, whites took the front seats of the bus, while blacks went to the back. As the bus filled up, blacks had to give up their seats to whites.

When Rosa Parks, a 42-year-old African-American woman and secretary of the Montgomery NAACP, was told she would have to stand so white folks could sit, she refused (Bray 1995). She

Until the 1960s, the South's public facilities were racially segregated. Some were reserved for whites only, others for blacks only. This apartheid was broken by blacks and whites who worked together and risked their lives to bring about a fairer society. Shown here is a 1963 sit-in at a Woolworth's lunch counter in Jackson, Mississippi. Sugar, ketchup, and mustard are being poured over the heads of the demonstrators.

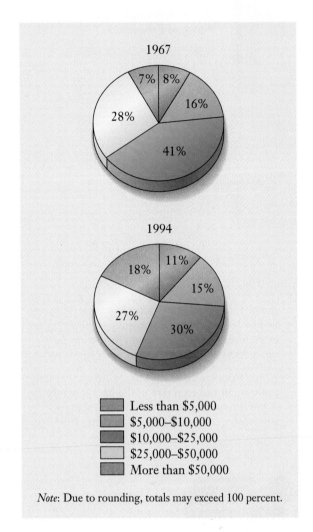

1967

1994

Less than $5,000
$5,000–$10,000
$10,000–$25,000
$25,000–$50,000
More than $50,000

Note: Due to rounding, totals may exceed 100 percent.

Sources: Barringer 1992; *Statistical Abstract* 1995:Table 49.

FIGURE 9.6

Changes in African-American Family Income (in 1993 dollars)

stubbornly sat there while the bus driver fumed and whites felt insulted. Her arrest touched off mass demonstrations, led fifty thousand blacks to boycott the city's buses for a year, and thrust an otherwise unknown preacher into a historic role.

Rev. Martin Luther King, Jr., who had majored in sociology at Morehouse College in Atlanta, Georgia, took control. He organized car pools and preached nonviolence. Incensed at this radical organizer and at the stirrings in the normally compliant African-American community, segregationists also put their beliefs into practice—by bombing homes and dynamiting churches.

Rising Expectations and Civil Strife The barriers came down slowly, but they did come down. Not until 1964 did Congress pass the Civil Rights Act, making it illegal to discriminate in hotels, theaters, and other public places. Then in 1965, Congress passed the Voting Rights Act, banning the fraudulent literacy tests that had been used to keep African Americans from voting.

Encouraged by such gains, African Americans experienced what sociologists call **rising expectations;** that is, they believed better conditions would soon follow. The lives of the poor among them, however, changed little, if at all. Frustrations built up, finally exploding in Watts in 1965, when people living in that African-American ghetto of central Los Angeles took to the streets in the first of what have been termed "the urban revolts." When King was assassinated by a white supremacist on April 4, 1968, ghettos across the nation again erupted in fiery violence. Under threat of the destruction of U.S. cities, Congress passed the sweeping Civil Rights Act of 1968.

Continued Gains Since then, African Americans have made remarkable political, educational, and economic gains. At 9 percent, African Americans have *quadrupled* their membership in the U.S. House of Representatives in the past 20 years (Rich 1986; *Statistical Abstract* 1995:Table 444). As enrollment in colleges increased, the middle class expanded, and it now holds three times the proportion of African Americans than it did in 1940. As shown in Figure 9.6, the proportion of African-American families making over $50,000 has more than doubled since 1967.

The extent of African-American political prominence was highlighted when Jesse Jackson (another sociology major) competed for the Democratic presidential nomination in 1984 and 1988. In 1989, this progress was further confirmed when L. Douglas Wilder of Virginia became the nation's first elected African-American governor (Perry 1990). The political prominence of African Americans came to the nation's attention again in 1991 at the televised Senate hearings held to confirm the appointment of Clarence Thomas to the Supreme Court. After grueling questioning concerning sexual harassment charges brought by Anita Hill, a former employee, Thomas was confirmed as the nation's second African-American Supreme Court Justice.

Current Reversals In spite of these gains, African Americans continue to lag behind in politics, eco-

Table 9.2

Race and Ethnicity and Comparative Well-Being

	Median Family Income	Percentage of White Income	Percentage Unemployed	Percentage of White Unemployment	Percentage Below Poverty Line	Percentage of White Poverty	Percentage Owning Their Homes	Percentage of White Home Ownership
White Americans[a]	$39,308	—	5.3%	—	12.1%	—	68%	—
African Americans	21,548	55%	11.5	217%	32.9	272%	42	62%
Latinos	23,912	61	10.6	200	29.3	242	40	59
Country of origin								
Mexico	23,714	60	10.7	202	30.1	249	44	65
Puerto Rico	20,301	52	12.8	242	36.5	317	23	34
Cuba	31,015	79	7.8	147	18.1	150	53	78
Central and South America	23,649	60	NA[c]	NA	26.7	221	26	38
Asian Americans[b]	44,456	113	4.1	77	15.2	126	52	76
Native Americans	21,619	55	NA	NA	31.2	258	NA	NA

Note: The racial and ethnic groups are listed from largest to smallest.
[a]Non-Latino.
[b]Includes Pacific Islanders.
[c]Not available.
Source: Statistical Abstract 1995:Tables 49, 50, 52, 53, 997.

---

nomics, and education. Only one U.S. Senator is African American, when by ratio in the population we would expect about 12. As Table 9.2 shows, African Americans average only 55 percent of white income, have much more unemployment and poverty, and are much less likely to own their home. As Table 9.3 shows, only 13 percent graduate from college. The increase in families with incomes over

---

Table 9.3

Education and Race or Ethnicity

	Less than High School	High School Graduates	1–3 Years College	College Graduates	Number of Doctorates Awarded	Percentage of Doctorates Awarded
White Americans	18%	34%	25%	23%	23,996	83.8%
African Americans	27	36	24	13	1,288	4.5
Latinos	47[a]	44	NA	9	973	3.4
Asian Americans	15	25	19	41	2,004	7.0
Native Americans	35[a]	56	NA	9	114	0.4

Note: NA = not available. Totals except for doctorates refer to persons 25 years and over.
[a]Totals for Latinos and Native Americans are not listed in the same way in the source as they are for other groups.
Source: Statistical Abstract 1995:Tables 50, 52, 53, 997.

$50,000 mentioned earlier is also only part of the story, for as Figure 9.6 on page 230 also shows, the number of African-American families making less than $5,000 has also increased.

Race or Social Class? A Sociological Debate Controversy has swirled around the conclusions of sociologist William Wilson (1978, 1987), who argues that social class has become more important than race in determining the life chances of African Americans. Wilson notes that prior to civil rights legislation, the African-American experience was dominated by race. Throughout the United States, African Americans were systematically excluded from avenues of economic advancement—denied good schools and good jobs. When civil rights legislation opened new opportunities, middle-class African Americans seized them. As they advanced economically, they left the inner city, following the path taken by other ethnic groups. Unfortunately, just as legal remedies began to open doors to African Americans, opportunities for unskilled labor declined: manufacturing jobs dried up and many other blue-collar jobs were transferred to the suburbs. As a result, while better-educated African Americans were able to obtain middle-class, white-collar jobs, a large group of African Americans—those with poor education and lack of skills—was left behind, trapped by poverty in the inner city.

The result, says Wilson, is two worlds of African-American experience. Those who are stuck in the inner city live in poverty, attend underfunded schools, face dead-end jobs or welfare, and are filled with hopelessness and despair, combined with apathy or hostility. Here is concentrated the violence that so often dominates the evening news. African-American males are more than *seven* times as likely to be homicide victims as are white males, and African-American females are more than *four* times as likely as white females to be murdered (*Statistical Abstract* 1995:Table 133). Homicide is now the leading cause of death for African-American males ages 15 to 24. Each year, more African-American males are killed by other African Americans than died in the entire nine years of the war in Vietnam.

In contrast, African Americans who have moved up the social class ladder live in good housing in secure neighborhoods, work at well-paid jobs that offer advancement, and send their children to good schools. Their middle-class experiences and lifestyle have changed their views on life, and their aspirations and values no longer have much in common with those of African Americans who remain poor.

As discussed in the text, sociologists disagree about the relative significance of race and social class in determining social and economic conditions of African Americans. William Julius Wilson, shown here, is an avid proponent of the social class side of this debate.

According to Wilson, then, social class—not race—has become the most significant factor in the lives of African Americans today.

Many sociologists point out that this analysis omits the vital element—ongoing discrimination—that continues to underlie the relative impoverishment of African Americans. Sociologist Charles Willie (1991), for example, notes that even when they do the same work, whites average more income than do African Americans. This, he argues, points to racial discrimination, not to social class. He and other critics are concerned that Wilson's analysis can be used by people who want to turn back affirmative action. Willie is referring to the many humiliations that African Americans continue to experience because of the color of their skin. Many middle-class and wealthy African Americans, for example, report being pulled over in traffic by police who assume their expensive cars must be stolen. A *New York Times* reporter recounts how she was rushing to catch a plane. She was stopped by a white security officer, who concluded that since she was black and in such a hurry, she must be carrying drugs (Cose 1993).

What is the answer to this sociological debate? It is likely that *both* discrimination and social class are significant in the African-American experience. It is also likely that African Americans who enjoy greater opportunities and occupy higher statuses face considerably less discrimination—although what they do face is no less painful.

Latinos (Hispanic Americans)

Numbers, Origins, and Location When birds still nestled in the trees from which the *Mayflower* was made, there were Latino settlements in Florida and New Mexico (Bretos 1994). Today, Latinos, or Hispanic Americans—people of Spanish origin—are the second-largest minority group in the United States. As shown in Figure 9.7, about 18 million people trace their origins to Mexico (**Chicanos**), almost 3 million to Puerto Rico, over 1 million to Cuba, and almost 4 million people to Central or South America.

Latino immigration has been so large that today about as many Latinos live in the United States as there are Canadians in Canada (28 million). To midwesterners, such a comparison often comes as a surprise, for Latinos are virtually absent from vast stretches of Middle America. As shown in Figure 9.8, 70 percent are concentrated in just four states: California, Texas, New York, and Florida. Most Latinos from Puerto Rico live in New York City, and Cuban Americans are concentrated in the Miami area. In less than ten years, Latinos are expected to become the largest minority group in the United States (*Statistical Abstract* 1996:Table 19).

Spanish Language The Spanish language distinguishes Latinos from other U.S. ethnic minorities. With its large numbers of Latinos, the United States has become one of the largest Spanish-speaking nations in the world (*Statistical Abstract* 1995:Table 57). Because almost half of Latinos are unable to speak English, or can do so only with difficulty, many face a major obstacle to getting good jobs.

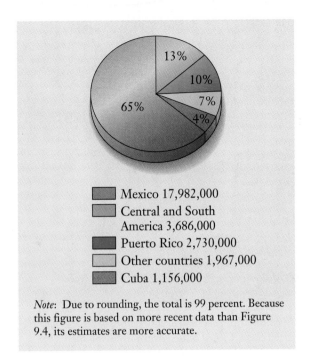

Mexico 17,982,000
Central and South America 3,686,000
Puerto Rico 2,730,000
Other countries 1,967,000
Cuba 1,156,000

Note: Due to rounding, the total is 99 percent. Because this figure is based on more recent data than Figure 9.4, its estimates are more accurate.

Source: Statistical Abstract 1996:Table 53.

FIGURE 9.7
Country of Origin of U.S. Latinos

Politics and Disunity For Latinos, country of origin is highly significant. Puerto Ricans, for example, feel little in common with Latinos from Mexico, Venezuela, or El Salvador—just as last century's immigrants from Germany, Sweden, and England felt little in common with one another. A sign of these

FIGURE 9.8
Where U.S. Latinos Live

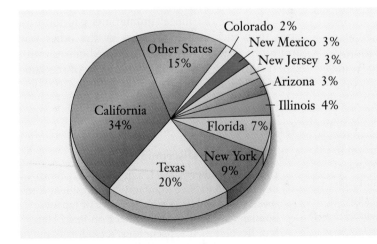

Source: Statistical Abstract 1995:Table 38.

When the U.S. government took control of what is now the southwestern United States, Mexicans living there were transformed from the dominant group into a minority group. As shown in this fiesta in San Antonio, Texas, some Mexican Americans celebrate their ethnic identity with depictions from their rich cultural heritage.

divisions among Latinos is the preference of many to refer to themselves by country of origin, such as Puerto Rican or Cuban American, rather than as Latino or Hispanic (Otten 1994).

As with other ethnic groups, Latinos, too, are separated by social class. The half-million Cubans who fled Castro's rise to power in 1959, for example, were mostly well-educated, well-to-do professionals or businesspeople. In contrast, the 100,000 "boat people" from Cuba who fled in 1980 were mostly lower-class refugees, people with whom the earlier arrivals would not even have associated in Cuba. The earlier arrivals, firmly established in Florida and in control of many businesses and financial institutions, continue to distance themselves from the more recent immigrants.

These divisions of national origin and social class are a major obstacle to Latino political unity. One consequence is a severe underrepresentation in politics. Although they make up at least 8 percent of the U.S. population (perhaps 10 or 11 percent, depending on the statistics used), Latinos hold only 3 percent of the seats in the U.S. Congress and just 1½ percent of the elected state and local offices (*Statistical Abstract* 1995:Tables 444, 456).

Fragmented among themselves, Latinos also find that a huge gulf separates them from African Americans (Skerry and Hartman 1991). With highly distinct cultures and differing ideas about life, these two minorities often avoid each other. As Latinos have become more visible in U.S. society and more vocal in their demands for equality, they have come face to face with African Americans who fear that Latino gains in jobs and at the ballot box will come at their expense (Chavez 1990).

Comparative Conditions Compared with non-Hispanic whites and with Asian Americans, Latinos are worse off on the indicators of well-being shown in Table 9.2 (page 231). Compared with African Americans, however, Latinos are better off on most of these indicators. This table also illustrates the significance of country of origin. You can see that Cuban Americans score much better on these indicators of well-being, while conditions are considerably worse for Puerto Rican Americans. Table 9.3 (page 231) shows that almost half of Latinos do not complete high school, and only 9 percent graduate from college. In a postindustrial society that increasingly stresses advanced skills, these figures indicate growing problems.

The Immigrant Backlash The large numbers of illegal immigrants have led to growing resentment, especially in southern California and New York City, where they are concentrated (Mydans 1993; Miller 1995). Some are convinced that the immigrants are taking jobs away from citizens, others that they are an economic drag on taxpayers through their use of welfare and other social services. Many are disturbed that the United States has lost control over its borders. Whether the illegal immigrants pay more in taxes than they cost in benefits or the other way around has become a matter of heated debate, with experts differing in their interpretations of the same statistics (Huddle 1993; James 1993; Simon 1993).

Asian Americans

A Background of Discrimination

It was December 7, 1941, a quiet Sunday morning destined to "live in infamy," as President Roosevelt described it. Wave after wave of Japanese bombers began their dawn attack on Pearl Harbor. Beyond their expectations, the pilots found the Pacific fleet anchored like sitting ducks.

234

By pushing the United States into World War II, this attack changed the world political order. As the nation readied for war, no American was untouched. Millions left home to battle overseas. Other millions left the farm to work in factories to support the war effort. Everyone lived with the rationing of food, gasoline, coffee, sugar, meat, and other essentials.

Just as waves of planes had rolled over Pearl Harbor, so waves of suspicion and hostility rolled over the Japanese Americans. Many feared that Japan would invade the United States and that the Japanese Americans would fight on Japan's side (Daniels 1975). They also feared that they would sabotage military installations on the West Coast.

Although no Japanese American had been involved in even a single act of sabotage, on February 1, 1942, President Roosevelt signed Executive Order 9066, authorizing the removal of anyone considered a threat from specified military areas. All people on the West Coast who were *one-eighth Japanese or more* were imprisoned, sent to what were termed "relocation camps." They were charged with no crime. There were no indictments, no trials. Japanese ancestry was sufficient cause for being imprisoned.

This was not the first time that Asian Americans had met discrimination. Lured by gold strikes in the West and a vast need for unskilled workers, 200,000 Chinese had immigrated between 1850 and 1880. Feeling threatened by competing cheap labor, Anglo mobs and vigilantes intimidated the Chinese, and in 1882 Congress passed the Chinese Exclusion Act, suspending all Chinese immigration for ten years. Four years later, the Statue of Liberty was dedicated. The tired, the poor, and the huddled masses it was to welcome were obviously not Chinese.

Spillover Bigotry When immigrants from Japan began to arrive, they encountered "spillover bigotry," a stereotype that lumped Asians together, depicting them as sneaky, lazy, and untrustworthy. In 1913 California passed the Alien Land Act, prohibiting anyone ineligible for citizenship from owning land. Federal law, which initially had allowed only whites to be citizens, had been amended in the 1870s to extend that right to African Americans and some Native Americans—although most Native Americans were not granted citizenship in their own land until 1924 (Amott and Matthaei 1991). The Supreme Court ruled that since Asians had not been mentioned in these amendments, they could not become citizens

(Schaefer 1979). In 1943, Chinese residents were finally allowed to become citizens, but those born in Japan were excluded from citizenship until 1952.

A World of Striking Contrasts Today, Asian Americans are the fastest-growing minority in the United States, doubling in just the past ten years (Chun and Zalokar 1992). Most Asian Americans live in the West, as can be seen in Figure 9.9. The three largest groups of Asian Americans—of Chinese, Filipino, and Japanese descent—are concentrated in Los Angeles, San Francisco, Honolulu, and New York City.

Contrary to stereotypes, it is inaccurate to characterize Asian Americans as a single group. They are diverse peoples divided by separate cultures. Like Latinos, Asian Americans from different countries feel little in common with one another and are divided by social class. From Table 9.2 (page 231), you can see that Asian Americans score higher than whites on almost all indicators of well-being. Such

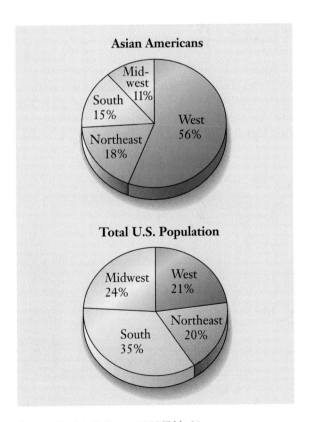

Sources: Statistical Abstract 1995:Table 31.

FIGURE 9.9

Residence of Asian Americans

figures have led to the stereotype that all Asian Americans are successful, a stereotype that masks huge ethnic differences. For example, with more than 30 percent of all households depending on welfare for survival, Southeast Asians have the highest rate of welfare dependency of any racial or ethnic group in the United States (Dunn 1994).

The reason that most Asian Americans have done so well can be traced to four major factors: family life, supportive community, educational achievement, and assimilation into mainstream culture.

Family life gives Asian Americans their basic strength, for they socialize their children into cultural values that stimulate cohesiveness and the motivation to succeed (Bell 1991). Most Asian-American children grow up in close-knit families that stress self-discipline, thrift, and industry (Suzuki 1985). The second factor, supportive community, means that the community supports the parents' efforts. For example, if a child is impolite, other adults will admonish the child and report the situation to the parents (McLemore 1994). This consistent socialization within a framework of encouragement and strict limits provides strong motivation for doing well in school. Their high rate of college graduation, shown in Table 9.3 (page 231), paves the way for high-paying professional and technical work, which, in turn, affords them better-than-average housing and health care. Assimilation, the fourth element, is indicated by their high intermarriage rate, shown in Figure 9.10.

Recent Immigrants In 1975, after the United States was defeated in Vietnam, 130,000 Vietnamese, fearful for their lives because they had sided with the United States, were evacuated. Scattered to various locations across the United States, they were denied an avenue of adjustment used by previous immigrant groups, the ethnic community. On their own, however, most Vietnamese moved to California and Texas, where they established such communities.

Another group of Vietnamese arrived later, termed by the media and the public "the boat people." This group, too, barely escaped with their lives. Fleeing in leaky boats, they were attacked by pirates who robbed them and raped the women. Although no one knows the exact number, it is estimated that 200,000 drowned (McLemore 1994).

In spite of their trauma and a huge language barrier, these immigrants adjusted well. Their children have done remarkably well in school, with three-fourths earning overall GPAs of *A*'s and *B*'s, and over 60 percent scoring in the top half on the standardized California Achievement Test (McLemore 1994). Their high rate of interracial marriage is an indication of their assimilation: 35 percent of Vietnamese Americans born in the United States marry non-Asian Americans (Lee and Yamanaka 1990).

Native Americans

Diversity of Groups Thanks to countless grade B Westerns, many Americans hold stereotypes of Native Americans on the frontier as wild, uncivilized savages, a single group of people subdivided into separate bands. The European immigrants of this period, however, encountered diverse groups of people with a variety of cultures, from nomadic hunters and gatherers to people living in wooden houses in settled agricultural communities. Each group had its own set of norms and values—and the usual ethnocentric pride in its own culture. Consider the following event:

> In 1744, the colonists of Virginia offered college scholarships for "savage lads." They were somewhat taken aback, however, when the Iroquois replied, "Several of our young people were formerly brought up at the colleges of Northern Provinces. They were instructed in all your sciences. But when they came back to us, they were bad runners, ignorant of every means of living in the woods, unable to bear either cold or hunger, knew neither how to build a cabin, take a deer, or

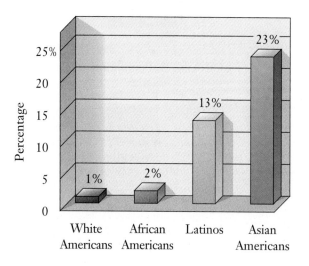

Sources: Lee and Yamanaka 1990.

FIGURE 9.10
U.S. Interracial Marriages

kill an enemy. . . . They were totally good for nothing."

They then added, "If the English gentlemen would send a dozen or two of their children to Onondaga, the great Council would take care of their education, bring them up in really what was the best manner and make men of them." (Nash 1974; in McLemore 1994)

Perhaps numbering 5 million, the Native Americans had no immunity to the diseases the Europeans brought with them. With deaths due to disease—and to warfare, a much lesser cause—their number was reduced to about *one-twentieth* its size, reaching a low point of about a half million at the turn of the century. Native Americans, who now number about 2 million (see Figure 9.4 on page 228), still represent diverse groups. Like Latinos and Asian Americans, Native Americans—who speak 150 different languages—do not think of themselves as a single people that justifies a single label (McLemore 1994).

From Treaties to Genocide and Population Transfer At first, relations between the European settlers and the Native Americans were by and large peaceful. The Native Americans accommodated the strangers, as there was plenty of land for both. As wave after wave of settlers continued to arrive, however, Pontiac, an Ottawa chief, saw the future—and didn't like it. He convinced several tribes to unite in an effort to push the Europeans into the sea. He al-

most succeeded, but failed when the English were reinforced by fresh troops (McLemore 1994).

A pattern developed. The U.S. government made treaties to buy some of a tribe's land, with the promise to honor forever the tribe's right to what it had not sold. European immigrants, who continued to pour into the United States, disregarded these boundaries. The tribes would resist, with death tolls on both sides. Washington would then intervene—not to enforce the treaty—but to force the tribe off its lands. In its relentless drive westward, the U.S. government embarked on a policy of genocide. The U.S. cavalry was assigned the task of "pacification," which translates as slaughtering tens of thousands of Native Americans who "stood in the way" of this territorial expansion.

The acts of cruelty perpetrated by the Europeans against Native Americans appear endless, but two of the most grisly were the distribution of blankets contaminated with smallpox under the guise of a peace offering, and the Trail of Tears, a forced march of a thousand miles from the Carolinas and Georgia to Oklahoma. Poorly clad, 15 thousand Cherokees were forced to make this midwinter march. Four thousand died. The symbolic end to Native American resistance came in 1890 with a massacre at Wounded Knee, South Dakota. Of 350 Native Americans, the U.S. cavalry gunned down 300 men, women, and children (Thornton 1987; Lind 1995). These acts took place after the U.S.

Of all the oppressive acts perpetrated against the Native Americans by the dominant Anglos, it is difficult to choose a single example. Among the top candidates, however, is the Trail of Tears. This painting is a sanitized version, as most victims walked, some were barefoot, although it was winter, and dead bodies were left strewn along the trail. Also, it is unlikely that any Native American was allowed to possess a rifle.

government changed its policy from genocide to population transfer and began to confine Native Americans to specified areas called *reservations.*

The Invisible Minority and Self-Determination

Native Americans can truly be called the invisible minority. Because about 50 percent live in rural areas—one-third in just Oklahoma, California, and Arizona—most other Americans are hardly conscious of a Native American presence in the United States. The isolation of two of every five Native Americans on reservations further reduces their visibility (Thornton 1987; *Statistical Abstract* 1995:Table 51).

The systematic attempts of European Americans to destroy the Native Americans' way of life and their resettlement onto reservations continue to have deleterious effects. Of all U.S. minorities, Native Americans are the worst off. As Table 9.2 on page 231 shows, the poverty rate of Native Americans is high. In addition, their life expectancy is lower than that of the nation as a whole, and their rates of suicide and alcoholism are higher (U.S. Department of Health and Human Services 1990). As Table 9.3 on page 231 shows, their education lags behind the nation's and only 9 percent graduate from college. The percentage of doctorates earned by Native Americans also remains below their proportion of the population.

These negative conditions are the consequence of Anglo domination. In the 1800s, U.S. courts determined that Native Americans did not own the land on which they had been settled and had no right to develop their resources. Native Americans were made wards of the state and treated like children by the Bureau of Indian Affairs (Mohawk 1991). Then, in the 1960s, Native Americans won a series of legal victories that restored their control over the land and their right to determine economic policy. As a result, several Native American tribes have opened businesses on their lands—ranging from industrial parks serving major metropolitan areas to fish canneries. Perhaps the development that has attracted the most attention is the opening of casinos, which for some tribes offers an exit from poverty. More than 200 tribes operate gambling businesses that generate about $2.5 billion a year (McLemore 1994).

A highly controversial issue is *separatism.* Because Native Americans were independent peoples when the Europeans arrived and they never willingly joined the United States, many tribes maintain the right to remain separate from the U.S. government and U.S. society. The chief of the Onondaga tribe in New York, a member of the Iroquois Federation, summarizes the issue this way:

> For the whole history of the Iroquois we have maintained that we are a separate nation. We have never lost a war. Our government still operates. We have refused the U.S. government's reorganization plans for us. We have kept our language and our traditions, and when we fly to Geneva to UN meetings, we carry Hau de no sau nee passports. We made some treaties that lost some land, but that also confirmed our separate-nation status. That the U.S. denies all this doesn't make it any less the case. (Mander 1992)

Like families, groups in societies also retell their past—with the retelling representing a particular point of view. The victors of wars gain a tremendous advantage in such retelling, for their versions become official history. As this photo depicts, even art is part of history. And like official history, art is also far from neutral, as this painting illustrates. Supposedly, this is the "most authentic" depiction of the Battle at Little Bighorn available, but note that the artist uses the perspective of those who lost the battle but won the war. The U.S. cavalry is dominantly portrayed, not the Native Americans. Also note Custer's exaggerated bravery. In the artist's rendering, Custer remains a symbol of "glorious" defeat.

One of the most significant changes is **pan-Indianism,** an emphasis on common elements that run through Native American cultures in the attempt to develop a self-identity that goes beyond the individual tribe. Whether Native Americans wish to work together as in pan-Indianism or to stress separatism and to identify solely with their own tribes, to assimilate into the dominant culture or to remain apart from it, to move to cities or to remain on reservations, to manufacture electronics or to engage only in traditional activities—"such decisions must be ours," say the Native Americans. "We are to be sovereign, not dictated to by the victors of the last centuries' wars."

Looking toward the Future

Race and ethnic relations constitute one of the most volatile issues facing the United States. As we approach the year 2000, two issues we will be grappling with are immigration and affirmative action.

The Immigration Debate

Both immigration and the fear of its consequences are central to U.S. history. The gates opened wide (numerically, if not in attitude) for a massive wave of immigrants who arrived in the late nineteenth and early twentieth centuries. Since 1980, a second great wave of immigration has brought some 15 million new residents to the United States (*Statistical Abstract* 1995:Tables 5, 100). Unlike the first wave, which was almost exclusively from western Europe, this second wave has brought with it much greater variety. In fact, it is changing the U.S. racial/ethnic mix (Henry 1990; Stevenson 1992; Lind 1995). If current trends in immigration (and birth) persist, somewhere between the years 2056 and 2080 the "average" American will trace his or her ancestry to Africa, Asia, South America, the Pacific Islands, the Middle East— to almost anywhere but white Europe.

In some states, the future is arriving much more quickly than this. In just a couple of years, California is expected to be the first state in which ethnic and racial minorities together constitute the majority. Already this is true in California's schools, where Latino, Asian-American, and African-American students outnumber non-Hispanic white students. Californians who request new telephone service from Pacific Bell can speak to customer service representatives in English, Spanish, Korean, Vietnamese, Mandarin, or Cantonese.

As in the past, there is a widespread concern that "too many" immigrants will alter the character of the United States. "Throughout the history of American immigration," write sociologists Alejandro Portés and Ruben Rumbaut (1990), "a consistent thread has been the fear that the 'alien element' would somehow undermine the institutions of the country and would lead it down the path of disintegration and decay." A widespread fear held by native-born European Americans in the early part of the century was that immigrants would subvert the democratic system in favor of communism. Today, some fear that the primacy of the English language is threatened. In addition, the age-old fear that immigrants will take jobs away from native-born Americans remains strong. Finally, minority groups that struggled for political representation fear that newer groups will gain political power at their expense.

Affirmative Action

The role of affirmative action in our multicultural society lies at the center of a national debate about how to steer a course in race and ethnic relations. In affirmative action, quotas based on race (and gender) are used in hiring and college admissions. Liberals, both white and minority, defend affirmative action, saying that it is the most direct way to level the playing field of economic opportunity. If whites are passed over, this is an unfortunate cost we must pay if we are to make up for past discrimination. Conservatives, in contrast, both white and minority, agree that opportunity should be open to all, but say that putting race (or sex) ahead of people's ability to perform a job is reverse discrimination. Because of their race (or sex), qualified people who had nothing to do with past discrimination are being discriminated against. They add that affirmative action stigmatizes the people who benefit from it because it suggests that they hold their jobs because of race (or sex), rather than merit.

This national debate crystallized with several controversial rulings. In 1995, the U.S. Supreme Court declared that quotas by race and sex in hiring are unconstitutional. The regents of the University of California then eliminated the race quotas they had been following in hiring and student admissions. Other states did the same. Then in 1996, California voters went further by passing Proposition 209, which abolished all state affirmative action programs. Federal courts immediately declared the law unconstitutional, ruling that quotas and affirmative

Ethnic work *refers to efforts to establish or to maintain ethnic identity. Ethnic festivals are one form of ethnic work. Their resurgence, as in this Puerto Rican festival in East Harlem, New York, is an indication of a growing sense of ethnic identity among many Americans.*

action are not the same (Lederman 1996; Wirpsa 1996). Evidently the issue of the proper role of affirmative action in a multicultural society will remain center stage for quite some time.

Toward a True Multicultural Society

The potential is for the United States to become a society not only in which different racial/ethnic groups co-exist, but where they respect one another and work for mutually beneficial goals. The idea of a multicultural society is for the various minority groups that make up the United States to participate fully in the social institutions of the country while maintaining their individual cultural integrity. This, however, is only a potential. To reach it will require that groups with different histories and cultures accept one another. Among other things, this means a rethinking of U.S. history as citizens—especially those who belong to the group that has taken its dominance for granted since the founding of the nation—grapple with their "unalterable" beliefs and other national symbols. For example, does the Alamo represent the heroic action of dedicated Americans struggling against huge odds—or the death of extremists bent on wresting territory from Mexico? Was the West settled by individuals determined to find economic opportunity and freedom from oppression—or was it a savage conquest, another brutal expression of white imperialism? Such issues are the focus of the Thinking Critically section that concludes this chapter.

Thinking Critically about Social Controversy

Whose History?

AS SYMBOLIC INTERACTIONISTS stress, the events of life do not come with built-in meaning. Instead, they are given meaning by being placed within a framework that interprets them. Consequently, the victors and the vanquished don't view events in the same way.

Consider the Battle of Little Bighorn. U.S. history books usually recount the massacre of an outnumbered, brave band of cavalrymen, with Gen. George Custer going down to a sad but somehow glorious defeat. When Joe Marshall, a Lakota Sioux, heard this version as a fourth-grader, he mustered all the courage he could, raised his hand, and told the class the version he had heard as he was growing up among the descendants of survivors of the battle. This version refers to an armed group invading Native American lands. When the young boy finished, his teacher smiled indulgently and said, "That's nice, but we'll stick to the real story."

The U.S. history books say there were no survivors of this battle. Think about this for a moment, and the point about perspectives in history will become even more obvious. For the Native Americans, there were *many* survivors. Indeed, those survivors kept the memory of the battle alive, using what is called "oral tradition" to pass to the next generation what took place during that battle. Their descendants have written a book that recounts those events, but the white officials who head the Little Bighorn Battlefield National Monument won't let the book be sold there—only books that recount the event from the European-American perspective may be sold.

It is this issue of perspective that underlies the current controversy surrounding the teaching of history in U.S. schools. The question of *what* should be taught was always assumed, for the school boards, teachers, and textbook writers were united by a background of shared assumptions. For example, it was unquestioningly assumed that George Washington was the general-hero-founder of the nation. No question was raised about whether school curricula should mention that he owned slaves. In the first place, most white school board members, teachers, and textbook writers were ignorant of such facts, and, secondly, on learning of them, thought them irrelevant.

But no longer. The issue now is multiculturalism, how to make certain that the accomplishments of both genders and our many racial and ethnic groups are included. Around the nation, teachers, principals, school boards, and publishers are wrestling with a slew of difficult questions. How much space should be given to Harriet Tubman in comparison to George Washington? Is enough attention paid to discrimination against Asian Americans? to Latinos? Is the attempted genocide of Native Americans sufficiently acknowledged? What about the contributions to U.S. society of women? How about those of white ethnics—Poles, Russians, and so on?

The answers to such questions will give birth to new images of history, which, rather than consisting of established past events, as is commonly supposed, is a flowing, winding, and sometimes twisted perception that takes place in the present.

Sources: Glazer 1991; Charlier 1992.

Summary and Review

Laying the Sociological Foundation

How is race both a reality and a myth?

In the sense that different groups inherit distinctive physical characteristics, race is a reality. There is, however, no agreement regarding what constitutes a particular race, or of how many races there are. In the sense of one race being superior to another, and of there being pure races, however, race is a myth. Nonetheless, the *idea* of race is powerful, shaping basic relationships among people. Pp. 212–214.

How do race and ethnicity differ?

Race refers to inherited biological characteristics, **ethnicity** to cultural ones. Ethnic groups identify with one another on the basis of common ancestry and cultural heritage. P. 214.

What are minority and dominant groups?

Minority groups are people singled out for unequal treatment by members of the **dominant group,** the group with more power, privilege, and social status. Minorities originate with migration and the expansion of political boundaries. Pp. 214–215.

Are prejudice and discrimination the same thing?

Prejudice refers to an attitude, **discrimination** to an act. Some people who are prejudiced do not discriminate, while others who are not prejudiced, do. Pp. 215–219.

How do individual and institutional discrimination differ?

Individual discrimination is the negative treatment of one person by another, while **institutional discrimination** is discrimination built into a society's social institutions. Institutional discrimination often occurs without the awareness of either the perpetrator or the object of discrimination. Referral rates for coronary bypass surgery are but one example. Pp. 219–220.

Theories of Prejudice

How do psychologists explain prejudice?

Psychological theories of prejudice stress **authoritarian personalities** and frustration displaced toward **scapegoats.** Pp. 220–221.

How do sociologists explain prejudice?

Sociological theories focus on how different social environments increase or decrease prejudice. Functionalists stress the benefits and costs that come from discrimination. Conflict theorists look at how the groups in power exploit racial and ethnic group divisions in order to hold down wages and otherwise maintain power. Symbolic interactionists stress how labels create **selective perception** and self-fulfilling prophecies. Pp. 221–223.

Patterns of Intergroup Relations

What are the major patterns of minority and dominant group relations?

Beginning with the least humane, they are **genocide, population transfer, internal colonialism, segregation, assimilation,** and **multiculturalism (pluralism).** Pp. 223–227.

Race and Ethnic Relations in the United States

What are the major ethnic groups in the United States?

From largest to smallest, the major ethnic groups are European Americans, African Americans, Latinos, Asian Americans, and Native Americans. Pp. 227–228.

What heightens ethnic identity, and what is "ethnic work"?

A group's size, power, physical characteristics, and amount of discrimination heighten or reduce ethnic identity. **Ethnic work** is the process of constructing an ethnic identity. For people with strong ties to their culture of origin, ethnic work involves enhancing and maintaining group distinctions. For those without a firm ethnic identity, ethnic work is an attempt to recover one's ethnic heritage. P. 227.

What are some issues in race relations and characteristics of minority groups today?

African Americans are increasingly divided into middle and lower classes, with two sharply contrasting worlds of experience. Illegal immigration has led to a backlash against Latinos. On many measures, Asian Americans are better off than white Americans, but their well-being varies by country of origin. For Native Americans, the primary issues are poverty, nationhood, and settling treaty obligations. The overarching issue for all groups is overcoming discrimination. Pp. 229–239.

Looking toward the Future

What main issues dominate racial/ethnic relations?

The main issues are immigration, affirmative action, and how to develop a true multicultural society. Much of our future hinges on how we address these issues. Pp. 239–241.

Where can I read more on this topic?

Suggested readings for this chapter are listed on page 440.

Glossary

assimilation the process of being absorbed into the mainstream culture (p. 225)

authoritarian personality Theodor Adorno's term for people who are prejudiced and rank high on scales of conformity, intolerance, insecurity, respect for authority, and submissiveness to superiors (p. 221)

Chicanos Latinos whose country of origin is Mexico (p. 233)

compartmentalize to separate acts from feelings or attitudes (p. 224)

discrimination an act of unfair treatment directed against an individual or a group (p. 216)

dominant group the group with the most power, greatest privileges, and highest social status (p. 215)

ethnic cleansing a policy of population elimination, including forcible expulsion and genocide (p. 225)

ethnicity (and **ethnic**) having distinctive cultural characteristics (p. 214)

ethnic work activities designed to discover, enhance, or maintain ethnic and racial identification (p. 227)

genocide the systematic annihilation or attempted annihilation of a race or ethnic group (p. 213)

individual discrimination the negative treatment of one person by another on the basis of that person's perceived characteristics (p. 219)

institutional discrimination negative treatment of a minority group that is built into a society's institutions (p. 219)

internal colonialism the systematic economic exploitation of a minority group (p. 225)

melting pot the idea that Americans of various backgrounds would melt (or merge), leaving behind their distinctive previous ethnic identities and forming a new ethnic group (p. 227)

minority group people who are singled out for unequal treatment on the basis of their physical and cultural characteristics, and who regard themselves as objects of collective discrimination (p. 214)

multiculturalism (also called **pluralism**) a policy that permits or encourages groups to express their individual, unique racial and ethnic identities (p. 227)

pan-Indianism an emphasis on common elements in Native-American culture in order to develop a mutual self-identity and to work toward the welfare of all Native Americans (p. 239)

pluralism another term for multiculturalism (p. 227)

population transfer involuntary movement of a minority group (p. 225)

prejudice an attitude of prejudging, usually in a negative way (p. 216)

race inherited physical characteristics that distinguish one group from another (p. 212)

racism prejudice and discrimination on the basis of race (p. 216)

reserve labor force the term used by conflict theorists for the unemployed, who can be put to work during times of high production and then discarded when no longer needed (p. 222)

rising expectations the sense that better conditions are soon to follow, which, if unfulfilled, creates mounting frustration (p. 230)

scapegoat an individual or group unfairly blamed for someone else's troubles (p. 221)

segregation the policy of keeping racial or ethnic groups apart (p. 225)

selective perception seeing certain features of an object or situation, but remaining blind to others (p. 222)

split labor market a term used by conflict theorists for the practice of weakening the bargaining power of workers by splitting them along racial, ethnic, sex, age, or any other lines (p. 222)

WASP a white Anglo-Saxon Protestant; narrowly, an American of English descent; broadly, an American of western European ancestry (p. 227)

white ethnics white immigrants to the U.S. whose culture differs from that of WASPs (p. 227)

Sociology and the Internet

All URLs listed are current as of the printing of this book. URLs are often changed. Please check our Website http://www.abacon.com/henslin for updates.

1. Effects of Inequality

The Internet allows us to observe without being observed. Let's use this characteristic of the Internet to better understand what inequalities of race and ethnicity mean to group members. Go to Gravity (http://www.newsavanna.com/gravity/gb.acgi$azone.21zz21), a Web site at which African Americans chat with each other. Click on the button beside "List all topics." Choose a topic that seems to be related to feelings or experiences of inequality, and read the exchanges. Look for indications of how inequality, real or perceived, affect people. Do this with several topics, making notes from the pertinent comments. Return to the site once a day for several days to check on current exchanges.

Now write a brief paper answering three questions: (1) Is the exchange similar to what *you* think and talk about? If not, how does it differ? (2) What kinds of experiences do you think lie behind the discussion? (3) Are discussion styles and topics similar to what you would expect within other Internet groups, such as a site dedicated to child abuse or one on fly fishing? Take both your paper and your notes to class, where you will meet in a discussion with other students to exchange ideas. (*Instructor:* It would be good to include people from different racial or ethnic groups in as many of the discussion groups as possible.)

2. Multiculturalism and Assimilation

The author of *The Promised Land*, Nicholas Lemann, is one of the leading U.S. writers on race, class, and poverty. I would like you to become better acquainted with his ideas.

Lemann is a contributing editor for *Harper's Monthly*, so we want to access that journal's home page. First, go to http://www.theAtlantic.com/atlantic/, then page down to "Search the Atlantic Monthly Web site." In the search blank, type "Nicholas Lemann" (without the quotation marks). You should now see a list of topics. First select "biography" and read this brief introduction to the author. Now go back to the previous page (the list of topics). If you can't get there, start over with the home page and repeat the search. First, you should read the article "The Origins of the Underclass." (The article is in two parts, which are not indicated in your search results; you will have to select both "The Origins of the Underclass" entries to find which is Part I.) After you have read both parts of the article, go back to the search results and find "The Unfinished War" (another two-part article). Read both parts of this article. Return to your search results and select "Philadelphia: Black Nationalism on Campus."

Write a paper summarizing each of the articles; then integrate the ideas into a single statement. To do this, you will have to draw your own conclusions about relationships among the ideas. Include your views on whether multiculturalism and assimiliation are incompatible. (*Instructor:* To create a briefer project, you may want to assign the articles to separate students or groups.)

Deidre Scherer, The Sisters, 1991.

C H A P T E R

10

*Inequalities of
Gender and Age*

*I*N TUNIS, THE CAPITAL OF TUNISIA, *on Africa's northern coast, I met some U.S. college students, with whom I spent a couple of days. When they said that they wanted to see Tunis's red light district, I wondered if it would be worth the trip. I already had seen other red light districts, including the unusual one in Amsterdam where the state licenses the women, requires medical checkups (certificates available for customers to inspect), sets the prices, and pays prostitutes social security at retirement. The women sit behind lighted picture windows while customers, strolling along canalside streets, browse from the outside.*

This time the sight turned my stomach.

We ended up on a narrow street opening onto the Mediterranean. Each side was lined with a row of one-room wooden shacks, the structures touching one another, side wall to side wall. In front of each open door stood a young woman. Peering from outside into the dark interior, I could see a tiny room with a well-worn bed.

The street was crowded with men looking at the women. Many of them wore sailor uniforms from countries that I couldn't identify.

As I looked more closely, I could see that some of the women had runny sores on their legs. Incredibly, with such visible evidence of their disease, customers still entered. Evidently the low price (at that time $2) was too much to resist.

With a sickening feeling in my stomach and the desire to vomit, I kept a good distance between myself and the beckoning women. One tour of the two-block area was more than sufficient.

Out of sight, I knew, was a group of men, their wealth coming from these exploited women who were condemned to a short life marked by fear and misery.

In the previous chapter we considered how people are treated differently due to their race and ethnicity. In this chapter, we examine how being classified by sex and age makes significant differences for people's lives. Our primary focus is **gender stratification**—males' and females' unequal access to power, prestige, and property on the basis of sex, but we also examine **ageism,** the prejudice, discrimination, and even hostility directed against people because of their age.

Gender and age are especially significant because they are master statuses that cut across all aspects of social life. No matter what we may attain in life, such as our education, we are labeled *male or female and assigned some age category.* Each label carries an image and a set of expectations about how a person should act. Those images and expectations not only guide our behavior but also serve as the basis of power relations (Rotundo 1983).

INEQUALITIES OF GENDER

Let's begin by considering the distinction between sex and gender.

Issues of Sex and Gender

When we consider how females and males differ, the first thing that usually comes to mind is **sex,** the *biological characteristics* that distinguish males and females. *Primary sex characteristics* consist of a vagina or a penis and other organs related to reproduction; *secondary sex characteristics* are the physical distinctions between males and females that are not directly connected with reproduction. Secondary sex characteristics become clearly evident at puberty, when males develop more muscles, a lower voice, and more hair and height while females form more fatty tissue, broader hips, and larger breasts.

Gender, in contrast, is a *social,* not a biological characteristic. Gender varies from one society to another, for it is what a group considers proper for its males and females. Whereas *sex* refers to male or female, *gender* refers to masculinity or femininity. In short, you inherit your sex, but you learn your gender as you are socialized into specific behaviors and attitudes.

As examined in this chapter's opening vignette, one form of the exploitation of women is prostitution. Another is dangerous, low-paying work that brings health problems. The problem is sometimes misconceptualized, however. For example, the young women working on this construction project in Burma—are they an example of gender exploitation? At first, it may appear so. But if young men also do heavy, dangerous work on this construction project— as they do—the matter moves beyound gender to another global issue of exploitation, that of wealth and social class oppression, one in which both women and men are victims.

The sociological significance of gender is that it is a device by which society controls its members. Gender sorts us, on the basis of sex, into different life experiences. It opens and closes access to power, property, and even prestige. Like social class, gender is a structural feature of society.

Before examining inequalities of gender, let's consider why the behaviors of men and women differ.

Biology or Culture? The Continuing Controversy

Why are most males more aggressive than most females? Why do women enter "nurturing" occupations such as nursing in such far greater numbers than men? To answer such questions, many people respond with some variation of "They're just born that way."

Is this the correct answer? Certainly biology plays a significant role in our lives. Each of us begins as a fertilized egg. The egg, or ovum, is contributed by our mother, the sperm that fertilizes the egg by our father. At the very moment the egg is fertilized, our sex is determined. Each of us receives twenty-three pairs of chromosomes from the ovum and twenty-three from the sperm. The egg has an X chromosome. If the sperm that fertilizes the egg also has an X chromosome, we become female (XX). If the sperm has a Y chromosome, we become male (XY).

That's the biology. Now, the sociological question is, Does this biological difference control our behavior? Does it, for example, make females more comforting and more nurturing, and males more aggressive and domineering? Almost all sociologists take the side of "nurture" in this "nature versus nurture" controversy, but a few do not. The dominant sociological position is represented by the symbolic interactionists. They stress that the visible differences of sex do not come with meanings built into them. Rather, each society gives its own interpretation to these physical differences, and on that basis assigns males and females to separate groups. Here they learn what is expected of them and are given different access to their society's privileges.

Most sociologists find the argument compelling that if biology were the principal factor in human behavior, around the world we would find women to be one sort of person and men another. In fact, however, ideas of gender vary greatly from one culture to another—and, as a result, so do male–female behaviors.

The Tahitians in the South Pacific, for example, provide an interesting contrast to our own gender expectations. They don't give their children names that are identifiable as male or female, and they don't divide their labor on the basis of gender. They expect both men and women to be passive, yielding, and to ignore slights. Neither males nor females are competitive in trying to attain material possessions (Gilmore 1990).

Opening the Door to Biology

The matter of nature versus nurture is not so easily settled, however, and some sociologists acknowledge that biological factors may be involved in some human behaviors other than reproduction and child-bearing. Alice Rossi, a feminist sociologist and former president of the American Sociological Association, has suggested that women are better prepared biologically for "mothering" than are men. She (1977, 1984) says that women are more sensitive to the infant's soft skin and their nonverbal communications. Her basic point is that the issue is not biology *or* society. It is that nature provides biological predispositions, which are then overlaid with culture.

To see why the door to biology is opening, just slightly, in sociology, let's consider a medical accident and a study of Vietnam veterans.

A Medical Accident The drama began in 1963, when 7-month-old identical twins were taken to a doctor for a routine circumcision (Money and Ehrhardt 1972). The inept physician, who was using electrocautery (a heated needle), turned the electric current too high and accidentally burned off the penis of one of the boys. You can imagine the parents' reaction of disbelief—followed by horror, as the truth sank in.

What can be done in a situation like this? The damage was irreversible. The parents were told that the child could never have sexual relations. After months of soul-wrenching agonies and tearful consultations with experts, the parents decided that their son should have a sex-change operation. When he was 17 months old, surgeons used the boy's own skin to construct a vagina. The parents then gave the child a girl's name, dressed him in frilly clothing, let his hair grow long, and began to treat him as a girl. Later, physicians gave the child female steroids to promote female pubertal growth.

At first the results were extremely promising. When the twins were 4½ years old, the mother said

(remember that the children are biologically identical),

> One thing that really amazes me is that she is so feminine. I've never seen a little girl so neat and tidy. . . . She likes for me to wipe her face. She doesn't like to be dirty, and yet my son is quite different. I can't wash his face for anything. . . . She is very proud of herself, when she puts on a new dress, or I set her hair. . . . She seems to be daintier. (Money and Ehrhardt 1972)

About a year later, the mother described how their daughter imitated her while their son copied his father:

> I found that my son, he chose very masculine things like a fireman or a policeman. . . . He wanted to do what daddy does, work where daddy does, and carry a lunch kit. . . . And [my daughter] didn't want any of those things. She wants to be a doctor or a teacher. . . . But none of the things that she ever wanted to be were like a policeman or a fireman, and that sort of thing never appealed to her. (Money and Ehrhardt 1972)

If the matter were this clear-cut, we could use this case to conclude that gender is entirely up to nurture. Seldom are things in life so simple, however, and a twist occurred in this story. In spite of this promising start and her parents' coaching, the twin whose sex had been reassigned did not adapt well to femininity. She rejected dolls and tried to urinate standing up. Classmates called her a "cavewoman" because she walked like a boy. At age 14, after she tried to commit suicide in despair over her inner turmoil, in a tearful confrontation her father told her about her birth and sex change. She then chose to stop her hormone therapy, and later had extensive surgery to partially reconstruct a penis. At age 25 he married a woman and adopted her children (Diamond 1982; Gorman 1997; "Sexual Identity . . . ." 1997).

The Vietnam Veterans Study In 1985, the U.S. government began a health study of Vietnam veterans. To be certain the study was representative, the researchers chose a random sample of 4,462 men. Among the data they collected was a measurement of testosterone for each veteran. Until this time, research on testosterone and human behavior was based on very small samples. Now, unexpectedly, sociologists had a large random sample available, which is turning out to hold surprising clues about human behavior.

This sample supports earlier studies showing that men who have higher levels of testosterone tend to be more aggressive and to have more problems as a consequence. These veterans, when they were boys, were more likely to get in trouble with parents and teachers and to become delinquents. As adults, they are more likely to use hard drugs, to get into fights, to end up in lower-status jobs, and to have more sexual partners. With this history, you probably won't find it surprising to learn that they also are less likely to marry. Certainly their low-paying jobs and trouble with authorities make them less appealing candidates for marriage. Those who do marry are less likely to share problems with their wives. They also are more likely to have affairs, to hit their wives, and to get divorced (Dabbs and Morris 1990; Booth and Dabbs 1993).

The Vietnam veterans study does not leave us solely with biology. Not all men with high testosterone get in trouble with the law, do poorly in school, or mistreat their wives. A chief difference, in fact, is social class. High-testosterone men from higher social classes are less likely to be involved in antisocial behaviors than are high-testosterone men from lower social classes (Dabbs and Morris 1990). *Social* factors (socialization, life goals, self-definitions), then, must also be at work. Uncovering them and discovering how they work in combination with testosterone will be of high sociological interest.

Sociologists stress the social factors that underlie human behavior, the experiences that mold us, funneling us into different directions in life. The study of Vietnam veterans discussed in the text is one indication of how the sociological door is slowly opening to also consider biological factors in human behavior.

▼ **In Sum** We shall have to await further studies, but the initial findings are intriguing, indicating that some behavior that we sociologists usually assume to be due entirely to socialization is, in fact, also influenced by biology. The findings are preliminary, but extremely significant. In the years to come, this should prove to be an exciting—and controversial—area of sociological research. One level will be to document differences that are clearly due to biology. The second level, of much greater sociological significance, is, in sociologist Janet Chafetz's (1990:30) phrase, to determine "how 'different' becomes translated into 'unequal.' "

Global Considerations: How Females Became a Minority Group

Around the world gender is *the* primary division between people. Each society sets up barriers to provide unequal access to power, property, and prestige on the basis of sex. Consequently, sociologists classify females as a *minority group*. Since females outnumber men, you may think this strange, but since this term refers to people who are discriminated against on the basis of physical or cultural characteristics, this concept applies to females (Hacker 1951).

Have females always been a minority group? Some analysts speculate that in some earlier societies women and men may have been social equals. Apparently the horticultural and hunting and gathering societies reviewed in Chapter 4 had much less gender discrimination than does our contemporary world. In these societies, women may have been equal partners with men, and they may have contributed about 60 percent of the group's total food (Lerner 1986).

How did it happen, then, that around the world women came to be systematically discriminated against? Let's consider the primary theory that has been developed.

Childbirth and Social Experiences

This theory points to social consequences of the biology of human reproduction (Lerner 1986; Friedl

1990). In early human history, life was short and to reproduce the human group many children had to be born. Because only females get pregnant, carry a child nine months, give birth, and nurse, women were limited in activities for a considerable part of their lives. To survive, an infant needed a nursing mother. With a child at her breast or in her uterus, or one carried on her hip or on her back, women were physically encumbered. Consequently, around the world women assumed tasks associated with the home and child care, while men took over the hunting of large animals and other tasks that required greater speed and absence from the base camp for longer periods of time (Huber 1990).

As a consequence, males became dominant. It was the men who left camp to hunt animals, who made contact with other tribes, who traded with these other groups, and who quarreled and waged war with them. It was also men who made and controlled the instruments of death, the weapons used for hunting and warfare. It was they who accumulated possessions in trade, and gained prestige by triumphantly returning with prisoners of war or with large animals to feed the tribe. In contrast, little prestige was given to the ordinary, routine, taken-for-granted activities of women—who were not seen as risking their lives for the group. Eventually, men took over society. Their weapons, items of trade, and knowledge gained from contact with other groups became sources of power. Women became second-class citizens, subject to men's decisions.

Evaluating the Theory

Is this theory correct? Remember that the answer lies buried in human history, and there is no way of testing it. Male dominance may be due to some entirely different cause. For example, anthropologist Marvin Harris proposed that because most men are stronger than most women and hand-to-hand combat was necessary in tribal groups, men became the warriors and women the reward to entice them to do battle. Frederick Engels proposed that **patriarchy** (male dominance of a society) developed with the origin of private property (Lerner 1986). He could not explain why private property should have produced patriarchy, however. Gerda Lerner (1986) suggests that patriarchy may even have had different origins in different places. And then, we cannot rule out biology altogether.

Whatever its origins, a circular system of thought evolved. Men developed notions of their own inherent superiority—based on the evidence of their dominant position in society. They surrounded many of their activities with secrecy, and constructed elaborate rules and rituals to avoid "contamination" by females, whom they now openly deemed inferior. Even today, patriarchy is always surrounded with cultural supports to justify male dominance.

As tribal societies developed into larger groups, men, enjoying their power and privileges, maintained their dominance. Long after hunting and hand-to-hand combat ceased to be routine, and even after

One theory about the origin of patriarchy is that because of childbirth women assumed tasks associated with home and child care, while men hunted and performed other tasks requiring greater strength, speed, and absence from home. Shown here is a Yali woman performing the traditional gender tasks assigned her.

large numbers of children were no longer needed to reproduce the human group, males held on to their power. Male dominance in contemporary societies, then, is a continuation of a millennia-old pattern whose origin is lost in history.

The Glass Ceiling and the Glass Escalator: Gender Inequality in the United States

Rather than some accidental hit-or-miss affair, the institutions of each society work together to maintain the group's particular forms of inequality. Customs, venerated by history, both justify and maintain arrangements of gender inequality. Although men have resisted sharing their privileged positions with women, change has come.

Fighting Back: The Rise of Feminism

To see how far we have come, it is useful to see where we used to be. In early U.S. society, the second-class status of women was taken for granted. A husband and wife were legally one person—him (Chafetz and Dworkin 1986). Women could not serve on juries, nor could they vote, make legal contracts, or hold property in their own name. How could times have changed so much that these conditions sound like fiction?

A central lesson of conflict theory is that power yields privilege; that, like a magnet, it draws to the elite the best resources available. Because men held tenaciously on to their privileges and used social institutions to maintain their position, basic rights for women came only through a prolonged and bitter struggle (Offen 1990).

Feminism, the view that biology is not destiny, and, therefore, stratification by gender is wrong and should be resisted, met strong opposition—both by men who had privilege to lose and by many women who accepted their status as morally correct. In 1916, feminists, then known as *suffragists*, founded the National Women's Party. In January 1917, they threw a picket line around the White House. After picketing continuously for six months, the picketers were arrested. Hundreds went to prison, including Lucy Burns and Alice Paul, two leaders of the National Women's Party. The extent to which these women had threatened male prerogatives is demonstrated by their treatment in prison.

Two men brought in Dorothy Day [the editor of a periodical that espoused women's rights], twisting her arms above her head. Suddenly they lifted her and brought her body down twice over the back of an iron bench. . . . They had been there a few minutes when Mrs. Lewis, all doubled over like a sack of flour, was thrown in. Her head struck the iron bed and she fell to the floor senseless. As for Lucy Burns, they handcuffed her wrists and fastened the handcuffs over [her] head to the cell door. (Cowley 1969)

This "first wave" of the women's movement had a radical branch that wanted to reform all the institutions of society and a conservative branch that concentrated on winning the vote for women (Chafetz and Dworkin 1986). The conservative branch dominated, and after the vote was won in 1920 the movement basically dissolved.

Foot binding, a form of violence against women, was practiced in China. This painting of a wealthy woman at her makeup table is from the late 1700s. The woman's tiny feet, which made it difficult for her to walk, was a "marker" of status, indicating that her husband was wealthy and did not need her labor.

The women's struggle for equal rights has been long and hard. During what is known as "the first wave" of the women's movement, against enormous opposition from men women won the right to vote in the United States. They first voted in national elections in 1920.

The "second wave" began in the 1960s. Sociologist Janet Chafetz (1990) points out that up to this time most women thought of work as a temporary activity to fill the time between completing school and getting married. When larger numbers of women began to work, however, they began to compare their working conditions with those of men. This shift in reference group created a different view of working conditions, launching a second wave of protest and struggle against gender inequalities. The goals of this second wave are broad—from changing work roles to changing policies on violence against women.

This second wave of the women's movement also has its liberal and conservative branches. Although each holds a different picture of what gender equality should look like, they share several goals, including nondiscrimination in job opportunities and pay. Both liberals and conservatives have a radical wing. The radicals on the liberal side call for hostility toward men, radicals on the conservative side a return to traditional family roles. All factions—whether radical or conservative—claim to represent the "real" needs of today's women. It is from these claims and counterclaims that the women's movement will continue to take shape and affect public policy.

Although women enjoy fundamental rights today, gender inequality continues to play a central role in social life. Let's look at gender relations in education, in medicine, and at work.

Gender Inequality in Education

Gender inequality in education is not readily apparent. More women than men are enrolled in U.S. colleges and universities, and women earn 54 percent of all bachelor's degrees. A closer look, however, reveals gender tracking. Women earn 89 percent of bachelor's degrees in home economics, while men earn 86 percent of bachelor's degrees in military "science." Similarly, men earn 86 percent of bachelor's degrees in the "masculine" field of engineering, while women are awarded 84 percent of bachelor's degrees in the "feminine" field of health sciences (*Statistical Abstract* 1995:Table 300). Because socialization gives males and females different orientations to life, they enter college with sex-linked aspirations. It is this socialization—rather than any presumed innate characteristics—that channels males and females into different educational paths.

If we follow students into graduate school, we see that with each passing year the proportion of women decreases. Table 10.1 gives us a snapshot of doctoral programs in the sciences. Note how aspirations (enrollment) and accomplishments (doctorates conferred) are sex linked. In all but two of the doctoral programs men outnumber women, and in *all* of them women are less likely to complete the doctorate.

If we follow those who earn doctoral degrees back into colleges and universities, we find gender stratification in rank and pay. Throughout the United States, women are less likely to be full professors, the highest rank. In addition, women full professors average less pay than men full professors. The higher the prestige of the university, the greater the discrimination, and women are most likely to be full professors in community colleges (DePalma 1993).

Although we still are a long way from equality, encouraging changes have taken place. As Figure 10.1 illustrates, the proportion of professional degrees earned by women has increased sharply. The most startling change is in dentistry, where in 1970 across the entire United States only 34 women earned this degree. That annual total is now over 1,200 (*Statistical Abstract* 1996:Table 304).

Table 10.1

Doctorates in Science, by Sex

Field	Students Enrolled in Doctoral Programs		Doctorates Conferred		Completion Ratio*a* (higher or lower than expected)	
	Women	Men	Women	Men	Women	Men
Computer Sciences	22%	78%	13%	87%	−41	+12
Agriculture	32%	68%	21%	79%	−34	+16
Mathematics	31%	69%	21%	79%	−32	+14
Engineering	14%	86%	10%	90%	−28	+5
Health Sciences	76%	24%	58%	42%	−24	+75
Social Sciences	44%	56%	34%	66%	−23	+18
Physical Sciences	25%	75%	22%	78%	−12	+4
Psychology	67%	33%	60%	40%	−10	+21
Biological Sciences	46%	54%	42%	58%	−9	+7

*a*The difference between the proportion enrolled in a program and the proportion granted doctorates divided by the proportion enrolled in the program. Data for enrollment are from 1993, for doctorates granted data are from 1992.
Source: Statistical Abstract 1995:Tables 301, 995.

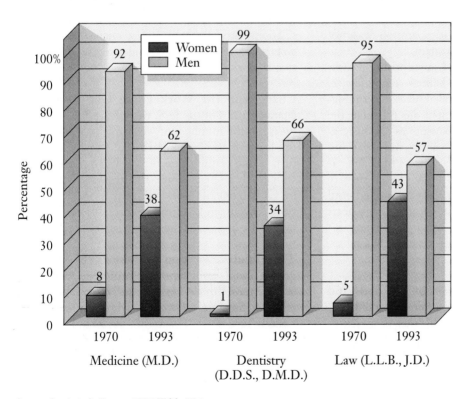

Source: Statistical Abstract 1996:Table 304.

FIGURE 10.1
Gender Changes in Professional Degrees

Gender Inequality in Health Care

A Matter of Life and Death

Medical researchers were perplexed. Reports were coming in from all over the country indicating that women were twice as likely to die after coronary bypass surgery. Researchers at Cedars-Sinai Medical Center in Los Angeles checked their own records. They found that of almost 2,300 coronary bypass patients, 4.6 percent of the women died as a result of the surgery, compared with only 2.6 percent of the men.

These findings presented a sociological puzzle. To solve it, medical researchers first turned to biology (Bishop 1990). In coronary bypass surgery, a blood vessel is taken from one part of the body and stitched to a coronary artery on the surface of the heart. Perhaps this operation was more difficult to perform on women because of their smaller hearts and coronary arteries. To find out, researchers measured the amount of time that surgeons kept patients on the heart–lung machine while they operated. They were surprised, for women spent *less* time on the machine than men, indicating that the operation was not more difficult to perform on women.

As the researchers probed, a surprising answer unfolded. It lay in neither biology nor lifestyle. Rather, the culprit was unintended sexual discrimination. Referring physicians simply did not take the chest pains of their women patients as seriously as those of their men patients. Physicians were *ten* times more likely to give men exercise stress tests and radioactive heart scans. They also sent men to surgery on the basis of abnormal stress tests, but waited until women showed clear-cut symptoms of coronary heart disease before sending them to surgery. Being referred for surgery after the disease is further along reduces the chances of survival.

Women's Organs as Sources of Disease—and Profit

Sociologist Sue Fisher (1986), who did participant observation in a hospital, was surprised to hear surgeons recommend total hysterectomy (removal of both the uterus and the ovaries) *when no cancer was present*. When she asked why, she found that men doctors regard the uterus and ovaries as "potentially disease producing," and also as unnecessary after the childbearing years. Underlying their eagerness to slice away these organs is another motive—greed. Surgeons make money by performing this surgery, and they "sell" the operation. Here is

how one resident explained the hard sell to sociologist Diana Scully (1994):

You have to look for your surgical procedures; you have to go after patients. Because no one is crazy enough to come and say, "Hey, here I am. I want you to operate on me." You have to sometimes convince the patient that she is really sick—if she is, of course [laughs], and that she is better off with a surgical procedure.

The way the doctor "convinces" the woman is to say that, unfortunately, the examination has turned up fibroids in her uterus—and they *might* turn into cancer. This statement is often sufficient, for it frightens women, who can picture themselves at their own funeral ready to be buried. What the surgeon withholds is the rest of the truth—that the fibroids probably will not turn into cancer and there are a variety of nonsurgical alternatives.

Gender Inequality in the Workplace

To examine the work setting is to make visible basic relations between men and women. Let's look at changes in the work force and examine discrimination at work.

Changes in the Work Force One of the chief characteristics of the U.S. work force is a steady increase in the numbers of women who work outside the home for wages. Figure 10.2 shows that at the turn of the century one of five U.S. workers was a woman. By 1940, this ratio had grown to one of four, by 1960 to one of three, and today it is almost one of two. As you can see from Figure 10.3, this ratio is one of the highest in the industrialized world.

The Quiet Revolution Because its changes are so gradual but its implications so profound, sociologists use the term **"quiet revolution"** to refer to the increasing numbers of women who have joined the ranks of paid labor. This trend, shown in Figure 10.4 on page 256, means a transformation of consumer patterns, relations at work, self-concepts, and relationships with boyfriends, husbands, and children. For immigrants, too, the entry of women into the workplace can have profound effects on family relationships. As discussed in the Immigrant Experience box on p. 258, this is particularly true when the immigrants are from cultures in which women are expected to remain subservient to men.

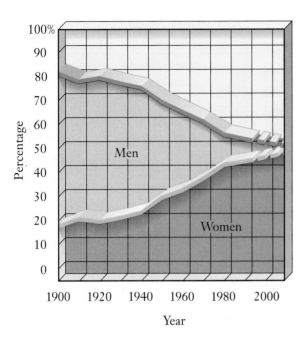

Broken lines indicate the author's projections.

Source: Statistical Abstract—Various years and 1995: Table 627.

FIGURE 10.2

Men's and Women's Proportion of the U.S. Labor Force

One of the most significant aspects of the quiet revolution is indicated by Figure 10.4c. Note that since 1960 the proportion of married women with preschool children who work for wages has tripled. It now equals the average of all U.S. women.

These materials provide a background of historical change, but they do not show inequality. For that, let's look at the pay gap.

The Pay Gap How would you like to earn an extra $800,000 to $900,000 on your job? If this sounds attractive, all you have to do is average an extra $22,000 a year between the ages of 25 and 65.

This must be almost impossible, you say? On the contrary, it's easy if you are a *male* college graduate. As Figure 10.5 on page 257 shows, this is how much more the *average man* with a bachelor's degree or higher will earn. Hardly any single factor pinpoints gender discrimination better than this total. Figure 10.5 also shows that the gender gap in earnings applies to all levels of education. In fact, if we consider all year-round, full-time workers in all fields, we find that women's wages average only 74 percent of men's (*Statistical Abstract* 1996:Table 725). As Figure 10.6 on page 257 shows, until 1985 women's earnings hovered between 58 and 61 percent of men's, so being paid three-fourths of what men make is actu-

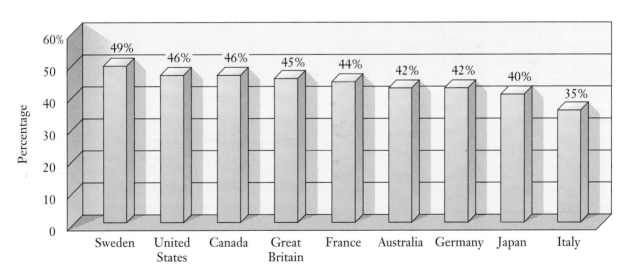

Source: Statistical Abstract 1995:Tables 649, 1386.

FIGURE 10.3

Women as a Percentage of Total Civilian Workers

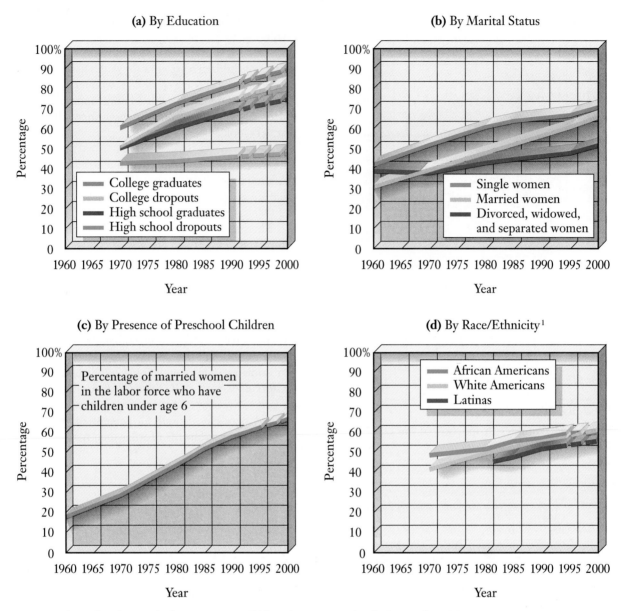

(a) By Education

(b) By Marital Status

(c) By Presence of Preschool Children

(d) By Race/Ethnicity[1]

[1]Data for other racial/ethnic groups unavailable in the source; no data for Latinas for 1970–1980.

Broken lines indicate the author's projections.

Source: Statistical Abstract 1993:Tables 622, 633.

FIGURE 10.4

Percentage of Women in the U.S. Labor Force by Education, Marital Status, Preschool Children, and Race/Ethnicity

ally an improvement. A gender gap in pay character-izes all industrialized nations, but only in Japan is the gap larger than in the United States (Blau and Kahn 1992).

What logic can underlie the gender pay gap? Earlier we saw that college degrees are gender linked, so perhaps this gap is due to career choices. Maybe more women choose lower-paying jobs, such

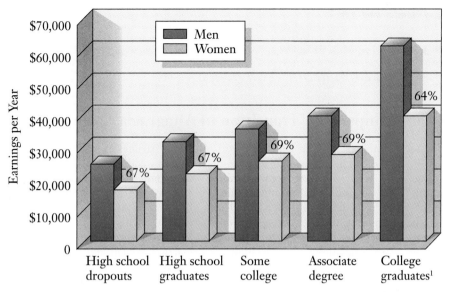

FIGURE 10.5

The Gender Pay Gap, by Education

¹Includes bachelor's and all higher degrees.

Source: Statistical Abstract 1996: Table 728.

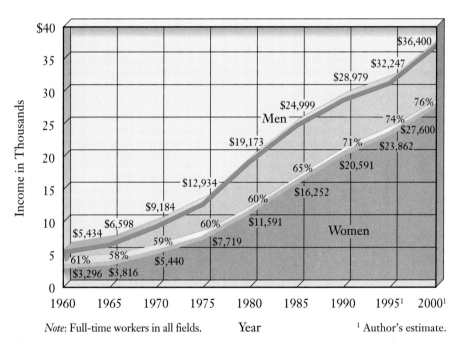

FIGURE 10.6

The Gender Pay Gap: What Percentage of Men's Income Do Women Earn?

Note: Full-time workers in all fields.   Year   ¹ Author's estimate.

Source: Beeghley 1989: 239 *Statistical Abstract* 1996: Table 725.

as grade school teaching, whereas men are more likely to go into better-paying fields, such as business, law, and engineering. Actually, this is true, and researchers have found that about *half* the pay gap is due to such factors. The balance, however, is due to gender discrimination (Kemp 1990).

Depending on your sex, then, you are likely either to benefit from gender discrimination—or to be its vic-

tim. Because the pay gap will be so important in your own work life, let's follow some college graduates to see how it actually takes place. Economists Rex Fuller and Richard Schoenberger (1991) examined the starting salaries of the business majors at the University of Wisconsin, of whom 47 percent were women. They found that the women graduates began work with an average salary that was 11 percent ($1,737) less than the men's.

The Immigrant Experience

Changing Relationships: The Transition of Altagracia Ortiz

ALTAGRACIA ORTIZ EMIGRATED to New York City from Santiago in 1971 at the age of 26, leaving her husband and children temporarily behind with his parents. An accomplished seamstress, Altagracia easily found work through a cousin in a unionized apparel factory. By 1977, she had accumulated sufficient savings to successfully sponsor her husband, Carlito's, migration.

The couple's problems began almost from the moment Carlito stepped off the plane. "Maybe I had changed after so many years of being on my own, being my own boss," she stated. "When I left Santo Domingo [the Dominican Republic], I was an innocent who was totally dependent on my husband's wages. Here it was different, and he couldn't stomach it."

Altagracia said that she and her husband struggled constantly over household budgeting and socializing. "He wanted me to give him my salary, and then he would give me a small household allowance. I knew he would use my hard-earned money for heavy drinking and who knows what else. I insisted that we pool our wages and decide together on all household expenses. . . . He would get furious when I used some of my money to go out with some girl friends, but he saw nothing wrong

with staying out all night with some of his friends."

The breaking point came when Carlito had trouble finding a job a few years after they had brought their children to New York. Yet he refused "to help me with the housework and children, even though he was staying home and sleeping the whole day. So finally I said to him, you are no man. You want me to be both *el jefe de casa* (male household head) and *la ama de casa* (housewife). I told him to move in with his sister, and he did; our marriage of more than twenty-five years was over. . . . Maybe if he had tried harder to find work; or maybe if he had tried to help even a little, we would still be together, but, imagine, he just refused to help."

Altagracia was acutely aware of the social and economic ramifications of her decision to end the marriage. She explained, "In my country all little girls, no matter how rich or poor they may be, dream of a church wedding with the bride all dressed in white lace. This means the girl has respect and social standing. She is not like the woman who lives without a man and has children with whomever—like they say in my country 'one poor hen with lots of chicks all fathered by different roosters!' So here I was after so

much struggling to have that church wedding, to bring my family together in New York, only to be a woman left alone without a husband. . . . It was one of the saddest days in my life. Not only did I lose the respect I once had as a married woman, but my children and I lost the material support Carlito was able to provide. And here we are today, *pobrecitos* ("poor little ones"), as you can see."

Altagracia's situation worsened when only five months after her separation, she was permanently laid off from her long-standing job at the apparel factory. After experiencing problems both in gaining another job through the union and in obtaining unemployment benefits, Altagracia decided to apply for welfare. She combined this income with wages she received, "working off the books" in a neighborhood sweatshop. Her average weekly wage of $80 plus $135 in welfare has allowed Altagracia to pay the rent on the apartment she shares with her children and to afford the most basic necessities.

Patricia R. Pessar
Yale University
A Visa for a Dream: Dominicans in New York, Allyn and Bacon (1996)

You might be able to think of valid reasons for this initial pay gap. For example, the women might have been less qualified. Perhaps their grades were lower. Or maybe they did fewer internships. If so, they would deserve lower salaries. To find out, Fuller and Schoenberger reviewed the students' college records. To their surprise, they found that the women had *higher* grades and *more* internships. In

other words, if women were equally qualified, they were offered lower salaries—and if they were more qualified, they were offered lower salaries—a classic lose–lose situation.

What happened after these graduates were on the job? Did their starting salaries wash out, so that after a few years the women and men earned about the same? Fuller and Schoenberger checked their salaries five years later. Instead of narrowing, the pay gap had grown even wider. By this time, the women earned 14 percent ($3,615) less than the men.

As a final indication of the extent of the U.S. gender pay gap, consider this. As noted in Chapter 8, the CEOs of the 350 largest U.S. corporations average $1.8 million a year. I examined the names of these CEOs, and *not one of them is a woman.* Your best chance to reach the top is to be named John, Robert, James, William, or Charles, in that order. Edward, Lawrence, and Richard are also very helpful. Amber, Candace, Leticia, and María, however, apparently bring a penalty.

The Glass Ceiling or the Glass Escalator? What keeps women from breaking through the *glass ceiling*, the mostly invisible barrier that keeps women from reaching the executive suite? Researchers have identified a "pipeline" that leads to the top—marketing, sales, and production—positions that directly add to the corporate bottom line (Reich 1995). Women, however, stereotyped as better at "support," are steered into human resources or public relations. There successful projects are not appreciated the same as those that bring in corporate profits—and bonuses for their managers. Felice Schwartz, founder of Catalyst, an organization that focuses on women's issues in the workplace, put it this way: men, who dominate the executive suite, stereotype potential leaders as people who look like themselves (Lopez 1992).

Another reason that the glass ceiling is so powerful is that women lack mentors, successful executives who take an interest in them and teach them the ropes. Some men executives fear gossip and sexual harassment charges if they get close to a woman in a subordinate position. Others don't mentor women because of stereotypes of women as weak (Lancaster 1995; Reich 1995). To lack a mentor is no trivial matter, for supposedly all top executives have had a coach or mentor (Lancaster 1995).

The contrast becomes all the more apparent from research by sociologist Christine Williams (1995), who studied nurses, elementary school teachers, librarians, and social workers. Interviewing both men and women in these traditionally women's occupations, she found that instead of bumping into a glass ceiling, the men climbed aboard a "glass escalator." That is, compared with women the men were accelerated into more desirable work assignments, higher-level positions, and larger salaries. The motor that drives the glass escalator is gender, the

stereotype that because someone is male he is more capable.

Sexual Harassment

In a third-floor hallway at a convention of Navy pilots at the Las Vegas Hilton, male officers lined up against the walls. When female pilots tried to walk by, the men pushed, touched, and rubbed the women. One female officer reported that a male officer grabbed her buttocks with both hands, then grabbed her breasts. Other women reported similar incidents (*U.S. News & World Report*, July 13, 1992).

When the women complained, male officers shrugged their shoulders and said with a wink that "boys will be boys." They felt that the women were being too sensitive. "What do you expect when you're around a bunch of drunk pilots, anyway?" A Navy investigation found no fault. When the female officers complained to the media, pressures mounted, and the Secretary of the Navy resigned.

Sexual harassment—unwelcome sexual attention that affects someone's job or creates a hostile working environment, whether from management or by fellow employees if management permits the behavior—was not recognized as a problem until the 1970s. Before this, women considered unwanted sexual statements, touches, looks, and pressures to have sex as a personal matter.

With the prodding of feminists, women began to see unwanted sexual advances at work as part of a *structural* problem. That is, they began to see them not simply as a man here and there doing obnoxious things because he was attracted to a woman, but, rather, as men using their positions of authority to force unwanted sexual activities on women. Today, with the changes in the work force that we just reviewed, women are also sexual harassers.

As symbolic interactionists stress, terms affect our perception. So it is with *sexual harassment*, and because we have this term we now see the same behaviors in a different light from our predecessors. This term has hit such a nerve that it has been exported around the world, as is discussed in the Global Glimpse box on the next page.

▶ Gender and Violence

The high rate of violence in U.S. society shocks foreigners and frightens Americans. Only a couple of generations back, many Americans left their homes and cars unlocked. Today, fearful of carjackings, they

A Global Glimpse

Sexual Harassment in Japan

THE PUBLIC RELATIONS department had come up with an eye-catcher: each month, the cover of the company's magazine would show a woman taking off one more piece of clothing. The men were pleased, looking forward to each new issue.

Six months later, with the cover girl poised to take off her tank top in the next edition, the objections of women employees had grown too loud to ignore. "We told them it was a lousy idea," said Junko Takashima, assistant director of the company's women's affairs division. The firm dropped the striptease act.

The Japanese men didn't get the point. "What's all the fuss about?" they asked. "Beauty is beauty. We're just admiring the ladies. It's a wish, or maybe a hope. It's nothing serious. It just adds a little spice to boring days at the office."

"It's degrading to us, and it must stop," responded female workers, who, encouraged by the U.S. feminist movement, have broken their tradition of passive silence.

The Japanese have no word of their own to describe this situation, so they have borrowed the English phrase "sexual harassment." They now are struggling to apply it to their own culture. In Japan, a pat on the bottom has long been taken for granted as a boss's way of getting his secretary's attention.

Differing cultural expectations have led to problems when Japanese executives—always male—have been sent to overseas factories. A managing director of Honda learned this the hard way. During business meetings he repeatedly put his hand on the knee of a U.S. employee. When she threatened to sue, he was transferred back to Japan.

The Japanese expectation that everyone will work together harmoniously does not make it easy to complain. But some women are now speaking out, and discovering how to apply the Western concept of "sexual harassment."

Source: Based on Graven 1990.

even lock their cars while driving, and, fearful of rape and kidnappings, escort their children to school. Lurking behind these fears is the gender inequality of violence—that females are most likely to be victims of males, not the other way around. Let's briefly review this almost one-way street in gender violence.

Violence against Females

Because rape was the recurring theme of our review of research methods in Chapter 1, here we shall just mention a couple of its primary features. Rape has become so common in the United States that each year 1 of every 1,000 females 12 years of age and over in the entire country is raped. Rapists are almost exclusively young males. Although males aged 15 to 24 make up only about 15 percent of the U.S. male population, about 34 percent of those arrested for rape are in this age group (*FBI Uniform Crime Reports* 1994:Table 39; *Statistical Abstract* 1994:Table 15).

A form of rape that has been given much media attention is date rape. What has shocked so many about date rape (also known as *acquaintance rape*) is

studies showing that it is not an isolated event here and there. For example, about 21 percent of women taking the introductory psychology courses at Texas A&M University reported that they had been forced to have sexual intercourse. Date rape most commonly occurs not between relative strangers on first dates, but between couples who have known each other about a year (Muehlenhard and Linton 1987). Most date rapes go unreported. Those that are reported are difficult to prosecute, for juries tend to believe that if a woman knows the accused she wasn't "really" raped (Bourque 1989).

Table 10.2 summarizes U.S. patterns of murder and gender. Note that although females make up about 51 percent of the U.S. population, they don't even come close to making up 51 percent of the nation's killers. Note also that when a female is the victim, nine times out of ten the killer is a male.

Women are also disproportionate victims of family violence. Spouse battering, marital rape, and incest are discussed in Chapter 12, while genital circumcision is the focus of the Global Glimpse box on page 262.

Table 10.2

Killers and Their Victims

	The Killers	
	Male	*Female*
The Victims		
Male	88%	12%
Female	91%	9%

Source: Sourcebook 1995:Table 3-123.

Table 10.3

U.S. Women in Political Office, 1995

	Percentage and Number Held by Women	
	Percentage	*Number*
National Office		
U.S. Senate	9%	9
U.S. House of Representatives	11%	47
State Office		
Governors	2%	1
Attorneys General	22%	11
Secretaries of State	28%	14
Treasurers	32%	16
State Auditors	8%	4
State Legislature	21%	1,536
Local Office		
Mayors[a]	18%	177

Note: Does not include women elected to the judiciary, appointed to state cabinet-level positions, elected to executive posts by the legislature, or members of a university board of trustees.

[a]Of cities with a population over 30,000.

Source: National Women's Political Caucus 1995.

A Feminist Understanding of Gender Patterns in Violence

Feminist sociologists have been especially effective in bringing violence against women to the public's attention. Some use symbolic interactionism, pointing out that to associate strength and virility with violence—as is done in so many areas of U.S. culture—is to produce violence. Others use conflict theory. They argue that as gender relations change males are losing power, and that some males become violent against females as a way to reassert their declining power and status.

Solutions

There is no magic bullet for this problem, but to be effective any solution must break the connection between violence and masculinity. This would require an educational program that incorporates school, churches, homes, and the media. Given such aspects of U.S. history as gun-slinging heroes of the West, and current messages in the mass media, it is difficult to be optimistic that a change will come soon.

Our next topic, women in politics, however, gives us much more reason for optimism.

The Changing Face of Politics

Why don't women, who outnumber men, take political control of the nation? Eight million more women than men vote in U.S. national elections (*Statistical Abstract* 1995:Table 459). As Table 10.3 shows, however, men officeholders greatly outnumber women. Despite the political gains women have made in recent elections, since 1789 1,800 men have served in the U.S. Senate, but only 24 women, including nine current senators. Not until 1992 was the first African-American woman (Carol Moseley-Braun) elected to the U.S. Senate (National Women's Political Caucus 1994; *Statistical Abstract* 1995:Table 444).

The Reasons for Women's Underrepresentation in Politics

Why are women underrepresented in U.S. politics? First, women are still underrepresented in law and business, the careers from which most politicians come. Further, most women do not perceive themselves as a class of people who need bloc political action in order to overcome domination. Most women also find the irregular hours needed to run for office incompatible with their role as mothers. Fathers, in contrast, whose ordinary roles are more likely to take them away from home, do not feel this same conflict.

▲ ▲ ▲ ▲ ▲ ▲ ▲ ▲ ▲ ▲ ▲ ▲ ▲ ▲ ▲ ▲ ▲ ▲ ▲ ▲

A Global Glimpse

Female Circumcision

FEMALE CIRCUMCISION IS common in parts of Muslim Africa and in some parts of Malaysia and Indonesia. This custom, often called *female genital mutilation* (FGM) by Westerners, is also known as *clitoral excision, clitoridectomy, infibulation,* and *labiadectomy,* depending largely on how much of the tissue is removed. Worldwide, between 100 million and 200 million females have been circumcised.

In some cultures only the girl's clitoris is cut off, in others the clitoris and both the labia majora and the labia minora. The Nubia in the Sudan cut away most of the girl's genitalia, then sew together the remaining outer edges with silk or catgut. The girl's legs are bound from ankles to waist for several weeks while scar tissue closes up the vagina almost completely. They leave a very small opening—variously described as the size of a matchstick or a pinhole—for the passage of urine and menstrual fluids. In East Africa the vaginal opening is not sutured shut, but the clitoris and both sets of labia are cut off.

Among most groups, the surgery takes place between the ages of 4 and 8. In some cultures it occurs seven to ten days after birth, while in others it is not performed until girls reach adolescence. It is often done without anesthesia, and the pain is so excruciating that adults sometimes must hold the girl down. In urban areas, the operation is sometimes performed by physicians; in rural areas, it is usually performed by a neighborhood woman.

Some of the risks are shock, extensive bleeding, infection, infertility, and death. Ongoing complications include vaginal spasms, painful intercourse, and lack of orgasms. The tiny opening makes

This preadolescent girl is being circumcised without anesthesia. As discussed in this box, female circumcision has become a major issue in violence against females.

urination and menstruation difficult. Frequent urinary tract infections result from urine and menstrual flow building up behind the little opening.

When the woman marries, the opening is cut wider to permit sexual intercourse. In some groups, this is the husband's responsibility. Before a woman gives birth, the opening is enlarged further. After birth, the vagina is again sutured shut, a cycle of surgically closing and opening that begins anew with each birth.

One woman, circumcised at 12, described it this way:

"Lie down there," the excisor suddenly said to me, pointing to a mat stretched out on the ground. No sooner had I laid down than I felt my frail, thin legs tightly grasped by heavy hands and pulled wide apart. I lifted my head. Two women on each side of me pinned me to the ground. My arms were also immobilized. Suddenly I felt some strange substance being spread over my genital area. . . . It was supposed to facilitate the excision. . . . I would have given anything at that moment to be a thousand miles away; then a shooting pain brought me back to reality. . . . I underwent the ablation of the labia minor and then of the clitoris. The operation seemed to go on forever . . . I was in the throes of agony, torn apart both physically and psychologically. It was the rule that girls of my age did not weep in this situation. I broke the rule. I reacted immediately with tears and screams of pain. . . . Never have I felt such excruciating pain!

[After the operation] they forced me, not only to walk back to join the other girls who had already been excised, but to dance with them . . . I was doing my best . . . then I fainted. . . . It was a month before I was completely healed. . . . When I was better, everyone mocked me, as I hadn't been brave, they said. (Walker and Parmar 1993:107–108)

What are the reasons for this custom? Some groups believe that it reduces female sexual desire, thus making it more likely that a woman will be a virgin at marriage, and, afterward, remain faith-

(continued)

▲ ▲ ▲ ▲ ▲ ▲ ▲ ▲ ▲ ▲ ▲ ▲ ▲ ▲ ▲ ▲ ▲ ▲

A Global Glimpse (Continued)

ful to her husband. Others believe that it enhances female fertility, prevents the clitoris from getting infected, and enhances vaginal cleanliness.

Feminists, who call female circumcision a form of ritual torture to control female sexuality, point out that the societies that practice it are male dominated. Mothers cooperate with the circumcision because in these societies an unmarried woman has virtually no rights, and an uncircumcised woman is considered impure and is not allowed to marry. Grandmothers insist that the custom continue out of concern that their granddaughters marry well.

Immigrants from Africa have brought the custom with them. Although the practice is specifi-cally banned only in three states (Minnesota, New York, and North Dakota), U.S. physicians will not perform it because they could be charged with child abuse. Some immigrant families pool their money and fly in an excisor who then performs the surgery on several girls. Others take their daughters to the homeland for the operation.

For Your Consideration

Do you think that Western nations should try to make African nations stop this custom? Or would this be ethnocentric, the imposition of Western values on other cultures? As one Somali woman said, "The Somali woman doesn't need an alien woman telling her how to treat her pri-vate parts." What legitimate basis do you think there is for members of one culture to interfere with another? What if people from some other nation did not like a U.S. custom because it violated their values—such as surgery to enlarge or reduce breasts, remove fat, or change the shape of one's nose—would they have a legitimate basis for interfering with us? Or does female circumcision belong to some special category that justifies intervention? If so, what category?

Sources: Based on Mahran 1978, 1981; Ebomoyi 1987; Lightfoot-Klein 1989; Merwine 1993; Walker and Parmar 1993; James 1994; Burstyn 1995; Waldman 1995b.

Women are also less likely to have a supportive spouse who is willing to play an unassuming background role while providing solace, encouragement, child care, and voter appeal. Finally, preferring to hold tightly on to their positions of power, men have been reluctant to incorporate women into centers of decision making or to present them as viable candidates.

These factors are changing, however, and we can expect more women to seek and gain political office. As we saw in Figure 10.1, more women are going into law, where they are doing more traveling and making statewide and national contacts. The same is true for business. Increasingly, child care is seen as a mutual responsibility of both mother and father. And in some areas, such as my own political district, party heads are searching for qualified candidates (read "people with voter appeal and without skeletons in their closets"), without regard to sex. The primary concern in at least some areas today is not gender, but whether a candidate can win. This generation, then, is likely to mark a fundamental change in women's political participation, and it appears only a matter of time until a woman occupies the Oval Office.

Glimpsing the Future—with Hope

By playing a fuller role in the decision-making processes of our social institutions, women are breaking the stereotypes and role models that lock males into exclusively male activities and push females into roles considered feminine. As structural barriers fall and more activities become degenderized, both males and females will be free to pursue activities more compatible with their abilities and desires as *individuals*.

As they develop a new consciousness of themselves and of their own potential, relationships between females and males will change. Certainly distinctions between the sexes will not disappear. There is no reason, however, for biological differences to be translated into social inequalities. The reasonable goal is appreciation of sexual differences coupled with equality of opportunity—which may well lead to a transformed society (Gilman 1911/1971; Offen 1990). If so, as sociologist Alison Jaggar (1990) observed, gender equality can become less a goal than a background condition for living in society.

In recent years, women have become much more prominent in politics, yet they remain only a minority of elected and appointed U.S. officials. Shown in this 1997 photo are eight of the nine women senators in the 105th Congress. Although the highest number ever to serve in the Senate, they represent only 9 percent of U.S. Senators.

INEQUALITIES OF AGING

In 1928, Charles Hart, who was working on his Ph.D. in anthropology, did fieldwork with the Tiwi, a preliterate people who live on an island off the northern coast of Australia. Because every Tiwi belongs to a clan, they assigned Hart to the bird (Jabijabui) clan and told him that a particular woman was his mother. Hart describes the woman as "toothless, almost blind, withered," who was "physically quite revolting and mentally rather senile." He then describes this remarkable event:

> [T]oward the end of my time on the islands an incident occurred that surprised me because it suggested that some of them had been taking my presence in the kinship system much more seriously than I had thought. I was approached by a group of about eight or nine senior men all of whom I knew. They were all senior members of the Jabijabui clan and they had decided among themselves that the time had come to get rid of the decrepit old woman who had first called me son and whom I now called mother. As I knew, they said, it was Tiwi custom, when an old woman became too feeble to look after herself, to "cover her up." This could only be done by her sons and her brothers and all of them had to agree beforehand, since once it was done they did not want any dissension among the brothers or clansmen,

as that might lead to a feud. My "mother" was now completely blind, she was constantly falling over logs or into fires, and they, her senior clansmen, were in agreement that she would be better out of the way. Did I agree?

> I already knew about "covering up." The Tiwi, like many other hunting and gathering peoples, sometimes got rid of their ancient and decrepit females. The method was to dig a hole in the ground in some lonely place, put the old woman in the hole and fill it in with earth until only her head was showing. Everybody went away for a day or two and then went back to the hole to discover to their surprise, that the old woman was dead, having been too feeble to raise her arms from the earth. Nobody had "killed" her; her death in Tiwi eyes was a natural one. She had been alive when her relatives last saw her. I had never seen it done, though I knew it was the custom, so I asked my brothers if it was necessary for me to attend the "covering up." They said no and they would do it, but only after they had my agreement. Of course I agreed, and a week or two later we heard in our camp that my "mother" was dead, and we wailed and put on the trimmings of mourning. (Hart 1970:154)

Apart from the morality of agreeing that the old woman should be "covered up" (and Hart seems more concerned about not having to watch the act than acquiescing to it), what is of interest is how the

Tiwi treated their frail elderly—or, more specifically, their frail *female* elderly. (You may have noticed that the Tiwi "covered up" only old women. As noted earlier, throughout the world females are discriminated against. As this case makes evident, in some places that discrimination extends even to death.)

Aging in Global Perspective

Every society must deal with the problem of people growing old, some of whom grow very frail. Although few societies choose to bury them alive, all must decide how to allocate limited resources among their citizens. As the proportion of the population that is old increases, as is happening in many nations, those decisions become more complex and the tensions they generate among the generations deepen.

The Social Construction of Aging

The example of how the Tiwi treat their frail female elderly reflects one extreme in how societies cope with aging. An extreme in a different direction is illustrated by the Abkhasians, an agricultural people who live in a mountainous region of Georgia, a republic of the former Soviet Union. Rather than "covering up" their elderly, the Abkhasians give them high respect and look to them for guidance. They would no more dispense with one of their elderly in this manner than we would "cover up" a sick child.

The Abkhasians may be the longest-lived people on earth. Many claim to live past 100—some beyond 120 and even 130 (Benet 1971). Although it is difficult to document the accuracy of these claims (Haslick 1974; Harris 1990), government records indicate that an extraordinary number of Abkhasians do live to a very old age.

Three main factors appear to account for their long lives. The *first* is their diet, which consists of little meat, much fresh fruit, vegetables, garlic, goat cheese, cornmeal, buttermilk, and wine. The *second* is their lifelong physical activity. They do slow down after age 80, but even after the age of 100 they still work about four hours a day. The *third* factor—a highly developed sense of community—goes to the very heart of Abkhasian culture. From childhood, each individual is highly integrated into a primary group, and remains so throughout life. There is no such thing as a nursing home, nor do the elderly live alone. Because even into old age they continue to

work and contribute to the group's welfare, they aren't a burden to anyone. They don't vegetate, nor do they find a need to "fill time" with bingo and shuffleboard. In short, the elderly feel no sudden rupture between what they "were" and what they "are."

The examples of the Tiwi and the Abkhasians reveal an important sociological principle—that aging is *socially constructed*. That is, nothing in the nature of aging summons forth any particular set of attitudes. Rather, attitudes toward the aged are rooted in society, and therefore differ from one social group to another. As we shall also see, even when people are considered old depends not on biology, but on culture.

Central to a group's culture are ways of viewing reality. Living for centuries in isolation on Bathurst and Melville Islands off the northern coast of Australia, the Tiwi, featured in the nearby vignette, developed a unique culture. Shown here is Wurarbuti, prior to leading a funeral dance. To be certain that his late uncle's ghost will not recognize him, Wurarbuti is wearing a "shirt" painted with ocher and clay, a topknot of cockatoo feathers, and a beard of goose feathers.

Effects of Industrialization

As noted in previous chapters, industrialization is a worldwide trend. Along with a higher standard of living, industrialization also brings a more plentiful food supply, better public health measures, especially a purer water supply, and a largely successful fight against the diseases that kill people at younger ages. Consequently, when a country industrializes more of its people reach older ages. Look at Table 10.4. You can see that the last four countries listed on the table, which are not industrialized, have only one-eighth to one-half the proportion of elderly of the Most Industrialized Nations.

As a nation's elderly population increases, so, too, does the bill its younger citizens pay to provide for their needs. In the Most Industrialized Nations, this bill has become a major social issue. Although Americans commonly complain that Social Security taxes are too high, Table 10.4 shows that the U.S. rate is comparatively low. In the Least Industrialized Nations, there are no social security taxes, and families are expected to take care of their own elderly.

With industrialization continuing without letup and the proportions of the elderly continuing to increase, future liabilities for care of the elderly have alarmed analysts. The most outstanding case is Germany, where by the year 2020 about 30 percent of the population will be over the age of 60. As projected, Germany's tax burden for the elderly will absorb nearly *all* the lifetime income of its future workers (Wessel 1995). Obviously, this is impossible, but no one has yet come up with a workable solution to the problem. Although the other Most Industrialized Nations trail Germany, they are walking the same perilous path.

The Graying of America

Figure 10.7 shows how U.S. life expectancy has grown throughout this century. To me, and perhaps to you, it is startling to realize that less than a hundred years ago the average American would not even see age 50. Since then, **life expectancy** has increased so greatly that Americans born today can expect to live until their 70s or 80s.

The term **graying of America** has been coined to refer to this increasing proportion of older people in the U.S. population. Look at Figure 10.8 on page 268. In 1900, only 4 percent of Americans were aged 65 and over. Today almost 13 percent are. In 1900, the average 65-year-old lived another twelve years; today a 65-year-old can expect to live seventeen more years (Treas 1995). U.S. society has become so "gray" that there are now eight million *more* elderly Americans than teenagers (*Statistical Abstract* 1995: Table 22). We also can note that we have a long way to go, for on a global scale U.S. women rank just

---

Table 10.4

The Elderly in Cross-Cultural Perspective

Country	Total Population	Percentage over 65	Number over 65	Percentage of Payroll Taxes Paid to Support the Elderly
Sweden	9,000,000	18.0%	1,600,000	19.8%
Germany	79,000,000	15.0	12,000,000	17.5
Italy	58,000,000	14.7	8,500,000	28.2
France	57,000,000	14.6	8,320,000	17.2
United States	255,000,000	12.6	32,000,000	12.4
Japan	124,000,000	11.9	14,800,000	14.5
Canada	27,000,000	11.5	3,100,000	5.0
China	1,134,000,000	5.8	65,800,000	N/A
Mexico	88,000,000	3.8	3,300,000	N/A
Egypt	54,000,000	3.4	1,800,000	N/A
Kenya	24,000,000	2.2	500,000	N/A

Sources: Kinsella and Taeuber 1993; *Statistical Abstract* 1995:Table 1384.

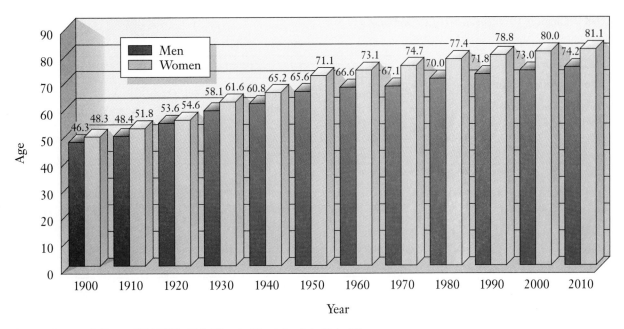

Sources: *Statistical Abstract* 1993:Table 115; *Historical Statistics of the United States, Colonial Times to 1970*, Bicentennial Edition, Part 1, Series B:107–115.

FIGURE 10.7

U.S. Life Expectancy by Year of Birth

fifteenth in life expectancy at birth, men only twenty-third (Treas 1995).

Can we expect this march to longer lives to continue? Very likely, but a warning flag is up. Between 1992 and 1993, U.S. life expectancy fell slightly, apparently due to so many deaths of young people from AIDS. The 1994 total didn't move back upward (Brody 1995). This could be a trend or merely a blip on an upward march. To see which, we must await more data.

It is important to keep in mind that the maximum length of life, the **life span,** has not increased. Experts disagree, however, on what that maximum is. Certainly it is at least 122, for this is the well-documented age of Jeanne Louise Calment of France, shown in the photo on this page. If the reports on the Abkhasians are correct, a matter of controversy, the human life span may exceed even this number by a comfortable margin.

Jeanne Calment, who turned 122 in February 1997, is shown here celebrating her birthday. The Guinness Book of Records lists Calment as the world's oldest living person whose age can be authenticated.

FIGURE 10.8

The Graying of America

Source: Statistical Abstract, various editions.

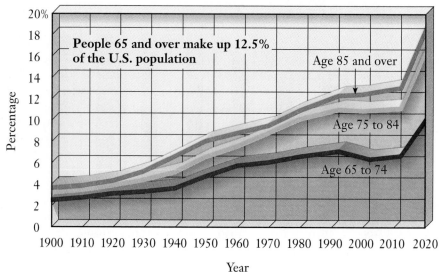

People 65 and over make up 12.5% of the U.S. population

Age 85 and over

Age 75 to 84

Age 65 to 74

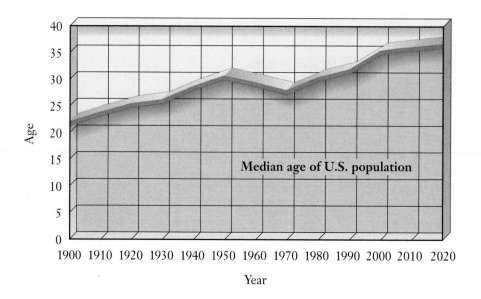

Median age of U.S. population

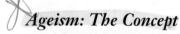

The Symbolic Interactionist Perspective

To apply symbolic interactionism, let's consider ageism and how negative stereotypes of the elderly developed.

Ageism: The Concept

At first, the audience sat quietly as the developers explained their plans for a high-rise apartment building. After a while, people began to shift uncomfortably in their seats. Now they were showing open hostility.

"That's too much money to spend on those people," said one.

"You even want them to have a swimming pool?" asked another incredulously.

Finally, one young woman put it all in a nutshell when she asked, "Who wants all those old people around?"

When physician Robert Butler (1975, 1980) heard these responses to plans to construct an apartment building for senior citizens, he began to realize how deeply feelings against the elderly run. He coined the term **ageism** to refer to prejudice, discrimination, and hostility directed against people because of their age. Let's see how ageism developed in U.S. society.

Shifting Meanings

Although old age means different things to different people, its general image is negative, and none of us wants the label "old" applied to us. We have "old and sick," "old and helpless," "old and crabby," "old and useless," and "old and dependent." Take your choice. None is pleasant.

As we have seen, there is nothing inherent in old age to summon forth negative attitudes. Some researchers even suggest that in early U.S. society old age had positive meanings (Cottin 1979; Kart 1990; Clair et al. 1993). Due to high death rates, they point out, not many people made it to old age. Consequently, growing old was seen as an accomplishment, and the younger generation listened to the elderly's advice about how to live a long life. With no pensions (this was before industrialization), the elderly continued to work at jobs that changed little over time, making them a storehouse of knowledge about work skills.

The coming of industrialization eroded, however, these bases of respect. With improved sanitation and medical care, more people reached old age, removing the distinction of being elderly. Then, too, the new forms of mass production made young workers as productive as the elderly. Coupled with mass education, this stripped away the mystique that the elderly possessed superior knowledge (Cowgill 1974). For a similar process now occurring in China, see the Global Glimpse box on the next page.

We have seen a basic principle of symbolic interactionism, that symbols, though powerful, are subject to change. Because most U.S. elderly can take care of themselves financially—and many are very well off—the meaning of old age is changing once again. In addition, the baby boom generation, the first of whom have now turned 50, has begun to confront the realities of aging. With their vast numbers and better health and finances, they are destined to positively affect our images of the elderly. Books and articles have already begun to appear that celebrate old age as a time of renewal, change, and challenge—not simply as a period that precedes death but, rather, as another stage of growth.

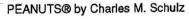

PEANUTS® by Charles M. Schulz

Stereotypes, which characterize all people and play such a profound role in social life, are a basic area of sociological investigation. In contemporary society, the mass media are a major source of stereotypes.

▲ ▲

A Global Glimpse

China: Changing Sentiment about the Elderly

As she contemplates her future, Zhao Chunlan, a 71-year-old widow, smiles shyly, but with evident deep satisfaction. She has heard about sons abandoning their aged parents. She has even heard whispering about brutality.

But Zhao has no such fears.

It is not that her son is such an exceptionally devoted man that he would never swerve from his traditional duty to his mother. Instead, it is a piece of paper that puts Zhao's mind at ease. Her 51-year-old son has signed a support agreement: He will cook her special meals, take her to regular medical checkups, even give her the largest room in his house and put the family's color television in it. (Sun 1990)

The elderly have always occupied a high status in China. The outline is well known: they are considered

sources of wisdom, given honored seating at both family and public gatherings, even venerated after death in ancestor worship.

Although this outline often may have represented more ideal than real culture, it appears to have been generally true. As China industrializes, however, the bonds between generations are weakening. Also contributing to this change is a longer life expectancy and a national birth policy that allows families to have only one child. Consequently, the over-65 population is mushrooming. Now about 66 million, or 6 percent of the population, the elderly may soar to 40 percent in just fifty years (Sun 1990; Kinsella and Taeuber 1993).

With no national social security system, it is essential that children remain providers for the elderly. To make sure, and alarmed by signs that bonds are weakening, many local officials insist that adult children sign support agreements for their aged parents. One province has hit on an ingenious device: in order to get a marriage license, the couple must sign a contract pledging to support their parents after they reach 60 (Sun 1990).

"I'm sure he would do right by me, anyway," says Zhao, "but this way I know he will."

The Functionalist Perspective

Functionalists examine how the various parts of society work together. We can consider an **age cohort,** people born at roughly the same time who pass through the life course together, as a component of society. This component affects other parts. For example, if the age cohort nearing retirement is large (a "baby boom" generation), many jobs will open at roughly the same time. If it is small (a "baby bust" generation), fewer jobs will open. A smooth transition at retirement requires a good adjustment among the parts of society.

Disengagement theory and activity theory, which we shall now examine, focus on the mutual adjustments necessary among those who are retiring and society's other components.

Disengagement Theory

Elaine Cumming and William Henry (1961) developed **disengagement theory** to explain how society

prevents disruption when the elderly vacate (or disengage from) their positions of responsibility. It would be disruptive if the elderly left their positions only because of emergency circumstances such as death or because they became incompetent. Consequently, societies use pensions to encourage the elderly to hand over their positions to younger people. Thus, disengagement is a mutual agreement between two parts of society that facilitates a smooth transition between the generations.

Cumming (1976) also examined disengagement from the individual's perspective. She pointed out that disengagement begins during middle age, long before retirement, when a person senses that the end of life is closer than its start. The individual does not immediately disengage, however, but, realizing that time is limited, begins to assign priority to goals and tasks. Disengagement begins in earnest when children leave home, then increases with retirement and eventually widowhood.

Evaluation of the Theory Disengagement theory has come under attack. Anthropologist Dorothy Jer-

The social position of the elderly differs from one society to another. In Asian cultures, the elderly usually enjoy high respect. Shown here is a Vietnamese-American boy intently learning from his grandfather how to do calligraphy.

rome (1992) points out that it contains an implicit bias against older people—assumptions that the elderly disengage from productive social roles, and then sort of sink into oblivion. Her own research shows that, instead of disengaging, the elderly actually *exchange* one set of roles for another. The new roles, which center around friendship, are no less satisfying than the earlier roles—although they are less visible to researchers, who tend to have a youthful orientation, and who show their bias by assuming that productivity is the measure of self-worth.

Activity Theory

Does retirement increase or decrease people's satisfaction with life? Are intimate activities more satisfying than formal ones? Such questions are the focus of **activity theory**, in which the central hypothesis is that the more activities that elderly people engage in, the more they find life satisfying. Although we could consider this theory under other perspectives, because its focus is how disengagement is functional or dysfunctional, it, too, can be considered from the functionalist perspective.

Evaluation of the Theory The research results are mixed. In general, as the theory suggests, more active people are more satisfied with life. But not always. For example, a study of retired people in

France found that some people are happier when they are very active, others when they are less involved (Keith 1982). Similarly, most people find informal, intimate activities, such as spending time with friends, to be more satisfying than formal activities. But not everyone. In one study, 2,000 retired U.S. men reported formal activities to be as important as more intimate ones. Even solitary activities, such as doing home repairs, had about the same impact as intimate activities on these men's life satisfaction (Beck and Page 1988).

With such mixed results, researchers need to search for key variables that underlie people's activities. I suggest three: finances, health, and individual orientations. The first may be related directly to social class, for older people with adequate finances are usually more satisfied with life (Atchley 1975; Krause 1993). The second is health, for healthier people are more active (Jerrome 1992; Johnson and Barer 1992). Third, the French and U.S. studies just mentioned indicate the significance of individual orientations. Just as some people are happier doing less, others are satisfied only if they are highly involved. Similarly, some people prefer informal activities, while others derive greater satisfaction from more formal ones. To simply count people's activities, then, is far from adequate, and these variables, as well as others, may provide the key to understanding the relationship between disengagement, activities, and life satisfaction.

The Conflict Perspective

From the conflict perspective, the guiding principles of social life are competition, disequilibrium, and change. So it is with society's age groups. As conflict theorists stress, whether the young and old recognize it or not, they are part of a basic struggle that threatens to throw society into turmoil. The passage of Social Security legislation is an example of this struggle.

Social Security Legislation

In the 1920s, before Social Security provided an income for the aged, two-thirds of all citizens over 65 had no savings and could not support themselves (Holtzman 1963; Hudson 1978). The Great Depression made matters even worse, and in 1930 Francis Townsend, a social reformer, started a movement to rally older citizens. He soon had one-third of all Americans over 65 enrolled in his Townsend clubs, demanding that the federal government impose a national sales tax of 2 percent to provide $200 a month for every person over 65—the equivalent of about $2,000 a month today. In 1934, the Townsend Plan went before Congress. Because it called for such high payments and many were afraid that it would remove younger people's incentive to save for the future, Congress looked for a way to reject the plan without appearing to oppose old age pensions. When President Roosevelt announced his own, more modest Social Security plan in June 1934, Congress embraced it (Schottland 1963; Amenta et al. 1992).

This legislation required that workers retire at 65. It did not matter how well people did their work, nor how much they needed an income. For decades, the elderly protested. Finally, in 1978 Congress raised the mandatory retirement age to 70, and eliminated it in 1986. Today, almost 90 percent of Americans retire by age 65, but they do so voluntarily. No longer can they be forced out of their jobs simply because of their age.

Conflict theorists point out that the retirement benefits Americans have today are not the result of generous hearts in Congress. They are, rather, the result of a struggle between competing interest groups. As conflict theorists stress, equilibrium is only a temporary balancing of social forces, one that is always ready to come apart. Perhaps, then, more direct conflict will emerge in the future. Let's consider that possibility.

FIGURE 10.9

Costs of Social Security

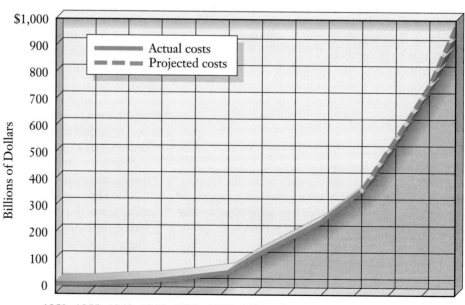

Sources: Statistical Abstract, various years. Recent years are from 1991:Table 592 and 1995:Table 520. Broken line indicates the author's estimates.

The Question of Intergenerational Conflict

Will the future bring conflict between the elderly and the young? Although violence is not likely to result, the grumblings have begun—complaints about the elderly getting more than their share of society's dwindling resources in an era of high taxes, reduced services, and gigantic budget deficits (Hunt 1995). The huge costs of Social Security have become a national concern. As Figure 10.9 on the previous page shows, Social Security taxes were only $784 million in 1950, but now they run almost *500* times higher.

Some form of conflict seems inevitable. As the United States grays, the number of people who collect Social Security grows, but the proportion of working people—those who pay for these benefits out of their wages—shrinks. Some see this shift in the **dependency ratio**, the number of workers it takes to pay one person's Social Security, as especially troubling. Presently, five working-age Americans pay Social Security taxes to support each person who is over 65—but shortly this ratio will drop to less than three to one, and by the year 2035, to two to one.

As Figure 10.10 shows, medical costs for the elderly have soared. Because of this, some fear that the health care of children is being shortchanged and Congress will be forced to "choose between old people and kids." Are the elderly and children, then, on a collision course? What especially alarms some are the data shown in Figure 10.11 on the next page. As the condition of the elderly improved, that of children worsened. Although critics are glad that the elderly are better off than they were, they are bothered that this improvement has come at the cost of the nation's children.

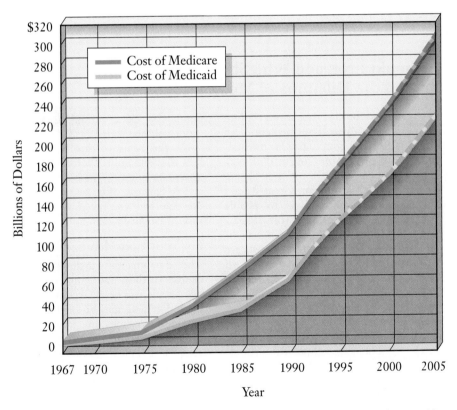

FIGURE 10.10

Health Care Costs for the Elderly and Disabled

Note: Medicare is intended for the elderly and disabled, Medicaid for the poor. Almost one-third of Medicaid payments ($31 billion) goes to the elderly (*Statistical Abstract* 1995: Table:166). Broken lines indicate the author's projections.

Source: Statistical Abstract, various years. Recent years are from 1995: Tables 159, 166.

FIGURE 10.11

Trends in Poverty: The Percentage of U.S. Youth and Elderly in Poverty

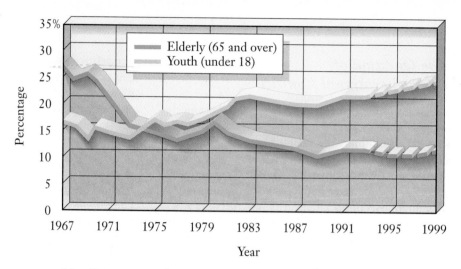

Note: For some years the government figures for youth refer to people under 18, for other years to people under 16 or 15. Broken lines indicate the author's projections.

Source: Congressional Research Service; *Statistical Abstract* 1995:Table 747.

Sociology and the New Technology

Who Should Live, and Who Should Die? Technology and the Dilemma of Medical Rationing

OUR NEW TECHNOLOGY has taken us to a new level of medical care. We now can cure many medical conditions that just a short time ago doomed people to early death. In other instances, the medical condition remains, but the patient is able to live a long life.

And therein lies the rub. Some technology is limited, and there isn't enough to go around to everyone who needs it. Other technology is so costly that society would go bankrupt if it were made available to everyone who has a particular condition. Who, then, should receive the benefits of our new medical technology?

Consider dialysis, the use of artificial kidneys to cleanse the blood of people suffering from kidney disease. Currently, dialysis is available to anyone who needs it, and the cost runs several billion dollars a year. Four percent of all Medicare goes to pay for the dialysis of just one-fourth of 1 percent of Medicare patients. Facing this same problem, Great Britain now rations dialysis to people under the age of 55 (Volti 1995).

Open heart surgery is a technological marvel, but its costs are astounding. One percent of all the money the nation spends on its medical bills goes to pay for the bypass surgeries of just four-hundredths of 1 percent of the population.

The costs of medical technology at the end of people's lives help us understand the issue. Of all Medicare money, about one-fourth is spent to maintain patients during just the last year of their lives. Almost a third of this amount is spent during the last month of life (Volti 1995).

At the heart of this issue of how to spend limited resources lie questions not only of costs, but also of fairness, of how to distribute equitably the benefits of advanced medical technology.

For Your Consideration

The dilemma is harsh: If we choose medical rationing, many sick people will be allowed to die. If we don't, we may go bankrupt. Use ideas, concepts, and principles from this and other chapters to develop a reasoned answer to this pressing issue. Also note how this dilemma changes shape if you view it from the contrasting perspectives of conflict theory, functionalism, and symbolic interactionism.

But has it really? Conflict sociologists Meredith Minkler and Ann Robertson (1991) say that while the figures themselves are true, the comparison is misleading. The money that went to the elderly did *not* come from the children. Would anyone say that the money the government gives to flood or earthquake victims comes from the children? Of course not. The government makes choices about where to spend money, and it could very well have decided to increase spending on *both* the elderly and the children. It simply has not done so. To frame the issue as money going to one at the expense of the other is an attempt to divide the working class. If the working class can be made to think that it must choose between suffering children and suffering old folks, it will be divided and unable to work together to change U.S. society.

Yet another area of conflict is emerging. Before our current technology, medical care was relatively inexpensive. Today its cost has become such a major social issue that, as discussed in the new technology box on the previous page, it soon may be rationed.

A Concluding Note

As these materials make evident, if our goal is to have a more equitable society, we have a long way to go. As we saw in the previous chapter, inequalities by race and ethnicity abound. As we have seen in this chapter, relations between the sexes and age groups are also marked by inequalities of many kinds.

The first task is to pinpoint a problem, to specify its dimensions. For this, we now have ample sociological data. The second task is to develop solutions, the third to implement them. Many solutions to these problems have been proposed already, and some, though imperfect, are being implemented. Perhaps a reader of this text will be introduced to basic sociological ideas and become an applied sociologist who will develop better solutions. The third step requires political action, for these problems are not individual, but structural, and they demand vast social resources for their solution.

Summary and Review

Issues of Sex and Gender

What is gender stratification?

The term **gender stratification** refers to unequal access to power, prestige, and property on the basis of sex. Each society establishes a structure that, on the basis of sex and gender, opens and closes access to the group's privileges. P. 246.

How do sex and gender differ?

Sex refers to biological distinctions between males and females. It consists of both primary and secondary sex characteristics. **Gender,** in contrast, is what a society considers proper behaviors and attitudes for its male and female members. Sex physically distinguishes males from females; gender defines what is "masculine" and "feminine." Pp. 246–247.

Why do the behaviors of males and females differ?

In the "nature versus nurture" debate—whether differences between the behaviors of males and females are caused by inherited (biological) or learned (cultural) characteristics—almost all sociologists take the side of nurture. In recent years, however, sociologists have begun to cautiously open the door to biology. Pp. 247–249.

Global Considerations: How Females Became a Minority Group

How did females become a minority group?

Patriarchy, or male dominance, appears to be universal. The origin of discrimination against females is lost in history, but the primary theory of how females became a minority group in their own societies focuses on the physical limitations imposed by childbirth. Pp. 249–251.

Gender Inequality in the United States

Is the feminist movement new?

In what is called the "first wave," feminists made demands for social change in the early 1900s—and were met with much hostility, and even violence. The "second wave" began in the 1960s and continues today. Pp. 251–252.

What forms does gender stratification in education take?

Although more women than men now attend college, each tends to select "feminine" or "masculine" fields. In addition, men outnumber women in all but two scientific fields. Change is indicated by the growing numbers of women in such fields as law and medicine. Pp. 252–254.

Gender Relations in the Workplace

How does gender inequality show up in the workplace?

Over the last century, women have made up an increasing proportion of the work force. Nonetheless, the gender gap in pay characterizes all occupations. For college graduates, the lifetime pay gap runs about $800,000 in favor of men. **Sexual harassment** also continues to be a reality of the workplace. Pp. 254–259.

Gender and Violence

What forms does violence against women take?

Females are overwhelmingly the victims of battering, rape, incest, and murder. Female circumcision is a special case of violence against females. Conflict theorists point out that men use violence to maintain their power. Pp. 259–261.

The Changing Face of Politics

What is the trend in gender inequality in politics?

A strict division of gender roles—women as child care providers and homemakers, men as workers outside the home—has traditionally kept women out of politics. Although women continue to be underrepresented in U.S. politics, the trend toward greater political equality is firmly in place. Pp. 261–263.

Glimpsing the Future—with Hope

What progress has been made in reducing gender inequality?

In the United States, women are playing a fuller role in the decision-making processes of our social institutions. The reasonable goal is appreciation of sexual differences coupled with equality of opportunity. P. 263.

Aging in Global Perspective

How are the elderly treated around the world?

There is no single set of attitudes, beliefs, or policies regarding the aged that characterizes the world's nations. Rather, they vary from exclusion and killing to integration and honor. The global trend is for more people to live longer. Pp. 264–265.

What does the social construction of aging mean?

Nothing in the nature of aging summons forth any particular set of attitudes. Rather, attitudes toward the elderly are rooted in society, differing from one social group to another. Even when people are considered old depends not on biology, but on culture. Pp. 265–267.

The Symbolic Interactionist Perspective

What factors influence perceptions of aging?

Symbolic interactionists stress the **social construction of aging,** emphasizing that no age has any particular built-in meaning. **Ageism,** negative reactions to the elderly, is based on stereotypes. Pp. 268–270.

The Functionalist Perspective

How is retirement functional for society?

Functionalists focus on how the withdrawal of the elderly from positions of responsibility benefits society. **Disengagement theory** examines retirement as a device for ensuring that a society's positions of responsibility will be passed smoothly from one generation to the next. **Activity theory** examines how people adjust when they disengage from productive roles. Pp. 270–271.

The Conflict Perspective

Is there conflict between different age groups?

Social Security legislation is an example of one generation making demands on another generation for limited resources. As the **dependency ratio**—the number of workers who support one retired person—decreases, workers may become resentful. The argument that benefits to the elderly come at the cost of benefits to children is fallacious. Pp. 272–275.

Where can I read more on these topics?

Suggested readings for this chapter are listed on page 440.

Glossary

activity theory the view that satisfaction during old age is related to a person's level and quality of activity (p. 271)

age cohort people born at roughly the same time who pass through the life course together (p. 270)

ageism prejudice, discrimination, and hostility directed against people because of their age; can be directed against any age group, including youth (pp. 246, 269)

dependency ratio the number of workers required to support one person on Social Security (p. 273)

disengagement theory the view that society prevents disruption by having the elderly vacate their positions of responsibility so the younger generation can step into their shoes (p. 270)

feminism the philosophy that men and women should be politically, economically, and socially equal, and organized activity on behalf of this principle (p. 251)

gender the social characteristics that a society considers proper for its males and females; masculinity or femininity (p. 247)

gender stratification males' and females' unequal access to power, prestige, and property on the basis of their sex (p. 246)

graying of America older people making up an increasing proportion of the U.S. population (p. 266)

life expectancy the age that someone can be expected to live to (p. 266)

life span the maximum length of life (p. 267)

patriarchy a society in which authority is vested in men; control by men of a society or group (p. 250)

quiet revolution the fundamental changes in society that follow when vast numbers of women enter the work force (p. 254)

sex biological characteristics that distinguish females and males, consisting of primary and secondary sex characteristics (p. 246)

sexual harassment unwanted sexual advances, usually within an occupational or educational setting (p. 259)

Sociology and the Internet

All URLs listed are current as of the printing of this book. URLs are often changed. Please check our Website http://www.abacon.com/henslin for updates.

1. Date Rape

The section in this chapter headed "Gender and Violence" notes that there are several types of violence involving men and women and that overwhelmingly men are the aggressors and women the victims. As a college student, the frequency of date rape should be of great concern to you.

To study date rape, we need to look at the more general category of acquaintance rape. Go to the "Sexual assault information page" at (http://www.cs.utk.edu/~bartley/saInfoPage.html). Click on "Acquaintance Rape," and you should see a list of ten or twelve links to sites having information or other resources. Gather information from six of these sites: "Acquaintance Rape" (the first listing, not the second); "Connecticut Sexual Assault Crisis Services"; "'Friends' Raping Friends"; "Myths and Facts about Acquaintance Rape"; and "Sexual Assault and Rape: Advice to Men."

When you finish with your research, you should be able to write a short paper on the incidence, characteristics, and prevention of date rape, as well as on some resources for women who are victims. If you want to gather more information, follow the links given at the various sites you visit.

2. The Elderly and the Government

You have read in this chapter about the controversy surrounding Social Security, only one of the government's many programs for the elderly. This project will allow you to explore some of those programs.

The Administration on Aging (AoA) is the executive branch's chief agency aimed at the elderly. Go to the agency's home page (http://www.aoa.dhhs.gov/), and select "About" at the bottom of the screen. Select "Fact Sheet" on the new screen. Learn what you can about the AoA by reading what is on the page. You may find the organization chart of the agency interesting. When you finish, go back to the "About" page. (If you get lost, just start over with the AoA home page, and select "About" again.) Three other topics besides the "Fact Sheet" are available: "The Older American Act," "The Administration on Aging," and "The Aging Network." Follow some of the links under each of these headings. Your instructor will tell you how extensive and in what form your report on the research should be. (*Instructor:* Consider assigning one segment of the project to each of several groups of students for a panel; allow students to prepare a written report on one area; or assign a major written report on the entire project.)

Pacita Abad, Masters of the Universe, 1992.

11

Politics and the Economy: Leadership and Work in the Global Village

N THE 1930s, GEORGE ORWELL wrote 1984, *a book about a future in which the government, known as "Big Brother," dominates society, dictating almost every aspect of everyone's life. To even love someone is considered a sinister activity, a betrayal of the first love and unquestioning allegiance that all citizens owe Big Brother.*

Two characters, Winston and Julia, fall in love. They meet furtively, always with the threat of discovery hanging over their heads. When informers turn them in, interrogators separate Julia and Winston. They swiftly proceed to break their affection—to restore their loyalty to Big Brother.

Then follows a remarkable account of Winston and his tormentor, O'Brien. Winston is strapped so tightly into a chair that he can't even move his head. O'Brien explains that inflicting pain is not always enough, but that everyone has a breaking point, some worst thing that will push them over the edge.

O'Brien tells Winston that he has discovered his worst fear. Then he sets a cage with two giant, starving sewer rats on the table next to Winston. O'Brien picks up a hood connected to the door of the cage and places it over Winston's head. He then explains that when he presses the lever, the door of the cage will slide up, and the rats will shoot out like bullets and bore straight into Winston's face. Winston's eyes, the only part of his body that he can move, dart back and forth, revealing his terror. Speaking so quietly that Winston has to strain to hear him, O'Brien adds that the rats sometimes attack the eyes first, but sometimes they burrow through the cheeks and devour the tongue. When O'Brien places his hand on the lever, Winston realizes that the only way out is for someone to take his place. But who? Then he hears his own voice screaming, "Do it to Julia! . . . Tear her face off, strip her to the bones. Not me! Julia! Not me!"

Orwell does not describe Julia's interrogation, but when Julia and Winston see each other later they realize that each has betrayed the other. Their love is gone. Big Brother has won.

Winston's misplaced loyalty had made him a political heretic, for it was the obligation of every citizen to place the state above all else in life. To preserve the state's dominance over the individual, Winston's allegiance had to be taken away from Julia. As you see, it was.

Although seldom this dramatic, politics is always about power and authority.

POLITICS: ESTABLISHING LEADERSHIP

For a society to exist, it must have a system of leadership. Some people will have to have power over others. Let's explore this topic that is so significant for our lives.

Power, Authority, and Violence

As Max Weber (1913/1947) pointed out, we perceive **power**—the ability to get your way, even over the resistance of others—as either legitimate or illegitimate. Legitimate power is called **authority.** This is power that people accept as right. In contrast, illegitimate power—called **coercion**—is power that people do not accept as just.

Imagine that you are on your way to buy a CD player on sale for $250. As you approach the store, a man jumps out of an alley and shoves a gun in your face. He demands your money. Frightened for your life, you hand it over. After filing a police report, you head back to college to take a sociology exam. You are running late, so you step on the gas. As the needle hits 85, you see flashing blue and red lights in your rearview mirror. Your explanation about the robbery doesn't faze the officer—nor the judge who hears your case a few weeks later. She first lectures you on safety and then orders you to pay $50 court costs plus $10 for every mile an hour over 65 mph. You pay the $250.

What's the difference? The mugger, the police officer, and the judge—each has power, and in each case you part with $250. The difference is that the mugger has no authority. His power is illegitimate— he has no *right* to do what he did. In contrast, you acknowledge that the officer has the right to stop you and that the judge has the right to fine you. Theirs is authority, or legitimate power.

Authority and Legitimate Violence

As sociologist Peter Berger observed, it makes little difference whether you willingly pay the fine that the judge levies against you, or refuse to pay it. The court will get its money one way or another.

> There may be innumerable steps before its application [violence], in the way of warnings and reprimands. But if all the warnings are disregarded, even in so slight a matter as paying a traffic ticket, the last thing that will happen is that a couple of cops show up at the door with handcuffs and a Black Maria. Even the moderately courteous cop who hands out the initial traffic ticket is likely to wear a gun—just in case. (Berger 1963)

The *government*, then, also called the **state**, claims a monopoly on legitimate force or violence. This point, made by Max Weber (1946, 1922/1968)—that the state claims the exclusive right to use violence and the right to punish everyone else who does—is crucial to our understanding of politics. If someone owes you a debt, you cannot imprison that person or even forcibly take the money. The state can. The ultimate proof of the state's authority is that you cannot kill someone because he or she has done something that you consider absolutely horrible—but the state can. As Berger (1963) summarized this matter, *"Violence is the ultimate foundation of any political order."*

But why do people accept power as legitimate? Max Weber (1922/1968) identified three sources of authority: traditional, rational-legal, and charismatic. Let's examine each.

Traditional Authority

Throughout history, the most common form of authority has been tradition. **Traditional authority,** which is based on custom, is the hallmark of preliterate groups. In these societies, custom dictates basic relationships. For example, because of birth a particular individual becomes the chief, king, or queen. As

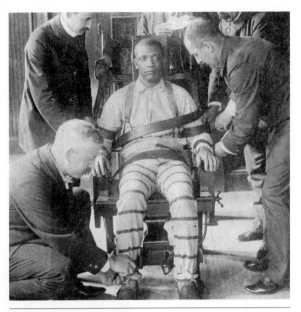

The ultimate foundation of any political order is violence. Nowhere is this more starkly demonstrated than when a government takes human life. Shown in this 1910 photo from Sing Sing Prison is a man about to be executed.

far as members of that society are concerned, this is the right way to determine a ruler because "this is the way it always has been done."

Traditional authority declines with industrialization, but it never dies out. In postindustrial societies, for example, parents exercise authority over their children *because* parents always have had such authority. From generations past, we inherit the idea that parents should discipline their children, choose their doctors and schools, and teach them religion and morality.

Rational-Legal Authority

The second type of authority, **rational-legal authority,** is based, not on custom, but on written rules. *Rational* means reasonable, and *legal* means part of law. Thus *rational-legal* refers to matters agreed to by reasonable people and written into law (or regulations of some sort). The matters agreed to may be as broad as a constitution that specifies the rights of all members of a society or as narrow as a contract between two individuals. Because bureaucracies are based on written rules, rational-legal authority is also called *bureaucratic authority.*

George Washington, shown here at the Constitutional Convention at Philadelphia in 1787, is an example of rational-legal authority. That is, he took office according to a system of rules that people had agreed on, in this case, the new Constitution of the United States.

Rational-legal authority comes from the position that an individual holds, not from the person who holds the position. In a democracy, for example, the president's authority comes from the office, as specified in a written constitution, not from custom or the individual's personal characteristics. In rational-legal authority, everyone—no matter how high the office—is subject to the organization's written rules. In governments based on traditional authority, the ruler's word may be law, but in those based on rational-legal authority, the ruler's word is subject to the law.

Charismatic Authority — Based on Personality unstable People

A few centuries back, in 1429, the English controlled large parts of France. When they prevented the coronation of a new French king, a farmer's daughter heard a voice telling her that God had a special assignment for her—that she should put on men's clothing, recruit an army, and go to war against the English. Inspired, Joan of Arc raised an army, conquered cities, and vanquished the English. Later that year, her visions were fulfilled as she stood next to Charles VII while he was crowned king of France. (Bridgwater 1953)

Joan of Arc is an example of **charismatic authority,** the third type of authority Weber identified. (*Charisma* is a Greek word that means a gift freely and graciously given [Arndt and Gingrich 1957].) A charismatic individual is someone to whom people are drawn because they believe that person has been touched by God or has been endowed by nature with exceptional qualities (Lipset 1993). The armies did not follow Joan of Arc because it was the custom to do so, as in traditional authority. Nor did they risk their lives alongside her because she held a position defined by written rules, as in rational-legal authority. Instead, people followed her because they were drawn to her outstanding traits. They saw her as a messenger of God, fighting on the side of justice, and accepted her leadership because of these appealing qualities.

The Threat Posed by Charismatic Leaders A king owes allegiance to tradition, and a president to written laws. To what, however, does a charismatic leader owe allegiance? Because their authority is based only on their personal ability to attract followers, charismatic leaders pose a threat to the established political system. They direct followers solely according to personal preference, not according to the paths of tradition or the regulations of law. Accordingly, they can inspire followers to disregard—or even to overthrow—traditional and rational-legal authorities.

This means that charismatic leaders pose a threat to the established order. Consequently, traditional and rational-legal authorities are often quick to oppose charismatic figures. If they are not careful, however, their opposition may create a martyr, arousing even higher sentiment in favor of the charismatic leader. Occasionally the Roman Catholic church

One of the best examples of charismatic authority is Joan of Arc, shown here at the coronation of Charles VII, whom she was instrumental in making king. Uncomfortable at portraying Joan of Arc wearing only a man's coat of armor, the artist has not only made certain she is wearing plenty of makeup but also added a ludicrous skirt.

rational-legal systems of authority, the rules of succession are firm.

Charismatic authority, however, has no such rules of succession, making it inherently less stable than either traditional or rational-legal authority. Because charismatic authority is built around a single individual, the death or incapacitation of a charismatic leader can mean a bitter struggle for succession. Consequently, some charismatic leaders make arrangements for an orderly transition of power by appointing a successor. This does not guarantee orderly succession, of course, for the followers may not perceive the designated heir in the same way as they did the charismatic leader. A second strategy is for the charismatic leader to build an organization, which then develops a system of rules or regulations, thus transforming itself into a rational-legal leadership. Weber used the term **routinization of charisma** to refer to the transfer of authority from a charismatic leader to either traditional or rational-legal authority.

faces such a threat when a priest claims miraculous powers, a claim perhaps accompanied by amazing healings. As people flock to this individual, they bypass parish priests and the formal ecclesiastical structure. To transfer allegiance from the organization to an individual threatens the church bureaucracy. Consequently, the church hierarchy may encourage the priest to withdraw from the public eye, perhaps to a monastery, to rethink matters. Thus the threat is defused, rational-legal authority reasserted, and the stability of the organization maintained.

The Transfer of Authority

The orderly transfer of authority from one leader to another is crucial for social stability. Under traditional authority, people know who is next in line. Under rational-legal authority, people may not know who the next leader will be, but they do know *how* that person will be selected. In both traditional and

Charismatic authorities can be of any morality, from the saintly to the most bitterly evil. Like Joan of Arc, Adolf Hitler attracted throngs of people, providing the stuff of dreams and arousing them from disillusionment to hope. This poster from the 1930s entitled Es Lebe Deutschland *("Long Live Germany") illustrates the qualities of leadership that Germans of that period saw in Hitler.*

Types of Government

How do the various types of government—monarchies, democracies, dictatorships, and oligarchies—differ? As we compare them, let's also look at how the institution of the state arose, and how the idea of citizenship was revolutionary.

Monarchies: The Rise of the State

Early societies were small and needed no extensive political system. They operated more like an extended family, with decisions being made as they became necessary. As surpluses developed and societies grew larger, cities evolved—perhaps about 3500 B.C. (Fischer 1976). **City-states** then came into being, with power radiating outward from a city like a spider's web. Although the city controlled the immediate area around it, the areas between cities remained in dispute. Each city-state had its own **monarchy,** a king or queen whose right to rule was passed on to the children.

City-states often quarreled, and wars were common. The victorious ones extended their rule, and eventually a single city-state was able to wield power over an entire region. As the size of these regions grew, the people slowly developed an identity with the larger region. That is, they began to see distant inhabitants as a "we" instead of a "they." What we call the **state**—the political entity that claims a monopoly on the use of violence within a territory—came into being.

Democracies: Citizenship as a Revolutionary Idea *the people decide*

The United States had no city-states. Each colony, however, like a city-state, was small and independent. After the American Revolution, the colonies united. With the greater strength and resources that came from political unity, they conquered almost all of North America, bringing it under the power of a central government.

The government formed in this new country was called a **democracy.** (Derived from two Greek words —*kratos* [power], and *demos* [common people]—*democracy* literally means "power to the people.") Because of the bitter antagonisms associated with the revolution against the British king, the founders of the new country were distrustful of monarchies. They wanted to put political decisions into the hands

of the people. This was not the first democracy the world had seen, but such a system had been tried before only with smaller groups. Athens, a city-state of Greece, practiced democracy two thousand years ago, with each free male above a certain age having the right to be heard and to vote. Members of Native American tribes also were able to elect a chief, and in some, women were able to vote and to hold the office of chief.

Because of their small size, tribes and cities were able to practice **direct democracy.** That is, they were small enough for the eligible voters to meet together, express their opinions, and then vote publicly—much like a town hall meeting today. As populous and spread out as the United States was, however, direct democracy was impossible, and **representative democracy** was invented. Certain citizens (at first only white landowners) voted for men to represent them in Washington. Later the vote was extended to nonowners of property, to African-American men, then to women, and to others. Our new communications technologies, which make "electronic town meetings" possible, may also allow a new form of direct democracy. This issue is explored in the Sociology and the New Technology box on the next page.

Today we take the idea of citizenship for granted. What is not evident to us is that the idea had to be conceived in the first place. There is nothing natural about citizenship—it is simply one way in which people choose to define themselves. Throughout most of human history, people were thought to belong to a clan, to a tribe, or even to a ruler. The idea of **citizenship**—that by virtue of birth and residence people have basic rights—is quite new to the human scene (Turner 1990).

The concept of representative democracy based on citizenship, perhaps the greatest gift the United States has given to the world, was revolutionary. Power was to be vested in the people themselves, and government was to flow from the people. That this concept was revolutionary is generally forgotten, but its implementation meant *the reversal of traditional ideas, for the government was to be responsive to the people's wishes, not the people to the wishes of the government.*

The idea of **universal citizenship**—of *everyone* having the same basic rights by virtue of being born in a country (or by immigrating and becoming a naturalized citizen)—flowered very slowly, and came into practice only through fierce struggle. When the United States was founded, for example, this idea was still in its infancy. Today it seems inconceivable to us

Sociology and the New Technology

Politics and Democracy in a Technological Society

"Politics is just like show business." —RONALD REAGAN

IS THE NEW TECHNOLOGY a threat to democracy? Politicians and their pollsters use computers, sophisticated telephone link-ups, faxes, and online services such as the Internet to take the pulse of the public—and to convey their platforms and their biases. Instead of tuning in and passively listening to a politician's speech, we now can interact with—talk back to—candidates and leaders via online computer forums, "electronic town meetings," and call-in radio and TV talk shows.

This shift to more interactive communications technologies lies at the heart of a debate over the health and future of our democracy. Critics charge that when elected officials use the new technology to constantly "take the public's temperature," they give more attention to minute shifts in

public opinion than to the business of governing. Politicians use poll results to "fine tune" their public posturing, to take sides on issues with no personal conviction of what is right. In other words, politicians now campaign nonstop.

Critics worry that our new interactive communications have only begun to undermine the process of governing. "Televoting" (voting from home with the push of a button), they fear, may replace our current form of representational democracy with a form of direct democracy. Some welcome this possibility, for it would allow the voters to directly make laws and decide a wide variety of social issues, rather than having politicians do this for them. Others, however, fear that televoting may be a detour around the U.S. Constitution's careful system of checks

and balances designed to safeguard us from the "tyranny of the majority." To determine from a poll that 51 percent of adults hold a certain opinion on an issue is one thing—it can give guidance to leaders. But to have 51 percent of televoters determine a law or an issue is not the same as having elected representatives publicly argue a proposed law or an issue and then try to balance the interests of the many groups that make up their constituents.

Visual image over substance, reasoned leadership replaced by nonstop campaigning, even a fundamental change in our current form of democracy—these are some of the issues that the new technologies bring to today's politics.

Sources: "Democracy and Technology," 1995; Diamond and Silverman 1995; L. Grossman 1995.

---

that anyone on the basis of gender or race/ethnicity should not have the right to vote, hold office, make a contract, testify in court, or own property. For earlier generations of Americans, however, it seemed just as inconceivable that the poor, women, African Americans, Native Americans, and Asian Americans should have such rights.

Dictatorships and Oligarchies: The Seizure of Power

If an individual seizes power and then dictates his will onto the people, the government is known as a **dictatorship.** If a small group seizes power, the government is called an **oligarchy.** The frequent coups in Central and South America, in which a few military leaders seize control of a country, are examples of oligarchies. Although one individual may be named

president, it often is a group of high-ranking officers, working behind the scenes, that makes the decisions. If their designated president becomes uncooperative, they remove him from office and designate another.

If a monarchy, dictatorship, or oligarchy exerts almost total control over a people, it is called **totalitarianism.** As our opening vignette demonstrated, totalitarian regimes tolerate no opposing opinion. In Nazi Germany, for example, Hitler used a ruthless secret police force, the Gestapo, to maintain control over the people. Spies even watched moviegoers' reactions to newsreels, reporting those who did not respond "appropriately" (Hipler 1987).

People around the world find the ideas of citizenship and representative democracy appealing. Those who have no say in their government's decisions, or who face prison for expressing dissent, find in these ideas the hope for a brighter future. With today's electronic communications, people no longer remain ignorant of whether they are more or less privileged politically than others. This knowledge produces pressure for greater citizen participation in government. With continued developments in communications, the future will continue to step up this pressure.

The U.S. Political System

With this global background, let's examine the U.S. political system. We shall consider the two major political parties, voting patterns, and the role of lobbyists and PACs.

Political Parties and Elections

After the founding of the United States, numerous political parties emerged, but by the time of the Civil War, two parties dominated U.S. politics (Burnham 1983): the Democrats, who in the public mind are associated with the working class, and the Republicans, who are associated with wealthier people. Each party nominates candidates, and in pre-elections, called *primaries*, the voters decide which candidates will represent their party. Each candidate then campaigns, trying to appeal to the most voters. Table 11.1 shows how Americans align themselves with political parties.

Although the Democrats and Republicans represent different philosophical principles, each party appeals to such a broad membership that it is difficult to distinguish a conservative Democrat from a liberal Republican. The extremes, however, are easy to discern. Deeply committed Democrats support legislation that transfers income from one group to another or that controls wages, working conditions, and competition. Dyed-in-the-wool Republicans oppose such legislation.

Those elected to Congress may cross party lines. That is, some Democrats vote for legislation proposed by Republicans, and vice versa. This happens because officeholders support their party's philosophy but not necessarily its specific proposals. Thus when it comes to a specific bill, such as raising the minimum wage, some conservative Democrats may view the measure as unfair to small employers, or too costly, and vote with the Republicans against the bill. At the same time, liberal Republicans—feeling that the proposal is just, or sensing a changing sentiment in voters back home—may side with its Democratic backers.

Regardless of their differences, however, the Democrats and Republicans represent *different slices*

Table 11.1

How Americans Identify with Political Parties

	1960	1970	1980	1990	1994
Democrats					
Strong Democrat	20%	20%	18%	20%	15%
Weak Democrat	25	24	23	19	19
Independent Democrat	6	10	11	12	13
Total	51	54	52	51	47
Republicans					
Strong Republican	16	9	9	10	16
Weak Republican	14	15	14	15	15
Independent Republican	7	8	12	12	12
Total	37	32	35	37	43
Other					
Independent	10	13	13	11	10
Not Political	3	1	2	2	1
Total	13	14	15	13	11

Note: Due to rounding, the totals do not always equal 100 percent.

Sources: Statistical Abstract 1991:Table 452; 1996:Table 455.

of the center. Although each may ridicule its opposition and promote different legislation, each party firmly supports such fundamentals of U.S. political philosophy as free public education, a strong military, freedom of religion, speech, and assembly, and, of course, capitalism—especially the private ownership of property.

Third parties also play a role in U.S. politics, but to have any influence they, too, must support these centrist themes. To advocate their radical change is to doom a third party to a short life of little political consequence. Because most Americans consider a vote for a third party a waste, third parties do notoriously poorly at the polls. Two exceptions are Theodore Roosevelt's Bull Moose party, which won more votes in 1912 than Taft, the Republican presidential candidate, and the United We Stand (now Reform) party, headed by billionaire political hopeful Ross Perot, which won 19 percent of the vote in 1992 (Bridgwater 1953; *Statistical Abstract* 1995:Table 437).

Voting Patterns

Year after year, Americans show consistent voting patterns. From Table 11.2 on the next page, you can see that the percentage of people who vote increases with age. This table also shows the significance of race and ethnicity. Non-Hispanic whites are more likely to vote than are African Americans or Asian Americans, while Latinos are the least likely to vote. The significance of race/ethnicity is so great that non-Hispanic whites are more than twice as likely to vote as are Latinos. A crucial aspect of the socialization of newcomers to the United States is to learn the U.S. political system, which is the topic of the Immigrant Experience box on page 289.

Table 11.2 also shows that voting increases with education. College graduates are more than twice as likely to vote as those who complete only grade school. Employment and income are also significant. People who make over $35,000 a year are twice as likely to vote as those who make less than $5,000. Finally, note that men and women are about equally as likely to vote.

Social Integration How can we explain the voting patterns shown in Table 11.2? The people most likely to vote are older, more educated, affluent, employed whites, while those least likely to vote are poor, younger, ill-educated, unemployed Latinos. From these patterns, we can draw this principle: *The more that people feel they have a stake in the political sys-*

The essence of a democracy is people being able to elect their leaders. Although the United States gave the world representative democracy, the vote was withheld from many on the basis of property, sex, and race. As reviewed in the text, minorities are still underrepresented. Shown here is Ben Nighthorse Campbell, Senator from Colorado. Campbell, a Northern Cheyenne, is the first Native American to serve in the U.S. Senate in 60 years.

tem, the more likely they are to vote. They have more to protect, and feel that voting can make a difference. In effect, people who have been rewarded by the political system feel more socially integrated. They vote because they perceive that elections directly affect their own lives and the type of society in which they and their children live.

Alienation In contrast, those who gain less from the system—in terms of education, income, and jobs—are more likely to be alienated. They feel that their vote will not affect their lives one way or another, that "next year will bring more of the same, regardless of who is president," that "all politicians lie to us." Similarly, minorities who feel the U.S. political system is a "white" system are less motivated to vote.

Voter Apathy Table 11.2 also indicates that many people who do have jobs, high education, and good

Table 11.2

Percentage of Eligible U.S. Voters Who Vote

	For President				For Congress
	1980	*1984*	*1988*	*1992*	*1994*
Overall					
Americans Who Vote	59%	60%	57%	61%	45%
Age					
18–20	36	37	33	39	17
21–24	43	44	38	46	22
25–34	55	55	48	53	32
35–44	64	64	61	64	46
45–64	69	70	68	70	56
65 and up	65	68	69	70	61
Sex					
Male	59	59	56	60	44
Female	59	61	58	62	45
Race or Ethnicity					
Whites	61	61	59	64	47
African Americans	51	56	52	54	37
Latinos	30	33	29	29	19
Asian Americans and Pacific Islanders	NA	NA	NA	50	NA
Education					
Grade school only	43	43	37	35	23
High school dropout	46	44	41	41	27
High school graduate	59	59	55	58	41
College dropout	67	68	65	69	49
College graduate	80	79	78	81	63
Labor Force					
Employed	62	62	58	64	45
Unemployed	41	44	39	46	28
Income					
Under $5,000	38	39	35	NA	NA
$5,000 to $9,999	46	49	41	NA	NA
$10,000 to $14,999	54	55	48	NA	NA
$15,000 to $19,999	57	60	54	NA	NA
$20,000 to $24,999	61	67	58	NA	NA
$25,000 to $34,999	67	74	64	NA	NA
$35,000 and over	74	74	70[a]	NA	NA

[a]For 1988, the percentage is an average of $35,000 to $49,900 and over $50,000.

Sources: Statistical Abstract 1991:Table 450; 1995:Table 459; *Current Population Reports*, Series P-20, vol. 440; U.S. Bureau of the Census, "Voting and Registration in the Election of November 1992," no. 466, p. 20.

incomes also stay away from the polls. Many people do not vote because of **voter apathy,** or indifference. Like the alienated, they feel that their vote will not affect the outcome. A common attitude is "What difference does my one vote make when there are millions of voters?" Although they are not alienated,

Ethnicity and Class as the Path to Political Participation

THAT THE UNITED STATES is the land of immigrants is a truism; every schoolchild knows that since the English Pilgrims first landed on Plymouth Rock, successive groups —among them Germans, Scandinavians, Italians, Poles, and Greeks —crossed the Atlantic Ocean to reach U.S. shores.

Some, such as the Irish immigrants in the late 1800s and early 1900s, left to escape brutal poverty and famine. Others, such as the Jews of czarist Russia, fled a government that singled them out for persecution. Some fled as refugees or asylum seekers from lands ravaged by war. Others, called *entrepreneurial immigrants*, sought economic opportunities absent in their native lands. Still others came as *sojourners*, planning to return home after a temporary stay.

Today the United States witnesses its second large wave of immigration of the twentieth century. The first, in the early 1900s, in which immigrants came to account for 13.2 percent of the population, consisted largely of Europeans. Today, the mix of immigrants—currently about 7.9 percent of the population—is far more diverse, with most coming from South and Central America and Asia. Since 1980, over 11 million legal immigrants have settled in the United States. About another 4 million are here illegally.

A widespread fear held by U.S.-born Americans in the early part of the century was that immigrants would subvert the democratic system in favor of socialism or communism. Today some fear that the primacy of the English language is threatened. In addition, the age-old fear that immigrants will take jobs away from U.S.-born Americans remains strong. Finally, minority groups that struggled for political representation fear that newer groups will gain political power at their expense.

What route to political participation do immigrants take? In general, they first organize as a group on the basis of *ethnicity* rather than *class*. In response to common problems, especially discrimination, they reaffirm their cultural identity. "This represents the first effective step in their social and political incorporation," note sociologists Alejandro Portes and Ruben Rumbaut. "By mobilizing the collective vote and by electing their own to office, immigrant minorities have learned the rules of the democratic game and absorbed its values in the process."

Irish immigrants to Boston illustrate this pattern of banding together on the basis of ethnicity. They built a power base that put the Irish in political control of the city, and, ultimately, saw one of their own sworn in as president of the United States.

As Portes and Rumbaut observe, "Assimilation as the rapid transformation of immigrants into Americans 'as everyone else' has never happened." Instead, all immigrant groups began by fighting for their own interests as Irish, Italians, and so on. Only when they had attained enough political power to overcome discrimination did they become "like everyone else"—that is, like others who had power.

Thus, only when a certain level of political power is achieved, when groups gain political representation somewhat proportionate to their numbers, does the issue of class grow in significance. This, then, is the path that immigrants follow in their socialization into the U.S. political system.

Sources: Portes and Rumbaut 1990; Salholz 1990; Prud'Homme 1991; James 1993; *Statistical Abstract* 1995: Tables 5, 10, 54, 1364.

many of the apathetic see little difference between the two major political parties.

The result of alienation and apathy is that two of five eligible voters do not vote for president, and that most of the nation's eligible voters do not bother to vote for candidates for Congress.

Lobbyists and Special-Interest Groups

Suppose you are president of the United States, and you want to make dairy products more affordable for the poor. As you check into the matter, you find that prices for milk and cheese are high because the government is paying dairy farmers $150 million a year in price supports (*Statistical Abstract* 1995:Table 1113). You therefore propose to eliminate these subsidies.

Immediately, large numbers of people leap into action. They send telegrams to your office, contact their senators and representatives, and call reporters for news conferences. The news media report that your proposal will put dairy farmers out of business. The Associated Press distributes pictures of a farm family—their Holsteins grazing contentedly in the background—informing readers how this healthy, happy family of good Americans struggling to make a living will be destroyed by your harsh proposal. President or not, you don't have a chance of getting your legislation passed.

What happened? The dairy industry went to work to protect its special interests. A **special-interest group** consists of people who think alike on a particular issue and who can be mobilized for political action. The dairy industry is just one of thousands of such groups that employ **lobbyists,** people paid to influence legislation on behalf of their clients. Special-interest groups and lobbyists have become a major force in U.S. politics. Members of Congress who are interested in being reelected must pay attention to them, for they represent blocs of voters who have a vital interest in the outcome of specific bills. Well financed and able to contribute huge sums, lobbyists can deliver votes to you—or to your opponent.

Because so much money was being passed under the table by special-interest groups to members of Congress, in the 1970s legislation limited the amount that any individual, corporation, or special-interest group could give a candidate, and required all contributions over $1,000 to be reported. Special-interest groups immediately did an end sweep around the new laws by forming **political action committees (PACs),** organizations that solicit contributions from many donors—each contribution within the allowable limit—and then use the large total to influence legislation.

PACs have become a powerful influence in Washington, for they bankroll lobbyists and legislators. About four thousand PACs disburse over $400 million (*Statistical Abstract* 1995:Tables 465, 466). A few PACs represent broad social interests such as environmental protection, but most stand for narrow financial concerns, such as the dairy, oil, banking, and construction industries. Those PACs with the most clout in terms of money and votes gain the ear of Congress. In short, to politicians the sound of money talking sounds like the voice of the people (Ferguson 1995).

Criticism of Lobbyists and PACs The major criticism leveled against lobbyists and PACs is that their money, in effect, buys votes. Rather than representing the people who elected them, legislators support the special interests of groups able to help them stay in power. The influence of foreign lobbyists has been a target of especially harsh criticism. As shown in Figure 11.1, the top ten foreign lobbyists spend

FIGURE 11.1

Foreign Lobbyists: The Top 10 Spenders

1. Japan — $60 million
2. Canada — $23 million
3. Germany — $13 million
4. France — $12.8 million
5. Mexico — $11 million
6. Hong Kong — $10.5 million
7. Kuwait — $9.5 million
8. Taiwan — $8 million
9. Australia — $8 million
10. Ireland — $7.8 million

Source: Engelberg and Tolchin 1993.

$163 million annually to influence votes. Japan has hired over 100 former U.S. government officials to pressure members of Congress to reduce quotas and duties on imports of its products. During election years, Japan contributes to *both* presidential candidates. Critics argue that the playing field is not level, for Japan has made it illegal for foreigners to influence *its* legislation (Judis 1990; Duffy 1992).

Even if the United States were to outlaw PACs, special-interest groups would not disappear from the U.S. political process. Lobbyists walked the corridors of the Senate long before PACs, and for good or ill, they play an essential role in the U.S. political system.

Who Rules the United States?

With lobbyists and PACs, just whom do U.S. senators and representatives really represent? This question has led to lively debate among sociologists.

The Functionalist Perspective: Pluralism

Functionalists view the state as having arisen out of the basic needs of the social group. To protect themselves from would-be oppressors, people formed a government and gave it the monopoly on violence. The risk is that the state can turn that force against its own citizens. To return to the example used earlier, states have a tendency to become muggers. Thus, people must perform a balancing act between having no government—which would lead to **anarchy,** a state in which disorder and violence reign—and having a government to protect them from violence, but that may itself turn against them. When functioning well, then, the state is a balanced system that protects its citizens—from one another *and* from government.

 What keeps the U.S. government from turning against its citizens? Functionalists say that **pluralism,** a diffusion of power among many interest groups, prevents any one group from gaining control of the government and using it to oppress the people (Polsby 1959; Huber and Form 1973; Dahl 1961, 1982). To keep the government from coming under the control of any one group, the founders of the United States set up three branches of government: the executive (president), judiciary (courts), and legislative (the Senate and House of Representatives). Each is sworn to uphold the Constitution, which guarantees rights to citizens, and each can nullify the actions of the other two. This system of **checks and balances** was designed to ensure that power remains distributed and that no one branch of government dominates.

From the functionalist perspective, ethnic groups, women, men, farmers, office workers, bosses, religious groups, bankers, the unemployed, and the retired, as well as the broader categories of the rich, middle class, and poor, are all parts of our pluralist society. As each group pursues its own interests, it is balanced by other groups pursuing theirs. As special-interest groups negotiate with one another and reach compromises, conflict is minimized, and the resulting policies gain wide support. Consequently, no one group rules, and the political system is responsive to the people.

The Conflict Perspective: The Power Elite, or Ruling Class

Conflict theorists disagree. If you focus on the lobbyists scurrying around Washington, they say, you get a blurred image of superficial activities. What really counts is the big picture, not its fragments. The important question is who holds the power that determines the overarching policies of the United States. For example, who determines how many Americans will be out of work by raising or lowering interest rates? Who sets policies that transfer jobs from the United States to countries with low-cost labor? And the ultimate question of power: Who is behind decisions to go to war?

C. Wright Mills (1956) took the position that the most important matters are not decided by lobbyists,

As conflict theorists stress, capitalist economies need a reserve labor force *that can be put to work in boom times and laid off during economic downturns. A good example is silver mining in Idaho, depicted in this photo. When silver prices fall below the cost of producing silver, workers are laid off. This miner, and other members of the reserve labor force, will then survive on unemployment, and when that runs out, on low-paying, part-time work or welfare. When silver prices again rise, they will be called back to work, again putting in gruelling hours like this—until the next reduction in silver prices leads to a repetition of the process.*

nor even by Congress. Rather, the decisions that have the greatest impact on the lives of Americans—and people across the face of the globe—are made by a **power elite.** As depicted in Figure 11.2, the power elite consists of the top leaders of the largest corporations, the most powerful generals and admirals of the armed forces, and certain elite politicians—the president, his cabinet, and select senior members of Congress who chair the major committees. It is they who wield power, who make the decisions that direct the country—and shake the world (Hellinger and Judd 1991; Ferguson 1995).

Are the three groups that make up the power elite—the top political, military, and corporate leaders—equal in power? Mills said they were not, but for his choice of dominance he did not point to the president and his staff or even to the generals and admirals, but rather to the corporate heads. Because all three segments of the power elite view capitalism as essential to the welfare of the country, business interests, he said, come foremost in setting national policy.

Sociologist William Domhoff (1967, 1990) uses the term *ruling class* to refer to the power elite. He focuses on the 1 percent of Americans who belong to the super-rich, the powerful capitalist class studied in Chapter 8. Members of this class control our top corporations and foundations, even the boards that oversee our major universities. It is no accident, says Domhoff, that from this group the president chooses most members of his cabinet and appoints the top ambassadors to the most powerful countries of the world.

Conflict theorists point out that we should not think of this ruling class as a group that meets together and agrees on specific matters. Rather, it consists of people whose backgrounds and orientations to life are so similar—they attend prestigious private schools, belong to exclusive private clubs, and are millionaires many times over—that they automatically share the same values and goals. Their behavior stems not from some grand conspiracy to control the country, but rather from a mutual interest in solving the problems that face large businesses (Useem 1984). With their political connections extending to the top centers of power, this powerful group sets the economic and political conditions under which the rest of the country operates (Domhoff 1990).

Which View Is Right?

The functionalist and conflict views of power in U.S. society cannot be reconciled. Either competing interests block the dominance of any single group, as functionalists assert, or a power elite oversees the major decisions of the United States, as conflict theorists maintain. Perhaps at the middle level of Mills's model, depicted in Figure 11.2, the competing interest groups do keep each other at bay, and none is able to dominate. If so, the functionalist view would apply to this middle level, as well as the lowest level of power. Perhaps functionalists have just not looked high enough, however, and activities at the peak remain invisible to them. If so, on that level lies the key to U.S. power, the dominance by an elite as it follows its mutual interests.

The answer, however, is not yet conclusive. For that, we must await more research.

FIGURE 11.2

Power in the United States: The Model Proposed by C. Wright Mills

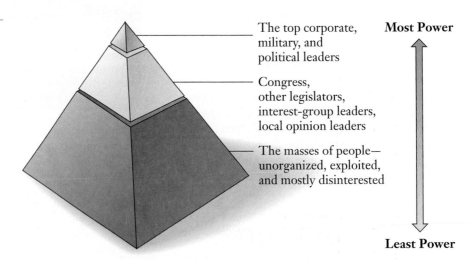

The top corporate, military, and political leaders

Congress, other legislators, interest-group leaders, local opinion leaders

The masses of people— unorganized, exploited, and mostly disinterested

Most Power

Least Power

Source: Based on Mills 1956.

THE ECONOMY: WORK IN THE GLOBAL VILLAGE

How will radical shifts in our economy affect your chances of getting a good job? The materials we shall now review can shed some light on this question. Let's begin with a story about Kim.

> The alarm pounded in Kim's ears. "Not Monday already," she groaned. "There must be a better way of starting the week." She pressed the snooze button on the clock (from Germany) to sneak another ten minutes' sleep. In what seemed just thirty seconds, the alarm shrilly insisted she get up and face the week.
>
> Still bleary-eyed after her shower, Kim peered into her closet and picked out a silk blouse (from China), a plaid wool skirt (from Scotland), and leather shoes (from India). She nodded, satisfied, as she added a pair of simulated pearls (from Taiwan). Running late, she hurriedly ran a brush (from Mexico) through her hair. As Kim wolfed down a bowl of cereal (from the United States), topped with milk (from the United States), bananas (from Costa Rica), and sugar (from the Dominican Republic), she turned on her kitchen television (from Korea) to listen to the weather forecast.
>
> Gulping the last of her coffee (from Brazil), Kim grabbed her briefcase (from Wales), purse (from Spain), and jacket (from Malaysia), and quickly climbed into her car (from Japan). As she glanced at her watch (from Switzerland), she hoped the traffic would be in her favor. She muttered to herself as she glimpsed the gas gauge at a street light (from Great Britain). She muttered again when she paid for the gas (from Saudi Arabia), for the price had risen over the weekend. "My check never keeps up with prices," she moaned to herself as she finished the drive to work.
>
> The office was abuzz. Six months ago, New York headquarters had put the company up for sale, but there had been no takers. The big news this Monday was that both a Japanese and a Canadian corporation had put in bids over the weekend. No one got much work done that day, as the whole office speculated about how things might change.
>
> As Kim walked to the parking lot after work, she saw a tattered "Buy American" bumper sticker on the car next to hers. "That's right," she said to herself. "If people were more like me, this country would be in better shape."

The Transformation of Economic Systems

Although this vignette may be slightly exaggerated, many of us are like Kim—using a multitude of products from around the world, and yet concerned about our country's ability to compete in global markets. Today the **economy**—a system of producing and distributing goods and services—differs radically from all but our most recent past. The products Kim uses make it apparent that today's economy knows no national boundaries. To better understand what has happened, let's begin with a review of sweeping historical changes.

Preindustrial Societies: From Equality to Inequality

The earliest human groups, *hunting and gathering societies*, had a simple **subsistence economy.** Groups of perhaps twenty-five to forty people lived off the land, gathering what they could find and moving from place to place as their food supply ran low. Because there was little or no excess food or other items, they did little trading with other groups. With no excess to accumulate, everybody possessed about the same as everyone else.

Then something unexpected happened, which produced a surplus and ushered in social inequality: people discovered how to breed animals and cultivate plants. Due to the more dependable food supply in *pastoral and horticultural societies*, humans settled down in a single place. Human groups grew larger, and for the first time some individuals could devote their energies to tasks other than producing food. Some people became leather workers, others weapon makers, and so on. This new division of labor produced a variety of items that were available for trade. The primary sociological significance of surplus and trade was that they fostered *social inequality*, for some people now accumulated more possessions than others. The effects of that change remain with us today.

The next major change was due to the invention of the plow, which made land much more productive. As *agricultural societies* developed, even more people were freed from food production and more specialized divisions of labor followed. Trade expanded, and trading centers developed. As trading centers turned into cities, power passed from the heads of families and clans to a ruling elite. The result was even greater social, political, and economic inequality.

One of the negative consequences of early industrialization in the West was the use of child labor. In the photo on the left, of the U.S. textile industry in the 1800s, you can see spindle boys at work in a Georgia cotton mill. Today's Least Industrialized Nations are experiencing the same negative consequence as they industrialize. The photo on the right shows boys at work in a contemporary textile factory in Varanas, India.

Industrial Societies: The Birth of the Machine

Industrial societies, which are based on machines powered by fuels, created a surplus unlike anything the world had seen. The invention of the steam engine in 1765, which resulted in this vast surplus of manufactured goods, stimulated trade between nations. The Industrial Revolution also magnified social inequality, for it permitted a handful of individuals to exploit the labor of vast numbers of others.

As the surplus increased, the emphasis changed from the production of goods to their consumption. Sociologist Thorstein Veblen (1912) used the term **conspicuous consumption** to describe this fundamental change in people's orientations. By this term, Veblen meant that the Protestant ethic identified by Weber—an emphasis on hard work, savings, and a concern for salvation (discussed in Chapter 13)—had been replaced by an eagerness to show off wealth by the "elaborate consumption of goods."

Postindustrial Societies: The New Technology Gives Birth to the Information Age

To understand this new type of society, we should note that there are three types of work: primary, sec-

ondary, and tertiary. In the *primary sector*, which is central to preindustrial societies, workers extract natural resources from the environment. People who fish for a living or who mine copper work in the primary sector. So do hunters, cattle raisers, farmers, and lumberjacks. In the *secondary sector*, which dominates industrial societies, workers turn raw materials into manufactured goods. They package fish, process copper into electrical wire, and turn trees into lumber and paper. In contrast, providing services is the main focus of the *tertiary sector*. Computer technicians and automobile mechanics install or service products, while others, such as private detectives and cab drivers, provide personal services.

In 1973, sociologist Daniel Bell noted that the United States had become dominated by the tertiary sector, that more people worked in this sector than in the other two. Other countries such as Japan and Germany soon followed. Finding this change highly significant, an indication that *an entirely new type of society was emerging*, Bell coined the term *postindustrial society*. He identified six characteristics of the postindustrial society: (1) a service sector so large that it employs the majority of workers; (2) a huge surplus of goods; (3) even more extensive trade among nations; (4) a wider variety and quantity of goods available to the average person; (5) an "information explosion"; and (6) a "global village"—that is, the globe becomes linked by instantaneous communications.

Figure 11.3 illustrates our transition to this new society. From this figure, you can see the decline of employment in farming (the primary sector), where most of our ancestors once worked. During the 1800s, a typical farmer could produce only enough food for five people, but with today's powerful farming machinery and hybrid seeds he or she now feeds about eighty. In the 1800s over 50 percent of U.S. workers were engaged in farming, today only about 1 percent (*Statistical Abstract* 1995:Tables 649, 1098). As the number of farmers declined during the early and mid-1900s, manufacturing (the secondary sector) picked up the slack. Then blue-collar work (the secondary sector) rapidly declined, being replaced by white-collar work (the tertiary sector).

Although *most* of the labor force in postindustrial societies work in the tertiary sector, all three sectors exist side by side. Take the common lead pencil as an example. People who extract lead and cut timber work in the primary sector, those who turn the wood and lead into pencils are in the secondary sector, and those who advertise and sell the pencils work in the tertiary sector.

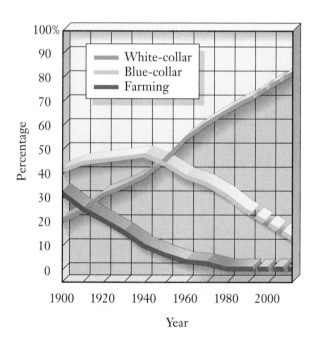

Broken lines are the author's estimates.

Source: Statistical Abstract, various years and 1995:Table 652.

FIGURE 11.3

Percentage of U.S. Workers in Three Types of Work

Perhaps the "information explosion" is the key element of the postindustrial society. Although few people are needed to produce food or basic materials and few people to process them, the information explosion demands that large numbers of people do "knowledge work"—managing information and designing and servicing products. Almost all of us who graduate from college will be doing some form of "knowledge work."

The consequences of this information explosion that is transforming the world are extremely uneven. Most of us who graduate from college will become as comfortable with the new society as our predecessors became with theirs. But not everyone will find a comfortable niche in this new global village.

You can think of the village as divided into three large neighborhoods—the three worlds of development, which we reviewed in Chapter 7. Due to political and economic arrangements, some nations are socially destined to live in the poor part of the village, where citizens barely eke out a living from menial work. Some will even starve to death while fellow villagers in another neighborhood feast on the best that the globe has to offer.

Within each neighborhood in the village, gross inequalities also show up, for both the wealthy and poor neighborhoods have citizens who are well off and those who are poor. Since the United States is the global economic leader, occupying a mansion in the best neighborhood, let's look at U.S. trends.

Ominous Trends in the United States

After U.S. workers unionized, one of their first demands was a shorter work week. For about the past hundred years or so their work week grew consistently shorter. Then in the 1960s this trend reversed course (Schor 1991). U.S. workers now average 1,948 hours of work a year, matched only by workers in Great Britain. They are soundly beaten, however, by Japanese workers, who average 2,120 hours a year (Ono and Schlesinger 1992; MacShane 1993).

A primary reason that the average work week of U.S. workers increased is the attempt by U.S. firms to remain competitive in the global marketplace. By paying overtime to their regular workers, companies can add fewer full-time workers and thus avoid paying additional unemployment, medical, and retirement benefits. For the same reason, they are *"downsizing"* (reducing their staff) and hiring temporary workers (whom they can release at will). Even col-

FIGURE 11.4

The Inverted Income Pyramid: The Proportion of Income Received by Each Fifth of the U.S. Population

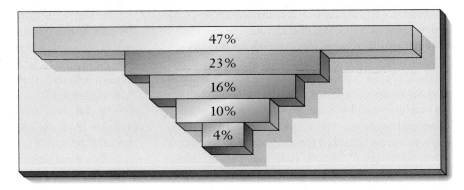

47%

23%

16%

10%

4%

Source: Statistical Abstract 1996:Table 719.

leges and universities are not exempt from this trend, and increasing numbers of instructors are part-timers. Hired to teach specific courses, they are exempt from tenure, promotion, sick leave, and retirement benefits. Some analysts are concerned that these patterns may be permanent, foreshadowing an era of easily discharged workers who live with insecurity, low pay, and few benefits.

Certainly the inequalities are great. The inverted pyramid shown in Figure 11.4 is a snapshot of how the nation's income is divided. Each rectangle represents a fifth of the U.S. population. The proportion that goes to the nation's wealthiest fifth is at the top, the proportion going to the poorest fifth at the bottom. Note that *47 percent* of the whole country's income goes to just one-fifth of Americans, while only *4 percent* goes to the poorest fifth. Rather than bringing equality, then, the postindustrial economy has perpetuated the income inequalities of the industrial economy.

Although the United States remains a land of vast opportunities—such as those seized by the Chinese immigrants featured in The Immigrant Experience box on page 297—many Americans find that their standard of living is stagnating or even declining. Look at Figure 11.5. The gold bars show current dollars, the dollars the average worker finds in his or her paycheck. From this, it seems that U.S. workers are making a lot more than they used to. The green bars, which show the *buying power* of these earnings, however, strip away the illusion. They show that inflation has whittled away the value of those dollars, and workers can't buy as much with their $11 today as they could with the "measly" $3 they made in 1970. The question is not "How could you live on just $3 an hour back in 1970?" but, rather, "How can you live on just $11 an hour today?"

Bennett Harrison and Barry Bluestone (1988) call these shrinking paychecks *the great American U-turn.* Underlying this U-turn is a surge in imports and a decline in exports. The United States used to sell (export) more than it purchased (imports). One

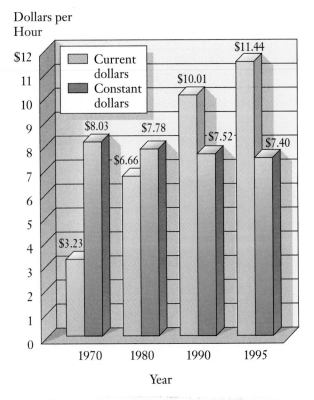

Dollars per Hour

Current dollars

Constant dollars

$12
11
10
9
8
7
6
5
4
3
2
1
0

$3.23

$8.03

$6.66

$7.78

$10.01

$7.52

$11.44

$7.40

1970   1980   1990   1995

Year

Source: Statistical Abstract 1993:Table 667; 1996:Table 659.

FIGURE 11.5

Average Hourly Earnings of U.S. Workers in Current and Constant (1982) Dollars

▼▲▼▲▼▲▼▲▼▲▼▲▼▲▼▲▼▲▼▲▼▲▼▲▼▲▼▲▼▲▼▲▼

The Immigrant Experience

The Economic Success of the New Chinese Immigrants

AS WE SAW on Table 9.2 on page 227, the average annual income of Chinese immigrants is higher than that of white Americans. Why have Chinese immigrants been so economically successful?

The first factor is their general background. Most of the new immigrants had lived in urban areas such as Hong Kong, Macao, and Taipei, and had attained a good education. Some had business experience. The second common theme of the immigrants, even those with low education, was to work within a family unit and to seize each opportunity in the new land.

The garment industries of New York City, San Francisco, and Los Angeles provide an example of their economic adaptation and allow us to see some of the factors in their success. Some of the immigrants saw the potential of this business, and family and kin pooled their savings and worked together to begin small factories. They hired recently arrived immigrants as seamstresses, women who knew how to sew and needed cash badly. These women

work at low wages as second wage earners to supplement their family incomes, in turn, saving what they can so they, too, can move upward. These family-run enterprises are small and flexible enough to weather the seasonal nature of the fashion industry.

A second example is the Chinese restaurants that dot the landscape of the United States. These businesses require ethnic expertise, and thus rule out competition from non-Chinese. They also are labor intensive, requiring long hours of preparation and efficient organization. In the typical case, these restaurants are family enterprises, with parents, relatives, and children all working to reach the goal of their mutual success. In general, the Chinese restaurant is a business preferred by first-generation immigrants. They stress to their children the benefits of a good education, and their children tend to pass up their parents on the social class ladder by entering such fields as law, engineering, and computer science.

Families working together for a common goal, willing to spend

long hours in intensive labor, saving as much as they can for the future, and pushing their children to succeed in school, then, are the primary keys in the success of Chinese immigrants. For them, the "American Dream" is alive and well.

The immigrants are not immune to the emerging global economy. NAFTA is a special concern for those in the garment industry, for in the search for cheaper labor, many manufacturers may move their production out of the United States to South and Central America. If this happens, many of the Chinese immigrants will be denied employment in what has been for them the first step on the social class ladder. Granted the dedication and tenacity that they have shown so far, however, it is likely that they will adjust successfully to any changes.

Bernard Wong
San Francisco State University
Ethnicity and Entrepreneurship among the Immigrant Chinese, Allyn and Bacon (1996)

---

result was hefty annual profits that could be plowed back into building new factories and machinery—which brought higher wages and a growing standard of living. For the last twenty years or so, however, the United States has had a voracious, uncontrolled appetite, importing much more than it has exported (*Statistical Abstract* 1993:Table 1344; 1995:Table 1320). In addition, Americans are saving less. In 1980, Americans saved almost 7 percent of their income. Today it is less than 4 percent (*Statistical Abstract* 1995:Tables 710, 711).

This is a formula for disaster. With spiraling debt, the United States has less money to invest in wages, education, factories, parks, or any other ways that in-

crease a people's quality of life. Like an individual, if a nation spends more each year than it takes in, economic problems are inevitable. In just a few short years the United States went from being the world's largest creditor to the world's largest debtor. Today the national debt is so huge that the interest payments alone run more than all the money the U.S. government spends on health, science, space, agriculture, housing, protecting the environment, and the entire justice system (Kennedy 1993).

If these trends continue, the result could be a *"two-thirds society"* (Glotz 1986). An upper third would consist of well-educated and prosperous technocrats who would be in charge. In the middle third would be workers who, though insecure in their jobs, earn a more-or-less adequate income. At the bottom, however, would be another third of the entire population consisting of the unemployed and the underemployed—migrant workers, the physically and mentally handicapped, teenagers who cannot find their way into the job market, and older people who have been pushed out of the job market—with minorities a disproportionate share of this bottom third.

World Economic Systems

To understand where the United States stands in the world economic order, we need to compare capitalism and socialism, the two main economic systems in force today.

Capitalism

People who live in a capitalist society are immersed in details that blur its essentials. It is difficult to see beyond the local shopping mall and fast-food chains. If we distill the many businesses of the United States to their basic components, however, we see that **capitalism** has three essential features: (1) *private ownership of the means of production* (individuals own the land, machines, and factories, and decide what shall be produced); (2) *the pursuit of profit* (trying to sell something for more than it cost); and (3) *market competition* (an exchange of items between willing buyers and sellers).

Welfare (or State) Capitalism versus Laissez-Faire Capitalism Many people believe the United States is an example of pure capitalism. Pure capitalism, however (also called **laissez-faire capitalism**—literally, "hands off" capitalism), means that market forces operate without interference from the government. Such is not the case in the United States. The current form of U.S. capitalism is **welfare** or **state capitalism.** Private citizens own the means of production and pursue profits, but they do so within a vast system of laws designed to protect the welfare of the population.

Suppose you have discovered what you think is a miracle tonic: It will grow hair, erase wrinkles, and dissolve excess fat. If your product works, you will become an overnight sensation—not only a millionaire, but also the toast of television talk shows.

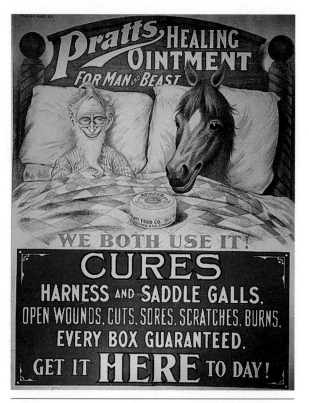

This advertisement from 1885 represents an earlier stage of capitalism when individuals were free to manufacture and market products with little or no interference from the government. Today, the production and marketing of goods take place under detailed, complicated government regulations.

Before you count your money—and your fame—however, you must reckon with **market restraints,** the laws and regulations of welfare capitalism that limit your capacity to sell what you produce. First, you must comply with local and state rules. You must obtain a charter of incorporation, a business license, and a state tax number that allows you to buy without paying sales taxes. Then come the federal regulations. You cannot simply take your item to local stores and ask them to sell it; you first must seek approval from federal agencies that monitor compliance with the Pure Food and Drug Act. This means you must prove that your product will not cause harm to the public. In addition, you must be able to substantiate your claims—or else face being shut down by state and federal agencies that monitor the market for fraud. Your manufacturing process is also subject to government regulations: state and local laws concerning cleanliness and state and federal rules for the storage and disposal of hazardous wastes.

Suppose you succeed in overcoming these obstacles, your business prospers, and the number of your employees grows. Other federal agencies will monitor your compliance with regulations concerning racial and sexual discrimination, the payment of minimum wages, and the remittance of Social Security taxes. State agencies will also examine your records to see that you have paid unemployment compensation taxes on your employees and sales taxes on items that you sell at retail. Finally, the Internal Revenue Service will constantly look over your shoulder. In short, the highly regulated U.S. economic system is far from an example of laissez-faire capitalism.

Socialism

Socialism also has three essential components: (1) the public ownership of the means of production; (2) central planning; and (3) the distribution of goods without a profit motive.

The government owns the means of production—not only the factories, but also the land, railroads, oil wells, and gold mines. Unlike capitalism, in which **market forces**—supply and demand—determine what shall be produced and the prices that will be charged, a central committee decides that the country needs *X* number of toothbrushes, *Y* toilets, and *Z* shoes. This group decides how many of each shall be produced, which factories will produce them, the prices that will be charged for the items, and where they will be distributed.

Socialism is designed to eliminate competition, for goods are sold at predetermined prices regardless of demand for an item, its quality, or the cost to produce it. Profit is not the goal, nor is encouraging consumption of goods in low demand (by lowering the price), nor limiting the consumption of hard-to-get goods (by raising the price). Rather, the goal is to produce goods for the general welfare and to distribute them according to people's needs, not their ability to pay.

In a socialist economy, *everyone* in the economic chain works for the government. The members of the central committee who determine production are government employees, as are supervisors who implement their plans, the factory workers who do the producing, the truck drivers who move the merchandise, and the clerks who sell it. Although those who purchase the items work at entirely different jobs—in

offices, on farms, in day care centers—they, too, are government employees.

Just as capitalism does not exist in a pure form, neither does socialism. Although the ideology of socialism calls for resources to be distributed according to need and not position, in line with the functionalist argument of social stratification presented in Chapter 8, socialist countries found it necessary to offer higher salaries for some jobs in order to entice people to take greater responsibilities. For example, factory managers always earn more than factory workers. By narrowing the huge pay gaps that characterize capitalist nations, however, socialist nations established considerably greater equality of income.

Democratic Socialism   Dissatisfied with the greed and exploitation of capitalism and the lack of freedom and individuality of socialism, some Western nations (most notably Sweden and Denmark) developed **democratic socialism,** or welfare socialism. In this form of socialism, both the state and individuals engage in production and distribution. Although the government owns and runs the steel, mining, forestry, and energy concerns, as well as the country's telephones, television stations, and airlines, remaining in private hands are the retail stores, farms, manufacturing concerns, and most service industries.

Ideologies of Capitalism and Socialism

Capitalism and socialism not only have different approaches to producing and distributing goods, but they also represent distinct ideologies. *Capitalists* hold that market forces should determine both products and prices. They also believe it is healthy for people to strive after profits, for this encourages them to develop and produce products desired by the public. *Socialists*, in contrast, believe that profits are immoral. Because an item's value represents the work that goes into it, profit is an amount withheld from workers. The government, then, should own the means of production, using them not for profit, but to produce and distribute items according to people's needs, not their ability to pay.

These ideologies paint each other in such stark colors that *each sees the other as a system of exploitation.* Capitalists see socialists as violating basic human rights of freedom of decision and opportunity, while socialists see capitalists as violating basic human rights of freedom from poverty. With each side painting itself in moral colors while viewing the other as a threat to its very existence, this century witnessed the world split into two main blocs. The West armed itself to defend capitalism, the East to defend socialism. Prior to the collapse of the Soviet Union in 1989, the remaining "nonaligned" nations often were able to extort vast sums of economic and military aid by playing the West and the East off against one another.

Criticisms of Capitalism and Socialism

The primary criticism leveled against capitalism is that it leads to social inequality. Capitalism, say its critics, produces a tiny top layer consisting of wealthy people, who exploit a vast bottom layer of poorly paid workers. Those few who own the means of production accrue power, and they get legislation passed that goes against the public good merely to further their own interests.

The primary criticism leveled against socialism is that it does not respect individual rights (Berger 1991). Others (in the form of some government body) make decisions about where people will work, live, and go to school. In the case of China, they even decide how many children women may bear (Mosher 1983). Critics also argue that central planning is grossly inefficient (Kennedy 1993), that socialism is not capable of producing much wealth. They say that its supposedly greater equality really amounts to giving almost everyone an equal chance to be poor.

If politics make strange bedfellows, so do economics. The animosity of U.S. politicians to Vietnam's economic system was once so fierce they sacrificed hundreds of thousands of lives and billions of dollars in a wasted effort to extinguish "the enemy." This photo from Ho Chi Minh City, the capital of Vietnam, illustrates how this former "enemy to death" is now in the process of becoming an economic partner of the United States. How do convergence theory and globalization explain this billboard?

Convergence: A Developing Hybrid

Clark Kerr (1960, 1983) suggested that as nations industrialize they grow alike. They produce similar divisions of labor (such as professionals and skilled technicians), encourage higher education, and urbanize. Similar values also emerge, uniting its various groups. By themselves, these tendencies would make capitalist and socialist nations grow more alike, but some sociologists, such as William Form (1979), have identified another factor that brings these nations closer to one another: Despite their incompatible ideologies, both capitalist and socialist systems have adopted features of the other. Known as **convergence theory**, this view points to a possible hybrid or mixed economy for the future.

Convergence theory is given support by the new emphasis on profit in socialist countries. Suffering from shoddy goods and plagued by shortages, with standards of living that severely lag behind those of the West, Russia and China have begun to reinstate market forces, including the private own-

ership of property and profits for those who produce and sell goods. They solicit Western investments, encourage farmers to cultivate their own plots on the communal farms, allow credit cards, and even permit a stock market.

Changes in U.S. capitalism also support this theory, for the United States has adopted many socialist practices. In each instance, money is extracted from some to pay for benefits received by others. Consider the following: unemployment compensation (taxes paid by workers are distributed to those who no longer produce a profit); subsidized housing (shelter, paid for by the many, is distributed to the poor and elderly, with no motive of profit); welfare (taxes from the many are distributed to the needy); the minimum wage (the government, not the employer, determines the minimum that a worker shall be paid); and Social Security (the retired do not receive what they paid into the system, but, rather, money collected from current workers). Such embrace of socialist principles means that the United States has produced its own version of a mixed type of economy.

Perhaps, then, the upheavals now occurring in the world's economic systems indicate that the hybrid is closer than ever. On the one hand, not even staunch capitalists want a system that does not provide at least minimum support during unemployment, extended illness, and old age. On the other hand, socialist leaders have reluctantly admitted that profit does motivate people to work harder.

Capitalism in a Global Economy

To understand today's capitalism, we need to consider the corporation within the context of a global economy.

The Corporation — Protect the owners

The corporation is a legal entity that protects its owners. Treated in law as an individual, the **corporation** is the joint ownership of a business enterprise, whose liabilities and obligations are separate from those of its owners. For example, each shareholder of Xerox—whether the owner of one or 100,000 shares—owns a portion of the company. As a legal entity, Xerox can buy and sell, sue and be sued, make contracts, and incur debts. The corporation, however, not its individual owners, is responsible for the firm's liabilities—such as paying its debts and fulfilling its contracts.

Corporations have so changed capitalism that the term **corporate capitalism** has emerged to indicate that giant corporations dominate the economic system. Of its hundreds of thousands of businesses and tens of thousands of corporations, a mere 500 dominate the U.S. economy. Called the "Fortune 500" (derived from *Fortune* magazine's annual profile of the largest 500 companies), the annual profits of these firms represent one-quarter of the entire U.S. gross national product (*Statistical Abstract* 1995:Tables 706, 884).

One of the most significant aspects of corporations is the *separation of ownership and management.* Unlike in most businesses, it is not the owners, those who own the company's stock, who run the day-to-day affairs of the company (Walters 1995). Rather, a corporation is run by managers who are able to treat it *as though it were their own.* The result is the "ownership of wealth without appreciable control, and control of wealth without appreciable ownership" (Berle

and Means 1932). Sociologist Michael Useem (1984) put it this way:

> When few owners held all or most of a corporation's stock, they readily dominated its board of directors, which in turn selected top management and ran the corporation. Now that a firm's stock [is] dispersed among many unrelated owners, each holding a tiny fraction of the total equity, the resulting power vacuum allow[s] management to select the board of directors; thus management [becomes] self-perpetuating and thereby acquire[s] de facto control over the corporation.

Because of this power vacuum, at the annual meeting stockholders ordinarily rubber-stamp management's recommendations. It is so unusual for this not to happen that when it does not the outcome is called a **stockholders' revolt.** The irony of this term is generally lost, but remember that in such cases it is not the workers but the owners who are rebelling!

Interlocking Directorates

One way in which the wealthy use corporations to wield power is by means of **interlocking directorates** (Mizruchi and Koenig 1991). The elite serve as directors of several companies. Their fellow members on those boards also sit on the boards of other companies, and so on. Like a spider's web that starts at the center and then fans out in all directions, the top companies in the country are incorporated into a network (Mintz and Schwartz 1985). The chief executive officer of a firm in England, who sits on the board of directors of half a dozen other companies, noted,

> If you serve on, say, six outside boards, each of which has, say, ten directors, and let's say out of the ten directors, five are experts in one or another subject, you have a built-in panel of thirty friends who are experts who you meet regularly, automatically each month, and you really have great access to ideas and information. You're joining a club, a very good club. (Useem 1984)

This concentration of power minimizes competition, for a director is not going to approve a plan that will be harmful to another company in which he or she (mostly he) has a stake.

Global Capitalism: The Case of Multinational Corporations

Kim, in the vignette on page 293, illustrates the new distribution patterns of our global marketplace. The

multinational corporations—companies that operate across national boundaries—move investments and production from one part of the globe to another. Their search for profits across national boundaries has brought a flood of low-priced goods to consumers. Like Kim, we consume these items without being aware of where they are produced.

The variety and cheaper prices, though, come at a cost. On the more visible side are the millions of jobs that have been yanked out from under U.S. workers and moved to Mexico, Indonesia, and other countries with low labor costs. On the less visible side, as conflict theorists stress, is the exploitation of workers in the Least Industrialized Nations. Some of the items we consume are produced by children toiling long hours in sweat shops, others by young women whose health is hurt by their working conditions (Ehrenreich and Fuentes 1997). There also is a high environmental cost, for, unlike in the Most Industrialized Nations, in these countries few regulations govern the disposal of toxic waste.

With profit their moral guide, the conscience of multinational corporations is ruled by dollar signs.

A New World Order?

Underlying today's almost frantic globalization of capitalism is the new technology that allows a worldwide flow of information, capital, and goods. In the race for profits have come alliances that one day may bring the unexpected bonus of world peace. The United States, Canada, and Mexico have formed a North American Free Trade Association (NAFTA), to which all of South America will eventually belong.

GATT, the General Agreement on Tariffs and Trade, incorporates 124 nations in the World Trade Organization. Most European nations are united in an economic and political unit called the European Union (EU). Each nation retains its own legislature, courts, army, and head of state; there also is a European Parliament, a European court, a coming single currency (the Eurodollar), and, as proposed, a single military.

We cannot separate global political and economic events, for they have become wedded—and their marriage is of utmost significance for our own future. Consider just the global interconnections of the multinational corporations. With their allegiance to profits, national boundaries have become increasingly meaningless. The sociological significance of this trend is that multinational corporations have become more and more detached from the interests and values of their country of origin. As a U.S. executive said, "The United States does not have an automatic call on our resources. There is no mind-set that puts the country first" (Kennedy 1993).

As these global giants grow, their elites are likely to become more and more interconnected. To forge international trade agreements, they also court the partnership of national elites—who benefit in exchange for their cooperation. This process may ultimately interlace the elites of the world's nations. If so, far removed from the tribal loyalties of national boundaries, the multinational corporations and their new trade agreements will be a force for peace.

The price for world peace, for economic and political unity, however, may come at a high cost. If we end up with a new world order dominated by a handful of the world's top corporate leaders, our everyday life with Big Brother could be like that of Winston and Julia in our opening vignette.

Summary and Review

Power, Authority, and Violence

How are authority and coercion related to power?

Authority is power that people view as legitimately exercised over them, while **coercion** is power they consider unjust. The **state** is a political entity that claims a monopoly on violence over a particular territory. If enough people consider a state's power illegitimate, revolution is possible. Pp. 280–281.

What kinds of authority are there?

Max Weber identified three types of authority. Power in **traditional authority** derives from custom—patterns set down in the past are the rules for the present. Power in **rational-legal authority** (also called *bureaucratic authority*) is based on law and written procedures. In **charismatic authority,** power is based on loyalty to an individual to whom people are attracted. Charismatic authority, which undermines traditional and rational-legal authority, has built-in problems in transferring authority to a new leader. Pp. 281–283.

Types of Government

How are the types of government related to power?

In a **monarchy,** power is based on hereditary rule; in a **democracy,** power is given the ruler by citizens; and in a **dictatorship,** power is seized by an individual or small group. Pp. 284–286.

The U.S. Political System

What are the main characteristics of the U.S. political system?

The United States has two main political parties, each trying to win the center of the political spectrum. Voter turnout is higher among people who are more socially integrated, those who sense a greater stake in the outcome of elections, such as the more educated and well-to-do. **Lobbyists** and **special-interest groups,** such as **political action committees (PACs)**, play a significant role in U.S. politics. Pp. 286–290.

Who Rules the United States?

Is the United States controlled by a ruling class?

In a view known as **pluralism,** functionalists say that no one group holds power, that the country's many competing interest groups balance one another. Conflict theorists, who focus on the top level of power, say that the United States is governed by a **power elite,** a *ruling class* made up of the top corporate, military, and political leaders. At this point, the matter is not settled. Pp. 290–292.

The Transformation of Economic Systems

How are economic systems linked to types of societies?

The earliest societies, hunting and gathering, were **subsistence economies:** Small groups lived off the land and produced little or no surplus. Economic systems grew more complex as people discovered how to domesticate and cultivate (pastoral and horticultural societies), farm (agricultural societies), and manufacture (industrial societies). Each of these methods allowed people to produce a *surplus*, which fostered trade. Trade, in turn, brought social inequality as some people began to accumulate more than others. Pp. 293–298.

World Economic Systems

How do the major economic systems differ?

The world's two major economic systems are capitalism and socialism. In **capitalism,** private citizens own the means of production and pursue profits. In **socialism,** the state owns the means of production and determines production with no goal of profit. Adherents of each have developed ideologies that defend their own systems and paint the other as harmful. Following **convergence theory,** in recent years each system has adopted features of the other. Pp. 298–301.

Capitalism in a Global Economy

What is the role of the corporation in capitalism?

The term **corporate capitalism** indicates that giant corporations dominate capitalism. **Interlocking directorates** tie these companies together. The profit goal of **multinational corporations** removes their allegiance from any particular nation. Pp. 301–302.

A New World Order?

Is humanity headed toward a one-world political order?

The global expansion of capitalism due to new technology, accompanied by the trend toward larger political unions, may indicate that a world political order is developing. This may bring world peace, but perhaps at a high cost of personal freedom. P. 302.

Where can I read more on this topic?

Suggested readings for this chapter are listed on pages 441–442.

Glossary

anarchy a condition of lawlessness or political disorder caused by the absence or collapse of governmental authority (p. 291)

authority power that people accept as rightly exercised over them (p. 280)

capitalism an economic system characterized by the private ownership of the means of production, the pursuit of profit, and market competition (p. 298)

charismatic authority authority based on an individual's outstanding traits, which attract followers (p. 282)

checks and balances separation of powers among the three branches of U.S. government—legislative, executive, and judicial—so that each is able to nullify the actions of the other two, thus preventing the domination of any single branch (p. 291)

citizenship the concept that birth (and residence) in a country impart basic rights (p. 284)

city-state an independent city whose power radiates outward, bringing the adjacent area under its rule (p. 284)

coercion power that people do not accept as just (p. 280)

conspicuous consumption Thorstein Veblen's term for a change from the Protestant ethic to an eagerness to show off wealth by the elaborate consumption of goods (p. 294)

convergence theory the view that as both capitalist and socialist economic systems adopt features of the other, a hybrid (or mixed) economic system will emerge (p. 300)

corporate capitalism the domination of the economic system by giant corporations (p. 301)

corporation the joint ownership of a business enterprise, whose liabilities and obligations are separate from those of its owners (p. 301)

democracy a system of government in which authority derives from the people (p. 284)

democratic socialism a hybrid economic system in which capitalism is mixed with state ownership (p. 299)

dictatorship a form of government in which power is seized by an individual (p. 285)

direct democracy a form of democracy in which voters meet together to discuss issues and make their decisions (p. 284)

economy a system of distribution of goods and services (p. 293)

interlocking directorates individuals serving on the board of directors of several companies (p. 301)

laissez-faire capitalism unrestrained manufacture and trade (literally "hands off" capitalism) (p. 298)

lobbyists people who try to influence legislation on behalf of their clients or interest groups (p. 290)

market forces the law of supply and demand (p. 299)

market restraints laws and regulations that govern the manufacture and sale of products (p. 298)

monarchy a form of government headed by a king or a queen (p. 284)

multinational corporations companies that operate across national boundaries (p. 302)

oligarchy a form of government in which power is held by a small group of individuals; the rule of the many by the few (p. 285)

pluralism diffusion of power among many interest groups, preventing any single group from gaining control of the government (p. 291)

political action committees (PACs) an organization formed by one or more special-interest groups to solicit and spend funds for the purpose of influencing legislation (p. 290)

power the ability to get your way, even over the resistance of others (p. 280)

power elite C. Wright Mills's term for the top leaders of U.S. corporations, military, and politics who make the nation's major decisions (p. 292)

rational-legal authority authority based on law or written rules and regulations (also called bureaucratic authority) (p. 281)

representative democracy a form of democracy in which voters elect representatives to govern and make decisions on their behalf (p. 284)

routinization of charisma the transfer of authority from a charismatic figure to either a traditional or a rational-legal form of authority (p. 283)

socialism an economic system characterized by the public ownership of the means of production, central planning, and the distribution of goods without a profit motive (p. 299)

special-interest group people who share views on a particular issue and who can be mobilized for political action (p. 290)

state a government; the political entity that claims a monopoly on the use of violence within a territory (pp. 281, 284)

stockholders' revolt the refusal of a corporation's stockholders to rubber-stamp decisions made by its managers (p. 301)

subsistence economy a type of economy in which human groups live off the land with little or no surplus (p. 293)

totalitarianism a form of government that exerts almost total control over the people (p. 285)

traditional authority authority based on custom (p. 281)

universal citizenship the idea that everyone has the same basic rights by virtue of being born in a country (or by immigrating and becoming a naturalized citizen) (p. 284)

voter apathy indifference and inaction with respect to the political process (p. 288)

welfare (or state) capitalism an economic system in which individuals own the means of production but the state regulates many economic activities for the welfare of the population (p. 298)

Sociology and the Internet

All URLs listed are current as of the printing of this book. URLs are often changed. Please check our Website http://www.abacon.com/henslin for updates.

1. Postindustrial Society

In this chapter, Henslin talks about three eras in the history of economic systems: preindustrial, industrial, and postindustrial. Perhaps the most crucial for all of us is the one we are living in, "Postindustrial Societies: The New Technology Gives Birth to the Information Age."

To learn more about this vital topic, first, read the section headed "The Transformation of Economic Systems," paying special attention to the nature of postindustrial society. Next, go to the Web page of "The Millennial Files" (http://www.mmmfiles.com) and read the entire article. (You might want to print each section so it is easier to take notes.)

When you finish, write a five- or six-page paper on the background, characteristics, problems, and future of postindustrial society.

2. Special-Interest Groups

In this chapter, you have read about the controversy surrounding lobbyists, special-interest groups, and political action committees (PACs). Let's see what we can find out about them on the Internet.

Go to Yahoo's list of sites under "Politics" (http://www.yahoo.com/Government/Politics). Select "Interest Groups." You should now see three categories. "Lobbying Firms" points to firms advertising their services. You might want to look at a few of these just to see what is being offered. The second category, "Political Action Committees," leads to several sites, most of them dealing with single issues at the state level (California's Ecovote Line, for example). If you are doing this project in an election year, you will find a fascinating CNN site that lists all the contributions to major candidates (by state). It's interesting to see who supports whom, and for how much. The third category is "Public Interest Groups." Under this heading you will find several links to single-issue groups: abortion issues, animal rights, and so on. Look at several areas that you think are controversial or that particularly interest you.

A report on this excursion will have to be very broad, so let's use a journal approach. Write a narrative of where you went and what you found, along with personal reactions along the way. Organize your report in diary form. Don't forget to include a general introduction and a conclusion.

Carmen Lomas Garza, Making Tamales, 1987.

C H A P T E R

12

Marriage and Family

"H OLD STILL. WE'RE GOING TO BE LATE," said Sharon as she tried to put shoes on 2-year-old Michael, who kept squirming away.

Finally succeeding with the shoes, Sharon turned to 4-year-old Brittany, who was trying to pull a brush through her hair. "It's stuck, Mom," Brittany said.

"Well, no wonder. Just how did you get gum in your hair? I don't have time for this, Brittany. We've got to leave."

Getting to the van fifteen minutes behind schedule, Sharon strapped the kids in, and then herself. Just as she was about to pull away, she remembered that she had not checked the fridge for messages.

"Just a minute, kids. I'll be right back."

Running into the house, she frantically searched for a message from Tom. She vaguely remembered him mumbling something about being held over at work. She grabbed the Post-It and ran back to the van.

"He's picking on me," complained Brittany when her mother climbed back in.

"Oh, shut up, Brittany," Sharon said. "He's only 2. He can't pick on you."

"Yes, he did," Brittany said, crossing her arms defiantly, as she stretched out her foot to kick her brother's seat.

"Oh, no! How did Mikey get that smudge on his face in the car seat? Did you do that, Brit?"

Brittany crossed her arms again, pushing out her lips in her classic pouting pose.

As Sharon drove to the day care center, she tried to calm herself. "Only two more days of work this week, and then the weekend. Then I can catch up on housework and have a little relaxed time with the kids. And Tom can finally cut the lawn and buy the groceries," she thought. "And maybe we'll even have time to make love. Boy, that's been a long time."

At a traffic light, Sharon found time to read Tom's note. "Oh, no. That's what he meant. He has to work Saturday. Well, there go those plans."

What Sharon didn't know was that her boss also had made plans for Sharon's Saturday. And that their emergency Saturday baby-sitter would be unavailable. And that the van would break down on the way home from work. That Michael was coming down with chicken pox. That Brittany would follow next. That . . .

Marriage and Family in Global Perspective

To better understand U.S. patterns of marriage and family, let's first look at how they differ around the world. This will give us a context for interpreting our own experience in this vital social institution.

Defining Family

"What is a family, anyway?" asked William Sayres (1992) at the beginning of an article on this topic. By this question, he meant that although the family is so significant to humans that it is universal—every human group in the world organizes its members in families—the world's cultures display so much variety that the term *family* is difficult to define. For example, although the Western world regards a family as consisting of a husband, wife, and children, other groups have family forms in which men have more than one wife (**polygyny**) or women more than one husband (**polyandry**). Or to try define the family as the approved group into which children are born overlooks the Banaro of New Guinea. Among this group a young woman must give birth before she can marry, and she *cannot* marry the father of her child (Murdock 1949).

And so it goes. For just about every element you might consider essential to marriage or family, some group has a different custom. Even the sex of the bride and groom may not be what you expect. Although in almost every instance the bride and groom are female and male, there are rare exceptions. In some Native-American tribes, for example, a man or woman who wanted to be a member of the opposite sex went through a ceremony (*berdache*) and was *declared* a member of the opposite sex. From then on, not only did the "new" man or woman do the tasks associated with his or her new sex, but the individual also was allowed to marry. In this instance, the husband and wife were of the same biological sex. In the contemporary world, Denmark, Norway, and Sweden have legalized homosexual marriages.

Such remarkable variety means settling for a very broad definition. A **family** consists of two or more people who consider themselves related by blood, marriage, or adoption. A **household,** in contrast, consists of all people who occupy the same housing unit—a house, apartment, or other living quarters.

We can classify families as **nuclear** (husband, wife, and children) and **extended** (including people such as grandparents, aunts, uncles, and cousins in ad-dition to the nuclear unit). Sociologists also refer to the **family of orientation** (the family in which an individual grows up) and the **family of procreation** (the family formed when a couple have their first child). Finally, regardless of its form, **marriage** can be viewed as a group's approved mating arrangements—usually marked out by a ritual of some sort (the wedding) to indicate the couple's new public status.

Common Cultural Themes

In spite of this diversity, several common themes do run through marriage and family. As illustrated in Table 12.1, all societies use marriage and family to establish patterns of mate selection, descent, inheritance, and authority. Let's look at these themes.

Norms of Mate Selection Each human group establishes norms to govern who marries whom. Norms of **endogamy** specify that people should marry within their own group. Groups may prohibit interracial marriages, for example. In contrast, norms

---

Table 12.1

Common Cultural Themes: Marriage in Traditional and Industrial Societies

Characteristic	Traditional Societies	Industrial (and Postindustrial) Societies
What is the structure of marriage?	*Extended* (marriage embeds spouses in a large kinship network of explicit obligations)	*Nuclear* (marriage brings fewer obligations toward the spouse's kin)
What are the functions of marriage?	Encompassing (see the six functions listed on p. 311)	More limited (many functions are fulfilled by other social institutions)
Who holds authority?	Highly *patriarchal* (authority is held by males)	Although patriarchal features remain, authority is more evenly divided
How many spouses at one time?	Most have one spouse (*monogamy*), while some have several (*polygamy*)	One spouse
Who selects the spouse?	The spouse is selected by the parents, usually the father	Individuals choose their own spouse
Where does the couple live?	Couples most commonly reside with the groom's family (*patrilocal residence*), less commonly with the bride's family (*matrilocal residence*)	Couples establish a new home (*neolocal residence*)
How is descent figured?	Most commonly figured from male ancestors (*patrilineal kinship*), less commonly from female ancestors (*matrilineal kinship*)	Figured from male and female ancestors equally (*bilateral kinship*)
How is inheritance figured?	Rigid system of rules; either patrilineal or matrilineal	Highly individualistic; usually bilateral

of **exogamy** specify that people must marry outside their group. The best example is the **incest taboo,** which prohibits both sex and marriage among specified relatives. In some societies these norms are written into law, but in most cases they are informal. For example, in the United States most whites marry whites and most African Americans marry African Americans—not because of any laws but because of informal norms.

Reckoning Descent How are you related to your father's father or to your mother's mother? The explanation is found in your society's **system of descent,** how people trace kinship over generations. To us, a **bilateral system** seems logical—and natural— for we think of ourselves as related to people on *both* the mother's and father's sides of the family. "Doesn't everyone?" you might ask. Interestingly, this is only one logical way to reckon descent. In a **patrilineal system,** descent is traced only to the father's side, and children are not considered related to their mother's relatives. In a **matrilineal system,** descent is figured only on the mother's side, and children are not considered related to their father's relatives.

Rights of Inheritance Marriage and family—in whatever form is customary in a society—are also used to compute rights of inheritance. In the bilateral

system, property is passed to both males and females, in the patrilineal system only to males, and in the matrilineal system (the rarest form) only to females. Each system matches a people's ideas of justice and logic.

Patterns of Authority Historically, some form of **patriarchy,** a social system in which men dominate women, has formed a thread running through all societies. Contrary to what many think, there are no historical records of a true **matriarchy,** a social system in which women as a group dominate men as a group. Our marriage and family customs, then, developed within a framework of patriarchy. Although family patterns in the United States are becoming more *egalitarian,* or equal, many customs practiced today point to their patriarchal origin. Naming patterns, for example, reflect patriarchy. In spite of recent trends, the typical bride still takes the groom's last name; children, too, are usually given the father's last name. For information on a society that systematically promotes equality in marriage, see the Global Glimpse box opposite.

Marriage and Family in Theoretical Perspective

When we consider marriage from a global perspective, then, we see that our own forms of marriage and

Patterns of marriage vary around the world. As each group adjusts to life's circumstances, it adopts its own patterns, which then become embedded in the culture. Succeeding generations view their particular customs not as mere adaptations, but as morally right. Worldwide, the most common marital pattern is monogamy. *The second most common patten is* polygyny, *one man having more than one wife. Shown here is a polygynous family in Iran, consisting of one husband, three wives, and ten children. If the man continues to be economically successful, he may marry yet another wife, as part of his prestige in the community is based on his being able to support a large family.*

family are just one of a wide variety of patterns that humans have chosen. Let's see what picture emerges when we apply the three sociological theories.

The Functionalist Perspective: Functions and Dysfunctions

Functionalists stress that to survive, a society must meet certain basic needs, or functions. When functionalists look at family, they examine how it is related to other parts of society, especially how the family contributes to the well-being of society.

Why the Family Is Universal Functionalists note that although the form of marriage and family varies from one group to another, the family is universal because it fulfills six needs basic to every society's well-being. These needs, or functions, are (1) economic production, (2) socialization of children, (3) care of the sick and aged, (4) recreation, (5) sexual control, and (6) reproduction. To make certain that these functions are performed, every human group has found it necessary to adopt some form of the family.

Functions of the Incest Taboo Functionalists note that the incest taboo helps families avoid *role confusion*. This, in turn, facilitates the socialization of children. For example, if father–daughter incest were allowed, how should a wife treat her daughter—as a daughter, as a subservient second wife, or

---

A Global Glimpse

Family Life in Sweden

SWEDISH LAWMAKERS HOLD a strong image of what good family life is. That image is of total equality in marriage and the welfare of children. They bolster this image with laws designed to put women and men on equal footing in marriage, to have mothers and fathers share responsibility for the home and children, and to protect the financially weaker party in the event of divorce.

At the center of family laws is the welfare of children. Health care for mothers and children, for example, is free. This includes all obstetric care and all health care during pregnancy. Maternity centers offer free health checks and courses in preparation for childbirth. Fathers are encouraged to attend the childbirth classes.

When a child is born, the parents are eligible for fifteen months' leave of absence with pay. Both cannot receive compensation at the same time, and the parents decide how they will split the leave between them. For the first twelve months the state pays 90 percent of gross income, and then a generous fixed rate for the remaining three months. The paid leave need not be taken all at once, but can be spread over eight years. The parents can stay at home full time, or they can work part time for a longer period. Because mothers were taking all the leave, the law now includes a "father's month," one month that cannot be transferred to the mother.

The government also guarantees other benefits. All fathers are entitled to ten days' leave of absence with full pay when a child is born. When a child is sick, either parent can care for the child and receive full pay for missed work— up to sixty days a year per child. Moreover, by law local governments must offer child care. And if a husband becomes violent or threatens his wife, the woman can have a security alarm installed in their home free of charge.

The divorce laws have been drawn up with a view to what is best for the child. Local governments are required to provide free counseling to any parent who requests it. If both parties agree and if they have no children under the age of 16, a couple is automatically entitled to a divorce. Otherwise the law requires a six-month cooling-off period, so they can more calmly consider what is best for their children. Joint custody of children is automatic, unless one of the parents opposes it. The children may live with only one of the parents. The parent who does not live with the children is required to pay child support in proportion to his or her finances. If the parent fails to do so, the social security system makes the payments.

For Your Consideration

How does the Swedish system compare with that of the United States? What "system" for watching out for the welfare of children does the United States have, anyway?

Source: Based on The Swedish Institute 1992; Froman 1994.

In 1937, Mary Frances Grimes, an 11-year-old bride, and her 67-year-old husband, William H. Grimes, received national publicity. Married "in the woods" near Neelyville, Missouri, the bride said that she regretted the marriage and did not "love anyone but my doll." Is this an example of gender age, as symbolic interactionists might say? Or, as conflict theorists would say, of gender exploitation?

even as a rival? And should the daughter act toward her mother as her mother or as a rival wife? Would the father be her father or her lover? And would the wife be the husband's main wife, a secondary wife—or even "the mother of the other wife" (whatever role that might be)? Maternal incest would also lead to complications every bit as confusing as these.

Another function of the incest taboo is to force people to look outside the family for marriage partners. Anthropologists theorize that exogamy was especially functional in tribal societies, for it forged alliances between tribes that otherwise might have killed each other off. Today, exogamy extends a bride's and groom's social networks beyond the nuclear family, building relationships with their spouse's family.

Isolation and Emotional Overload Functionalists also analyze the dysfunctions that arise from the relative isolation of the nuclear family. Unlike members of extended families, who are enmeshed in kinship networks, members of nuclear families can count on fewer people for material and emotional support.

This makes the members of a nuclear family vulnerable to "emotional overload." That is, because the stress that comes with crises such as the loss of a job—or even the routine pressures of a harried life, as depicted in our opening vignette—is spread around fewer people, greater strain is placed on each family member (Zakuta 1989; DiGiulio 1992). In addition, the relative isolation of the nuclear family makes it vulnerable to a "dark side"—incest and various other forms of abuse, matters we examine later in this chapter.

The Conflict Perspective: Gender and Power

As you recall, central to conflict theory is the struggle over scarce resources. The recurring struggle over who does housework is actually a struggle over scarce resources—time, energy, and the leisure to pursue interesting activities.

The Power Struggle over Housework Most men resist doing housework. As Figure 12.1 shows, working wives end up doing almost all of it. The little effort that husbands make seems so great to them, however, that even when his wife does 81 percent of the cooking, 78 percent of the cleaning, and so on, the husband is likely to see himself as splitting the work fifty–fifty (Galinsky et al. 1993). Things are so one-sided that wives are eight times more likely to feel that the division of housework is unfair (Sanchez 1994).

And no wonder. Sociologist Arlie Hochschild (1989) found that in the *typical* case, after returning home from an eight-hour day of work for wages, the wife puts in a "second shift" doing cooking, cleaning, and child care. She calculated the difference in time spent on housework and found that in two-paycheck families wives average fifteen hours more work each week than their husbands. This means that wives work an *extra month of twenty-four-hour days a year.* Hochschild (1989) quoted the one-sided nature of the second shift, as satirized by Garry Trudeau in the *Doonesbury* comic strip:

> A "liberated" father is sitting at his word processor writing a book about raising his child. He types, "Today I wake up with a heavy day of work ahead of me. As Joannie gets Jeffry ready for day care, I ask her if I can be relieved of my usual household responsibilities for the day. Joannie says, 'Sure, I'll make up the five minutes somewhere.'"

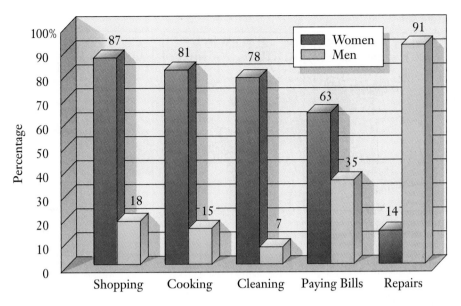

FIGURE 12.1

In Two-Paycheck Marriages, Who Has More Responsibility for Housework?

Source: Galinsky et al. 1993.

Not surprisingly, the burden of the second shift creates deep discontent among wives. These problems, as well as how wives and husbands cope with them, are discussed in the following Thinking Critically section.

▼▲▼▲▼▲▼▲▼▲▼▲▼▲▼▲

Thinking Critically about
Social Controversy

The Second Shift—
Strains and Strategies

To FIND OUT what life is like in two-paycheck families, for nine years sociologist Arlie Hochschild (1989) and her research associates interviewed and reinterviewed fifty-some families. Hochschild also did participant observation with a dozen of them. She "shopped with them, visited friends, watched television, ate with them, and came along when they took their children to day care."

Hochschild notes that women have no more time in a day than when they stayed home, but now there is twice as much to get done. Most wives and husbands in her sample felt that the *second shift*—the household duties that follow the day's work for pay—is the wife's responsibility. But as they cook, vacuum, and take care of the children after their job at the office or factory, many wives feel tired, emotionally drained, and resentful. Not uncommonly, these feelings show up in the bedroom, where the wives show a lack of interest in sex.

It isn't that men do nothing around the house. But since they see household responsibilities as the wife's duty, they "help out" when they feel like it—or when they get nagged into it. And since most of us prefer to tend to our children than to clean house, men are more likely to "help out" on the second shift by taking children to do "fun" things—to see movies, or to go for outings in the park. In contrast, the woman's time with the children is more likely to be "maintenance"—feeding and bathing them, taking them to the doctor, and so on.

The strains from working the second shift affect not only the marital relationship, but also the self-concept. Here is how one woman tried to buoy her flagging self-esteem:

> After taking time off for her first baby, Carol Alston felt depressed, "fat," "just a housewife," and for a while became the supermarket shopper who wanted to call down the aisles, "I'm an MBA! I'm an MBA!"

Most wives feel strongly that the second shift should be shared, but many feel it is hopeless to try to get their husbands to change. They work the second shift, but they resent it. Others have a "showdown" with their husbands, some even giving the ultimatum, "It's share the second shift, or it's divorce." Still others try to be the "supermom" who can do it all.

Some men cooperate and cut down on their commitment to a career. Others cut back on movies, seeing friends, doing hobbies. Most men, however, engage in what Hochschild describes as "strategies of resistance." She identified the following:

- *Waiting it out.* Many men never volunteer to do household chores, forcing their wives to ask them.

ARLO & JANIS ® by Jimmy Johnson

The cartoonist has beautifully captured the reduction of needs strategy discussed by Hochschild.

Since many wives dislike asking because it feels like "begging," this strategy often works. Some men make this strategy even more effective by showing irritation or becoming glum when they are asked, discouraging the wife from asking again.

- *Playing dumb.* When they do housework, some men become incompetent. They can't cook rice without burning it; when they go to the store, they forget grocery lists; they can never remember where the broiler pan is. Hochschild did not claim that husbands do these things on purpose, but, rather, by withdrawing their mental attention from the task, they "get credit for trying and being a good sport"— but in such a way that they are not chosen next time.
- *Needs reduction.* An example of this strategy is a father of two who explained that he never shopped because he didn't "need anything." He didn't need to iron his clothes because he "[didn't] mind wearing a wrinkled shirt." He didn't need to cook because "cereal is fine." As Hochschild observed, "Through his reduction of needs, this man created a great void into which his wife stepped with her 'greater need' to see him wear an ironed shirt . . . take his shirts to the cleaners . . . and cook his dinner."
- *Substitute offerings.* Expressing appreciation to the wife for being so organized that she can handle both work for wages and the second shift at home can be a substitute for helping—and subtle encouragement for her to keep on working the second shift.

For Your Consideration

Hochschild (1991) is confident such problems can be resolved. Use these materials to

1   Identify the underlying *structural* causes of the problem of the second shift.

2   Based on your answer to number 1, identify *structural* solutions to this problem.

3   Determine how a working wife and husband might best reconcile this problem.

The Symbolic Interactionist Perspective: Gender and Housework

As noted in Chapter 1, symbolic interactionists focus on the meanings that people give their experiences. Let's apply the symbolic interactionist perspective to some surprising findings about husbands and housework.

Housework, Paychecks, and Masculinity   The first finding is probably what you expect—the closer a husband's and wife's earnings are, the more likely they are to share housework. Although husbands in such marriages don't share housework equally, they do share more than most other husbands. These two findings, however, may be surprising: When husbands get laid off, most *decrease* their housework. And *husbands who earn less than their wives do the least housework.*

How can we explain this? It would seem that husbands who get laid off or who earn less than their wives would want to balance things out by doing more around the house, not less. Researchers suggest that the key is gender role. If a wife earns more than her husband, it threatens his masculinity—he takes it as a sign that he has failed in his traditional gender role of provider. To do housework—"women's work" in his eyes—threatens it even further. By avoiding housework, he "reclaims" his masculinity (Hochschild 1989; Brines 1994).

The Family Life Cycle

Thus far we have seen that the forms of marriage and family vary widely and have examined marriage and family from the three sociological perspectives. Now let's discuss love, courtship, and the family life cycle.

Love and Courtship in Global Perspective

Until recently, social scientists thought that romantic love originated in western Europe during the medieval period (Mount 1992). When anthropologists William Jankowiak and Edward Fischer (1992) surveyed the data available on 166 societies around the world, they found that this was not so. **Romantic love**—people being sexually attracted to one another and idealizing the other—showed up in 88 percent (147) of these groups. The role of love, however, differs sharply from one society to another. As the Global Glimpse box on the next page details, for example, Indians don't expect love to occur until *after* marriage—if then.

Because love plays such a significant role in Western life—and often is thought to be the *only* proper basis for marriage—social scientists have probed this concept with the tools of the trade: laboratory experiments, questionnaires, interviews, and systematic observations. One of the more interesting experiments was conducted by psychologists Donald Dutton and Arthur Aron, who discovered that "fear breeds love" (Rubin 1985). Across a rocky gorge, about 230 feet above the Capilano River in North Vancouver, a rickety footbridge sways in the wind. Another footbridge, a solid structure, crosses only ten feet above a shallow stream. A young, attractive woman approached men who were crossing these bridges and told them she was studying "the effects of exposure to scenic attractions on creative expression." She showed them a picture, and they wrote down their associations. The sexual imagery in their stories showed that the men on the unsteady, frightening bridge were more sexually aroused than the men on the solid bridge. More of these men also called the young woman afterward—supposedly to get more information about the study.

This research, of course, was really about sexual attraction, not love. The point, however, is that romantic love usually begins with sexual attraction. We find ourselves sexually attracted to someone and spend time with that person. If we discover mutual interests, we may label our feelings "love." Apparently, then, romantic love has two components. The first is emotional, a feeling of sexual attraction. The second is cognitive, a label that we attach to our feelings. If we do attach this label, we describe ourselves as being "in love."

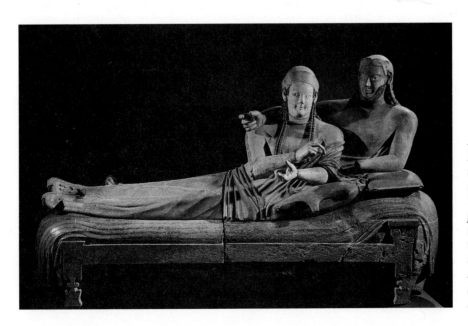

Romantic love reaches far back into history, as illustrated by this Etruscan sarcophagus. The Etruscans, reaching their peak of civilization in 500 B.C. in what is now Italy, were vanquished by Rome about one hundred years later. The artist has portrayed the couple's mutual affection and satisfaction.

East Is East and West Is West . . . :
Love and Arranged Marriage in India

AFTER ARUN BHARAT RAM returned to India with a degree from the University of Michigan, his mother announced that she wanted to find him a wife. Arun would be a good "catch" anywhere: 27 years old, well educated, well mannered, intelligent, handsome—and, not incidentally, heir to one of the largest fortunes in India.

Arun's mother already had someone in mind. Manju, who came from a solid, middle-class family, was also a college graduate. Arun and Manju met in a coffee shop in a luxury hotel—along with both sets of parents. He found her pretty and quiet. He liked that. She was impressed that he didn't boast about his background.

After four more meetings, one with the two alone, the parents asked their children if they were willing to marry. Neither had any major objections.

The Prime Minister of India and fifteen hundred other guests came to the wedding.

"I didn't love him," Manju says. "But when we talked, we had a lot of things in common." She then adds, "But now I couldn't live without him. I've never thought of another man since I met him."

Although India has undergone extensive social change, Indian sociologists estimate that about 95 percent of marriages are still arranged by the parents. Today, however, as with Arun and Manju, couples have veto power over their parents' selection. Another innovation is that the couple are allowed to talk to each other before the wedding—unheard of just a generation ago.

The fact that arranged marriages are the norm in India does not mean that this ancient land is without a tradition of passion and love. Far from it. The *Kamasutra* is world renowned for its explicit details about lovemaking, and the erotic sculptures at Khajuraho still startle Westerners today. Indian mythology extols the copulations of gods, and every Indian schoolchild knows the love story of the god Krishna and Radha, the beautiful milkmaid he found irresistible.

Why, then, does India have arranged marriages, and why does this practice persist today, even among the educated and upper classes? We can also ask why the United States has such an individualistic approach to marriage.

To answer these questions takes us to a basic sociological principle—that *a group's marriage practices match its values and patterns of social stratification.* Individual mate selection matches U.S. values of individuality and independence, while arranged marriages match Indian values of children deferring to parental authority. In addition, arranged marriages reaffirm caste lines by channeling marriage within the same caste.

To Indians, to practice unrestricted dating would be to trust important matters to inexperienced young people. It would encourage premarital sex, which, in turn, would break down family lines that virginity at marriage assures the upper castes. Consequently, Indian young people are socialized to think that parents have cooler heads and superior wisdom in these matters. In the United States, family lines are much less important, and caste is an alien concept.

Even ideas of love differ. For Indians, love is a peaceful emotion, based on long-term commitment and devotion to family. Indians also think of love as something that can be "created" between two people. To do so, one needs to arrange the right conditions—and marriage is one of those right conditions.

Thus, Indian and U.S. cultures have produced not just different, but opposite, approaches to love and marriage. For Indians, marriage produces love—while for Americans, love produces marriage. Americans see love as having a mysterious element, a passion that "grabs" the individual. Indians see love as a peaceful feeling that develops when a man and a woman are united in intimacy and share common interests and goals in life.

Sources: Based on Cooley 1962; Gupta 1979; Weintraub 1988; Bumiller 1992; Sprecher and Chandak 1992; Whyte 1992.

Marriage

In the typical case, marriage in the United States is preceded by "love," but contrary to folklore, whatever love is, it certainly is not blind. That is, love does not hit anyone willy-nilly, as if Cupid had shot darts blindly into a crowd. If it did, marital patterns would be unpredictable. An examination of who marries whom, however, reveals that love is socially channeled.

The Social Channels of Love and Marriage. The most highly predictable social channels are age, education, social class, race, and religion (Tucker and Mitchell-Kernan 1990; Kalmijn 1991). For example, a Latina with a college degree whose parents are both physicians is likely to fall in love with and marry a Latino slightly older than herself who has graduated from college. Similarly, a female high school dropout whose parents are on welfare is likely to fall in love with and marry a male who comes from a background similar to hers.

Sociologists use the term **homogamy** to refer to the tendency of people with similar characteristics to marry one another. Homogamy occurs largely as a result of *propinquity*, or spatial nearness. That is, we tend to "fall in love with" and marry people who live near us or whom we meet at school, church, or work. The people with whom we associate are far from a random sample of the population, for social filters produce neighborhoods, schools, and churches that follow racial and social class lines.

As with all social patterns, there are exceptions. Although 94 percent of Americans who marry choose someone of their same race, this means 6 percent do not. Since there are 54 million married couples in the United States, those 6 percent add up, totaling three million couples. As Figure 12.2 shows, interracial marriages also show distinct patterns. Asian Ameri-

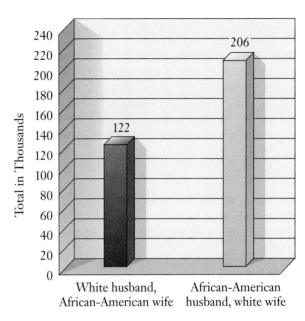

Source: *Statistical Abstract* 1996:Table 62.

FIGURE 12.3

The Racial Background of Husbands and Wives in Marriages between Whites and African Americans

cans are the most likely to marry someone of a different race, white Americans the least likely to do so.

There is no doubt that interracial marriages have become more acceptable. For example, during the past twenty-five years the number of married couples increased only 22 percent, but the number of marriages between African Americans and whites increased 450 percent—20 times as fast. This total is still relatively small, however, representing only ½ percent (296,000) of the 54 million U.S. married couples (*Statistical Abstract* 1995:Table 61). As Figure 12.3 shows, these particular interracial marriages also exhibit distinct patterns.

Childbirth

Marital Satisfaction Sociologist Martin Whyte (1992), who interviewed wives in the greater Detroit area, found that marital satisfaction usually decreases with the birth of a child. To explain why, recall from Chapter 5 that a dyad (just two persons) provides greater intimacy than a triad (after adding a third person, interaction must be shared). To move from the theoretical to the practical, think about the implications of coping with a newborn—heavy ex-

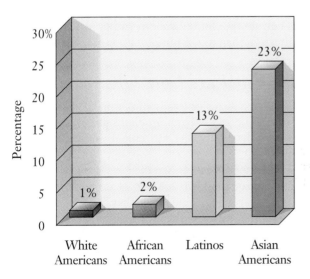

Source: Lee and Yamanaka 1990.

FIGURE 12.2

What Percentage of Americans Marry Outside Their Racial/Ethnic Group?

penses, less free time (feeding, soothing, and diapering), less sleep, even a decrease in sexual relations (Rubenstein 1992).

Social Class Sociologist Lillian Rubin (1976, 1992b) compared fifty working-class couples with twenty-five middle-class couples. She found that social class is a key to how couples adjust to the arrival of children. For the average working-class couple, the first baby arrived just nine months after marriage. They hardly had time to adjust to being husband and wife before they were thrust into the demanding roles of mother and father. The result was financial problems, bickering, and interference from in-laws. The young husbands weren't ready to "settle down" and resented getting less attention from their wives. A working-class husband who became a father just five months after getting married made a telling remark to Rubin when he said, "There I was, just a kid myself, and I finally had someone *to take care of me.* Then suddenly, I had to take care of a kid, and she was too busy with him *to take care of me.*" (italics added)

In contrast, the middle-class couples postponed the birth of their first child, which gave them more time to adjust to each other. On average, their first baby arrived three years after marriage. Their greater financial resources also worked in their favor, making life a lot easier and marriage more pleasant.

Child Rearing

Who's minding the kids while the parents are at work? A while back such a question would have been ridiculous, for the mother was at home taking care of the children. As with Sharon in our opening vignette, however, that assumption no longer holds. With three of five U.S. mothers working for wages, who is taking care of the children?

Married Couples and Single Mothers Figure 12.4 compares the child care arrangements of married couples and single mothers. As you can see, their overall child care arrangements are similar. For each, about one-third of preschoolers are cared for in the child's home. The main difference is the role of the child's father while the mother is at work. For married couples, almost one of four children is cared for by the father, while for single mothers such child care plummets to only one of fourteen. As you can see, grandparents step in to help fill the gap left by the absent father.

Birth Order Birth order is also significant. Parents tend to discipline their firstborns more than their later children, and to give them more attention. When the second child arrives, the firstborn competes to maintain the attention. Researchers suggest that this instills in firstborns a greater drive for success, which is why they are more likely than their siblings to earn higher grades in school, to go to college, and to go further in college. Firstborns are even more likely to become astronauts, to appear on the cover of *Time* magazine, and to become president of the United States. Although subsequent children may not go as far, most are less anxious about being successful, and more relaxed in their relationships (Forer 1976; White et al. 1979; Snow et al. 1981; Goleman 1985).

Social Class Social class is also important in child rearing. Sociologist Melvin Kohn (1963, 1977; Kohn and Schooler 1969) found that parents socialize their children into the norms of their work worlds. Because members of the working class are more closely supervised and are expected to follow explicit rules laid down for them by others, their concern is less with their children's motivation and more with outward conformity. They are more apt to use physical punishment. In contrast, middle-class parents, who are expected to take more initiative on the job, are more concerned that their children develop curiosity, self-expression, and self-control. They also are more likely to withdraw privileges or affection than to use physical punishment.

The Family in Later Life

The later stages of family life bring their own pleasures to be savored and problems to be solved. Let's look at the empty nest, retirement, and widowhood.

The Empty Nest When the last child leaves home, the husband and wife are left, as at the beginning of their marriage, "alone together." This situation, sometimes called the **empty nest,** is thought to signal a difficult time of adjustment for women because they have devoted so much energy to a child-rearing role that is now gone. Sociologist Lillian Rubin (1992a), who interviewed both career women and homemakers, found that this picture is largely a myth. Contrary to the stereotype, she found that women's satisfaction generally *increases* when the last child leaves home. A typical statement was made by

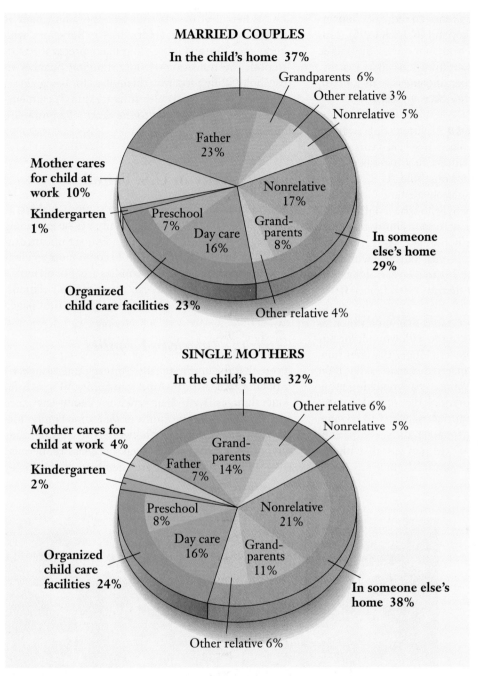

MARRIED COUPLES

In the child's home 37%
Grandparents 6%
Other relative 3%
Nonrelative 5%

Father 23%

Mother cares for child at work 10%

Kindergarten 1%

Preschool 7%

Day care 16%

Nonrelative 17%

Grand-parents 8%

In someone else's home 29%

Organized child care facilities 23%

Other relative 4%

SINGLE MOTHERS

In the child's home 32%
Other relative 6%
Nonrelative 5%

Mother cares for child at work 4%

Kindergarten 2%

Father 7%

Grand-parents 14%

Preschool 8%

Day care 16%

Nonrelative 21%

Grand-parents 11%

In someone else's home 38%

Organized child care facilities 24%

Other relative 6%

Source: O'Connel 1993.

FIGURE 12.4
Who Takes Care of Preschoolers While the Mother Is at Work?

a 45-year-old woman, who leaned forward in her chair as though to tell Rubin a secret:

> To tell you the truth, most of the time it's a big relief to be free of them, finally. I suppose that's awful to say. But you know what, most of the women I know feel the same way. It's just that

they're uncomfortable saying it because there's all this talk about how sad mothers are supposed to be when the kids leave home.

Similar findings have come from other researchers, who report that most mothers feel relieved at being able to spend more time on themselves.

Many couples also report a renewed sense of companionship at this time (Mackey and O'Brien 1995). This closeness appears to stem from four causes: the couple is free of the many responsibilities of child rearing, they have more leisure, their income is at its highest, and their financial obligations are reduced.

The Not-So-Empty Nest An interesting twist on leaving home has taken place in recent years. With prolonged education, an uncertain job market, and a higher cost to establish a household, U.S. children are leaving home later (Goldscheider and Goldscheider 1994). In addition, many who struck out on their own have found the cost or responsibility too great and are returning to the home nest. As a result, 53 percent of all U.S. 18- to 24-year-olds live with their parents, and one of eight 25- to 34-year-olds is still living at home (*Statistical Abstract* 1995:Table 63).

Widowhood Women are more likely than men to face the problem of adjusting to widowhood, for not only does the average wife live longer than her husband but she also has married a man older than herself. The death of a spouse is a wrenching away of identities that had merged through the years (DiGiulio 1992). Now that the one who had become an essential part of the self is gone, the survivor, as in adolescence, is forced once again to wrestle with the perplexing question "Who am I?"

When death is unexpected, the adjustment is much more difficult (Hiltz 1989). Survivors who know that death is impending make preparations to smooth the transition—from arranging finances to psychologically preparing themselves for being alone. Saying good-bye and cultivating treasured last memories help them to adjust to the death of an intimate companion.

Diversity in U.S. Families

It is important to note that there is no such thing as *the* American family. Rather, family life varies widely throughout the United States. The significance of social class, noted earlier, will become more evident as we see how diverse U.S. families are. For an example of how immigration can affect family relations, see the Immigrant Experience box on the next page.

African-American Families

Note that the heading reads "African-American *families*," not "*The* African-American family." There is no such thing as *the* African-American family, any more than there is *the* white family or *the* Latino family. The primary distinction is not between African Americans and other groups, but between social classes. Because African Americans who are members of the upper

There is no such thing as the *African-American family, any more than there is* the *Native-American, Asian-American, Latino, or Irish-American family. Rather, each racial-ethnic group has different types of families, with the primary determinant being social class.*

This African-American family is observing Kwanzaa, a new festival that celebrates their African heritage. Can you explain how Kwanzaa is an example of ethnic work, *a concept introduced in Chapter 9?*

▼▲▼

The Immigrant Experience

Russian Jews in the United States

AROUND THE WORLD, Jews have faced various forms of persecution, and around the world the family has offered a place of refuge. So it also was in the former Soviet Union. It was in the family that they could disagree with a repressive regime that demanded allegiance, and it was the family that used its connections with government officials to help their children get admitted to good schools and begin good career tracks in spite of regulations and other obstacles designed to hold back Jews.

The family was also the reason that the Jews I interviewed left the Soviet Union. Although the parents had to give up careers and retirement benefits, they saw this as worthwhile in order to help assure a better future for their children. The family is also at the center of helping the immigrants adjust to their new land. Through a network of extended families, refugees obtain a variety of resources—from their initial sponsorship to the U.S. to job referrals, even the investment capital needed to open a small business.

Relatives who have arrived earlier provide support and advice to newcomers. This family-based exchange of information and resources goes a long way toward softening the economic and emotional trauma of the immigration experience.

The immigration experience, however, creates problems for Jewish families by driving a wedge between the generations. Because children master U.S. customs and the English language much more quickly than their parents, some teenagers end up managing the family's affairs. This may include meeting the emotional, social, and economic needs of parents, grandparents, and siblings. After being socialized into the U.S. lifestyle, with its emphasis on independence, many younger immigrants resent such responsibilities. They feel deprived of the extended adolescence and consumption patterns common to the United States. Some try to escape the responsibilities thrust upon them by spending little time at home, refusing to eat their mother's cooking (not "that kind"

of food!), and adopting social and political values that contradict those of their parents.

The parents and grandparents, who had planned on guiding their children, find their Soviet-based experiences to be of little value in the United States. As a woman who had been a concert pianist in Odessa said: "I cannot tell my daughter 'when I was 15,' because she says, 'when you were 15, you were in Russia.' " Similarly, in the Soviet Union it was taken for granted that parents would guide their children in making choices of job and spouse. Here, in contrast, what the parents see as support, the children see as an attempt to control them, an infringement on their personal freedom. As a UCLA student said, "My parents don't understand that I am an American now. Nobody lives with their parents after marriage. I want to have my own life."

Steven Gold
Michigan State University
From the Workers' State to the Golden State: Russian Jews in California, Allyn and Bacon (1996)

---

class follow the class interests reviewed in Chapter 8—preservation of privilege and family fortune—they are especially concerned about the family background of those whom their children marry (Gatewood 1990). To them, marriage is viewed as a merger of family lines. Children of this class marry later than children of other classes.

Middle-class African-American families focus on achievement and respectability. Both husband and wife are likely to work outside the home. Their concerns are that the family stay intact and that their children go to college, get good jobs, and marry well—that is, marry people like themselves, respect-

able and hardworking, who want to get ahead in school and pursue a successful career.

African-American families in poverty face all the problems that cluster around poverty (Franklin 1994). Because the men are likely to have few skills and to be unemployed, it is difficult for them to fulfill the cultural roles of husband and father. Consequently, these families are likely to be headed by a woman and to have a high rate of unwed motherhood. Divorce and desertion are also more common than among other classes. Sharing scarce resources and stretching kinship are primary survival mechanisms. That is, people who have helped out in hard times are considered brothers, sisters, or cousins, to whom one owes obligations as though they were blood relatives (Stack 1974). Sociologists use the term *fictive kin* to refer to this stretching of kinship.

From Figure 12.5, you can see that, compared with whites and Latinos, African-American families are less likely to be headed by married couples and more likely to be headed by women. Because of a *marriage squeeze*—an imbalance in the sex ratio, in this instance fewer unmarried men per 100 unmarried women—African-American women are more likely than other racial groups to marry men who are less educated than themselves, who are unemployed, or who are divorced (South 1991).

Latino Families

As Figure 12.5 shows, the proportion of Latino families headed by married couples and women falls in between those of whites and African Americans. The effects of social class on families, just sketched, also apply to Latinos. In addition, families differ by country of origin. Families from Cuba, for example, are much more likely to be headed by a married couple than are families from Puerto Rico (*Statistical Abstract* 1995:Table 53).

What really distinguishes Latino families, however, is culture—especially the Spanish language, the

Roman Catholic religion, and a strong family orientation with a disapproval of divorce. Although there is some debate among the experts, another characteristic seems to be **machismo**—an emphasis on male strength and dominance. In Chicano families (those originating from Mexico), the husband/father plays a stronger role than in either white or African-American families (Vega 1990). Machismo apparently decreases with each generation in the United States (Hurtado et al. 1992). In general, however, the wife/mother makes most of the day-to-day decisions for the family and does the routine disciplining of the children. She usually is more family centered than her husband, displaying more warmth and affection for her children.

Generalizations have limits, of course, and as with other ethnic groups individual Latino families vary considerably from one another (Baca Zinn 1994; Carrasquillo 1994).

Asian-American Families

As you can see from Figure 12.5, the structure of Asian-American families is almost identical to that of white families. Apart from this broad characteristic, because Asian Americans come from twenty countries, their family life varies considerably, reflecting their many different cultures. In addition, as with Latino families, the more recent the immigration, the

FIGURE 12.5

Family Structure: The Percentage of U.S. Households Headed by Men, Women, and Married Couples

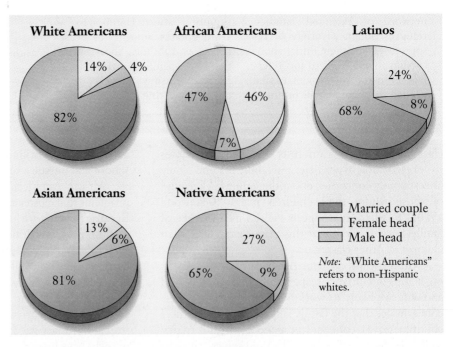

Source: Statistical Abstract 1996:Table 74; except O'Hare 1992 for Native Americans.

closer their family life reflects the family life of their country of origin (Kibria 1993; Glenn 1994).

In spite of such differences, sociologist Bob Suzuki (1985), who studied Chinese-American and Japanese-American families, identified several distinctive characteristics. Although Asian Americans have adopted the nuclear family, they have retained Confucian values that provide a distinct framework for family life: humanism, collectivity, self-discipline, hierarchy, respect for the elderly, moderation, and obligation. Obligation means that each individual owes respect to other family members and is responsible to never bring shame on the family. Asian Americans tend to be more permissive than Anglos in child rearing and more likely to use shame and guilt rather than physical punishment to control their children's behavior.

Native-American Families

Perhaps the single most significant issue that Native-American families face is whether to follow traditional values or to assimilate (Yellowbird and Snipp 1994). This primary distinction makes for vast differences in families. The traditionals speak native languages and emphasize distinctive Native-American values and beliefs. Those who have assimilated into the broader culture do not.

Figure 12.5 depicts the structure of Native-American families. You can see how it is almost identical to that of Latinos. In general, Native-American parents are permissive with their children and avoid physical punishment. Elders play a much more active role in their children's families than is true of most U.S. families: they not only provide child care, but they also teach and discipline children. Like others, Native-American families differ by social class.

▼ **In Sum** From this brief review of African-American, Latino, Asian-American, and Native-American families, you can see that race/ethnicity signifies little for understanding family life. Rather, social class and culture hold the keys. The more resources a family has, the more it assumes the characteristics of a middle-class nuclear family. Compared with the poor, middle-class families have fewer children and fewer unmarried mothers, and place greater emphasis on educational achievement and deferred gratification.

One-Parent Families

From TV talk shows to government officials, one-parent families have become a matter of general concern. The increase is no myth. Since 1970, the number of one-parent families has tripled, while the number of two-parent families has actually decreased by 250,000 (*Statistical Abstract* 1995:Table 71). Two primary reasons underlie this change. The first is the high divorce rate, which each year forces a million children from two-parent homes to one-parent

Although there is no such thing as the *Latino family, in general Latinos place high emphasis on extended family relationships.*

homes (*Statistical Abstract* 1995: Table 146). The second is a sharp increase in unwed motherhood. Overall, 30 percent of U.S. children are born to women who are not married, a 50 percent increase in just ten years (*Statistical Abstract* 1995:Table 94).

The primary reason for the concern, however, may have less to do with children being reared by one parent than the fact that most one-parent families are poor. This poverty is not a coincidence. Most one-parent families are headed by women. Although 90 percent of children of divorce live with their mothers, most divorced women earn less than their former husbands. In the case of unwed mothers, most have little education and few marketable skills, which condemns them to bouncing from one minimum-wage job to another, with welfare sandwiched in between.

To understand the typical one-parent family, then, we need to view it through the lens of poverty; for that is its primary source of strain. The results are serious, not just for these parents and their children, but for society as a whole. Children from single-parent families are more likely to drop out of high school, to get arrested, to have emotional problems, and to get divorced (Wallerstein and Blakeslee 1992; Whitehead 1993; O'Neill 1993; McLanahan and Sandefur 1994). If female, they are more likely to bear a child while still a teenager and to bear children outside marriage. The cycle of poverty is so powerful that *nearly half* of all welfare recipients are current or former teenage parents (Corbett 1995).

Families without Children

Overall, about 11 percent of U.S. married couples never have children. The percentage, however, varies with education. The more education a woman has, the more likely she is to expect to bear no children (*Statistical Abstract* 1995:Tables 102, 104). Race/ethnicity is also significant, and Latinas are much less likely to expect to remain childless than are white and African-American women.

Why do some couples choose to not have children? Sociologist Kathleen Gerson (1985) found that some women view their marriage as too fragile to withstand the strains that a child would bring. Other women believe that if they have children they will be stuck at home—bored, lonely, and losing career opportunities. Many couples simply see a child as too expensive. With more education and careers for women, abortion, technological advances in contraception, and the growing costs of rearing children, the proportion of women who never bear children is likely to increase.

Blended Families

An increasingly significant type of family in the United States is the **blended family,** one whose members once were part of other families. Two divorced people who marry and each bring their children into a new family unit become a blended family. With divorce common, millions of children spend some of their childhood in blended families. One result is more complicated family relationships, exemplified by the following description written by one of my students:

> I live with my dad. I should say that I live with my dad, my brother (whose mother and father are also my mother and father), my half sister (whose father is my dad, but whose mother is my father's last wife), and two stepbrothers and stepsisters (children of my father's current wife). My father's wife (my current stepmother, not to be confused with his second wife, who, I guess, is no longer my stepmother) is pregnant, and soon we all will have a new brother or sister. Or will it be a half brother or half sister?

> If you can't figure this out, I don't blame you. I have trouble myself. It gets very complicated around Christmas. Should we all stay together? Split up and go to several other homes? Who do we buy gifts for, anyway?

Gay Families

In 1989, Denmark was the first country to legalize marriage between people of the same sex. Since then, two neighbors, Norway and Sweden, have also made same-sex marriages legal (Ingrassia 1996). Although such marriages remain illegal in the United States, same-sex couples in several major cities can register as "domestic partners," publicly agreeing to be jointly responsible for their basic living expenses. The city offers health benefits to the domestic partners of its employees, and the employee can take paid bereavement leave if the partner dies. More than seventy major corporations such as Ben & Jerry's, Lotus, and Apple have made similar arrangements for their employees (Jefferson 1994).

What are gay marriages like? As with everything else in life, same-sex couples cannot be painted with a single brush stroke (Allen and Demo 1995). As with opposite-sex couples, social class is highly significant, and orientations to life differ according to education, occupation, and income. Sociologists Blumstein and Schwartz (1985) interviewed same-sex couples and found their main struggles to be housework, money, careers, problems with relatives, and sexual adjust-

Homosexuals in the West are contesting laws that limit marriage to heterosexuals. When the lawsuit of the two women shown in the foreground of this photo reached Hawaii's Supreme Court, the court declared the state's limitation of marriage to heterosexuals unconstitutional. In Denmark, Sweden, and Norway, marriages between people of the same sex are now legal.

ment—the same as for heterosexual couples. Same-sex couples are much more likely to break up, however, probably because of a combination of higher levels of sexual infidelity and a lack of legal and broad social support.

Trends in U.S. Families

As is apparent from this discussion, patterns of marriage and family life in the United States are undergoing a fundamental shift. Other indicators of this change, which we shall now examine, include the postponement of marriage, cohabitation, single motherhood, divorce, and remarriage.

Postponing Marriage

Figure 12.6 illustrates one of the most significant trends in U.S. marriages. As you can see, the average age of first-time brides and grooms declined from 1890 to about 1950. In 1890 the typical first-time bride was 22, but by 1950 she had just left her teens. For about twenty years there was little change. Then in 1970 the average age started climbing rapidly upward. Today the age of the average first-time groom is back to where it was in 1890, and *the average first-time bride is older than at any other time in U.S. history*. Because Americans are postponing marriage, the proportion of never-married younger Americans has grown. As Figure 12.7 shows, the percentage of unmarried young women is now about *double* what it was in 1970.

Why did this change occur? As sociologist Larry Bumpass points out, if we were to count cohabitation, we would find that this average age has changed

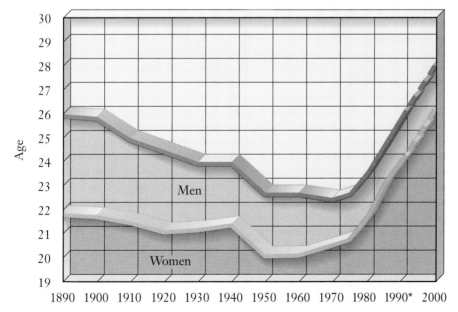

FIGURE 12.6

The Median Age at Which Americans Marry for the First Time

*Latest year available; data after this year are author's projections.

Source: Statistical Abstract 1996: Table 149, and earlier years.

FIGURE 12.7

Americans Ages 20–24 Who Have Never Married

*Author's estimate.

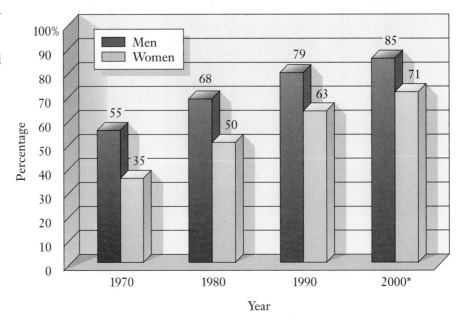

Source: Statistical Abstract 1993:Table 60; 1996:Table 59.

little (Bumpass et al. 1991). Although Americans have postponed the age at which they first marry, they have *not* postponed the age at which they first set up housekeeping with someone of the opposite sex. Let's look at this trend in cohabitation.

Cohabitation

As Figure 12.8 shows, **cohabitation,** adults living together in a sexual relationship without being married, has increased about *seven times* in just over two decades. Cohabitation has become so common that about half of the couples who marry have cohabited (Bumpass 1995). With this change in behavior have come changed attitudes. For example, when hiring executives, some corporations now pay for live-in partners to attend orientation sessions.

Commitment is the essential difference between cohabitation and marriage. Whereas the assumption of marriage is permanence, cohabiting couples agree to remain together for "as long as it works out." Marriage requires public vows—and a judge to authorize its termination; cohabitation requires only that a couple move in together—if the relationship sours, they simply move out. Sociologists have found that couples who cohabit before marriage are more likely to divorce than couples who do not first cohabit (Bennett et al. 1988; Whyte 1992). The reason, they conclude, is that cohabiting couples have a weaker commitment to marriage and to relationships.

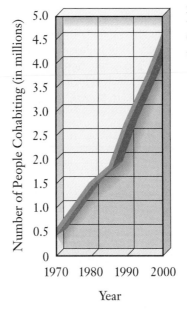

FIGURE 12.8

Cohabitation in the United States

Source: Statistical Abstract 1996:Table 61.

Unmarried Mothers in Global Perspective

Earlier we discussed the steady increase in births to unmarried U.S. mothers. To better understand this trend, we can place it in global perspective. As Figure 12.9 shows, the United States is not alone in this increase. Of the ten industrial nations for which we have data, all

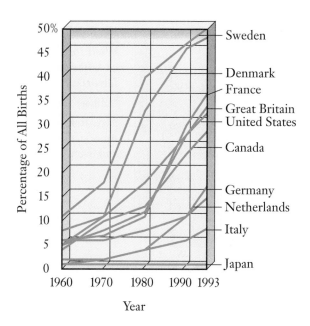

Source: *Statistical Abstract* 1996:Table 1330.

FIGURE 12.9

Births to Unmarried Women in Ten Industrialized Nations

except Japan have experienced sharp increases in births to unmarried mothers. Far from the highest, the U.S. rate falls in the middle third of these nations.

From this figure, it seems fair to conclude that industrialization sets in motion social forces that encourage out-of-wedlock births. There are several problems with this conclusion, however. Why was the rate so low in 1960? Industrialization had been in process for many decades prior to that time. Why are the rates in the bottom four nations only a fraction of those in the top six nations? Why does Japan's rate remain so consistently low? Why are Sweden's and Denmark's so high? With but a couple of minor exceptions, the ranking of these nations in the 1990s is the same as in 1960. By itself, then, industrialization is too simple an answer. A fuller explanation would have to focus on customs and values embedded within the particular cultures. For that answer, we will have to await further research.

The Sandwich Generation and Elder Care

The *sandwich generation* refers to people who find themselves sandwiched between two generations, responsible for the care of their children and for their own aging parents. Typically between the ages of 40 and 55, these people find themselves pulled in two equally compelling directions. Feeling responsible both for their children and their parents, they are plagued with guilt and anger because they can be in only one place at a time (Shellenbarger 1994a).

Concerns about elder care have gained the attention of the corporate world, and about 25 percent of large companies offer elder care assistance to their employees (Hewitt Associates 1995). This assistance includes seminars, referral services, and flexible work schedules in order to help employees meet their responsibilities without missing so much work (Shellenbarger 1994b). Because of their own experiences, CEOs may respond more positively to their workers' problems with elder care than to child day care. Most CEOs are older men whose wives stayed home to take care of their children, so they lack an understanding of the stresses of balancing work and child care. Nearly all have aging parents, however, and many have faced the turmoil of trying to cope with their needs.

With people living longer, this issue is likely to become increasingly urgent as we enter the twenty-first century.

▶ Divorce and Remarriage

The topic of family life would not be complete without considering divorce. Let's first try to determine how much divorce there really is.

The pregnancy of unmarried teenagers, common in the United States and most of the Western world, complicates social life. Among other problems is a much higher dropout rate from high school. To combat this problem, New Futures High School in Albuquerque, New Mexico, allows teen mothers to take their children to class.

Problems in Measuring Divorce

You probably have heard that the U.S. divorce rate is 50 percent, a figure popular with reporters. The statistic is true in the sense that each year about half as many divorces are granted as marriages are performed. In 1996, for example, 2,344,000 U.S. couples married and 1,156,000 couples divorced ("Population Update" 1996).

With these statistics, what is wrong with saying that the divorce rate is 50 percent? The real question is why these two figures should be compared in the first place. The couples who divorced do not—with rare exceptions—come from the group who married that year. The one set of figures has nothing to do with the other, so these statistics in no way establish the divorce rate.

What figures should we compare, then? Couples who divorce are drawn from the entire group of married people in the country. Since the United States has 54,937,000 married couples, and only 1,156,000 of them obtained divorces in 1996, the divorce rate is 2.1 percent, not 50 percent (*Statistical Abstract* 1996: Table 66). A couple's chances of still being married at the end of a year are 98 percent—not bad odds—and certainly much better than the mass media would have us believe.

Over time, of course, those annual 2.1 percentages add up. A third way of measuring divorce, then, is to ask, "Of all U.S. adults, what percentage are divorced?" Figure 12.10 shows the increase. Again, a cross-cultural comparison helps to place U.S. statistics in perspective—but the news is not good. As Table 12.2 illustrates, the United States has—by far—the highest divorce rate in the industrialized world. If current trends persist, it is likely that half or even more of all U.S. marriages will end in divorce (Milbank 1996).

One hopeful note is that the U.S. divorce rate leveled off about 1980, and as Table 12.2 shows, has even declined since then. The Down-to-Earth Sociology box on the next page reports some "curious" findings about divorce, and factors that make marriage successful are summarized at the end of this chapter.

Children of Divorce

Each year, over one million U.S. children discover that their parents are divorcing (*Statistical Abstract* 1995: Table 146). Most divorcing parents become so wrapped up in their own problems that they are unable to prepare their children for the divorce—even if they

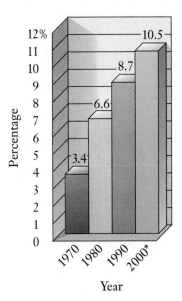

FIGURE 12.10

What Percentage of Americans Are Divorced?

*Author's estimate.

Note: Refers to Americans age 18 and over.

Source: *Statistical Abstract* 1996: Table 58.

knew how to do so in the first place. When the break comes, children become confused and insecure. For security, many cling to the unrealistic idea that their parents will be reunited (Wallerstein and Kelly 1992).

A surprising finding, although still tentative, is that grown children of divorce feel more distant from their parents than do children from intact families—

Table 12.2

Divorce Rates in Ten Industrialized Nations per Thousand Married Women

	1960	1970	1980	1990	1994
United States	9	15	23	21	21
Canada	2	6	11	12	13
Denmark	6	8	11	13	13
Great Britain	2	5	12	12	13
Sweden	5	7	11	12	13
Netherlands	2	3	8	8	9
France	3	3	6	8	8
Germany	4	5	6	8	7
Japan	4	4	5	5	6
Italy	NA	1	1	2	2

Note: Strangely, the source gives data only per 1,000 women. The last reporting year is not consistent. Italy, for example, is 1992.

Sources: Statistical Abstract 1992: Table 1364; 1996: Table 1329.

Down-to-Earth Sociology

You Be the Sociologist: Curious Divorce Patterns

SOCIOLOGISTS ALEX HECKERT, Thomas Nowak, and Kay Snyder (1995) did secondary analysis (see pages 25, 27) of data gathered on a nationally representative sample of 5,000 households. Here are three of their findings:

1. If the wife earns more than her husband, the marriage is more likely to break up; if the husband earns more than his wife, divorce is less likely.

2. If the wife's health is poorer than her husband's, the marriage is more likely to break up; if the husband's health is poorer than his wife's, divorce is less likely.

3. The more housework a wife does, the less likely a couple is to divorce.

Can you explain these findings? You be the sociologist. Please develop your own explanations before you turn the page.

continued

---

even from the parent they lived with (Lye et al. 1993). Compared with adults who grew up in intact families, grown-up children of divorced parents are also less likely to have contact with either their father or their mother (Webster and Herzog 1995). A study of college students at McGill University showed that those whose mothers did not remarry, who remarried and then divorced again, or who had interfered with the children's relationship with their father had the most problems. Those whose mothers entered a single, stable, intimate relationship after the divorce had the best adjustment—including a better ability to build an intimate relationship (Bolgar et al. 1995).

Researchers have identified several factors that help children adjust to divorce. Adjustment is better if (1) both parents show understanding and affection; (2) the child lives with a parent who is making a good adjustment; (3) family routines are consistent; (4) the family has adequate money for its needs; and (5) at least according to preliminary studies, the child lives with the parent of the same sex (Lamb 1977; Clingempeel and Repucci 1982; Peterson and Zill 1986; Wallerstein and Kelly 1992). Sociologist Urie Bronfenbrenner (1992) reports that children adjust better if there is a second adult who can be counted on for support. This person makes the third leg of a stool, giving stability to the smaller family unit. Any adult can be the third leg, he says—a relative, friend, mother-in-law, or even co-worker—but the most powerful stabilizing third leg is the father, the ex-husband.

The Absent Father and Serial Fatherhood

With divorce common and mothers usually being given custody of the children, a new fathering pattern has emerged. In this pattern, known as **serial fatherhood**, divorced fathers tend to maintain high contact with their children during the first year or two after divorce. As the men develop a relationship with

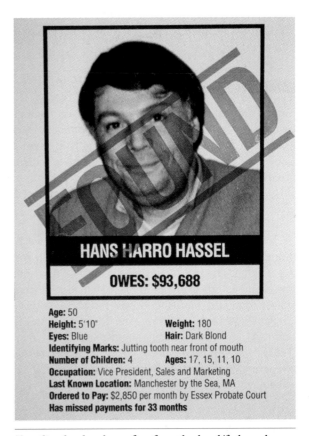

HANS HARRO HASSEL

OWES: $93,688

Age: 50
Height: 5'10" **Weight:** 180
Eyes: Blue **Hair:** Dark Blond
Identifying Marks: Jutting tooth near front of mouth
Number of Children: 4 **Ages:** 17, 15, 11, 10
Occupation: Vice President, Sales and Marketing
Last Known Location: Manchester by the Sea, MA
Ordered to Pay: $2,850 per month by Essex Probate Court
Has missed payments for 33 months

Families that break up often face a husband/father who does not want to pay child support. After pressure from women's groups, courts in recent years have taken a tougher attitude toward "deadbeat dads." Shown here is part of the warrant packet of a successful investigation.

▲▼▲▼▲▼▲▼▲▼▲▼▲▼▲▼▲▼▲▼▲▼▲▼▲▼▲▼▲▼▲▼▲▼

Down-to-Earth Sociology *(Continued)*

Heckert, Nowak, and Snyder suggest these explanations:

1. A wife who earns more than her husband has more alternatives to an unsatisfying marriage; a wife who earns less is more dependent.

2. Social pressure is greater for a wife to take care of a husband in poor health than it is for a husband to take care of a wife in poor health.

3. Who does the most housework is an indication of a husband's and wife's relative bargaining power. Wives with the most bargaining power are the least likely to put up with unsatisfying marriages.

---

another woman, they begin to play an active role with the woman's children and reduce contact with their own children. With another breakup, this pattern may repeat. Only about one-sixth of children who live apart from their fathers see them as often as every week. Actually, most divorced fathers stop seeing their children altogether (Ahlburg and De Vita 1992; Furstenberg and Harris 1992; Seltzer 1994). Apparently, for many men fatherhood has become a short-term commitment.

The Ex-Spouses

Anger, depression, and anxiety are common feelings at divorce. But so is relief. Women are more likely than men to feel that the divorce is giving them a "new chance" in life. A few couples manage to remain friends through it all—but they are the exception. The spouse who initiates the divorce usually gets over it sooner (E. Stark 1989; Kelly 1992).

After divorce, a couple's cost of living increases—two homes, two utility bills, and so forth. But the financial impact is very different for men and for women. Divorce often spells economic hardship for women, especially mothers of small children, whose standard of living drops about 37 percent (Seltzer 1994). In contrast, the former husband's standard of living is likely to increase (Weitzman 1985). The higher a woman's education, the better prepared she is to survive financially after divorce (Dixon and Rettig 1994).

Remarriage

Despite the number of people who emerge from the divorce court swearing "Never again!" most do. But they aren't remarrying as quickly as they used to. In the 1960s, the average woman remarried in about

two years. Today she waits about five years to remarry (*Statistical Abstract* 1995:Table 147). Comparable data are not available for men.

As Figure 12.11 shows, most divorced people remarry other divorced people. You may be surprised that the women most likely to remarry are young mothers and those who have not graduated from high school (Glick and Lin 1986). Apparently women who are more educated and more independent (no children) can afford to be more selective. Men are more likely than women to remarry, perhaps because they have a larger pool of potential mates from which to select.

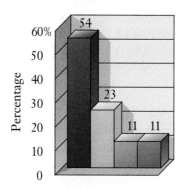

First marriage of bride and groom

Remarriage of bride and groom

First marriage of bride, remarriage of groom

First marriage of groom, remarriage of bride

Source: Statistical Abstract 1996:Table 147.

FIGURE 12.11

The Marital History of U.S. Brides and Grooms

How do remarriages work out? The divorce rate of remarried people *without* children is the same as that of first marriages. Those who bring children into a new marriage, however, are more likely to divorce again. To understand why, we need further research on the dynamics of remarriages (MacDonald and DeMaris 1995). As sociologist Andrew Cherlin (1989) notes, we have not developed adequate norms for remarriages. For example, we lack satisfactory names for stepmothers, stepfathers, stepbrothers, stepsisters, stepaunts, stepuncles, stepcousins, and stepgrandparents. At the very least, these are awkward terms to use, but they also represent ill-defined relationships.

Two Sides of Family Life

Let's first look at situations in which marriage and family have gone seriously wrong and then try to answer the question of what makes marriage work.

The Dark Side of Family Life: Battering, Marital Rape, and Incest

The dark side of family life deals with events that the people involved would rather keep in the dark. We shall look at battering, rape, and incest.

Battering To determine the amount and types of violence in U.S. homes, sociologists have interviewed nationally representative samples of U.S. couples (Straus 1980; Straus, Gelles, and Steinmetz 1980; Straus and Gelles 1988; Straus 1992). Although not all sociologists agree (Dobash et al. 1992, 1993; Pagelow 1992), Murray Straus concludes that husbands and wives are about equally likely to attack one another. When it comes to the effects of violence, however, gender equality certainly vanishes (Gelles 1980; Straus 1980, 1992). As Straus points out, even though *she* may throw the coffeepot first, it is generally *he* who lands the last and most damaging blow. Consequently, many more wives than husbands seek medical attention because of marital violence. A good part of the reason, of course, is that most husbands are bigger and stronger than their wives, putting women at a disadvantage in this literal battle of the sexes.

Straus (1992) emphasizes that gender inequality underlies much marital violence. That is, the sexist structure of society makes some men think that they are superior and have a right to force their will on their wives. Violence between husbands and wives, however, is not equally distributed among the social classes. Rather, it follows certain "social channels," making some people much more likely to be abusers—or victims—than others. The highest rates of marital violence (Gelles 1980) are found among

- Families with low incomes
- Blue-collar workers
- People under 30
- Families in which the husband is unemployed
- Families with above-average numbers of children
- Families living in large urban areas
- Individuals who have no religious affiliation
- Parents with low education

Marital Rape How common is marital rape? Sociologist Diana Russell (1990), who used a sampling technique that allows generalization, found that 14 percent of married women report that their husbands

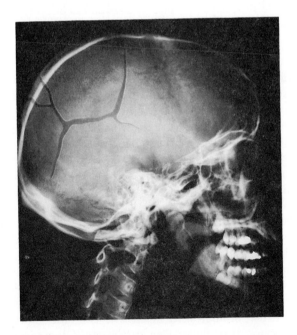

Some men break more than their girlfriends' hearts.
A bad relationship can hurt more than your feelings.

With spouse battering a focus of national attention, a publicity-educational campaign is being run to try to break what is often called the cycle of violence. Shown here is one of the attention-getting posters used in this campaign.

have raped them. Similarly, 10 percent of a representative sample of Boston women interviewed by sociologists David Finkelhor and Kersti Yllo (1983, 1989) reported that their husbands had used physical force to compel them to have sex. Finkelhor's and Yllo's in-depth interviews with fifty of these victims showed that marital rape most commonly occurs during separation or during the breakup of a marriage. They found three types of marital rape:

- *Nonbattering rape* (40 percent). The husband forces his wife to have sex, with no intent to hurt her physically. These instances generally involve conflict over sex, such as the husband feeling insulted when his wife refuses to have sex.
- *Battering rape* (48 percent). In addition to sexually assaulting his wife, the husband intentionally inflicts physical pain to retaliate for some supposed wrongdoing on her part.
- *Perverted rape* (6 percent). These husbands, apparently sexually aroused by the violent elements of rape, force their wives to submit to unusual sexual acts. Anger and hostility can also motivate this type of rape. (The remaining 6 percent are mixed, containing elements of more than one type.)

Incest Incest is more likely to occur in families that are socially isolated (Smith 1992), and is much more common than ordinarily thought (Russell 1986, 1990). Sociologist Diana Russell (n.d.), who interviewed women in San Francisco, found that the incest victims who experience the most difficulty are those who have been victimized the most often, over longer periods of time, and whose incest was "more intrusive"—for example, sexual intercourse as opposed to sexual touching.

Who are the offenders? Russell found that uncles are the most common offenders, followed by first cousins, then fathers (stepfathers especially), brothers, and, finally, relatives ranging from brothers-in-law to stepgrandfathers. Other researchers report that brother–sister incest is several times more common than father–daughter incest (Canavan et al. 1992). Incest between mothers and sons is rare.

The Bright Side of Family Life: Successful Marriages

Successful Marriages After examining divorce and family abuse, one could easily conclude that marriages seldom work out. That would be far from the truth, however, for about two of every three married Americans report that they are "very happy" with their marriages (Cherlin and Furstenberg 1988; Whyte 1992). To find out what makes marriage successful, sociologists Jeanette and Robert Lauer (1992) interviewed 351 couples who had been married fifteen years or longer. Fifty-one of these marriages were unhappy, but the couple stayed together for religious reasons, family tradition, or "for the sake of the children." Of the others, the 300 happy couples, all:

1. Think of their spouse as their best friend
2. Like their spouse as a person
3. Think of marriage as a long-term commitment
4. Believe that marriage is sacred
5. Agree with their spouse on aims and goals
6. Believe that their spouse has grown more interesting over the years
7. Strongly want the relationship to succeed
8. Laugh together

Sociologist Nicholas Stinnett (1992) used interviews and questionnaires to study 660 families from all regions of the United States and parts of South America. He found that happy families

1. Spend a lot of time together
2. Are quick to express appreciation
3. Are committed to promoting one another's welfare
4. Do a lot of talking and listening to one another
5. Are religious
6. Deal with crises in a positive manner

Symbolic Interactionism and the Misuse of Statistics Many of my students express concern about their own marital future, a wariness born out of the divorce of their parents, friends, neighbors, relatives—even pastors and rabbis. They wonder what chance they really have. Since sociology is not just an abstract discipline, but is really about our lives, it seems valuable in this context to stress that we are individuals, not statistics. That is, if the divorce rate were 33 percent or 50 percent, this does *not* mean that if we marry our chances of getting divorced are 33 percent or 50 percent. That is a misuse of statistics, and a very common one at that. Divorce statistics represent all marriages, and have absolutely *nothing* to do with any individual marriage. Our own chances depend on our own situation—especially the way we approach marriage.

To make this point clearer, let's apply symbolic interactionism. From a symbolic interactionist perspective, we create our own worlds. That is, experiences don't come with built-in meanings. Rather, we interpret our experiences, and act accordingly. Simply put, if we think of marriage as likely to fail, we increase the likelihood that it will fail; if we think that our marriage will work out well, the chances of a good marriage increase. In other words, we tend to act according to our ideas, creating a sort of self-fulfilling prophecy. The folk saying "There are no guarantees in life" is certainly true, but it does help to have a *vision* that a good marriage is possible and that it is worth achieving.

The Future of Marriage and Family

What can we expect of marriage and family in the future? Despite its many problems, marriage is in no danger of becoming a relic of the past. Marriage is so functional that it exists in every society. Conse-

quently, the vast majority of Americans will continue to find marriage vital to their welfare.

Certain trends are firmly in place. Cohabitation, births to single women, and age at first marriage will increase. More married women will join the work force, and they will continue to gain marital power. Equality in marriage, however, is not even on the horizon. The number of elderly will continue to increase, and more couples will find themselves sandwiched between caring for their parents and their own children. The plateauing of the divorce rate is another matter entirely. At this point we don't know if the plateau is just a breather, from which an even higher rate will be launched, the prelude to a decline, or even an indication that we have reached the saturation point and divorce will remain flat.

Finally, our culture will continue to be haunted by distorted images of marriage and family: the bleak ones portrayed in the mass media and the rosy ones painted by cultural myths. Sociological research can help correct these distortions, allowing us to see how our own family experiences fit into the patterns of our culture. Sociological research also can help to answer the big question of how to formulate social policy that will support and enhance family life.

Summary and Review

Marriage and Family in Global Perspective

What is a family—and what themes are universal?

Family is difficult to define. For just about every element one might consider essential, there are exceptions. Consequently, **family** is defined broadly—as two or more people who consider themselves related by blood, marriage, or adoption. Universally, **marriage** and family are mechanisms for governing mate selection, reckoning descent, and establishing inheritance and authority. Pp. 308–311.

Marriage and Family in Theoretical Perspective

What is the functionalist perspective on marriage and family?

Functionalists examine the functions of families, analyzing such matters as the **incest taboo.** They also examine consequences of weakening family functions, and the dysfunctions of the family. Pp. 311–312.

What is the conflict perspective on marriage and family?

Conflict theorists examine how marriage and family help perpetuate inequalities, especially the subservience of women. Power struggles in marriage, such as those over housework, are an example. Pp. 312–314.

What is a symbolic interactionist perspective on marriage and family?

Symbolic interactionists examine how the contrasting perspectives of men and women are played out in marriage—for example, how the meaning of housework affects who does what. Pp. 314–315.

The Family Life Cycle

What are the major elements of the family life cycle?

The major elements are love and courtship, marriage, childbirth, child rearing, and the family in later life.

Most marriages follow predictable patterns of age, social class, race, and religion. Childbirth and child-rearing patterns also vary by social class. Pp. 315–320.

Diversity in U.S. Families

How significant are race and ethnicity in family life?

The primary distinction is social class, not race or ethnicity. Families of the same social class are likely to be similar, regardless of their racial or ethnic makeup. Pp. 320–324.

What other diversity in U.S. families is there?

Also discussed were one-parent, childless, **blended,** and gay families. Although each has its own unique characteristics, social class is also significant in determining their primary characteristics. Poverty is especially significant for one-parent families, most of which are headed by women. Pp. 324–325.

Trends in U.S. Families

What major changes characterize U.S. families?

Two changes are postponement of first marriage and an increase in **cohabitation.** With more people living longer, many middle-aged people find themselves sandwiched between caring for their own children and their own parents. Pp. 325–327.

Divorce and Remarriage

What is the current divorce rate?

Depending on what figures you choose to compare, you can produce almost any rate you wish, from 75 percent to just 2.1 percent. However you figure it, the U.S. divorce rate is higher than in any other industrialized nation. Pp. 327–328.

How do children and their parents adjust to divorce?

Divorce is especially difficult for children, whose adjustment problems often continue into adulthood. Most divorced fathers do not maintain ongoing relationships with their children. Financial problems are usually greater for the former wives. Although most divorced people remarry, their rate of remarriage has slowed considerably. Pp. 328–331.

Two Sides of Family Life

What are the two sides of family life?

The dark side is family abuse—spouse battering, marital rape, and incest, activities that revolve around the misuse of power. The bright side is families that provide intense satisfaction for spouses and their children. Pp. 331–333.

The Future of Marriage and Family

What is the likely future of marriage and family?

We can expect cohabitation, births to unmarried mothers, and age at first marriage to increase. The growing numbers of women in the work force will likely continue to shift the marital balance of power. P. 333.

Where can I read more on this topic?

Suggested readings for this chapter are listed on pages 442–443.

Glossary

bilateral system a system of reckoning descent that counts both the mother's and the father's side (p. 310)

blended family a family whose members were once part of other families (p. 324)

cohabitation unmarried people living together in a sexual relationship (p. 326)

empty nest a married couple's domestic situation after the last child has left home (p. 318)

endogamy the practice of marrying within one's own group (p. 309)

exogamy the practice of marrying outside one's group (p. 310)

extended family a nuclear family plus other relatives, such as grandparents, uncles, and aunts, who live together (p. 309)

family two or more people who consider themselves related by blood, marriage, or adoption (p. 309)

family of orientation the family in which a person grows up (p. 309)

family of procreation the family formed when a couple's first child is born (p. 309)

homogamy the tendency of people with similar characteristics to marry one another (p. 317)

household all people who occupy the same housing unit (p. 309)

incest taboo rules specifying the degrees of kinship that prohibit sex or marriage (p. 310)

machismo an emphasis on male strength and dominance (p. 322)

marriage a group's approved mating arrangements, usually marked by a ritual of some sort (p. 309)

matriarchy a society or group in which authority is vested in women (p. 310)

matrilineal system a system of reckoning descent that counts only the mother's side (p. 310)

nuclear family a family consisting of a husband, wife, and child(ren) (p. 309)

patriarchy a society or group in which authority is vested in men (p. 310)

patrilineal system a system of reckoning descent that counts only the father's side (p. 310)

polyandry a marriage in which a woman has more than one husband (p. 308)

polygyny a marriage in which a man has more than one wife (p. 308)

romantic love feelings of erotic attraction accompanied by an idealization of the other (p. 315)

serial fatherhood a pattern of parenting in which a father, after divorce, reduces contact with his own children, serves as a father to the children of the woman he marries or lives with, then ignores them after moving in with or marrying another woman; this pattern repeats (p. 329)

system of descent how kinship is traced over the generations (p. 310)

Sociology and the Internet

All URLs listed are current as of the printing of this book. URLs are often changed. Please check our Website http://www.abacon.com/henslin for updates.

1. The World's Children

When sociologists look at the problems faced by families, they usually include the special difficulties faced by children, often in a global perspective. This project will involve your participating in a panel reporting on the state of the world's children and introduce you to the world's largest organization devoted to them, the United Nations agency UNICEF.

Go to their home page at http://www. unicef.org, page down to "Organization," and click on "About UNICEF." Read about the agency to give yourself some background on its purpose, goals, and activities. Return to the UNICEF home page and click on "The State of the World's Children," an annual report published by UNICEF. On the new page, click on "Summary." Note the important issues and the most crucial problems facing children throughout the world. Go back to "The State of the World's Children" page, and click on fact sheets. If you do not have an Acrobat reader, you will have to download a copy. Click on "Download the Reader," and follow the instructions for installing it on your machine. Back at the Report page, click on "Fact Sheets," and click on the "Download fact sheets as a PDF." (Because servers change aspects of their sites from time to time, you may find that UNICIF no longer uses the Acrobat [PDF] reader, but instructions will be given on how to use the reader currently employed.) Now go back to the Report page

and click on "Download the PDF version" to get the entire report. It will be your main source of information.

This seems like a great deal of reading, but in forming a panel, each of you can focus on a different aspect of the report. (Everyone, however, should read all the materials.)

2. Kinship Systems

As you have read in this chapter, there are universal needs that every society meets with some kind of family arrangements. Anthropologists have studied hundreds of these societies and have created concepts to refer to various kinship patterns. You have been introduced to a number of these terms, such as *polygyny, exogamy,* and *matrilineal.*

Now explore the fascinating world of kinship patterns by working through a brief Internet tutorial, "Principles of Kinship." Access the site at http://www. umanitoba.ca/anthropology/tutor/. You should see a list of topics, beginning with "Kin Fundamentals." Select this and follow it through. At the bottom of the page marked "Bilateral Kinship," select "Return to Main Menu," then select topic 2, "Systems of Descent." Go through all five areas, including the subtopics under 4, "Marriage Systems." Then look at the two ethnographic examples listed under 6: "A Turkish Peasant Village" and "Ancient Hebrews."

Write an essay describing the kinship systems in the Turkish village and among the Hebrews. Then analyze the U.S. system (based on your own experience), applying what you have learned in the tutorial.

Jessie Coates, Take Me to the Water, 1994.

C H A P T E R

13

Education and Religion

WENDY STILL FEELS RESENTMENT WHEN she recalls the memo that greeted her that Monday morning:

With growing concern about international competition for our products, the management is upgrading several positions. The attached listing of jobs states the new qualifications that must be met.

Wendy quickly scanned the list. The rumors had been right, after all. The new position the company was opening up—the job she had been slated to get—was listed.

After regaining her composure somewhat, but still angry, Wendy marched to her supervisor's office. "I've been doing my job for three years," she said. "You told me I'd get that new position."

"I know, Wendy. You'd be good at it. Believe me, I gave you a high recommendation. But what can I do? You know what the higher-ups are like. If they decide they want someone with a college degree, that's just what they'll get."

"But I can't go back to college now, not with all my responsibilities. It's been five years since I was in college, and I still have a year to go."

The supervisor was sympathetic, but she insisted that her hands were tied. Wendy would have to continue working at the lower job classification—and stay at the lower pay.

It was Wendy's responsibility to break in Melissa, the newcomer with the freshly minted college degree. Those were the toughest two weeks Wendy ever spent at work—especially since she knew that Melissa was already being paid more than she was.

EDUCATION: TRANSFERRING KNOWLEDGE AND SKILLS

Without a college degree, like Wendy you haven't a chance of landing some jobs—even though you would be good at them. Why? Let's look at the main characteristics of education.

Today's Credential Society

Sociologist Randall Collins (1979) observed that industrialized nations have become **credential societies,** that employers use diplomas and degrees to determine who is eligible for a job. In many cases the diploma or degree is irrelevant for the work that must be performed. The new job that Wendy wanted, for example, did not suddenly change into a task requiring a college degree. Her immediate supervisor knew Wendy's abilities and was sure she could handle the responsibility just fine—but the new company policy required a credential that Wendy didn't have. Similarly, is a high school diploma necessary to pump gas or to sell shoes? Yet employers routinely require such credentials.

In fact, it is often on the job, not at school, that employees learn the particular knowledge or skills that a job requires. A high school diploma teaches no one how to sell tacos or to be polite to customers. Wendy had to teach Melissa the ropes. Why, then, do employers insist on diplomas and degrees? Why don't they simply use on-the-job training?

A major reason credentials are required is the larger size, urbanization, and consequent anonymity of industrial societies. Diplomas and degrees serve as automatic sorting devices. Because employers don't know potential workers, they depend on schools to weed out the capable from the incapable. By hiring college graduates, the employer assumes the individuals are responsible people, for evidently they have shown up on time for numerous classes, have turned in scores of assignments, and have demonstrated basic writing and thinking skills. The specific job skills a position requires can then be grafted onto this base certified by the college.

In other cases, specific job skills must be mastered before an individual is allowed to do certain work. As a result of change in technology and in knowledge, simple on-the-job training will not do for physicians, engineers, and airline pilots. That is precisely why doctors so prominently display their

In hunting and gathering societies, there was no separate social institution called education. *As with this 4-year-old Kalahari boy in South Africa, children learned their adult economic roles from their parents and other kin.*

credentials. Their framed degrees declare that they have been certified by an institution of higher learning, that they are qualified to work on our bodies.

Without the right credentials, you won't get hired. It does not matter that you can do the job better than someone else. You will never have the opportunity to prove what you can do, for, like Wendy, you lack the credentials even to be considered for the job.

Education in Global Perspective

To gain an idea of the variety of education around the world, and how education is directly related to a nation's economy, let's look at an example from each of the three worlds of development. Keep in mind that these are just examples, that no single nation represents the wide variety of educational approaches that characterizes each of these three worlds.

Education in the Most Industrialized Nations: Japan

A central sociological principle of education is that a nation's education reflects its culture. Since a core Japanese value is solidarity with the group, competition among individuals is downgraded. For example, in the work force people who are hired together work as a team. They even are promoted collectively (Ouchi 1993). Japanese education reflects this group-centered ethic. Children in grade school work as a group, all mastering the same skills and materials. Teachers stress cooperation and respect for elders

and others in positions of authority. By law, Japanese schools even use the same textbooks.

In a fascinating cultural contradiction, college admission procedures are highly competitive (Cooper 1991). Like the Scholastic Assessment Test (SAT) required of U.S. college-bound high school seniors, Japanese seniors who want to attend college must take a national test. Only the top scorers in Japan, however—rich and poor alike—are admitted to college. In contrast, even a U.S. high school graduate who performs poorly on these tests can find some college to attend—as long as his or her parents can pay the tuition.

Just how highly do the Japanese value education? One way to tell how much a society values something is to see how much money it chooses to spend on it. By law, Japanese teachers are paid 10 percent more than the highest-paid civil service workers, putting teachers in the top 10 percent of the country's wage earners (Richburg 1985). Because the Japanese reward schoolteaching with both high pay and high prestige, each teaching opening is met by a barrage of eager, highly qualified applicants.

Education in the Industrializing Nations: Post-Soviet Russia

After the Revolution of 1917, the Soviet Communist party attempted to upgrade the nation's educational system. At that time, as in most other countries, education was limited to the elite. Following the sociological principle that education reflects culture, the new central government made certain that socialist values dominated its schools, for it saw education as a means to undergird the new political system. As a result, schoolchildren were taught that capitalism was evil and that communism was the salvation of the world.

Just as the economy was directed from central headquarters, so education was totally centralized, with orders issued out of a remote educational bureaucracy in Moscow. Schools throughout the country followed the same state-prescribed curriculum, and all students in the same grade used the same textbooks. Students memorized the materials, and, to prevent the development of thinking contrary to communism, were discouraged from discussing them (Bridgman 1994).

Post-Soviet Russians are now in the midst of "reinventing" education. For the first time, private, religious, and even foreign-run schools are allowed, and teachers can encourage students to question and to think for themselves. The problems confronting the Russians are mind-boggling. Not only do they have to retrain tens of thousands of teachers used to teaching pat political answers, but school budgets are also shrinking, while inflation is spiraling. Urban teachers are stampeding out of education into fields that, with the new capitalism, pay ten times the going rate for instructors (Bridgman 1994).

Because it is true of education everywhere, we can safely conclude that Russia is developing an educational system designed to reflect its culture. This system will glorify its historical exploits and reinforce its values and world views. One difficulty for the Rus-

sians at this point is that their values and world views are rapidly changing. Due to the transition to a competitive market system, basic ideas about profit and private property are being transformed—and their educational system is destined to reflect those changed values.

Education in the Least Industrialized Nations: Egypt

Education in the Least Industrialized Nations stands in sharp contrast to that in the industrialized world. Even if the Least Industrialized Nations have mandatory attendance laws, they are not enforced. Because most of their people work the land or take care of families, they find little need for education. In addition, most of these nations simply cannot afford extensive formal education. As we saw from Figure 7.1 (pp. 172–173), most people in the Least Industrialized Nations live on less than $1,000 a year. Consequently, in some nations most children do not go to school beyond the first couple of grades. As was once common around the globe, it is primarily the wealthy in the Least Industrialized Nations who have either the means or the leisure for formal education—especially anything beyond the basics. As an example, let's look at education in Egypt.

Several centuries before the birth of Christ, Egypt's world-renowned centers of learning produced such acclaimed scientists as Archimedes and Eukleides. The primary areas of study during this

The poverty of some of the Least Industrialized Nations defies the imagination of most people who have been reared in the industrialized world. Their educational systems are similarly marked by poverty. This photo depicts rural education in Eritrea, a former Italian colony on the Red Sea in Northeast Africa.

classic period were physics, astronomy, geometry, geography, mathematics, philosophy, and medicine. The largest library in the world was at Alexandria. Fragments from the papyrus manuscripts of this library, which burned to the ground, have been invaluable in deciphering ancient manuscripts. After defeat in war, however, education declined, never again to rise to its former prominence.

On the positive side, today's education is free at all levels, including college. On the negative side, qualified teachers are few, classrooms are crowded, many peasant children receive no education at all, and children of the wealthy are several times as likely to get a college education. Those who go beyond the five years of grade school attend a preparatory school for three years. High school also lasts for three years. During the first two years, all students take the same required courses, and during their third year they specialize in arts, science, or mathematics. Examinations are held monthly, and a national exam is given at the end of the senior year (El-Meligi 1992).

The Functionalist Perspective: Providing Social Benefits

A central position of functionalism is that when the parts of society are working properly, each contributes to the well-being or stability of that society. The intended consequences of people's actions are known as **manifest functions,** while those that are not intended are called **latent functions.** Let's examine the functions of education. *not Intended*

Teaching Knowledge and Skills

Education's most obvious manifest function is to teach knowledge and skills, whether the traditional three *R's* or their more contemporary version, such as computer literacy. Each society must train the next generation to fulfill its significant positions. Because our postindustrial society needs highly educated people, the schools supply them.

Cultural Transmission of Values

At least as significant as teaching knowledge and skills is a function of education called **cultural transmission,** a process by which schools pass a society's core values from one generation to the next. Consequently, schools in a socialist society stress values of socialism, while schools in a capitalist society teach

values that support capitalism. U.S. schools, for example, stress respect for private property, individualism, and competition.

Regardless of the economic system, loyalty to the state is a cultural value, and schools around the world teach patriotism. U.S. schools teach that the United States is the best country in the world; Russians learn that no country is better than Russia; and French, German, Japanese, Afghani, and Egyptian students all learn the same about their respective countries. To instill patriotism, grade school teachers in every country extol the virtues of the society's founders, their struggle for freedom from oppression, and the goodness of the country's basic social institutions.

Social Integration

Schools also perform the function of *social integration,* helping to mold students into a more or less cohesive unit. For example, when students salute the flag and sing the national anthem, they become aware of the "greater government," and gain a sense of national identity. One of the best indicators of how education promotes political integration is the millions of immigrants who have attended U.S. schools, learned mainstream ideas, and given up their earlier national and cultural identities as they became Americans (Violas 1978; Rodriguez 1995).

The sociological significance of this integrative function of education goes far beyond similarities of appearance or speech. *To forge a national identity is to stabilize the political system itself.* If people identify with a society's social institutions and *perceive them as the basis of their welfare,* they have no reason to rebel. This function is especially significant when it comes to the lower social classes, the groups from which social revolutionaries ordinarily would be drawn. The wealthy already have a vested interest in maintaining the status quo, but to get the lower classes to identify with a social system *as it is* goes a long way to preserving that system as it is.

Gatekeeping — Sorting Students by merit

Gatekeeping, or determining which people will enter what occupations, is another major function of education. Credentialing, the subject of the opening vignette, is an example of gatekeeping. Because Wendy did not have the credentials, but Melissa did, education closed the door to the one and opened it to the other.

Functionalists analyze both the manifest and latent functions of education. One of education's latent functions is to produce social integration. In this classroom, students of contrasting backgrounds are not just learning to play musical instruments, but they also are being socially integrated.

Essential to gatekeeping is **tracking,** sorting students into different educational programs on the basis of real or perceived abilities. U.S. high schools, for example, often funnel students into one of three tracks: general, college prep, or honors. Those in the lowest track are most likely to go to work after high school, although some attend community colleges; those in the highest track usually enter the more prestigious colleges around the country; and those in between most often attend a local college or regional state university.

Gatekeeping sorts people on the basis of merit, say functionalists. Sociologists Talcott Parsons (1940) and Kingsley Davis and Wilbert Moore (1945), who pioneered this view, also known as **social placement,** argue that a major task of society is to fill its positions with capable people. Some positions, such as that of physician, require high intelligence and many years of arduous education. Consequently, to motivate capable people to postpone immediate gratification and to submit to many years of rigorous education, high income and prestige are held out as rewards. Other jobs require far fewer skills and can be performed by people of lesser intelligence. Thus, functionalists look on education as a system that, to the benefit of society, sorts people according to their abilities.

Mainstreaming

A new function of education is **mainstreaming,** incorporating people with disabilities into regular social activities. As a matter of routine policy, students with disabilities used to be placed in special schools. Educators later concluded that in these settings disabled students learned to adjust only to a world of the disabled, leaving them ill prepared to cope with the dominant world. The educational philosophy then changed to having disabled students attend regular schools. For people who cannot walk, wheelchair ramps are provided; for those who cannot hear, "signers" (interpreters who use their hands) may attend classes with them. Most blind students still attend special schools, as do people with severe learning disabilities. Overall, one of three disabled students attends school in regular classrooms, one of three splits the day between regular and special classrooms, and one of three spends most of the day in special classrooms (*Statistical Abstract* 1995:Table 263).

Replacing Family Functions

U.S. education has become a rival for some family functions. Child care is an example. Grade schools do double duty as baby-sitters for parents who both work, or for single mothers in the work force. Child care always has been a *latent* function of formal education, for it was an unintended consequence of schooling. Now, however, since most families have two wage earners, child care has changed into a manifest function. Some schools even offer child care both before and after formal classes. Another example is providing sex education, which has stirred controversy, for some families resent this function being taken from them.

The Conflict Perspective: Reproducing the Social Class Structure

Unlike functionalists, who see education as a social institution that performs functions for the benefit of society, conflict theorists see the educational system as a tool used by the elite to maintain their dominance. Education, they stress, *reproduces the social class structure.* By this, they mean that education promotes the interests of a society's power elite and perpetuates a society's social class divisions. For example, regardless of children's abilities, the more well-to-do are likely to be placed in college-bound tracks, the poor into vocational tracks, and each to inherit matching life opportunities laid down before they were born.

Let's see how education reproduces the social class structure.

The Hidden Curriculum

The term **hidden curriculum** refers to the unwritten rules of behavior and attitudes, such as obedience to authority and conformity to cultural norms, that are taught in the schools in addition to the formal curriculum (Gillborn 1992). Conflict theorists note how this hidden curriculum perpetuates existing social inequalities. For example, the elite need people to run their business empires, and they are more comfortable if their managers possess "refined" language and manners. Consequently, middle-class schools, whose teachers know where their pupils are headed, stress "proper" English and "good" manners. In contrast, because few children from inner-city schools will occupy managerial positions, their teachers allow ethnic and street language in the classroom. To reproduce the class structure—that is, to take the same kind of position their parents have—these children do not need "refined" speech and manners; they simply need to be taught to obey rules so they can take their place in the closely supervised, low-status positions for which they are destined—and for which the schools prepare them (Bowles and Gintis 1976; Olneck and Bills 1980).

Tilting the Tests: Discrimination by IQ

Even intelligence tests play their part in keeping the social class system intact. For example, how would you answer this question?

> *A symphony is to a composer as a book is to a(n)____ .*
> ___ *paper*   ___ *sculptor*   ___ *musician*
> ___ *author*   ___ *man*

You probably had no difficulty coming up with "author" as your choice. Wouldn't any intelligent person have done so?

In point of fact, this question raises a central issue in intelligence testing. Not all intelligent people would know how to answer it, because it contains *cultural biases*. In other words, children from some backgrounds are more familiar with the concepts of symphonies, composers, sculptors, and musicians than are other children. Consequently, the test is tilted in their favor (Turner 1972; Ashe 1992).

Perhaps asking a different question will make the bias clearer. How would you answer this question?

> *If you throw dice and "7" is showing on the top, what is facing down?*
> ___ *seven*   ___ *snake eyes*   ___ *box cars*
> ___ *little Joes*   ___ *eleven*

This question, suggested by Adrian Dove (n.d.), a social worker in Watts, is slanted toward a lower-class experience. It surely is obvious that this *particular* cultural bias tilts the test so that children from some social backgrounds will perform better than others.

It is no different with IQ (intelligence quotient) tests that use such words as *composer* and *symphony*. A lower-class child may have heard about rap, rock, hip hop, or jazz, but not about symphonies. In other words, IQ tests measure not only intelligence but also culturally acquired knowledge. Whatever else we can say, the cultural bias built into IQ tests is clearly *not* tilted in favor of the lower class. One consequence is that disproportionate numbers of minorities and the poor are assigned to noncollege tracks (Kershaw 1992). This destines them for lower-paying jobs in adult life. Thus, conflict theorists view IQ tests as another weapon in the arsenal designed to maintain the social class structure over the generations (Postman 1992).

Stacking the Deck: Unequal Funding

Conflict theorists also stress how each state's funding for education stacks the deck against the poor. Because public schools are largely supported by local property taxes, the more well-to-do communities (where property values are higher) have more to spend on their children, while the poorer communities end up with much less. Consequently, the richer communities offer higher salaries (and take their pick of the most highly qualified and motivated teachers), buy the latest textbooks and microcomputers, as well as teach courses in foreign language, music, and so on. Because U.S. schools so closely reflect the U.S. social class system, then, the children of the privileged emerge from grade school best equipped for success in high school. In turn, they come out of high school best equipped for success in college.

The Bottom Line: Family Background

Because of the hidden curriculum, IQ tests, and unequal funding, college attendance is closely linked with social class. If you rank families from the poorest to the richest, at each income level the likelihood that children will attend college increases (Bowles 1977; Manski 1992–1993). College attendance is also closely related to race and ethnicity. In Figure 13.1, which shows the *funneling effect* of education, you can see that, compared with whites, African Americans and Latinos are less likely to complete high school, less likely to go to college, and if they go to college, less likely to graduate.

In short, because education's doors of opportunity swing open wide for some, but have to be hammered down if others are to enter, conflict theorists say that the educational system reproduces (or perpetuates) the social class structure.

The Symbolic Interactionist Perspective: Teacher Expectations

Whereas functionalists look at how education functions to benefit society and conflict theorists examine how education perpetuates social inequality, symbolic interactionists study face-to-face interactions inside the classroom. They have found that the expectations of teachers have profound consequences for their students.

The Rist Research

Symbolic interactionists have uncovered some of the dynamics of educational tracking. In what has become a classic study, sociologist Ray Rist (1970) did participant observation in an African-American grade school with an African-American faculty. Rist found that after only eight days in the classroom, the kindergarten teacher felt she knew the children's abilities well enough to assign them to three separate work tables. To Table 1 Mrs. Caplow assigned those she considered to be "fast learners." They sat at the front of the room, closest to her. Those whom she saw as "slow learners" she assigned to Table 3, located at the back of the classroom. She placed "average" students at Table 2, in between the other tables.

This seemed strange to Rist. He knew that the children had not been tested for ability, yet the teacher was certain she could differentiate between bright and slow children. Investigating further, Rist found that social class was the underlying basis for assigning the children to the different tables. Middle-class students were separated out for Table 1, children from poorer homes to Tables 2 and 3. The teacher paid the most attention to the children at Table 1, who were closest to her, less to Table 2, and the least to Table 3. As the year went on, children from Table 1

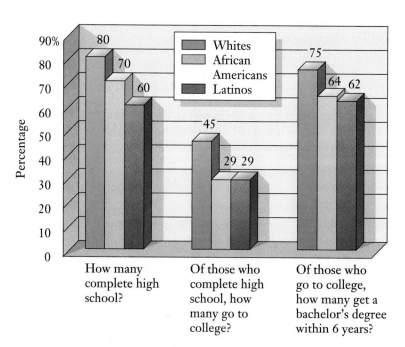

FIGURE 13.1

The Funneling Effects of Education: Race and Ethnicity

Legend: Whites, African Americans, Latinos

How many complete high school? — Whites 80, African Americans 70, Latinos 60

Of those who complete high school, how many go to college? — Whites 45, African Americans 29, Latinos 29

Of those who go to college, how many get a bachelor's degree within 6 years? — Whites 75, African Americans 64, Latinos 62

Note: Totals are available in the source only for these three racial-ethnic groups.

Source: Statistical Abstract 1995: Tables 269, 297.

perceived that they were treated better and came to see themselves as smarter. They became the leaders in class activities and even ridiculed children at the other tables, calling them "dumb." Eventually, the children at Table 3 disengaged themselves from many class-room activities. Not surprisingly, at the end of the year only the children at Table 1 had completed the lessons that prepared them for reading.

This early tracking stuck. When these students entered the first grade, their new teacher looked at the work they had accomplished and placed students from Table 1 at her Table 1. She treated her tables much as the kindergarten teacher had, and the children at Table 1 again led the class. In the second grade, the teacher reviewed the children's scores. She assigned the highest performing children to a group called the "Tigers." Befitting their name, she gave them challenging readers. Not surprisingly, the Tigers came from the original Table 1 in kinder-garten. The second group, called the "Cardinals," came from the original Tables 2 and 3. Her third group consisted of children she had failed the previ-ous year, whom she called the "Clowns." The Cardi-nals and Clowns were given less advanced readers.

Rist concluded that *the child's journey through school was preordained from the eighth day of kinder-garten!* This research, as with the Saints and the Roughnecks reported in Chapter 6, demonstrates the power of labels, how they can set people on courses of action that affect the rest of their lives.

How Do Teacher Expectations Work?

Sociologist George Farkas (1990a, 1990b) led a team of researchers in probing how teacher expectations affect grades. Using a stratified sample of students in a large urban school district in the Southwest, they discovered that students who scored similarly on course materials did not necessarily receive the same grade for the course. Females and Asian Americans averaged higher course grades than males, African Americans, Latinos, and whites—even though they all had scored the same on the course work.

To explain this, the first conclusion most of us might jump to would be discrimination. In this case, however, such an explanation does not seem to fit, for it is most unlikely that the teachers would be preju-diced against males and whites. Farkas used symbolic interactionism to interpret these unexpected results. He noted that some students "signal" to their teach-ers that they are "good students" by being more docile (being eager to cooperate and accept what the

teacher says) and showing that they are "trying hard." The teachers pick up these "signals" and reward such people with better grades. Females and Asian Amer-icans, the researchers concluded, are most likely to display these characteristics.

We do not yet have enough information on how teachers form their expectations, how they commu-nicate them to students, or exactly how these expec-tations influence teacher–student interaction. Nor do we know very much about how students "signal" messages to teachers. Perhaps you will become the educational sociologist who will shed more light on this significant area of human behavior.

◢ Problems in U.S. Education—and Their Solutions

To conclude this section, let's examine two of the major problems facing U.S. education today—and consider their potential solutions.

Problems: Mediocrity and Violence

The Rising Tide of Mediocrity Perhaps nothing so captures what is wrong with U.S. schools than this event, reported by sociologist Thomas Sowell (1993b):

> [A]n international study of 13-year-olds . . . found that Koreans ranked first in mathematics and Americans last. When asked if they thought they were "good at mathematics," only 23 percent of the Korean youngsters said "yes"—compared to 68 percent of American 13-year-olds. The Ameri-can educational dogma that students should "feel good about themselves" was a success in its own terms—though not in any other terms.

In 1983, a blue-ribbon presidential panel gave a grim assessment of U.S. education, warning of a "rising tide of mediocrity that threatens our very future as a nation and as a people." Even the title of the report, *A Nation at Risk*, sounded an alarm. What especially upset panel members was a decline in scores on the Scholastic Assessment Test (SAT). As Figure 13.2 shows, the math scores have recovered a good part of the lost ground. The verbal scores, however, are hold-ing at their lows. Both are lower than they were al-most thirty years ago.

The president of the American Federation of Teachers has come up with a unique defense of the decline in SAT scores—they indicate that teachers are doing a *better* job! The low test scores, he says, mean that teachers are getting more students to stay

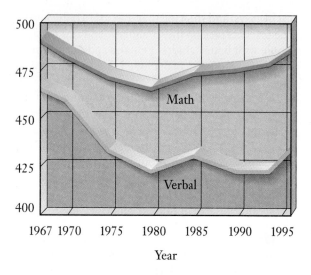

Year

Sources: Stecklow 1975; *Statistical Abstract* 1996:Table 274.

FIGURE 13.2

National Results of the Scholastic Assessment Test (SAT)

in high school and to go on to college. These students from poorer academic backgrounds, who used to drop out, now become part of the test results (Sowell 1993). Perhaps this is the reason. But if it is, it indicates not success, but a severe underlying problem—teachers giving inferior education to disadvantaged students (Murray and Hernstein 1992).

Others suggest that SAT scores have declined because children find television and video games more appealing than reading (Rigdon and Swasy 1990). Students who read little acquire a smaller vocabulary and less rigor in thought and verbal expression. Sociologists Donald Hayes and Loreen Wolfer (1993a, 1993b) are convinced that the culprit is the "dummied down" textbooks that pervade U.S. schools. Some point their fingers at other low standards: "frill" courses, less homework, fewer term papers, grade inflation, and burned-out teachers who are more interested in collecting paychecks than in educating their students.

You may have noticed on Figure 13.2 that there is a sharp increase in verbal scores between 1994 and 1995. Unfortunately, this increase does not indicate that students are better prepared. Rather, the SAT was shortened, students given more time to answer the fewer questions, and the verbal part made easier (the antonym portion was dropped) (Manno 1995; Stecklow 1995). This "dummying down" of the SAT

is yet another form of grade inflation, to which we shall now turn.

Grade Inflation, Social Promotion, and Functional Illiteracy At the same time that SAT scores went down, grades went up. In the 1960s, high school teachers gave out about twice as many *C*'s as *A*'s, but now the *A*'s exceed the *C*'s. **Grade inflation** in the face of declining standards has been accompanied by **social promotion,** the practice of passing students from one grade to the next even though they have not mastered basic materials. One unfortunate result is **functional illiteracy,** difficulty with reading and writing even though one has graduated from high school. Some high school graduates cannot fill out job applications; others can't figure out if they are given the right change at the grocery store.

Violence in Schools

James Murphy was teaching his government class at Dartmouth High, in a quiet university town 50 miles south of Boston, when two Dartmouth students and a third teenager suddenly burst through the door. One brandished a bat, another a billy club, and the third a hunting knife. When they asked for Shawn Pina, Jason Robinson made the fatal mistake of asking why they wanted him. When Murphy saw one go after Robinson with the bat, he wrestled the assailant to the floor. Another plunged his knife into Robinson's stomach, killing him. (Toch 1993)

Many U.S. schools have deteriorated to the point that basic safety is an issue, putting students' lives at risk, a condition that only a few years back would have been unimaginable. Consequently, in some schools uniformed guards have become a fixture, while in others students can gain entrance only after passing through metal detectors. Some schools even supplement the traditional fire drills with "drive-by shooting drills" (Toch 1993; L. Grossman 1995).

Solutions: Safety, Standards, and Other Reforms

It is one thing to identify problems, quite another to find solutions for them. Let's consider solutions to the problems we just reviewed.

A Safe Learning Environment The first criterion for a good education is a safe learning environment. Granted the high rate of violence in U.S. society, some violence is bound to spill over into the schools, but basic steps can be taken to minimize that spillover. Fortunately, most U.S. schools are not yet violent, and those that are can be changed. School administrators and teachers can reclaim the schools by expelling all students who threaten the welfare of others and by refusing to tolerate threats, violence, drugs, and weapons (Toby 1992).

Higher Standards A study by sociologists James Coleman and Thomas Hoffer (1987) provides helpful guidelines for improving the quality of education. They wanted to see why the test scores of students in Catholic schools run 15 to 20 percent higher than those of students in public schools. Is it because they attract better students, while the public schools have to put up with everyone? To find out, Coleman and Hoffer tested 15,000 students in public and Catholic high schools, and three years later tested them again.

Their findings? From their sophomore through their senior years, students at Catholic schools pull ahead of public school students by about a full grade in verbal and math skills. The superior test performance of students in Catholic schools, they concluded, is due not to better students, but to higher standards. Catholic schools have not watered down their curricula as have public schools. The researchers also identified parental involvement as important, that parents and teachers in Catholic schools reinforce each other's commitment to learning.

To raise standards is really to apply the principle of teacher expectations: It means that we shall expect more of students, and this should yield excellent results. To expect more of *teachers* also matches this principle. These two expectations are combined in the following Thinking Critically section, where it becomes apparent that the problem is not the ability of the students, but, rather, the educational system itself.

Thinking Critically about Social Controversy

Breaking through the Barriers: The Jaime Escalante Approach to Restructuring the Classroom

CALLED "THE BEST TEACHER in America," Jaime Escalante taught in an East Los Angeles inner-city school plagued with poverty, crime, drugs, gangs, and the usual miser-

ably low student scores. In this self-defeating environment, he taught calculus. His students scored so highly on national tests that test officials, suspecting cheating, asked his students to retake the test. They did. Again they passed—this time with even higher scores.

Escalante's school ranks fourth in the nation in the number of students who have taken and passed the Advanced Placement SAT Calculus examination. For students to even take the test, they must complete algebra I, geometry, algebra II, trigonometry or math analysis, and calculus for first-year college and/or calculus for second-year college.

How did Escalante overcome such odds? His success is *not* due to a recruitment of the brightest students. Students' poor academic performance does not stand in the way of being admitted to the math program. The *only* requirement is an interest in math. What did Escalante do right, and what can we learn from his approach?

"Success starts with attitude" could be Escalante's motto. Few Latino students were taking math. Most were tracked into craft classes where they made jewelry and birdhouses. "Our kids are just as talented as anyone else. They just need the opportunity to show it. And for that, they must be motivated," he said. "They just don't think about becoming scientists or engineers."

Here are the keys to what Escalante accomplished. First, teaching and learning can't take place unless there is discipline. For that the teachers, not gangs, must control the classroom. Second, the students must believe in themselves. The teacher must inspire students with the idea that they *can* learn. (Remember teacher expectations.) Third, the students must be motivated to perform, in this case to see learning as a way out of the barrio, the path to good jobs.

Escalante uses a team approach. He has his students think of themselves as a team, of him as the coach, and the national exams as a sort of Olympics for which they are preparing. To stimulate team identity, the students wear team jackets, caps, and T-shirts with logos that identify them as part of the team. Before class, his students do "warmups" (hand clapping and foot stomping to a rock song).

His team has practice schedules as rigorous as a championship football team. Students must sign a contract that binds them to participate in the summer program he has developed, to complete the daily homework, and to attend Saturday morning and after-school study sessions. To get in his class, even the students' parents have to sign the contract. To keep before his students the principle that self-discipline pays off, Escalante covers his room with posters of sports figures in action—Jerry West, Magic Johnson, Michael Jordan, and Babe Ruth.

"How have I been successful with students from such backgrounds?" he asks. "Very simple. I use a time-

To say that today's school-children can't learn as well as previous schoolchildren is a case of blaming the victim. As discussed in the text, Jaime Escalante (shown here) demonstrated that teachers can motivate even highly deprived students to study hard and to excel in learning. His experience challenges us to rethink our approach to education.

honored tradition—hard work, lots of it, for teacher and student alike."

The following statement helps us understand how Escalante challenges his students to think of what is possible in life, instead of problems that destroy the possible:

> The first day when these kids walk into my room, I have a bunch of names of schools and colleges on the chalkboard. I ask each student to memorize one. The next day I pick one kid and ask, "What school did you pick?" He says USC or UCLA or Stanford, MIT, Colgate, and so on. So I say, "Okay, keep that in mind. I'm going to bring in somebody who'll be talking about the schools."

Escalante then has a college adviser talk to the class. But more than this, he also has arranged foundation money to help the students get to the colleges of their choice.

The sociological point is that the problem was *not* the ability of the students. Their failure to do well in school was not due to something *within* them. The problem was the *system*, the way classroom instruction is arranged. When Escalante changed the system of instruction, both attitudes and performance changed. Escalante makes this very point—that student performance does not depend on the charismatic personality of a single person, but on how we structure the learning setting.

For Your Consideration

What principles discussed in this or earlier chapters did Escalante apply? What changes do you think we can make in education to bring about similar results all over the country?

Sources: Based on Barry 1989; Meek 1989; Escalante and Dirmann 1990; Hilliard 1991.

RELIGION: ESTABLISHING MEANING

Let's look at the main characteristics of a second significant social institution.

▶ What Is Religion?

Sociologists who do research on religion analyze the relationship between society and religion and study the role that religion plays in people's lives. They do not seek to make value judgments about religious beliefs. Nor is their goal to verify or disprove anyone's faith. As mentioned in Chapter 1, sociologists have no tools for deciding that one course of action is more moral than another, much less that one religion is "the" correct one. Religion is a matter of faith; sociologists deal with empirical matters, things they can observe or measure. Thus sociologists can analyze how religion is related to stratification systems, measure the extent to which people are religious, and study the effects of religious beliefs and practices on people's lives. Unlike theologians, however, they cannot evaluate the truth of a religion's teachings.

In 1912 Emile Durkheim published an influential book, *The Elementary Forms of the Religious Life*, in which he tried to identify the elements common to all religions. After surveying religions around the world, Durkheim discovered no specific belief or practice that they all shared. He did find, however, that all religions, regardless of their name or teaching, separate the sacred from the profane. By **sacred,** Durkheim referred to aspects of life having to do with the supernatural that inspire awe, reverence, deep respect, even fear. By **profane,** he meant aspects of life that are not concerned with religion or religious purposes but are, instead, part of the ordinary aspects of everyday life. Durkheim also found that all religions develop a community around their practices and beliefs. He (1912/1965) concluded:

> A religion is a unified system of beliefs and practices relative to sacred things, that is to say, things set apart and forbidden—beliefs and practices which unite into one single moral community called a Church, all those who adhere to them.

Thus, Durkheim said, a **religion** is defined by three elements:

1 *Beliefs* that some things are sacred (forbidden, set off from the profane)

2 *Practice* (rituals) based on the things considered sacred

3 A *moral community* (a church) resulting from a group's beliefs and practices

Durkheim used the word **church** in an unusual sense, to refer to any "moral community" centered on beliefs and practices regarding the sacred. In Durkheim's sense, *church* refers to Buddhists bowing before a shrine, Hindus dipping in the Ganges River, and Confucianists offering food to their ancestors. Similarly, the term *moral community* does not imply morality in the sense familiar to most of us. A moral community is simply people united by their religious practices—and that would include Aztec priests who each day gathered around an altar to pluck out the beating heart of a virgin.

To better understand the sociological approach to religion, let's see what pictures emerge when we apply the three theoretical perspectives.

The Functionalist Perspective

Functionalists stress that religion is universal because it meets basic human needs. Let's look at some of the functions—and dysfunctions—of religion.

From his review of world religions, Durkheim concluded that all religions have beliefs, practices, and a moral community. Part of Hindu belief is that the Ganges is a holy river and bathing in it imparts spiritual benefits. Each year, millions of Hindus participate in this rite of ablution (purification).

Functions of Religion

Around the world, religions provide answers to perplexing questions about ultimate meaning—such as the purpose of life, why people suffer, and the existence of an afterlife. Religion fosters social solidarity by uniting believers into a community that shares values and perspectives ("we Jews," "we Christians," "we Muslims"). The religious rituals that surround marriage, for example, link the bride and groom with a broader community that wishes them well. So do other religious rituals, such as those that celebrate birth and mourn death.

The teachings of religion help people adjust to life's problems and provide guidelines for daily life. Six of the Ten Commandments, for example, contain warnings about lying, stealing, adultery, and how to get along with parents, employers, and neighbors. Religion also can help people adapt to new environments. For example, immigrants find the customs of a new land confusing. By keeping their native language alive and preserving familiar rituals and teachings,

349

Religion can promote social change, as was evident with the U.S. civil rights movement in the 1950s and 1960s. The foremost leader of this movement was Dr. Martin Luther King, Jr., a Baptist minister, shown in this 1963 photo making a speech in Washington, D.C. King's repetition of the phrase "I have a dream" helped to make this speech memorable. He was referring to his dream of the end of racial discrimination, when "all God's children" would live in harmony and peace. Although King was assassinated on April 4, 1968, his dream lives on in the hearts of many.

religion provides continuity with the immigrants' cultural past.

Just as education instills the value of patriotism, so do most religions. The most obvious example is the U.S. flag so prominently displayed in many churches. For its part, governments reciprocate by supporting God—as witnessed by the inaugural speeches of U.S. presidents, who invariably ask God to bless the nation.

Although religion is often so bound up with the prevailing social order that it resists social change, occasionally religion spearheads change. In the 1960s, for example, the civil rights movement, which fought to desegregate public facilities and abolish racial discrimination at southern polls, was led by religious leaders, especially leaders of African-American churches such as Martin Luther King, Jr. Churches also served as centers at which demonstrators were trained and rallies were organized (Jones 1992).

Dysfunctions of Religion

Functionalists also examine ways in which religion can be *dysfunctional*, that is, how it can bring harmful results. Two main dysfunctions are war and religious persecution.

War History is filled with accounts of wars based on religion—commingled with politics. Between the eleventh and fourteenth centuries, for example, Christian monarchs conducted nine bloody Crusades in an attempt to wrest control of the Holy Land from the Muslims. Unfortunately, such wars are not just a relic of the past. Even in recent years we have seen Protestants and Catholics kill one another in Northern Ireland, while Jews and Muslims in Israel and Christians and Muslims in Bosnia have done the same thing.

Religion as Justification for Persecution Beginning in the 1200s and continuing into the 1800s, in what has become known as the Inquisition, special commissions of the Roman Catholic church tortured women to elicit confessions that they were witches and then burned them at the stake. In 1692, Protestant leaders in Salem, Massachusetts, drowned women who were accused of being witches. (The last execution for witchcraft was in Scotland in 1722 [Bridgwater 1953].) Similarly, it seems fair to say that the Aztec religion had its dysfunctions—at least for the virgins offered to appease angry gods. In short, religion has been used to justify oppression and any number of brutal acts.

One of the most infamous examples of the dysfunction of religion is the Spanish Inquisition. Begun in 1478 under King Ferdinand and Queen Isabella, this Inquisition was not ended until 1820. With its liberal use of torture to elicit confessions of heresy, no Spaniard was safe.

The Symbolic Interactionist Perspective

Symbolic interactionists focus on the meanings that people give their experiences, especially how they use symbols. Let's apply this perspective to religious symbols, rituals, and beliefs to see how they help forge a community of like-minded people.

Religious Symbols

Suppose that it is about two thousand years ago and you have just joined a new religion. You have come to believe that a recently crucified Jew named Jesus is the Messiah, the Lamb of God offered for your sins. The Roman leaders are persecuting the followers of Jesus. They hate your

religion because you and your fellow believers will not acknowledge Caesar as God.

Christians are few in number, and you are eager to have fellowship with other believers. But how can you tell who is a believer? Spies are all over. The government has sworn to destroy this new religion, and you do not relish the thought of being fed to lions in the Coliseum.

You use a simple technique. While talking with a stranger, as though doodling absentmindedly in the sand or dust, you casually trace out the outline of a fish. Only fellow believers know the hidden symbolism—that, taken together, the first letter of the words in the Greek sentence "Jesus (is) Christ the Son of God" spell the Greek word for *fish*. If the other person gives no response, you rub out the outline and continue the interaction as normal. If there is a response, you eagerly talk about your new faith.

All religions use symbols to provide identity and social solidarity for their members. For Muslims, the primary symbol is the crescent moon and star, for Jews the Star of David, for Christians the cross. For members, these are not ordinary symbols, but sacred symbols that evoke feelings of awe and reverence. In Durkheim's terms, religions use symbols to specify what is sacred and to separate the sacred from the profane.

A symbol is a condensed way of communicating. Worn by a fundamentalist Christian, for example, the cross says, "I am a follower of Jesus Christ. I believe that He is the Messiah, the promised Son of God, that He loves me, that He died to take away my sins, that He rose from the dead and is going to return to earth, and that through Him I will receive eternal life."

That is a lot to pack into one symbol—and it is only part of what the symbol means to a fundamentalist believer. To people in other traditions of Christianity, the cross conveys somewhat different meanings—but to all Christians the cross is a shorthand way of expressing many meanings. So it is also with the Star of David, the crescent moon and star, the cow (expressing to Hindus the unity of all living things), and the various symbols of the world's many other religions.

Rituals

Rituals, ceremonies or repetitive practices, are also symbols that help unite people into a moral community. Some rituals, such as the bar mitzvah of Jewish

Symbolic interactionists stress that a basic characteristic of humans is that they attach meaning to objects and events and then use representations of those objects or events to communicate with one another. Some religious symbols are used to communicate feelings of awe and reverence. Michelangelo's Pietà, depicting Mary tenderly holding her son Jesus after his crucifixion, is one of the most acclaimed such symbols in the Western world, admired for its beauty by believers and nonbelievers alike.

boys and Holy Communion of Christians, are designed to create in the devout a feeling of closeness with God and unity with one another. Rituals include kneeling and praying at set times, bowing, crossing oneself, singing, lighting candles and incense, a liturgy, Scripture readings, processions, baptisms, weddings, funerals, and so on.

Beliefs

Symbols, including rituals, develop from beliefs. The belief may be vague ("God is") or highly specific ("God wants us to prostrate ourselves and face Mecca five times each day"). Religious beliefs include not only *values* (what is considered good and desirable in

life—how we ought to live) but also a **cosmology,** a unified picture of the world. For example, the Jewish, Christian, and Muslim belief that there is only one God, the creator of the universe, who is concerned about the actions of humans and who will hold us accountable for what we do, is a cosmology. It presents a unifying picture of the universe.

Religious Experience

The term **religious experience** refers to a sudden awareness of the supernatural or a feeling of coming in contact with God. Some people undergo a mild version, such as feeling closer to God when they look at a mountain or listen to a certain piece of music. Others report a life-transforming experience; for example, St. Francis of Assisi became aware of God's presence in every living thing.

Some Protestants use the term **born again** to describe people who have undergone such a life-transforming religious experience. These people say they came to the realization that they had sinned, that Jesus had died for their sins, and that God wants them to live a new life. Henceforth their worlds become transformed, they look forward to the Resurrection and a new life in heaven, and they see relationships with spouses, parents, children, and even bosses in a new light. They also report a need to make changes in how they interact with others, so that their lives reflect their new, personal commitment to Jesus as their "Savior and Lord." They describe a feeling of beginning life again, hence the term *born again.*

The Conflict Perspective

As we saw earlier, conflict theorists examine how education supports the status quo. They do the same in their analysis of religion.

Opium of the People

In general, conflict theorists are highly critical of religion. Karl Marx, an avowed atheist who believed that the existence of God was an impossibility, set the tone for conflict theorists with his most famous statement on this subject: "Religion is the sigh of the oppressed creature, the sentiment of a heartless world. . . . It is the opium of the people" (Marx 1844/1964). By this statement, Marx meant that oppressed workers, sighing for release from their suffering, escape

As the text explains, all major religious groups draw members from various ethnic groups and social classes. Individual congregations, however, are likely to be segregated by race, and to a great extent, by social class. These two photos are typical of worship practices in the United States.

into religion. For them, religion is like a drug that helps them forget their misery. By diverting their eyes to future happiness in a coming world, religion takes their eyes off their suffering in this one, thereby greatly reducing the possibility that they will rebel against their oppressors.

A Legitimation of Social Inequalities

Just as they do with education, conflict theorists examine how religion legitimates the social inequalities of society. By this, they mean that religion teaches that the existing social arrangements of a society represent what God desires. For example, during the Middle Ages Christian theologians decreed the "divine right of kings." This doctrine meant that God determined who would become king and set him on the throne. The king ruled in God's place, and it was the duty of a king's subjects to be loyal to him (and to pay their taxes). To disobey the king was to disobey God.

In what is perhaps the supreme technique of legitimating the social order, going even a step further than the "divine right of kings," the religion of ancient Egypt held that the Pharaoh was a god. The Emperor of Japan was similarly declared divine. If this were so, who could even question his decisions? How many of today's politicians would give their right arm for such a religious teaching!

Conflict theorists point to many other examples of how religion legitimates the social order. One of the more remarkable took place in the decades before the American Civil War. Southern ministers used Scripture to defend slavery, saying that it was God's

will—while northern ministers legitimated *their* region's social structure and used Scripture to denounce slavery as evil (Ernst 1988; Nauta 1993; White 1995). In India, Hinduism supports the caste system by teaching that an individual who tries to change caste will come back in the next life as a member of a lower caste—or even as an animal.

Religion and the Spirit of Capitalism

Max Weber disagreed with the conflict perspective that religion impedes social change by encouraging people to focus on the afterlife. In contrast, Weber saw religion's focus on the afterlife as a source of profound social change.

Like Marx, Weber personally observed the European countries industrialize. Weber was intrigued with the question of why some societies embraced capitalism, while others clung to their traditional ways. As he explored this problem, he concluded that religion held the key to **modernization**—the transformation of traditional societies into industrial societies.

To explain his conclusions, Weber wrote *The Protestant Ethic and the Spirit of Capitalism* (1904–1905/1958). He said that

1 Capitalism is not just a superficial change. Rather, capitalism represents a fundamentally different way of thinking about work and money. Traditionally, people worked just enough to meet their

basic needs, and it was a radical departure to accumulate a surplus, capital. Yet people's ideas changed so much that some even came to consider it a duty to invest money in order to make profits, which, in turn, they reinvested to make more profits. Weber called this new approach to work and money **the spirit of capitalism.**

2 Why did the spirit of capitalism develop in Europe, and not, for example, in China or India, where the people had similar intelligence, material resources, education, and so on? According to Weber, *religion was the key.* The religions of China and India, and indeed Roman Catholicism in Europe, encouraged a traditional approach to life, not thrift and investment. Capitalism appeared when Protestantism came on the scene.

3 What was different about Protestantism, especially Calvinism? John Calvin taught that God had predestined some people to heaven, others to hell, and that in this life you couldn't know where you were headed. People could depend neither on church membership nor on feelings about their relationship with God to know they were saved.

4 This doctrine made people anxious. "Am I predestined to hell or to heaven?" Calvinists wondered. As they wrestled with this question, they concluded that church members had a duty to prove that they were God's elect, and to live as though they were predestined to heaven—for good works were a demonstration of salvation.

5 This conclusion motivated Calvinists to lead highly moral lives *and* to work hard, to not waste time, and to be frugal—for idleness and needless spending were signs of worldliness. Weber called this self-denying approach to life **the Protestant ethic.**

6 The hard work, combined with spending money only on necessities (with luxuries narrowly defined), meant they had money left over. This accumulated capital, in turn, since it couldn't be spent, was invested—which led to a surge in production.

7 Thus, a change in religion (from Catholicism to Protestantism, especially Calvinism) led to a fundamental change in thought and behavior (the *Protestant ethic*). The result was the *spirit of capitalism*. Thus capitalism originated in Europe, and not in places where religion did not encourage capitalism's essential elements: the accumulation of capital through frugality and hard work, and its investment and reinvestment.

At this point in history, the Protestant ethic and the spirit of capitalism are not confined to any specific religion or even part of the world. Rather, they have become cultural traits that have spread to societies around the world (Greeley 1964; Yinger 1970). U.S. Catholics have about the same approach to life as do U.S. Protestants, and the Southeast Asian nations (Hong Kong, Japan, Malaysia, Singapore, South Korea, and Taiwan) have embraced capitalism—not exactly Protestant countries (Levy 1992).

Types of Religious Groups

Sociologists have identified four types of religious groups: cult, sect, church, and ecclesia. The typology presented here is a modification of analyses by sociologists Ernst Troeltsch (1931), Liston Pope (1942), and Benton Johnson (1963). Figure 13.3 illustrates the relationship between each of these four types of religious groups.

Cult

The word *cult* conjures up bizarre images—shaven heads, weird music, brainwashing—even images of ritual murder may come to mind. Cults, however, are not necessarily weird, and few practice "brainwashing" or bizarre rituals. In fact, *all religions began as cults* (R. Stark 1989). A **cult** is simply a new or different religion, whose teaching and practices put it at odds with the dominant culture and religion. Cults often begin with the appearance of a **charismatic leader,** an individual who inspires people because he or she seems to have extraordinary qualities. **Charisma** refers to an outstanding gift or an exceptional quality. Finding something highly appealing about such an individual, people feel drawn to both the person and the message.

The most popular religion in the world today began as a cult. Its handful of followers believed that an unschooled carpenter who preached in remote villages in a backwater country was the Son of God, that he was killed and came back to life. Those beliefs made the early Christians a cult, setting them apart from the rest of their society. Persecuted by both religious and political authorities, these early believers clung to one another for support, many cutting off associations with their unbelieving families and friends. To others, the early Christians must have seemed deluded and brainwashed.

Most cults fail. Not many people believe the new message, and the cult fades into obscurity. If large numbers of people become followers of the religion,

FIGURE 13.3

A Cult–Sect–Church–Ecclesia Continuum

Characteristics of the Group
1. Number of members
2. Wealth of organization
3. Wealth of members ("worldly success")
4. Formal training of clergy

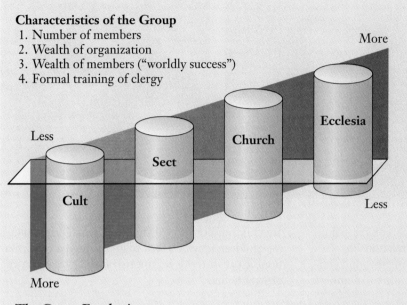

The Group Emphasizes
1. The need to reject society (the culture is a threat to true religion)
2. That it is rejected by society (the group feels hostility)
3. Hostility toward other religions
4. Hostility from other religions
5. Personal salvation
6. Emotional expression of religious beliefs
7. Revelation (God speaks directly to people)
8. God's direct intervention in people's lives (such as providing guidance or healing)
9. A duty to spread the message (evangelism)
10. A literal interpretation of Scripture
11. A literal heaven and hell
12. That a conversion experience is necessary

Note: Any religious organization can be placed somewhere on this continuum, based on its having "more" or "less" of these characteristics.

Sources: Based on Troeltsch 1931; Pope 1942; Johnson 1963.

however, the new religion changes from a cult to a sect. For more information on cults, see the box on page 356.

Sect

A **sect** is larger than a cult. Its members still feel tension with the prevailing beliefs and values of the broader society, but if a sect grows, that tension fades. To appeal to the new, broader base, the sect shifts some of its doctrines, redefining matters to remove some of the rough edges that created tension between it and the rest of society. The members then become more respectable in the eyes of the majority, and they feel less hostility and little, if any, isolation. If a sect follows this course, as it grows and becomes more integrated into society it changes into a church.

Church

At this point, the religious group is highly bureaucratized—probably with national and international headquarters that give directions to the local congregations. The group's worship service is likely to have grown more sedate, with much less emphasis on personal salvation and emotional expression. Writ-

The sociological and common-sense meanings of the term cult *differ radically. Shoko Asahara of Japan, left, matches the public's image of a crazed cult leader. Asahara headed a cult that on March 20, 1995, released a nerve gas, sarin, in the Tokyo subway during rush hour. The attack left ten people dead and 4,700 injured. As the text explains, the socio-logical meaning of* cult, *in contrast, is neutral.*

ten prayers may be read before the congregation, sermons are more formal, and the relationship with God is less intense. Rather than joining through con-version—seeing the new truth—most new members are children born to existing members. When older, the children may be asked to go through a confirma-tion or bar mitzvah ceremony in order to affirm the group's beliefs.

Down-to-Earth Sociology

Heaven's Gate and Other Cults

THE NEWS MADE INSTANT head-lines around the world. Thirty-nine bodies in an exclusive San Diego neighborhood draped in purple, diamond-shaped shrouds. Some of the men had been cas-trated. No sign of a struggle.

Then followed reports of their beliefs. A spaceship was hiding be-hind the Hale-Bopp comet ready to transport them to a new life. To be beamed aboard, they had to commit suicide. For their space travels, each cult member put on new Nike sneakers. Each also packed a bag with clothing, $5 bills and quarters—and a passport.

Then there is the garbage-eat-ing Brotherhood led by a an ex-Marine who claims he is Jesus. His long-haired followers rummage through dumpsters, carefully re-moving the mold before dining on rotting scraps of the material world they so disdain. They blame their stomachaches on Satan (O'Neill 1997).

Other Messiahs have appeared. Back in the 1970s, hundreds fol-lowed Jim Jones to Guyana. More than 900 committed suicide—or were murdered. Recently, 74 members of the Solar Temple in Switzerland, France, and Canada arranged themselves in the shape of a cross and burned themselves to death. They believed they would be transported to the star Sirius (Lacayo 1997).

Why would anyone fall for such messages? As this chapter's subti-tle indicates, providing *meaning* to life lies at the center of reli-gion. Always there are unsatisfied spiritual longings. And with to-day's rapid social change our tra-ditional meanings are constantly challenged and sometimes up-rooted. Most significantly, the teachings take place within a com-munity of people who fill needs of belonging. Members become isolated, cut off from family and friends who would provide a bal-ancing perspective on reality. Grad-ually the bizarreness of the views wear off as they are affirmed by people one likes and respects. Cult members become "insiders" to a secret message beyond the grasp of ordinary people.

Heaven's Gate, and its many counterparts throughout the world, matches the public's image of cults—bizarre people with strange teachings whose followers act in repugnant ways. As this chapter stresses, however, the *sociological* meaning of cult is different. All new religions begin as cults. Some grow and become sects. Others even develop into churches and ecclesias.

None that do so, however, have mass suicide as part of their mes-sage. That sort of eliminates the possibility of moving up the con-tinuum illustrated on page 355.

Ecclesia

Finally, some groups become so well integrated into a culture, and so strongly allied with their government, that it is difficult to tell where one leaves off and the other takes over. In these state religions, also called **ecclesia,** the government and religion work together to try to shape society. There is no recruitment of members, for citizenship makes everyone a member. The majority of the society, however, may belong to the religion in name only. The religion is part of cultural identification, not an eye-opening experience. In Sweden, for example, all citizens in the 1860s had to memorize Luther's *Small Catechism* and be tested on it yearly (Anderson 1995). Today, Lutheranism is still the state religion, but most Swedes come to church only for baptisms, marriages, and funerals.

Variations in Patterns

Obviously, not all religious groups go through all these stages—from cult to sect to church to ecclesia. Some die out because they fail to attract enough members. Others, such as the Amish, remain sects. And, as is evident from the few countries that have state religions, very few religions ever become ecclesias.

In addition, these classifications are not perfectly matched in the real world. For example, although the Amish are a sect, they place little or no emphasis on recruiting others. The early Quakers, another sect, shied away from emotional expressions of their beliefs. They would quietly meditate in church, with no one speaking, until God gave someone a message to share with others. Finally, some groups that become churches may retain a few characteristics of sects, such as an emphasis on evangelism or a personal relationship with God.

Although all religions began as cults, not all varieties of a particular religion have done so. For example, some denominations—"brand names" within a major religion, such as Methodism or Reform Judaism—may begin as splinter groups. A large group within a church may disagree with some aspects of the church's teachings (not its major message) and break away to form its own organization. An example is the Southern Baptist Convention, formed in 1845 to defend the right to own slaves (Ernst 1988; Nauta 1993; White 1995).

Characteristics of Religion in the United States

Although many think religion is less important to Americans than it used to be, the growth in religious

---

Table 13.1

Growth in Religious Membership: The Percentage of Americans Who Belong to a Church or Synagogue

	Percentage Who Claim Membership
1776	17%
1860	37%
1890	45%
1926	58%
1975	71%
1994	68%

Sources: Finke 1992; *Statistical Abstract* 1996:Table 88.

---

membership does not support such an assumption. As Table 13.1 shows, the proportion of Americans who belong to a church or synagogue is now *four* times higher than it was when the country was founded. Ninety-four percent of Americans believe there is a God, and 77 percent believe there is a heaven. On any given weekend, two of every five Americans attend a church or synagogue (Woodward 1989; Gallup 1990; *Statistical Abstract* 1996:Table 88).

Characteristics of Members

Let's look at the characteristics of the 68 percent of Americans who belong to a church or synagogue.

Region Membership is not evenly distributed around the country. As shown on Table 13.2, membership is highest in the South, followed by the Midwest and the East. Perhaps membership is so much lower in the West because the West both is the newest region in the nation and has the highest net

---

Table 13.2

Church and Synagogue Membership, Percentage of Population by Region

South	75%
Midwest	72%
East	68%
West	55%

Source: Statistical Abstract 1996:Table 88.

migration. If so, when its residents have put down firmer roots, the West's proportion of religious membership will increase.

Social Class Religion in the United States is stratified by social class. As Figure 13.4 illustrates, each religious group draws members from all social classes, but some are "top-heavy" and others "bottom-heavy." The most top-heavy are the Episcopalians and Jews, the most bottom-heavy the Baptists and Evangelicals. This figure is further confirmation that churchlike groups tend to appeal more to the successful, the more sectlike to the less successful.

Race and Ethnicity All major religious organizations draw from the nation's various racial and ethnic groups. Like social class, however, race and ethnicity tend to cluster. People of Latino or Irish descent are likely to be Roman Catholics, those of Greek origin to belong to the Greek Orthodox church. African Americans are likely to be Protestants, more specifically Baptists, or to belong to fundamentalist sects.

Although many churches are integrated, it is not without cause that Sunday morning between 10 and 11 A.M. has been called "the most segregated hour in the United States." African Americans tend to belong to African-American churches, while most whites see only whites in theirs. The segregation of churches is based not on law, but on custom.

Table 13.3

Age and Church or Synagogue Membership

Age	Membership
18–29	61%
30–49	65%
50+	77%

Source: Statistical Abstract 1996:Table 88.

Age As shown on Table 13.3, the chances that an American belongs to a church or synagogue increase with age. Possibly this is because people become more concerned about an afterlife as they age. Another explanation is that membership is seen as part of the adult role, and as people marry, become parents, or become more established, they are more likely to join.

Characteristics of Religious Groups

Let's examine major characteristics of the religious organizations in the United States.

Diversity With its quarter of a million congregations and hundreds of denominations, the United States does not even come close to being dominated

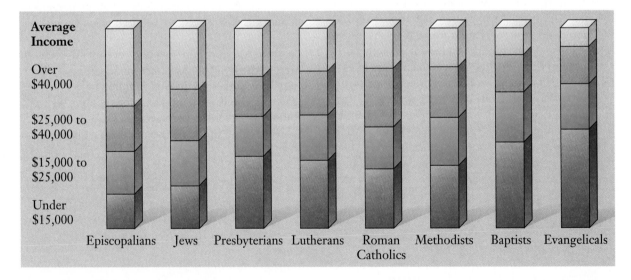

Source: Compiled from data in *Gallup Opinion Index* 1987:20–27, 29.

FIGURE 13.4
Income and Religious Affiliation

by any single religious group (*Statistical Abstract* 1995:Table 85). Table 13.4 illustrates some of this remarkable diversity, as does the box on U.S. Islam on page 361.

Competition and Recruitment The many religious groups of the United States compete for clients. The groups even advertise in the Yellow Pages of the telephone directory and insert appealing advertising—under the guise of news—in the religious section of the Saturday or Sunday edition of the local newspapers.

Table 13.4

U.S. Churches with at Least 100,000 Members

Roman Catholic	59,860,000
Baptist	36,400,000
Methodist	13,560,000
Pentecostal	10,020,000
Lutheran	8,350,000
Islam	5,500,000
Church of God in Christ	5,000,000
Mormon	4,670,000
Jews	4,300,000
Presbyterian	4,275,000
Eastern Orthodox	3,490,000
Episcopal Church	2,500,000
Reformed Churches	2,080,000
Churches of Christ	1,650,000
Christian Churches	1,070,000
Disciples of Christ	960,000
Jehovah's Witnesses	930,000
Hindu	910,000
Adventist	790,000
Church of the Nazarene	590,000
Community Churches	590,000
Salvation Army	450,000
Christian and Missionary Alliance	300,000
Churches of God	260,000
Mennonite	260,000
Buddhist	230,000
Evangelical Free Church	230,000
Unitarian Universalist	140,000
Baha'i Faith	130,000
Christian Congregation	110,000

Source: World Almanac and Book of Facts 1994:726–727; 1996:644–645.

Fundamentalist Revival The fundamentalist churches are undergoing a revival. They teach that the Bible is literally true and that salvation comes only through a personal relationship with Jesus Christ. They also decry what they see as the permissiveness of U.S. culture: sex on television and in movies, abortion, corruption in public office, premarital pregnancy, cohabitation, and drugs. Their answer to these problems is firm, simple, and direct: people whose hearts are changed through religious conversion will change their lives. The approach of the mainstream churches, which offer a remote God and a corresponding lack of emotional involvement, fails to meet the basic religious needs of large numbers of Americans. Consequently, as Figure 13.5 shows, the mainstream churches have been losing members, while the fundamentalists have been gaining. The exception is the Roman Catholics, whose growth is primarily due to heavy immigration from Catholic countries.

The Electronic Church What began as a ministry to shut-ins and those who do not belong to a church has blossomed into its own type of church. Its preachers, called "televangelists," reach millions of viewers and raise millions of dollars. Some of its most famous ministries are those of Robert Schuler (the "Crystal Cathedral") and Pat Robertson (the 700 Club).

An interesting combination of local congregations and the electronic church has emerged. Some independent fundamentalist groups now subscribe to the electronic church. They pay a fee in return for having "name" ministers piped "live" into their local congregation. They build services around these electronic messages, supplementing them with songs and adding other "local touches."

Secularization and the Splintering of U.S. Churches

As the model, fashionably slender, paused before the head table of African-American community leaders, her gold necklace glimmering above the low-cut bodice of her emerald-green dress, the hostess, a member of the Church of God in Christ, said, "It's now OK to wear more revealing clothes—as long as it's done in good taste." Then she added, "You couldn't do this when I was a girl, but now it's OK—and you can still worship God." (Author's files)

With increased immigration from Muslim countries, Islam has become more visible in the United States. Shown here are adherents praying on New York City's Madison Avenue during the Muslim Day Parade.

When I heard these words, I grabbed a napkin and quickly jotted them down, my sociological imagination stirred at their deep implication. As strange as it may seem, this simple event pinpoints the essence of why the Christian churches in the United States have splintered. Let's see how that could possibly be.

The simplest answer to why Christians don't have just one church, or at most several, instead of the hundreds of sects and denominations that dot the U.S. landscape, is disagreements about doctrine (church teaching). As theologian and sociologist Richard Niebuhr pointed out, however, there are many ways of settling doctrinal disputes besides splin-

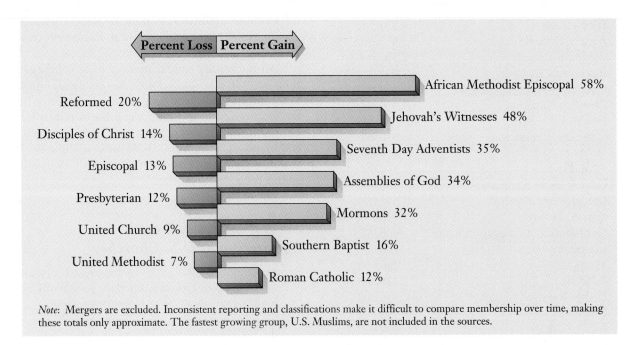

Percent Loss | Percent Gain

African Methodist Episcopal 58%

Reformed 20%

Jehovah's Witnesses 48%

Disciples of Christ 14%

Seventh Day Adventists 35%

Episcopal 13%

Assemblies of God 34%

Presbyterian 12%

Mormons 32%

United Church 9%

Southern Baptist 16%

United Methodist 7%

Roman Catholic 12%

Note: Mergers are excluded. Inconsistent reporting and classifications make it difficult to compare membership over time, making these totals only approximate. The fastest growing group, U.S. Muslims, are not included in the sources.

Sources: Yearbook of American and Canadian Churches 1993:Table 2; *Statistical Abstract* 1985:Table 74; 1995:Table 84.

FIGURE 13.5

U.S. Churches: Gains and Losses in Ten Years

Our Multicultural Society

The New Neighbor: Islam in the United States

IT IS SUNDAY morning, and across the nation Americans are on their way to church. Instead of going into a Baptist or a Roman Catholic church or a Jewish synagogue, many Americans now enter mosques. In a scene that is growing increasingly familiar, they take off their shoes, face Mecca, and kneel with their faces to the floor.

Called by some the fastest growing religion in the United States—perhaps numbering 6 million—Islam is making its presence felt. Islam's growth is fueled by two main sources. The primary source is the millions of immigrants from the Middle East and Asia who have arrived in the United States since the 1980s. Like the immigrants before them, these refugees from Muslim countries brought their religion as part of their culture. Slightly more than half of America's Muslims are foreign-born immigrants from Muslim countries (Brooke 1995). The second source is growth among African Americans. Although believers represent a cross-section of African Americans, the call of Islam is heard most loudly in the inner city (Peart 1993).

The appeal of Islam to African Americans is the message of

black pride, self-improvement, and black power. Although U.S. Muslims are divided among about twenty groups, the appeal is similar: morality (no drugs, crime, or extramarital sex), respect for women, and black empowerment. Among all groups, modest clothing is required. Among some, ultraconservative codes are in effect: men and women sit separately in public, women wear robes that cover them from head to toe, and one-on-one dating is prohibited (Tapia 1994). Many men embrace the authority that Islam ascribes to them. For many, both men and women, Islam is a way to connect with African roots.

For many Americans, Louis Farrakhan is synonymous with U.S. Islam. Although he is the most visible and vocal Muslim leader, the group he heads, the Nation of Islam, has only about 10,000 members (Brooke 1995). The other 97 percent of Black Muslims belong to other organizations. One, headed by W. Dean Mohammed, claims over a million members.

Just as their organizations are diverse, so their opinions are wide-ranging. On race, for example, they vary from the idea that

the races are equal to the belief that African Americans are superior and whites are devils. Similarly, some groups stress black separatism, while others emphasize the need to enter the U.S. mainstream and identify with the ideas of the country's founding fathers.

Alarmed that Islam has gained so many converts, some African-American Christians have begun a counterattack. They hold Muslim Awareness seminars in order to warn Christians away from Islam (Tapia 1994). A former Black Muslim, who is now a Christian evangelist and sees it his duty to counter Islam, says the difference is grace. "Islam is a works-oriented religion, but Christianity is built on God's grace in Jesus."

"His is just a slave religion," retort some Muslims.

In spite of tension and confrontation, it is apparent that the Muslim presence is not temporary, that the face of U.S. religion is being fundamentally altered. Mosques are taking their place in the midst of churches and synagogues, a true sign of a multicultural society.

tering off and forming another religious organization. Niebuhr (1929) suggested that the answer lies more in *social* change than in *religious* conflict.

The explanation goes like this. As noted earlier, when a sect becomes more churchlike, tension between it and the main culture lessens. Quite likely, its founders and first members were poor, or at least not very successful in worldly pursuits. Feeling estranged from their general culture, they received a good part of their identity from their religion. Their

services and customs stressed differences between their values and those of the dominant culture. Typically, their religion also stressed the joys of the coming afterlife, when they would be able to escape from their present pain.

As time passes, the group's values—such as frugality and the avoidance of gambling, alcohol, and drugs—help later generations become successful. As they attain more education and become more middle class, they grow more respectable in the eyes of society. They no longer experience the alienation felt by the founders of their group. Life's burdens don't seem as heavy, and the need for relief through an afterlife doesn't seem as pressing. Similarly, the pleasures of the world no longer appear as threatening to the "true" belief. Then, as in the preceding example of the fashion show, there follows an attempt to harmonize religious beliefs with their changing orientation to the culture.

This process is called the **secularization of religion**—a group shifting its focus from spiritual matters to the affairs of this world. (The term *secular* means "belonging to the world and its affairs.") Such accommodation with the secular culture, however, displeases the group's members who have had less worldly success. They still feel estranged from the broader culture. For them, tension and hostility continue to be real. They see secularization as giving up the group's fundamental truths, a "selling out" to the secular world. After futile attempts to bring the group back to its senses, they break away, forming a sect that once again stresses its differences from the world, the need for more personal, emotional religious experiences, and salvation from the pain of living in this world. The cycle then repeats itself.

The secularization of religion also occurs on a much broader scale. As societies *modernize* (industrialize, urbanize, develop mass education, adopt advanced technology, and transform from *Gemeinschaft* to *Gesellschaft*), people depend much less on religious explanations for the problems of life (Berger 1967). Even religious leaders may turn to answers provided by sociology, philosophy, psychology, science, medicine, and so on. In some churches, sermons are based on novels and academic studies instead of the Bible, psychological encounter groups replace repentance and prayer, and "sin" is redefined as "less than optimum choices." Abandoning its religious beliefs, the church nonetheless retains its rituals, which some now find devoid of the meaning they once held. This

dissatisfaction with the accommodation to the general culture, in turn, provides fertile ground for the formation of splinter groups.

The Future of Religion

Despite secularization, religion thrives in even the most advanced scientific nations. Humans are inquiring creatures, and one of the questions people develop as they reflect on life is the purpose of it all. Why are we born? Is there an afterlife? If so, where are we going? Out of these concerns arises this question: If there is a God, what does God want of us in this life? Does God have a preference about how we should live?

Science, including sociology, cannot answer such questions. By its very nature, science cannot tell us about four main concerns that many people have: (1) the existence of God, (2) the purpose of life, (3) the existence of an afterlife, and (4) morality. About the first, science has nothing to say (no test tube has either isolated God or refuted God's existence). For the second, while science can provide a definition of life and describe the characteristics of living organisms, it has nothing to say about ultimate purpose. For the third, science can offer no information, for it has no tests to prove or disprove a "hereafter." For the fourth, science can demonstrate the consequences of behavior but not the moral superiority of one action compared with another. This means that science cannot even prove that loving your family and neighbor is superior to hurting and killing them. It can describe death and compute consequences, but it cannot dictate the *moral* superiority of any action, even in such an extreme example.

There is no doubt that religion will last as long as humanity lasts—for what could replace it? And if something did, and answered such questions, would it not be religion under another name?

Summary and Review

Today's Credential Society

What is a credential society, and how did it develop?

A **credential society** is one in which employers use diplomas and degrees to determine who is eligible for a job. One reason that credentialism developed is that large, anonymous societies lack the personal knowledge common to smaller groups; educational certification provides evidence of a person's ability. Pp. 338–339.

Education in Global Perspective

How does education compare in the three worlds of development?

In general, formal education reflects a nation's economy. Education is extensive in the Most Industrialized Nations. It undergoes vast change in the Industrializing Nations, and is very spotty in the Least Industrialized Nations. Japan, post-Soviet Russia, and Egypt provide examples of education in the three worlds of development. Pp. 339–341.

The Functionalist Perspective: Providing Social Benefits

What is the functionalist perspective on education?

Among the functions of education are the teaching of knowledge and skills, **cultural transmission** of values, social integration, **gatekeeping,** and **mainstreaming.** Functionalists also note that education has replaced some traditional family functions. Pp. 341–342.

The Conflict Perspective: Reproducing the Social Class Structure

What is the conflict perspective on education?

The basic view of conflict theorists is that education *reproduces the social class structure;* that is, through such mechanisms as unequal funding and operating different schools for the elite and for the masses, education reinforces a society's basic social inequalities. Pp. 342–344.

The Symbolic Interactionist Perspective: Teacher Expectations

What is the symbolic interactionist perspective on education?

Symbolic interactionists focus on face-to-face interaction. In examining what occurs in the classroom, they have found a self-fulfilling prophecy, that student performance tends to conform to teacher expectations, whether they are high or low. Pp. 344–345.

Problems in U.S. Education— and Their Solutions

What are the chief problems that face U.S. education?

In addition to violence, the major problem is mediocrity, as shown by low SAT scores, **grade inflation, social promotion,** and **functional illiteracy.** Pp. 345–346.

What are the primary solutions to these problems?

The primary solution is to restore high educational standards, which can be done only after providing basic security for students. Any solution for improving quality must be based on raising standards and expecting more of students and teachers alike. Pp. 346–348.

Religion: Establishing Meaning

What is religion?

Durkheim identified three essential characteristics of **religion:** beliefs that set the **sacred** apart from the **profane,** rituals, and a moral community (a **church**). Pp. 348–349.

The Functionalist Perspective

What are the functions and dysfunctions of religion?

Among the functions of religion are answering questions about ultimate meaning, providing social solidarity, guidelines for everyday life, adaptation, support for the government, and fostering social change. Among the dysfunctions of religion are war and religious persecution. Pp. 349–350.

The Symbolic Interactionist Perspective

What aspects of religion do symbolic interactionists study?

Symbolic interactionists focus on the meanings of religion for its followers. They examine religious symbols, **rituals,** beliefs, **religious experiences,** and the sense of community provided by religion. Pp. 351–352.

The Conflict Perspective

What aspects of religion do conflict theorists study?

Conflict theorists examine the relationship of religion to social inequalities, especially how religion is a conservative force that reinforces a society's stratification system. Pp. 352–353.

Religion and the Spirit of Capitalism

What does the spirit of capitalism have to do with religion?

Max Weber disagreed with Marx's conclusion that religion impedes social change. In contrast, Weber saw religion as a primary source of social change. He analyzed how Protestantism gave rise to **the Protestant ethic,** which stimulated what he called **the spirit of capitalism.** The result was capitalism, which transformed society. Pp. 353–354.

Types of Religious Groups

What types of religious groups are there?

Sociologists divide religious groups into cults, sects, churches, and ecclesias. All religions began as **cults.** Those that survive tend to develop into **sects** and eventually into **churches.** Sects, often led by **charismatic leaders,** are unstable. Some are perceived as a threat and are persecuted by the state. **Ecclesias,** or state religions, are rare. Pp. 354–356.

Characteristics of Religion in the United States

What are the main characteristics of religion in the United States?

Religious membership varies by region, social class, age, and race or ethnicity. Among the major characteristics are diversity, competition, a fundamentalist revival, and the electronic church. Pp. 356–359.

What is the connection between secularization of religion and the splintering of churches?

Secularization of religion, a change in a religious group's focus from spiritual matters to concerns of "this world," is the key to understanding why churches divide. Basically, as a cult or sect changes to accommodate its members' upward social class mobility, it changes into a church. Left dissatisfied, members who are not upwardly mobile tend to splinter off and form a new cult or sect, and the cycle repeats itself. Cultures permeated by religion also secularize. This, too, leaves many dissatisfied and promotes social change. Pp. 359–362.

The Future of Religion

What is the future of religion?

Although industrialization led to the secularization of culture, this did not spell the end of religion, as many social analysts assumed it would. Because science and education cannot answer questions of ultimate meaning, the existence of God or an afterlife, or provide guidelines for morality, the need for religion will remain. In any foreseeable future, religion will prosper. P. 362.

Where can I read more on this topic?

Suggested readings for this chapter are listed on pages 443–444.

Glossary

born again a term describing Christians who have undergone a life-transforming religious experience so radical that they feel they have become a "new person" (p. 352)

charisma literally, an extraordinary gift from God; more commonly, an outstanding, "magnetic" personality (p. 354)

charismatic leader literally, someone to whom God has given an extraordinary gift; more commonly, someone who exerts extraordinary appeal to a group of followers (p. 354)

church according to Durkheim, one of the three essential elements of religion—a moral community of believers (p. 349); used by other sociologists to refer to a highly bureaucratized religious organization (p. 356)

cosmology teachings or ideas that provide a unified picture of the world (p. 352)

credential society a group that uses diplomas and degrees to determine who is eligible for jobs, even though the diploma or degree may be irrelevant to the actual work (p. 338)

cult a new religion with few followers, whose teachings and practices put it at odds with the dominant culture and religion (p. 354)

cultural transmission in reference to education, the ways by which schools transmit a society's culture, especially its core values (p. 341)

ecclesia a religious group so integrated into the dominant culture that it is difficult to tell where the one begins and the other leaves off (p. 356)

functional illiterate a high school graduate who has difficulty with basic reading and math (p. 346)

gatekeeping the process by which education opens and closes doors of opportunity; another term for the social placement function of education (p. 341)

grade inflation giving higher grades for the same work; a general rise in student grades without a corresponding increase in learning or test scores (p. 346)

hidden curriculum the unwritten goals of schools, such as teaching obedience to authority and conformity to cultural norms (p. 343)

latent functions the unintended consequences of people's actions that help to keep a social system in equilibrium (p. 341)

mainstreaming helping people to become part of the mainstream of society (p. 342)

manifest functions the intended consequences of people's actions designed to help some part of a social system (p. 341)

modernization the transformation of traditional societies into industrial societies (p. 353)

profane Durkheim's term for common elements of everyday life (p. 349)

Protestant ethic Max Weber's term to describe the ideal of a self-denying highly moral life, accompanied by hard work and frugality (p. 354)

religion according to Emile Durkheim, beliefs and practices that separate the profane from the sacred and unite its adherents into a moral community (p. 349)

religious experience an awareness of the supernatural or a feeling of coming in contact with God (p. 352)

rituals ceremonies or repetitive practices; in this context, religious observances or rites, often intended to evoke a sense of awe of the sacred (p. 352)

sacred Durkheim's term for things set apart or forbidden, that inspire fear, awe, reverence, or deep respect (p. 349)

sect a group larger than a cult whose members feel substantial hostility from and toward society (p. 355)

secularization of religion the replacement of a religion's "otherworldly" concerns with concerns about "this world" (p. 362)

social placement a function of education; funneling people into a society's various positions (p. 342)

social promotion passing students to the next grade even though they have not mastered the basic materials (p. 346)

spirit of capitalism Weber's term for the desire to accumulate capital as a duty—not to spend it, but as an end in itself—and to constantly reinvest it (p. 354)

tracking the sorting of students into educational programs on the basis of real or perceived abilities (p. 342)

Sociology and the Internet

All URLs listed are current as of the printing of this book. URLs are often changed. Please check our Website http://www.abacon.com/henslin for updates.

1. Inequality in Education

This project will allow you to analyze data on the theories of education discussed in this chapter.

Go to the National Center for Educational Statistics site (http://www. ed.gov/NCES), and click on "Publications." On the new page click on "General Publications." On the general publications page, move down near the bottom and click on "Mini-Digest of Educational Statistics: (date)" where you should see a chart labeled "The Mini-Digest of Education Statistics: (date)" and an extensive list of data locations. Under "Educational Outcomes," click on "Dropouts" and print or download the figure and table you find there. Note the trends between 1970 and the present in Figure 7. Does this suggest anything to you about educational inequalities? Look at the details in Table 16. Are the trends constant through the years, or do they fluctuate greatly from year to year? Next, back up to the previous screen ("Mini-Digest . . ."), look under "Elementary and Secondary Schools," click on "Enrollment by Race and Ethnicity," and print or download Table 6. The table shows the percentage of children in school for three racial or ethnic groups. What can you conclude from the table? Look at the distribution as functionalists, conflict theorists, and symbolic interactionists might. (You might need to read again the sections in the first half of this chapter.) How would each explain the patterns revealed in the table? To continue the project, browse among other topics on the Mini-Digest page. Look for evidence of educational inequalities involving race, gender, or other meaningful variables you might discover.

On the basis of your research, write a paper on educational inequalities. Attempt to interpret each of the patterns you found by using the three theories you encountered earlier.

2. Churches, Cults, and Sects

As you have discovered, sociologists use the terms *cult* and *sect* differently from the way they are often used in the media or in everyday conversation. To begin this project, first write sociological definitions of church and sect. Now go to the Yahoo site on cyberspace religions (http://www.yahoo.com/society_and_culture/ cyberculture/religions/). (If you have trouble with this long address, go to http://www.yahoo.com and follow the path through each page.) You will see a number of links. Go through each of them and determine which are meant to be taken seriously. Of those, how many are representative of churches? For the remainder, use the definitions you wrote at the beginning of the project to determine the characteristics that indicate whether they are more sectlike or cultlike. Write a brief analysis of your findings, and compare them with the conclusions of other students in the class.

Kindred McLeary, Lower East Side from Scenes of New York, 1938.

C H A P T E R

14

Population and Urbanization

THE IMAGE STILL HAUNTS ME. There stood Celia, age 30, her distended stomach obvious proof that her thirteenth child was on its way. Her oldest was only 14 years old! A mere boy by our standards, he already had gone as far in school as he ever would. Each morning, he joined the men to work in the fields. Each evening around twilight, we saw him return home, exhausted from hard labor in the subtropical sun.

My wife and I, who were living in Colima, Mexico, had eaten dinner in Celia and Angel's home, which clearly proclaimed the family's poverty. A thatched hut consisting of only a single room served as home for all fourteen members of the family. At night, the parents and younger children crowded into a double bed, while the eldest boy slept in a hammock. As in many other homes in the village, the others slept on mats spread on the dirt floor.

The home was meagerly furnished. It had only a gas stove, a cabinet where Celia stored her cooking utensils and dishes, and a table. There being no closets, clothes were hung on pegs in the walls. There were no chairs, not even one. This really startled us. The family was so poor that they could not afford even a single chair.

Celia beamed as she told us how much she looked forward to the birth of her next child. Could she really mean it? It was hard to imagine that any woman would want to be in her situation.

Yet Celia meant every word. She was as full of delightful anticipation as she had been with her first child—and with all the others in between.

How could Celia have wanted so many children—especially when she lived in such poverty? That question bothered me. I couldn't let it go until I had the solution.

This chapter helps provide an answer.

POPULATION IN GLOBAL PERSPECTIVE

Celia's story takes us into the heart of **demography,** the study of the size, composition, growth, and distribution of human populations. It brings us face to face with the question of whether we are doomed to live in a world so filled with people that there will be practically no space for anybody. Will our planet be able to support its growing population? Or is chronic famine and mass starvation the sorry fate of most earthlings? Let's look at how this concern first began, and then at what today's demographers say about it.

A Planet with No Space to Enjoy Life?

Sometimes the cultural diffusion of a simple item can have far-reaching consequences on nations. An example is the potato, which the Spanish Conquistadors found among the natives of the Andes. When the Spanish brought this food back to Europe, Europeans first viewed it suspiciously, but they gradually came to accept it. Eventually, the potato became the principal food of the lower classes. With more abundant food, fertility increased, and the death rate dropped. As a result, Europe's population soared, almost doubling during the 1700s (McKeown 1977).

This rapid growth alarmed Thomas Malthus (1766–1834), an English economist. He saw it as a sign of coming doom. In 1798, he wrote a book that became world famous, *An Essay on the Principle of Population.* In it, Malthus proposed what became known as the **Malthus theorem.** He argued that while population grows geometrically (from 2 to 4 to 8 to 16 and so forth), the food supply increases only arithmetically (from 1 to 2 to 3 to 4 and so on). This meant, he claimed, that if births go unchecked, the population of a country, or even of the world, will outstrip its food supply.

The New Malthusians

Was Malthus right? This question has become a matter of heated debate among demographers. One group, which can be called the "New Malthusians," is

In earlier generations, large farm families were common. (My own father came from a Minnesota farm family of ten children.) As the country industrialized and urbanized, having many children changed from a function (many hands to help with crops and food production) to a dysfunction (family members who were expensive, non-producing). Consequently, the size of families shrank as we entered Stage 3 of the demographic transition, and today U.S. families of this size are practically nonexistent.

convinced that today's situation is at least as grim as, if not grimmer than, Malthus ever imagined. Figure 14.1 shows how fast the world's population is growing. *In just the time it takes you to read this chapter, another fifteen thousand to twenty thousand babies will be born!* By this time tomorrow, the earth will have an additional quarter of a million people to support. This increase goes on hour after hour, day after day, without letup.

The New Malthusians point out that the world's population is following an **exponential growth curve.** In other words, if growth doubles during approximately equal intervals of time, it suddenly accelerates. To illustrate the far-reaching implications of exponential growth, sociologist William Faunce (1981) told a parable about a man who saved a rich man's life. The rich man was grateful and said that he wanted to reward the man for his heroic deed.

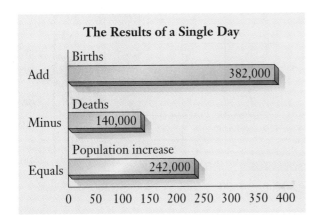

The Results of a Single Day

Add	Births	382,000
Minus	Deaths	140,000
Equals	Population increase	242,000

0   50   100   150   200   250   300   350   400

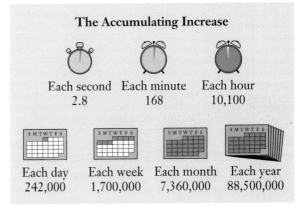

The Accumulating Increase

Each second	Each minute	Each hour
2.8	168	10,100

Each day	Each week	Each month	Each year
242,000	1,700,000	7,360,000	88,500,000

Source: Crews 1995:5.

FIGURE 14.1

How Fast Is the World's Population Growing?

The man replied he would like his reward to be spread out over a four-week period, with each day's amount being twice what he received on the preceding day. He also said he would be happy to receive only one penny on the first day. The rich man immediately handed over the penny and congratulated himself on how cheaply he had gotten by. At the end of the first week, the rich man checked to see how much he owed and was pleased to find that the total was only $1.27. By the end of the second week he owed only $163.83. On the twenty-first day, however, the rich man was surprised to find that the total had grown to $20,971.51. When the twenty-eighth day arrived the rich man was shocked to discover that he owed $1,342,177.28 for that day alone and that the total reward had jumped to $2,684,354.56!

This is precisely what alarms the New Malthusians. They claim that humanity has just entered the "fourth week" of an exponential growth curve. Figure 14.2 shows why they think the day of reckoning is just around the corner. They point out that it took all of human history for the world's population to reach its first billion, around 1800. It then took about one hundred thirty years (until 1930) to add the second billion. Just thirty years later (1960), the world population hit three billion. The time needed to reach the fourth billion was cut in half, to only fifteen years (1975). It then took just twelve more years (1987) for the total to hit five billion. Right now, the world population is closing in on six billion (Cohen 1996).

To illustrate this increase, the new Malthusians have come up with some mind-boggling statistics. They note that before the Industrial Revolution it took 1,600 years for the world's population to double, but that the most recent doubling took just 40 years—40 times as fast (Cohen 1996). They also point out that between 8000 B.C. and A.D. 1750 the world added an average of only 67,000 people a year—but now that many people are being added *every six to seven hours* (Weeks 1994).

It is obvious, claim the New Malthusians, that there is going to be less and less for more and more.

The Anti-Malthusians

This does seem obvious, and no one wants to live in a shoulder-to-shoulder world and fight for scraps. How, then, can anyone argue with the New Malthusians?

A much more optimistic group of demographers, whom we can call the "Anti-Malthusians," claim that such an image of the future is ridiculous. "Ever since Malthus reached his faulty conclusions,"

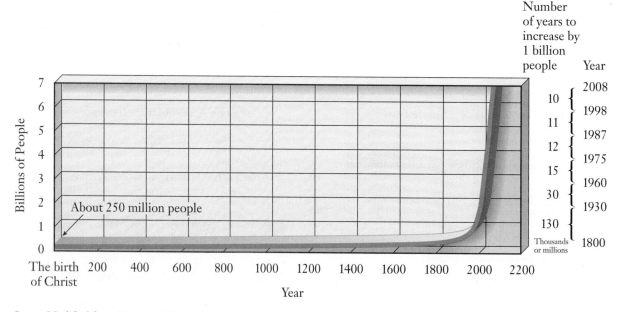

Source: Modified from Piotrow 1973:4.

FIGURE 14.2

World's Population Growth over 2,000 Years

The New Malthusians doubt that families in the Least Industrialized Nations will reduce their birth rate without strong government intervention, such as that being done in China. The Anti-Malthusians, in contrast, say that there is nothing to be concerned about, that as nations industrialize they will follow the same demographic transition *that occurred in Europe and North America.*

they argue, "people have been claiming that the sky is falling—that it is only a matter of time until the world is overpopulated and we all starve to death." The New Malthusians erroneously think that people breed like germs in a bucket, as illustrated by the following example.

> Assume there are two germs in the bottom of a bucket, and they double in number every hour. . . . If it takes one hundred hours for the bucket to be full of germs, at what point is the bucket one-

half full of germs? A moment's thought will show that after ninety-nine hours the bucket is only half full. The title of this volume [*The 99th Hour*] is not intended to imply that the United States is half full of people but to emphasize that it is possible to have "plenty of space left" and still be precariously near the upper limit. (Price 1967)

Anti-Malthusians, such as economist Julian Simon (1981, 1992), regard this image as dead wrong. In their view, people do not blindly reproduce until there is no room left. They say that it is ridiculous to project the world's current population growth into the indefinite future, for this fails to take into account people's intelligence and rational planning when it comes to having children. To understand human reproduction, we need to look at the historical record more closely.

The Anti-Malthusians believe that Europe's **demographic transition** provides a more accurate picture of the future. This transition is diagrammed in Figure 14.3. During most of its history, Europe was in Stage 1. High birth rates offset by high death rates led to a fairly stable population. Then came Stage 2, the "population explosion" that so upset Malthus. Europe's population surged because birth rates remained high, while death rates went down. Finally, Europe made the transition to Stage 3—the population stabilized as people brought their birth rates into line with their lower death rates.

This, continue the Anti-Malthusians, is precisely what will happen in the Least Industrialized Nations. Their current surge in growth simply indicates that

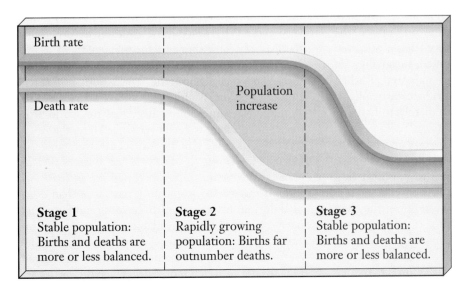

FIGURE 14.3

The Demographic Transition

they have reached the second stage of the demographic transition. Hybrid seed and modern medicine imported from the Most Industrialized Nations have cut their death rates, but their birth rates remain high. When they move into the third stage, as surely they will, we will wonder what all the fuss was about.

The Anti-Malthusians point out that Europe's demographic transition has been so successful that now their governments are concerned that their citizens *are not having enough babies.* They worry about **population shrinkage,** not producing enough children to replace people who die. Already, workers from the Least Industrialized Nations have migrated to Europe to fill this gap, which has created a volatile mixture of ethnic groups in Germany, France, and Italy. Japan is another Most Industrialized Nation that is not reproducing itself.

Who Is Correct?

As you can see, both the New Malthusians and the Anti-Malthusians project trends into the future. The New Malthusians project world growth trends and are alarmed. The Anti-Malthusians project the demographic transition onto the Least Industrialized Nations and are reassured.

Only the future will prove the accuracy of these projections. There is no question that the Least Industrialized Nations are in Stage II of the demographic transition. The question is, will these countries ever enter Stage III? After World War II, Western medicine, techniques of public hygiene, hybrid seeds, herbicides, and farm machinery were exported around the globe. Death rates plummeted as the food supply increased and health improved. At first, almost everyone was ecstatic. As the birth rates of the Least Industrialized Nations stayed high, however, and their populations mushroomed, misgivings set in. Demographers such as Paul and Anne Ehrlich (1972, 1978) predicted worldwide catastrophe if something were not done immediately to halt the population explosion.

The conflict perspective helps explain what happened when this message reached the leaders of the industrialized world. They saw the mushrooming populations of the Least Industrialized Nations as a force that could upset the balance of power they had so carefully worked out. Fearing that the poorer countries, with swollen populations, might demand a larger share of the earth's resources, they used the United Nations to spearhead global efforts to reduce

world population growth. At first, those efforts looked as though they were doomed to fail as populations in the Least Industrialized Nations continued to surge. Then, gradually, the birth rates in countries such as China, India, South Korea, and Sri Lanka began to fall. Their populations did not decrease, but the rate at which they were growing slowed down, dropping from an average 2.1 percent a year in the late 1960s to 1.9 percent today.

The New Malthusians and Anti-Malthusians greeted this news with significantly different interpretations. The New Malthusians stressed, as they still do, that this was but a dent in the increase. The populations of the Least Industrialized Nations are still increasing, they point out, only not as fast as they were. A slower growth rate still spells catastrophe—it just takes a little longer for it to hit. For the Anti-Malthusians, however, this decrease in the rate of growth is the signal that Stage III of the demographic transition is arriving. First the death rates of the Least Industrialized Nations fell—now, just as expected, their birth rates are falling.

Who is right? It simply is too early to tell. Like the proverbial pessimists who call the glass of water half empty, the New Malthusians interpret changes in world population growth negatively. And like the optimists who call the same glass half full, the Anti-Malthusians view the figures positively. Sometime during our lifetimes we should know the answer.

Why Are People Starving?

Pictures of starving children haunt us. They gnaw at our conscience; we live in such abundance, while these children and their parents starve before our very eyes. Why don't these children have enough food? Is it because there are too many of them, as the New Malthusians claim, or simply that the abundant food produced around the world does not reach them, as the Anti-Malthusians argue?

The basic question is this: Does the world produce enough food to feed everyone? Here, the Anti-Malthusians make a point that seems irrefutable. As Figure 14.4 shows, *the amount of food produced for each person in the world is now more than it was in 1950.* Although the world's population has more than doubled during this time, improved seeds and fertilizers have made more food available for each person on earth. And even more food is on the way, add the Anti-Malthusians, for chemists have now discovered how to split nitrogen molecules. Since the earth's at-

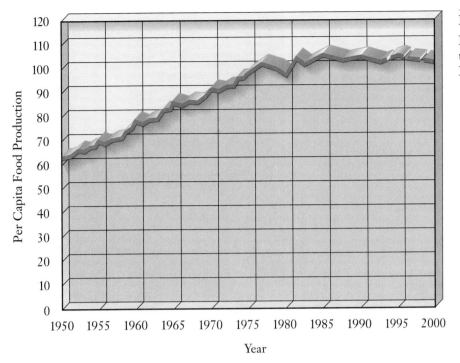

FIGURE 14.4

How Much Food Does the World Produce Per Person?

Note: 1979–1981 = 100. Years 1975 to 1991 are U.N. figures; years prior to 1975 have been recomputed from Simon to 1979–1981 base; years beyond 1993 are the author's projections.

Sources: Simon 1981:58; *United Nations Statistical Yearbook* 1985–1986:Table 7; and 1990–1991:Table 4; *Statistical Abstract* 1995:Table 1401.

mosphere is 78 percent nitrogen, in a few years we will be able to produce chemical compounds—including fertilizers—out of thin air (Naj 1995).

Then why do people die of hunger? From Figure 14.4, we can conclude that starvation does not occur because the earth produces too little food, but because particular places lack food. Some countries produce more food than their people can consume, others less than they need for survival. In short, the cause of starvation is an imbalance between supply and demand. One of the most notable examples is that at the same time as widespread famine is ravishing West Africa, the U.S. government is paying farmers to *reduce* their crops. The United States's problem is too much food; West Africa's, too little.

The New Malthusians counter with the argument that the world's population is continuing to grow and that we do not know how long the earth will continue to produce enough food. They remind us of the penny doubling each day, as well as the germs multiplying in a bucket. It is only a matter of time, they say, until the earth no longer produces enough food—not "if," but "when."

The way in which governments view this matter is crucial for deciding social policy. If the problem is too many people, a government may call for one course of action, whereas an imbalance of resources would indicate another solution entirely. Where the New Malthusians would attempt to reduce the number of people in the world, the Anti-Malthusians would try to distribute food more equitably.

Both the New Malthusians and the Anti-Malthusians have contributed significant ideas, but theories will not eliminate the problem of famines. Starving children are going to continue to peer out at us from our televisions and magazines, their tiny, shriveled bodies and bloated stomachs calling for us to do something. It is important to understand the underlying cause of such human misery, some of which could certainly be alleviated by transferring food from nations that have a surplus.

Pictures of starving people, such as this mother and her child, haunt Americans and other members of the Most Industrialized Nations. Many of us wonder why, when others are starving, we should live in the midst of such abundance, often overeating and even having extra food that we casually scrape into the garbage. The text discusses the causes for such unconscionable disparities.

These pictures of starving Africans give the impression that Africa is overpopulated. Why else would all those people be starving? The truth, however, is very different. Africa has 22 percent of the earth's land surface, but only 10.5 percent of the earth's population (Nsamenang 1992). The reason for famines in Africa, then, certainly is *not* too many people living on too little land. Rather, these famines are due to two primary causes: outmoded farming techniques and ongoing political instability—revolutions and other warfare—that disrupt harvests and food distribution.

Population Growth

The Least Industrialized Nations are growing *nine times faster* than the Most Industrialized Nations (1.9 percent a year compared with 0.2 percent). At these rates, it will take 350 years for the average Most Industrialized Nation to double its population, but just 37 years for the average Least Industrialized Nation to do so (Population Reference Bureau 1995). Why do those who can least afford it have so many children?

Why Do the Least Industrialized Nations Have So Many Children?

To understand why the population is increasing so much more rapidly in the Least Industrialized Na-

tions, let's figure out why Celia is so happy about having her thirteenth child. To do so, we need to apply the symbolic interactionist perspective, to try to understand the world of Celia and Angel as they see it. Celia and Angel's culture tells them that twelve children are *not* enough, that they ought to have a thirteenth—as well as a fourteenth and fifteenth. How can that be? Let us consider three reasons that bearing many children plays a central role in their lives—and in the lives of millions of poor people around the world.

First is the status of parenthood. In the Least Industrialized Nations, motherhood is the most exalted status a woman can achieve. The more children a woman bears, the more she is thought to have achieved the purpose for which she was born. Similarly, a man proves his manhood by fathering children. The more children he fathers, especially sons, the better—for through them his name lives on.

Second, the community supports this view. Celia and those like her live in *Gemeinschaft* communities, where people share values and closely identify with one another. Their community awards or withholds status. And everyone agrees that children are a sign of God's blessing and that a couple should have many children. As people produce children, then, they achieve status in one of the primary ways held out by their community. The barren woman, not the woman with a dozen children, is to be pitied.

While these factors provide strong motivations for bearing many children, there is yet a third incentive. Poor people in the Least Industrialized Nations consider children economic assets. They have no social security or medical and unemployment insurance. As a result, they are motivated to bear *more* children, not fewer, for when parents become sick or too old to work—or when no work is to be found—they rely on their families to take care of them. The more children they have, the broader their base of support. Moreover, like the eldest son of Celia and Angel, children begin contributing to the family income at a young age. See Figure 14.5.

To those of us who live in the Most Industrialized Nations, it seems irrational to have many children. And *for us it would be.* To understand life from the framework of people who are living it, however—the essence of the symbolic interactionist perspective—reveals how it makes perfect sense to have many children. Consider this report by an Indian government worker:

Thaman Singh (a very poor man, a water carrier). . . . welcomed me inside his home, gave me a cup of tea (with milk and "market" sugar, as he proudly pointed out later), and said: "You were trying to convince me in 1960 that I shouldn't have any more sons. Now, you see, I have six sons and two daughters and I sit at home in leisure. They are grown up and they bring me money. One even works outside the village as a laborer. *You told me I was a poor man and couldn't support a large family. Now, you see, because of my large family I am a rich man.*" (Mamdani 1973, italics added)

Conflict theorists offer a different view of why women in the poor nations bear so many children. They stress that in these cultures men dominate women in all spheres of life, including that of reproduction. Conflict theorists would argue that Celia has internalized values that support male dominance. For example, in Latin America **machismo** is common. This emphasis on male virility and dominance includes fathering many children, especially sons, as

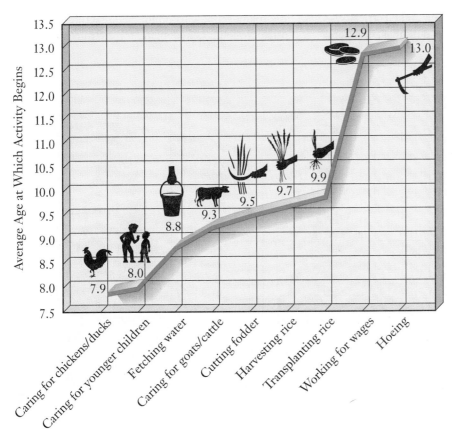

FIGURE 14.5

Why the Poor Need Children. Surviving children are an economic asset in the Least Industrialized Nations. Based on a survey in Indonesia, this figure shows that boys and girls can be net income earners for their families by the age of 9 or 10.

Source: U.N. Fund for Population Activities.

a means of achieving status in the community. From a conflict perspective, then, the reason poor people have so many children is that men continue to control women's reproductive choices.

Implications of Different Rates of Growth

The result of Celia and Angel's desire for many children—and of the millions of Celias and Angels like them—is that Mexico's population will double in thirty-four years. In contrast, Sweden's population is growing at only 0.1 percent a year, and it will take 990 years to double. To illustrate a country's population dynamics, demographers use **population pyramids,** depicting a population by age and sex. Figure 14.6 contrasts Mexico, in Stage 2 of the demographic transition, with the United States, in advanced Stage 3.

The implications of a doubled population are mind-boggling. *Just to stay even*, within thirty–four years Mexico must double its jobs, food production, and factories; hospitals and schools; transportation, communication, water, gas, sewer, and electrical systems; housing, churches, civic buildings, theaters,

stores, and parks. If Mexico fails to double them, its already meager standard of living will drop even further.

A declining standard of living poses the threat of political instability—protests, riots, even revolution, and, in response, severe repression by the government. As conflict theorists point out, this possibility is one reason that the Most Industrialized Nations keep pressuring the United Nations to support worldwide birth control. Political instability in one country can spill over into others, threatening an entire region's balance of power. Consequently, to help preserve political stability, with one hand the Most Industrialized Nations give agricultural aid, IUDs, and condoms to the masses in the Least Industrialized Nations—while with the other they sell arms and munitions to the elites in these countries. Both actions serve the same purpose, say conflict theorists.

Estimating Population Growth: The Three Demographic Variables

To accurately project the future of human populations is obviously important. Educators want to know how many schools to build. Manufacturers want to anticipate changes in demand for their products. The

FIGURE 14.6

Population Pyramids of Mexico and the United States

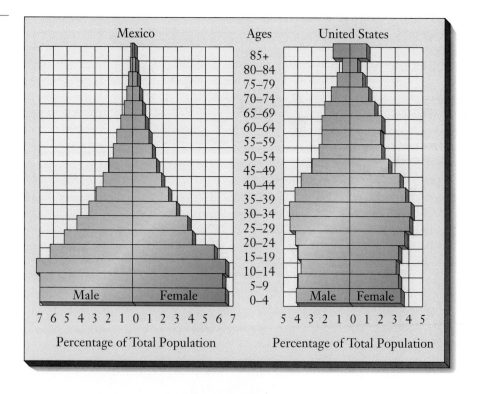

Demographics: study of human Population ✓

government needs to know how many doctors, engineers, and executives to train, as well as how many people will be paying taxes and how many young people will be available to fight a war.

To project population trends, demographers use three basic **demographic variables:** fertility, mortality, and migration. Let's look at each.

Fertility The **fertility rate** is the number of children the average woman bears. A term sometimes confused with fertility is *fecundity*, the number of children women are *capable* of bearing. The fecundity of women around the world is around twenty children each. Their fertility rate, however (the actual number of children they bear), is much lower. The world's overall fertility rate is 3.1, which means that the average woman in the world bears 3.1 children during her lifetime. At 2.0, the fertility rate of U.S. women is considerably less.

The region of the world that has the highest fertility rate is Africa, where the average woman gives birth to 5.8 children; the lowest is Europe, where the average woman bears only 1.5 children. The record for the lowest rate is held by tiny San Marino in Europe, where the average woman gives birth to only 1.1 children. The world's highest rate is 8.1, a record held by Gaza is Asia. This means that the average woman in Gaza gives birth to *seven* times as many children as the average San Marino woman (Population Reference Bureau 1995).

To compute the fertility rate of a country, demographers usually depend on a government's records of births. From these, they figure the country's **crude birth rate,** the annual number of live births per 1,000 population. There may be considerable slippage here, of course. The birth records in many of the Least Industrialized Nations are haphazard.

From Figure 14.6, you can see how a country's age structure affects its birth rate. If by some miracle Mexico were transformed overnight into a nation as industrialized as the United States, its birth rate would continue to be higher—simply because a much higher percentage of Mexican women are in their childbearing years.

Mortality The second demographic variable, **crude death rate,** refers to the number of deaths per 1,000 population. It, too, varies widely around the world. The highest death rate is 22, a record held by the Central African Republic, while the lowest is just 2, a record jointly held by the oil-rich nations of Kuwait and Qatar is Asia (Population Reference Bureau 1995). Recall Figure 7.1 (on page 172–173) for the incredible differences in standards of living and quality of life that underlie these death rates.

Migration The third major demographic variable is the **net migration rate,** the difference between the number of *immigrants* (people moving in) and *emigrants* (people moving out) per 1,000 population. Unlike fertility and mortality rates, this rate does not affect the global population, for people are simply shifting their residence from one country to another.

As is apparent, immigrants are seeking a better life. To find it, they are willing to give up the security of their family and friends and to move to a country with a strange language and unfamiliar customs. What motivates people to embark on such a venture? To understand migration, we need to look at both *push* and *pull* factors. The push factors are what people want to escape—poverty, the lack of religious and political freedoms, even political persecution. The pull factors are the magnets that draw people to a new land, such as a chance for higher wages and better jobs.

Around the world, the flow of migration is from the Least Industrialized Nations to the industrialized countries (Kalish 1994). After "migrant paths" are established, immigration often accelerates as networks of kin and friends become further magnets that attract more people from the same nation—and even from the same villages. As discussed in the Multicultural Society box on the next page, immigration is contributing to a shifting U.S. racial/ethnic mix.

By far, the United States is the world's number one choice of immigrants, and this nation admits more immigrants each year than all the other nations of the world combined. Twenty million—one of every 12 Americans—were born in another country. Table 14.1 shows where U.S. immigrants were born. In an attempt to escape the poverty experienced by Celia and Angel, large numbers of people also enter the United States illegally. The U.S. government puts their number at 3.4 million, of whom 2 million are thought to have come from Central and South America, mostly from Mexico (*Statistical Abstract* 1995:Table 10, 1364).

As mentioned in Chapter 9, experts cannot agree whether immigrants are a net contributor to or a drain on the U.S. economy. Economist Julian Simon (1986, 1993) claims that the net results benefit the country. After subtracting what immigrants collect in welfare and adding what they produce in jobs and

Where the U.S. Population Is Headed— The Shifting Racial/Ethnic Mix

DURING THE NEXT fifty years, the population of the United States is expected to grow by about 44 percent. To see what the population will look like in fifty years, can we simply multiply the current racial/ethnic mix by 44 percent?

The answer is a resounding no. During the next fifty years some groups will increase much more than others, giving us a different-looking United States. Let's try to catch a glimpse of the future.

As you can see from the table below, except for Native Americans all groups are expected to in-crease in size. With low U.S. birth rates, however, most of this growth will come from immigration, especially from Asia and Latin America. These vastly differing growth rates mean that most groups' proportion of the U.S. population will change, in some cases dramatically. African Americans are an exception, for there is little immigration from Africa. The change is so extensive that in fifty years about one in every ten Americans will be from an Asian background, and one of six of Hispanic background. At that time, there will still be more whites than all other groups combined, but their majority will be much smaller, dropping from about 76 percent of the U.S. population to about 60 percent.

For Your Consideration

This shifting racial/ethnic mix is one of the most significant events occurring in the United States. Use the conflict perspective to identify the groups most likely to be threatened and to anticipate their likely responses.

Projecting the Future

Racial/Ethnic Group	Current Size	Expected Size in 50 Years	Growth Rate	Percentage of U.S. Population Now	in 50 Years
Asian Americans	8,000,000	40,000,000	500%	2.9%	10.1%
Latinos	23,000,000	69,000,000	300%	8.4%	17.4%
African Americans	33,000,000	48,000,000	47%	12.0%	12.1%
White Americans	210,000,000	237,000,000	13%	76%	59.9%
Native Americans	2,000,000	2,000,000	0%	0.7%	0.5%
Total	276,000,000	396,000,000	44%	100%	100%

Sources: Modified from Crispell 1992; *Statistical Abstract* 1995: Tables 49, 50, 52, 53, 56.

---

taxes, he concludes that immigrants make an overall positive contribution to the U.S. economy. Other economists such as Donald Huddle (1993) produce figures showing that immigrants are a huge drain on taxpayers. At this point, not enough evidence is in to allow us to come to a rational conclusion.

The Demographic Equation and Problems in Forecasting Population Growth

The total of the three demographic variables—fertility, mortality, and net migration—gives us a country's **growth rate,** the net change after people have been added to and subtracted from a population. What demographers call the **basic demographic equation** is quite simple:

Growth rate = births − deaths + net migration

If population increase depended only on biology, the demographer's job would be simple. But social factors—economic booms and busts, wars, plagues, and famines—push birth rates up or down. As shown in the Global Glimpse box on page 380, even infanticide affects them. Government programs also complicate projections. Some governments take steps to

Table 14.1

Immigrants to the United States, by Region and Country, 1981–1993

North America		Lebanon	59,000	Europe	1,145,000
North America	4,378,000	Israel	50,000	*Europe*	1,145,000
Mexico	2,940,000	Jordan	46,000	Former Soviet Union	243,000
Dominican Republic	381,000	Taiwan	44,000	Great Britain	195,000
Jamaica	274,000	Bangladesh	33,000	Poland	170,000
Haiti	209,000	Iraq	29,000	Germany	94,000
Cuba	195,000	Syria	29,000	Ireland	63,000
Canada	165,000	Turkey	28,000	Romania	59,000
Trinidad and Tobago	62,000	*Central and South America*	1,288,000	Portugal	49,000
Barbados	21,000	El Salvador	315,000	Italy	41,000
Asia	3,891,000	Colombia	170,000	Greece	35,000
Philippines	683,000	Guatemala	136,000	France	32,000
Vietnam	594,000	Guyana	125,000	Yugoslavia	27,000
China	526,000	Peru	101,000	Spain	21,000
Korea	403,000	Ecuador	81,000	*Africa*	283,000
India	384,000	Nicaragua	78,000	Nigeria	52,000
Iran	202,000	Honduras	75,000	Egypt	44,000
Laos	172,000	Brazil	41,000	Ethiopia	42,000
Cambodia	124,000	Panama	39,000	Ghana	22,000
Pakistan	101,000	Argentina	36,000		
Hong Kong	93,000	Chile	30,000		
Thailand	86,000				
Japan	66,000				

Note: Because only the countries of largest emigration are listed, the total of the countries is less than the total given for the region.

Source: Statistical Abstract 1995:Table 8.

get women to bear more children, others to reduce the size of families. When Hitler decided that Germany needed more "Aryans" and the German government outlawed abortion and offered cash bonuses for women who gave birth, the population increased.

In contrast, when Chinese authorities decided that their population should not grow any larger, they not only launched a "One couple, one child" advertising campaign, but they fined couples who had a second child. They also instituted a severe abortion policy. Steven Mosher (1983, 1993), an anthropologist who did fieldwork in China, reports,

> Each population unit, such as a rural collective, is limited to a certain number of births per year, which it allots to couples who have yet to have children. Women who have had their allotted quota of one who get pregnant are forced to attend round-the-clock study courses until they submit to an abortion. In some cases abortions are physically forced on resisting women, some of whom are nine months pregnant. (Erik 1982)

Letting such policies pass without comment, we can see that a government's efforts to change a country's growth rate complicate the demographer's task of projecting future populations.

The primary factor that influences a country's growth rate, however, is its rate of industrialization. *In every country that industrializes, the growth rate declines.* Not only does industrialization open up economic opportunities, but it also makes children more expensive. They require more education and remain dependent longer. Significantly, the basis for conferring status also changes—from having children to attaining education and displaying material wealth. People like Celia and Angel then begin to see life differently, and their motivation to have many children drops sharply. Not knowing how rapidly industrialization will progress, or how quickly changes in values and reproductive behavior will follow, adds to the difficulty of making accurate projections.

Because of such complications, demographers play it safe by making *several* projections of popula-

▲ ▲ ▲ ▲ ▲ ▲ ▲ ▲ ▲ ▲ ▲ ▲ ▲ ▲ ▲ ▲ ▲ ▲

A Global Glimpse

Killing Little Girls: An Ancient and Thriving Practice

"THE MYSTERIOUS CASE of the Missing Girls" could have been the title of this box. Around the globe, for every 100 girls about 105 boys are born. In China, however, for every 100 baby girls, there are 111 baby boys. With China's huge population, this imbalance indicates that about 400,000 baby girls are missing each year. What is happening to them?

The answer is *female infanticide*, the killing of girl babies. When a Chinese woman goes into labor, village midwives sometimes grab a bucket of water. If the newborn is a girl, she is plunged into the water before she can draw her first breath.

At the root of this infanticide is economics. The people are extremely poor, and they have no pensions. When parents can no longer work, sons support them. In contrast, a daughter must be married off, at great expense, and at that point her obligations transfer to her husband and his family.

In the past few years, the percentage of boy babies has grown. The reason, again, is economics, but this time with a new twist. As China opened the door to capitalism, travel and trade opened up—but primarily to men, for it is not thought appropriate for women to travel alone. Thus men find themselves in a better position to bring profits home to the family—one more push toward preferring male children.

By no means is female infanticide limited to China. Although the British banned this practice in India in 1870, it still continues there. Western technology has even been put to work. Many Indian women use amniocentesis to learn the sex of their child, and then decide whether or not to abort. In 99.9 percent of cases, the aborted fetus is female.

This use of amniocentesis for sex selection led to a public outcry in India. The outrage was not about female infanticide, however, nor was it due to some antiabortion movement. Rather, the public became indignant when a physician mistakenly gave the parents wrong information and aborted a *male* baby!

It is likely that the preference for boys, and the consequent female infanticide, will not disappear until the social structures that perpetuate sexism are dismantled. This will not take place until women hold as much power as men, a time, should it ever occur, that apparently lies far in the future.

Sources: Lagaipa 1990; McGowan 1991; Polumbaum 1992; Renteln 1992; Greenhalgh and Li 1995.

---

tion growth. For example, what will the population of the United States be in the year 2010? Perhaps we will be at **zero population growth,** with every 1,000 women giving birth to 2,100 children (the extra 100 children make up for those who do not survive). Will a larger proportion of women go to college? (The more education women have, the fewer children they bear.) How will immigration change during the coming years? Will AIDS come under control? Will some other horrible disease appear? What will happen to the economy? With such huge variables, it is easy to see why demographers make the three projections of the U.S. population shown in Figure 14.7.

URBANIZATION

Let's look at a different aspect of population, where people live. Since the world is rapidly becoming urban, we shall concentrate on urban trends and urban life. To better understand urban life, let's first find out how the city itself came about.

The Development of Cities

Cities are not new to the world scene. Perhaps as early as seven to ten thousand years ago people built small cities with massive defensive walls, such as Catal Hüyük (Schwendinger and Schwendinger 1983) and biblically famous Jericho (Homblin 1973).

Cities on a larger scale originated about 3500 B.C., about the same time as the invention of writing (Chandler and Fox 1974; Hawley 1981). At that time, cities appeared in several parts of the world—first in Mesopotamia (Iran) and later in the Nile, Indus, and Yellow River valleys, in West Africa, around the Mediterranean, in Central America, and the Andes (Fischer 1976; Flanagan 1990).

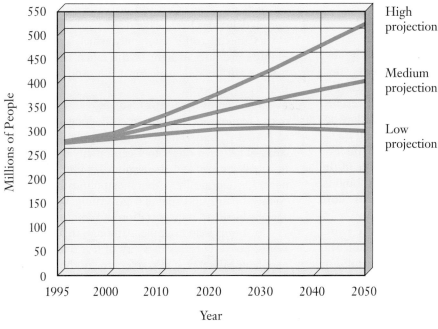

High projection

Medium projection

Low projection

FIGURE 14.7
Population Projections of the United States

Year

Millions of People

Source: Statistical Abstract 1996: Table 17.

The key to the origin of cities is the development of more efficient agriculture (Lenski and Lenski 1987). Only when farming produces a surplus can some people stop being food producers and gather in cities to spend time in other pursuits. A **city,** in fact, can be defined as a place in which a large number of people are permanently based and do not produce their own food. The invention of the plow between five and six thousand years ago created widespread agricultural surpluses, stimulating the development of towns and cities (Curwin and Hart 1961).

Early cities were small economic centers surrounded by walls to keep out enemies. These cities had to be fortresses, for they were constantly threatened by armed, roving tribesmen and by nearby leaders of city-states who raised armies to enlarge their domain and enrich their coffers by sacking neighboring cities. Pictured here is Carcasonne, a restored medieval city in southern France.

The Industrial Revolution and the Size of Cities

Most early cities were tiny by comparison with those of today, merely a collection of a few thousand people in agricultural centers or on major trade routes. The most notable exceptions are two cities that reached one million for a brief period of time before they declined—Changan in China about A.D. 800 and Baghdad in Persia about A.D. 900 (Chandler and Fox 1974). Even Athens at the peak of its power in the fifth century B.C. had less than 200,000 inhabitants. Rome, at its peak, may have had a million or more (Flanagan 1990).

Even 200 years ago, the only city in the world that had a population of more than a million was Peking (now Beijing), China (Chandler and Fox 1974). Then in just 100 years, by 1900, the number of such cities jumped to sixteen. The reason is the Industrial Revolution, which drew people to cities by providing work. It also stimulated the invention of mechanical means of transportation and communication, and allowed people, resources, and products to be moved efficiently—all essential factors (called "infrastructure") on which large cities depend. Today almost 300 cities have a million or more people (Frisbie and Kasarda 1988).

Urbanization, Metropolises, and Megalopolises

Although cities are not new to the world scene, urbanization is. **Urbanization** refers to masses of people moving to cities and to these cities having a growing influence on society. Urbanization is worldwide. In 1800, only 3 percent of the world's population lived in cities (Hauser and Schnore 1965). Today about 43 percent do: about 75 percent of people in the industrialized world and 35 percent of those who live in the Least Industrialized Nations. Each year the world's urban population grows by about 0.5 percent, and soon most people will live in cities (Palen 1987; Population Reference Bureau 1995). Without the Industrial Revolution this remarkable growth could not have taken place, for an extensive infrastructure is needed to support hundreds of thousands and even millions of people in a relatively small area.

To understand the city's attraction, we need to consider the "pull" of urban life. Due to its exquisite division of labor, the city offers incredible variety—music ranging from rock and rap to country and classic, diets for vegetarians and diabetics as well as imported delicacies from around the world for the rest of us. Cities also offer anonymity, which so many find highly refreshing in light of the much tighter controls of village and small-town life. And, of course, the city offers work.

Some cities have grown so large and influential over a region that the term *city* is no longer adequate to describe them. The term **metropolis** is used instead. This term refers to a central city surrounded by smaller cities and their suburbs. They are connected economically, sometimes politically through county boards and regional governing bodies, and socially by ties of transportation and communication.

St. Louis is an example. Although this name, St. Louis, properly refers to a city of less than 400,000 people in Missouri, it also refers to another two million people living in over a hundred separate towns in both Missouri and Illinois, vaguely known as the "St. Louis or Bi-State Area." Although these towns are independent politically, they form an economic unit. They are united by work (many people in the smaller towns work in St. Louis, or are served by industries from St. Louis), by communications (the same area newspaper and radio and television stations), and by transportation (the same interstates, "Bi-State Bus" system, and international airport). As symbolic interactionists would note, a common identity also arises from the area's shared symbols (the Arch, the Mississippi River, Busch Brewery, the Cardinals, the Rams, the Blues—both the hockey team and the music). Most of the towns run into one another, and if you were to drive through this metropolis you would not know that you were leaving one town and entering another—unless you had lived here some time and were aware of the fierce small-town identifications and rivalries that exist side by side with this larger metropolitan identification.

Some metropolises have grown so large and influential that the term **megalopolis** is used to describe them. This term refers to an overlapping area consisting of at least two metropolises and their many suburbs. Of the twenty or so megalopolises in the United States, the three largest are the eastern seaboard running from Maine to Virginia, the area in Florida between Miami, Orlando, and Tampa, and California's coastal area between San Francisco and San Diego.

This process of urban areas turning into a metropolis and metropolises developing into a megalopolis is also worldwide. Table 14.2 lists the sixteen

Table 14.2

The World's Sixteen Largest Cities

Rank	City	Country	Population (in millions)
1	Tokyo-Yokohama	Japan	28
2	Mexico City	Mexico	24
3	São Paulo	Brazil	22
4	Seoul	South Korea	19
5	New York	United States	15
6	Osaka–Kobe–Kyoto	Japan	14
7	Bombay	India	14
8	Calcutta	India	13
9	Rio de Janeiro	Brazil	13
10	Buenos Aires	Argentina	12
11	Tehran	Iran	12
12	Manila	Philippines	11
13	Cairo	Egypt	11
14	Jakarta	Indonesia	11
15	Moscow	Russia	11
16	Los Angeles	United States	10

Source: Statistical Abstract 1994:Table 1355.

largest cities in the world. Note that most are located in the Least Industrialized Nations.

U.S. Urban Patterns

When the United States was founded, it was almost exclusively rural. Figure 14.8 illustrates the country's change to an urban population. In 1790, only about 5 percent of Americans lived in cities. By 1920, this figure had jumped to 50 percent. Urbanization has continued without letup, and today somewhere between 75 and 80 percent of Americans live in cities.

The U.S. Census Bureau has divided the country into 269 metropolitan statistical areas (MSAs). Each MSA consists of a central city and the urbanized county areas linked to it. As Table 14.3 shows, over half of the entire U.S. population lives in just 40 or so MSAs.

With its history rooted in immigration, the United States has been marked by restlessness. Today, millions of Americans pack up and leave family and familiar surroundings in a relentless search for work and better lifestyles. One result is shown on Figure 14.9. As you can see, people are fleeing the Northeast, while the South is currently the most desirable destination.

Table 14.4, which compares the fastest and slowest growing U.S. cities, presents another picture of this migration. As is apparent, all the fastest growing cities are in the West or in the South. Of the declining and slowest growing cities, ten are in the Northeast, while the South and West have one each.

As Americans migrate and businesses move, to serve them **edge cities** have developed. This term refers to a clustering of shopping malls, hotels, office parks, and residential areas near the intersection of major highways (Walker 1991; Garreau 1992). Although this clustering of services may overlap the boundaries of several cities or towns, it provides a sense of place to those who live, work, or shop there.

Another major U.S. urban pattern is **gentrification,** the movement of middle-class people into run-down areas of a city. They are attracted by the low prices for quality housing that, though deteriorated, can be restored. One consequence is an improvement in the appearance of urban neighborhoods—freshly painted buildings, well-groomed lawns, and the absence of boarded-up windows. Another consequence is that the poor residents are displaced as the more well-to-do newcomers move in. Tension often arises between these groups (E. Anderson 1990; 1995).

FIGURE 14.8

Urban Makeup of the U.S. Population, 1790–2010

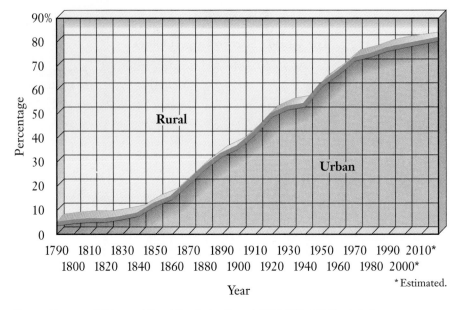

Sources: Patterns of Urban and Rural Population Growth 1980:159–162; *Statistical Abstract* 1988:Table 33; 1995:Table 440.

Models of Urban Growth

In the 1920s, Chicago was a vivid mosaic of newly arrived immigrants, gangsters, prostitutes, the homeless, the rich, and the poor—much as it is today. Sociologists at the University of Chicago studied these contrasting ways of life. One of these sociologists, Robert Park, coined the term **human ecology** to describe how people adapt to their environment (Park and Burgess 1921; Park 1936). (This concept is also known as *urban ecology*.) The process of urban growth is of special interest to human ecol-

ogists. Let's look at the three main models they have developed.

The Concentric Zone Model To explain how cities expand, sociologist Ernest Burgess (1925) proposed a *concentric zone model*. As shown in part A of Figure 14.10, Burgess noted that a city expands outward from its center. Zone 1 is the central business district. Encircling this downtown area is a zone in transition (Zone 2). It contains deteriorating housing and rooming-houses, which, as Burgess noted, breed poverty, disease, and vice. Zone 3 is the area to which thrifty

Table 14.3

Metropolitan Statistical Areas over 1 Million			
Census Year	*Number of MSAs*	*Population (millions)*	*Percentage of U.S. Population*
1950	14	45	30%
1960	22	64	36
1970	31	84	41
1980	35	104	46
1990	39	125	50
1995[a]	44	150	57
2000[a]	50	170	63

[a]Author's estimate.
Source: U.S. Census Bureau 1991:2.

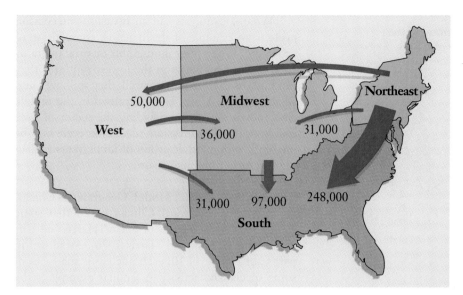

FIGURE 14.9
Net Migration Flows between Regions, 1993–1994

Source: Statistical Abstract 1996:Table 32.

workers have moved to escape the zone in transition and yet maintain easy access to their work. Zone 4 contains more expensive apartments, residential hotels, single-family dwellings, and exclusive areas where the wealthy live. Still farther out, beyond the city limits, is Zone 10, a commuter zone consisting of suburban areas or satellite cities that have developed around rapid transit routes.

Burgess intended this model to represent "the tendencies of any town or city to expand radially from its central business district." He noted, however, that no "city fits perfectly this ideal scheme." Some cities have physical obstacles, such as a lake, river, or railroad, which cause their expansion to depart from the model. Although Burgess also noted in 1925 that businesses were deviating from the model

---

Table 14.4

The Twelve Fastest and Slowest Growing (and declining) U.S. Cities

Fastest		Slowest	
1. Las Vegas, NV	26.2%	1. Salinas, CA	−1.1%
2. McAllen, TX	20.2	2. Binghamton, NY	−1.0
3. Boise City, ID	17.5	3. Scranton, PA	−0.2
4. Bremerton, WA	16.2	4. Jersey City, NJ	−0.1
5. Olympia, WA	16.1	5. Utica, NY	−0.1
6. Brownsville, TX	15.2	6. Pittsburgh, PA	0.3
7. Colorado Springs, CO	14.0	7. New York, NY	0.4
8. Austin, TX	13.9	8. Bridgeton, NJ	0.5
9. Atlanta, GA	12.6	9. Dayton, OH	0.5
10. Killeen, TX	12.5	10. Philadelphia, PA	0.5
11. Knoxville, TN	12.5	11. Shreveport, LA	0.5
12. El Paso, TX	12.4	12. Youngstown, OH	0.5

Note: Population change 1990–1994. A minus sign indicates a loss of population. At 12.4, Raleigh, NC, ties El Paso, but lost out due to alphabetizing.
Source: Statistical Abstract 1995:Table 43.

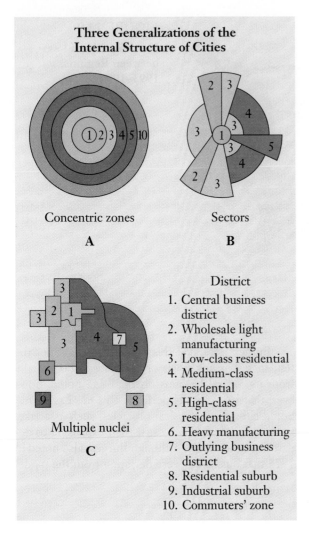

Three Generalizations of the Internal Structure of Cities

Concentric zones

A

Sectors

B

Multiple nuclei

C

District
1. Central business district
2. Wholesale light manufacturing
3. Low-class residential
4. Medium-class residential
5. High-class residential
6. Heavy manufacturing
7. Outlying business district
8. Residential suburb
9. Industrial suburb
10. Commuters' zone

Source: Cousins and Nagpaul 1970.

FIGURE 14.10

Models of Urban Growth

by locating in outlying zones, he was unable to anticipate the extent of this trend—the suburban shopping malls that replaced downtown stores and now account for more than half the country's retail sales (Palen 1987; Milbank 1995).

The Sector Model Sociologist Homer Hoyt (1939, 1971) noted that a city's concentric zones do not form a complete circle, and he modified Burgess's model of urban growth. As shown in part B of Figure 14.10, a concentric zone can contain several sectors—one of working-class housing, another of expensive homes, a third of businesses, and so on, all competing for the same land.

What sociologists call an **invasion–succession cycle** is an example of this dynamic competition of urban life. When poor immigrants or rural migrants enter a city, they settle in the lowest-rent area they can find. As their members swell, they spill over into adjacent areas. Upset at their presence, the middle class moves out, thus expanding the sector of low-cost housing. The invasion–succession cycle may be ongoing, with another group of immigrants replacing this earlier one, and so on.

The Multiple-Nuclei Model Geographers Chauncey Harris and Edward Ullman noted that some cities have several centers or nuclei (Harris and Ullman 1945; Ullman and Harris 1970). As shown in part C of Figure 14.10, each nucleus is the focus of some specialized activity. A familiar example is the clustering of fast-food restaurants in one area and automobile dealerships in another. Sometimes similar activities are grouped together because they profit from cohesion; retail districts, for example, draw more customers if there are more stores. Other clustering occurs because some activities, such as factories and expensive homes, are incompatible with one another. Thus, push–pull factors separate areas by activities, and services are not evenly spread throughout an urban area.

Critique of the Models These models tell only part of the story of how cities develop. They are time bound, for medieval cities didn't follow these patterns (see the photo on page 381). They also are geography bound, as Americans visiting Europe can attest. England, for example, has planning laws that preserve greenbelts (trees, farmlands) around the cities. This prevents urban sprawl: Wal-Mart cannot buy land outside the city and put up a store, but instead must locate in the downtown area with the other stores. Norwich, for example, has 250,000 people; yet the city suddenly ends, and in its greenbelt pheasants skitter across plowed fields while sheep graze in endless meadows (Milbank 1995). The models, then, do not account for urban planning policies.

The models also fall short when it comes to the cities of the Least Industrialized Nations. Here, too, U.S. visitors are surprised: the wealthy often claim the inner city, where fine restaurants and other services are readily accessible. Tucked behind tall walls and protected from public scrutiny, they enjoy luxurious homes and gardens. In contrast, the poor, especially rural migrants, settle unclaimed fringe areas outside the city (see the Global Glimpse box on the next page).

▲ ▲ ▲ ▲ ▲ ▲ ▲ ▲ ▲ ▲ ▲ ▲ ▲ ▲ ▲ ▲ ▲ ▲

A Global Glimpse

Urbanization in the Least Industrialized Nations

IMAGES OF LEAST Industrialized Nations that portray serene pastoral scenes distort today's reality. In these nations, poor rural people have flocked to the cities in such numbers that, as we saw in Table 14.2, these nations now contain most of the world's largest cities. In general, the world's industrialization preceded urbanization, but here urbanization is preceding industrialization. Their limited technology makes it difficult to support the mushrooming urban populations.

When rural migrants and immigrants move to U.S. cities, they usually settle in low-rent districts, areas of deteriorated housing usually located near the city's center. The wealthy reside in exclusive suburbs and in luxurious city enclaves. In contrast, migrants in the Least Industrialized Nations settle in squatter settlements outside the city. There they build shacks from scrap boards, cardboard, and bits of corrugated metal. Even flattened tin cans are considered valuable building material. The squatters enjoy no city facilities—roads, transportation lines, water, sewers, or garbage pickup. After thousands of squatters have settled in an area, the city runs bus lines to it, acknowledging their de facto right to live there. Eventually the city runs a water line to the area and several hundred people use a single spigot. About 4 *million* of Mexico City's inhabitants live in such conditions.

Why are people rushing to these cities? Basically, the rural way of life is breaking down. As the second leg of the demographic transition kicks in—low death rates and high birth rates—rural populations are multiplying, and no longer is there enough land to divide up among descendants. There also are the pull factors discussed in this chapter—from jobs, education, and better housing to a more stimulating life.

Will cities in the Least Industrialized Nations satisfy the people's longing for a better life? As miserable as life is for the poor in these cities, for many it is an improvement over what they left behind. If not, they would flee the city to return to pastoral pleasures. If the Anti-Malthusians are right, this second stage of the demographic transition will come to an end, and the population of the Least Industrialized Nations will stabilize. In the meantime, however, the Least Industrialized Nations cannot catch up with their population explosion—or their urban growth.

Sources: Based on Palen 1987; Singh 1988; Huth 1990; Kasarda and Crenshaw 1991; Chen 1996.

The Least Industrialized Nations are facing massive upheaval as they rapidly urbanize, resulting in disparities such as those depicted here. Lacking the infrastructure to support their many newcomers, cities of the Least Industrialized Nations, already in poverty, face the anguish of developing jobs, housing, sewage and electrical systems, roads, schools, and so on.

City Life

Beyond food, shelter, and safety, we humans also need **community,** a sense of belonging—feeling that others care what happens to us, and that we can depend on the people around us. Some people find community in the city; others find only its opposite, **alienation,** a sense of not belonging, and a feeling that no one cares what happens to you. Let's look at these two aspects of city life.

Alienation

> Twenty-eight-year-old Catherine Genovese, who was called Kitty by almost everyone in her Queens neighborhood, was returning home from work. After she had parked her car, a man grabbed her. She screamed, "Oh my God, he stabbed me! Please help me! Please help me!"
>
> For more than half an hour, thirty-eight respectable, law-abiding citizens looked out their windows and watched as the killer stalked and stabbed Kitty in three separate attacks. Twice the sudden glow from their bedroom lights interrupted him and frightened him off. Each time he returned, sought her out, and stabbed her again. Not one person telephoned the police during the assault. (*New York Times*, March 26, 1964)

When the police interviewed them, some witnesses said, "I didn't want to get involved." Others said, "We thought it was a lovers' quarrel." Some simply said, "I don't know." People throughout the country were shocked. It was as though Americans awoke one morning to discover that the country had changed overnight. They took this event as a sign that people could no longer trust one another, that the city was a cold, lonely place.

Why should the city be alienating? In a classic essay, "Urbanism as a Way of Life," sociologist Louis Wirth (1938) argued that the city undermines kinship and neighborhood, which are the traditional bedrock of social control and social solidarity. Urban dwellers live in anonymity, he pointed out. They go from one superficial encounter to another. This causes them to grow aloof, to become indifferent to other people's problems—as did the neighbors of Kitty Genovese. In short, the personal freedom that the city provides comes at the cost of alienation.

Wirth's explanation is built on two contrasting ideas we discussed in Chapter 4. *Gemeinschaft,* the sense of community that comes from everyone knowing everyone else, is ripped apart when a country industrializes. A new society emerges, characterized by *Gesellschaft,* secondary, impersonal relationships. The end result can be alienation so deep that people can sit by while someone else is being murdered. Lacking identification with one another, people develop the attitude, "It's simply none of *my* business."

Community

The city, however, is more than a mosaic of strangers who feel disconnected and distrustful of one another. It also consists of a series of smaller worlds, within which people find community. People come to know the smaller areas of the city where they live, work, shop, and play. Even slums, which to outsiders seem so threatening, can provide a sense of belonging. In a classic study of the "slums" of Boston, sociologist Herbert Gans notes,

> After a few weeks of living in the West End (of Boston), my observations—and my perceptions of the area—changed drastically. The search for an apartment quickly indicated that the individual units were usually in much better condition than the outside or the hallways of the buildings. Subsequently, in wandering through the West End, and in using it as a resident, I developed a kind of selective perception, in which my eye focused only on those parts of the area that were actually being used by people. Vacant buildings and boarded-up stores were no longer so visible, and the totally deserted alleys or streets were outside the set of paths normally traversed, either by myself or by the West Enders. . . .
>
> Since much of the area's life took place on the street, faces became familiar very quickly. I met my neighbors on the stairs and in front of my building. And, once a shopping pattern developed, I saw the same storekeepers frequently, as well as the area's "characters" who wandered through the streets every day on a fairly regular route and schedule. In short, the exotic quality of the stores and the residents also wore off as I became used to seeing them.

Living in the West End, Gans gained an insider's perspective. He found that in spite of its narrow streets, substandard buildings, and even piled-up garbage, most West Enders had chosen to live there: *to them the West End was a low-rent district, not a slum.* Gans had located a community in the West End, discovering that its residents visited back and forth with relatives and were involved in networks of friendships and acquaintances. Gans therefore titled his

The city dwellers whom Gans identified as ethnic villagers find community in the city. Living in tightly knit neighborhoods, they know many other residents. Some first-generation immigrants have even come from the same village in the "old country."

book *The Urban Villagers* (1962). The residents of the West End were extremely upset when well-intentioned urban planners embarked on an urban renewal scheme to get rid of the "slum." And their distrust proved well founded, for with the gleaming new buildings came invaders with more money who took over the area. Its former residents were dispossessed, their intimate patterns destroyed.

Types of Urban Dwellers

Whether you find alienation or community in the city depends on who you are, for the city offers both. People from different backgrounds experience the city differently. Gans (1962, 1968, 1991) identified five types of people who live in the city. The first

three types live in the city by choice, finding in it a valued sense of community.

The Cosmopolites The cosmopolites are the city's students, intellectuals, professionals, artists, and entertainers. They have been drawn to the city because of its conveniences and cultural benefits.

The Singles Young, unmarried people come to the city seeking jobs and entertainment. Businesses and services such as singles bars, singles apartment complexes, and computer dating cater to their needs. Their stay in the city often reflects a stage in their life course, for most move to the suburbs after they marry and have children.

The Ethnic Villagers United by race, ethnicity, and social class, these people live in tightly knit neighborhoods that resemble villages and small towns. Moving

Men like this one, who has just drunk himself into a stupor, are not an unfamiliar sight in some parts of U.S. cities. The text describes various types of urban dwellers. What type is this man?

within a close circle of family and friends, the ethnic villagers try to isolate themselves from what they view as the harmful effects of city life.

The next two groups are the deprived and the trapped, outcasts of industrial society, with little choice about where they live. They are alienated and always skirting the edge of disaster.

The Deprived The deprived live in blighted neighborhoods more like urban jungles than urban villages. Consisting of the very poor, the emotionally disturbed, and the handicapped, they represent the bottom of society in terms of income, education, social status, and work skills. Some of them stalk their jungle in search of prey, their victims usually deprived people like themselves. Their future holds little chance for anything better in life, either for themselves or their children.

The Trapped The trapped can find no escape either. They consist of people who could not afford to move when their neighborhood was "invaded" by another ethnic group, elderly people who are not wanted elsewhere, alcoholics and other drug addicts, and the downwardly mobile. Like the deprived, the trapped also suffer high rates of assault, mugging, robbery, and rape.

Urban Sentiment: Finding a Familiar World

Sociologists have analyzed how urban dwellers build community in the city. Part of it comes by personalizing their shopping. They shop in the same stores, and after a period of time customers and clerks greet each other by name. Particular taverns, restaurants, and shops become more than just buildings in which to purchase items and services. They become meeting places where neighborhood residents build social relationships with one another and share informal news about the community (Stone 1954; Gans 1970).

Spectator sports also help urban dwellers find a familiar world in the city (Hudson 1991). When the Cardinals won the World Series, for example, the entire St. Louis metropolitan area celebrated the victory of "our" team—even though less than one in seven of the area's 2.5 million people lives in the city. Sociologists David Karp and William Yoels (1990) note that such identification is so intense that long after moving to other parts of the country many people maintain an emotional allegiance to the sports teams of the city in which they grew up.

As sociologists Richard Wohl and Anselm Strauss (1958) pointed out, city dwellers also develop strong feelings for particular objects and locations in the city, such as buildings, rivers, lakes, parks, and even trees and street corners. In some cases objects become a type of logo that represents the city:

> We need only show persons New York's skyline, or San Francisco's Golden Gate Bridge, or New Orleans's French Quarter, and the city will be quickly identified by most. For those who live in these respective cities, such objects and places do not merely identify the city; they are also sources for personal identification *with* the city. (Karp et al. 1991, italics added)

The Norm of Noninvolvement and the Diffusion of Responsibility

Urban dwellers try to avoid intrusions from strangers. As they traverse everyday life in the city, they follow a *norm of noninvolvement.*

A fundamental drama being played out in various areas of American life is the struggle between the haves and the have-nots. As much as possible, the haves segregate themselves from the have-nots. Urban life, however, often makes their paths cross, at least momentarily, as captured in this photo.

To do this, we sometimes use props such as news-papers to shield ourselves from others and to indi-cate our inaccessibility for interaction. In effect, we learn to "tune others out." In this regard, we might see the Walkman as the quintessential urban prop in that it allows us to be tuned in and tuned out at the same time. It is a device that al-lows us to enter our own private world and thereby effectively to close off encounters with others. The use of such devices protects our "per-sonal space," along with our body demeanor and facial expression (the passive "mask" or even scowl that persons adopt on subways). (Karp et al. 1991)

Recall Kitty Genovese, whose story was re-counted on page 388. That troubling case disturbed social psychologists John Darley and Bibb Latané (1968), who ran the series of experiments featured in Chapter 5, pp. 123–124. As you may recall, they found that the *more* bystanders there are, the *less* likely people are to help. As a group grows, people's sense of responsibility becomes diffused, with each person assuming that *another* will do the responsible thing. "With these other people here, it is not *my* re-sponsibility," they reason.

The norm of noninvolvement and the diffusion of responsibility help to explain the response to Kitty Genovese's murder. The bystanders at her death were *not* uncaring, alienated people. They *did* care that a woman was being attacked. They simply were abiding by an urban norm—one helpful in getting them through everyday city life, but, unfortunately, dysfunctional in some crucial situations. This norm, combined with killings, carjackings, muggings, and the generalized fear that the city now engenders in many Americans, underlies a desire to retreat to a safe haven. This topic is discussed in the Down-to-Earth Sociology box on the next page.

The Decline of the City

The poverty, decay, and general decline of U.S. cities are among the primary problems of urban life today. Let's examine underlying reasons for these condi-tions and consider how to develop social policy to solve urban problems and improve our quality of life.

Suburbanization

On Suburbs and Ghettos Suburbanization, which refers to people moving from cities to **suburbs,** the communities located just outside a city, is not new. The dream of a place of one's own with green grass, a few trees, and kids playing in the yard was not discov-ered by this generation (Riesman 1970). For the past hundred years or so, as transportation became more efficient, especially with the development of automo-biles, white Americans have moved to towns next to the cities in which they work. Minorities joined this movement about 1970. The extent to which Ameri-cans have left the city in search of their dreams is re-markable. In 1957, only 37 million Americans lived in the suburbs (Karp et al. 1991), but today over half of all Americans live in them (Gans 1991).

The U.S. city has been the loser in this transi-tion. As people moved out of the city, businesses and jobs followed. As the city's tax base shrank, the result-ing budget squeeze affected not only parks, zoos, li-braries, and museums, but even the city's basic services—its schools, streets, sewer and water sys-tems, and police and fire departments.

As this shift in population and resources took place, left behind were people who had no choice but to stay in the city. The net result, says sociologist William Wilson (1987), was the transformation of the inner city into a ghetto. Left behind were fami-lies and individuals who were trapped by poverty, welfare dependency, lack of training and skills, per-sistent unemployment, along with people who prey on others through street crime. The term *ghetto*, says Wilson, "suggests that a fundamental social trans-formation has taken place . . . that groups repre-sented by this term are collectively different from and much more socially isolated from those that lived in these communities in earlier years" (quoted in Karp et al. 1991).

Barriers to Mutual Identification: City versus Suburb Having made the move out of the city, suburbanites prefer the city to keep its problems to itself. They reject proposals to share suburbia's rev-enues with the city and oppose measures that would allow urban and suburban governments joint control over what has become a contiguous mass of people and businesses. Suburban leaders generally see it as in their best interests to remain politically, economi-cally, and socially separate from their nearby city. They do not mind going to the city to work, or ven-turing there on weekends for the diversions it of-fers, but they do not want to help shoulder the city's burdens.

It is likely that the mounting bill will come due ultimately, however, and that eventually suburbanites will have to pay for their uncaring attitude toward the urban disadvantaged. Karp et al. (1991) put it this way:

Down-to-Earth Sociology

Urban Fear and the Gated Fortress

GATED NEIGHBORHOODS—WHERE a gate on a street literally opens and closes access to a neighborhood—are not new. They always have been available to the rich. What is new is the upper middle class's rush to towns where the residents pay heavy taxes to keep private the town's entire facilities, including its streets.

Towns cannot discriminate on the basis of religion or ethnicity/race, but they can—and do—discriminate on the basis of social class. Klahanie, Washington, is an excellent example. Begun in 1985, it was supposed to take twenty years to develop. With its safe streets, 300 acres of open space, and its ban on satellite dishes, flagpoles, and even basketball hoops on garages, demand for the $300,000-plus homes in this private, lake-nestled community has exceeded supply (Egan 1995).

The future will bring many more such private towns as the upper middle class flees crime-ridden urban areas and attempts to build a bucolic dream. A strong sign of the future is that Walt Disney Company is building Celebration, a planned town of 20,000 people just south of Orlando, Florida (Egan 1995). With the new technology, the residents of these new private communities will be able to communicate with the outside world while remaining securely locked within their gated fortresses.

Community always involves a sense of togetherness, of identity with one another. Apparently it also contains the idea of separateness from others. If we become a nation of gated communities, where homeowners withdraw into private domains, separating themselves from the rest of the nation, this will be another declaration that the urban experiment has failed.

The U.S. economic system has proven highly beneficial to most citizens, but it also has left many in poverty. To protect themselves, primarily from the poor, the upper middle class increasingly seeks sanctuary behind gated residential enclaves.

It may be that suburbs can insulate themselves from the problems of central cities, at least for the time being. In the long run, though, there will be a steep price to pay for the failure of those better off to care compassionately for those at the bottom of society.

The Los Angeles riots, and the sporadic riots since then, may be part of that bill—perhaps just the down payment.

Disinvestment

Already by the 1940s, the movement out of cities to suburbs had begun to undermine the cities' tax base, a problem only accelerated as poor rural migrants, mostly African American, moved in large numbers to northern cities (Lemann 1994). As the tax base eroded, services declined—from garbage pickup to education. Buildings deteriorated, and banks began **redlining:** afraid of loans going bad, banks drew a line on a map around a problem area and refused to make loans for housing or businesses there. The **disinvestment** (withdrawal of investment) pushed these areas into further decline. Not unconnected, youth gangs, murders, and robberies are high in these areas, while education, employment, and income are low.

Deindustrialization and Globalization

The development of a global market has also left a heavy footprint on U.S. cities (Rodríguez 1994). To compete in the global market, many U.S. industries have abandoned local communities and moved their factories to countries where labor costs are lower. Although this makes their products more competitive, it also has eliminated millions of U.S. manufacturing jobs. With no jobs and no training in the new information technologies, many poor people are locked out of the benefits of the postindustrial economy that is engulfing the United States. Left behind in the inner cities, many live in despair as a distant economy charges into the uncharted waters of a brave new world without them.

Social Policy: Failure and Potential

The Failure Social policy usually takes one of two forms. The first is to tear down and rebuild in the fancifully named effort called **urban renewal.** The

Like the phoenix, luxury hotels and apartments, along with exclusive restaurants and shops, have arisen from the ashes of urban decay. Urban renewal, a benefit for the privileged, has displaced the poor, often shoving them into adjacent areas every bit as deprived as those in which they previously lived.

result is the renewal of an area—but not for its inhabitants. Stadiums, high-rise condos, luxury hotels, and expensive shops are built. Outpriced, the area's inhabitants are displaced. They flow into adjacent areas, adding to their problems. The second is some sort of **enterprise zone,** economic incentives such as reduced taxes to encourage businesses to move into the area. Although the intention is good, failure is usually the result. Most businesses refuse to locate in high-crime areas. Those that do may find that the costs of additional security and losses from crime run higher than the tax savings. If workers are hired from the problem area, and the jobs pay a decent wage, which most do not, the workers move to better neighborhoods, frustrating the purpose of establishing an enterprise zone (Lemann 1994). After all, who chooses to live with the fear of violence?

The Potential: An Urban Manhattan Project Despite the problems facing U.S. cities—problems so severe that they are discussed not only around dinner tables in New York and Los Angeles, but also in Tokyo and London—government policies remain uncoordinated and ineffective (Flanagan 1990; Lemann 1994).

A "nothing works" mentality will solve nothing. U.S. cities can be revitalized and made into safe and decent places to live. There is nothing in their nature that turns cities into dangerous, deteriorating slums. Most cities of Europe, for example, are both safe and pleasant. If U.S. cities are to change, they must become top agenda items of the U.S. government, with adequate resources in terms of money and human talents focused on overcoming urban woes.

Granted the deplorable condition of many U.S. cities, and the flight of the middle classes—both whites and minorities—to greener pastures, an urban Manhattan Project seems in order. During World War II the United States and the Allies faced a triumphant Hitler in Europe and Tojo in Asia. The United States gathered its top scientific minds, gave them all the resources they needed, and produced the atomic bomb. Today, a similar gathering of top social scientists and similar resources may be required to triumph over urban ills.

Guiding Principles Sociologist William Flanagan (1990) suggests three guiding principles for working out specific solutions to our pressing urban problems:

- *Scale.* Regional and national planning is necessary. Currently, the many local jurisdictions, with their many rivalries, competing goals, and limited resources, lead to a hodgepodge of mostly unworkable solutions. A positive example is Portland, Oregon, where a regional government prohibits urban sprawl and ensures a greenbelt (Ortega 1995).

- *Livability.* Growth must be channeled in such a way that cities are appealing and meet human needs, especially the need of community discussed earlier. This will attract the middle classes into the city and increase the tax base. In turn, this will help finance the services that make the city more livable.

- *Social justice.* In the final analysis, social policy must be evaluated by its effects on people. "Urban renewal," for example, that displaces the poor for the benefit of the middle class and wealthy does not pass this standard. The same would apply to solutions that create "livability" for select groups but neglect the poor and the homeless.

Unless the *root* causes of urban problems are addressed—housing, education, and jobs—solutions, at best, will be only Band-Aids that cover up problems, or, at worst, window dressing for politicians who want to *appear* as though they are doing something about the problems that affect our quality of life.

Summary and Review

A Planet with No Space to Enjoy Life?

What debate did Thomas Malthus initiate?

In 1798, Thomas Malthus analyzed the surge in Europe's population. His conclusion, called the **Malthus theorem,** was that because the population grows geometrically but food only arithmetically, the world will outstrip its food supply. The debate between today's New Malthusians and those who disagree, the Anti-Malthusians, continues. Pp. 368–372.

Why are people starving?

Starvation is not due to a lack of food in the world, for there now is more food for each person in the entire world than there was fifty years ago. Starvation, rather, is due to a maldistribution of food. Pp. 372–374.

Population Growth

Why do the poor nations have so many children?

In the Least Industrialized Nations children generally are viewed as gifts from God, cost little to rear, and represent the parents' social security. Consequently, people are motivated to have large families. Pp. 374–376.

What are the three demographic variables?

To compute population growth, demographers use *fertility, mortality,* and *migration.* The **basic demographic**

equation is births minus deaths plus net migration equals growth rate. Pp. 376–378.

Why is forecasting population difficult?

A nation's growth rate is affected by unanticipated variables—from economic conditions, wars, plagues, and famines to government policies and industrialization. Pp. 378–380.

The Development of Cities

What is the relationship of cities to farming?

Cities can develop only if there is a large agricultural surplus, which frees people from food production. The primary impetus to the development of cities was the invention of the plow about five or six thousand years ago. Pp. 380–381.

How did the Industrial Revolution affect the size of cities?

Almost without exception, throughout history cities have been small. After the Industrial Revolution stimulated mechanical transportation and communication, the infrastructure on which modern cities depend, cities grew quickly and much larger. P. 382.

What are metropolises and megalopolises?

Urbanization is so extensive that some cities have become **metropolises,** dominating the areas adjacent to them. The areas of influence of some metropolises have merged, forming a **megalopolis.** Pp. 382–383.

Models of Urban Growth

What models of urban growth have been proposed?

The primary models are the concentric zone model, a sector model, and a multiple-nuclei model. These models fail to account for medieval cities, as well as many European cities and those in the Least Industrialized Nations. Pp. 384–387.

City Life

Is the city inherently alienating?

Some people experience alienation in the city; others find community in it. What people find depends largely on their background and urban networks. Five major types of people who live in cities are cosmopolites, singles, ethnic villagers, the deprived, and the trapped. Pp. 388–391.

The Decline of the City

Why have U.S. cities declined?

Three primary reasons for their decline are **suburbanization** (as people moved to the suburbs, the tax base of cities eroded and services deteriorated), **disinvestment** (financial institutions withdrawing their financing), and deindustrialization (which has caused a loss of jobs). Pp. 391–393.

What social policy can salvage U.S. cities?

A Manhattan Project on Urban Problems could likely produce workable solutions. Three guiding principles for developing social policy are scale, livability, and social justice. Pp. 393–394.

Where can I read more on this topic?

Suggested readings for this chapter are listed on page 444.

Glossary

alienation a sense of not belonging, and a feeling that no one cares what happens to you (p. 388)

basic demographic equation growth rate = births – deaths + net migration (p. 378)

city a place in which a large number of people are permanently based and do not produce their own food (p. 381)

community a place people identify with, where they sense that they belong and that others care what happens to them (p. 388)

crude birth rate the annual number of births per 1,000 population (p. 377)

crude death rate the annual number of deaths per 1,000 population (p. 377)

demographic transition a three-stage historical process of population growth: first, high birth rates and high death rates; second, high birth rates and low death rates; and third, low birth rates and low death rates (p. 371)

demographic variables the three factors that influence population growth: fertility, mortality, and net migration (p. 377)

demography the study of the size, composition, growth, and distribution of human populations (p. 368)

disinvestment the withdrawal of investments by financial institutions, which seals the fate of an urban area (p. 393)

edge city a large clustering of service facilities and residences near a highway intersection that provides a sense of place to people who live, shop, and work there (p. 383)

enterprise zone the use of economic incentives in a designated area with the intention of encouraging investment there (p. 393)

exponential growth curve a pattern of growth in which numbers double during approximately equal intervals, thus accelerating in the latter stages (p. 369)

fertility rate the number of children that the average woman bears (p. 377)

gentrification the displacement of the poor in a section of a city by the relatively affluent, who renovate the former's homes (p. 383)

growth rate the net change in a population after adding births, subtracting deaths, and either adding or subtracting net migration (p. 378)

human ecology Robert Park's term for the relationship between people and their environment (natural resources, such as land) (p. 384)

invasion–succession cycle the process of one group of people displacing a group whose racial/ethnic or social class characteristics differ from their own (p. 386)

Malthus theorem an observation by Thomas Malthus that although the food supply increases only arithmetically, population grows geometrically (p. 368)

megalopolis an urban area consisting of at least two metropolises and their many suburbs (p. 382)

metropolis a central city surrounded by smaller cities and their suburbs (p. 382)

net migration rate the difference between the number of immigrants and emigrants per 1,000 population (p. 377)

population pyramid a graphic representation of a population, divided into age and sex (p. 376)

population shrinkage the process by which a country's population becomes smaller because its birth rate and immigration are too low to replace those who die and emigrate (p. 372)

redlining the officers of a financial institution deciding not to make loans in a particular area (p. 393)

suburbanization the movement from the city to the suburbs (p. 391)

suburbs the communities adjacent to the political boundaries of a city (p. 391)

urbanization an increasing proportion of a population living in cities and those cities having an increasing influence on their society (p. 382)

urban renewal the rehabilitation of a rundown area of a city, which usually results in the displacement of the poor who are living in that area (p. 393)

zero population growth a demographic condition in which women bear only enough children to reproduce the population (p. 380)

Sociology and the Internet

All URLs listed are current as of the printing of this book. URLs are often changed. Please check our Website http://www.abacon.com/henslin for updates.

1. World Hunger

To learn more about world hunger, first read the section in your text entitled "A Planet with No Space to Enjoy Life?" (pp. 368–374) and take special note of "Why are people starving?" (pp. 372–374). What are the main arguments of the New Malthusians and Anti-Malthusians regarding world hunger? If the main problem is distribution of food and not its production, which of the two seems more nearly correct?

In looking at information on the Internet, you will be comparing two sites dedicated to research on and the elimination of starvation around the world. Go to "The

30 Hour Famine" page (http://www. 30hourfamine.org/whats.html) and browse the site. Then go to "The HungerWeb" (http://www.brown. edu/Departments/World_Hunger_Program) and read through the page. When you have finished, go back to the top of the page and click on "Alan Shawn Feinstein World Hunger Program" (overview). Follow the links by clicking on items in the list.

Write a brief paper in which you include both the theories and patterns of world hunger. Elaborate on the efforts to solve the problem.

2. Social Inequality in Your Town

Sometimes studying demography can seem very abstract. Even when the implications for poverty and starvation are dealt with, the problems may appear very far from the relative safety of our own lives. In this project, you will be bringing the study of population to your own world.

First, go to the U.S. Census Bureau's Population Division site (http://www.census.gov/ftp/pub/population/www/). Select "1990 Census Data," and then page down to "1990 Census Lookup." Select "STF3a (detailed geography)." On the new page, you should find "Retrieve the areas you've selected" marked. Click on "Go to level: state—place" to mark it instead. Now page down, select your home state, and click on the Select bar. When the next page comes up, scroll down to select your home town, and again click on the Select bar. On the new page, "Choose tables" should already be marked, so just click on Select. Now you should see a heading telling you to "Select the tables you wish to receive." For now, mark "P1 Persons" and "P7 Sex (2)." Click on "Submit." There should already be a dot before "HTML Format," so just click on "Submit" again. You should now see the two tables you asked for. You can print or save them.

Now that you know how to get the data, go back to the "Select the tables . . ." page. Pick tables that will tell you about the social conditions of your town. Do you have a large minority population? What is the state of the housing? Explore so that you can write a report on what just knowing about demographic variations tells you about your home town.

Christian Pierre, Power Book Girl, 1996.

C H A P T E R

15

Social Change: Technology, Social Movements, and the Environment

THE MORNING OF JANUARY 28, 1986, *dawned clear but near freezing, strange weather for subtropical Florida. At the Kennedy Space Center, launch pad 39B was lined with three inches of ice. Icicles 6 to 12 inches long hung like stalactites from the pad's service structure.*

Shortly after 8 A.M., the crew took the elevator to the white room, where they entered the crew module. By 8:36 A.M., the seven members of the crew were strapped in their seats. They were understandably disappointed when liftoff, scheduled for 9:38 A.M., was delayed because of the ice.

Due to a strong public relations campaign, public interest in the flight ran high. Attention focused on Christa McAuliffe, a 37-year-old high school teacher from Concord, New Hampshire, the first private citizen to fly aboard a space shuttle. Across the nation, schoolchildren watched with great anticipation, for Mrs. McAuliffe, selected from thousands of applicants (including the author of this text), was to give two televised lessons during the flight. The first was to describe life aboard a spacecraft in orbit, the second to discuss the prospects of using space's microgravity to manufacture new products.

At the viewing site, thousands of spectators had joined the families and friends of the crew eagerly awaiting the launch. They were delighted to see Challenger's *two solid-fuel boosters ignite and broke into cheers as this product of technical innovation thundered majestically into space.*

The time was 11:38 A.M. Seventy-three seconds later, the Challenger, *racing skyward at 2,900 feet per second, had reached an altitude of 50,000 feet and was 7 miles from the launch site. Suddenly, a brilliant glow appeared on one side of the external tank. In seconds, the glow blossomed into a gigantic fireball. Screams of horror arose from the crowd as the* Challenger, *now 19 miles away, exploded, and bits of debris began to fall from the sky.*

In classrooms across the country, children burst into tears. Adult Americans stared at their televisions in stunned disbelief. (Based on Broad 1986; Magnuson 1986; Lewis 1988; Maier 1993.)

If any characteristic describes social life today, it is rapid social change. As we shall see in this chapter, technology, such as that which made the *Challenger* first a reality and then a disaster, is a driving force behind this change. To understand social change is to better understand today's society—and our own lives.

An Overview of Social Change

Social change, a shift in the characteristics of culture and society, is such a vital part of social life that it has been a theme throughout this book. To make this theme more explicit, let's review the main points about social change made in the preceding chapters.

The Four Social Revolutions

The rapid, far-reaching social change that the world is currently experiencing did not "just happen."

Rather, it is the result of fundamental forces set in motion thousands of years ago, beginning with the gradual domestication of plants and animals. This first social revolution allowed hunting and gathering societies to develop into horticultural and pastoral societies (see pages 90–91). The plow brought about the second social revolution, from which agricultural societies emerged. Then the invention of the steam engine ushered in the Industrial Revolution, and now we are witnessing the fourth social revolution, stimulated by the invention of the microchip.

From Gemeinschaft to Gesellschaft

Although our lives are being vitally affected by this fourth revolution, we have seen only the tip of the iceberg. By the time this social revolution is full blown, little of our way of life will be left untouched. We can assume this because that is how it was with the first three social revolutions. For example, the change from agricultural to industrial society meant not only that people moved from villages to cities, but also that intimate, lifelong relationships were replaced by impersonal, short-term associations. Paid work, contracts, and especially money replaced the reciprocal obligations required by kinship, social position, and friendship. As reviewed on pages 93–95, sociologists use the terms *Gemeinschaft* and *Gesellschaft* to indicate this fundamental shift in society.

Capitalism and Industrialization

Just why did societies change from *Gemeinschaft* to *Gesellschaft?* Karl Marx pointed to a social invention called *capitalism*. He analyzed how the breakup of feudal society threw people off the land, creating a surplus of labor. Moving to cities, these masses were exploited by the owners of the means of production (factories, machinery, tools), setting in motion antagonistic relationships between capitalists and workers that remain today.

Max Weber agreed that capitalism was changing the world, but he traced capitalism to the Protestant Reformation (see pp. 353–354). He noted that the Reformation stripped from Protestants the assurance that church membership saved them. As they agonized over heaven and hell, they concluded that God did not intend to leave the elect in uncertainty, that God would provide visible evidence for people predestined to heaven. That sign, they decided, was prosperity. An unexpected consequence of the Reformation, then, was to make Protestants work hard and be thrifty. The result was an economic surplus and capitalism, which laid the groundwork for the Industrial Revolution that transformed the world.

Modernization

The term given to the sweeping changes ushered in by the Industrial Revolution is **modernization.**

The Protestant Reformation ushered in not only religious change, but as Max Weber analyzed, also fundamental social-economic change. This painting by Hans Holbein, the Younger, shows the new prosperity of the merchant class—previously only the nobility had such possessions.

Table 15.1 reviews these changes. This table is an *ideal type* in Weber's sense of the term, for no society comprises to the maximum degree all the traits listed here. For example, although most Americans now work in the tertiary sector of the economy, many millions still work in the primary and secondary sectors. Thus all characteristics shown in Table 15.1 should be interpreted as "more" or "less" rather than "either/or."

Traditional, or *Gemeinschaft*, societies are small and rural, slow-changing, with little stress on formal education. Most illnesses are treated at home. People live in extended families, look to the past for guide-

lines to the present, usually show high respect for elders, and have rigid social stratification and much inequality between the sexes. Life and morals tend to be seen in absolute terms, and few differences are tolerated. Modern societies, in contrast, are large, more urbanized, and fast-changing. They stress formal education, are future oriented, and are less religiously oriented. In the third stage of the demographic transition, people have small families, low rates of infant mortality, longer lives, higher incomes, and vastly more material possessions.

As technology from the industrialized world is introduced into traditional societies, we are able to

Table 15.1

A Typology of Traditional and Modern Societies

Characteristics	Traditional Societies	Modern Societies
General Characteristics		
Social change	Slow	Rapid
Size of group	Small	Large
Religious orientation	More	Less
Formal education	No	Yes
Place of residence	Rural	Urban
Demographic transition	First stage	Third stage
Family size	Larger	Smaller
Infant mortality	High	Low
Life expectancy	Short	Long
Health care	Home	Hospital
Temporal orientation	Past	Future
Material Relations		
Industrialized	No	Yes
Technology	Simple	Complex
Division of labor	Simple	Complex
Income	Low	High
Material possessions	Few	Many
Social Relationships		
Basic organization	*Gemeinschaft*	*Gesellschaft*
Families	Extended	Nuclear
Respect for elders	More	Less
Social stratification	Rigid	More open
Statuses	More ascribed	More achieved
Gender equality	Less	More
Norms		
View of reality, life, and morals	Absolute	Relativistic
Social control	Informal	Formal
Tolerance of differences	Less	More

For centuries, Western society remained virtually unchanged. As in this 15th-century painting, work, which was passed from parents to children, was based on personal relationships and revolved around the seasons. How this long-standing traditional way of life gave way to Gesellschaft *society has been a primary topic of sociological investigation.*

witness how far-reaching the changes are. Take just modern medicine as an example. Its introduction into the Least Industrialized Nations helped to usher in the second stage of the demographic transition. As death rates dropped and birth rates remained high, the population exploded, bringing hunger, starvation, and mass migration to cities. This rush to cities that have little industrialization, new to the world scene, is creating a host of problems yet to be solved. (See the Global Glimpse box on page 387.)

Technology and Shifts in the Global Map

Already during the sixteenth century, today's global divisions had begun to emerge. Trade alliances, forged by those nations with the most advanced technology of the time (the swiftest ships and the most powerful armaments), created a division into rich and poor nations. Then, according to *dependency theory*, as capitalism emerged, the nations that industrialized exploited the resources of those that did not. This led to the nonindustrialized nations becoming dependent on those that had industrialized (see page 175). Today's information revolution will have similar consequences on global stratification. Those nations that take the fast lane on the information superhighway, primarily the Most Industrialized Nations, are destined to dominate in the coming generation.

Since World War II, a realignment of national and regional powers (called *geopolitics*) has resulted in a triadic division of the world: a Japan-centered East, a Germany-centered Europe, and a United States-centered western hemisphere (Robertson 1992). These three global powers, along with four lesser ones—Canada, France, Great Britain, and Italy—dominate today's globe. Known as G7 (meaning *the* "Group of 7"), these industrial giants hold annual meetings at which they decide how to divide up the world's markets and regulate global economic policy, such as interest rates, tariffs, and currency exchanges. Their goal is to perpetuate their global dominance, which includes keeping prices down on raw materials from the Least Industrialized Nations. Cheap oil is essential for this goal, which requires the domination of the Mideast, whether that be accomplished through peaceful means or by a joint war effort of the United Nations.

Because of Russia's nuclear arsenal, the G7 has carefully courted Russia—giving Russia observer status at its annual summits and providing loans and expertise to help Russia's transition to capitalism. The breakup of the Soviet Union has been a central consideration in G7's plans for a new world order, and events there will help determine the shape of future global stratification.

The Resurgence of Ethnic Conflicts

Threatening the global map so carefully partitioned by the G7 is the resurgence of ethnic conflicts. The breakup of the Soviet empire lifted the cover that had held in check the centuries-old hatreds and frustrated nationalistic ambitions of many ethnic groups. With the Soviet military and the KGB in disarray, these groups turned violently on one another. In Africa, similar seething hatreds have brought warfare to groups only formally united by artificial political boundaries. In Europe, the former Yugoslavia divided, with parts self-destructing as pent-up fury was unleashed. Ethnic conflicts threaten to erupt in Germany, France, Italy, the United States, and Mexico. At what point these resentments and hatreds will play themselves out, if ever, is unknown.

For the most part, the Most Industrialized Nations care little if the entire continent of Africa self-destructs in ethnic slaughter, but they could not tolerate interethnic warfare in Bosnia. If it had spread, an inferno could have engulfed Europe. For global control, the G7 must be able to depend on political and economic stability in its own neighborhood, as well as in those countries that provide the essential raw materials for its industrial machine.

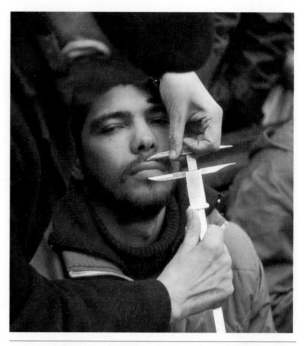

In spite of the vast social change occurring around the globe, race-ethnicity remains a fundamental distinction among human groups. Shown here is a Ukrainian being measured to see if he is really "full lipped" enough to be called a Tartar.

How Technology Changes Society

As you may recall from Chapter 2, **technology** carries a double meaning. It refers both to *tools*, items used to accomplish tasks, and to the skills or procedures to make and use those tools. This broad concept includes tools as simple as a comb as well as those as complicated as computers. Technology's second meaning—the skills or procedures to make and use tools—refers in this case not only to the procedures used to manufacture combs and computers but also to those required to "produce" an acceptable hairdo or to gain access to the Internet. Apart from its particulars, technology always refers to *artificial means of extending human abilities*.

All human groups make and use technology, but the chief characteristic of postindustrial societies (also called **postmodern societies**) is technology that greatly extends our abilities to analyze information, to communicate, and to travel. These *new technologies*, as they are called, allow us to do what had never been done in history: to probe space and other

Technology, which drives much social change, is at the forefront of our information revolution. This revolution, based on the computer chip, allows reality to cross with fantasy, a merging that sometimes makes it difficult to tell where one ends and the other begins. Shown here is an example of "performance animation," or "morphing," in the David Byrnes video "She's Mad."

planets, to communicate almost instantaneously anywhere on the globe, to travel greater distances faster, and to store, retrieve, and analyze vast amounts of information.

This level of accomplishment, although impressive, is really very superficial. Of much greater significance is a level beyond this, how technology changes people's way of life. *Technology is much more than the apparatus.* On a very obvious level, without automobiles, telephones, televisions, computers, and the like, our entire way of life would be strikingly different. As we look at how technology spreads, I shall stress this sociological aspect of technologyy, how it affects people's lives.

Ogburn's Theory of Social Change

Sociologist William Ogburn (1922/1938, 1961, 1964) identified three processes of social change. Technology, he said, can lead to social change through invention, discovery, and diffusion.

Invention Ogburn defined **invention** as a combining of existing elements and materials to form new ones. Whereas we think of inventions as being only material, such as computers, there also are *social* inventions, such as bureaucracy and capitalism. As we saw in these instances (pp. 114–121 and 353–354),

social inventions can have far-reaching consequences for a society. Later on, we will explore ways in which the computer is transforming society.

Discovery Ogburn's second process of change is **discovery,** a new way of seeing reality. The reality is already present, but people now see it for the first time. An example is Columbus's "discovery" of North America, which had consequences so huge that it even altered the course of history. This example also illustrates another principle: A discovery brings extensive change only when it comes at the right time. Other groups, such as the Vikings, had already "discovered" America in the sense of learning that a new land existed (the land, of course, was no discovery to the Native Americans already living in it). Viking settlements disappeared into history, however, and Norse culture was untouched by the discovery.

Diffusion The spread of an invention or discovery from one area to another, called **diffusion,** can have far-reaching effects on human relationships. For example, when missionaries introduced steel axes to the Aborigines of Australia, it upset their whole society. Before this, the men controlled the making of axes, using a special stone available only in a remote region and passing axe-making skills from one man to another. Women had to request permission to use the stone axe. When steel axes became common, women also possessed them, and the men lost both status and power (Sharp 1995).

Diffusion also includes the spread of ideas. The idea of citizenship, for example, changed the political structure, for no longer was the monarch an unquestioned source of authority. Today, the concept of gender equality is circling the globe, with the basic idea that it is wrong to withhold rights on the basis of someone's sex. This idea, though now taken for granted in a few parts of the world, is revolutionary. Like citizenship, it is destined to transform basic human relationships and entire societies.

Cultural Lag Ogburn coined the term **cultural lag** to refer to how some elements of a culture adapt to an invention or discovery more rapidly than others. Technology, he suggested, usually changes first, followed by culture. In other words, we play catch-up with changing technology, adapting our customs and ways of life to meet its needs.

Culture contact *is the source of* diffusion, *the spread of an invention or discovery from one area to another. Shown here are two children of the Huli tribe in Papua New Guinea amused at a Polaroid shot of themselves.*

The computer provides a good example. Let's consider how it is changing our way of life.

The Impact of the Computer

The ominous wail seemed too close for comfort. Sally looked in her rear-view mirror and realized that the flashing red lights and the screaming siren might be for her. She felt confused. "I'm just on my way to Soc class," she thought. "I'm not speeding or anything." After she pulled over, an angry voice over a loudspeaker ordered her out of the car.

As she got out, someone barked the command, "Back up with your hands in the air!" Bewildered, Sally stood frozen for a moment. "Put 'em up now! Right now!" She did as she was told.

The officer crouched behind his open door, his gun drawn. When Sally reached the police car—still backing up—the officer grabbed her, threw her to the ground, and handcuffed her hands behind her back. She heard words she would never forget, "You are under arrest for murder. You have the right to remain silent. Anything you say can and will be used against you in a court of law. You have the right to an attorney. If you cannot afford one, one will be provided for you."

Traces of alarm still flicker across Sally's face when she recalls her arrest. She had never even had a traffic ticket, much less been arrested for anything. The nightmare that Sally experienced happened because of a "computer error." With the inversion of two numbers, her car's license number had been entered instead of that of a woman wanted for a brutal killing earlier that day.

None of us is untouched by the computer, but it is unlikely that many of us have felt its power as directly and dramatically as Sally did. For most of us, the computer's control lies quietly behind the scenes. Although the computer has intruded into our daily lives, most of us never think about it. Our grades are computerized, and probably our paychecks as well. When we buy groceries, a computer scans our purchases and presents a printout of the name, price, and quantity of each item. Essentially the computer's novelty has given way to everyday routine; it is simply another tool.

Many people rejoice over the computer's capacity to improve their quality of life. They are pleased with the quality control of manufactured goods and the reduction of drudgery. Records are much easier to keep, and we can type just one letter and let the computer print and address it to ten individuals—or to ten thousand. With ease, I can modify this sentence, this paragraph, or any section of this book.

Some people, however, worry about errors that can creep into computerized records, aware that something like Sally's misfortune may happen to them. Others fear that confidentiality of computerized data will be abused, in the way that Orwell's Big Brother used information to achieve total control.

As is apparent from the design of this 1903 car, which looks like a horse buggy, *new technology builds on existing technology*. At this point, the automobile was an inefficient novelty. Only after supporting technology came into being, especially graveled and paved roads, was the automobile a serious contender with other forms of transportation. At the time this photo was taken, who could have imagined that this strange instrument was destined to transform society?

These are legitimate concerns, but space does not permit us to pursue them further.

At this point, let's consider how the computer is changing medicine, education, and the workplace, then its likely effects on social inequality.

Medicine

The patient's symptoms were mystifying. After exercise, one side of his face and part of his body turned deep red, the other chalky white. He looked as though someone had taken a ruler and drawn a line down the middle of his body.

Stumped, the patient's physician consulted a medical librarian who punched a few words into a personal computer to search for clues in the world's medical literature. Soon, the likely answer flashed on the screen: Harlequin's disease. (Winslow 1994)

The computer was right, and a neurosurgeon was able to correct the patient's nervous system. With computers, physicians can peer within the body's hidden recesses to determine how its parts are functioning or to see if surgery is necessary. Surgeons can operate on unborn babies and on previously inaccessible parts of the brain. In a coming "lab-on-a-chip," one million tiny fragments of genetic DNA can be crammed onto a disposable microchip. Read by a laser scanner, in just a few minutes the chip reveals such things as whether a patient carries the cystic fibrosis gene or has grown resistant to AIDS drugs. The chip will sell for only $10 (King 1994).

As the future rushes in, the microchip is bringing even more technological wonders. In what is

called *telemedicine*, patients have their heart and lungs checked with a stethoscope—by doctors who are hundreds of miles away. The data are transmitted by fiber-optic cable (Richards 1996). Soon a surgeon in Boston or San Francisco, using a remote-controlled robot and images relayed via satellite to computers, will be able to operate on a wounded soldier in a battlefield hospital on the other side of the world (Associated Press 1995).

Will the computer lead to "doctorless" medical offices? Will we perhaps one day feed vital information about ourselves into a computer—sex, age, race, family medical history, symptoms, and test results—and receive a printout of what is wrong with us (and, of course, a prescription)? Somehow "Take two aspirins and key me in the morning" doesn't sound comforting.

Although computers do outperform physicians in diagnostics (Waldholz 1991), such an office is likely to remain only a concept in some futurist's fanciful imagination, for physicians will vigorously repel such an onslaught on their expertise. Many patients are also likely to resist, for they would miss interacting with their doctors, especially the assurances and other psychological support that good physicians provide. It is likely, then, that the computer will remain a diagnostic tool for physicians, not a replacement for them.

Education Almost every grade school in the United States introduces its students to the computer. Children learn how to type on it, as well as how to use mathematics and science software. Successful educational programs use a gamelike format that makes students forget they are "studying." Classrooms are being wired to the Internet; students in schools that have no teachers knowledgeable in Russian are able to take courses in Russian—as well as the sociology of baseball ("Cyberschool" 1996).

The unequal funding we discussed in Chapter 13 is significant in this context. Those schools able to afford the latest in computer technology are able to better prepare their students for the future. That advantage, of course, goes to students of private schools and the richest public school districts, thus helping to perpetuate social inequalities that arise from the chance of birth.

The computer will transform the college of the future. Each office and dormitory room and off-campus residence will be connected by fiber-optic cable, and a professor will be able to transmit a 250-page book directly from his or her office to a student's bedroom, or back the other way, in *less* time than it took to read this sentence ("Harvard Wired" 1994). To help students and professors do research or prepare reports, computers will search millions of pages of text. Digital textbooks will replace printed versions such as this one. You will be able to key in the terms *social interaction* and *gender*, and select your preference of historical period and geographical area—and the computer will spew out maps, moving images, and sounds. It will be the same for riots and Los Angeles, sexual discrimination in the military, even the price of marijuana. If you wish, the computer will give you a test—at your chosen level of difficulty—so you can immediately check your mastery of the material.

The Workplace The computer is also transforming the workplace. The simplest level is how we do work. For example, I am composing this book on a computer, which will immediately print what I write. A series of archaic, precomputer processes follows, however, in which the printed copy is sent via the postal service to an editor, who physically handles the manuscript and sends it to others who do the same. The manuscript is eventually returned to me via the postal service for final corrections—a rather primitive process, much as would have occurred during Benjamin Franklin's day. Eventually I will be able to zap my manuscript electronically from my computer to my editor's computer—when practice catches up with potential.

The computer is also changing things on a deeper level, for it alters social relationships. For example, no longer do I bring my manuscript to a university secretary, wait, and then retrieve it several days later. Since I make the corrections directly at the computer, the secretary is bypassed entirely. In this instance, the computer enhances social relationships, for the department secretary has much less work, and this new process eliminates the necessity of excuses when a manuscript is not ready on time—and the tensions in the relationship that this brings.

The computer's effects may be so radical that it reverses the historical change in work location. As discussed earlier, industrialization caused work to shift from home to factory and office. Since workers now can be "networked" (linked via computers), this fundamental change may be reversed. Already millions of workers remain at home, where they perform their work on computers.

On the negative side are increased surveillance of workers and depersonalization. As a telephone information operator said,

> The computer knows everything. It records the minute I punch in, it knows how long I take for each call.... I am supposed to average under eighteen seconds per call.... Everything I do is reported to my supervisor on his computer, and if I've missed my numbers I get a written warning. I rarely see the guy.... It's intense. It's me and the computer all day. I'm telling you, at the end of the day I'm wiped out. Working with computers is the coal mining of the nineties. (Mander 1992:57)

▼ **In Sum** A change in technology inevitably leads to a change in culture. To some, such changes as those we just discussed are threatening, for, always, established ways of life must be modified. Consequently, while some welcome new technology, others resist it, the topic of the New Technology box on the next page.

Cyberspace and Social Inequalities

The term **information superhighway** carries the idea of information traveling at a high rate of speed among homes and businesses. Just as a highway allows physical travel from one place to another, so homes and businesses will be connected by the rapid flow of information. Already 40+ million people around the world are able to communicate by Internet, while other services such as Prodigy, America Online, and CompuServe allow electronic access to libraries of information. Some programs sift, sort, and transmit scanned images, sound, even video

Sociology and the New Technology

From the Luddites to the Unabomber: Opposition to Technology

BECAUSE EVERY NEW technology replaces some existing technology, technology always threatens someone. Consequently, opposition to technology is common; on occasion, the opposition even grows violent. The classic example occurred in the British textile industry in the early 1800s when owners introduced machines that made stockings. The workers, whose jobs were being automated away, smashed the machines. Twelve thousand troops had to be called out to restore order. Some of the Luddites (named after Ned Ludlum, an apprentice stocking maker who destroyed his machine) were shipped off to Australia; others were executed (Volti 1995). Today, the term "Luddite" means someone who opposes new technology.

Opposition is usually directed at a specific new technology, but sometimes it is a protest against technology in general. Jacques Ellul (1965), for example, a French sociologist, warned that technology was destroying traditional values. Humans, he said, are becoming "a single tightly integrated and articulated component" of technology. Technology, he added, is producing a monolithic world culture in which "variety is mere appearance."

The message of Ellul and others like him, such as Neil Postman (1992), reached but a few intellectuals who discussed the matter in faculty seminars and wrote obscure papers on the subject. In contrast, the Unabomber's message came thundering into our consciousness, for he chose to send his warning signals not via books and articles, but via the mail—in explosives that maimed and killed their unsuspecting recipients. For seventeen years, the man sent bombs, with no apparent message behind his seemingly random attacks. Then unexpectedly, in 1995, he sent a verbal message, promising to stop his terror if his 35,000-word essay against technology were published. The *New York Times* and the *Washington Post* duly printed it. His message, in its essence, was not dissimilar to Ellul's: Technology is destroying us.

For Your Consideration

What do the Luddites, Jacques Ellul, and the Unabomber have in common? Use concepts presented in this and earlier chapters to analyze the effects of technology on society. Given your conclusions, should we fear new technologies?

---

among participants. Using electronic mail (e-mail), people are able to zap messages without regard to national boundaries. This is the future, a world linked by almost instantaneous communications, with information readily accessible around the globe, and few places to be called remote.

The implications of the information superhighway (also called the *Infobahn*) for national and global stratification are severe. On the national level, we can end up with information have-nots among inner-city and rural residents, thus perpetuating present inequalities (Carey and Lewyn 1994). On the global level, the question is, Who will control the information superhighway? The answer, of course, should be obvious, for it is the Most Industrialized Nations that are developing the communications system. This leads to one of the more profound issues of the twenty-first century—will such control destine the Least Industrialized Nations to a perpetual pauper status?

Other Theories of Social Change

Although technology certainly is a driving force in social change, let's look at other explanations of why societies change. Let's first consider two major types of theories—evolutionary and cyclical—and then look at conflict theory.

Evolutionary Theories

Evolutionary theories can be classified as unilinear, multilinear, and cyclical. Let's consider each.

Unilinear Evolution *Unilinear* evolutionary theories assume that all societies follow the same path. Evolving from simpler to more complex forms, they go through uniform sequences (Barnes 1935). Many different versions have been proposed, but one that once dominated Western thought was Lewis Morgan's (1877) theory that societies go through three stages: savagery, barbarism, and civilization. In his eyes English society served as the epitome of civilization, which all others were destined to follow.

Since the basic assumption of this theory, that all preliterate groups have the same form of social organization, has been found to be untrue, unilinear evolution has been discredited. In addition, to see one's own society as the top of the evolutionary ladder is now considered unacceptably ethnocentric.

still goes through similar stages but end up at the same place

Multilinear Evolution *Multilinear* views of evolution have replaced unilinear theories. Instead of assuming that all societies follow the same path, multilinear theories presuppose that different routes can lead to a similar stage of development. Thus, to become industrialized, societies need not pass through the same sequence of stages (Sahlins and Service 1960; Lenski and Lenski 1987).

Evaluating Evolutionary Theories Central to evolutionary theories, whether unilinear or multilinear, is the idea of *progress*, that preliterate societies evolve from a simple form of organization toward a higher state. Growing appreciation of the rich diversity—

and complexity—of traditional cultures has discredited this idea. Moreover, Western culture is now in crisis (poverty, racism, discrimination, war, terrorism, alienation, violent sexual assaults, unsafe streets, rampant fear) and no longer regarded as holding the answers to human happiness. Consequently, the assumption of progress has been cast aside and evolutionary theories have been rejected (Eder 1990; Smart 1990).

Cyclical Theories *entire civilization*

Cyclical theories attempt to account for the rise of entire civilizations, not a particular society. Why, for example, did Egyptian, Greek, and Roman civilizations rise to a peak of power and then disappear? Cyclical theories assume that civilizations are like organisms: they are born, see an exuberant youth, come to maturity, then decline as they reach old age, and finally die (Hughes 1962).

To explain this pattern, historian Arnold Toynbee (1946) proposed that each time a society successfully meets a challenge, oppositional forces are set up. At its peak, when a civilization has become an empire, the ruling elite loses its capacity to keep the masses in line "by charm rather than by force." As the oppositional forces are set loose, the fabric of society is ripped apart. Although force may hold the empire together for hundreds of years, the civilization is doomed.

In a book that provoked widespread controversy, *The Decline of the West* (1926–1928), Oswald Spengler, a German teacher and social critic, proposed that Western civilization had passed its peak and was in decline. Although the West succeeded in overcoming the crises provoked by Hitler and Mussolini that so disturbed Spengler, as Toynbee noted, civilizations do not necessarily end in a sudden and total collapse. Since the decline can last hundreds of years, some analysts think that the crisis in Western civilization mentioned earlier (poverty, rape, murder, and so on) may indicate that Spengler was right.

Conflict Theory

Long before Toynbee, Marx identified a recurring process in human history. He said that each *thesis* (a current arrangement of power) contains its own *antithesis* (contradiction or opposition). A struggle develops between the thesis and its antithesis, leading

The dominating assumption during the 1800s and in the earlier part of this century was that European and European-derived cultures represented the pinnacle of human evolution. Consequently, other groups represented a lesser stage of development. When they evolved, they, too, would become like the Europeans. Such an assumption may underlie this 1828 portrait of Hoowaunneka, a Native American of the Winnebago tribe, as the painter, C. B. King (inadvertently) gave Hoowaunneka European features.

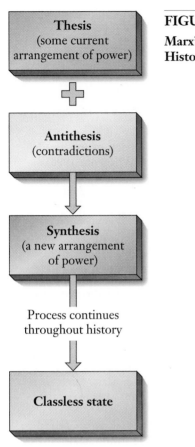

FIGURE 15.1

Marx's Model of Historical Change

Process continues throughout history

ment of power and must at some point be resolved into a synthesis, and so on.

Because these contradictions, which are built into arrangements of power, create huge discontent, they can lead to social movements. As social movements are very significant for our lives, let's examine them.

Social Movements as a Source of Social Change

Social movements consist of large numbers of people who organize to promote or resist social change. Examples of such deliberate and sustained efforts include the temperance movement, the civil rights movement, the white supremacist movement, the women's movement, the animal rights crusade, the nuclear freeze movement, and the environmental movement.

At the heart of social movements lie grievances and dissatisfactions. Some people find a current condition of society intolerable, and their goal is to *promote* social change. Theirs is called a **proactive social movement.** In contrast, others feel threatened because some condition of society is changing, and they organize to *resist* that change. Theirs is a **reactive social movement.**

To further their goals, people develop **social movement organizations.** Those whose goal is to promote social change develop such organizations as the National Organization for Women (NOW) and the National Association for the Advancement of Colored People (NAACP). In contrast, for those who are trying to resist these changes, the Stop-ERA and the Ku Klux Klan serve the same purpose. To recruit followers and sympathizers, leaders of social movements use various attention-getting devices, from marches and rallies to sit-ins and boycotts. To publicize their grievances, they also may stage "media events." Some do so very effectively (see Our Multicultural Society box on the next page).

Social movements are like a rolling sea, says sociologist Mayer Zald (1992). During one period of time, few social movements appear, but shortly afterward a wave of them rolls in, each competing for the public's attention. Zald suggests that a *cultural crisis* can give birth to a wave of social movements. By this, he means that there are times when a society's institutions fail to keep up with social changes, many people's needs go unfulfilled, massive unrest follows,

to a *synthesis* (a new arrangement of power). This new social order, in turn, becomes a thesis that will be challenged by its own antithesis, and so on. Figure 15.1 gives a visual summary of this process.

According to Marx's view (called a **dialectical process** of history), each ruling group sows the seeds of its own destruction. Consider capitalism. Marx said that capitalism (the thesis) is built on the exploitation of workers (an antithesis, or built-in opposition). With workers and owners on a collision course, the dialectical process will not stop until workers establish a classless state (the synthesis).

The analysis of G7 on pages 403–404 follows conflict theory. The current division of global resources and markets is a thesis. An antithesis is resentment on the part of have-not nations. If one of the Least Industrialized Nations gains in relative wealth or military power, that nation will press for a redistribution of resources. Any new arrangement, or synthesis, will contain its own antithesis (such as ethnic hostilities), contradictions that haunt the arrange-

▼▲▼▲▼▲▼▲▼▲▼▲▼▲▼▲▼▲▼▲▼▲▼▲▼▲▼▲▼▲▼▲▼▲▼▲▼

Our Multicultural Society

The Million-Man March: Another Step in an Unfinished Social Movement

THE CIVIL RIGHTS MOVEMENT of the 1950s and 1960s did not end in the year 1970. This movement brought huge gains: integrated public facilities, schools, voting booths, housing, and workplaces. Or, rather, the right to such aspects of social life, for they always seemed to be elusive, to somehow disappear just when they seemingly were on the verge of being fulfilled.

The inner city, with all of its ills, from unemployment to violent crime, has become the single most powerful symbol that this social movement is unfinished. The nightly headlines not only nurture the fears of both African Americans and whites—and of everyone else—but also proclaim the unfinished nature of the civil rights movement.

The Million-Man March—consisting of thousands of African-American males from all over the country who gathered on the Mall in Washington, D.C., in the fall of 1995—picked up where this move-

ment stalled. It had two essential features. The first is an outward direction: protest at continued obstacles; the insistence that the walls of racism come down; voter registration drives; a sense of optimism and determination that good can be accomplished. And overriding all else, a sense of black unity arising from twin sources—shared pain and a glimpse of a promising future.

This first feature is a direct reflection of the old civil rights movement.

The second feature, an inward-turning, is a redirecting of the civil rights movement. It is a conservative, proactive stance, a desire by African Americans to make changes in the African-American community. As stressed by the march's organizers, this feature underscores the need to build greater respect between men and women, to reduce spouse abuse, and to assume the obligations of fatherhood—including marriage, nurturing and supporting one's

children, and giving them a positive role model of responsible masculinity (Whetstone 1996).

This desire for inward change, to be manifested in personal relationships, reflects the religious orientation of the march's organizers. The emphases are on repentance, atonement, and changed behavior. Although a religious orientation to the civil rights movement is not new—for central to this movement has been a dedication to religious principles motivated by moral outrage over grievous wrongs—this inward direction of the religious orientation is new.

The Million-Man March, then, did not begin with a figurative march to Washington. Nor did it end with the departure of the buses. Rather, the march is one facet of an interrupted social movement—one destined to take other forms in the future, for its goals have been but partially reached.

and social movements spring into action to bridge this gap.

Types of Social Movements

Since social change is always their goal, we can classify social movements according to their *target* and the *amount of change* they seek. Figure 15.2 summarizes the classification developed by sociologist David Aberle (1966). If you read across, you will see that the target of the first two types of social movements is *individuals*. **Alterative social movements** seek only to *alter* some particular behavior of people. An example is a powerful social movement of

the early 1900s, the Women's Christian Temperance Union (WCTU), whose goal was to get people to stop drinking alcohol. Its members were convinced that if they could close the saloons, such problems as poverty and wife abuse would go away. **Redemptive social movements** also target individuals, but here the aim is for *total* change. An example is a religious social movement that stresses conversion. In fundamentalist Christianity, for example, when someone converts to Christ, the entire person is supposed to change, not just some specific behavior. Self-centered acts are to be replaced by loving behaviors toward others as the convert becomes, in their terms, a "new creation."

Amount of Change

	Partial	Total
Individual	Alterative 1	Redemptive 2
Society	3 Reformative	4 Transformative

(Target of Change)

Source: Aberle 1966.

FIGURE 15.2

Types of Social Movements

The target of the next two types of social movements is *society*. **Reformative social movements** seek to *reform* some specific aspect of society. The environmental movement, for example, seeks to reform the ways society treats the environment, from its disposal of garbage and nuclear wastes to its use of forests and water. **Transformative social movements,** in contrast, seek to *transform* the social order itself and to replace it with a new version of the good society. Revolutions, such as those in the American colonies, France, Russia, and Cuba, are examples.

Propaganda and the Mass Media

Aware of how influential the mass media are, the leaders of social movements try to manipulate the media in order to influence **public opinion,** how people think about some issue. The right kind of publicity enables them to arouse a sympathetic public and to lay the groundwork for recruiting more members. Pictures of bloodied, dead baby seals, for example, go a long way to getting a group's message across.

A key to understanding social movements, then, is **propaganda.** Although this word often evokes negative images, it actually is neutral. Propaganda is simply the presentation of information in the attempt to influence people. Its original meaning was positive, for *propaganda* referred to a committee of cardinals of the Roman Catholic church whose assignment was the care of foreign missions. (They were to *propagate* the faith.) The term has traveled a long way since then, however, and today it usually refers to a one-sided presentation of information that distorts reality.

Propaganda, in the sense of organized attempts to manipulate public opinion, is a regular part of modern life. Advertisements, for example, are a form of propaganda, for they present a one-sided version of reality.

The use of propaganda *is popular among people committed to the goals of a social movement. They can see only one side to the social issue about which they are so upset. Do you think there is another side to this social issue?*

▲▼▲▼▲▼▲▼▲▼▲▼▲▼▲▼▲▼▲▼▲▼▲▼▲▼▲▼▲▼

Down-to-Earth Sociology

"Tricks of the Trade"—The Fine Art of Propaganda

SOCIOLOGISTS ALFRED AND ELIZABETH LEE (1939) found that propaganda relies on seven basic techniques, which they termed "tricks of the trade." To be effective, the techniques should be subtle, with the audience remaining unaware of just which part of their mind or emotions is being manipulated. If propaganda is effective, people will not know *why* they support something, only that they do—as they fervently defend it.

1. *Name calling.* This technique aims to arouse opposition to the competing product, candidate, or policy by associating it with a negative image. By comparison, one's own product, candidate, or policy appears attractive. Political candidates who call an opponent "soft on crime" are using this technique.

2. *Glittering generality.* Essentially the opposite of the first, this technique surrounds the product, candidate, or policy with "virtue words," phrases that arouse positive feelings. "She's a *real* Democrat" has little meaning, but it makes the audience feel something has been said. "He stands for individualism" is so general that it is meaningless, yet the audience thinks it has heard a specific message about the candidate.

3. *Transfer.* In its positive form, this technique associates the product, candidate, or policy with something that the public respects or approves; in its negative form, with something of which it disapproves. Let's look at the positive form: You might not be able to get by with saying, "Coors is patriotic," but surround a beer with the U.S. flag, and beer drinkers will get the idea that it is more patriotic to drink this brand of beer than another.

4. *Testimonials.* Famous and admired individuals are used to endorse a product, candidate, or policy. Elizabeth Taylor hawks perfume while other movie stars extol the relief offered by hemorrhoid ointments. Candidates for political office may solicit the endorsement of movie stars—who may know next to nothing about the candidate, or even about politics itself. In the negative form of this technique, a despised person is associated with the competing product. If propagandists could get by with it, they would show Saddam Hussein drinking a competing beer or announcing support for an opposing candidate.

5. *Plain folks.* Sometimes it pays to associate the product, candidate, or policy with "just plain folks." "If Mary or John Q. Public likes it, you will, too." A political candidate who kisses babies, dons a hard hat, and has lunch at McDonald's while photographers "catch him or her in the act"—is using the "plain folks" strategy. "I'm just a regular person" is the message of the presidential candidate posing for photographers in jeans and work shirt—while making certain that the Mercedes and chauffeur do not show up in the background.

6. *Card stacking.* The aim of this technique is to present only positive information about what you support, only negative information about what you oppose. Make it sound as though there is only one conclusion that a rational person can draw. Use falsehoods, distortions, and illogical statements if you must.

7. *Bandwagon.* "Everyone is doing it" is the idea behind this technique. Emphasizing how many others buy the product or support the candidate or policy conveys the message that anyone who doesn't join in is on the wrong track. After all, "20 million Frenchmen can't be wrong," can they?

The Lees (1939) added, "Once we know that a speaker or writer is using one of these propaganda devices in an attempt to convince us of an idea, we can separate the device from the idea and see what the idea amounts to on its own merits."

Underlying effective propaganda are seven basic techniques, discussed in the Down-to-Earth Sociology box above. Perhaps by understanding these techniques, you will be able to resist one-sided appeals—whether they come from social movements or from hawkers of some new product.

The mass media have become, in effect, the gatekeepers to social movements. If those who control and work in the mass media—from owners to reporters—are sympathetic to some particular "cause," you can be sure that it receives sympathetic treatment. If the social movement goes against their own views, it will be ignored or given unfavorable treatment. If you ever get the impression that the media are trying to manipulate your opinions and attitudes on some particular social movement—or some social issue—you probably are right. Far from doing unbiased reporting, the media are under the control and influence of people who have an agenda to get across. To the materials in the Down-to-Earth Sociology box on propaganda, then, we need to add the biases of the media establishment, the issues to which it chooses to give publicity, those it ignores, and its favorable and unfavorable treatment of issues and movements.

Sociology can be a liberating discipline (Berger 1963/1997). It sensitizes us to the existence of *multiple realities;* that is, for any single point of view on some topic, there likely are competing points of view, which some find equally as compelling. Each represents reality as the individual sees it, but different experiences lead to different perceptions. Consequently, although the committed members of a social movement are sincere, and perhaps even sacrifice for "the cause," theirs is but one view of the way the world is. If other sides were presented, the issue would look quite different.

The Stages of Social Movements

Sociologists have identified five stages in the growth and maturity of social movements (Lang and Lang 1961; Mauss 1975; Spector and Kitsuse 1977; Tilly 1978; Jaspar 1991). They are

1 *Initial unrest and agitation.* During this first stage, people are upset about some condition in society and want to change it. Leaders emerge who verbalize people's feelings and crystallize issues. Most social movements fail at this stage. Unable to gain enough support, after a brief flurry of activity they quietly die.

2 *Resource mobilization.* The crucial factor that enables social movements to make it past the first stage is **resource mobilization.** By this term, sociologists mean the mobilization of resources such as time, money, people's skills, technologies such as direct mailing and fax machines, and attention by the mass media (Oliver and Marwell 1992; Buechler 1993). In some cases, an indigenous leadership arises to mobilize available resources. Other groups, having no capable leadership of their own, turn to outsiders, "specialists for hire."

As sociologists John McCarthy and Mayer Zald (1977; Zald and McCarthy 1987) point out, even though large numbers of people may be upset over some condition of society, without resource mobilization they are only upset people, perhaps even agitators, but not a social movement.

3 *Organization.* A division of labor is set up. The leadership makes policy decisions, and the rank and file carry out the daily tasks necessary to keep the movement going. There is still much collective excitement about the issue, the movement's focal point of concern.

4 *Institutionalization.* At this stage, the movement has developed a bureaucracy, the type of formal hierarchy described in Chapter 5. The collective excitement is gone, and control lies in the hands of career officers, who may care more about their own position in the organization than the movement for which the organization's initial leaders made sacrifices.

5 *Organizational decline and possible resurgence.* As managing the day-to-day affairs of the organization comes to dominate the leadership, their attention is diverted away from the issues around which the movement originated. No longer a collection of committed people who share a common cause, the movement may decline at this point.

Decline is not inevitable, however. More idealistic and committed leaders may emerge, step to the forefront, and reinvigorate the movement. Or, as in the case of abortion, groups in conflict with each other may fight on opposite sides of the issue, each continuously invigorating the other and preventing the movement's decline. The following Thinking Critically section contrasts the two opposing groups in regard to abortion.

Thinking Critically about Social Controversy

Which Side of the Barricades? Prochoice and Prolife as a Social Movement

NO ISSUE SO DIVIDES Americans as abortion does. Although most Americans take a more moderate view, on one side are some who feel that abortion should be permitted under any circumstance, even during the last

Activists in social movements become committed to "the cause." The social movement around abortion, currently one of the most dynamic in the United States, has split Americans, is highly visible, and has articulate spokespeople on both sides.

month of pregnancy. They are matched by some on the other side who are convinced that abortion should never be allowed, not even during the first month of pregnancy. This polarization constantly breathes new life into the movement.

When the U.S. Supreme Court determined in its 1973 decision, *Roe* v. *Wade*, that states could not restrict abortion, the prochoice side relaxed. Victory was theirs, and they thought their opponents would quietly disappear. Instead, large numbers of Americans were disturbed by what they saw as gross immorality. For them, the legal right to abortion amounted to the right to murder unborn children.

The two sides see matters in totally incompatible ways. On the one hand, those in favor of choice view the 1.5 million abortions performed annually in the United States as examples of women exercising their basic reproductive rights. On the other, those who gather under the prolife banner see them as legalized murder. To the prochoice side, those who oppose abortion stand in the way of women's rights, forcing women to continue pregnancies they desire to terminate. To the prolife forces, those who advocate choice are seen as condoning murder, as putting their own desires for school, career, or convenience ahead of the lives of unborn children.

There is no way to reconcile such opposing views. Each sees the other as unreasonable and extremist. And each uses propaganda by focusing on worst-case scenarios: prochoice images of young women, raped at gunpoint, forced to bear the children of rapists; prolife images of women who are eight months pregnant killing their babies instead of nurturing them.

These views are in permanent conflict. And as each side fights for what it considers basic rights, it reinvigorates the other. When in 1989 the U.S. Supreme Court decided in *Webster* v. *Reproductive Services* that states could restrict abortion, one side mourned it as a defeat, the other hailed it as a victory. Seeing the political battle going against them, the prochoice side regrouped for a determined struggle. The prolife side, sensing judicial victory within its grasp, gathered forces for a push to complete the overthrow of *Roe* v. *Wade*.

This goal of the prolife side came close to becoming reality in *Casey* v. *Planned Parenthood*. On June 30, 1992, in a 6-to-3 decision the Supreme Court upheld a Pennsylvania law that requires a woman to wait 24 hours between the confirmation of pregnancy and abortion, girls under 18 to obtain the consent of one parent to have an abortion, and women to be informed about alternatives to abortion and to be given materials that describe the fetus. In the same case, by a 5-to-4 decision, the Court ruled that a wife does not have to inform her husband if she intends to have an abortion.

Because the two sides do not see the same reality, this social movement cannot end unless the vast majority of Americans commit to one side or the other. Otherwise, all legislative and judicial outcomes—whether the overthrow of *Roe* v. *Wade* or such extremes as a constitutional amendment declaring abortion either murder or a woman's right—are victories to one and defeats to the other. Nothing, then, to these activists is ever complete, but each action is only a way station in a hard-fought, bitter moral struggle.

For Your Consideration

Typically, the last stage of a social movement is decline. Why does this last stage not apply to this social movement? Under what conditions will this social movement decline?

The longer the pregnancy, the smaller the proportion of Americans who approve abortion. Does your opinion about abortion change depending on the length of pregnancy? For example, how do you feel about abortion during the second month versus the eighth month? What do you think about abortion in cases of rape and incest? Can you identify some of the *social* reasons that underlie your opinions?

Sources: Luker 1984, Neikirk and Elsasser 1992; McKenna 1995; *Statistical Abstract* 1995:Table 111; Rhys Williams 1995; Henslin 1996.

Social Change and the Natural Environment

Of all the changes swirling around us, perhaps those affecting the natural environment hold the most serious implications for human life. I shall close the book with a short overview of this pressing matter.

Before looking at the social movement that has grown around this issue, let's examine environmental problems in the three worlds of development.

Environmental Problems in the Most Industrialized Nations

Although even preliterate groups produced pollution, the frontal assault on the natural environment did not begin in earnest until nations industrialized. The more extensive the industrialization, the better it was considered for a nation's welfare, and the slogan for the Most Industrialized Nations has been "Growth at any cost."

Industrial growth did come, but at a high cost to the natural environment. Today, for example, formerly pristine streams are polluted sewers, the water supply of many cities is unfit to drink, and Los Angeles announces "smog days" on radio and television: schoolchildren are kept inside during recess, and everyone is warned to stay indoors. Of all the consequences of pollution that we could discuss—such as the depletion of the ozone layer in order to have the convenience of spray bottles and air conditioners, which may yet prove to be a folly that harms all hu-

manity—due to space we shall consider just the implications of fossil fuels.

Fossil Fuels and Environmental Degradation

The burning of fossil fuels for factories, motorized vehicles, and power plants has been especially harmful. Fish can no longer survive in some lakes in Canada and the northeastern United States because of **acid rain**—the burning fossil fuels release sulfur dioxide and nitrogen oxide, which react with moisture in the air to become sulfuric and nitric acids (Luoma 1989).

An invisible but infinitely more serious consequence is the greenhouse effect. Like the glass of a greenhouse, the gases emitted from burning fossil fuels allow sunlight to enter the earth's atmosphere freely, but inhibit the release of heat. It is as though the gases have closed the atmospheric window through which our planet breathes. Some scientists say that the resulting global warming may melt the polar ice caps and inundate the world's shorelines, cause the climate boundaries to move north about four hundred miles, and make many animal and plant species extinct (Smith and Tirpak 1988; Thomas 1988; Weisskopf 1992). Not all scientists agree with this scenario, however; some even doubt that a greenhouse effect exists (Harper 1995). The most recent measurements, however, strongly indicate that the earth is warming (Bishop 1995).

The Energy Shortage, Internal Combustion Engines, and Multinational Corporations

If you ever read about an energy shortage, you can be sure it is false. There is no energy shortage, nor can there ever be. The earth holds the potential of producing unlimited low-cost power, which can help to raise the living standards of humans across the globe. The sun, for example, produces more energy than humanity could ever need. Boundless energy is also available from the tides and the winds. In some cases, we need better technology to harness these sources of energy, while in others we need only to apply technology we already have.

Since burning fossil fuels in internal combustion engines is the main source of pollution in the Most Industrialized Nations, and vast sources of alternative energy are available, why don't we develop the technology to use these alternative sources of energy? From a conflict perspective, these abundant sources of energy present a threat to the multinationals' oil monopoly. To maintain their profits, these corporations make certain that internal combustion engines remain dominant. The practical development and widespread use of alternative sources of power will wait until the multinationals have cornered the market on the technology that will harness them—so they can continue to reap huge profits.

Environmental Racism and Social Class Pollution in the United States has a racial and social class bias (Cushman 1993; Noah 1994). Racial minorities and the poor are disproportionately exposed to air pollution, hazardous wastes, pesticides, and the like. The basic reasons are that the land where the poor live sells cheaply, and the rich will not stand for factories to spew pollution near their homes. For the same reasons, hazardous waste landfills are likely to be located in predominantly African-American or Latino communities. To deal with this issue, a new specialty, environmental poverty law, is developing (Hayes 1992).

Environmental Problems in the Industrializing Nations

Severe consequences of industrialization, such as ozone depletion, the greenhouse effect, and global warming, cannot be laid solely at the feet of the Most Industrialized Nations. With their rush to be contenders in the global competition, a lack of funds to pay for pollution controls, and few anti-pollution laws, the Industrializing Nations have made their own enormous contributions to this problem. Breathing the air of Mexico City, for example, is the equivalent of smoking two packs of cigarettes a day (Durbin 1995).

The former Soviet Union is a special case. Until this empire broke up, pollution had been treated as a state secret. Scientists and journalists were forbidden to mention pollution in public. Even peaceful demonstrations to call attention to pollution could net participants two years in prison (Feshbach 1992). With protest stifled and no environmental protection laws, environmental pollution was rampant: Almost half of Russia's arable land has been made unsuitable for farming, about a third of Russians live in cities where air pollution is over ten times greater than levels permitted in the United States, and half of Russia's tap water is unfit to drink. Pollution is so severe that the life expectancy of Russians has dropped, a lesson that should not be

lost on the rest of us as we make decisions on how to treat our environment.

Environmental Problems in the Least Industrialized Nations

With its greater poverty and swelling populations, the Least Industrialized Nations have an even greater incentive to industrialize at any cost. These pressures, combined with almost nonexistent environmental regulations, destine the Least Industrialized Nations to become the earth's major source of pollution.

Their lack of environmental protection laws has not gone unnoticed by opportunists in the Most Industrialized Nations, who have begun to use these countries as a garbage dump for hazardous wastes and for producing chemicals that their own people will no longer tolerate (LaDou 1991; Smith 1995). Alarmed at the growing environmental destruction, the World Bank, a monetary arm of the Most Industrialized Nations, has placed pressure on the Least Industrialized Nations to reduce pollution and soil erosion (Lachica 1992). Understandably, the basic concern of these nations is to produce food and housing first, and to worry about the environment later.

Rain Forests and Extinction Holding unknown consequences for the future of humanity is the extinction of numerous plant and animal species as tropical rain forests are relentlessly cleared for lumber, farms, and pastures. Although the rain forests cover just 7 percent of the planet's land area, they are home to half of all its plant species. With the rain forests disappearing at a rate of nearly *2,500 acres every hour* (McCuen 1993), it is estimated that ten thousand species are made extinct each year—about one per hour (Durning 1990). As the rain forests are destroyed, so are the Indian tribes who live in them. With their extinction goes their knowledge of the environment, the topic of the Global Glimpse box on the next page.

The Bottom Line: The Growth Machine versus the Earth

Underlying today's environmental decay is the globalization of capitalism that I have stressed throughout this text. To maintain their dominance and increase their wealth, the Most Industrialized Na-

▲ ▲ ▲ ▲ ▲ ▲ ▲ ▲ ▲ ▲ ▲ ▲ ▲ ▲ ▲ ▲ ▲ ▲

A Global Glimpse

The Rain Forests: Lost Tribes, Lost Knowledge

SINCE 1900, NINETY of Brazil's 270 Indian tribes have disappeared. As settlers have taken over their lands, other tribes have settled in villages. With village life comes a loss of tribal knowledge.

Tribal groups are not just "wild" people barely surviving in spite of their ignorance. On the contrary, they possess intricate forms of social organization and knowledge accumulated over thousands of years. The 2,500 Kayapo Indians, for example, belong to one of the Amazon's endangered tribes. The Kayapo use 250 types of wild fruit and hundreds of nut and tuber species. They cultivate thirteen distinct bananas, eleven kinds of manioc (cassava), sixteen strains of sweet potatos, and seventeen kinds of yams. Many of these varieties are unknown to non-Indians. The Kayapo also use thousands of medicinal plants, one of which contains a drug effective against intestinal parasites.

Until recently, Western scientists dismissed tribal knowledge as superstitious and worthless. Now, however, the West is coming to realize that to lose tribes is to lose knowledge. In the Central African Republic, a man whose chest was being eaten away by a subcutaneous amoeboid infection lay dying because he did not respond to drugs. Out of desperation, the Catholic nuns who were treating him sought the advice of a native doctor, who applied crushed termites to the open wounds. The "dying" man made a remarkable recovery.

The disappearance of the rain forests destroys many species yet unknown that may hold healing properties. Of the earth's 265,000 species of plants, only 1,100 have been thoroughly studied by Western scientists. Yet 40,000 may possess medicinal or undiscovered nutritional value for humans. For example, scientists have recently discovered that the leaves of *Taxus baccata*, a Himalayan tree found in mountainous parts of India, contain taxol, a drug effective against ovarian cancer.

On average, one tribe of Amazonian Indians has been lost each year of this century—due to violence against them, greed by non-Indians for their native lands, and exposure to infectious diseases against which they have little resistance. Ethnocentrism underlies much of this assault. Perhaps the extreme is represented by the cattle ranchers in Colombia who killed eighteen Cueva Indians. The cattle ranchers were perplexed when they were put on trial for murder. They asked why they should be charged with a crime, since everyone knew that the Cuevas were animals, not people. They pointed out that there was even a verb in Colombian Spanish, *cuevar*, which means "to hunt Cueva Indians." So what was their crime, they asked? The jury found them innocent because of "cultural ignorance."

Sources: Durning 1990; Gorman 1991; Linden 1991; Stipp 1992; Simons 1995.

tions, spurred by the multinational corporations, continue to push for economic growth. At the same time, the Industrializing Nations, playing catch-up, are striving to develop their economies. Meanwhile, the Least Industrialized Nations are anxious to enter the race; because they start from even farther behind, they have to push for even faster growth.

Many scientists are convinced that the earth cannot withstand such an onslaught (Krupp 1995). Already our economic production creates extensive pollution, and faster-paced production means faster-paced destruction of our environment. If the goal is a **sustainable environment,** a world system in which we use our physical environment to meet our needs without destroying the future, we cannot continue to trash the earth's natural resources. In short, the ecological message is incompatible with an economic message that it is OK to rape the environment for the sake of profits.

The Environmental Movement

Concern about the world's environmental problems has produced a worldwide social movement. In some countries, political parties whose central issue is the environment, called *green parties*, campaign in local and national elections. Germany's Green party has even won seats in the national legislature (Kiefer 1991).

Activists in the environmental movement generally seek solutions in politics, education, and legislation. Despairing that pollution continues, the rain forests are still being cleared, and species are swiftly becoming extinct, some activists are convinced that the planet is doomed unless immediate steps are taken. Choosing a more radical course, they use extreme tactics to try to arouse indignation among the public and thus force the government to act. Convinced that they stand for true morality, many are willing to break the law and go to jail for their actions. Such activists are featured in the following Thinking Critically section.

▼▲▼▲▼▲▼▲▼▲▼▲▼▲▼▲

Thinking Critically about Social Controversy

Ecosabotage

Blocking a logging road by standing in front of a truck; climbing atop a giant Douglas fir slated for cutting; pouring sand down the gas tank of a bulldozer; tearing down power lines and ripping up survey stakes; driving spikes into redwood trees and sinking whaling vessels— are these the acts of dangerous punks, intent on vandalism and with little understanding of the needs of modern society, or of brave men and women willing to put their freedom, and even their lives, on the line on behalf of the earth itself?

To get some idea of why ecosabotage is taking place, consider the Medicine Tree, a 3,000-year-old redwood in the Sally Bell Grove near the northern California coast. Georgia Pacific, a lumber company, was determined to cut down the Medicine Tree, the oldest and largest of the region's redwoods, which rests on an ancient sacred site of the Sinkyone Indians. Members of Earth First! chained themselves to the tree. After they were arrested, the sawing began. Other protesters jumped over the police-lined barricade and planted themselves in front of the axes and chain saws. A logger swung an axe and missed a demonstrator. At that moment, the sheriff radioed a restraining order, and the cutting stopped.

How many 3,000-year-old trees remain on this planet? Do fences and picnic tables for backyard barbecues justify cutting them down? It is questions like these, as well as the slaughter of seals, the destruction of the rain forests, and the drowning of dolphins in mile-long drift nets that spawned Earth First! and other organizations, such as Greenpeace and Sea Shepherds, which are devoted to preserving the environment at any cost.

"We feel like there are insane people who are consciously destroying our environment, and we are compelled to fight back," explains a member of one of the militant groups. "No compromise in defense of Mother Earth!" says another. "With famine and death approaching, we're in the early stages of World War III," adds another.

As concern about the environment has grown, a social movement has developed to try to change the course of events. Earth First!, one group within this movement, is featured in the text.

The dedication of some of these activists has brought them close to martyrdom. When Paul Watson, founder of the Sea Shepherds, sprayed seals with green dye, which destroys the value of their pelts but doesn't hurt the animals, hunters hogtied him, dragged him across the ice, and threatened to toss him into the sea. "It's no big deal," says Watson, "when you consider that 100 million people in this century have died in wars over real estate."

Radical environmentalists represent a broad range of activities and purposes. They are united neither on tactics nor goals. Some want to stop a specific action, such as the killing of whales, or to destroy all nuclear weapons and dismantle nuclear power plants. Others want everyone to become vegetarians. Still others want the earth's population to be reduced to one billion, roughly what it was in 1800. Some even want humans to return to hunting and gathering bands. Most espouse a simpler lifestyle that will consume less energy and place less pressure on the earth's resources. These groups are so splintered that the founder of Earth First!, Dave Foreman, quit his own organization when it became too confrontational for his tastes.

Among their successes, the radical groups count a halt to the killing of dolphins off Japan's Iki Island, a ban on whaling, trash recycling in many communities, hundreds of thousands of acres of uncut trees, and, of course, the Medicine Tree.

For Your Consideration

Who, then, are these people? Should we applaud ecosaboteurs or jail them? As symbolic interactionists stress, it all depends on your definition. And as conflict theorists emphasize, your definition likely depends on your location in the economic structure. That is, if you are the owner of a lumber company you will see ecosaboteurs differently from the way a camping enthusiast would. How does your own view of ecosaboteurs depend on your life situation? What effective alternatives to ecosabotage are there for people who are convinced that we are destroying the very life support system of our planet?

Sources: Russell 1987; Borrelli 1988; Guha 1989; Carpenter 1990; Eder 1990; Foote 1990; Martin 1990; Parfit 1990; Reed and Benet 1990; Courtney 1995.

Environmental Sociology

Environmental sociology, which examines the relationship between human societies and the environment, emerged as a subdiscipline of sociology about 1970 (Dunlap and Catton 1979, 1983; Albrecht and Murdoch 1986; Buttel 1987; Freudenburg and Gramling 1989; Laska 1993). These are its main assumptions:

1 The physical environment is a significant variable in sociological investigation.

2 Human beings are but one species among many that depend on the natural environment.

3 Because of intricate feedbacks to nature, human actions have many unintended consequences.

4 The world is finite, so there are potential physical limits to economic growth.

5 Economic expansion requires increased extraction of resources from the environment.

6 Increased extraction of resources leads to ecological problems.

7 These ecological problems place restrictions on economic expansion.

8 Governments create environmental problems by trying to create conditions for the profitable accumulation of capital.

As you can see, the goal of environmental sociology is not to stop pollution or nuclear power, but rather to study how human cultures, values, and behavior affect the physical environment and how the physical environment affects human activities. Environmental sociologists, however, are generally also environmental activists, and the Section on Environment and Technology of the American Sociological Association tries to influence governmental policies (American Sociological Association n.d.).

Technology and the Environment: The Goal of Harmony

It is inevitable that humans will continue to develop new technologies. But the abuse of our environment by those technologies is not inevitable. To understate the matter, the destruction of our planet is an unwise choice.

If we are to have a world that is worth passing on to coming generations, we must seek harmony between technology and the natural environment. This will not be easy. At one extreme are people who claim that to protect the environment we must eliminate industrialization and go back to some sort of preindustrialized way of life. At the other extreme are people unable to see the harm being done to the natural environment, who want the entire world to continue industrializing at full speed. Somewhere, there must be a middle ground, one that recognizes that industrialization is here to stay but that we *can* control it, for it is our creation. Industrialization, controlled, can enhance our quality of life; uncontrolled, it will destroy us.

As a parallel to the development of technologies, then, we must develop systems to greatly reduce or eliminate their harm to the environment. This includes mechanisms to oversee the production, use, and disposal of technology. The question, of course, is whether we have the resolve to take the steps to preserve the environment for future generations. The stakes—no less than the welfare of the entire planet—are surely high enough to motivate us to make the wise choices.

Summary and Review

An Overview of Social Change

What are the major trends in social change over the course of human history?

The primary changes in human history are the four social revolutions (domestication, agriculture, industrialization, and information), the change from *Gemeinschaft* to *Gesellschaft* types of societies, capitalism and industrialization, **modernization,** and global stratification. Ethnic conflicts and social movements indicate cutting edges of social change. Pp. 400–405.

What is Ogburn's theory of social change?

Ogburn identified technology as the basic cause of social change, which comes through three processes: **invention, discovery,** and **diffusion.** Pp. 405–406.

What types of technology are there, and what effects does a changed technology have on society?

Because technology is an organizing force of social life, when technology changes its effects can be profound. The computer, for example, is changing the way we practice medicine, learn, work, and even think. The **information superhighway** is likely to perpetuate social inequalities on both national and global levels. Pp. 406–409.

Besides technology, capitalism, modernization, and so on, what other theories of social change are there?

Evolutionary theories presuppose that societies are moving from the same starting point to some similar ending point. *Unilinear* theories, which assume the same path for everyone, have been replaced with *multilinear* theories, which assume that different paths can lead to the same stage of development. *Cyclical* theories, in contrast, view civilizations as going through a process of birth, youth, maturity, decline, and death. Conflict theorists view social change as inevitable, for each *thesis* (basically an arrangement of power) contains an *antithesis* (contradictions). A new *synthesis* develops to resolve these contradictions, but it, too, contains contradictions that will have to be resolved, and so on. This is called a **dialectical process.** Pp. 409–411.

Social Movements as a Source of Social Change

What types of social movements are there?

Social movements consist of large numbers of people who organize to promote or resist social change. Depending on their target (individuals or society) and the amount of social change desired (partial or complete), social movements can be classified as **alterative, redemptive, reformative,** and **transformative.** Pp. 411–413.

How are the mass media related to social movements?

Because the mass media are gatekeepers for social movements, their favorable or unfavorable coverage greatly affects social movements. Social movements make use of **propaganda** to further their causes. Pp. 413–415.

What stages do social movements go through?

Sociologists have identified these stages of social movements: initial unrest and agitation, mobilization, organization, institutionalization, and, finally, decline. Resurgence is also possible, if, as in the case of abortion, opposing sides revitalize one another. Pp. 415–417.

Social Change and the Natural Environment

What are the environmental problems of the Most Industrialized Nations?

The environmental problems of the Most Industrialized Nations are severe, ranging from city smog and **acid rain** to the **greenhouse effect.** Scientists debate whether the greenhouse effect is real; if it is, it may cause **global warming** that will fundamentally affect our lives. The burning of fossil fuels in internal combustion engines lies at the root of many environmental problems, but alternative sources of energy are unlikely to be developed until the multinational corporations can turn them into a profit. Because of the location of polluting factories and hazardous waste sites, environmental problems have a greater impact on minorities and the poor (sometimes called *environmental racism*). Pp. 417–418.

What are the environmental problems of the Industrializing and Least Industrialized Nations?

The worst environmental problems are found in the former Soviet Union, a legacy of the unrestrained exploitation of resources by the Communist party. The rush of the Least Industrialized Nations to industrial-

ize, in the absence of environmental laws, destines them to become a major source of environmental destruction. The world is facing a basic conflict between the lust for profits through the exploitation of the earth's resources and the need to produce a **sustainable environment.** Pp. 418–419.

What is the environmental movement?

The environmental movement is an attempt to restore a healthy environment for the world's people. This global movement takes many forms, from peacefully influencing the political process to *ecosabotage*, sabotaging the efforts of people thought to be legally harming the environment. Pp. 419–421.

What is environmental sociology?

Environmental sociology is not an attempt to change the environment, but a study of the relationship between humans and the environment. Environmental sociologists are generally also environmental activists. Pp. 421–422.

Where can I read more on this topic?

Suggested readings for this chapter appear on pages 444–445.

Glossary

acid rain rain containing sulfuric and nitric acid (p. 417)

alterative social movement a social movement that seeks to alter only particular aspects of people (p. 412)

cultural lag William Ogburn's term for human behavior lagging behind technological innovations (p. 405)

dialectical process a view of history and power in which each arrangement, or thesis, contains contradictions, or antitheses, which must be resolved; the new arrangement, or synthesis, contains its own contradictions; and so on (p. 411)

diffusion the spread of invention or discovery from one area to another; identified by William Ogburn as a major process of social change (p. 405)

discovery a new way of seeing reality; identified by William Ogburn as a major process of social change (p. 405)

environmental sociology a subdiscipline of sociology that examines how human activities affect the physical environment and how the physical environment affects human activities (p. 421)

global warming an increase in the earth's temperature due to the greenhouse effect (p. 417)

greenhouse effect the buildup of carbon dioxide in the earth's atmosphere that allows light to enter but inhibits the release of heat; believed to cause global warming (p. 417)

ideal type a composite of characteristics based on many specific examples; "ideal" in this case means a description of the abstracted characteristics, not what one desires to exist (p. 402)

information superhighway the developing, worldwide electronic network; carries the idea of information traveling at a high rate of speed among homes and businesses (p. 408)

invention the combination of existing elements and materials to form new ones; identified by William Ogburn as a major process of social change (p. 405)

modernization the transformation of traditional societies into industrial societies (p. 401)

postmodern society another term for postindustrial society (p. 404)

proactive social movement a social movement that promotes some social change (p. 411)

propaganda in its broad sense, the presentation of information in the attempt to influence people; in its narrow sense, one-sided information used to try to influence people (p. 413)

public opinion how people think about some issue (p. 413)

reactive social movement a social movement that resists some social change (p. 411)

redemptive social movement a social movement that seeks to change people totally (p. 412)

reformative social movement a social movement that seeks to reform some specific aspect of society (p. 413)

resource mobilization a stage that social movements succeed or fail based on their ability to mobilize resources such as time, money, and people's skills (p. 415)

social change the alteration of culture and societies over time (p. 400)

social movement large numbers of people who organize to promote or resist social change (p. 411)

social movement organization an organization developed to further the goals of a social movement (p. 411)

sustainable environment a world system in which we use our physical environment to meet the needs of humanity without destroying our environment (p. 419)

technology often defined as the applications of science, but can be thought of as tools, items used to accomplish tasks, along with the skills or procedures to make and use those tools (p. 404)

transformative social movement a social movement that seeks to change society totally (p. 413)

Sociology and the Internet

All URLs listed are current as of the printing of this book. URLs are often changed. Please check our Website http://www.abacon.com/henslin for updates.

1. Social Movements

Read the section "Social Movements as a Source of Social Change" (pp. 411–417). You will be using this information to analyze several social movements having Web pages.

Go to Calyx's Activist Groups (http://www.calyx. net/activist. html), and investigate several of the groups listed. For each group, try to determine if it has the characteristics of a social movement, what type of movement it is, and whether or not you think it will be successful.

Although you probably have your own ideas about what will or will not work, base your discussion (or paper, if one is assigned) on the text section "The Stages of Social Movements" (p. 415). Compare your findings with others in your class.

2. The Growth Machine versus the Earth

This chapter's summary of the impact of social change on the environment in the Most Industrialized Nations suggests that the "bottom line" involves a decision for the global growth machine or the earth. Attempts at balancing these concerns, especially among the Least Industrialized Nations, are referred to as "sustainable environment."

To learn more about this, first read the section "Social Change and the Natural Environment" (pp. 417–421). Then look at a collection of efforts at creating sustainable environments by accessing Solstice (http://solstice.crest.org). Read the information on Solstice itself, then click on the "Related net sites" to see a large and varied list of sites dedicated to environmental concerns. Browse several of them.

Following your instructor's assignment, either write a paper on or prepare for a discussion on these topics: Is the sustainable environment theme aimed only at Least Industrialized Nations, or is it global? What are some policies and practices that you think might work with nations at different levels of industrialization? Are there any that would be practical in nearly all countries? How likely is it that any of the policies will be adopted by the United States? What do you think the future holds: growth machine or the earth? Or a compromise enabling a sustainable environment?

GLOSSARY

achieved statuses positions that are earned, are accomplished, or involve at least some effort or activity on the individual's part (p. 86)

acid rain rain containing sulfuric and nitric acid (p. 417)

activity theory the view that satisfaction during old age is related to a person's level and quality of activity (p. 267)

age cohort people born at roughly the same time who pass through the life course together (p. 266)

ageism prejudice, discrimination, and hostility directed against people because of their age; can be directed against any age group, including youth (p. 242)

agents of socialization people and groups that influence our self-concept, emotions, attitudes, and behavior (p. 68)

aggregate people who temporarily share the same physical space but do not see themselves as belonging together (p. 108)

alienation Marx's term for the experience of being cut off from the product of one's labor, which results in a sense of powerlessness and normlessness (pp. 117, 388)

alterative social movement a social movement that seeks to alter only particular aspects of people (p. 412)

anarchy a condition of lawlessness or political disorder caused by the absence or collapse of governmental authority (p. 291)

applied sociology the use of sociology to solve problems—from the micro level of family relationships to the macro level of war and pollution (p. 12)

ascribed statuses positions an individual either inherits at birth or receives involuntarily later in life (p. 86)

assimilation the process of being absorbed into the mainstream culture (p. 221)

authoritarian leader a leader who leads by giving orders (p. 124)

authoritarian personality Theodor Adorno's term for people who are prejudiced and rank high on scales of conformity, intolerance, insecurity, respect for authority, and submissiveness to superiors (p. 217)

authority power that people accept as rightly exercised over them; also called legitimate power (pp. 17, 280)

background assumptions deeply embedded common understandings, or basic rules, concerning our view of the world and of how people ought to act (p. 97)

basic (or pure) sociology sociological research whose only purpose is to make discoveries about life in human groups, not to make changes in those groups (p. 30)

basic demographic equation growth rate = births – deaths + net migration (p. 378)

bilateral system a system of reckoning descent that counts both the mother's and the father's side (p. 310)

blended family a family whose members were once part of other families (p. 324)

born again a term describing Christians who have undergone a life-transforming religious experience so radical that they feel they have become a "new person" (p. 352)

bourgeoisie Karl Marx's term for capitalists, those who own the means of production (p. 163)

bureaucracies formal organizations with a hierarchy of authority, a clear division of labor, impersonality of positions, and emphasis on written rules, communications, and records (p. 114)

capitalism an economic system characterized by the private ownership of the means of production, the pursuit of profit, and market competition (p. 298)

capitalist class the wealthy who own the means of production and buy the labor of the working class (p. 148)

capitalist world economy the dominance of capitalism in the world, along with an interdependence of the world's nations that capitalism has created (p. 174)

caste system a form of social stratification in which one's status is determined by birth and is lifelong (p. 161)

category people who have similar characteristics (p. 108)

charisma literally, an extraordinary gift from God; more commonly, an outstanding, "magnetic" personality (p. 354)

charismatic authority authority based on an individual's outstanding traits, which attract followers (p. 282)

charismatic leader literally, someone to whom God has given an extraordinary gift; more commonly, someone who exerts extraordinary appeal to a group of followers (p. 354)

checks and balances separation of powers among the three branches of U.S. government—legislative, executive, and judicial—so that each is able to nullify the actions of the other two, thus preventing the domination of any single branch (p. 291)

Chicanos Latinos whose country of origin is Mexico (p. 229)

church according to Durkheim, one of the three essential elements of religion—a moral community of believers (p. 349); used by other sociologists to refer to a highly bureaucratized religious organization (p. 356)

citizenship the concept that birth (and residence) in a country impart basic rights (p. 284)

city a place in which a large number of people are permanently based and do not produce their own food (p. 381)

city-state an independent city whose power radiates outward, bringing the adjacent area under its rule (p. 284)

class conflict Karl Marx's term for the struggle between owners (the bourgeoisie) and workers (the proletariat) (p. 7)

class consciousness Karl Marx's term for awareness of a common identity based on one's position in the means of production (p. 163)

class system a form of social stratification based primarily on the possession of money or material possessions (p. 162)

clinical sociology the direct involvement of sociologists in bringing about social change (p. 12)

clique a cluster of people within a larger group who choose to interact with one another; an internal faction (p. 113)

coalition the alignment of some members of a group against others (p. 122)

coercion power that people do not accept as just (p. 280)

cohabitation unmarried people living together in a sexual relationship (p. 326)

colonialism the process by which one nation takes over another nation, usually for the purpose of exploiting its labor and natural resources (p. 174)

community a place people identify with, where they sense that they belong and that others care what happens to them (p. 388)

compartmentalize to separate acts from feelings or attitudes (p. 220)

conflict theory a theoretical framework in which society is viewed as composed of groups competing for scarce resources (p. 17)

conspicuous consumption Thorstein Veblen's term for a change from the Protestant ethic to an eagerness to show off wealth by the elaborate consumption of goods (p. 294)

contradictory class locations Erik Wright's term for a position in the class structure that generates contradictory interests (p. 187)

control theory the idea that two control systems—inner controls and outer controls—work against our tendencies to deviate (p. 140)

convergence theory the view that as both capitalist and socialist economic systems adopt features of the other, a hybrid (or mixed) economic system will emerge (p. 300)

corporate capitalism the domination of the economic system by giant corporations (p. 301)

corporate culture the orientations that characterize corporate work settings (p. 118)

corporation the joint ownership of a business enterprise, whose liabilities and obligations are separate from those of its owners (p. 301)

cosmology teachings or ideas that provide a unified picture of the world (p. 352)

counterculture a subculture whose values place its members in opposition to the values of the broader culture (p. 45)

credential society a group that uses diplomas and degrees to determine who is eligible for jobs, even though the diploma or degree may be irrelevant to the actual work (p. 338)

crime the violation of norms that are written into law (p. 135)

criminal justice system the system of police, courts, and prisons set up to deal with people who are accused of having committed a crime (p. 148)

crude birth rate the annual number of births per 1,000 population (p. 377)

crude death rate the annual number of deaths per 1,000 population (p. 377)

cult a new religion with few followers, whose teachings and practices put it at odds with the dominant culture and religion (p. 354)

cultural diffusion the spread of cultural characteristics from one group to another (p. 51)

cultural goals the legitimate objectives held out to the members of a society (p. 145)

cultural lag William Ogburn's term for human behavior lagging behind technological innovations (pp. 51, 405)

cultural leveling the process by which cultures become similar to one another, especially by which Western industrial culture is imported and diffused into the Least Industrialized Nations (p. 53)

cultural relativism understanding a people from the framework of their own culture (p. 39)

cultural transmission in reference to education, the ways by which schools transmit a society's culture, especially its core values (p. 341)

culture the language, beliefs, values, norms, behaviors, and even material objects that are passed from one generation to the next (p. 37)

culture contact when people from different cultures come into contact with one another (p. 42)

culture of poverty the values and behaviors of the poor that are assumed to make them fundamentally different from other people; these factors are assumed to be largely responsible for their poverty, and parents are assumed to perpetuate poverty across generations by passing these characteristics on to their children (pp. 175, 200)

culture shock the disorientation that people experience when they come in contact with a fundamentally different culture and can no longer depend on their taken-for-granted assumptions about life (p. 37)

deferred gratification forgoing something in the present in the hope of achieving greater gains in the future (p. 202)

degradation ceremony a term coined by Harold Garfinkel to describe rituals designed to strip an individual of his or her identity as a group member; for example, a court martial or the defrocking of a priest (p. 71)

democracy a system of government in which authority derives from the people (p. 284)

democratic leader a leader who leads by trying to reach a consensus (p. 124)

democratic socialism a hybrid economic system in which capitalism is mixed with state ownership (p. 299)

demographic transition a three-stage historical process of population growth: first, high birth rates and high death rates; second, high birth rates and low death rates; and third, low birth rates and low death rates (p. 371)

demographic variables the three factors that influence population growth: fertility, mortality, and net migration (p. 377)

demography the study of the size, composition, growth, and distribution of human populations (p. 368)

dependency ratio the number of workers required to support one person on Social Security (p. 269)

dependency theory the view that the Least Industrialized Nations have been unable to develop their economies because they grew dependent on the Most Industrialized Nations (p. 175)

deterrence creating fear so people will refrain from an act (p. 150)

deviance the violation of rules or norms (p. 135)

dialectical process a view of history and power in which each arrangement, or thesis, contains contradictions, or antitheses, which must be resolved; the new arrangement, or synthesis, contains its own contradictions; and so on (p. 411)

dictatorship a form of government in which power is seized by an individual (p. 285)

differential association Edwin Sutherland's term to indicate that associating with some groups results in learning an "excess of definitions" of deviance (attitudes favorable to committing deviant acts), and, by extension, in a greater likelihood that their members will become deviant (p. 138)

diffusion the spread of invention or discovery from one area to another; identified by William Ogburn as a major process of social change (p. 405)

direct democracy a form of democracy in which voters meet together to discuss issues and make their decisions (p. 284)

discovery a new way of seeing reality; identified by William Ogburn as a major process of social change (p. 405)

discrimination an act of unfair treatment directed against an individual or a group (p. 212)

disengagement theory the view that society prevents disruption by having the elderly vacate their positions of responsibility so the younger generation can step into their shoes (p. 266)

disinvestment the withdrawal of investments by financial institutions, which seals the fate of an urban area (p. 393)

divine right of kings the idea that the king's authority comes directly from God (p. 167)

division of labor how work is divided among the members of a group (p. 93)

dominant group the group with the most power, greatest privileges, and highest social status (p. 211)

downward social mobility movement down the social class ladder (p. 195)

dramaturgy an approach, pioneered by Erving Goffman, analyzing social life in terms of drama or the stage (p. 96)

dyad the smallest possible group, consisting of two persons (p. 122)

ecclesia a religious group so integrated into the dominant culture that it is difficult to tell where the one begins and the other leaves off (p. 356)

economy a system of distribution of goods and services (p. 293)

edge city a large clustering of service facilities and residences near a highway intersection that provides a sense of place to people who live, shop, and work there (p. 383)

ego Freud's term for a balancing force between the id and the demands of society (p. 65)

electronic community people who more or less regularly interact with one another on the Internet (p. 113)

empty nest a married couple's domestic situation after the last child has left home (p. 318)

endogamy the practice of marrying within one's own group (pp. 161, 309)

enterprise zone the use of economic incentives in a designated area with the intention of encouraging investment there (p. 393)

environmental sociology a subdiscipline of sociology that examines how human activities affect the physical environment and how the physical environment affects human activities (p. 421)

ethnic cleansing a policy of population elimination, including forcible expulsion and genocide (p. 221)

ethnic work activities designed to discover, enhance, or maintain ethnic and racial identification (p. 223)

ethnicity (and **ethnic**) having distinctive cultural characteristics (p. 210)

ethnocentrism the use of one's own culture as a yardstick for judging the ways of other individuals or societies, generally leading to a negative evaluation of their values, norms, and behaviors (p. 38)

ethnomethodology the study of how people use background assumptions to make sense of life (p. 97)

exchange mobility about the same numbers of people moving up and down the social class ladder, such that, on balance, the social class system shows little change (p. 196)

exogamy the practice of marrying outside one's group (p. 310)

exponential growth curve a pattern of growth in which numbers double during approximately equal intervals, thus accelerating in the latter stages (p. 369)

expressive leader an individual who increases harmony and minimizes conflict in a group; also known as a *socioemotional leader* (p. 124)

extended family a nuclear family plus other relatives, such as grandparents, uncles and aunts, who live together (p. 309)

face-saving behavior techniques used to salvage a performance that is going sour (p. 96)

false consciousness Karl Marx's term to refer to workers identifying with the interests of capitalists (p. 164)

family two or more people who consider themselves related by blood, marriage, or adoption (p. 309)

family of orientation the family in which a person grows up (p. 309)

family of procreation the family formed when a couple's first child is born (p. 309)

feminism the philosophy that men and women should be politically, economically, and socially equal, and organized activity on behalf of this principle (p. 247)

feminization of poverty a trend in U.S. poverty whereby most poor families are headed by women (p. 198)

fertility rate the number of children that the average woman bears (p. 377)

folkways norms that are not strictly enforced (p. 44)

functional analysis a theoretical framework in which society is viewed as composed of various parts, each with a function that, when fulfilled, contributes to society's equilibrium; also known as functionalism and structural functionalism (p. 15)

functional illiterate a high school graduate who has difficulty with basic reading and math (p. 346)

gatekeeping the process by which education opens and closes doors of opportunity; another term for the social placement function of education (p. 341)

Gemeinschaft a type of society in which life is intimate; a community in which everyone knows everyone else and people share a sense of togetherness (p. 93)

gender the social characteristics that a society considers proper for its males and females; masculinity or femininity (p. 243)

gender socialization the ways in which society sets children onto different courses in life because they are male or female (p. 66)

gender stratification males' and females' unequal access to power, prestige, and property on the basis of their sex (p. 242)

generalized other taking the role of a large number of people (p. 63)

genetic predisposition inborn tendencies (p. 137)

genocide the systematic annihilation or attempted annihilation of a race or ethnic group (p. 209)

gentrification the displacement of the poor in a section of a city by the relatively affluent, who renovate the former's homes (p. 383)

Gesellschaft a type of society dominated by impersonal relationships, individual accomplishments, and self-interest (p. 95)

gestures the ways in which people use their bodies to communicate with one another (p. 40)

global warming an increase in the earth's temperature due to the greenhouse effect (p. 417)

globalization the extensive interconnections among nations due to the expansion of capitalism (p. 174)

goal displacement a goal displaced by another, such as an organization adopting new goals (p. 115)

grade inflation giving higher grades for the same work; a general rise in student grades without a corresponding increase in learning or test scores (p. 346)

graying of America older people making up an increasing proportion of the U.S. population (p. 262)

greenhouse effect the buildup of carbon dioxide in the earth's atmosphere that allows light to enter but inhibits the release of heat; believed to cause global warming (p. 417)

group people who regularly and consciously interact with one another; in a general sense, people who have something in common and who believe that what they have in common is significant (p. 88)

group dynamics the ways in which individuals affect groups and groups influence individuals (p. 121)

groupthink Irving Janis's term for a narrowing of thought by a group of people, leading to the perception that there is only one correct answer, in which the suggestion of alternatives becomes a sign of disloyalty (p. 128)

growth rate the net change in a population after adding births, subtracting deaths, and either adding or subtracting net migration (p. 378)

halfway house community support facilities where ex-prisoners supervise many aspects of their own lives, such as household tasks, but continue to report to authorities (p. 150)

hidden curriculum the unwritten goals of schools, such as teaching obedience to authority and conformity to cultural norms (p. 343)

homogamy the tendency of people with similar characteristics to marry one another (p. 317)

Horatio Alger myth belief that anyone can get ahead if only he or she tries hard enough; encourages people to strive to get ahead and deflects blame for failure from society to the individual (p. 203)

horticultural society a society based on cultivating plants by the use of hand tools (p. 90)

household all people who occupy the same housing unit (p. 309)

human ecology Robert Park's term for the relationship between people and their environment (natural resources, such as land) (p. 384)

hunting and gathering society a society dependent on hunting and gathering for survival (p. 90)

id Freud's term for the individual's inborn basic drives (p. 65)

ideal culture the ideal values and norms of a people, the goals held out for them (p. 49)

ideal type a composite of characteristics based on many specific examples; "ideal" in this case means a description of the abstracted characteristics, not what one desires to exist (p. 402)

ideology beliefs about the way things ought to be that justify social arrangements (p. 160)

illegitimate opportunity structure opportunities for crimes that are woven into the texture of life (p. 146)

impression management the term used by Erving Goffman to describe people's efforts to control the impressions that others receive of them (p. 96)

in-groups groups toward which one feels loyalty (p. 111)

incapacitation the removal of offenders from "normal" society; taking them "off the streets," thereby removing their capacity to commit crimes against the public (p. 150)

incest taboo rules specifying the degrees of kinship that prohibit sex or marriage (p. 310)

individual discrimination the negative treatment of one person by another on the basis of that person's perceived characteristics (p. 215)

Industrial Revolution the third social revolution, occurring when machines powered by fuels replaced most animal and human power (p. 92)

information superhighway the developing, worldwide electronic network; carries the idea of information traveling at a high rate of speed among homes and businesses (p. 408)

inner control capacity to withstand pressures and tendencies to deviate (p. 140)

institutional discrimination negative treatment of a minority group that is built into a society's institutions (p. 215)

institutionalized means approved ways of reaching cultural goals (p. 145)

instrumental leader an individual who tries to keep the group moving toward its goals; also known as a *task-oriented leader* (p. 124)

intergenerational mobility the change that family members make in social class from one generation to the next (p. 195)

interlocking directorates individuals serving on the board of directors of several companies (p. 301)

internal colonialism the systematic economic exploitation of a minority group (p. 221)

invasion–succession cycle the process of one group of people displacing a group whose racial/ethnic or social class characteristics differ from their own (p. 386)

invention the combination of existing elements and materials to form new ones; identified by William Ogburn as a major process of social change (p. 405)

iron law of oligarchy Robert Michels's term for the tendency of formal organizations to be dominated by a small, self-perpetuating elite (p. 110)

labeling theory the view, developed by symbolic interactionists, that the labels people are given affect their own and others' perceptions of them, thus channeling their behavior either into deviance or into conformity (p. 141)

laissez-faire capitalism unrestrained manufacture and trade (literally "hands off" capitalism) (p. 298)

laissez-faire leaders individuals who lead by being highly permissive (p. 124)

language a system of symbols that can be combined in an infinite number of ways to communicate abstract thought (p. 41)

latent functions the unintended consequences of people's actions that help to keep a social system in equilibrium (p. 341)

leader someone who influences other people (p. 124)

leadership styles ways in which people express their leadership (p. 124)

life course the stages of our life as we go from birth to death (p. 73)

life expectancy the age that someone can be expected to live to (p. 262)

life span the maximum length of life (p. 263)

lobbyists people who try to influence legislation on behalf of their clients or interest groups (p. 290)

looking-glass self a term coined by Charles Horton Cooley to refer to the process by which our self develops through internalizing others' reactions to us (p. 62)

machismo an emphasis on male strength and dominance (p. 322)

macro-level analysis an examination of large-scale patterns of society (p. 18)

macrosociology analysis of social life focusing on broad features of social structure, such as social class and the relationships of groups to one another; an approach usually used by functionalists and conflict theorists (p. 83)

mainstreaming helping people to become part of the mainstream of society (p. 342)

Malthus theorem an observation by Thomas Malthus that although the food supply increases only arithmetically, population grows geometrically (p. 368)

manifest functions the intended consequences of people's actions designed to help some part of a social system (p. 341)

marginal working class the most desperate members of the working class, who have few skills, have little job security, and are often unemployed (p. 148)

market forces the law of supply and demand (p. 299)

market restraints laws and regulations that govern the manufacture and sale of products (p. 298)

marriage a group's approved mating arrangements, usually marked by a ritual of some sort (p. 309)

mass media forms of communication directed to huge audiences (p. 67)

master status a status that cuts across the other statuses that an individual occupies (p. 86)

material culture the material objects that distinguish a group of people, such as their art, buildings, weapons, utensils, machines, hairstyles, clothing, and jewelry (p. 37)

matriarchy a society or group in which authority is vested in women (p. 310)

matrilineal system a system of reckoning descent that counts only the mother's side (p. 310)

means of production the tools, factories, land, and investment capital used to produce wealth (p. 163)

mechanical solidarity Durkheim's term for the unity or shared consciousness that comes from being involved in similar occupations or activities (p. 93)

medicalization of deviance to make some deviance a medical matter, a symptom of some underlying illness that needs to be treated by physicians (p. 151)

megalopolis an urban area consisting of at least two metropolises and their many suburbs (p. 382)

melting pot the idea that Americans of various backgrounds would melt (or merge), leaving behind their distinctive previous ethnic identities and forming a new ethnic group (p. 223)

meritocracy a form of social stratification in which all positions are awarded on the basis of merit (p. 165)

metropolis a central city surrounded by smaller cities and their suburbs (p. 382)

micro-level analysis an examination of small-scale patterns of society (p. 18)

microsociology analysis of social life focusing on social interaction; an approach usually used by symbolic interactionists (p. 83)

minority group people who are singled out for unequal treatment on the basis of their physical and cultural char-

acteristics, and who regard themselves as objects of collective discrimination (p. 210)

modernization the transformation of traditional societies into industrial societies (pp. 353, 401)

monarchy a form of government headed by a king or a queen (p. 284)

mores norms that are strictly enforced because they are thought essential to core values (p. 44)

multiculturalism (also called **pluralism**) a policy that permits or encourages groups to express their individual, unique racial and ethnic identities (p. 223)

multinational corporations companies that operate across many national boundaries (pp. 176, 302)

negative sanction an expression of disapproval for breaking a norm; ranging from a mild, informal reaction such as a frown to severe formal reactions such as a prison sentence, banishment, or death (p. 44, 136)

neocolonialism the economic and political dominance of the Least Industrialized Nations by the Most Industrialized Nations (p. 176)

net migration rate the difference between the number of immigrants and emigrants per 1,000 population (p. 377)

networking the process of consciously using or cultivating networks for some gain (p. 113)

new technology a technology introduced into a society that has a significant impact on that society (p. 50)

nonmaterial culture (also called *symbolic culture*) a group's ways of thinking (including its beliefs, values, and other assumptions about the world) and doing (its common patterns of behavior, including language and other forms of interaction) (p. 37)

nonverbal interaction communication without words through gestures, space, silence, and so on (p. 18)

norms the expectations, or rules of behavior, that develop out of values (p. 44)

nuclear family a family consisting of a husband, wife, and child(ren) (p. 309)

oligarchy a form of government in which power is held by a small group of individuals; the rule of the many by the few (p. 285)

organic solidarity Durkheim's term for the interdependence that results from people needing others to fulfill their jobs; solidarity based on the division of labor (p. 93)

out-groups groups toward which one feels antagonisms (p. 111)

outer control groups and individuals, such as family, friends, and police, that influence us to avoid deviance (p. 140)

pan-Indianism an emphasis on common elements in Native-American culture in order to develop a mutual self-identity and to work toward the welfare of all Native Americans (p. 235)

pastoral society a society based on the pasturing of animals (p. 90)

patriarchy a society in which authority is vested in men; control by men of a society or group (pp. 246, 310)

patrilineal system a system of reckoning descent that counts only the father's side (p. 310)

peer group a group of individuals of roughly the same age who are linked by common interests (p. 69)

personality disorders as a theory of deviance, the view that a personality disturbance of some sort causes an individual to violate social norms (p. 137)

pluralism diffusion of power among many interest groups, preventing any single group from gaining control of the government (p. 291)

pluralistic society a society made up of many different groups (p. 46)

political action committees (PACs) an organization formed by one or more special-interest groups to solicit and spend funds for the purpose of influencing legislation (p. 290)

polyandry a marriage in which a woman has more than one husband (p. 308)

polygyny a marriage in which a man has more than one wife (p. 308)

population pyramid a graphic representation of a population, divided into age and sex (p. 376)

population shrinkage the process by which a country's population becomes smaller because its birth rate and immigration are too low to replace those who die and emigrate (p. 372)

population transfer involuntary movement of a minority group (p. 221)

positive sanction a reward or positive reaction for following norms, ranging from a smile to a prize (pp. 44, 136)

positivism the application of the scientific approach to the social world (p. 6)

postmodern society another term for postindustrial society (p. 404)

poverty line the official measure of poverty; calculated as three times a low-cost food budget (p. 197)

power the ability to get your way, even over the resistance of others (pp. 183, 280)

power elite C. Wright Mills's term for the top leaders of corporations, military, and politics who make the nation's major decisions (pp. 183, 292)

prejudice an attitude of prejudging, usually in a negative way (p. 212)

prestige respect or regard (p. 184)

primary group a group characterized by intimate, long-term, face-to-face association and cooperation (p. 108)

proactive social movement a social movement that promotes some social change (p. 411)

profane Durkheim's term for common elements of every-day life (p. 349)

proletariat Karl Marx's term for the people who work for those who own the means of production (p. 163)

propaganda in its broad sense, the presentation of information in the attempt to influence people; in its narrow sense, one-sided information use to try to influence people (p. 413)

Protestant ethic Max Weber's term to describe the ideal of a self-denying highly moral life, accompanied by hard work and frugality (p. 354)

public opinion how people think about some issue (p. 413)

quiet revolution the fundamental changes in society that follow when vast numbers of women enter the work force (p. 250)

race inherited physical characteristics that distinguish one group from another (p. 208)

racism prejudice and discrimination on the basis of race (p. 212)

(the) rationalization of society the increasing influence of bureaucracies in society, which makes the "bottom line" of results dominant in social life (p. 116)

rational-legal authority authority based on law or written rules and regulations (also called bureaucratic authority) (p. 281)

reactive social movement a social movement that resists some social change (p. 411)

real culture the norms and values that people actually follow (p. 49)

recidivism rate the proportion of people who are rearrested (p. 149)

redemptive social movement a social movement that seeks to change people totally (p. 412)

redlining the officers of a financial institution deciding not to make loans in a particular area (p. 393)

reference group Herbert Hyman's term for the groups we use as standards to evaluate ourselves (p. 111)

reformative social movement a social movement that seeks to reform some specific aspect of society (p. 413)

rehabilitation the resocialization of offenders so that they can become conforming citizens (p. 150)

religion according to Emile Durkheim, beliefs and practices that separate the profane from the sacred and unite its adherents into a moral community (p. 349)

religious experience a sudden awareness of the supernatural or a feeling of coming in contact with God (p. 352)

representative democracy a form of democracy in which voters elect representatives to govern and make decisions on their behalf (p. 284)

reserve labor force the term used by conflict theorists for the unemployed, who can be put to work during times of high production and then discarded when no longer needed (p. 218)

resocialization the process of learning new norms, values, attitudes, and behaviors (p. 71)

resource mobilization a theory that social movements succeed or fail based on their ability to mobilize resources such as time, money, and people's skills (p. 415)

retribution the punishment of offenders in order to restore the moral balance upset by an offense (p. 149)

rising expectations the sense that better conditions are soon to follow, which, if unfulfilled, creates mounting frustration (p. 225)

rituals ceremonies or repetitive practices; in this context, religious observances or rites, often intended to evoke a sense of awe of the sacred (p. 352)

role the behaviors, obligations, and privileges attached to a status (p. 87)

role conflict conflicts that someone feels between roles because the expectations attached to one role are incompatible with the expectations of another role (p. 96)

role strain conflicts that someone feels within a role (p. 96)

romantic love feelings of erotic attraction accompanied by an idealization of the other (p. 315)

routinization of charisma the transfer of authority from a charismatic figure to either a traditional or a rational-legal form of authority (p. 283)

sacred Durkheim's term for things set apart or forbidden, that inspire fear, awe, reverence, or deep respect (p. 349)

sanction an expression of approval or disapproval given to people for upholding or violating norms (p. 44)

Sapir–Whorf hypothesis Edward Sapir and Benjamin Whorf's hypothesis that language creates ways of thinking and perceiving (p. 44)

scapegoat an individual or group unfairly blamed for someone else's troubles (p. 217)

secondary group compared with a primary group, a larger, relatively temporary, more anonymous, formal, and impersonal group based on some interest or activity (p. 109)

sect a group larger than a cult whose members feel substantial hostility from and toward society (p. 355)

secularization of religion the replacement of a religion's "otherworldly" concerns with concerns about "this world" (p. 362)

segregation the policy of keeping racial or ethnic groups apart (p. 221)

selective perception seeing certain features of an object or situation, but remaining blind to others (p. 218)

self the concept, unique to humans, of being able to see ourselves "from the outside"; to gain a picture of how others see us (p. 61)

serial fatherhood a pattern of parenting in which a father, after divorce, reduces contact with his own children, serves as a father to the children of the woman he marries or lives with, then ignores them after moving in with or marrying another woman; this pattern repeats (p. 329)

sex biological characteristics that distinguish females and males, consisting of primary and secondary sex characteristics (p. 242)

sexual harassment unwanted sexual advances, usually within an occupational or educational setting (p. 255)

significant other an individual who significantly influences someone else's life (p. 63)

slavery a form of social stratification in which some people own other people (p. 159)

small group a group small enough so everyone can interact directly with all the other members (p. 122)

social change the alteration of culture and societies over time (p. 400)

social class a large number of people with similar amounts of income and education who work at jobs that are roughly comparable in prestige (pp. 84, 163, 180)

social cohesion the degree to which members of a group or a society feel united by shared values and other social bonds (p. 93)

social construction of reality the use of background assumptions and life experiences to define what is real (p. 100)

social construction of technology the view (opposed to *technological determinism*) that culture (people's values and special interests) shape the development and use of technology (p. 52)

social environment the entire human environment, including direct contact with others (p. 58)

social institution the organized, usual, or standard ways by which society meets its basic needs (p. 88)

social integration the degree to which people feel a part of social groups (p. 8)

social interaction what people do when they are in one another's presence (pp. 18, 83)

social location people's group memberships because of their location in history and society (p. 4)

social mobility movement up or down the social class ladder (p. 162)

social movement large numbers of people who organize to promote or resist social change (p. 411)

social movement organization an organization developed to further the goals of a social movement (p. 411)

social network the social ties radiating outward from the self, that link people together (p. 113)

social order a group's usual and customary social arrangements (p. 134)

social placement a function of education; funneling people into a society's various positions (p. 342)

social promotion passing students to the next grade even though they have not mastered the basic materials (p. 346)

social stratification the division of people into layers according to their relative power, property, and prestige; applies to both a society and nations (p. 158)

social structure the relationship of people and groups to one another (p. 83)

socialism an economic system characterized by the public ownership of the means of production, central planning, and the distribution of goods without a profit motive (p. 299)

socialization the process by which people learn the characteristics of their group—the attitudes, values, and actions thought appropriate for them (pp. 61)

society a group of people who share a culture and a territory (pp. 4, 88)

sociological perspective an approach to understanding human behavior by placing it within its broader social contexts (p. 4)

sociology the scientific study of society and human behavior (p. 6)

special-interest group people who share views on a particular issue and who can be mobilized for political action (p. 290)

spirit of capitalism Weber's term for the desire to accumulate capital as a duty—not to spend it, but as an end in itself—and to constantly reinvest it (p. 354)

split labor market a term used by conflict theorists for the practice of weakening the bargaining power of workers by splitting them along racial, ethnic, sex, age, or any other lines (p. 218)

state a government; the political entity that claims a monopoly on the use of violence within a territory (pp. 281, 284)

status the position that someone occupies in society or a social group; one's social ranking (p. 85, 187)

status consistent people ranking high or low on all three dimensions of social class (p. 187)

status inconsistency a contradiction or mismatch between statuses; a condition in which a person ranks high on some dimensions of social class and low on others (pp. 87, 187)

status symbols items used to identify a status (p. 86)

stigma "blemishes" that discredit a person's claim to a "normal" identity (p. 136)

stockholders' revolt the refusal of a corporation's stockholders to rubber-stamp decisions made by its managers (p. 301)

strain theory Robert Merton's term for the strain engendered when a society socializes large numbers of people to desire a cultural goal (such as success) but withholds from many the approved means to reach that goal; one adaptation to the strain is deviance, including crime, the choice of an innovative means (one outside the approved system) to attain the cultural goal (p. 145)

street crime crimes such as mugging, rape, and burglary (p. 148)

structural mobility movement up or down the social class ladder that is attributable to changes in the structure of society, not to individual efforts (p. 195)

subculture the values and related behaviors of a group that distinguish its members from the larger culture; a world within a world (p. 45)

subsistence economy a type of economy in which human groups live off the land with little or no surplus (p. 293)

suburbanization the movement from the city to the suburbs (p. 391)

suburbs the communities adjacent to the political boundaries of a city (p. 391)

superego Freud's term for the conscience, which consists of the internalized norms and values of our social groups (p. 65)

sustainable environment a world system in which we use our physical environment to meet the needs of humanity without destroying our environment (p. 419)

symbol something to which people attach meanings and then use to communicate with others (p. 40)

symbolic culture another term for nonmaterial culture (p. 40)

symbolic interactionism a theoretical perspective in which society is viewed as composed of symbols that people use to establish meaning, develop their views of the world, and communicate with one another (p. 13)

system of descent how kinship is traced over the generations (p. 310)

taboo a norm so strong that it brings revulsion if violated (p. 45)

taking the role of the other putting oneself in someone else's shoes; understanding how someone else feels and thinks and thus anticipating how that person will act (p. 62)

teamwork the collaboration of two or more persons who, interested in the success of a performance, manage impressions jointly (p. 96)

techniques of neutralization ways of thinking or rationalizing that help people deflect society's norms (p. 141)

technological determinism the view that technology is the driving force behind culture; in its extreme form, technology is seen as taking on a life of its own, forcing human behavior to follow (p. 52)

technology in its narrow sense, tools; in its broader sense, the skills or procedures necessary to make and use those tools (pp. 50, 404)

theory a general statement about how some parts of the world fit together and how they work; an explanation of how two or more facts are related to one another (p. 13)

Thomas theorem basically, that people live in socially constructed worlds; that is, people jointly build their own realities; summarized in William I. Thomas's statement "If people define situations as real, they are real in their consequences." (p. 99)

total institution a place in which people are cut off from the rest of society and are almost totally controlled by the officials who run the place (p. 71)

totalitarianism a form of government that exerts almost total control over the people (p. 285)

tracking the sorting of students into different educational programs on the basis of real or perceived abilities (p. 342)

traditional authority authority based on custom (p. 281)

transformative social movement a social movement that seeks to change society totally (p. 413)

triad a group of three persons (p. 122)

underclass a small group of people for whom poverty persists year after year and across generations (p. 191)

universal citizenship the idea that everyone has the same basic rights by virtue of being born in a country (or by immigrating and becoming a naturalized citizen) (p. 284)

upward social mobility movement up the social class ladder (p. 195)

urban renewal the rehabilitation of a rundown area of a city, which usually results in the displacement of the poor who are living in that area (p. 393)

urbanization an increasing proportion of a population living in cities and those cities having an increasing influence on their society (p. 382)

value cluster a series of interrelated values that together form a larger whole (p. 48)

value contradiction values that contradict one another; to follow the one means to come into conflict with the other (p. 48)

values the standards by which people define what is desirable or undesirable, good or bad, beautiful or ugly (p. 44)

voluntary association a group made up of volunteers who organize on the basis of some mutual interest; the Girl Scouts, Baptists, and Alcoholics Anonymous are examples (p. 109)

voter apathy indifference and inaction with respect to the political process (p. 288)

WASP a white Anglo-Saxon Protestant; narrowly, an American of English descent; broadly, an American of western European ancestry (p. 223)

wealth property and income (p. 181)

welfare (or state) capitalism an economic system in which individuals own the means of production but the state regulates many economic activities for the welfare of the population (p. 298)

white ethnics white immigrants to the U.S. whose culture differs from that of WASPs (p. 223)

white-collar crime Edwin Sutherland's term for crimes committed by people of respectable and high social status in the course of their occupations (p. 147)

working class people who sell their labor to the capitalist class (p. 148)

world system economic and political connections that tie the world's countries together (p. 174)

zero population growth a demographic condition in which women bear only enough children to reproduce the population (p. 380)

CHAPTER 1   The Sociological Perspective

Berger, Peter L. *Invitation to Sociology: A Humanistic Perspective*. New York: Doubleday, 1963. This delightful analysis of how sociology applies to everyday life is highly recommended.

Charon, Joel M. *Symbolic Interactionism: An Introduction, an Interpretation, an Integration*, 5th ed. Englewood Cliffs, N.J.: Prentice Hall, 1995. As it lays out the main points of symbolic interactionism, this book provides an understanding of why symbolic interactionism is important in sociology.

Henslin, James M., ed. *Down to Earth Sociology: Introductory Readings*, 9th ed. New York: Free Press, 1997. This collection of readings about everyday life is designed to broaden the reader's understanding of society, and of the individual's place within it.

Mills, C. Wright. *The Sociological Imagination*. New York: Oxford University Press, 1959. This classic work provides an overview of sociology from the framework of conflict theory.

Straus, Roger, ed. *Using Sociology*. Bayside, N.Y.: General Hall, 1985. The author presents an overview of applied and clinical sociology.

Turner, Stephen Park, and Jonathan H. Turner. *The Impossible Science: An Institutional Analysis of American Sociology*. Newbury Park, Calif.: Sage, 1990. After tracing the history of U.S. sociology since the Civil War, the authors reflect on its future.

Journals

Applied Behavioral Science Review, Clinical Sociology Review, International Clinical Sociology, Journal of Applied Sociology, The Practicing Sociologist, and *Sociological Practice Review* report the experiences of sociologists who work in a variety of applied settings, from peer group counseling and suicide prevention to recommending changes to school boards.

Humanity & Society, the official journal of the Association for Humanist Sociology, publishes articles that "serve to advance the quality of life of the world's people."

Research Methods in Sociology

Bailey, Kenneth D. *Methods of Social Research*, 4th ed. New York: Free Press, 1994. A detailed explanation of the research methods that, due to limited space, we could only touch on in this chapter—plus much more.

Baker, Therese L. *Doing Social Research*, 2nd ed., New York: McGraw-Hill, 1994. This "how-to" book of sociological research describes the major ways in which sociologists gather data and the logic that underlies each method.

Burgess, Robert, ed. *Studies in Qualitative Sociology: Reflections on Field Experience*. London: JAI Press, 1990. First-person accounts by sociologists provide an understanding of the problems and rewards of fieldwork.

Jorgensen, D. L. *Participant Observation: A Methodology for Human Studies*. Newbury Park, Calif.: Sage, 1989. The book explains the value of participant observation and summarizes interesting studies. From it, you may understand why *you* are uniquely qualified for doing participant observation.

Merton, Robert K., Marjorie Fiske, and Patricia L. Kendall. *The Focused Interview: A Manual of Problems and Procedures*, 2nd ed. New York: Free Press, 1990. Interviewing techniques are outlined; of value primarily to more advanced students.

Scully, Diana. *Understanding Sexual Violence: A Study of Convicted Rapists*. New York: Routledge, 1994. The author's examination of the rationalizations of rapists helps us understand why some men rape and what they gain from it.

Webb, Eugene J., Donald T. Campbell, Richard D. Schwartz, Lee Sechrest, and Janet Below Grove. *Unobtrusive Measures: Nonreactive Research in the Social Sciences*. Boston: Houghton Mifflin, 1981. This clear overview of unobtrusive measures also contains concise summaries of a great deal of research.

Whyte, William Foote, and Kathleen King Whyte. *Learning from the Field: A Guide from Experience*. Beverly Hills, Calif.: Sage, 1984. Focusing on the extensive field experience of the senior author, this book provides insight into the critical involvement of the self in this research method.

Wiehe, Vernon R., and Ann L. Richards. *Intimate Betrayal: Understanding and Responding to the Trauma of Acquaintanceship Rape*. Newbury Park, Calif.: Sage, 1995. This examination of acquaintanceship rape and its impact on victims includes materials on intervention and prevention.

Journal

Visual Sociology Review. A specialized journal in qualitative sociology that focuses on the analysis of social life through visual means such as photos, movies, and videos.

Writing Papers for Sociology

Cuba, Lee J. *A Short Guide to Writing about Social Science.* Glenview, Ill.: Scott, Foresman, 1993. The author summarizes the various types of social science literature, presents guidelines on how to organize and write a research paper, and explains how to prepare an oral presentation.

The Sociology Writing Group. *A Guide to Writing Sociology Papers*, 3rd ed. New York: St. Martin's Press, 1994. The guide walks students through the steps in writing a sociology paper, from choosing the initial assignment to doing the research and turning in a finished paper. Also explains how to manage your time and correctly cite sources.

About a Career in Sociology

The following pamphlets or brochures are available free of charge from the American Sociological Association: 1722 N Street, N.W., Washington, DC 20036. Tel. (202) 833-3410. Fax (202) 785-0146. ASA_Executive_Office@MCI mail.com

Careers in Sociology. American Sociological Association. What can you do with sociology? You like the subject and would like to major in it, but. . . . This pamphlet provides information about jobs available for sociology majors.

Ferris, Abbott L. *How to Join the Federal Workforce and Advance Your Sociological Career.* American Sociological Association. This pamphlet gives tips on how to find employment in the federal government, including information on how to prepare a job application.

Majoring in Sociology: A Guide for Students. American Sociological Association. This brochure provides an overview of the programs offered in sociology departments, possible areas of specialization, and how to find information on jobs.

Miller, Delbert C. *The Sociology Major as Preparation for Careers in Business.* American Sociological Association. What careers can a sociology major pursue in business or industry? This brochure includes sections on job prospects, graduate education, and how to practice sociology in business careers.

These two books are also useful if you are considering a career as a sociologist: The first provides background information; the second is more specific.

Hess, Beth B. *Individual Voices, Collective Visions: Fifty Years of Women in Sociology.* Philadelphia: Temple University Press, 1995. During the past fifty years, women have played an increasingly larger role in sociology, which, like the other sciences, has been dominated by men. The author examines this change.

Stephens, W. Richard. *Careers in Sociology.* Boston: Allyn and Bacon, 1995. How can you make a living with a major in sociology? The author explores careers in sociology, from business and government to health care and the law.

CHAPTER 2 Culture

Chagnon, Napoleon A. *Yanomamo: The Fierce People*, 4th ed. New York: Holt, Rinehart & Winston, 1983. This fascinating account of a preliterate people whose customs are extraordinarily different from ours will help you to see the arbitrariness of choices that underlie human culture.

Edgerton, Robert B. *Sick Societies: Challenging the Myth of Primitive Harmony.* New York: Free Press, 1992. The author's thesis is that cultural relativism is misinformed, that we have the obligation to judge cultures that harm its members as inferior to those that do not.

Goodall, Jane, and Michael Nichols. *The Great Apes: Between Two Worlds.* Washington, D.C.: National Geographic Society, 1993. This account of Jane Goodall's research offers—as much as is possible—an insider's view of the behavior of chimpanzees.

Harris, Marvin. *Cannibals and Kings: The Origins of Cultures.* New York: Random House, 1977.

Harris, Marvin. *Good to Eat: Riddles of Food and Culture.* New York: Simon & Schuster, 1986.

To read Harris's books is to read about cultural relativism. Using a functional perspective, this anthropologist analyzes cultural practices that often seem bizarre to outsiders. He interprets those practices within the framework of the culture being examined.

Shames, Laurence. *The Hunger for More: Searching for Values in an Age of Greed.* New York: Vintage Books, 1991. A critical account of changing U.S. values.

Spindler, George, Louise Spindler, Henry T. Trueba, and Melvin D. Williams. *The American Cultural Dialogue and Its Transmission.* Bristol, Penn.: Falmer Press, 1990. The authors analyze values central to U.S. culture: individuality, freedom, community, equality, and success.

Tucker, David M. *The Decline of Thrift in America: Our Cultural Shift from Saving to Spending.* New York: Praeger, 1991. The author traces the change in U.S. values from thrift to spending and consumption, indicating how this change has affected the competitiveness of the United States in world markets.

Zellner, William W. *Countercultures: A Sociological Analysis.* New York: St. Martin's, Press, 1995. The author's analysis of skinheads, the Ku Klux Klan, survivalists, satanism, the Church of Scientology, and the Unification Church (Moonies) helps us understand why people join countercultures.

Journal

Urban Life, a sociological journal that focuses on social interaction, contains many detailed studies of the cultures of small, off-beat groups.

CHAPTER 3 Socialization

Ariès, Philippe. *Centuries of Childhood: A Social History of Family Life.* New York: Vintage Books, 1965. This pathbreaking study of childhood in Europe during the Middle Ages provides a sharp contrast to child-rearing patterns in modern society.

Elkin, Frederick, and Gerald Handel. *The Child and Society*, 5th ed. New York: Random House, 1991. This classic overview of the socialization of children emphasizes social class, race, sex, and place of residence as significant factors in socialization.

Epstein, Jonathan S., ed. *Adolescents and Their Music: If It's Too Loud, You're Too Old.* Hamden, Conn.: Garland Publishing, 1994. The type of music a particular age, ethnic, or religious group prefers is never an accident, but is a vital part of the group's relative place in society. This analysis clarifies that relationship between youth and society.

Gilmore, David D. *Manhood in the Making: Cultural Concepts of Masculinity.* New Haven, Conn.: Yale University Press, 1991. A survey of societies around the world aimed at determining if masculinity is constant; contains fascinating cross cultural data.

Lieberman, Alicia F. *The Emotional Life of the Toddler.* New York: Free Press, 1993. The author analyzes challenges in socializing young children and presents many interesting case materials on problems that toddlers confront.

Mead, George Herbert. *Mind, Self and Society from the Standpoint of a Social Behaviorist,* Charles W. Morris, ed. Chicago: University of Chicago Press, 1974. First published in 1934. Put together from notes taken by Mead's students, this book presents Mead's analysis of how mind and self are products of society.

Rymer, Russ. *Genie: An Abused Child's Flight from Silence.* New York: HarperCollins, 1993. This moving account of Genie includes the battles among linguists, psychologists, and social workers, who all claimed to have Genie's best interests at heart.

Sociological Studies of Child Development: A Research Annual. Greenwich, Conn.: JAI Press. Along with theoretical articles, this annual publication reports on sociological research on the socialization of children.

White, Merry. *The Material Child: Coming of Age in Japan and America.* New York: Free Press, 1993. Comparing adolescence in the United States and Japan, the author examines sexuality, friendship, plans for the future, and relationships with peers, family, and school.

CHAPTER 4 Social Structure and Social Interaction

Barber, Bernard. *Constructing the Social System.* New Brunswick, N.J.: Transaction Books, 1993. An example of the macrosociological approach to understanding human life; perhaps best suited for advanced students.

Goffman, Erving. *The Presentation of Self in Everyday Life.* New York: Doubleday, 1990. First published in 1959. This is the classic statement of dramaturgical analysis; it provides a different way of looking at everyday life.

Hardin, Russell. *One for All: The Logic of Group Conflict.* Princeton, N.J.: Princeton University Press, 1995. The author explores the social structure that underlies group conflict.

Hatfield, Elaine, and Susan Sprecher. *Mirror, Mirror . . . : The Importance of Looks in Everyday Life.* Albany: State University of New York Press, 1986. All of us consider appearance to be very important in everyday life. You may be surprised, however, at just how significant good looks are for determining what happens to us.

Helmreich, William B. *The Things They Say Behind Your Back: Stereotypes and the Myths Behind Them.* New Brunswick, N.J.: Transaction Books, 1984. Spiced with anecdotes and jokes, yet sensitively written, the book explores the historical roots of stereotypes. The author also illustrates how stereotypes help produce behaviors that reinforce the stereotypes.

Karp, David A., and William C. Yoels. *Sociology and Everyday Life.* Itasca, Ill.: Peacock, 1986. The authors examine how social order is constructed and how it provides the framework for our interactions.

Schellenberg, James A. *Exploring Social Behavior: Investigations in Social Psychology.* Boston: Allyn and Bacon, 1993. The author takes the reader on an intellectual journey, exploring such "mysteries" as identity, conscience, intelligence, attraction, and aggression.

Tönnies, Ferdinand. *Community and Society (Gemeinschaft und Gesellschaft).* New Brunswick, N.J.: Transaction Books, 1988. Originally published in 1887, this classic work, focusing on social change, provides insight into how society influences personality. Rather challenging reading.

Walker, Beverly M., ed. *Construction of Group Realities: Culture, Society, and Personal Construction Theory.* New York: Praeger, 1995. Our views of life, what we believe, even what we perceive have a group basis to them.

Whyte, William Foote. *Corner Boys: A Study of Clique Behavior.* New York: Irvington, 1993. Originally published in 1945. The author's analysis of interaction in a U.S. Italian slum demonstrates how social structure affects personal relationships.

Journals

The following three journals feature articles on symbolic interactionism and analyses of everyday life: *Qualitative Sociology, Symbolic Interaction,* and *Urban Life.*

CHAPTER 5 Social Groups in a Socially Diverse Society

Albrecht, Gary L. *The Disability Business: Rehabilitation in America.* Newbury Park, Calif.: Sage, 1992. This examination of how the megabillion-dollar rehabilitation industry functions focuses on how the desire for profit combines with marketing techniques to influence the quality of patient care.

Devereaux, James A. *Designing Bureaucracies: Institutional Capacity and Large-Scale Problem Solving.* Stanford, Calif.: Stanford University Press, 1995. Bureaucracies will remain a part of the foreseeable future. The author explains how they can live up to their potential.

Fleisher, Mark S. *Beggars and Thieves: Lives of Urban Street Criminals.* Madison: University of Wisconsin Press, 1995. Based on years of participant observation, the author presents an inside view of thieves, gangs, addicts, and lifelong criminals.

Forschi, Martha, and Edward J. Lawler, eds. *Group Processes: Sociological Analysis.* New York: Nelson-Hall, 1994. How do your associates, friends, family—and even strangers—influence you? Among other topics, these authors explore such influences.

Herkscher, Charles, and Anne Donnellon, eds. *The Post-Bureaucratic Organization.* Beverly Hills, Calif.: Sage, 1994. By any other name, is a bureaucracy still a bureaucracy? The authors of these articles explain how bureaucracies can be modified to better reach the organization's goals and to better meet human needs.

Homans, George. *The Human Group.* New York: Harcourt, Brace, 1950. Homans develops the idea that all human groups share common activities, interactions, and sentiments and examines various types of social groups from this point of view.

Howard, Philip K. *The Death of Common Sense: How Law Is Suffocating America.* New York: Randon House, 1995. One of the best examples of how bureaucracies can become impediments to the goals they are designed to achieve is the way law is practiced in the United States.

Hummel, Ralph P. *The Bureaucratic Experiment: A Critique of Life in the Modern Organization,* 4th ed. New York: St. Martin's Press, 1994. The author explores the perils and promises of bureaucracies, with an emphasis on how bureaucracies can become better tools for human needs.

Janis, Irving. *Victims of Groupthink.* Boston: Houghton Mifflin, 1972. Janis analyzes how groups can become cut off from alternatives, interpret evidence in light of their preconceptions, and embark on courses of action that they should have seen as obviously incorrect.

Kephart, William M., and William W. Zellner. *Extraordinary Groups: An Examination of Unconventional Lifestyles,* 4th ed. New York: St. Martin's Press, 1991. This sketch of the history and characteristics of eight groups—the Old Order Amish, Oneida Community, Gypsies, Shakers, Hasidim, Father Divine Movement, Mormons, and Jehovah's Witnesses—illustrates the effects of groups on their members.

Mills, Theodore M. *The Sociology of Small Groups.* Englewood Cliffs, N.J.: Prentice Hall, 1984. Mills provides an overview of research on small groups, focusing on the interaction that occurs within them (group dynamics).

CHAPTER 6 Deviance and Social Control

Adler, Patricia A., and Peter Adler, eds. *Constructions of Deviance: Social Power, Context, and Interaction.* Belmont, Calif.: Wadsworth, 1994. This collection of readings illustrates insights provided by the symbolic interactionist perspective.

Blomberg, Thomas G., and Stanley Cohen, eds. *Punishment and Social Control.* Hawthorne, N.Y.: Aldine de Gruyter, 1995. Focusing on prisons and criminal justice, the authors of these sixteen articles analyze why well-intentioned social policy often leads to bad results.

Jankowski, Martín Sánchez. *Islands in the Street: Gangs and American Urban Society.* Berkeley: University of California Press, 1991. The author's extensive participant observation of street gangs makes a fascinating and insightful introduction to this topic.

Mann, Coramae Richey. *Unequal Justice: A Question of Color.* Bloomington: Indiana University Press, 1994. The author examines a controversial issue: why our jails and prisons are so disproportionately filled with minorities.

Matza, David. *Delinquency and Drift.* New Brunswick, N.J.: Transaction Books, 1990. This analysis of how the delinquent subculture reflects the standards of conventional society explains how the drift toward delinquency is sometimes unwittingly aided by the enforcers of the social order.

Messner, Steven F., and Richard Rosenfeld. *Crime and the American Dream.* Belmont, Calif.: Wadsworth, 1994. Explains how the "American Dream" produces a strong desire to make money but fails to instill adequate desires to play by the rules. Supports Merton's strain theory featured in this chapter.

Rafter, Nicole Hahn. *Partial Justice: Women, Prisons, and Social Control,* 2nd ed. New Brunswick, N.J.: Transaction Books, 1990. The author documents the development of separate prisons for women, the goal of reform in women's prisons, and current concerns to produce more than "partial justice."

Scott, Kody. *Monster: The Autobiography of an L.A. Gang Member.* New York: Penguin Books, 1993. This intriguing inside view of gang life provides a rare glimpse of the power of countercultural norms.

Weisburd, David, Stanton Wheeler, Elin Waring, and Nancy Bode. *Crimes of the Middle Classes: White-Collar Offenders in the Federal Courts.* New Haven, Conn.: Yale University Press, 1991. This analysis of how opportunity—access to an organization's resources—leads to white-collar crime illustrates how crime is distributed throughout the social classes.

Wright, Richard T., and Scott Decker. *Burglars on the Job: Streetlife and Residential Break-ins.* Boston: Northeastern University Press, 1994. For an understanding of how burglars think, as well as how they "work," this book is highly recommended.

CHAPTER 7 Social Stratification in Global Perspective

Curtis, James, and Lorne Tepperman, eds. *Haves and Have-Nots: An International Reader on Social Inequality.* Englewood Cliffs, N.J.: Prentice Hall, 1994. The authors of these fifty-six articles explore economic, power, and status inequality among the world's nations.

Freedman, Robert. *The Mind of Karl Marx: Economic, Political, and Social Perspectives.* Chatham, N.J.: Chatham House, 1986. A conflict theorist provides an overview of social stratification from this perspective.

Harrison, Paul. *Inside the Third World: The Anatomy of Poverty*, 3rd ed. London: Penguin Books, 1993. The book's vivid examples make conditions in the Least Industrialized Nations come alive.

International Monetary Fund. *World Economic Outlook: A Survey*. Washington, D.C.: International Monetary Fund, 1992. Comparative data on the world's economies provide insight into the interrelationships of the three worlds of development.

Kennedy, Paul. *Preparing for the Twenty-First Century*. New York: Random House, 1993. A thorough analysis of the relationship among the three worlds of economic development.

Kibria, Nazli. *Family Tightrope: The Changing Lives of Vietnamese Americans*. Princeton, N.J.: Princeton University Press, 1993. To change one's culture challenges almost all aspects of the self. The author analyzes how Vietnamese families are adjusting to their new lives.

Lane, David, ed. *Russia in Flux: The Political and Social Consequences of Reform*. Brookfield, Vt.: Ashfield, 1992. The author analyzes the political and economic changes in Russia, the consequences of which are being felt throughout the world.

Miles, Rosalind. *The Woman's History of the World*. New York: HarperCollins, 1990. The author examines the importance of gender in human history.

Said, Edward W. *Culture and Imperialism*. New York: Knopf, 1993. The author analyzes the relationship of national power to cultural dominance, especially that of the Most Industrialized Nations to the Least Industrialized Nations.

Scheper-Hughes, Nancy. *Death without Weeping: The Violence of Everyday Life in Brazil*. Berkeley: University of California Press, 1992. As stressed in this chapter, global stratification leaves some nations in poverty—in spite of their possessing rich natural resources. The results can be a short and brutish life for the underprivileged of those nations, as documented in this report.

CHAPTER 8 Social Class in the United States

Berrick, Jill Duerr. *Faces of Poverty: Portraits of Women and Children on Welfare*. New York: Oxford University Press, 1995. With a focus on how welfare helps the poor survive from day to day, the author puts a human face on this stereotyped population.

Crompton, Rosemary. *Class and Stratification: An Introduction to Current Debates*. Cambridge, Mass.: Polity Press, 1993. Social stratification leads us into one of the most controversial of sociological topics, for it confronts us with the question of what to do about inequality. The author reviews issues discussed in this chapter—and much more.

Domhoff, G. William. *State Autonomy or Class Dominance? Case Studies on Policy Making in America*. Hawthorne, N.Y.: Aldine de Gruyter, 1996. The author, a conflict theorist, applies his analysis of social class and power to the development of major U.S. policy decisions.

Gatewood, Willard B. *Aristocrats of Color: The Black Elite, 1880–1920*. Bloomington: Indiana University Press, 1990. Analyzing the rise and decline of the African-American upper class that developed after the Civil War, the author focuses on marriage, occupations, education, religion, social clubs, and relationships with whites and with African Americans of lower classes.

Gilbert, Dennis, and Joseph A. Kahl. *The American Class Structure: A New Synthesis*, 4th ed. Belmont, Calif.: Wadsworth, 1993. Two sociologists provide an overview of social stratification in the United States.

Grusky, David B., ed. *Social Stratification: Class, Race, and Gender in Sociological Perspective*. Boulder, Colo.: Westview Press, 1994. The authors of these readings explain how social class, race, and gender are the primary elements underlying social stratification in contemporary society.

Hurst, Charles E. *Social Inequality: Forms, Causes, and Consequences*. 2nd ed. Boston: Allyn and Bacon, 1995. Hurst analyzes social stratification in the United States.

Jennings, James. *Understanding the Nature of Poverty in Urban America*. Westport, Conn.: Praeger, 1994. In this analysis of major characteristics of U.S. poverty, the author also analyzes why poverty persists.

Liebow, Elliot. *Tell Them Who I Am: The Lives of Homeless Women*. New York: Penguin Books, 1995. Based on participant observation in a Washington, D.C., shelter for homeless women, this study puts flesh and blood on those nameless faces we see on the news and on our city streets.

MacLeod, Jay. *Ain't No Makin' It: Aspirations and Attainment in a Low-Income Neighborhood*, expanded ed. Boulder, Colo.: Westview Press, 1995. Following two groups of high school boys into adulthood, the author documents how social class inequality is sustained from generation to generation, and how friendships and families, work and school experiences shape occupational aspirations.

Massey, Douglas S., and Nancy A. Denton. *American Apartheid: Segregation and the Making of the Underclass*. Cambridge, Mass.: Harvard University Press, 1993. The authors explain how the "underclass" developed and propose possible solutions to this pressing problem.

Mitchell, William C. *Beyond Politics: Markets, Welfare, and Bureaucracy*. New York: Westview, 1994. Welfare reform has become a popular political topic. This book explains how much of what is wrong with welfare is due to the bureaucracy set up to administer Washington's programs.

Rank, Mark Robert. *Living on the Edge: The Realities of Welfare in America*. New York: Columbia University Press, 1995. This account of what poor people do to make ends meet dispels many myths of welfare recipients.

Wilson, William Julius. *The Truly Disadvantaged: The Inner City, the Underclass, and Public Policy*. Chicago: University of Chicago Press, 1990. The author looks at how the conditions of the ghetto poor have deteriorated and suggests what can be done to improve matters.

CHAPTER 9 Inequalities of Race and Ethnicity

Browning, Christopher R. *Ordinary Men: Reserve Police Battalion 101 and the Final Solution in Poland.* New York: HarperPerennial, 1993. A startling account of how a government turned ordinary men into mass murderers.

Du Bois, W. E. B. *Black Reconstruction in America: An Essay Toward a History of the Part Which Black Folk Played in the Attempt to Reconstruct Democracy in America, 1860–1880.* New York: Harcourt, Brace 1935; London: Frank Cass, 1966. This analysis of the role of African Americans in the Civil War and in the years immediately following provides a glimpse into a neglected part of U.S. history.

Duneier, Mitchell. *Slim's Table: Race, Respectability, Masculinity.* Chicago: University of Chicago Press, 1994. Based on participant observation, the author analyzes the relationships of a group of working-class African-American men in Chicago, with an emphasis on how they maintain their sense of moral worth.

Feiner, Susan F., ed. *Race and Gender in the American Economy: Views from Across the Spectrum.* Englewood Cliffs, N.J.: Prentice Hall, 1994. The authors of these readings examine major issues in sexism and racism that confront Americans today.

Hagan, William Thomas. *American Indians.* Chicago: University of Chicago Press, 1993. This analysis of Native Americans has a focus on relationships between Native Americans and the U.S. government.

Khazanov, Anatoly M. *After the USSR: Ethnicity, Nationalism, and Politics in the Commonwealth of Independent States.* Madison: University of Wisconsin Press, 1996. This analysis of ethnic nationalism provides insight into the ethnic strife of the former USSR and the reasons for its downfall.

Lipset, Seymour Martin, and Earl Raab. *Jews and the New American Scene.* Cambridge, Mass.: Harvard University Press, 1995. The book centers on this question: With little antisemitism, reduced threat to Israel, low participation in formal religion, and high intermarriage (57 percent), what is going to hold the Jewish community together?

Mander, Jerry. *In the Absence of the Sacred: The Failure of Technology and the Survival of the Indian Nations.* San Francisco, Calif.: Sierra Club Books, 1992. With a focus on the impact of technology, the author analyzes past and present relations of Native Americans and the U.S. government.

Moore, Joan, and Raquel Pinderhughes, eds. *In the Barrios: Latinos and the Underclass Debate.* New York: Sage, 1993. With an emphasis on immigration, discrimination, and gangs, the authors of the nine essays in this volume examine the overall social and economic conditions of poor Latinos.

Parrillo, Vincent N. *Strangers to These Shores: Race and Ethnic Relations in the United States,* 4th ed. New York: Macmillan, 1994. A detailed summary of the racial and ethnic groups that make up the United States, with an emphasis on their history and relationships to Anglos.

Rodriguez, Clara. *Puerto Ricans: Born in the U.S.A.* Boston: Unwin Hyman, 1989. The author presents an overview of Puerto Rican Americans.

Trueba, Henry T., Lilly Cheng, and Kenji Ima. *Myth or Reality: Adaptive Strategies of Asian Americans in California.* Washington, D.C.: Falmer Press, 1993. With an emphasis on family, school, community, and work, the authors examine conflicts and adaptations of Asian-American immigrants.

CHAPTER 10 Inequalities of Gender and Age

Inequalities of Gender

Amott, Teresa. *Caught in the Crisis: Women and the U.S. Economy.* New York: Monthly Review Press, 1995. A short, readable overview of women's economic roles from a leftist perspective.

Anderson, Margaret L. *Thinking about Women: Sociological Perspectives on Sex and Gender,* 3rd ed. New York: Macmillan, 1993. An overview of the main issues of sex and gender in contemporary society, ranging from sexism and socialization to work and health.

Campbell, Anne. *Men, Women, and Aggression.* New York: Basic Books, 1993. This comparison of male–female differences in aggression includes fights, robbery, marital violence, and street gangs.

Chafetz, Janet Saltzman. *Gender Equity: An Integrated Theory of Stability and Change.* Newbury Park, Calif.: Sage, 1990. A theoretical overview of the women's movement.

Driscoll, Dawn-Marie, and Carol R. Goldberg. *Members of the Club: The Coming of Age of Executive Women.* New York: Free Press, 1993. Based on interviews with senior women executives, the authors suggest strategies for climbing to the top of the corporate ladder.

Farganis, Sondra. *The Social Reconstruction of the Feminine Character,* 2nd ed. Lanham, MD: Rowman & Littlefield, 1996. An overview of feminist theory that emphasizes how views of women are shaped by concrete situations.

Gay, Kathlyn. *The New Power of Women in Politics.* Hillside, N.J.: Enslow, 1994. The author examines how the face of politics is changing due to the changing role of women in U.S. society.

Gilman, Charlotte Perkins. *The Man-Made World or, Our Androcentric Culture.* New York: Charlton, 1911. Reprinted in 1971 by Johnson Reprint. This early book on women's liberation provides an excellent view of female–male relations at the beginning of this century.

Goldberg, Steven. *Why Men Rule: A Theory of Male Dominance.* Chicago: Open Court, 1993. A detailed explanation of the author's theory of male dominance featured in this chapter.

Jacobs, Jerry A., ed. *Gender Inequality at Work.* Thousand Oaks, Calif.: Sage, 1995. The authors of these articles review the main issues in gender discrimination in employment.

Kimmel, Michael S., and Michael A. Messner, eds. *Men's Lives,* 2nd ed. New York: Macmillan, 1993. These authors examine major issues of sex and gender as they affect men. An excellent companion, and often counterpoint, to the Anderson book.

Lorber, Judith. *Paradoxes of Gender.* New Haven, Conn.: Yale University Press, 1994. The author focuses on two vital issues: how gender is constructed and how gender is a primary component of social inequality.

Messner, Michael A., and Donald F. Sabo. *Sex, Violence, and Power in Sports: Rethinking Masculinity.* Freedom, Calif.: Crossing Press, 1994. The authors explore the connection between sports, pain, sexuality, and masculinity.

Tannen, Deborah. *You Just Don't Understand: Women and Men in Conversation.* New York: Morrow, 1990. A psycholinguist documents the extent to which speech patterns of men and women are related to basic differences in their social worlds.

Williams, Christine L. *Still a Man's World: Men Who Do Women's Work.* Berkeley: University of California Press, 1995. Based on in-depth interviews with men and women in nursing, elementary school teaching, librarianship, and social work, the author concludes that, due to the high value placed on masculinity, men who work in traditionally women's occupations find a "glass escalator" instead of a "glass ceiling."

Witt, Linda, Karen M. Paget, and Glenna Matthews. *Running as a Woman: Gender and Power in American Politics.* New York: Macmillan, 1994. This history of women in politics includes successful strategies for running for political office as a woman.

Journals

The following four journals focus on the role of gender in social life: *Feminist Studies, Gender & Society,* the official journal of Sociologists for Women in Society, *Sex Roles,* and *Signs: Journal of Women in Culture and Society.*

Inequalities of Age

Calmenson, George. [Video] *Growing toward Fulfillment: Learning and the Mature Body.* Ashland, Oregon: Southern Oregon State College Media Center, 1996. This 30-minute video proposes shifting the perception of aging from an industrial model to a biologically based model of development.

Clair, Jeffrey Michael, David A. Karp, and William C. Yoels. *Experiencing the Life Cycle: A Social Psychology of Aging,* 2nd ed. Springfield, Ill.: Thomas, 1993. The authors examine social factors that underlie the adjustments that the elderly make to life changes.

Cockerham, William C. *This Aging Society.* Englewood Cliffs, N.J.: Prentice Hall, 1991. The social consequences of the growing numbers of elderly in U.S. society are the focus of this book.

Cox, Harold G. *Late Life: The Realities of Aging,* 3rd ed. Englewood Cliffs, N.J.: Prentice Hall, 1993. Using a sym-

bolic interactionist framework, the author presents an overview of issues in aging.

Jerrome, Dorothy. *Good Company: An Anthropological Study of Old People in Groups.* Edinburgh, England: Edinburgh University Press, 1992. The author analyzes the day-to-day interactions that provide the primary bases for satisfying adjustment to old age.

National Center for Health Statistics. *Common Beliefs about the Rural Elderly: What Do National Data Tell Us?* Washington, D.C.: U.S. Government Printing Office, 1993. This book provides a broad overview of a neglected topic, U.S. elderly in rural areas.

Posner, Richard A. *Aging and Old Age.* Chicago: University of Chicago Press, 1995. The author, a federal judge and prolific social analyst, proposes that a biology of aging accounts for changes in intelligence and emotions, which, in turn, has surprising consequences for society.

Stoller, Eleanor Palo, and Rose Campbell Gibson. *Worlds of Difference: Inequality in the Aging Experience.* Thousand Oaks, Calif.: Pine Forge Press, 1994. The authors document extensive inequalities borne by the U.S. elderly and explain the social conditions that create those inequalities.

Journals

The Gerontologist, Journal of Aging and Social Policy, Journal of Aging Studies, Journal of Cross-Cultural Gerontology, Journal of Elder Abuse and Neglect, Journal of Gerontology, and *Journal of Women and Aging* focus on issues of aging, while *Youth and Society* examines adolescent culture.

CHAPTER 11 Politics and the Economy: Leadership and Work in the Global Village

Politics

Aho, James A. *This Thing of Darkness: A Sociology of the Enemy.* Seattle: University of Washington, 1994. This book provides insight into how people develop a collective perception that there is a broad conspiracy to destroy their way of life, and a shared, impassioned hatred of what they term "the enemy."

Allen, Oliver E. *The Tiger.* New York: Addison-Wesley, 1993. An entertaining account of Tammany Hall, the corrupt political group that controlled New York City from the 1800s to past the middle of this century.

Amnesty International. *Amnesty International Report.* London: Amnesty International Publications, published annually. The reports summarize human rights violations around the world, listing specific instances country by country.

Bills, David D., ed. *The New Modern Times: Factors Reshaping the World of Work.* Albany: State University of New York, 1994. The authors help us understand the global social changes that, forcing a restructuring of our economy, are vitally affecting our everyday lives.

Chavance, Bernard. *The Transformation of Communist Systems: Economic Reform since the 1950s,* Charles Hauss, trans.

Boulder, Colo.: Westview Press, 1994. This analysis provides a detailed background for understanding the extensive economic changes occurring in the formerly communist nations.

Chirot, Daniel. *Modern Tyrants: The Power and Prevalence of Evil in Our Age.* New York: Free Press, 1994. From Hitler and Stalin to Trujillo, Mao, and Pol Pot, the author analyzes the political expediency that underlies tyranny.

Ferguson, Thomas. *Golden Rule.* Chicago: University of Chicago Press, 1995. The title, based on the statement "to discover who rules, follow the gold (money)," gives support to the conflict perspective of U.S. politics.

Mills, C. Wright. *The Power Elite.* New York: Oxford University Press, 1956. This classic analysis elaborates the conflict thesis summarized in this chapter that U.S. society is ruled by the nation's top corporate leaders, together with an elite from the military and political institutions.

Porter, Bruce D. *War and the Rise of the State: The Military Foundations of Modern Politics.* New York: Free Press, 1994. The author presents an intriguing analysis of how war and the military underlie the creation of the state and of changed relations within it.

Stiglmayer, Alexandra, ed. *Mass Rape: The War against Women in Bosnia-Herzegovina*, Marion Faber, trans. Lincoln: University of Nebraska Press, 1994. Giving chilling accounts, the authors explain why mass rape sometimes accompanies war, as it did in Bosnia.

Journals

Most sociology journals publish articles on politics. Three that focus on this area of social life are *American Political Science Review*, *Journal of Political and Military Sociology*, and *Social Policy*.

Research in Political Sociology: A Research Annual. Greenwich, Conn.: JAI Press. This annual publication is not recommended for beginners, as the findings and theories are often difficult and abstract. It does, however, analyze political topics of vital concern to our well-being.

The Economy

Berger, Peter L. *The Capitalist Revolution: Fifty Propositions about Prosperity, Equality, and Liberty.* New York: Basic Books, 1991. Berger's explanation of why capitalism is highly productive and why it enhances personal liberty is especially useful in light of changes in the industrializing nations.

Drucker, Peter F. *Post-Capitalist Society.* New York: HarperCollins, 1993. A highly readable account of the fundamental changes that are transforming our society, including how we live, work, and even think.

Harrison, Bennett, and Barry Bluestone. *The Great U-Turn: Corporate Restructuring and the Polarizing of America.* New York: Basic Books, 1990. The authors investigate major changes taking place in the U.S. economy, focusing on the declining standard of living of the average American.

Marx, Karl. *Selected Writings in Sociology and Social Philosophy*, Thomas B. Bottomore and Maximilian Rubel, eds. New York: McGraw-Hill, 1964. If you are unfamiliar with Marx's ideas, you will benefit from this useful introduction, especially Marx's analysis of social class and alienation.

Morales, Rebecca, and Frank Bonilla, eds. *Latinos in a Changing U.S. Economy: Comparative Perspectives on Growing Inequality.* Newbury Park, Calif.: Sage, 1993. Some groups feel the negative consequences of a changing economy more than do other groups. The authors of these articles analyze why Latinos are falling behind.

Porter, Michael E. *The Competitive Advantage of Nations.* New York: Free Press, 1990. Based on research in ten countries, the author first examines how productivity is the key to a nation's competitive market position and then provides an explanation for the economic success of Japan and the decline of Great Britain.

Statham, Anne, Eleanor M. Miller, and Hans O. Mauksch, eds. *The Worth of Women's Work.* Albany: State University of New York Press, 1988. The authors examine women's work, both unpaid housework and paid work in the labor force.

Womack, James P., Daniel T. Jones, and Daniel Roos. *The Machine That Changed the World.* New York: HarperPerennial, 1991. This analysis of the international automobile industry stresses how the lean production techniques developed by Toyota revolutionized mass production.

Journals

Two journals that focus on issues presented in this chapter are *Insurgent Sociologist* and *Work and Occupations*.

CHAPTER 12 The Family: Initiation into Society

Conger, Rand D., and Glen H. Elder, Jr., eds. *Families in Troubled Times: Adapting to Change in Rural America.* Hawthorne, N.Y.: Aldine de Gruyter, 1994. An examination of how farm families adjusted during a precipitous economic decline.

Coontz, Stephanie. *The Way We Never Were: American Families and the Nostalgia Trap.* New York: Basic Books, 1992. This provocative analysis of family history shows that current concerns about marriage and families are not new.

Hochschild, Arlie. *The Second Shift: Working Parents and the Revolution at Home.* New York: Avon Books, 1989. Based on interviews and participant observation, the author provides an in-depth report on family life in homes where both husband and wife are employed full time.

Ingoldsby, Bron B., and Suzanna Smith, eds. *Families in Multicultural Perspective.* New York: Guilford, 1995. Provides an introduction to the rich diversity of the world's marriage and family forms.

McLanahan, Sarah, and Gary Sandefur. *Growing Up with a Single Parent: What Hurts, What Helps.* Cambridge, Mass.: Harvard University Press, 1994. One-parent families are of growing national concern, but not all single-parent families are the same. The authors analyze differences that affect children's chances of doing well—or poorly—in school, work, and marriage.

Roberts, Albert R., ed. *Helping Battered Women: New Perspectives and Remedies.* New York: Oxford University Press, 1996. The focus of this book is helping abused women escape and remain free from violent relationships.

Ross, Jacob Joshua. *The Virtues of the Family.* New York: Free Press, 1994. The author, a philosopher, argues that the family is not a rigid, static institution with inflexible roles, but, rather, a dynamic social structure from which human morality and human nature emerge.

Rubin, Lillian. *Families on the Faultline: America's Working Class Speaks about the Family, the Economy, Race and Ethnicity.* New York: HarperCollins, 1994. Based on interviews, this book maps primary concerns of the working class, allowing us to better understand the tensions they face.

Journals

Family Relations, International Journal of Sociology of the Family, Journal of Comparative Family Studies, Journal of Divorce, Journal of Family and Economic Issues, Journal of Family Issues, Journal of Family Violence, Journal of Marriage and the Family, and *Marriage and Family Review* publish articles on almost every aspect of marriage and family life.

CHAPTER 13 Education and Religion

Education

Cookson, Peter W. *School Choice: The Struggle for the Soul of American Education.* New Haven, Conn.: Yale University Press, 1994. This focus on school choice examines the controversy over educational reform, which, based on fundamentally different ideas about the philosophy and content of education, is not likely to be resolved soon.

Howe, Quincy, Jr. *Under Running Laughter: Notes from a Renegade Classroom.* New York: Free Press, 1990. A tenured professor of classics recounts his experiences and describes the unorthodox techniques he used to teach "throwaway" adolescents in the inner city.

Hurn, Christopher J. *The Limits and Possibilities of Schooling: An Introduction to the Sociology of Education,* 3rd ed. Boston: Allyn and Bacon, 1993. This overview of the sociology of education reviews in greater depth many of the topics discussed in this chapter.

Kozol, Jonathan. *Savage Inequalities.* New York: Crown Publishers, 1991. Kozol presents a journalistic account of educational inequalities that arise from social class.

Postman, Neil. *Technopoly: The Surrender of Culture to Technology.* New York: Knopf, 1992. An analysis of how technology is destroying vital aspects of social life and how education can lead the resistance against technological tyranny.

Schoolland, Ken. *Shogun's Ghost: The Dark Side of Japanese Education.* Westport, Conn.: Bergin & Garvey, 1990. The author, a college teacher in Japan for five years, shatters the myth of excellence in Japanese education in his account of unruly classrooms, general lack of discipline and study habits, truancy, and rampant cheating on exams.

Sowell, Thomas. *Inside American Education: The Decline, the Deception, the Dogmas.* New York: Free Press, 1993. The author, a thoroughgoing conservative, scathingly denounces most trends in U.S. education.

Trueba, Henry T., Lila Jacobs, and Elizabeth Kirton. *Cultural Conflict and Adaptation: The Case of Hmong Children in American Society.* Bristol, Penn.: Falmer Press, 1990. In examining problems of Hmong children living in California, the author probes the multiethnic challenges facing U.S. schools.

Journals

The following journals contain articles that examine almost every aspect of education: *Education and Urban Society, Harvard Educational Review,* and *Sociology of Education.*

Religion

Berger, Peter L. *The Sacred Canopy: Elements of a Sociological Theory of Religion.* New York: Anchor Books, 1990. Applying the functionalist, symbolic interactionist, and conflict perspectives to the analysis of religion, the author synthesizes the writings of Emile Durkheim, Max Weber, and Karl Marx.

Berger, Peter L. *A Far Glory: The Quest for Faith in an Age of Credulity.* New York: Free Press, 1992. A sociologist explains how faith is possible in an age of pluralistic relativism.

Finke, Roger, and Rodney Stark. *The Churching of America.* New Brunswick, N.J.: Rutgers University Press, 1992. An overview of the growth of formal religious membership in the United States, with an emphasis on how new religious organizations (sects, cults) fuel this growth.

Haddad, Yvonne Yazbeck, and Adair T. Lummis. *Islamic Values in the United States: A Comparative Study.* New York: Oxford University Press, 1987. Like the millions of immigrants before them, the large numbers of Muslims who have recently immigrated to the United States have brought their religion with them. The authors examine the adaptation of Islam to its new environment.

Lyden, John, ed. *Enduring Issues in Religion: Opposing Viewpoints.* San Diego, Calif.: Greenhaven, 1995. As these readings make evident, religion often represents emotion-laden social issues on which people have strong opinions.

Marty, Martin E., and R. Scott Appleby. *The Glory and the Power: The Fundamentalist Challenge to the Modern World.* Boston: Beacon Press, 1992. Examining fundamentalism in the United States, Israel, Egypt, and elsewhere, the authors explain why fundamentalism is enjoying a revival.

Nord, Warren A. *Religion and American Education: Rethinking a National Dilemma.* Chapel Hill: University of North Carolina Press, 1995. The author, a philosopher, argues that religious studies should be a part of the curricula of public schools.

Schoenherr, Richard A., and Lawrence A. Young. *Full Pews and Empty Altars: Demographics of the Priest Shortage.* Madison: University of Wisconsin Press, 1993. The authors analyze the implications of why, in spite of growing numbers of Roman Catholics, the number of priests is shrinking.

Stark, Rodney. *The Rise of Christianity: A Sociologist Reconsiders History.* Princeton, New Jersey: Princeton University Press, 1996. The author analyzes how a tiny messianic movement on the fringe of the Roman Empire became the dominant faith of Western civilization.

Journals

The following three journals publish articles that focus on the sociology of religion: *Journal for the Scientific Study of Religion, Review of Religious Research,* and *Sociological Analysis: A Journal in the Sociology of Religion.*

CHAPTER 14 Population and Urbanization

Anderson, Elijah. *StreetWise: Race, Class, and Change in an Urban Community.* Chicago: University of Chicago Press, 1992. A participant observation study that explores the relationships between those who are gentrifying an inner-city area and those who are being displaced.

Burgess, Ernest W., ed. *Urban Community.* New York: AMS Press, 1993. This reprint of a classic 1926 book provides a glimpse of earlier life in the United States.

Department of Agriculture. *Yearbook of Agriculture.* Washington, D.C.: Department of Agriculture, published annually. The yearbook focuses on specific aspects of U.S. agribusiness, especially international economies and trade.

Flora, Cornelia Butler, Jan L. Flora, Jacqueline D. Spears, and Louis E. Swanson. *Rural Communities: Legacy and Change.* Boulder, Colo.: Westview Press, 1992. The authors examine profound changes that are transforming rural life.

Haughton, Graham, and Colin Hunter. *Sustainable Cities.* Bristol, Penn.: Jessica Kingsley, 1994. While many despair about the quality of life in U.S. cities, these authors present proposals for how cities can be designed so they improve our quality of life.

Karp, David A., Gregory P. Stone, and William C. Yoels. *Being Urban: A Sociology of City Life,* 2nd ed. New York: Praeger, 1991. This overview of urban life stresses the everyday lives of city dwellers—what people *do* in cities, how they adjust and get along.

Kasinitz, Philip, ed. *Metropolis: Center and Symbol of Our Times.* New York: New York University Press, 1995. Urbanization, one of the main trends of the contemporary world and a primary factor in shaping our views of life, is the focus of these authors.

Liebow, Elliot. *Tally's Corner: A Study of Negro Streetcorner Men.* Boston: Little, Brown, 1967. This participant observation study of black street corner men and their families in Washington, D.C., has become a classic in sociology.

Phillips, E. Barbara. *City Lights: Urban-Suburban Life in a Global Society,* 2nd ed. New York: Oxford University Press, 1995. What major challenges do U.S. cities face in our coming global society? That is the primary question examined by this author.

Sennett, Richard. *Flesh and Stone: The Body and the City in Western Civilization.* New York: Norton, 1994. This analysis of cities through history focuses on an interesting relationship, that of dominant ideas about the human body and the layout of cities.

Weeks, John R. *Population: An Introduction to Concepts and Issues,* 5th ed. Belmont, CA: Wadsworth Publishing Company, 1994. Focusing on both the United States and the world, the author analyzes major issues in population.

Whyte, William Foote. *Street Corner Society: The Social Structure of an Italian Slum.* Chicago: University of Chicago Press, 1993. First published in 1943. Still quoted and reprinted, this classic participant observation study provides insight into the social organization of an area of a U.S. city that, from an outsider's perspective, appeared socially disorganized.

CHAPTER 15 Social Change: Technology, Social Movements, and the Environment

Baber, Zaheer. *This Vulnerable Planet: A Short Economic History of the Environment.* New York: Monthly Review Press, 1994. An overview of how production is related to environmental degradation, from earlier times to capitalism and socialism, with too many apologies for environmental destruction in the former Soviet Union.

Brown, Lester R., ed. *State of the World.* New York: Norton, published annually. Experts on environmental issues analyze environmental problems throughout the world; a New Malthusian perspective.

Butel, Frederick H. *Forcing the Spring: The Transformation of the American Environmental Movement.* Washington, D.C.: Island Press, 1993. A history of the rise, decline, and resurgence of perhaps the most important global movement.

Colborn, Theo, Dianne Dumanoski, and John Peterson Myers. *Our Stolen Future: Are We Threatening Our Fertility, Intelligence, and Survival—A Scientific Detective Story.* New York: Dutton, 1996. Using a detective-style narrative, the authors argue that the bombardment of people and wildlife by chemicals commonly found in plastics, pesticides, and industrial pollutants are threatening our capacity to reproduce, fight off disease, and develop normal intelligence.

Council on Environmental Quality. *Environmental Quality.* Washington, D.C.: U.S. Government Printing Office, published annually. Each report evaluates the condition of some aspect of the environment.

Cross, Gary, S., and Rick Szostak. *Technology and American Society: A History.* Englewood Cliffs, N.J.: Prentice Hall,

1995. The authors analyze how technology, a driving force in social change, is having fundamental effects on our lives.

Curtis, Russell L., Jr., and Benigno E. Aguirre, eds. *Collective Behavior and Social Movements*. Boston: Allyn and Bacon, 1993. The thirty-five readings in this collection, some at an advanced level, provide an overview of the major topics of this chapter.

Feshbach, Murray, and Alfred Friendly. *Ecocide in the USSR*. New York: Basic Books, 1992. The authors analyze the political repression of environmentalists and the government's willing sacrifice of the environment for the sake of "building a brighter, industrial future."

Gates, Bill. *The Road Ahead*. New York: Viking, 1995. Will the new technology bring us a wallet PC—which will dispense airline and concert tickets, and function as a checkbook and credit card, and communicate fax and e-mail messages? The chairman of Microsoft sees this—and many other surprises—as part of our trip down the information highway.

Gitlin, Todd. *The Sixties: Years of Hope, Days of Rage*. New York: Bantam, 1987. The author, now a sociologist, was a leader in the peace movement that arose during the social unrest of the 1960s. He combines personal experience with a sociological perspective.

Jasper, James M., and Dorothy Nelkin. *The Animal Rights Crusade: The Growth of a Moral Protest*. New York: Free Press, 1992. With an emphasis on philosophy, motivation, and tactics, the authors provide a kaleidoscopic overview of the animal rights movement, from its beginnings to its international participation.

Klee, Ernst, Willi Dressen, and Volker Riess. *"The Good Old Days": The Holocaust as Seen by Its Perpetrators and Bystanders*, Deborah Burnstone, trans. New York: Free Press, 1991. This chilling account of massacres by the SS is based on the photographs they took of their "work," their letters home, and their scrapbooks.

Larana, Enrique, Hank Johnston, and Joseph R. Gusfield, eds. *New Social Movements: From Ideology to Identity*. Philadelphia: Temple University Press, 1994. The authors explain how and why social movements have become an essential part of contemporary life in society.

McCuen, Gary E., ed. *Ecocide and Genocide in the Vanishing Forest: The Rainforests and Native People*. Hudson, Wis.: GEM Publications, 1993. Eighteen brief readings examine why the rainforests are vanishing and explore possible solutions to this problem.

Stead, W. Edward, and Jean Garner Stead. *Management for a Small Planet*. Newbury Park, Calif.: Sage, 1992. The authors examine how we can reconcile our need for economic production with our need to protect the earth's ecosystem.

Journals

Earth First! Journal and *Sierra*, magazines published by Earth First! and the Sierra Club respectively, are excellent sources for keeping informed of major developments in the environmental movement.

R E F E R E N C E S

Abdullah, Mohammed Nur. "Letter to the Editor." *Wall Street Journal*, November 2, 1995:A15.

Aberle, David. *The Peyote Religion among the Navaho*. Chicago: Aldine, 1966.

Abramson, Jill. "How Outsider Clinton Built a Potent Network of Insider Contacts." *Wall Street Journal*, March 12, 1992:A1, A4.

Addams, Jane. *Twenty Years at Hull House*. New York: Signet, 1981. First published in 1910.

Adler, Patricia A., Steven J. Kless, and Peter Adler. "Socialization to Gender Roles: Popularity among Elementary School Boys and Girls." *Sociology of Education*, 65, July 1992:169–187.

Adorno, Theodor W., Else Frenkel-Brunswick, D. J. Levinson, and R. N. Sanford. *The Authoritarian Personality*. New York: Harper & Row, 1950.

Ahlburg, Dennis A., and Carol J. De Vita. "New Realities of the American Family." *Population Bulletin*, 47, 2, August 1992:1–44.

Albrecht, Donald E., and Steven H. Murdoch. "Natural Resource Availability and Social Change." *Sociological Inquiry*, 56, 3, Summer 1986:381–400.

Aldrich, Nelson W., Jr. *Old Money: The Mythology of America's Upper Class*. New York: Vintage Books, 1989.

Allen, Katherine R., and David H. Demo. "The Families of Lesbians and Gay Men: A New Frontier in Family Research." *Journal of Marriage and the Family*, 57, February 1995:111–127.

Allport, Floyd. *Social Psychology*. Boston: Houghton Mifflin, 1954.

Amenta, Edwin, Bruce G. Carruthers, and Yvonne Zylan. "A Hero for the Aged? The Townsend Movement, the Political Mediation Model, and U.S. Old-Age Policy, 1934–1950." *American Journal of Sociology*, 98, 2, September 1992:308–339.

American Sociological Association. "Code of Ethics." Washington, D.C.: American Sociological Association, August 14, 1989.

American Sociological Association. "Section on Environment and Technology." Pamphlet, no date.

Amott, Teresa, and Julie Matthaei. *Race, Gender, and Work: A Multicultural Economic History of Women in the United States*. Boston: South End Press, 1991.

Anderson, Elijah. *A Place on the Corner*. Chicago: University of Chicago Press, 1978.

Anderson, Elijah. *Streetwise*. Chicago: University of Chicago Press, 1990.

Anderson, Elijah. "Streetwise." In *Down to Earth Sociology: Introductory Readings*, 8th ed., James M. Henslin, ed. New York: Free Press, 1995:168–177.

Anderson, Nels. *Desert Saints: The Mormon Frontier in Utah*. Chicago: University of Chicago Press, 1966. First published in 1942.

Anderson, Philip. "God and the Swedish Immigrants." *Sweden and America*, Autumn 1995:17–20.

Ansberry, Clare. "Despite Federal Law, Hospitals Still Reject Sick Who Can't Pay." *Wall Street Journal*, November 29, 1988:A1, A4.

"Anybody's Son Will Do." National Film Board of Canada, KCTS, and Films, 1983.

Ariés, Philippe. *Centuries of Childhood*. R. Baldick, trans. New York: Vintage Books, 1965.

Arlacchi, P. *Peasants and Great Estates: Society in Traditional Calabria*. Cambridge, England: Cambridge University Press, 1980.

Arndt, William F., and F. Wilbur Gingrich. *A Greek-English Lexicon of the New Testament and Other Early Christian Literature*. Chicago: University of Chicago Press, 1957.

Asch, Solomon. "Effects of Group Pressure upon the Modification and Distortion of Judgments." In *Readings in Social Psychology*, Guy Swanson, Theodore M. Newcomb, and Eugene L. Hartley, eds. New York: Holt, Rinehart and Winston, 1952.

Ashe, Arthur. "A Zero-Sum Game That Hurts Blacks." *Wall Street Journal*, February 27, 1992:A10.

Associated Press. "Future Medicine Looks Futuristic." December 2, 1995.

Atchley, Robert C. "Dimensions of Widowhood in Later Life." *Gerontologist*, 15, April 1975:176–178.

Baca Zinn, Maxine. "Adaptation and Continuity in Mexican-Origin Families." In *Minority Families in the United States: A Multicultural Perspective*, Ronald L. Taylor, ed. Englewood Cliffs, N.J.: Prentice Hall, 1994:64–81.

Bagguley, Paul, and Kirk Mann. "Idle Thieving Bastards? Scholarly Representations of the 'Underclass.' " *Work, Employment, and Society*, 6, 1, March 1992:113–126.

Bales, Robert F. "The Equilibrium Problem in Small Groups." In *Working Papers in the Theory of Action*, Talcott Parsons et al., eds. New York: Free Press, 1953:111–115.

Bales, Robert F. *Interaction Process Analysis*. Reading, Mass.: Addison-Wesley, 1950.

Baltzell, E. Digby. *Puritan Boston and Quaker Philadelphia*. New York: Free Press, 1979.

Baltzell, E. Digby, and Howard G. Schneiderman. "Social Class in the Oval Office." *Society*, September–October 1988:42–49.

Banerjee, Nela. "Debate over Measuring the Poverty Line Will Come to a Head in Senate Hearings." *Wall Street Journal*, May 12, 1994:A2.

Banfield, Edward C. *The Unheavenly City Revisited.* Boston: Little, Brown, 1974.

Barnes, Fred. "How to Rig a Poll." *Wall Street Journal*, June 14, 1995:A14.

Barnes, Harry Elmer. *The History of Western Civilization*, Vol. 1. New York: Harcourt, Brace, 1935.

Barringer, Felicity. "Rich–Poor Gulf Widens among Blacks." *New York Times*, September 25, 1992:A12.

Barry, Paul. "Strong Medicine: A Talk with Former Principal Henry Gradillas." *College Board Review*, Fall 1989:2–13.

Beck, Allen J., Susan A. Kline, and Lawrence A. Greenfeld. "Survey of Youth in Custody, 1987." Washington, D.C.: U.S. Department of Justice, September 1988.

Beck, Scott H., and Joe W. Page. "Involvement in Activities and the Psychological Well-Being of Retired Men." *Activities, Adaptation, & Aging*, 11, 1, 1988:31–47.

Becker, Howard S. *Outsiders: Studies in the Sociology of Deviance.* New York: Free Press, 1966.

Beeghley, Leonard. *The Structure of Social Stratification in the United States.* Boston: Allyn and Bacon, 1989.

Beeghley, Leonard. *The Structure of Social Stratification in the United States*, 2nd ed. Boston: Allyn and Bacon, 1996.

Begley, Sharon. "Twins: Nazi and Jew." *Newsweek*, 94, December 3, 1979:139.

Belcher, John R. "Are Jails Replacing the Mental Health System for the Homeless Mentally Ill?" *Community Mental Health Journal*, 24, 3, Fall 1988:185–195.

Bell, Daniel. *The Coming of Post-Industrial Society: A Venture in Social Forecasting.* New York: Basic Books, 1973.

Bell, David A. "An American Success Story: The Triumph of Asian-Americans." In *Sociological Footprints: Introductory Readings in Sociology*, 5th ed., Leonard Cargan and Jeanne H. Ballantine, eds. Belmont, Calif.: Wadsworth, 1991:308–316.

Bellah, Robert N., Richard Madsen, William M. Sullivan, Ann Swidler, and Steven M. Tipton. *Habits of the Heart: Individualism and Commitment in American Life.* Berkeley: University of California Press, 1985.

Benales, Carlos. "70 Days Battling Starvation and Freezing in the Andes: A Chronicle of Man's Unwillingness to Die." *New York Times*, January 1, 1973:3.

Bender, Sue. "Everyday Sacred: A Journey to the Amish." *Utne Reader*, September–October 1990:91–97.

Benet, Sula. "Why They Live to Be 100, or Even Older, in Abkhasia." *New York Times Magazine*, 26, December 1971.

Bennett, Neil G., Ann Klimas Blanc, and David E. Bloo. "Commitment and the Modern Union: Assessing the Link between Premarital Cohabitation and Subsequent Marital Stability." *American Sociological Review*, 53, 1988:127–138.

Benokraitis, Nijole V., and Joe R. Feagin. "Sex Discrimination—Subtle and Covert." In *Down to Earth Sociology: Introductory Readings*, 6th ed., James M. Henslin, ed. New York: Free Press, 1991:334–343.

Berger, Peter L. *The Capitalist Revolution: Fifty Propositions about Prosperity, Equality, and Liberty.* New York: Basic Books, 1991.

Berger, Peter L. *Invitation to Sociology: A Humanistic Perspective.* New York: Doubleday, 1963.

Berger, Peter L. "Invitation to Sociology." In *Down to Earth Sociology: Introductory Readings*, 9th ed., James M. Henslin, ed. New York: Free Press, 1997:3–7. First published in 1963.

Berger, Peter L. *The Sacred Canopy: Elements of a Sociological Theory of Religion.* Garden City, N.Y.: Doubleday, 1967.

Berk, Laura E. *Child Development*, 3rd ed. Boston: Allyn and Bacon, 1994.

Berle, Adolf, Jr., and Gardiner C. Means. *The Modern Corporation and Private Property.* New York: Harcourt, Brace and World, 1932. As cited in Useem 1980:44.

Bernard, Viola W., Perry Ottenberg, and Fritz Redl. "Dehumanization: A Composite Psychological Defense in Relation to Modern War." In *The Triple Revolution Emerging: Social Problems in Depth*, Robert Perucci and Marc Pilisuk, eds. Boston: Little, Brown, 1971:17–34.

Bernstein, Jonas. "How the Russian Mafia Rules." *Wall Street Journal*, October 26, 1994:A20.

Bernstein, Richard. "Play Penn." *New Republic*, August 2, 1993.

Besser, Terry L. "A Critical Approach to the Study of Japanese Management." *Humanity and Society*, 16, 2, May 1992:176–195.

Bijker, Wiehe E., ed. *The Social Construction of Technological Systems: New Directions in the Sociology and History of Technology.* Cambridge, Mass.: MIT Press, 1987.

Bishop, Jerry E. "Long-Ignored Cycle in Climate Suggests Worse Greenhouse Effect than Thought." *Wall Street Journal*, April 11, 1995:B5.

Bishop, Jerry E. "Study Finds Doctors Tend to Postpone Heart Surgery for Women, Raising Risk." *Wall Street Journal*, April 16, 1990:B4.

Blackwelder, Stephen P. "Duality of Structure in the Reproduction of Race, Class, and Gender Inequality." Paper presented at the 1993 meetings of the American Sociological Association.

Blau, Francine D., and Lawrence M. Kahn. "The Gender Earnings Gap: Some International Evidence." Working Paper No. 4224, National Bureau of Economic Research, December 1992.

Blau, Peter M., and Otis Dudley Duncan. *The American Occupational Structure.* New York: Wiley, 1967.

Blumstein, Alfred, and Jacqueline Cohen. "Characterizing Criminal Careers." *Science*, 237, August 1987:985–991.

Blumstein, Philip, and Pepper Schwartz. *American Couples: Money, Work, Sex.* New York: Pocket Books, 1985.

Bobo, Lawrence, and James R. Kluegel. "Modern American Prejudice: Stereotypes, Social Distance, and Perceptions of Discrimination toward Blacks, Hispanics, and Asians." Paper presented at the 1991 annual meeting of the American Sociological Association.

Bolgar, Robert, Hallie Zweig-Frank, and Joel Paris. "Childhood Antecedents of Interpersonal Problems in Young Adult Children of Divorce." *Journal of the American Acad-*

emy of Child and Adolescent Psychiatry, 34, 2, February 1995:143–150.

Booth, Alan, and James M. Dabbs, Jr. "Testosterone and Men's Marriages." *Social Forces, 72*, 2, December 1993: 463–477.

Borrelli, Peter. "The Ecophilosophers." *Amicus Journal*, Spring 1988:30–39.

"The Boss's Pay." *Wall Street Journal*, April 12, 1995:R13-R15.

Bourgois, Philippe. "Crack in Spanish Harlem." In *Haves and Have-Nots: An International Reader on Social Inequality*, James Curtis and Lorne Tepperman, eds. Englewood Cliffs, N.J.: Prentice Hall, 1994:131–136.

Bourque, L. B. *Defining Rape*. Durham, N.C.: Duke University Press, 1989.

Bowles, Samuel. "Unequal Education and the Reproduction of the Social Division of Labor." In *Power and Ideology in Education*, J. Karabel and A. H. Halsey, eds. New York: Oxford University Press, 1977.

Bowles, Samuel, and Herbert Gintis. *Schooling in Capitalist America*. New York: Basic Books, 1976.

Brajuha, Mario, and Lyle Hallowell. "Legal Intrusion and the Politics of Fieldwork: The Impact of the Brajuha Case." *Urban Life, 14*, 4, January 1986:454–478.

Brauchli, Marcus W. "A Satellite TV System Is Quickly Moving Asia into the Global Village." *Wall Street Journal*, May 10, 1993:A1, A8.

Bray, Rosemary L. "Rosa Parks: A Legendary Moment, a Lifetime of Activism." *Ms. Magazine, 6*, 3, November–December 1995:45–47.

Breen, Richard, and Christopher T. Whelan. "Gender and Class Mobility: Evidence from the Republic of Ireland." *Sociology, 29*, 1, February 1995:1–22.

Bretos, Miguel A. "Hispanics Face Institutional Exclusion." *Miami Herald*, May 22, 1994.

Bridgman, Ann. "Report from the Russian Front." *Education Week, 13*, 28, April 6, 1994:22–29.

Bridgwater, William, ed. *The Columbia Viking Desk Encyclopedia*. New York: Viking Press, 1953.

Brines, Julie. "Economic Dependency, Gender, and the Division of Labor at Home." *American Journal of Sociology, 100*, 3, November 1994:652–688.

Broad, William J. "The Shuttle Explodes." *New York Times*, January 29, 1986:A1, A5.

Broderick, Francis L. "W. E. B. Du Bois: History of an Intellectual." In *Black Sociologists*, James E. Blackwell and Morris Janowitz, eds. Chicago: University of Chicago Press, 1974.

Brody, Jane E. "Pause in Life-Expectancy Gains Tied to AIDS." *New York Times*, August 30, 1995:B6.

Bronfenbrenner, Urie, as quoted in Diane Fassel. "Divorce May Not Harm Children." In *Family in America: Opposing Viewpoints*, Viqi Wagner, ed. San Diego, Calif.: Greenhaven Press, 1992:115–119.

Brooke, James. "Amid U.S. Islam's Growth in the U.S., Muslims Face a Surge in Attacks." *New York Times*, August 28, 1995:A1, B7.

Browning, Christopher R. *Ordinary Men: Reserve Police Battalion 101 and the Final Solution in Poland*. New York: HarperPerennial, 1993.

Bryant, Clifton D. "Cockfighting: America's Invisible Sport." In *Down to Earth Sociology: Introductory Readings*, 7th ed., James M. Henslin, ed. New York: Free Press, 1993: 211–224.

Buechler, Steven M. "Beyond Resource Mobilization: Emerging Trends in Social Movement Theory." *Sociological Quarterly, 34*, 2, 1993:217–235.

Bumiller, Elisabeth. "First Comes Marriage—Then, Maybe, Love." In *Marriage and Family in a Changing Society*, 4th ed., James M. Henslin, ed. New York: Free Press, 1992:120–125.

Bumpass, Larry. "Forum II. Patterns, Causes, and Consequences of Out-of-Wedlock Childbearing: What Can Government Do?" *Focus, 17*, 1, Summer 1995:41–45.

Bumpass, Larry L., James A. Sweet, and Andrew Cherlin. "The Role of Cohabitation in Declining Rates of Marriage." *Journal of Marriage and the Family, 53*, November 1991:913–927.

Burgess, Ernest W. "The Growth of the City: An Introduction to a Research Project." In *The City*, Robert E. Park, Ernest W. Burgess, and Roderick D. McKenzie, eds. Chicago: University of Chicago Press, 1925:47–62.

Burnham, Walter Dean. *Democracy in the Making: American Government and Politics*. Englewood Cliffs, N.J.: Prentice Hall, 1983.

Burstyn, Linda. "Female Circumcision Comes to America." *Atlantic Monthly, 276*, 4, October 1995:28–35.

Bush, Diane Mitsch, and Robert G. Simmons. "Socialization Processes over the Life Course." In *Social Psychology: Sociological Perspectives*, Morris Rosenberg and Ralph H. Turner, eds. New Brunswick, N.J.: Transaction Books, 1990: 133–164.

Butler, Robert N. "Ageism: Another Form of Bigotry." *Gerontologist, 9*, Winter 1980:243–246.

Butler, Robert N. *Why Survive? Being Old in America*. New York: Harper & Row, 1975.

Buttel, Frederick H. "New Directions in Environmental Sociology." *Annual Review of Sociology, 13*, W. Richard Scott and James F. Short, Jr., eds. Palo Alto, Calif.: Annual Reviews, 1987:465–488.

Canavan, Margaret M., Walter J. Meyer III, and Deborah C. Higgs. "The Female Experience of Sibling Incest." *Journal of Marital and Family Therapy, 18*, 2, 1992:129–142.

Cardoso, Fernando Henrique. "Dependent Capitalist Development in Latin America." *New Left Review, 74*, July–August 1972:83–95.

Carey, John, and Mark Lewyn. "Yield Signs on the Info Interstate." *Business Week*, January 24, 1994:88–90.

Carpenter, Betsy. "Redwood Radicals." *U.S. News & World Report, 109*, 11, September 17, 1990:50–51.

Carr, Deborah, Carol D. Ryff, Burton Singer, and William J. Magee. "Bringing the 'Life' Back into Life Course Research: A 'Person-Centered' Approach to Studying the Life Course." Paper presented at the 1995 meetings of the American Sociological Association.

Carrasquillo, Hector. "The Puerto Rican Family." In *Minority Families in the United States: A Multicultural Perspective*, Ronald L. Taylor, ed. Englewood Cliffs, N.J.: Prentice Hall, 1994:82–94.

Carrington, Tim. "Developed Nations Want Poor Countries to Succeed on Trade, But Not Too Much." *Wall Street Journal*, September 20, 1993:A10.

Carroll, Peter N., and David W. Noble. *The Free and the Unfree: A New History of the United States.* New York: Penguin, 1977.

Cartwright, Dorwin, and Alvin Zander, eds. *Group Dynamics*, 3rd ed. Evanston, Ill.: Peterson, 1968.

Cerulo, Karen A., Janet M. Ruane, and Mary Chayko. "Technological Ties That Bind: Media-Generated Primary Groups." *Communication Research*, 19, 1, February 1992:109–129.

Chafetz, Janet Saltzman. *Gender Equity: An Integrated Theory of Stability and Change.* Newbury Park, Calif.: Sage, 1990.

Chafetz, Janet Saltzman, and Anthony Gary Dworkin. *Female Revolt: Women's Movements in World and Historical Perspective.* Totowa, N.J.: Rowman & Allanheld, 1986.

Chagnon, Napoleon A. *Yanomamo: The Fierce People*, 2nd ed. New York: Holt, Rinehart and Winston, 1977.

Chambliss, William J. "The Saints and the Roughnecks." In *Down to Earth Sociology: Introductory Readings*, 9th ed., James M. Henslin, ed. New York: Free Press, 1997: 246–260. First published in *Society*, 11, 1973.

Chandler, Daniel. "Technological or Media Determinism." Internet, "Media and Communication Studies Page," 1995. E-mail: dgc@aberystwyth.ac.

Chandler, Tertius, and Gerald Fox. *3000 Years of Urban Growth.* New York: Academic Press, 1974.

Chandra, Vibha P. "Fragmented Identities: The Social Construction of Ethnicity, 1885–1947." Unpublished paper, 1993a.

Chandra, Vibha P. "The Present Moment of the Past: The Metamorphosis." Unpublished paper, 1993b.

Charlier, Marj. "Little Bighorn from the Indian Point of View." *Wall Street Journal*, September 15, 1992:A12.

Chavez, Linda. "Rainbow Collision." *New Republic*, November 19, 1990:14–16.

Chen, Edwin. "Twins Reared Apart: A Living Lab." *New York Times Magazine*, December 9, 1979:112.

Chen, Kathy. "Chinese Are Going to Town as Growth of Cities Takes Off." *Wall Street Journal*, January 4, 1996: A1, A12.

Cherlin, Andrew. "Remarriage as an Incomplete Institution." In *Marriage and Family in a Changing Society*, 3rd ed., James M. Henslin, ed. New York: Free Press, 1989: 492–501.

Cherlin, Andrew, and Frank F. Furstenberg, Jr. "The American Family in the Year 2000." In *Down to Earth Sociology*, 5th ed., James M. Henslin, ed. New York: Free Press, 1988:325–331.

Childs, C. P., and Greenfield, P. M. "Informal Modes of Learning and Teaching: The Case of the Zinacanteco Weaving." *Advances in Cross-Cultural Psychology*, Vol. 2, N. Warren, ed. London: Academic Press, 1982:269–311.

Chodorow, Nancy J. "What Is the Relation between Psychoanalytic Feminism and the Psychoanalytic Psychology of Women?" In *Theoretical Perspectives on Sexual Difference*, Deborah L. Rhode, ed. New Haven, Conn.: Yale University Press, 1990:114–130.

Chun, Ki-Taek, and Jadja Zalokar. *Civil Rights Issues Facing Asian Americans in the 1990s.* Washington, D.C.: U.S. Commission on Civil Rights, February 1992.

Clair, Jeffrey Michael, David A. Karp, and William C. Yoels. *Experiencing the Life Cycle: A Social Psychology of Aging*, 2nd ed. Springfield, Ill.: Thomas, 1993.

Clark, Candace. "Sympathy in Everyday Life." In *Down to Earth Sociology: Introductory Readings*, 6th ed., James M. Henslin, ed. New York: Free Press, 1991:193–203.

Clingempeel, W. Glenn, and N. Dickon Repucci. "Joint Custody after Divorce: Major Issues and Goals for Research." *Psychological Bulletin*, 9, 1982:102–127.

Cloward, Richard A., and Lloyd E. Ohlin. *Delinquency and Opportunity: A Theory of Delinquent Gangs.* New York: Free Press, 1960.

Cnaan, Ram A. "Neighborhood-Representing Organizations: How Democratic Are They?" *Social Science Review*, December 1991:614–634.

Cohen, Erik. "Lovelorn Farangs: The Correspondence between Foreign Men and Thai Girls." *Anthropological Quarterly*, 59, 3, July 1986:115–127.

Cohen, Joel E. "How Many People Can the Earth Support?" *Population Today*, January 1996:4–5.

Cohen, Morris R. "Moral Aspects of the Criminal Law." *Yale Law Journal*, 49, April 1940:1009–1026.

Coleman, James William. *The Criminal Elite: The Sociology of White Collar Crime.* New York: St. Martin's Press, 1989.

Coleman, James, and Thomas Hoffer. *Public and Private Schools: The Impact of Communities.* New York: Basic Books, 1987.

Collins, Patricia Hill. "Learning from the Outsider Within: The Sociological Significance of Black Feminist Thought." *Social Problems*, 33, 6, December 1986:514–532.

Collins, Randall. *Conflict Sociology: Toward an Explanatory Science.* New York: Academic Press, 1974.

Collins, Randall. *The Credential Society: An Historical Sociology of Education.* New York: Academic Press, 1979.

Collins, Randall. *Theoretical Sociology.* San Diego, Calif.: Harcourt Brace Jovanovich, 1988.

Comstock, George, and Victor C. Strasburger. "Deceptive Appearances: Television Violence and Aggressive Behavior." *Journal of Adolescent Health Care*, 11, 1, January 1990:31–44.

Cooley, Charles Horton. *Human Nature and the Social Order.* New York: Scribner's, 1902.

Cooley, Charles Horton. *Social Organization.* New York: Scribner's, 1909.

Cooley, Charles Horton. *Social Organization.* New York: Schocken, 1962.

Cooper, Kenneth J. "New Focus Sought in National High School Exams: NEH Backs Approach Used in Europe and Japan to Assess Knowledge Rather than Aptitude." *Washington Post*, May 20, 1991:A7.

Corbett, Thomas. "Welfare Reform in the 104th Congress: Goals, Options, and Tradeoffs." *Focus*, 17, 1, Summer 1995:29–31.

Corcoran, Mary, Greg J. Duncan, Gerald Gurin, and Patricia Gurin. "Myth and Reality: The Causes and Persistence of Poverty." *Journal of Policy Analysis and Management*, 4, 4, 1985:516–536.

Cose, Ellis. *The Rage of the Privileged Class.* New York: HarperCollins, 1993.

Coser, Lewis A. *Masters of Sociological Thought: Ideas in Historical and Social Context,* 2nd ed. New York: Harcourt Brace Jovanovich, 1977.

Cottin, Lou. *Elders in Rebellion: A Guide to Senior Activism.* Garden City, N.Y.: Anchor Doubleday, 1979.

Couch, Carl J. *Social Processes and Relationships: A Formal Approach.* Dix Hills, N.Y.: General Hall, 1989.

Courtney, Kelly. "Two Sides of the Environmental Movement: Radical Earth First! and the Sierra Club." Paper presented at the 1995 meetings of the American Sociological Association.

Cousins, Albert N., and Hans Nagpaul. *Urban Man and Society: A Reader in Urban Sociology.* New York: McGraw-Hill, 1970.

Cowen, Emory L., Judah Landes, and Donald E. Schaet. "The Effects of Mild Frustration on the Expression of Prejudiced Attitudes." *Journal of Abnormal and Social Psychology,* January 1959:33–38.

Cowgill, Donald. "The Aging of Populations and Societies." *Annals of the American Academy of Political and Social Science, 415,* 1974:1–18.

Cowley, Joyce. *Pioneers of Women's Liberation.* New York: Merit, 1969.

Crews, Kimberly. "National Curricula Make Place for Population." *Population Today,* July–August 1995:4–5.

Crispell, Diane. "People Patterns." *Wall Street Journal,* March 16, 1992:B1.

Crosbie, Paul V., ed. *Interaction in Small Groups.* New York: Macmillan, 1975.

Crossen, Cynthia. *Wall Street Journal,* November 14, 1991:A1, A7.

Cumming, Elaine. "Further Thoughts on the Theory of Disengagement." In *Aging in America: Readings in Social Gerontology,* Cary S. Kart and Barbara B. Manard, eds. Sherman Oaks, Calif.: Alfred Publishing, 1976:19–41.

Cumming, Elaine, and William E. Henry. *Growing Old: The Process of Disengagement.* New York: Basic Books, 1961.

Curwin, E. Cecil, and Gudmond Hart. *Plough and Pasture.* New York: Collier Books, 1961.

Cushman, John H. "U.S. to Weigh Blacks' Complaints about Pollution." *New York Times,* November 19, 1993:A16.

"Cyberschool Makes Its Debut." *The American Schoolboard, 183,* 1, January 1996:A11.

Dabbs, James M., Jr., "Age and Seasonal Variation in Serum Testosterone Concentration Among Men." *Chronobiology International,* 7, 3, 1990:245–49.

Dabbs, James M., Jr., and Robin Morris. "Testosterone, Social Class, and Antisocial Behavior in a Sample of 4,462 Men." *Psychological Science,* 1, 3, May 1990:209–211.

Dahl, Robert A. *Dilemmas of Pluralist Democracy: Autonomy vs. Control.* New Haven, Conn.: Yale University Press, 1982.

Dahl, Robert A. *Who Governs?* New Haven, Conn.: Yale University Press, 1961.

Dahrendorf, Ralf. *Class and Class Conflict in Industrial Society.* Palo Alto, Calif.: Stanford University Press, 1959.

Daniels, Roger. *The Decision to Relocate the Japanese Americans.* Philadelphia: Lippincott, 1975.

Darley, John M., and Bibb Latané. "Bystander Intervention in Emergencies: Diffusion of Responsibility." *Journal of Personality and Social Psychology, 8,* 4, 1968:377–383.

Davis, Fred. "The Cabdriver and His Fare: Facets of a Fleeting Relationship." *American Journal of Sociology, 65,* September 1959:158–165.

Davis, Kingsley. "Extreme Isolation." In *Down to Earth Sociology: Introductory Readings,* 8th ed., James M. Henslin, ed. New York: Free Press, 1995:117–125.

Davis, Kingsley, and Wilbert E. Moore. "Reply to Tumin." *American Sociological Review, 18,* 1953:394–396.

Davis, Kingsley, and Wilbert E. Moore. "Some Principles of Stratification." *American Sociological Review, 10,* 1945:242–249.

Davis, L. J. "Medscam." In *Deviant Behavior 96/97,* Lawrence M. Salinger, ed. Guilford, Conn.: Dushkin, 1996:93–97.

Davis, Nancy J., and Robert V. Robinson. "Class Identification of Men and Women in the 1970s and 1980s." *American Sociological Review, 53,* February 1988:103–112.

Deck, Leland P. "Buying Brains by the Inch." *Journal of the College and University Personnel Association, 19,* 1968:33–37.

DeMause, Lloyd. "Our Forebears Made Childhood a Nightmare." *Psychology Today 8,* 11, April 1975:85–88.

"Democracy and Technology." *Economist,* June 17, 1995:21–23.

Denney, Nancy W., and David Quadagno. *Human Sexuality,* 2nd ed. St. Louis: Mosby Year Book, 1992.

DePalma, Anthony. "Rare in Ivy League: Women Who Work as Full Professors." *New York Times,* January 24, 1993:1, 23.

Diamond, Edwin, and Robert A. Silverman. *White House to Your House: Media and Politics in Virtual America.* Cambridge, Mass.: MIT Press, 1995.

Diamond, Milton. "Sexual Identity: Monozygotic Twins Reared in Discordant Sex Roles and a BBC Follow-Up." *Archives of Sexual Behavior, 11,* 2, 1982:181–186.

DiGiulio, Robert C. "Beyond Widowhood." In *Marriage and Family in a Changing Society,* 4th ed., James M. Henslin, ed. New York: Free Press, 1992:457–469.

Dixon, Celvia Stovall, and Kathryn D. Rettig. "An Examination of Income Adequacy for Single Women Two Years after Divorce." *Journal of Divorce and Remarriage, 22,* 1–2, 1994:55–71.

Doane, Ashley W., Jr. "Bringing the Majority Back In: Towards a Sociology of Dominant Group Ethnicity." Paper presented at the annual meetings of the Society for the Study of Social Problems, 1993.

Dobash, Russell P., R. Emerson Dobash, Margo Wilson, and Martin Daly. "Marital Violence Is Not Symmetrical: A Response to Campbell." *SSSP Newsletter, 24,* 3, Fall 1993:26–30.

Dobash, Russell P., R. Emerson Dobash, Margo Wilson, and Martin Daly. "The Myth of Sexual Symmetry in Marital Violence." *Social Problems, 39,* 1, February 1992:71–91.

Dobriner, William M. "The Football Team as Social Structure and Social System." In *Social Structures and Systems: A Sociological Overview.* Pacific Palisades, Calif.: Goodyear, 1969a:116–120.

Dobriner, William M. *Social Structures and Systems.* Pacific Palisades, Calif.: Goodyear, 1969b.

Dobyns, Henry F. *Their Numbers Became Thinned: Native American Population Dynamics in Eastern North America.* Knoxville: University of Tennessee Press, 1983.

Dollard, John, et al. *Frustration and Aggression.* New Haven, Conn.: Yale University Press, 1939.

Domhoff, G. William. "The Bohemian Grove and Other Retreats." In *Down to Earth Sociology: Introductory Readings,* 9th ed., James M. Henslin, ed. New York: Free Press, 1997:340–352.

Domhoff, G. William. *The Power Elite and the State: How Policy Is Made in America.* New York: Aldine de Gruyter, 1990.

Domhoff, G. William. *Who Really Rules? New Haven and Community Power Reexamined.* New Brunswick, N.J.: Transaction Books, 1978.

Domhoff, G. William. *Who Rules America?* Englewood Cliffs, N.J.: Prentice Hall, 1967.

Domhoff, G. William. *Who Rules America Now? A View of the '80s.* Englewood Cliffs, N.J.: Prentice Hall, 1983.

Dove, Adrian. "Soul Folk 'Chitling' Test or the Dove Counterbalance Intelligence Test." no date. (mimeo)

Du Bois, W. E. B. *The Autobiography of W. E. B. Du Bois: A Soliloquy on Viewing My Life from the Last Decade of Its First Century.* New York: International Press, 1968.

Du Bois, W. E. B. *Black Reconstruction in America, 1860–1889.* New York: Atheneum, 1992. First published in 1935.

Du Bois, W. E. B. *Black Reconstruction in America: An Essay Toward a History of the Part Which Black Folk Played in the Attempt to Reconstruct Democracy in America, 1860–1880.* New York: Cass, 1966. First published in 1935.

Du Bois, W. E. B. *The Souls of Black Folk: Essays and Sketches.* Chicago: McClurg, 1903.

Dudenhefer, Paul. "Poverty in the Rural United States." *Focus,* 15, 1, Spring 1993:37–46.

Duffy, Michael. "When Lobbyists Become Insiders." *Time,* November 9, 1992:40.

Dunlap, Riley E., and William R. Catton, Jr. "Environmental Sociology." *Annual Review of Sociology,* 5, 1979:243–273.

Dunlap, Riley E., and William R. Catton, Jr. "What Environmental Sociologists Have in Common Whether Concerned with 'Built' or 'Natural' Environments." *Sociological Inquiry,* 53, 2/3, 1983:113–135.

Dunn, Ashley. "Southeast Asians Highly Dependent on Welfare in U.S." *New York Times,* May 19, 1994:A1, A23.

Durbin, Stefanie. "Mexico." *Population Today,* July–August, 1995:7.

Durkheim, Emile. *The Division of Labor in Society.* George Simpson, trans. New York: Free Press, 1933. First published in 1893.

Durkheim, Emile. *The Elementary Forms of the Religious Life.* New York: Free Press, 1965. First published in 1912.

Durkheim, Emile. *The Rules of Sociological Method.* Sarah A. Solovay and John H. Mueller, trans.; George E. G. Catlin, ed. New York: Free Press, 1964. First published in 1893.

Durkheim, Emile. *Suicide: A Study in Sociology.* John A. Spaulding and George Simpson, trans. New York: Free Press, 1966. First published in 1897.

Durning, Alan. "Cradles of Life." In *Social Problems 90/91,* LeRoy W. Barnes, ed. Guilford, Conn.: Dushkin, 1990:231–241.

Ebomoyi, Ehigie. "The Prevalence of Female Circumcision in Two Nigerian Communities." *Sex Roles,* 17, 3/4, 1987:139–151.

Eder, Klaus. "The Rise of Counter-culture Movements against Modernity: Nature as a New Field of Class Struggle." *Theory, Culture & Society,* 7, 1990:21–47.

Edgerton, Robert B. *Deviance: A Cross-Cultural Perspective.* Menlo Park, Calif.: Benjamin/Cummings, 1976.

Edgerton, Robert B. *Sick Societies: Challenging the Myth of Primitive Harmony.* New York: Free Press, 1992.

Egan, Timothy. "Many Seek Security in Private Communities." *New York Times,* September 3, 1995:1, 22.

Ehrenreich, Barbara, and Annette Fuentes. "Life on the Global Assembly Line." In *Down to Earth Sociology: Introductory Readings,* 9th ed., James M. Henslin, ed. New York: Free Press, 1997:367–375.

Ehrlich, Paul R., and Anne H. Ehrlich. "Humanity at the Crossroads." *Stanford Magazine,* Spring–Summer 1978:20–23.

Ehrlich, Paul R., and Anne H. Ehrlich. *Population, Resources, and Environment: Issues in Human Ecology,* 2nd ed. San Francisco: Freeman, 1972.

Ekman, Paul, Wallace V. Friesen, and John Bear. "The International Language of Gestures." *Psychology Today,* May 1984:64.

Elder, Glen H., Jr. "Age Differentiation and Life Course." *Annual Review of Sociology,* 1, 1975:165–190.

Ellul, Jacques. *The Technological Society.* New York: Knopf, 1965.

El-Meligi, M. Helmy. "Egypt." In *Handbook of World Education: A Comparative Guide to Higher Education and Educational Systems of the World,* Walter Wickremasinghe, ed. Houston, Texas: American Collegiate Service, 1992: 219–228.

Engelberg, Stephen, and Martin Tolchin. "Foreigners Find New Ally in U.S. Industry." *New York Times,* November 2, 1993:A1, B8.

Epstein, Cynthia Fuchs. *Deceptive Distinctions: Sex, Gender, and the Social Order.* New Haven, Conn.: Yale University Press, 1988.

Erik, John. "China's Policy on Births." *New York Times,* January 3, 1982: IV, 19.

Ernst, Eldon G. "The Baptists." In *Encyclopedia of the American Religious Experience: Studies of Traditions and Movements,* Vol. 1, Charles H. Lippy and Peter W. Williams, eds. New York: Scribner's, 1988:555–577.

Escalante, Jaime, and Jack Dirmann. "The Jaime Escalante Math Program." *Journal of Negro Education,* 59, 3, Summer 1990:407–423.

Etzioni, Amitai. *An Immodest Agenda: Rebuilding America before the Twenty-First Century.* New York: McGraw-Hill, 1982.

Ezekiel, Raphael S. *The Racist Mind: Portraits of American Neo-Nazis and Klansmen.* New York: Viking, 1995.

Famighetti, Robert, ed. *The World Almanac and Book of Facts 1995.* Mahwah, N.J., 1994.

Faris, Robert E. L., and Warren Dunham. *Mental Disorders in Urban Areas.* Chicago: University of Chicago Press, 1939.

Farkas, George, Robert P. Grobe, Daniel Sheehan, and Yuan Shuan. "Cultural Resources and School Success: Gender,

Ethnicity, and Poverty Groups within an Urban School District." *American Sociological Review, 55*, February 1990a:127–142.

Farkas, George, Daniel Sheehan, and Robert P. Grobe. "Coursework Mastery and School Success: Gender, Ethnicity, and Poverty Groups within an Urban School District." *American Educational Research Journal, 27*, 4, Winter 1990b:807–827.

Faunce, William A. *Problems of an Industrial Society*, 2nd ed. New York: McGraw-Hill, 1981.

Featherman, David L. "Opportunities Are Expanding." *Society, 13*, 1979:4–11.

Featherman, David L., and Robert M. Hauser. *Opportunity and Change*. New York: Academic Press, 1978.

Feldman, Saul D. "The Presentation of Shortness in Everyday Life—Height and Heightism in American Society: Toward a Sociology of Stature." Paper presented at the 1972 meetings of the American Sociological Association.

Ferguson, Thomas. *Golden Rule*. Chicago: University of Chicago Press, 1995.

Feshbach, Murray, and Alfred Friendly, Jr. *Ecocide in the USSR: Health and Nature Under Siege*. New York: Basic Books, 1992.

Fialka, John J. "Demands on New Orleans's 'Big Charity' Hospital Are Symptomatic of U.S. Health-Care Problem." *Wall Street Journal*, June 22, 1993:A18.

Finke, Roger. *The Churching of America, 1776–1990: Winners and Losers in Our Religious Economy*. New Brunswick, N.J.: Rutgers University Press, 1992.

Finkelhor, David, and Kersti Yllo. *License to Rape: Sexual Abuse of Wives*. New York: Holt, 1985.

Finkelhor, David, and Kersti Yllo. "Marital Rape: The Myth versus the Reality." In *Marriage and Family in a Changing Society*, 3rd ed., James M. Henslin, ed. New York: Free Press, 1989:382–391.

Fischer, Claude S. *The Urban Experience*. New York: Harcourt, 1976.

Fisher, Sue. *In the Patient's Best Interest: Women and the Politics of Medical Decisions*. New Brunswick, N.J.: Rutgers University Press, 1986.

Flanagan, William G. *Urban Sociology: Images and Structure*. Boston: Allyn and Bacon, 1990.

Flavell, John H., et al. *The Development of Role-Taking and Communication Skills in Children*. New York: Wiley, 1968.

Foote, Jennifer. "Trying to Take Back the Planet." *Newsweek, 115*, 6, February 5, 1990:20–25.

Forer, Lucille K. *The Birth Order Factor: How Your Personality Is Influenced by Your Place in the Family*. New York: McKay, 1976.

Form, William. "Comparative Industrial Sociology and the Convergence Hypothesis." In *Annual Review of Sociology, 5*, 1, 1979, Alex Inkeles, James Coleman, and Ralph H. Turner, eds.

Fox, Elaine, and George E. Arquitt. "The VFW and the 'Iron Law of Oligarchy.' " In *Down to Earth Sociology: Introductory Readings*, 4th ed., James M. Henslin, ed. New York: Free Press, 1985:147–155.

Franklin, Clyde W., II. "Sex and Class Differences in the Socialization Experiences of African American Youth." *Western Journal of Black Studies, 18*, 2, 1994:104–111.

Freudenburg, William R., and Robert Gramling. "The Emergence of Environmental Sociology: Contributions of Riley E. Dunlap and William R. Catton, Jr." *Sociological Inquiry, 59*, 4, November 1989:439–452.

Friedl, Ernestine. "Society and Sex Roles." In *Conformity and Conflict: Readings in Cultural Anthropology*. James P. Spradley and David W. McCurdy, eds. Glenview, Ill.: Scott, Foresman, 1990:229–238.

Frisbie, W. Parker, and John D. Kasarda. "Spatial Processes." In *Handbook of Sociology*, Neil J. Smelser, ed. Newbury Park, Calif.: Sage, 1988:629–666.

Froman, Ingmarie. "Sweden for Women." *Current Sweden, 407*, November 1994:1–4.

Fuller, Rex, and Richard Schoenberger. "The Gender Salary Gap: Do Academic Achievement, Internship Experience, and College Major Make a Difference?" *Social Science Quarterly, 72*, 4, December 1991:715–726.

Furstenberg, Frank F., Jr., and Kathleen Mullan Harris. "The Disappearing American Father? Divorce and the Waning Significance of Biological Fatherhood." In *The Changing American Family: Sociological and Demographic Perspectives*, Scott J. South and Stewart E. Tolnay, eds. Boulder, Colo.: Westview Press, 1992:197–223.

Furtado, Celso. *The Economic Growth of Brazil: A Survey from Colonial to Modern Times*. Westport, Conn.: Greenwood Press, 1984.

Galbraith, John Kenneth. *The Nature of Mass Poverty*. Cambridge, Mass.: Harvard University Press, 1979.

Galinsky, Ellen, James T. Bond, and Dana E. Friedman. *The Changing Workforce: Highlights of the National Study*. New York: Families and Work Institute, 1993.

Gallup, George, Jr. *The Gallup Poll: Public Opinion 1989*. Wilmington, Del.: Scholarly Resources, 1990.

Gans, Herbert J. *People and Plans: Essays on Urban Problems and Solutions*. New York: Basic, 1968.

Gans, Herbert J. *People, Plans, and Policies: Essays on Poverty, Racism, and Other National Urban Problems*. New York: Columbia University Press, 1991.

Gans, Herbert J. *The Urban Villagers*. New York: Free Press, 1962.

Gans, Herbert J. "Urbanism and Suburbanism." In *Urban Man and Society: A Reader in Urban Ecology*, Albert N. Cousins and Hans Nagpaul, eds. New York: Knopf, 1970:157–164.

Garbarino, Merwin S. *American Indian Heritage*. Boston: Little, Brown, 1976.

Garfinkel, Harold. "Conditions of Successful Degradation Ceremonies." *American Journal of Sociology, 61*, 2, March 1956:420–424.

Garfinkel, Harold. *Studies in Ethnomethodology*. Englewood Cliffs, N.J.: Prentice Hall, 1967.

Garreau, Joel. *Edge City: Life on the New Frontier*. New York: Doubleday, 1992.

Gatewood, Willard B. *Aristocrats of Color: The Black Elite, 1880–1920*. Bloomington: Indiana University Press, 1990.

Gay, Jill. "The Patriotic Prostitute." *Progressive*, February 1985:34–36.

Gelles, Richard J. "The Myth of Battered Husbands and New Facts about Family Violence." In *Social Problems 80–81*, Robert L. David, ed. Guilford, Conn.: Dushkin, 1980.

Gerson, Kathleen. *Hard Choices: How Women Decide about Work, Career, and Motherhood.* Berkeley: University of California Press, 1985.

Gerth, H. H., and C. Wright Mills. *From Max Weber: Essays in Sociology.* New York: Galaxy, 1958.

Gilbert, Dennis, and Joseph A. Kahl. *The American Class Structure: A New Synthesis.* Homewood, Ill.: Dorsey Press, 1982.

Gilbert, Dennis, and Joseph A. Kahl. *The American Class Structure: A New Synthesis,* 4th ed. Homewood, Ill.: Dorsey Press, 1993.

Gillborn, David. "Citizenship, 'Race' and the Hidden Curriculum." *International Studies in the Sociology of Education,* 2, 1, 1992:57–73.

Gilman, Charlotte Perkins. *The Man-Made World or, Our Androcentric Culture.* New York: Johnson Reprint, 1971. First published in 1911.

Gilmore, David D. *Manhood in the Making: Cultural Concepts of Masculinity.* New Haven, Conn.: Yale University Press, 1990.

Glazer, Nathan. "In Defense of Multiculturalism." *New Republic,* September 2, 1991:18–22.

Glenn, Evelyn Nakano. "Chinese American Families." In *Minority Families in the United States: A Multicultural Perspective,* Ronald L. Taylor, ed. Englewood Cliffs, N.J.: Prentice Hall, 1994:115–145.

Glick, Paul C., and S. Lin. "More Young Adults Are Living with Their Parents: Who Are They?" *Journal of Marriage and Family,* 48, 1986:107–112.

Glotz, Peter. "Forward to Europe." *Dissent,* 33, 3, Summer 1986:327–339. (As quoted in Harrison and Bluestone 1988.)

Glueck, Sheldon, and Eleanor Glueck. *Physique and Delinquency.* New York: Harper & Row, 1956.

Goffman, Erving. *Asylums: Essays on the Social Situation of Mental Patients and Other Inmates.* Chicago: Aldine, 1961.

Goffman, Erving. *Stigma.* Englewood Cliffs, N.J.: Prentice Hall, 1963.

Gold, Ray. "Janitors versus Tenants: A Status–Income Dilemma." *American Journal of Sociology,* 58, 1952: 486–493.

Gold, Steven. *From the Workers' State to the Golden State: Russian Jews in California.* Boston: Allyn and Bacon, 1996.

Goldberg, Susan, and Michael Lewis. "Play Behavior in the Year-Old Infant: Early Sex Differences." *Child Development,* 40, March 1969:21–31.

Goldscheider, Frances, and Calvin Goldscheider. "Leaving and Returning Home in 20th Century America." *Population Bulletin,* 48, 4, March 1994:2–33.

Goleman, Daniel. "Pollsters Enlist Psychologists in Quest for Unbiased Results." *New York Times,* September 7, 1993: C1, C11.

Goleman, Daniel. "Spacing of Siblings Strongly Linked to Success in Life." *New York Times,* May 28, 1985:C1, C4.

Gordon, David M. "Class and the Economics of Crime." *The Review of Radical Political Economics,* 3, Summer 1971: 51–57.

Gorman, Christine. "A Boy Without a Penis." *Time,* March 24, 1997:83. "Sexual Identity is Inborn Trait, According to Study." *Alton Telegraph,* March 16, 1997:A6.

Gorman, Peter. "A People at Risk: Vanishing Tribes of South America." *The World & I,* December 1991:678–689.

Gottfredson, Michael R., and Travis Hirschi. *A General Theory of Crime.* Stanford, Calif.: Stanford University Press, 1990.

Gourevitch, Philip. "After the Genocide." *New Yorker,* December 18, 1995:78–94.

Graven, Kathryn. "Sex Harassment at the Office Stirs Up Japan." *Wall Street Journal,* March 21, 1990:B1, B7.

Greeley, Andrew M. "The Protestant Ethic: Time for a Moratorium." *Sociological Analysis,* 25, Spring 1964:20–33.

Greenhalgh, Susan, and Jiali Li. "Engendering Reproductive Policy and Practice in Peasant China: For a Feminist Demography of Reproduction." *Signs,* 20, 3, Spring 1995: 601–640.

Grossman, Laurie. "Desolate Housing Project Provides Profit and Lessons." *Wall Street Journal,* April 5, 1995: B1, B7.

Grossman, Lawrence K. *The Electronic Republic: Reshaping Democracy in the Information Age.* New York: Viking, 1995.

Groves, Melissa M., and Diane M. Horm-Wingerd. "Commuter Marriages: Personal, Family, and Career Issues." *Sociology and Social Research,* 75, 4, July 1991:212–217.

Guha, Ramachandra. "Radical American Environmentalism and Wilderness Preservation: A Third World Critique." *Environmental Ethics,* 11, 1, Spring 1989:71–83.

Gupta, Giri Raj. "Love, Arranged Marriage, and the Indian Social Structure." In *Cross-Cultural Perspectives of Mate Selection and Marriage,* George Kurian, ed. Westport, Conn.: Greenwood Press, 1979.

Haas, Jack. "Binging: Educational Control among High-Steel Iron Workers." *American Behavioral Scientist,* 16, 1972:27–34.

Hacker, Helen Mayer. "Women as a Minority Group." *Social Forces,* 30, October 1951:60–69.

Hall, Edward T. *The Hidden Dimension.* Garden City, N.Y.: Anchor Books, 1969.

Hall, Edward T. *The Silent Language.* New York: Doubleday, 1959.

Hall, G. Stanley. *Adolescence: Its Psychology and Its Relations to Physiology, Anthropology, Sociology, Sex, Crime, Religion, and Education.* New York: Appleton, 1904.

Hall, Peter M. "Interactionism and the Study of Social Organization." *Sociological Quarterly,* 28, November 1987:1–22.

Hardy, Quentin. "Fortunately, Many Japanese Have Training in the Art of Self-Defense." *Wall Street Journal,* June 29, 1993:B1.

Harlow, Harry F., and Margaret K. Harlow. "The Affectional Systems." In *Behavior of Nonhuman Primates: Modern Research Trends,* Vol. 2, Allan M. Schrier, Harry F. Harlow, and Fred Stollnitz, eds. New York: Academic Press, 1965:287–334.

Harlow, Harry F., and Margaret K. Harlow. "Social Deprivation in Monkeys." *Scientific American,* 207, 1962:137–147.

Harper, Charles L. "Time to Phase Out Fossil Fuels?" *Wall Street Journal,* December 26, 1995:A6.

Harrington, Michael. *The Other America: Poverty in the United States.* New York: Macmillan, 1962.

Harrington, Michael. *The Vast Majority: A Journey to the World's Poor.* New York: Simon & Schuster, 1977.

Harris, Chauncey, and Edward Ullman. "The Nature of Cities." *Annals of the American Academy of Political and Social Science, 242,* 1945:7–17.

Harris, Diana K. *The Sociology of Aging.* New York: Harper, 1990.

Harris, Marvin. *Cows, Pigs, Wars, and Witches: The Riddles of Culture.* New York: Vintage Books, 1974.

Harrison, Bennett, and Barry Bluestone. *The Great U-Turn: Corporate Restructuring and the Polarizing of America.* New York: Basic Books, 1988.

Harrison, Paul. *Inside the Third World: The Anatomy of Poverty,* 3rd ed. London: Penguin Books, 1993.

Hart, Charles W. M., and Arnold R. Pilling. *The Tiwi of North Australia.* New York: Holt, Rinehart and Winston, 1960.

Hart, Paul. "Groupthink, Risk-Taking and Recklessness: Quality of Process and Outcome in Policy Decision Making." *Politics and the Individual, 1,* 1, 1991:67–90.

Hartinger, Brent. "Homosexual Partners Are Changing the Family." In *Family in America: Opposing Viewpoints,* Viqi Wagner, ed. San Diego, Calif.: Greenhaven Press, 1992:55–62.

Hartley, Eugene. *Problems in Prejudice.* New York: King's Crown Press, 1946.

"Harvard Wired." *Economist,* February 5, 1994:87.

Haslick, Leonard. *Gerontologist, 14,* 1974:37–45.

Hauser, Philip, and Leo Schnore, eds. *The Study of Urbanization.* New York: Wiley, 1965.

Hawley, Amos H. *Urban Society: An Ecological Approach.* New York: Wiley, 1981.

Hayes, Arthur S. "Environmental Poverty Specialty Helps the Poor Fight Pollution." *Wall Street Journal,* October 9, 1992:B5.

Hayes, Donald P., and Loreen T. Wolfer. "Have Curriculum Changes Caused SAT Scores to Decline?" Paper presented at the annual meetings of the American Sociological Association, 1993a.

Hayes, Donald P., and Loreen T. Wolfer. "Was the Decline in SAT-Verbal Scores Caused by Simplified Schoolbooks?" Technical Report Series 93-8. Ithaca, N.Y.: Cornell University Press, 1993b.

Heckert, D. Alex, Thomas C. Nowak, and Kay A. Snyder. "The Impact of Husbands' and Wives' Relative Earnings on Marital Dissolution." Paper presented at the 1995 meetings of the American Sociological Association.

Heilbrun, Alfred B. "Differentiation of Death-Row Murderers and Life-Sentence Murderers by Antisociality and Intelligence Measures." *Journal of Personality Assessment, 64,* 1990:617–627.

Hellinger, Daniel, and Dennis R. Judd. *The Democratic Façade.* Pacific Grove, Calif.: Brooks/Cole, 1991.

Henley, Nancy, Mykol Hamilton, and Barrie Thorne. "Womanspeak and Manspeak." In *Beyond Sex Roles,* Alice G. Sargent, ed. St. Paul, Minn.: West, 1985.

Henry, William A., III. "Beyond the Melting Pot." *Time,* April 9, 1990:28–31.

Henslin, James M. *Introducing Sociology: Toward Understanding Life in Society.* New York: Free Press, 1975.

Henslin, James M. "On Becoming Male: Reflections of a Sociologist on Childhood and Early Socialization." In *Down to Earth Sociology: Introductory Readings* 9th Ed., James M. Henslin, ed. New York: Free Press, 1997a:130–140.

Henslin, James M. *Social Problems,* 4th ed. Englewood Cliffs, N.J.: Prentice Hall, 1996.

Henslin, James M. "The Survivors of the F-227." In *Down to Earth Sociology: Introductory Readings,* 9th ed., James M. Henslin, ed. New York: Free Press, 1997b:237–245.

Henslin, James M. "Trust and Cabbies." In *Down to Earth Sociology: Introductory Readings,* 7th ed., James M. Henslin, ed. New York: Free Press, 1993:183–196.

Henslin, James M., and Mae A. Biggs. "Behavior in Pubic Places: The Sociology of the Vaginal Examination." In *Down to Earth Sociology: Introductory Readings,* 9th ed., James M. Henslin, ed. New York: Free Press, 1997: 203–213.

Hewitt Associates, *Summary of Work and Family Benefits Report.* Lincolnshire, Ill.: Hewitt Associates, 1995.

Hibbert, Christopher. *The Roots of Evil: A Social History of Crime and Punishment.* New York: Minerva, 1963.

Higginbotham, Elizabeth, and Lynn Weber. "Moving with Kin and Community: Upward Social Mobility for Black and White Women." *Gender and Society, 6,* 3, September 1992:416–440.

Higley, John, Ursula Hoffmann-Lange, Charles Kadushin, and Gwen Moore. "Elite Integration in Stable Democracies: A Reconsideration." *European Sociological Review, 7,* 1, May 1991:35–53.

Hilliard, Asa, III. "Do We Have the *Will* to Educate All Children?" *Educational Leadership, 49,* September 1991:31–36.

Hiltz, Starr Roxanne. "Widowhood." In *Marriage and Family in a Changing Society,* 3rd ed., James M. Henslin, ed. New York: Free Press, 1989:521–531.

Hipler, Fritz. Interview in a television documentary with Bill Moyers in *Propaganda,* in the series "Walk through the 20th Century," 1987.

Hirschi, Travis. *Causes of Delinquency.* Berkeley: University of California Press, 1969.

Hochschild, Arlie. Note to the Author. 1991.

Hochschild, Arlie. *The Second Shift: Working Parents and the Revolution at Home.* New York: Viking, 1989.

Hochschild, Arlie Russell. "The Sociology of Feeling and Emotion: Selected Possibilities." In *Another Voice: Feminist Perspectives on Social Life and Social Science,* Marcia Millman and Rosabeth Moss Kanter, eds. Garden City, N.Y.: Anchor Books, 1975.

Holtzman, Abraham. *The Townsend Movement: A Political Study.* New York: Bookman, 1963.

Homblin, Dora Jane. *The First Cities.* Boston: Little, Brown, Time-Life Books, 1973.

Honeycutt, Karen. "Disgusting, Pathetic, Bizarrely Beautiful: Representations of Weight in Popular Culture." Paper presented at the 1995 meetings of the American Sociological Association.

Hornblower, Margot. "The Skin Trade." *Time,* June 21, 1993:45–51.

Horowitz, Irving Louis. *Three Worlds of Development: The Theory and Practice of International Stratification.* New York: Oxford University Press, 1966.

Horowitz, Ruth. "Community Tolerance of Gang Violence." *Social Problems, 34,* 5, December 1987:437–450.

Horowitz, Ruth. *Honor and the American Dream: Culture and Identity in a Chicano Community.* New Brunswick, N.J.: Rutgers University Press, 1983.

Horwitz, Tony. "Dinka Tribes Made Slaves in Sudan's Civil War." *Wall Street Journal*, April 11, 1989:A19.

Horwitz, Tony, and Craig Forman. "Immigrants to Europe from the Third World Face Racial Animosity." *Wall Street Journal*, August 14, 1990:A1, A9.

Hostetler, John A. *Amish Society*, 3rd ed. Baltimore: Johns Hopkins University Press, 1980.

Houtman, Dick. "What Exactly Is a 'Social Class'?: On the Economic Liberalism and Cultural Conservatism of the 'Working Class.'" Paper presented at the 1995 meetings of the American Sociological Association.

Howells, Lloyd T., and Selwyn W. Becker. "Seating Arrangement and Leadership Emergence." *Journal of Abnormal and Social Psychology, 64*, February 1962:148–150.

Hoyt, Homer. "Recent Distortions of the Classical Models of Urban Structure." In *Internal Structure of the City: Readings on Space and Environment*, Larry S. Bourne, ed. New York: Oxford University Press, 1971:84–96.

Hoyt, Homer. *The Structure and Growth of Residential Neighborhoods in American Cities.* Washington, D.C.: Federal Housing Administration, 1939.

Huber, Joan. "From Sugar and Spice to Professor." In *Down to Earth Sociology: Introductory Readings*, 5th ed., James M. Henslin, ed. New York: Free Press, 1988:92–101.

Huber, Joan. "Micro-Macro Links in Gender Stratification." *American Sociological Review, 55*, February 1990:1–10.

Huber, Joan, and William H. Form. *Income and Ideology.* New York: Free Press, 1973.

Huddle, Donald. "The Net National Cost of Immigration." Washington, D.C.: Carrying Capacity Network, 1993.

Hudson, James R. "Professional Sports Franchise Locations and City, Metropolitan and Regional Identities." Paper presented at the annual meetings of the American Sociological Association, 1991.

Hudson, Robert B. "The 'Graying' of the Federal Budget and Its Consequences for Old-Age Policy." *Gerontologist, 18*, October 1978:428–440.

Huggins, Martha K. "Lost Childhoods: Assassinations of Youth in Democratizing Brazil." Paper presented at the annual meetings of the American Sociological Association, 1993.

Hughes, H. Stuart. *Oswald Spengler: A Critical Estimate*, rev. ed. New York: Scribner's, 1962.

Hughes, Kathleen A. "Even Tiki Torches Don't Guarantee a Perfect Wedding." *Wall Street Journal*, February 20, 1990:A1, A16.

Humphreys, Laud. *Tearoom Trade: Impersonal Sex in Public Places.* Chicago: Aldine, 1970.

Humphreys, Laud. "Impersonal Sex and Perceived Satisfaction." In *Studies in the Sociology of Sex*, James M. Henslin, ed. New York: Appleton-Century-Crofts, 1971:351–374.

Humphreys, Laud. *Tearoom Trade: Impersonal Sex in Public Places*, enlarged ed. Chicago: Aldine, 1975.

Hunt, Albert R. "Democrats' Trade-Off: Kids or Seniors?" *Wall Street Journal*, May 25, 1995:A15.

Hurtado, Aída, David E. Hayes-Bautista, R. Burciaga Valdez, and Anthony C. R. Hernández. *Redefining California: Latino Social Engagement in a Multicultural Society.* Los Angeles: UCLA Chicano Studies Research Center, 1992.

Huth, Mary Jo. "China's Urbanization under Communist Rule, 1949–1982." *International Journal of Sociology and Social Policy, 10*, 7, 1990:17–57.

Huttenbach, Henry R. "The Roman *Porajmos:* The Nazi Genocide of Europe's Gypsies." *Nationalities Papers, 19*, 3, Winter 1991:373–394.

Ingrassia, Lawrence. "Danes Don't Debate Same-Sex Marriage, They Celebrate Them." In *Deviant Behavior 96/97*, Lawrence M. Salinger, ed. Guilford, Conn.: Dushkin, 1996:183–184.

Institute for Social Research. "Televised Violence and Kids: A Public Health Problem?" *ISR Newsletter, 18*, 1, February 1994:5–7.

Jacobs, Charles. "Letter to the Editor." *Wall Street Journal*, November 2, 1995:A15.

Jaggar, Alison M. "Sexual Difference and Sexual Equality." In *Theoretical Perspectives on Sexual Difference*, Deborah L. Rhode, ed. New Haven, Conn.: Yale University Press, 1990:239–254.

James, Daniel. "To Cut Spending, Freeze Immigration." *Wall Street Journal*, June 24, 1993:A13.

James, Stephen A. "Reconciling International Human Rights and Cultural Relativism: The Case of Female Circumcision." *Bioethics, 8*, January 1994:1–26.

Janis, Irving. *Victims of Groupthink.* Boston: Houghton Mifflin, 1972.

Jankowiak, William R., and Edward F. Fischer. "A Cross-Cultural Perspective on Romantic Love." *Journal of Ethnology, 31*, 2, April 1992:149–155.

Jankowski, Martín Sánchez. *Islands in the Street: Gangs and American Urban Society.* Berkeley: University of California Press, 1991.

Jaspar, James M. "Moral Dimensions of Social Movements." Paper presented at the annual meetings of the American Sociological Association, 1991.

Jefferson, David J. "Gay Employees Win Benefits for Partners at More Corporations." *Wall Street Journal*, March 18, 1994:A1, A2.

Jerrome, Dorothy. *Good Company: An Anthropological Study of Old People in Groups.* Edinburgh, England: Edinburgh University Press, 1992.

Johnson, Benton. "On Church and Sect." *American Sociological Review, 28*, 1963:539–549.

Johnson, Cathryn. "The Emergence of the Emotional Self: A Developmental Theory." *Symbolic Interaction, 15*, 2, Summer 1992:183–202.

Johnson, Colleen L., and Barbara M. Barer. "Patterns of Engagement and Disengagement among the Oldest Old." *Journal of Aging Studies, 6*, 4, Winter 1992:351–364.

Jones, Lawrence N. "The New Black Church." *Ebony*, November 1992:192, 194–195.

Jordon, Mary. "College Dorms Reflect Trend of Self-Segregation." In *Ourselves and Others*, 2nd ed., The Washington Post Writer's Group, eds. Boston: Allyn and Bacon, 1996:85–87.

Judis, John B. "The Japanese Megaphone." *New Republic, 202*, 4, January 22, 1990:20–25.

Kagan, Jerome. "The Idea of Emotions in Human Development." In *Emotions, Cognition, and Behavior*, Carroll E.

Izard, Jerome Kagan, and Robert B. Zajonc, eds. New York: Cambridge University Press, 1984:38–72.

Kalichman, Seth C. "MMPI Profiles of Women and Men Convicted of Domestic Homicide." *Journal of Clinical Psychology*, 44, 6, November 1988:847–853.

Kalish, Susan. "International Migration: New Findings on Magnitude, Importance." *Population Today*, 22, 3, March 1994:1–2.

Kalmijn, Matthijs. "Shifting Boundaries: Trends in Religious and Educational Homogamy." *American Sociological Review*, 56, December 1991:786–800.

Kanter, Rosabeth Moss. *The Change Masters: Innovation and Entrepreneurship in the American Corporation*. New York: Simon & Schuster, 1983.

Kanter, Rosabeth Moss. *Men and Women of the Corporation*. New York: Basic Books, 1977.

Karnow, Stanley, and Nancy Yoshihara. *Asian Americans in Transition*. New York: Asia Society, 1992.

Karp, David A., Gregory P. Stone, and William C. Yoels. *Being Urban: A Sociology of City Life*, 2nd ed. New York: Praeger, 1991.

Karp, David A., and William C. Yoels. "Sport and Urban Life." *Journal of Sport and Social Issues*, 14, 2, 1990:77–102.

Kart, Cary S. *The Realities of Aging: An Introduction to Gerontology*, 3rd ed. Boston: Allyn and Bacon, 1990.

Kasarda, John D., and Edward M. Crenshaw. "Third World Urbanization: Dimensions, Theories, and Determinants." *Annual Review of Sociology*, 17, 1991:467–501.

Katz, Michael B. *The Undeserving Poor: From the War on Poverty to the War on Welfare*. New York: Pantheon, 1989.

Katz, Sidney. "The Importance of Being Beautiful." In *Down to Earth Sociology: Introductory Readings*, 8th ed., James M. Henslin, ed. New York: Free Press, 1995:301–307.

Keith, Jennie. *Old People, New Lives: Community Creation in a Retirement Residence*, 2nd ed. Chicago: University of Chicago Press, 1982.

Kelly, Joan B. "How Adults React to Divorce." In *Marriage and Family in a Changing Society*, 4th ed., James M. Henslin, ed. New York: Free Press, 1992:410–423.

Kemp, Alice Abel. "Estimating Sex Discrimination in Professional Occupations with the *Dictionary of Occupational Titles*." *Sociological Spectrum*, 10, 3, 1990:387–411.

Keniston, Kenneth. *Youth and Dissent: The Rise of a New Opposition*. New York: Harcourt Brace Jovanovich, 1971.

Kennedy, Paul. *Preparing for the Twenty-First Century*. New York: Random House, 1993.

Kephart, William M., and William W. Zellner. *Extraordinary Groups: An Examination of Unconventional Life-Styles*, 5th ed. New York: St. Martin's Press, 1994.

Kerr, Clark. *The Future of Industrialized Societies*. Cambridge, Mass.: Harvard University Press, 1983.

Kerr, Clark, et al. *Industrialism and Industrial Man: The Problems of Labor and Management in Economic Growth*. Cambridge, Mass.: Harvard University Press, 1960.

Kershaw, Terry. "The Effects of Educational Tracking on the Social Mobility of African Americans." *Journal of Black Studies*, 23, 1, September 1992:152–169.

Kettl, Donald F. "The Savings-and-Loan Bailout: The Mismatch between the Headlines and the Issues." *PS*, 24, 3, September 1991:441–447.

Kibria, Nazli. *Family Tightrope: The Changing Lives of Vietnamese Americans*. Princeton, N.J.: Princeton University Press, 1993.

Kiefer, Francine S. "Radical Left Exits German Green Party after Sharp Dispute." *Christian Science Monitor*, April 29, 1991:4.

King, Ralph T., Jr. "Soon, a Chip Will Test Blood for Diseases." *Wall Street Journal*, October 25, 1994:B4.

Kinsella, Kevin, and Cynthia M. Taeuber. *An Aging World*. Washington, D.C.: U. S. Bureau of the Census, 1993.

Kluegel, James R., and Eliot R. Smith. *Beliefs about Inequality: America's Views of What Is and What Ought to Be*. Hawthorne, N.Y.: Aldine de Gruyter, 1986.

Kohlfeld, Carol W., and Leslie A. Leip. "Bans on Concurrent Sale of Beer and Gas: A California Case Study." *Sociological Practice Review*, 2, 2, April 1, 1991:104–115.

Kohn, Melvin L. *Class and Conformity: A Study in Values*, 2nd ed. Homewood, Ill.: Dorsey Press, 1977.

Kohn, Melvin L. "Occupational Structure and Alienation." *American Journal of Sociology*, 82, 1976:111–130.

Kohn, Melvin L. "Social Class and Parent–Child Relationships: An Interpretation." *American Journal of Sociology*, 68, 1963:471–480.

Kohn, Melvin L. "Social Class and Parental Values." *American Journal of Sociology*, 64, 1959:337–351.

Kohn, Melvin L., and Carmi Schooler. "Class, Occupation, and Orientation." *American Sociological Review*, 34, 1969:659–678.

Kohn, Melvin L., and Carmi Schooler. *Work and Personality: An Inquiry into the Impact of Social Stratification*. New York: Ablex Press, 1983.

Kohn, Melvin L., Kazimierz M. Slomczynski, and Carrie Schoenbach. "Social Stratification and the Transmission of Values in the Family: A Cross-National Assessment." *Sociological Forum*, 1, 1, 1986:73–102.

Krause, Neal. "Race Differences in Life Satisfaction among Aged Men and Women." *Journal of Gerontology*, 48, 5, 1993:235–244.

Kraybill, Donald B. *The Riddle of Amish Culture*. Baltimore: Johns Hopkins University Press, 1989.

Krupp, Helmar. "European Technology Policy and Global Schumpeter Dynamics: A Social Science Perspective." *Technological Forecasting and Social Change*, 48, 1995:7–26.

Krysan, Maria, and Reynolds Farley. "Racial Stereotypes: Are They Alive and Well? Do They Continue to Influence Race Relations?" Paper presented at the 1993 meeting of the American Sociological Association.

Kurian, George Thomas. *Encyclopedia of the First World*, Vols. 1, 2. New York: Facts on File, 1990.

Kurian, George Thomas. *Encyclopedia of the Second World*, New York: Facts on File, 1991.

Kurian, George Thomas. *Encyclopedia of the Third World*, Vols. 1, 2, 3. New York: Facts on File, 1992.

Lacayo, Richard. "The Lure of the Cult." *Time*, April 7, 1997:45–46.

Lachica, Eduardo. "Third World Told to Spend More on Environment." *Wall Street Journal*, May 18, 1992:A2.

LaDou, Joseph. "Deadly Migration: Hazardous Industries' Flight to the Third World." *Technology Review*, 94, 5, July 1991:46–53.

Lagaipa, Susan J. "Suffer the Little Children: The Ancient Practice of Infanticide as a Modern Moral Dilemma." *Issues in Comprehensive Pediatric Nursing, 13,* 1990:241–251.

Lancaster, Hal. "Managing Your Career." *Wall Street Journal,* November 14, 1995:B1.

Landtman, Gunnar. *The Origin of the Inequality of the Social Classes.* New York: Greenwood Press, 1968. First published in 1938.

Lang, Kurt, and Gladys E. Lang. *Collective Dynamics.* New York: Crowell, 1961.

Lannoy, Richard. *The Speaking Tree: A Study of Indian Culture and Society.* New York: Oxford University Press, 1975.

LaPiere, Richard T. "Attitudes versus Action." *Social Forces, 13,* December 1934:230–237.

Larson, Jeffry H. "The Marriage Quiz: College Students' Beliefs in Selected Myths about Marriage." *Family Relations,* January 1988:3–11.

Lauer, Jeanette, and Robert Lauer. "Marriages Made to Last." In *Marriage and Family in a Changing Society,* 4th ed., James M. Henslin, ed. New York: Free Press, 1992:481–486.

Lederman, Douglas. "Educators and Lawmakers in Texas Seek New Ways to Help Minority Students." *Chronicle of Higher Education, 43,* 13, November 22, 1996:A27.

Lee, Alfred McClung, and Elizabeth Briant Lee. *The Fine Art of Propaganda: A Study of Father Coughlin's Speeches.* New York: Harcourt Brace, 1939.

Lee, Sharon M., and Keiko Yamanaka. "Patterns of Asian American Intermarriage and Marital Assimilation." *Journal of Comparative Family Studies, 21,* 2, Summer 1990: 287–305.

Lemann, Nicholas. "The Myth of Community Development." *New York Times Magazine,* January 9, 1994:26–31.

Lemann, Nicholas. *The Promised Land: The Great Black Migration and How It Changed America.* New York: Random House, 1991.

Lenski, Gerhard. *Power and Privilege: A Theory of Social Stratification.* New York: McGraw-Hill, 1966.

Lenski, Gerhard. "Status Crystallization: A Nonvertical Dimension of Social Status." *American Sociological Review, 19,* 1954:405–413.

Lenski, Gerhard, and Jean Lenski. *Human Societies: An Introduction to Macrosociology,* 5th ed. New York: McGraw-Hill, 1987.

Lerner, Gerda. *Black Women in White America: A Documentary History.* New York: Pantheon Books, 1972.

Lerner, Gerda. *The Creation of Patriarchy.* New York: Oxford University Press, 1986.

Lessinger, Johanna. *From the Ganges to the Hudson: Indian Immigrants in New York City.* Boston: Allyn and Bacon, 1996.

Levinson, D. J. *The Seasons of a Man's Life.* New York: Knopf, 1978.

Levy, Marion J., Jr. "Confucianism and Modernization." *Society, 24,* 4, May–June 1992:15–18.

Lewis, Oscar. "The Culture of Poverty." *Scientific American, 113,* October 1966a:19–25.

Lewis, Oscar. *La Vida.* New York: Random House, 1966b.

Lewis, Richard S. *Challenger: The Final Voyage.* New York: Columbia University Press, 1988.

Liben, Paul. "Farrakhan Honors African Slavers." *Wall Street Journal,* October 20, 1995:A14.

Liebow, Elliot. *Tally's Corner: A Study of Negro Streetcorner Men.* Boston: Little, Brown, 1967.

Lightfoot-Klein, A. "Rites of Purification and Their Effects: Some Psychological Aspects of Female Genital Circumcision and Infibulation (Pharaonic Circumcision) in an Afro-Arab Society (Sudan)." *Journal of Psychological Human Sexuality, 2,* 1989:61–78.

Lin, Nan, Walter M. Ensel, and John C. Vaughn. "Social Resources and Strength of Ties: Structural Factors in Occupational Status Attainment." *American Sociological Review, 46,* 4, August 1981:393–405.

Lind, Michael. *The Next American Nation: The New Nationalism and the Fourth American Revolution.* New York: Free Press, 1995.

Linden, Eugene. "Lost Tribes, Lost Knowledge." *Time,* September 23, 1991:46, 48, 50, 52, 54, 56.

Linton, Ralph. *The Study of Man.* New York: Appleton-Century-Crofts, 1936.

Lippitt, Ronald, and Ralph K. White. "An Experimental Study of Leadership and Group Life." In *Readings in Social Psychology,* 3rd ed., Eleanor E. Maccoby, Theodore M. Newcomb, and Eugene L. Hartley, eds. New York: Holt, Rinehart and Winston, 1958:340–365. (As summarized in Olmsted and Hare 1978:28–31.)

Lipset, Seymour Martin. "Democracy and Working-Class Authoritarianism." *American Sociological Review, 24,* 1959:482–502.

Lipset, Seymour Martin. "The Social Requisites of Democracy Revisited." Presidential address to the American Sociological Association, Boston, Massachusetts, 1993.

Lipset, Seymour Martin, ed. *The Third Century: America as a Post-Industrial Society.* Stanford, Calif.: Hoover Institution Press, 1979.

Lipton, Michael. *Why Poor People Stay Poor: Urban Bias in World Development.* Cambridge, Mass.: Harvard University Press, 1979.

Lombroso, Cesare. *Crime: Its Causes and Remedies,* H. P. Horton, trans. Boston: Little, Brown, 1911.

Lopez, Julie Amparano. "Study Says Women Face Glass Walls as Well as Ceilings." *Wall Street Journal,* March 3, 1992:B1, B8.

Lopez, Julie Amparano. "Managing Your Career." *Wall Street Journal,* January 12, 1994.

Luker, Kristin. *Abortion and the Politics of Motherhood.* Berkeley: University of California Press, 1984.

Lundberg, Olle. "Causal Explanations for Class Inequality in Health—An Empirical Analysis." *Social Science and Medicine, 32,* 4, 1991:385–393.

Luoma, Jon R. "Acid Murder No Longer a Mystery." In *Taking Sides: Clashing Views on Controversial Environmental Issues,* 3rd ed., Theodore D. Goldfarb, ed. Guilford, Conn.: Dushkin, 1989:186–192.

Lye, Diane N., Daniel H. Klepinger, Patricia Davis Hyle, and Anjanette Nelson. "Childhood Living Arrangements and Adult Children's Relations with Their Parents." 1993 revisions of a paper presented at the annual meetings of the Population Association of America, 1992.

MacDonald, William L., and Alfred DeMaris. "Remarriage, Stepchildren, and Marital Conflict: Challenges to the Incomplete Institutionalization Hypothesis." *Journal of Marriage and the Family*, 57, May 1995:387–398.

Mackey, Richard A., and Bernard A. O'Brien. *Lasting Marriages: Men and Women Growing Together.* Westport, Conn.: 1995.

MacShane, Denis. "Lessons for Bosses and the Bossed." *New York Times*, July 19, 1993:A15.

Magnuson, E. "A Cold Soak, a Plume, a Fireball." *Time*, February 17, 1986:25.

Mahler, Sarah. Communication to the author. January 1995.

Mahoney, John S., Jr., and Paul G. Kooistra. "Policing the Races: Structural Factors Enforcing Racial Purity in Virginia (1630–1930)." Paper presented at the 1995 meetings of the American Sociological Association.

Mahran, M. "Medical Dangers of Female Circumcision." *International Planned Parenthood Federation Medical Bulletin, 2*, 1981:1–2.

Mahran, M. *Proceedings of the Third International Congress of Medical Sexology.* Littleton, Mass.: PSG Publishing, 1978.

Maier, Mark. "Teaching from Tragedy: An Interdisciplinary Module on the Space Shuttle *Challenger*." *T.H.E. Journal*, September 1993:91–94.

Mamdani, Mahmood. "The Myth of Population Control: Family, Caste, and Class in an Urban Village." New York: Monthly Review Press, 1973.

Mander, Jerry. *In the Absence of the Sacred: The Failure of Technology and the Survival of the Indian Nations.* San Francisco, Calif.: Sierra Club Books, 1992.

Manno, Bruno V. "The Real Score on the SATs." *Wall Street Journal*, September 13, 1995:A14.

Manski, Charles F. "Income and Higher Education." *Focus, 14*, 3, Winter 1992–1993:14–19.

Marger, Martin N. *Elites and Masses: An Introduction to Political Sociology*, 2nd ed. Belmont, Calif.: Wadsworth, 1987.

Markhusen, Eric. "Genocide in Cambodia." In *Down to Earth Sociology: Introductory Readings*, 8th ed., James M. Henslin, ed. New York: Free Press, 1995:355–364.

Marshall, Samantha. "It's So Simple: Just Lather Up, Watch the Fat Go down the Drain." *Wall Street Journal*, November 2, 1995:B1.

Martin, Michael. "Ecosabotage and Civil Disobedience." *Environmental Ethics, 12*, 4, Winter 1990:291–310.

Martin, William G. "The World-Systems Perspective in Perspective: Assessing the Attempt to Move beyond Nineteenth-Century Eurocentric Conceptions." *Review, 17*, 2, Spring 1994:145–185.

Marx, Karl. "Contribution to the Critique of Hegel's Philosophy of Right." In *Karl Marx: Early Writings*, T. B. Bottomore, ed. New York: McGraw-Hill, 1964:45. First published in 1844.

Marx, Karl, and Friedrich Engels. *Communist Manifesto.* New York: Pantheon, 1967. First published in 1848.

Massey, Douglas S., and Nancy A. Denton. *American Apartheid: Segregation and the Making of the Underclass.* Cambridge, Mass.: Harvard University Press, 1993.

Mauss, Armand. *Social Problems as Social Movements.* Philadelphia: Lippincott, 1975.

McCall, Michael. "Who and Where Are the Artists?" In *Fieldwork Experience: Qualitative Approaches to Social Research*, William B. Shaffir, Robert A. Stebbins, and Allan Turowetz, eds. New York: St. Martin's, 1980:145–158.

McCarthy, Colman. "America's Homeless: Three Days Down and Out in Chicago." *Nation, 236*, 9, March 5, 1983:1, 271.

McCarthy, John D., and Mayer N. Zald. "Resource Mobilization and Social Movements: A Partial Theory." *American Journal of Sociology, 82*, 6, 1977:1212–1241.

McCuen, Gary E., ed. *Ecocide and Genocide in the Vanishing Forest: The Rainforests and Native People.* Hudson, Wis.: GEM Publications, 1993.

McGowan, Jo. "Little Girls Dying: An Ancient & Thriving Practice." *Commonweal*, August 9, 1991:481–482.

McKenna, George. "On Abortion: A Lincolnian Position." *Atlantic Monthly*, September 1995:51–67.

McKeown, Thomas. *The Modern Rise of Population.* New York: Academic Press, 1977.

McLanahan, Sara, and Gary Sandefur. *Growing Up with a Single Parent: What Hurts, What Helps.* Cambridge, Mass.: Harvard University Press, 1995.

McLemore, S. Dale. *Racial and Ethnic Relations in America.* Boston: Allyn and Bacon, 1994.

McLuhan, Marshall. *Understanding Media: The Extensions of Man.* New York: Mentor, 1964.

Mead, George Herbert. *Mind, Self and Society.* Chicago: University of Chicago Press, 1934.

Meek, Anne. "On Creating 'Ganas': A Conversation with Jaime Escalante." *Educational Leadership, 46*, 5, February 1989:46–47.

Menzel, Peter. *Material World: A Global Family Portrait.* San Francisco: Sierra Club, 1994.

Merton, Robert K. "The Social-Cultural Environment and Anomie." In *New Perspectives for Research on Juvenile Delinquency*, Helen L. Witmer and Ruth Kotinsky, eds. Washington, D.C.: U.S. Department of Health, Education, and Welfare, 1956:24–50.

Merton, Robert K. *Social Theory and Social Structure*, enlarged ed. New York: Free Press, 1968.

Merwine, Maynard H. "How Africa Understands Female Circumcision." *New York Times*, November 24, 1993.

Meyrowitz, Joshua. "The Adultlike Child and the Childlike Adult: Socialization in an Electronic Age." *Daedalus, 113*, 1984:19–48.

Michael, Robert T. "Measuring Poverty: A New Approach." *Focus, 17*, 1, Summer 1995:2–13.

Michalowski, Raymond J. *Order, Law, and Crime: An Introduction to Criminology.* New York: Random House, 1985.

Milbank, Dana. "Guarded by Greenbelts, Europe's Town Centers Thrive." *Wall Street Journal*, May 3, 1995a:B1, B4.

Milbank, Dana. "No Fault Divorce Law Is Assailed in Michigan, and Debate Heats Up." *Wall Street Journal*, January 5, 1996:A1, A6.

Milbank, Dana. "Working Poor Fear Welfare Cutbacks Aimed at the Idle Will Inevitably Strike Them, Too." *Wall Street Journal*, August 9, 1995b:A10.

Milgram, Stanley. "Behavioral Study of Obedience." *Journal of Abnormal and Social Psychology, 67*, 4, 1963:371–378.

Milgram, Stanley. "The Small World Problem." *Psychology Today, 1*, 1967:61–67.

Milgram, Stanley. "Some Conditions of Obedience and Disobedience to Authority." *Human Relations, 18*, February 1965:57–76.

Miller, Dan E. "Milgram Redux: Obedience and Disobedience in Authority Relations." In *Studies in Symbolic Interaction*, Norman K. Denzin, ed. Greenwich, Conn.: JAI Press, 1986:77–106.

Miller, John J. "Don't Close Our 'Golden Door.'" *Wall Street Journal*, May 25, 1995:A14.

Miller, Michael W. "Survey Sketches New Portrait of the Mentally Ill." *Wall Street Journal*, January 14, 1994: B1, B10.

Miller, Walter B. "Lower Class Culture as a Generating Milieu of Gang Delinquency." *Journal of Social Issues, 14*, 3, 1958:5–19.

Mills, C. Wright. *The Power Elite*. New York: Oxford University Press, 1956.

Mills, C. Wright. *The Sociological Imagination*. New York: Oxford University Press, 1959.

Minkler, Meredith, and Ann Robertson. "The Ideology of 'Age/Race Wars': Deconstructing a Social Problem." *Ageing and Society, 11*, 1, March 1991:1–22.

Mintz, Beth A., and Michael Schwartz. *The Power Structure of American Business*. Chicago: University of Chicago Press, 1985.

Mizruchi, Mark S., and Thomas Koenig. "Size, Concentration, and Corporate Networks: Determinants of Business Collective Action." *Social Science Quarterly, 72*, 2, June 1991:299–313.

Mohawk, John C. "Indian Economic Development: An Evolving Concept of Sovereignty." *Buffalo Law Review, 39*, 2, Spring 1991:495–503.

Money, John, and Anke A. Ehrhardt. *Man and Woman, Boy and Girl*. Baltimore: Johns Hopkins University Press, 1972.

Montagu, M. F. Ashley. *Introduction to Physical Anthropology*, 3rd ed. Springfield, Ill.: Thomas, 1960.

Montagu, M. F. Ashley. *The Concept of Race*. New York: Free Press, 1964.

Morgan, Lewis Henry. *Ancient Society*. 1877.

Morgan, M. "Television and Adolescents' Sex-Role Stereotypes: A Longitudinal Study." *Journal of Personality and Social Psychology, 43*, 1982:947–955.

Morgan, M. "Television, Sex-Role Attitudes, and Sex-Role Behavior." *Journal of Early Adolescence, 7*, 3, 1987:269–282.

Morris, J. R. "Racial Attitudes of Undergraduates in Greek Housing." *College Student Journal, 25*, 1, March 1991: 501–505.

Mosher, Steven W. *A Mother's Ordeal: One Woman's Fight against China's One-Child Policy*. New York: Harcourt, Brace, 1993.

Mosher, Steven W. "Why Are Baby Girls Being Killed in China?" *Wall Street Journal*, July 25, 1983:9.

Mount, Ferdinand. *The Subversive Family: An Alternative History of Love and Marriage*. New York: Free Press, 1992.

Moynihan, Daniel Patrick. "Social Justice in the *Next* Century." *America*, September 14, 1991:132–137.

Muehlenhard, Charlene L., and Melaney A. Linton. "Date Rape and Sexual Aggression in Dating Situations: Incidence and Risk Factors." *Journal of Counseling Psychology, 34*, 2, 1987:186–196.

Muir, Donal E. "'White' Fraternity and Sorority Attitudes Toward 'Blacks' on a Deep-South Campus." *Sociological Spectrum, 11*, 1, January–March 1991:93–103.

Murdock, George Peter. *Social Structure*. New York: Macmillan, 1949.

Murray, Charles. "The Coming White Underclass." *Wall Street Journal*, October 29, 1993:A16.

Murray, Charles, and R. J. Hernstein. "What's Really Behind the SAT-Score Decline?" *Public Interest, 106*, Winter 1992:32–56.

Mydans, Seth. "Poll Finds Tide of Immigration Brings Hostility." *New York Times*, June 27, 1993:A1, A16.

Myrdal, Gunnar. *Challenge to Affluence*. New York: Pantheon Books, 1962.

Naj, Amal Kumar. "Some Manufacturers Drop Efforts to Adopt Japanese Techniques." *Wall Street Journal*, May 7, 1993:A1, A12.

Naj, Amal Kumar. "MIT Chemists Achieve Goal of Splitting Nitrogen Molecules in the Atmosphere." *Wall Street Journal*, May 12, 1995:B3.

Nakao, Keiko, and Judith Treas. "Occupational Prestige in the United States Revisited: Twenty-Five Years of Stability and Change." Paper presented at the annual meetings of the American Sociological Association, 1990. (As referenced in Kerbo, Harold R. *Social Stratification and Inequality: Class Conflict in Historical and Comparative Perspective*, 2nd ed. New York: McGraw-Hill, 1991:181.)

Nash, Gary B. *Red, White, and Black*. Englewood Cliffs, N.J.: Prentice Hall, 1974.

National Women's Political Caucus. "Fact Sheet on Women's Political Progress." Washington, D.C.: January 1993.

National Women's Political Caucus. "Factsheet on Women's Political Progress." Washington, D.C., June 1995.

Nauta, André. "That They All May Be One: Can Denominationalism Die?" Paper presented at the annual meetings of the American Sociological Association, 1993.

Neikirk, William, and Glen Elsasser. "Ruling Weakens Abortion Right." *Chicago Tribune*, June 30, 1992:1, 8.

Nelson, Ruth K. "Letter to the Editor." *Wall Street Journal*, November 2, 1989:A23.

Neugarten, Bernice L. "Middle Age and Aging." In *Growing Old in America*, Beth B. Hess, ed. New Brunswick, N.J.: Transaction Books, 1976:180–197.

Neugarten, Bernice L. "Personality and Aging." In *Handbook of the Psychology of Aging*, James E. Birren and K. Warren Schaie, eds. New York: Van Nostrand Reinhold, 1977: 626–649.

Newdorf, David. "Bailout Agencies Like to Do It in Secret." *Washington Journalism Review, 13*, 4, May 1991:15–16.

Niebuhr, H. Richard. *The Social Sources of Denominationalism*. New York: Holt, 1929.

Noah, Timothy. "White House Forms Panel to Investigate Cold War Radiation Tests on Humans." *Wall Street Journal*, January 4, 1994:A12.

Nsamenang, A. Bame. *Human Development in Cultural Context: A Third World Perspective.* Newbury Park, Calif.: Sage, 1992.

O'Connel, Martin. "Where's Papa? Father's Role in Child Care." Population Trends and Public Policy no. 20. Washington, D.C.: Population Reference Bureau, September 1993.

Offen, Karen. "Feminism and Sexual Difference in Historical Perspective." In *Theoretical Perspectives on Sexual Difference*, Deborah L. Rhode, ed. New Haven, Conn.: Yale University Press, 1990:13–20.

Ogburn, William F. "The Hypothesis of Cultural Lag." In *Theories of Society: Foundations of Modern Sociological Theory*, Vol. 2, Talcott Parsons, Edward Shils, Kaspar D. Naegele, and Jesse R. Pitts, eds. New York: Free Press, 1961: 1270–1273.

Ogburn, William F. *On Culture and Social Change: Selected Papers*, Otis Dudley Duncan, ed. Chicago: University of Chicago Press, 1964.

Ogburn, William F. *Social Change, with Respect to Culture and Original Nature.* New York: Viking Press, 1938. First published in 1922.

O'Hare, William P. "America's Minorities—The Demographics of Diversity." *Population Bulletin, 47,* 4, December 1992:1–46.

Oliver, Pamela E., and Gerald Marwell. "Mobilizing Technologies for Collective Action." In *Frontiers in Social Movement Theory*, Aldon D. Morris and Carol McClurg Mueller, eds. New Haven, Conn.: Yale University Press, 1992:251–272.

Olmsted, Michael S., and A. Paul Hare. *The Small Group*, 2nd ed. New York: Random House, 1978.

Olneck, Michael R., and David B. Bills. "What Makes Sammy Run? An Empirical Assessment of the Bowles-Gintis Correspondence Theory." *American Journal of Education, 89,* 1980:27–61.

O'Malley, Jeff. "Sex Tourism and Women's Status in Thailand." *Society and Leisure, 11,* 1, Spring 1988:99–114.

O'Neill, Helen. "Strange, Strange Worlds." *Alton Telegraph*, April 6, 1997:A10.

O'Neill, June. "Can Work and Training Programs Reform Welfare?" *Journal of Labor Research, 14,* 3, Summer 1993:265–281.

Ono, Yumiko, and Jacob M. Schlesinger. "With Careful Planning, Japan Sets Out to Be 'Life Style Superpower.'" *Wall Street Journal*, October 10, 1992:A1, A11.

Ortega, Bob. "Portland, Ore., Shows Nation's City Planners How to Guide Growth." *Wall Street Journal*, December 26, 1995:A1, A8.

Otten, Alan L. "People Patterns." *Wall Street Journal*, January 18, 1994a:B1.

Otten, Alan L. "People Patterns." *Wall Street Journal*, September 23, 1994b:B1.

Ouchi, William. *Theory Z: How American Business Can Meet the Japanese Challenge.* Reading, Mass.: Addison-Wesley, 1981.

Ouchi, William. "Decision-Making in Japanese Organizations." In *Down to Earth Sociology*, 7th ed., James M. Henslin, ed. New York: Free Press, 1993:503–507.

Pagelow, Mildred Daley. "Adult Victims of Domestic Violence: Battered Women." *Journal of Interpersonal Violence*, 7, 1, March 1992:87–120.

Palen, John J. *The Urban World*, 3rd ed. New York: McGraw-Hill, 1987.

Parfit, Michael, "Earth First!ers Wield a Mean Monkey Wrench." *Smithsonian, 21,* 1, April 1990:184–204.

Park, Robert Ezra. "Human Ecology." *American Journal of Sociology, 42,* 1, July 1936:1–15.

Park, Robert E., and Ernest W. Burgess. *Human Ecology.* Chicago: University of Chicago Press, 1921.

Parsons, Talcott. "An Analytic Approach to the Theory of Social Stratification." *American Journal of Sociology, 45,* 1940:841–862.

Pasztor, Andy. "U.S., Grumman Reach Accord in Pentagon Case." *Wall Street Journal*, November 23, 1993:A3.

Patterns of Urban and Rural Population Growth. Population Study no. 68. New York: United Nations Department of International and Economic Social Affairs, 1980.

Pearl, Daniel. "Futurist Schlock: Today's Cyberhype Has a Familiar Ring." *Wall Street Journal*, September 7, 1995a:A1, A6.

Pearl, Daniel. "Government Tackles a Surge of Smut on the Internet." *Wall Street Journal*, February 8, 1995b:B1, B8.

Pearlin, L. I., and Melvin L. Kohn. "Social Class, Occupation, and Parental Values: A Cross-National Study." *American Sociological Review, 31,* 1966:466–479.

Peart, Karen N. "Converts to the Faith." *Scholastic Update, 126,* 4, October 22, 1993:16–18.

Perry, James M. "Virginia's Wilder to Base Run for White House on Blend of Fiscal Conservatism and Compassion." *Wall Street Journal*, December 19, 1990:A18.

Persell, Caroline Hodges, Sophia Catsambis, and Peter W. Cookson, Jr. "Family Background, School Type, and College Attendance: A Conjoint System of Cultural Capital Transmission." *Journal of Research on Adolescence, 2,* 1, 1992:1–23.

Pessar, Patricia R. *A Visa for a Dream: Dominicans in New York.* Boston: Allyn and Bacon, 1966.

Peterson, James L., and Nicholas Zill. "Marital Disruption, Parent–Child Relationships, and Behavior Problems in Children." *Journal of Marriage and the Family, 48,* 1986:295–307.

Phillips, John L., Jr. *The Origins of Intellect: Piaget's Theory.* San Francisco: Freeman, 1969.

Piaget, Jean. *The Construction of Reality in the Child.* New York: Basic Books, 1954.

Piaget, Jean. *The Psychology of Intelligence.* London: Routledge & Kegan Paul, 1950.

Pines, Maya. "The Civilizing of Genie." *Psychology Today, 15,* September 1981:28–34.

Piotrow, Phylis Tilson. *World Population Crisis: The United States' Response.* New York: Praeger, 1973.

Piturro, Marlene. "Managing Diversity." *Executive Female*, May-June 1991:45–46, 48.

Platt, Tony. " 'Street' Crime—A View from the Left." *Crime and Social Justice: Issues in Criminology, 9,* 1978:26–34.

Polenberg, Richard. *One Nation Divisible: Class, Race, and Ethnicity in the United States since 1938.* New York: Penguin, 1980.

Polsby, Nelson W. "Three Problems in the Analysis of Community Power." *American Sociological Review, 24,* 6, December 1959:796–803.

Polumbaum, Judy. "China: Confucian Tradition Meets the Market Economy." *Ms.,* September–October 1992:12–13.

Pope, Liston. *Millhands and Preachers: A Study of Gastonia.* New Haven, Conn.: Yale University Press, 1942.

Population Reference Bureau. "World Information Data Sheet." Washington, D.C., May 1995.

"Population Update." *Population Today, 24,* 2, February 1996:6.

Portes, Alejandro, and Ruben G. Rumbaut. *Immigrant America.* Berkeley: University of California Press, 1990.

Postman, Neil. *Technopoly: The Surrender of Culture to Technology.* New York: Knopf, 1992.

Price, Daniel O., ed. *The 99th Hour.* Chapel Hill: University of North Carolina Press, 1967.

Prud'Homme, Alex. "Getting a Grip on Power." *Time,* July 29, 1991:15–16.

"Racial Balkanization at Cornell." *Wall Street Journal,* July 25, 1995:A10.

Ray, J. J. "Authoritarianism Is a Dodo: Comment on Scheepers, Felling and Peters." *European Sociological Review, 7,* 1, May 1991:73–75.

Raymond, Chris. "New Studies by Anthropologists Indicate Amish Communities Are Much More Dynamic and Diverse than Many Believed." *Chronicle of Higher Education,* December 19, 1990:A1, A9.

Read, Piers Paul. *Alive. The Story of the Andes Survivors.* Philadelphia: Lippincott, 1974.

Reckless, Walter C. *The Crime Problem,* 5th ed. New York: Appleton, 1973.

Reed, Susan, and Lorenzo Benet. "Ecowarrior Dave Foreman Will Do Whatever It Takes in His Fight to Save Mother Earth." *People Weekly, 33,* 15, April 16, 1990: 113–116.

Reich, Michael. "The Economics of Racism." In *The Capitalist System,* Richard C. Edwards, Michael Reich, and Thomas E. Weiskopf, eds. Englewood Cliffs, N.J.: Prentice Hall, 1972:313–321.

Reich, Robert B. *Good for Business: Making Full Use of the Nation's Human Capital, The Environmental Scan.* Washington, D.C.: U.S. Department of Labor, March 1995.

Reitman, Valerie, and Oscar Suris. "In a Cultural U-Turn, Mazda's Creditors Put Ford behind the Wheel." *Wall Street Journal,* November 21, 1994:A1, A4.

Renteln, Alison Dundes. "Sex Selection and Reproductive Freedom." *Women's Studies International Forum, 15,* 3, 1992:405–426.

Rich, Spencer. "Number of Elected Hispanic Officials Doubled in a Decade, Study Shows." *Washington Post,* September 19, 1986:A6.

Richards, Bill. "Doctors Can Diagnose Illnesses Long Distance, to the Dismay of Some." *Wall Street Journal,* January 17, 1996:A1, A8.

Ricks, Thomas E. "'New' Marines Illustrate Growing Gap between Military and Society." *Wall Street Journal,* July 27, 1995:A1, A4.

Riesman, David. "The Suburban Dislocation." In *Urban Man and Society: A Reader in Urban Ecology,* Albert N. Cousins and Hans Nagpaul, eds. New York: Knopf, 1970:172–184.

Rigdon, Joan E., and Alecia Swasy. "Distractions of Modern Life at Key Ages Are Cited for Drop in Student Literacy." *Wall Street Journal,* October 1, 1990:B1, B3.

Rist, Ray C. "Student Social Class and Teacher Expectations: The Self-Fulfilling Prophecy in Ghetto Education." *Harvard Educational Review, 40,* 3, August 1970:411–451.

Ritzer, George. *The McDonaldization of Society: An Investigation into the Changing Character of Contemporary Life.* Thousand Oaks, Calif.: Pine Forge Press, 1993.

Ritzer, George. *Sociological Theory,* 3rd ed. New York: McGraw-Hill, 1992.

Robertson, Ian. "Social Stratification." In *The Study of Anthropology,* David E. Hunter and Phillip Whitten, eds. New York: Harper & Row, 1976.

Robertson, Ian. *Sociology,* 3rd ed. New York: Worth, 1987.

Robertson, Roland. *Globalization: Social Theory and Global Culture.* London: Sage, 1992.

Rodriguez, Richard. "The Education of Richard Rodriguez." *Saturday Review,* February 8, 1975:147–149.

Rodriguez, Richard. *Hunger of Memory: The Education of Richard Rodriguez.* Boston: Godine, 1982.

Rodriguez, Richard. "The Late Victorians: San Francisco, AIDS, and the Homosexual Stereotype." *Harper's Magazine,* October 1990:57–66.

Rodriguez, Richard. "Mixed Blood." *Harper's Magazine, 283,* November 1991:47–56.

Rodriguez, Richard. "Searching for Roots in a Changing Society." In *Down to Earth Sociology: Introductory Readings,* 8th ed., James M. Henslin, ed. New York: Free Press, 1995: 486–491.

Rodríguez, Victor M. "Los Angeles, U.S.A. 1992: 'A House Divided against Itself . . .'" *SSSP Newsletter,* Spring 1994:5–12.

Rogers, Joseph W. *Why Are You Not a Criminal?* Englewood Cliffs, N.J.: Prentice Hall, 1977.

Rossi, Alice S. "A Biosocial Perspective on Parenting." *Daedalus, 106,* 1977:1–31.

Rossi, Alice S. "Gender and Parenthood." *American Sociological Review, 49,* 1984:1–18.

Rotundo, E. Anthony. "Changing Ideals of American Middle-Class Manhood, 1770–1920." *Journal of Social History, 16,* 4, Summer 1983:23–38.

Rubenstein, Carin. "Is There Sex after Baby?" In *Marriage and Family in a Changing Society,* 4th ed., James M. Henslin, ed. New York: Free Press, 1992:235–242.

Rubin, Lillian Breslow. "The Empty Nest." In *Marriage and Family in a Changing Society,* 4th ed., James M. Henslin, ed. New York: Free Press, 1992a:261–270.

Rubin, Lillian Breslow. "Worlds of Pain." In *Marriage and Family in a Changing Society,* 4th ed., James M. Henslin, ed. New York: Free Press, 1992b:44–50.

Rubin, Lillian Breslow. *Worlds of Pain: Life in the Working-Class Family.* New York: Basic Books, 1976.

Rubin, Zick. "The Love Research." In *Marriage and Family in a Changing Society,* 2nd ed., James M. Henslin, ed. New York: Free Press, 1985.

Ruggles, Patricia. "Short and Long Term Poverty in the United States: Measuring the American 'Underclass.'" Washington, D.C.: Urban Institute, June 1989.

Ruggles, Patricia. *Drawing the Line: Alternative Poverty Measures and Their Implication for Public Policy.* Washington, D.C.: Urban Institute, 1990.

Russell, Diana E. H. *The Secret Trauma: Incest in the Lives of Girls and Women.* New York: Basic Books, 1986.

Russell, Diana E. H. *Rape in Marriage.* Bloomington: Indiana University Press, 1990.

Russell, Dick. "The Monkeywrenchers." *Amicus Journal,* Fall 1987: 28–42.

"Russian Banker Is Killed in Apparent Poisoning." *Wall Street Journal,* April 7, 1995:A11.

Sahlins, Marshall D., and Elman R. Service. *Evolution and Culture.* Ann Arbor: University of Michigan Press, 1960.

Salholz, Eloise. "The Push for Power." *Newsweek,* April 9, 1990:19–20.

Samuelson, Paul A., and William D. Nordhaus. *Economics,* 13th ed. New York: McGraw-Hill, 1989.

Sanchez, Laura. "Gender, Labor Allocations, and the Psychology of Entitlement within the Home." *Social Forces, 13,* 2, December 1994:533–553.

Sandberg, Jared. "Electronic Erotica: Too Much Traffic." *Wall Street Journal,* February 8, 1995:B1, B8.

Sandefur, Gary D. "Children in Single-Parent Families: The Roles of Time and Money." *Focus, 17,* 1, Summer 1995: 44–45.

Sapir, Edward. *Selected Writings of Edward Sapir in Language, Culture, and Personality,* David G. Mandelbaum, ed. Berkeley: University of California Press, 1949.

Savells, Jerry. "Social Change among the Amish." In *Down to Earth Sociology: Introductory Readings,* 9th ed., James M. Henslin, ed. New York: Free Press, 1997:474–482.

Sawhill, Isabel V. "Poverty in the U.S.: Why Is It So Persistent?" *Journal of Economic Literature, 26,* 3, September 1988:1073–1119.

Saxe, G. B. "Candy Selling and Math Learning." *Educational Researcher, 17,* 6, 1995:14–21.

Sayres, William. "What Is a Family Anyway?" In *Marriage and Family in a Changing Society,* 4th ed., James M. Henslin, ed. New York: Free Press, 1992:23–30.

Scarce, Rik. "(No) Trial (But) Tribulations." *Journal of Contemporary Ethnography, 23,* 2, July 1994:123–149.

Scarce, Rik. "Rik Scarce Responds: A Clear-Cut Case of Academic Freedom at Risk." *Daily News* (Moscow-Pullman), June 12–13, 1993:1B.

Scarr, Sandra, and Marlene Eisenberg. "Child Care Research: Issues, Perspectives, and Results." *Annual Review of Psychology, 44,* 1963:613–644.

Schaefer, Richard T. *Racial and Ethnic Groups.* Boston: Little, Brown, 1979.

Schaefer, Richard T. *Sociology,* 3rd ed. New York: McGraw-Hill, 1989.

Schafran, Lynn Hecht. "Rape Is Still Underreported." *New York Times,* August 29, 1995:19.

Schlesinger, Jacob M., Michael Williams, and Craig Forman. "Japan Inc., Wracked by Recession, Takes Stock of Its Methods." *Wall Street Journal,* September 29, 1993:A1, A4.

Schor, Juliet B. "Americans Work Too Hard." *New York Times,* July 25, 1991:A21.

Schottland, Charles I. *The Social Security Plan in the U.S.* New York: Appleton, 1963.

Schwartz, Felice N. "Management Women and the New Facts of Life." *Harvard Business Review, 89,* 1, January–February 1989:65–76.

Schwendinger, Julia R., and Herman Schwendinger. *Rape and Inequality.* Beverly Hills, Calif.: Sage, 1983.

Scully, Diana. "Negotiating to Do Surgery." In *Dominant Issues in Medical Sociology,* 3rd ed., Howard D. Schwartz, ed. New York: McGraw-Hill, 1994:146–152.

Scully, Diana, and Joseph Marolla. "Convicted Rapists' Vocabulary of Motive: Excuses and Justifications." *Social Problems, 31,* 5, June 1984:530–544.

Scully, Diana, and Joseph Marolla. " 'Riding the Bull at Gilley's': Convicted Rapists Describe the Rewards of Rape." *Social Problems, 32,* 3, February 1985:251–263.

Searle, John R. *The Construction of Social Reality.* New York: Free Press, 1995.

Seidman, Steven A. "An Investigation of Sex-Role Stereotyping in Music Videos." *Journal of Broadcasting and Electronic Media,* Spring 1992:210–216.

Seltzer, Judith A. "Consequences of Marital Dissolution for Children." *Annual Review of Sociology, 20,* 1994:235–266.

Sharma, S. S. "Untouchables and Brahmins in an Indian Village." In *Haves and Have-Nots: An International Reader on Social Inequality,* James Curtis and Lorne Tepperman, eds. Englewood Cliffs, N.J.: Prentice Hall, 1994:299–303.

Sharp, Lauriston. "Steel Axes for Stone-Age Australians." In *Down to Earth Sociology: Introductory Readings,* 8th ed., James M. Henslin, ed. New York: Free Press, 1995: 453–462.

Shaw, Sue. "Wretched of the Earth." *New Statesman, 20,* March 1987:19–20.

Sheldon, William. *Varieties of Delinquent Youth: An Introduction to Constitutional Psychiatry.* New York: Harper, 1949.

Shellenbarger, Sue. "The Aging of America Is Making 'Elder Care' a Big Workplace Issue." *Wall Street Journal,* February 16, 1994a:A1, A8.

Shellenbarger, Sue. "How Some Companies Help with Elder Care." *Wall Street Journal,* February 16, 1994b:A8.

Shellenbarger, Sue. "Work and Family." *Wall Street Journal,* May 3, 1995:B1.

Sherif, Muzafer, and Carolyn Sherif. *Groups in Harmony and Tension.* New York: Harper & Row, 1953.

Sherman, Spencer. "The Hmong in America." *National Geographic,* October 1988:586–610.

Shill, Walt. "Lessons of the Japanese Mavericks." *Wall Street Journal,* November 1, 1993:A18.

Shirouzu, Norihiko, and Michael Williams. "Pummeled by Giants, Japan's Small Firms Struggle with Change." *Wall Street Journal,* July 25, 1995:A1, A5.

Shively, JoEllen. "Cowboys and Indians: Perceptions of Western Films among American Indians and Anglos." *American Sociological Review, 57,* December 1992:725–734.

Shively, JoEllen. "Cultural Compensation: The Popularity of Westerns among American Indians." Paper presented at the annual meetings of the American Sociological Association, 1991.

Signorielli, Nancy. "Children, Television, and Gender Roles: Messages and Impact." *Journal of Adolescent Health Care*, *11*, 1990:50–58.

Signorielli, Nancy. "Television and Conceptions about Sex Roles: Maintaining Conventionality and the Status Quo." *Sex Roles*, *21*, 5/6, 1989:341–360.

Silberman, Charles E. *Criminal Violence, Criminal Justice*. New York: Random House, 1978.

Sills, David L. *The Volunteers*. Glencoe, Ill.: Free Press, 1957.

Silver, Isidore. "Crime and Conventional Wisdom." *Society*, *14*, March–April 1977:9, 15–19.

Simmel, Georg. *The Sociology of Georg Simmel*, Kurt H. Wolff, ed. and trans. Glencoe, Ill.: Free Press, 1950. First published between 1902 and 1917.

Simon, David R., and D. Stanley Eitzen. *Elite Deviance*, 4th ed. Boston: Allyn and Bacon, 1993.

Simon, Julian L. "Population Growth Is Not Bad for Humanity." In *Taking Sides: Clashing Views on Controversial Social Issues*, Kurt Finsterbusch and George McKenna, eds. Guilford, Conn.: Dushkin, 1992:347–352.

Simon, Julian L. *Theory of Population and Economic Growth*. New York: Blackwell, 1986.

Simon, Julian L. *The Ultimate Resource*. Princeton, N.J.: Princeton University Press, 1981.

Simon, Julian L. "The Nativists Are Wrong." *Wall Street Journal*, August 4, 1993:A10.

Simons, Marlise. "The Amazon's Savvy Indians." In *Down to Earth Sociology: Introductory Readings*, 8th ed., James M. Henslin, ed. New York: Free Press, 1995:463–470.

Simpson, George Eaton, and J. Milton Yinger. *Racial and Cultural Minorities: An Analysis of Prejudice and Discrimination*, 4th ed. New York: Harper & Row, 1972.

Singh, Ajit. "Urbanism, Poverty, and Employment: The Large Metropolis in the Third World." Unpublished monograph, Cambridge University, 1988. As quoted in Giddens, Anthony. *Introduction to Sociology*. New York: Norton, 1991:690.

Skeels, H. M. *Adult Status of Children with Contrasting Early Life Experiences: A Follow-up Study*. Monograph of the Society for Research in Child Development, *31*, 3, 1966.

Skeels, H. M., and H. B. Dye. "A Study of the Effects of Differential Stimulation on Mentally Retarded Children." *Proceedings and Addresses of the American Association on Mental Deficiency*, *44*, 1939:114–136.

Skerry, Peter, and Michael Hartman. "Latin Mass." *New Republic*, June 10, 1991:18–20.

Smart, Barry. "On the Disorder of Things: Sociology, Postmodernity and the 'End of the Social.'" *Sociology*, *24*, 3, August 1990:397–416.

Smith, Beverly A. "An Incest Case in an Early 20th-Century Rural Community." *Deviant Behavior*, *13*, 1992:127–153.

Smith, Craig S. "China Becomes Industrial Nations' Most Favored Dump." *Wall Street Journal*, October 9, 1995:B1.

Smith, Joel B., and Dennis A. Tirpak. *The Potential Effects of Global Climate Change in the United States*. Washington, D.C.: U.S. Environmental Protection Agency, October 1988.

Snow, Margaret E., Carol Nagy Jacklin, and Eleanor E. Maccoby. "Birth-Order Differences in Peer Sociability at Thirty-Three Months." *Child Development*, *52*, 1981:589–595.

Sourcebook of Criminal Justice Statistics. Washington, D.C.: U.S. Government Printing Office, 1995.

South, Scott J. "Sociodemographic Differentials in Mate Selection Preferences." *Journal of Marriage and the Family*, *53*, November 1991:928–940.

Sowell, Thomas. "Effrontery and Gall, Inc." *Forbes*, September 27, 1993a:52.

Sowell, Thomas. *Inside American Education: The Decline, the Deception, the Dogmas*. New York: Free Press, 1993b.

Spector, Malcolm, and John Kitsuse. *Constructing Social Problems*. Menlo Park, Calif.: Cummings, 1977.

Speizer, Jeanne J. "Education." In *The Women's Annual, 1982–1983*, Barbara Haber, ed. Boston: Hall, 1983:29–54.

Spengler, Oswald. *The Decline of the West*, 2 vols., Charles F. Atkinson, trans. New York: Knopf, 1926–1928. First published in 1919–1922.

Spitzer, Steven. "Toward a Marxian Theory of Deviance." *Social Problems*, *22*, June 1975:608–619.

Sprecher, Susan, and Rachita Chandak. "Attitudes about Arranged Marriages and Dating among Men and Women from India." *Free Inquiry in Creative Sociology*, *20*, 1, May 1992:59–69.

Srisang, Koson. "The Ecumenical Coalition on Third World Tourism." *Annals of Tourism Research*, *16*, 1, 1989:119–121.

Srole, Leo, et al. *Mental Health in the Metropolis: The Midtown Manhattan Study*. New York: New York University Press, 1978.

Stack, Carol B. *All Our Kin: Strategies for Survival in a Black Community*. New York: Harper, 1974.

Stampp, Kenneth M. *The Peculiar Institution: Slavery in the Ante-Bellum South*. New York: Vintage Books, 1956.

Stark, Elizabeth. "Friends through It All." In *Marriage and Family in a Changing Society*, 3rd ed., James M. Henslin, ed. New York: Free Press, 1989:441–449.

Stark, Rodney. *Sociology*, 3rd ed. Belmont, Calif.: Wadsworth, 1989.

Starna, William A., and Ralph Watkins. "Northern Iroquoian Slavery." *Ethnohistory*, *38*, 1, Winter 1991:34–57.

Starrels, Marjorie. "The Evolution of Workplace Family Policy Research." *Journal of Family Issues*, *13*, 3, September 1992:259–278.

Statistical Abstract. See U.S. Bureau of the Census.

Stecklow, Steve. "Metal Detectors Find a Growing Market, But Not Many Guns." *Wall Street Journal*, September 7, 1993:A1, A8.

Stecklow, Steve. "SAT Scores Rise Strongly after Test Is Overhauled." *Wall Street Journal*, August 24, 1995: B1, B12.

Stepick, Alan. *Pride against Prejudice: Haitian Refugees in the U.S.* Boston: Allyn and Bacon, 1996.

Sterling, Claire. *Thieves' World*. New York: Simon & Schuster, 1994.

Stevenson, Richard W. "Catering to Consumers' Ethnic Needs." *New York Times*, January 23, 1992.

Stinnett, Nicholas. "Strong Families." In *Marriage and Family in a Changing Society*, 4th ed., James M. Henslin, ed. New York: Free Press, 1992:496–507.

Stipp, David. "Himalayan Tree Could Serve as Source of Anti-Cancer Drug Taxol, Team Says." *Wall Street Journal*, April 20, 1992:B4.

Stodgill, Ralph M. *Handbook of Leadership: A Survey of Theory and Research*. New York: Free Press, 1974.

Stone, Gregory P. "City Shoppers and Urban Identification: Observations on the Social Psychology of City Life." *American Journal of Sociology*, 60, November 1954:276–284.

Stone, Michael H. "Murder." *Psychiatric Clinics of North America*, 12, 3, September 1989:643–651.

Straus, Murray A. "Victims and Aggressors in Marital Violence." *American Behavioral Scientist*, 23, May–June 1980:681–704.

Straus, Murray A. "Explaining Family Violence." In *Marriage and Family in a Changing Society*, 4th ed., James M. Henslin, ed. New York: Free Press, 1992:344–356.

Straus, Murray A., and Richard J. Gelles. "Violence in American Families: How Much Is There and Why Does It Occur?" In *Troubled Relationships*, Elam W. Nunnally, Catherine S. Chilman, and Fred M. Cox, eds. Newbury Park, Calif.: Sage, 1988:141–162.

Straus, Murray A., Richard J. Gelles, and Suzanne K. Steinmetz. *Behind Closed Doors: Violence in the American Family*. New York: Anchor/Doubleday, 1980.

Stryker, Sheldon. "Symbolic Interactionism: Themes and Variations." In *Social Psychology: Sociological Perspectives*, Morris Rosenberg and Ralph H. Turner, eds. New Brunswick, N.J.: Transaction Books, 1990.

Sumner, William Graham. *Folkways: A Study in the Sociological Importance of Usages, Manners, Customs, Mores, and Morals*. New York: Ginn, 1906.

Sun, Lena H. "China Seeks Ways to Protect Elderly." *Washington Post*, October 23, 1990:A1.

Sutherland, Edwin H. *Criminology*. Philadelphia: Lippincott, 1924.

Sutherland, Edwin H. *Principles of Criminology*, 4th ed. Philadelphia: Lippincott, 1947.

Sutherland, Edwin H. *The Professional Thief*. Chicago: University of Chicago Press, 1937.

Sutherland, Edwin H. *White Collar Crime*. New York: Dryden Press, 1949.

Sutherland, Edwin H., and Donald Cressey. *Principles of Criminology*, 9th ed. Philadelphia: Lippincott, 1974.

Sutherland, Edwin H., Donald R. Cressey, and David F. Luckenbill. *Principles of Criminology*, 11th ed. Dix Hills, N.Y.: General Hall, 1992.

Suzuki, Bob H. "Asian-American Families." In *Marriage and Family in a Changing Society*, 2nd ed., James M. Henslin, ed. New York: Free Press, 1985:104–119.

Swedish Institute, The. "Fact Sheets on Sweden." February 1992.

Sweezy, Paul M., and Harry Magdoff. "Globalization—to What End? Part II." *Monthly Review*, 43, 10, March 1992:1–19.

Sykes, Gresham M., and David Matza. "Techniques of Neutralization." In *Down to Earth Sociology: Introductory Readings*, 5th ed., James M. Henslin, ed. New York: Free Press, 1988:225–231.

Szasz, Thomas S. "Mental Illness Is Still a Myth." In *Deviant Behavior 96/97*, Lawrence M. Salinger, ed. Guilford, Conn.: Dushkin, 1996:200–205.

Szasz, Thomas S. *The Myth of Mental Illness*, rev. ed. New York: Harper & Row, 1986.

Tapia, Andres. "Churches Wary of Inner-City Islamic Inroads." *Christianity Today*, 38, 1, January 10, 1994:36–38.

Thomas, Paulette. "Boston Fed Finds Racial Discrimination in Mortgage Lending Is Still Widespread." *Wall Street Journal*, October 9, 1992:A3.

Thomas, Paulette. "EPA Predicts Global Impact from Warming." *Wall Street Journal*, October 21, 1988:B5.

Thomas, R. Roosevelt, Jr. "From Affirmative Action to Affirming Diversity." *Harvard Business Review*, 90, March–April 1990:107–117.

Thornton, Russell. *American Indian Holocaust and Survival: A Population History since 1492*. Norman: University of Oklahoma Press, 1987.

Tilly, Charles. *From Mobilization to Revolution*. Reading, Mass.: Addison-Wesley, 1978.

Timerman, Jacobo. *Prisoner without a Name, Cell without a Number*. New York: Knopf, 1981.

Tobias, Andrew. "The 'Don't Be Ridiculous' Law." *Wall Street Journal*, May 31, 1995:A14.

Toby, Jackson. "To Get Rid of Guns in Schools, Get Rid of Some Students." *Wall Street Journal*, March 23, 1992:A12.

Toch, Thomas. "Violence in Schools." *U.S. News & World Report*, 115, 18, November 8, 1993:31–36.

Toffler, Alvin. *The Third Wave*. New York: Morrow, 1980.

Tolchin, Martin. "Mildest Possible Penalty Is Imposed on Neil Bush." *New York Times*, April 19, 1991:D2.

Tönnies, Ferdinand. *Community and Society (Gemeinschaft und Gesellschaft)*, with a new introduction by John Samples. New Brunswick, N.J.: Transaction Books, 1988. First published in 1887.

Tordoff, William. "The Impact of Ideology on Development in the Third World." *Journal of International Development*, 4, 1, 1992:41–53.

Toynbee, Arnold. *A Study of History*, D. C. Somervell, abridger and ed. New York: Oxford University Press, 1946.

Treas, Judith. "Older Americans in the 1990s and Beyond." *Population Bulletin*, 50, 2, May 1995:1–46.

Treiman, Donald J. *Occupational Prestige in Comparative Perspective*. New York: Academic Press, 1977.

Trice, Harrison M., and Janice M. Beyer. "Cultural Leadership in Organization." *Organization Science*, 2, 2, May 1991:149–169.

Troeltsch, Ernst. *The Social Teachings of the Christian Churches*. New York: Macmillan, 1931.

Trueba, Henry T., Lila Jacobs, and Elizabeth Kirton. *Cultural Conflict and Adaptation: The Case of Hmong Children in American Society*. Bristol, Penn.: Falmer Press, 1990.

Tucker, Belinda M., and Claudia Mitchell-Kernan. "New Trends in Black American Interracial Marriage: The Social Structural Context." *Journal of Marriage and the Family*, 52, 1990:209–218.

Tumin, Melvin M. "Some Principles of Stratification: A Critical Analysis." *American Sociological Review*, 18, 1953: 387–394.

Turk, Austin T. "Class, Conflict, and Criminalization." *Sociological Focus, 10,* 1977:209–220.

Turner, Bryan S. "Outline of a Theory of Citizenship." *Sociology, 24,* 2, May 1990:189–217.

Turner, Jonathan H. *American Society: Problems of Structure.* New York: Harper & Row, 1972.

Turner, Jonathan H. *The Structure of Sociological Theory.* Homewood, Ill.: Dorsey, 1978.

Ullman, Edward, and Chauncey Harris. "The Nature of Cities." In *Urban Man and Society: A Reader in Urban Ecology,* Albert N. Cousins and Hans Nagpaul, eds. New York: Knopf, 1970:91–100.

U.S. Bureau of the Census. *Statistical Abstract of the United States: The National Data Book.* Washington, D.C.: U.S. Government Printing Office. Published annually.

U.S. Department of Health and Human Services, Public Health Service. *Healthy People 2000.* Washington, D.C.: U.S. Government Printing Office, 1990.

Useem, Michael. *The Inner Circle: Large Corporations and the Rise of Business Political Activity in the U.S. and U.K.* New York: Oxford University Press, 1984.

Vande Berg, Leah R., and Diane Streckfuss. "Prime-Time Television's Portrayal of Women and the World of Work: A Demographic Profile." *Journal of Broadcasting and Electronic Media,* Spring 1992:195–208.

van den Haag, Ernest. *Punishing Criminals: Concerning a Very Old and Painful Question.* New York: Basic Books, 1975.

Veblen, Thorstein. *The Theory of the Leisure Class.* New York: Macmillan, 1912.

Vega, William A. "Hispanic Families in the 1980s: A Decade of Research." *Journal of Marriage and the Family, 52,* November 1990:1015–1024.

Vincent, Richard C., Dennis K. Davis, and Lilly Ann Boruszkowski. "Sexism on MTV: The Portrayal of Women in Rock Videos." *Journalism Quarterly 64,* 4, Winter 1987:750–755, 941–942.

Violas, P. C. *The Training of the Urban Working Class: A History of Twentieth Century American Education.* Chicago: Rand McNally, 1978.

Volti, Rudi. *Society and Technological Change,* 3rd ed. New York: St. Martin's Press, 1995.

Von Hoffman, Nicholas. "Sociological Snoopers." *Transaction 7,* May 1970:4, 6.

Wagley, Charles, and Marvin Harris. *Minorities in the New World.* New York: Columbia University Press, 1958.

Waldholz, Michael. " 'Computer Brain' Outperforms Doctors in Diagnosing Heart Attack Patients." *Wall Street Journal,* December 2, 1991:7B.

Waldman, Peter. "Riots in Bahrain Arouse Ire of Feared Monarchy As the U.S. Stands By." *Wall Street Journal,* June 12, 1995b:A1, A8.

Waldman, Peter. "Some Muslim Thinkers Want to Reinterpret Islam for Modern Times." *Wall Street Journal,* March 15, 1995a:A1, A8.

Walker, Alice, and Pratibha Parmar. *Warrior Marks: Female Genital Mutilation and the Sexual Blinding of Women.* New York: Harcourt Brace, 1993.

Walker, Tom. " 'Edge Cities' Represent a Quiet Social Revolution." *Atlanta Journal,* September 29, 1991:C1.

Wallerstein, Immanuel. *The Modern World System: Capitalist Agriculture and the Origins of the European World-Economy in the Sixteenth Century.* New York: Academic Press, 1974.

Wallerstein, Immanuel. *The Capitalist World-Economy.* New York: Cambridge University Press, 1979.

Wallerstein, Immanuel. *The Politics of the World-Economy: The States, the Movements, and the Civilizations.* Cambridge, England: Cambridge University Press, 1984.

Wallerstein, Immanuel. "Culture as the Ideological Battleground of the Modern World-System." In *Global Culture: Nationalism, Globalization, and Modernity,* Mike Featherstone, ed. London: Sage, 1990:31–55.

Wallerstein, Judith S., and Sandra Blakeslee. "Divorce Harms Children." In *Family in America: Opposing Viewpoints,* Viqi Wagner, ed. San Diego, Calif.: Greenhaven Press, 1992: 108–114.

Wallerstein, Judith S., and Joan B. Kelly. "How Children React to Parental Divorce." In *Marriage and Family in a Changing Society,* 4th ed., James M. Henslin, ed. New York: Free Press, 1992:397–409.

Walters, Alan. "Let More Earnings Go to Shareholders." *Wall Street Journal,* October 31, 1995:A23.

Watson, J. Mark. "Outlaw Motorcyclists." In *Down to Earth Sociology: Introductory Readings,* 5th ed., James M. Henslin, ed. New York: Free Press, 1988:203–213.

Weber, Max. "Politics as a Vocation." In *From Max Weber: Essays in Sociology,* Hans Gerth and C. Wright Mills, eds. New York: Oxford University Press, 1946:77–128.

Weber, Max. *The Theory of Social and Economic Organization,* A. M. Henderson and Talcott Parsons, trans., Talcott Parsons, ed. Glencoe, Ill.: Free Press, 1947. First published in 1913.

Weber, Max. *The Protestant Ethic and the Spirit of Capitalism.* New York: Scribner's, 1958. First published in 1904–1905.

Weber, Max. *Economy and Society.* Ephraim Fischoff, trans. New York: Bedminster Press, 1968. First published in 1922.

Webster, Pamela S., and A. Regula Herzog. "Effects of Parental Divorce and Memories of Family Problems on Relationships between Adult Children and Their Parents." *Journal of Gerontology, 50B,* 1, 1995:S24–S34.

Weeks, John R. *Population: An Introduction to Concepts and Issues,* 5th ed. Belmont, Calif.: Wadsworth, 1994.

Wei, William. *The Asian American Movement.* Philadelphia: Temple University Press, 1993.

Weintraub, Richard M. "A Bride in India." *Washington Post,* February 28, 1988.

Weisburd, David, Stanton Wheeler, and Elin Waring. *Crimes of the Middle Classes: White-Collar Offenders in the Federal Courts.* New Haven, Conn.: Yale University Press, 1991.

Weisskopf, Michael. "Scientist Says Greenhouse Effect Is Setting In." In *Ourselves and Others: The Washington Post Sociology Companion,* Washington Post Writers Group, eds. Boston: Allyn and Bacon, 1992:297–298.

Weitzman, Lenore J. *The Divorce Revolution.* New York: Free Press, 1985.

Wenneker, Mark B., and Arnold M. Epstein. "Racial Inequalities in the Use of Procedures for Patients with Ischemic Heart Disease in Massachusetts." *Journal of the American Medical Association, 261,* 2, January 13, 1989:253–257.

Wessel, David. "As Populations Age, Fiscal Woes Deepen." *Wall Street Journal*, September 11, 1995:A1.

"What's News." *Wall Street Journal*, December 4, 1995:A1.

Whetstone, Muriel L. "What Black Men and Women Should Do Now (about Black Men and Women)." *Ebony*, February 1996:135–138, 140.

White, Burton L., Barbara T. Kaban, and Jane S. Attanucci. *The Origins of Human Competence*. Lexington, Mass.: Heath, 1979.

White, Jack E. "Forgive Us Our Sins." *Time*, July 3, 1995:29.

Whitehead, Barbara Dafoe. "Dan Quayle Was Right." *Atlantic Monthly*, April 1993:47–84.

Whorf, Benjamin. *Language, Thought and Reality*. Cambridge, Mass.: MIT Press, 1956.

Whyte, Martin King. "Choosing Mates—The American Way." *Society*, March–April 1992:71–77.

Whyte, William H. *The City: Rediscovering the Center*. New York: Doubleday, 1989.

Willhelm, Sidney M. "Can Marxism Explain America's Racism?" *Social Problems*, 28, December 1980:98–112.

Williams, Christine L. *Still a Man's World: Men Who Do Women's Work*. Berkeley: University of California Press, 1995.

Williams, Rhys H. "Constructing the Public Good: Social Movements and Cultural Resources." *Social Problems*, 42, 1, February 1995:124–144.

Williams, Robin M., Jr. *American Society: A Sociological Interpretation*, 2nd ed. New York: Knopf, 1965.

Willie, Charles V. "Caste, Class, and Family Life Experiences." *Research in Race and Ethnic Relations*, 6, 1991: 65–84.

Wilson, James Q. "Is Incapacitation the Answer to the Crime Problem?" In *Taking Sides: Clashing Views on Controversial Social Issues*, 7th ed., Kurt Finsterbusch and George McKenna, eds. Guilford, Conn.: Dushkin, 1992:318–324.

Wilson, James Q. "Lock 'Em Up and Other Thoughts on Crime." *New York Times Magazine*, March 9, 1975:11, 44–48.

Wilson, James Q., and Richard J. Hernstein. *Crime and Human Nature*. New York: Simon & Schuster, 1985.

Wilson, William Julius. *The Declining Significance of Race: Blacks and Changing American Institutions*. Chicago: University of Chicago Press, 1978.

Wilson, William Julius. *The Truly Disadvantaged: The Inner City, the Underclass, and Public Policy*. Chicago: University of Chicago Press, 1987.

Winslow, Ron. "More Doctors Are Adding On-Line Tools to Their Kits." *Wall Street Journal*, October 7, 1994:B4.

Winslow, Ron. "Study Finds Blacks Get Fewer Bypasses." *Wall Street Journal*, March 18, 1992:B1.

Wirpsa, Leslie. "Proposition 209 Creates New Social Turbulence." *National Catholic Reporter*, 33, 5, November 22, 1996:5.

Wirth, Louis. "The Problem of Minority Groups." In *The Science of Man in the World Crisis*, Ralph Linton, ed. New York: Columbia University Press, 1945.

Wirth, Louis. "Urbanism as a Way of Life." *American Journal of Sociology*, 44, July 1938:1–24.

Wohl, R. Richard, and Anselm Strauss. "Symbolic Representation and the Urban Milieu." *American Journal of Sociology*, 63, March 1958:523–532.

Wolfgang, Marvin E., and Franco Ferracuti. *The Subculture of Violence: Toward an Integrated Theory in Criminology*. London: Tavistock, 1967.

Wong, Bernard. *Ethnicity and Entrepreneurship among the Immigrant Chinese*. Boston: Allyn and Bacon, 1996.

Woodward, Kenneth L. "Heaven." *Newsweek*, 113, 13, March 27, 1989:52–55.

Wouters, Cas. "On Status Competition and Emotion Management: The Study of Emotions as a New Field." *Theory, Culture & Society*, 9, 1992:229–252.

Wright, Erik Olin. *Class*. London: Verso, 1985.

Wright, Lawrence. "Double Mystery." *New Yorker*, August 7, 1995:45–62.

Wynter, Leon E. "Business and Race." *Wall Street Journal*, September 13, 1995:B1.

Yearbook of American and Canadian Churches. Nashville, Tenn.: Abingdon. Various editions.

Yellowbird, Michael, and C. Matthew Snipp. "American Indian Families." In *Minority Families in the United States: A Multicultural Perspective*, Ronald L. Taylor, ed. Englewood Cliffs, N.J.: Prentice Hall, 1994:179–201.

Yinger, J. Milton. *The Scientific Study of Religion*. New York: Macmillan, 1970.

Yinger, J. Milton. *Toward a Field Theory of Behavior: Personality and Social Structure*. New York: McGraw-Hill, 1965.

Zachary, G. Pascal. "Behind Stocks' Surge Is an Economy in Which Big U.S. Firms Thrive." *Wall Street Journal*, November 22, 1995:A1, A5.

Zakuta, Leo. "Equality in North American Marriages." In *Marriage and Family in a Changing Society*, 3rd ed., James M. Henslin, ed. New York: Free Press, 1989:105–114.

Zald, Mayer N. "Looking Backward to Look Forward: Reflections on the Past and the Future of the Resource Mobilization Research Program." In *Frontiers in Social Movement Theory*, Aldon D. Morris and Carol McClurg Mueller, eds. New Haven, Conn.: Yale University Press, 1992:326–348.

Zald, Mayer N., and John D. McCarthy, eds. *Social Movements in an Organizational Society*. New Brunswick, N.J.: Transaction Books, 1987.

Zawitz, Marianne W. *Report to the Nation on Crime and Justice*, 2nd ed. Washington, D.C.: U.S. Department of Justice, Bureau of Justice Statistics, July 1988.

Zellner, William W. *Countercultures: A Sociological Analysis*. New York: St. Martin's, 1995.

Zerubavel, Eviatar. *The Fine Line: Making Distinctions in Everyday Life*. New York: Free Press, 1991.

Zey, Mary. *Banking on Fraud: Drexel, Junk Bonds, and Buyouts*. Hawthorne, N.Y.: Aldine de Gruyter, 1993.

Ziegenhals, Gretchen E. "Confessions of an Amish Watcher." *Christian Century*, August 21–28, 1991:764–765.

Ziegler, Bart. "Banned by Comdex, Purveyors of Porn Put on Their Own Show." *Wall Street Journal*, November 14, 1995:B1, B8.

Zou, Heng Fu. "'The Spirit of Capitalism' and Long-Run Growth." *European Journal of Political Economy*, 10, 2, July 1994:279–293.

Nonmaterial culture, 37, 40, 51
Nonverbal interaction, 18
Norm of noninvolvement, 390–91
North American Free Trade Agreement (NAFTA), 194, 297, 302
Nuremberg, 213, 222

"Old boy" network, 113
Oligarchies, 285–86
Operational definitions, 21
Organic solidarity, 93
Out-groups, 111

PACs (Political Action Committees), 290
Participant observation, 25, 82
Past, the, 41–42
Patriarchy, 250, 310
Pay gap
  and gender inequality, 20, 119, 255–59
  and the "mommy track," 119
  and the "old boy" network, 11
Peer groups, 69–70, 139–40
Pelvic exams, 100–101
Perception, and language, 43–44
Personal space, 94, 96
Personality
  development of, 65
  disorders, 138
Pluralism. *See* Multiculturalism
Pluralistic society, 46
Politics
  African Americans in, 230
  and authority, 280–83
  and gender inequalities, 261–64
  Latinos in, 233–34
  overview of U.S., 280–92
  and participation of immigrants, 289
  and social class, 197
  and violence, 280–83
Polyandry, 308
Polygyny, 46, 308, 310
Poor, the. *See* Poverty
Population, 368–80. *See also* Population transfer
  conflict perspective on, 372, 375–76
  estimating growth of, 376–80
  and food production, 372–74

global aspects of, 368–80
growth of, 368–80, 81
and hunger, 372–74
shrinkage of, 372
symbolic interactionist perspective on, 374–75
trends in U.S., 377–78
and urbanization, 380–94
Population pyramids, 376
Population transfer, 225
Pornography, 143
Positivism, 6
Postindustrial societies. *See* Societies
Postmodern societies. *See* Societies
Poverty
  in the 1800s, 11
  in Brazil, 171
  and children, 202, 203–4, 171
  culture of, 175, 204–5
  of the elderly, 202
  explanations of, 205–6
  feminization of, 202
  and homelessness, 18
  and Hull-house, 10
  length of, 204–5
  line, 201–2
  and new technology, 393
  and race, 202, 203
  rural, 203, 204
  and single mothers, 204
  and social class, 201–7
  and wealth, 185
Power
  conflict perspective on, 148, 291–92, 312–14
  functionalist perspective on, 291
  of ideology, 167
  and inequality, 148
  overview of, 187–88
  seizure of, 285–86
  and social class, 164
  and social stratification, 166
  and wealth, 187–88
Power elite, 12, 187, 291–92
Prejudice. *See* Discrimination; Inequality; Race and ethnicity
Prestige, 164, 188–90
Primary groups, 108–9
Prisoners. *See* Imprisonment
Prisons. *See* Imprisonment

Progress, as a core value, 46
Proletariat, 7, 17, 163
Propaganda, 413–15
Property, 164, 185
Proposition 209, 239
Prostitution, 177
Protestant ethic, 354, 401
Protestantism
  and capitalism, 9, 353–54, 401
  and suicide, 7–8
Psychoanalysis, 65

Quality of life, 39
Questions used in research, 24–25
Quiet Revolution, the, 254–55

Race and ethnicity, 212–41
  African Americans and, 229–32
  Asian Americans and, 234–36
  classifications of, 213–14
  and education, 231, 344–45
  ethnic work and, 227
  global aspects of, 404
  and health, 220
  inequalities of, 212–41
  Latinos and, 233–34
  and mortgages, 219–20
  myth versus reality of, 212–13
  and Native Americans, 236–39
  outlook for future of, 239–41
  poverty and, 202, 203
  and relations among groups, 227–39
  religion and, 358, 361
  sociological foundation of, 212–20
  teacher expectations and, 344–45
  trends in U.S., 377–78
  and well-being, 231
  and white Europeans, 227–28
  in workplace, 119
Racism, 212–41. *See also* Discrimination; Inequality; Race and ethnicity
  in the 1800s, 11
  and African Americans, 229–32
  and Asian Americans, 234–35
  civil rights and, 229–32
  in-groups and, 111
  and intermarriage, 218
  out-groups and, 111
  slavery and, 160